To Aunt Jinny
for all of the love and support
you have given us over the years.
We are blessed to have you
in our lives

—MIKE

To Laura Cardinal,
who keeps the smiles
and joy coming.
I am indeed looking forward
to our next chapter together.

—CHET

To Jessica and Rebecca.
You make me proud
and you make me smile.

—ADRIENNE

about the authors

Michael A. Hitt

Texas A & M University

Michael Hitt is currently a Distinguished Professor of Management at Texas A&M University and holds the Joe B. Foster Chair in Business Leadership. He received his Ph.D. from the University of Colorado. Dr. Hitt has coauthored or co-edited 26 books and authored or coauthored many journal articles. A recent article listed him as one of the ten most cited authors in management over a 25-year period. The *Times Higher Education* listed him among the top scholars in economics, finance and management and tied for first among management scholars with the highest number of highly cited articles. He has served on the editorial review boards of multiple journals and is a former editor of the *Academy of Management Journal*. He is the current co-editor of the *Strategic Entrepreneurship Journal*. He received the 1996 Award for Outstanding Academic Contributions to Competitiveness and the 1999 Award for Outstanding Intellectual Contributions to Competitiveness Research from the American Society for Competitiveness. He is a Fellow in the Academy of Management and in the Strategic Management Society, a Research Fellow in the National Entrepreneurship Consortium and received an honorary doctorate from the Universidad Carlos III de Madrid for his contributions to the field. He is a former President of the Academy of Management, a Past President of the Strategic Management Society and a member of the Academy of Management Journals' Hall of Fame. He received awards for the best article published in the *Academy of Management Executive* (1999), *Academy of Management Journal* (2000), and the *Journal of Management* (2006). In 2001, he received the Irwin Outstanding Educator Award and the Distinguished Service Award from the Academy of Management. In 2004, Dr. Hitt was awarded the Best Paper Prize by the Strategic Management Society. In 2006, he received the Falcone Distinguished Entrepreneurship Scholar Award from Syracuse University.

C. Chet Miller

University of Houston

Dr. C. Chet Miller is the Bauer Professor of Organizational Studies at the Bauer School of Business, University of Houston. He received his Ph.D. from the University of Texas at Austin. He also received his B.A. from the University of Texas, where he was a member of Phi Beta Kappa and a Summa Cum Laude graduate.

Since working as a shift manager and subsequently completing his graduate studies, Dr. Miller has served on the faculties of Baylor University, Wake Forest University, and the University of Houston. He also has been a visiting faculty member at Cornell University and a guest instructor at Duke University. He is an active member of the Academy of

Management and the Strategic Management Society. He currently serves on the editorial boards of *Organization Science* and *Academy of Management Journal*, and is a past associate editor of *Academy of Management Journal*. Awards and honors include an outstanding young researcher award, nominations of several papers for honors, and teaching awards from multiple schools,

Dr. Miller has worked with a number of managers and executives. Through management-development programs, he has contributed to the development of individuals from such organizations as ABB, Bank of America, Krispy Kreme, La Farge, Red Hat, State Farm Insurance, and the U.S. Postal Service. His focus has been change management, strategic visioning, and high-involvement approaches to managing people.

Dr. Miller's published research focuses on the functioning of executive teams, the design of organizational structures and management systems, and the design of strategic decision processes. His publications have appeared in *Organization Science*, *Academy of Management Journal*, *Academy of Management Executive*, *Strategic Management Journal*, *Journal of Organizational Behavior*, and *Journal of Behavioral Decision Making*.

Dr. Miller teaches courses in the areas of organizational behavior, organization theory, and strategic management.

Adrienne Colella

Tulane University

Dr. Adrienne Colella is the A.B. Freeman Professor of Doctoral Studies and Research at the A.B. Freeman School of Business at Tulane University. She has also been a faculty member at the Mays Business School, Texas A&M University and at Rutgers University.

She received her Ph.D. and Masters degree from the Ohio State University in Industrial/ Organizational Psychology and her B.S. degree from Miami University. Dr. Colella is a fellow of the American Psychological Association and the Society for Industrial and Organizational Psychology, Division 14 of the APA. She will be the President of the Society of Industrial and Organizational Psychology in 2011.

Dr. Colella's main research focuses on treatment issues regarding persons with disabilities in the workplace and workplace accommodation. She has also published on a variety of other organizational behavior and human resources topics such as discrimination, pay secrecy, performance appraisal, motivation, socialization, and employee selection. Her research appears in the *Journal of Applied Psychology*, *Personnel Psychology*, *Academy of Management Journal*, *Academy of Management Review*, *Research in Personnel and Human Resource Management*, *Human Resource Management Review*, *Journal of Applied Social Psychology*, and the *Journal of Occupational Rehabilitation*, among other places. She is the editor of a Society of Industrial and Organizational Psychology Frontiers Series book on the psychology of workplace discrimination. Dr. Colella serves (or has served) on the editorial boards of *Personnel Psychology*, *Journal of Applied Psychology*, *Academy of Management Journal*, *Journal of Organizational Behavior*, *Human Resource Management Review*, *Human Performance*, *SIOP Frontier's Series*, *Human Resource Management*, and *Journal of Management*. She is an ad hoc reviewer for most other journals in the management field and federal funding agencies. Her research has been funded by a variety of national, state, and university sources.

Dr. Colella teaches undergraduate, masters-level, and Ph.D. level courses in Human Resource Management and Organizational Behavior.

brief contents

contents

preface

A few years ago, the following statement appeared on the cover of *Fast Company*, "The best leaders know where all of the great companies start. It's the people. ..." Despite all of the major technological advances made and the substantial increases in the power of computers (both hardware and software) that allow us to perform many functions more easily than in the past and to accomplish some tasks that we could not do in the past, all of this activity is driven by people. People developed Apple's iPod and iPad. People developed and implemented Twitter and Facebook. We communicate on cell phones and small laptop computers developed by people. Our automobiles are serviced by people; at restaurants we eat food prepared by people; we enjoy college and professional sports played by people. People are the drivers of organizations and make or break their success. Ed Breen, CEO of Tyco suggests that ideas provided by people are the basis of winning competitive battles because companies compete with their brains as well as their brawn. In support of this argument, Anne Mulcahy, former chairman of the board and former CEO of Xerox argues that people were the primary reason for Xerox's turnaround in performance. They attracted highly talented employees, motivated them and they were highly productive.[1]

Purpose

We wrote this book for several reasons. First, we wanted to communicate in an effective way the knowledge of managing people in organizations. The book presents up-to-date concepts of organizational behavior (OB) in a lively and easy-to-read manner. The book is based on classic and cutting-edge research on the primary topic of each chapter. Second, we wanted to emphasize the importance of people to the success of organizations. We do so by communicating how managing people is critical to implementing an organization's strategy, gaining an advantage over competitors, and ensuring positive organizational performance. This approach helps students to better understand the relevance of managing people, allowing the student to integrate these concepts with knowledge gained in other core business courses. To emphasize the importance of people, we use the term *human capital*. People are important assets to organizations; application of their knowledge and skills is necessary for organizations to accomplish their goals.

New to the Third Edition

A number of changes have been made to enrich the content of the book and to ensure that it is up-to-date with current organizational behavior research and managerial practice. For example, we have changed or updated all chapter opening cases (Exploring Behavior in Action), and all major case examples in the content of the chapters (e.g., Experiencing

Organizational Behavior, Managerial Advice). The few that were not changed represent classic examples (such as on the U.S. Civil War). Several of the major changes to the content are described below:

- New materials were added on the topic of firms gaining value from the knowledge learned by expatriates (Chapter 3).
- New materials were added on ethics and corruption (Chapter 3).
- Critical information was added on attractiveness and weight bias in our discussion of perception (Chapter 4).
- A new section focused on social dominance orientation as an individual difference was incorporated (Chapter 5).
- A new section was added on subconscious goals, an area of leading-edge research on goal setting (Chapter 6).
- Additional information was included on overload and job loss as important stressors (Chapter 7).
- Our discussion of communication networks was substantially modified and updated (Chapter 9).
- Building on our discussion of moods and emotions in Chapter 5, an explanation of how these characteristics of human functioning affect decision making was added to Chapter 10.
- New material was added in the crucial areas of workplace aggression and violence (Chapter 12).
- A new section was added on ambidextrous organizations, a topic of growing importance in OB (Chapter 13).
- A new section on top management changes was incorporated, along with new material on institutional changes and training (Chapter 14).

In addition to the above, we have added approximately 300 new references from the research literature and many more from popular press articles on managerial practice. Although we have made important revisions and updated materials to reflect current managerial practice, we have maintained all of the basic OB content that instructors found to be valuable and all of the pedagogical approaches that supported students' efforts to learn. Therefore, this third edition represents continued improvement of a high-quality teaching and learning tool. It continues to be written in an easy style and is user friendly, as were the first two editions of the book.

Value Provided by this Book

Managing OB involves acquiring, developing, managing, and applying the knowledge, skills, and abilities of people. A strategic approach to OB rests on the premise that people are the foundation for any firm's competitive advantage. Providing exceptionally high quality products and services, excellent customer service, best-in-class cost structure, and other advantages are based on the capabilities of the firm's people, its human capital. If organized and managed effectively, the knowledge and skills of the people in the firm are the basis for gaining an advantage over competitors and achieving long-term financial success.

Individual, interpersonal, and organizational characteristics determine the behavior and ultimately the value of an organization's people. Factors such as individuals' technical skills, personality characteristics, personal values, abilities to learn, and abilities to be self-managing are important bases for the development of organizational capabilities. At the interpersonal level, factors such as quality of leadership, communication within and between groups, and conflict within and between groups are noteworthy in the organization's ability to build important capabilities and apply them to achieve its goals. Finally, at the organizational level, the culture and policies of the firm are also among the most important factors, as they influence whether the talents and positive predispositions of individuals are effectively used. Thus, managing human capital is critical for an organization to beat its competition and to perform effectively.

This book explains how to effectively manage behavior in organizations. In addition, we emphasize how effective behavioral management relates to organizational performance. We link the specific behavioral topic(s) emphasized in each chapter to organizational strategy and performance through explicit but concise discussions. We also provide short cases and examples to highlight the relationships.

Therefore, we emphasize the importance of managing OB and its effect on the outcomes of the organization. This is highly significant because a number of organizations routinely mismanage their workforce. For example, some organizations routinely implement major reductions in the workforce (layoffs, downsizing) whenever they experience performance problems. How does an organization increase its effectiveness by laying off thousands of its employees? The answer is that it rarely does so.[2] Layoffs reduce costs but they also result in losses of significant human capital and valuable knowledge. These firms then suffer from diminished capabilities and their performance decreases further. Research shows that firms increasing their workforce during economic downturns enjoy much stronger performance when the economy improves.[3] These firms have the capabilities to take advantage of the improving economy, whereas firms that downsized must rebuild their capabilities and are less able to compete effectively. The firms listed annually in *Fortune's* "100 Best Companies to Work for" are consistently among the highest performers in their industries (e.g., Starbucks, Whole Foods Market, Marriott, American Express).

Concluding Remarks

The knowledge learned from a course in organizational behavior is important for managers at all levels: top executives, middle managers, and lower-level managers. While top executives may understand the strategic importance of managing human capital, middle and lower-level managers must also understand the linkage between managing behavior effectively and the organization's ability to formulate and implement its strategy. Managers do not focus solely on individual behavior. They also manage interpersonal, team, intergroup, and interorganizational relationships. Some refer to these relationships as "social capital." The essence of managing organizational behavior is the development and use of human capital and social capital.

Jack Welch, former CEO of GE, suggested that he and his management team used management concepts that energized armies of people allowing them to dream, dare, reach, and stretch their talents in order to do things they never thought possible. This book presents concepts that will help students to gain the knowledge needed to effectively manage behavior in organizations. This, in turn, helps in the implementation of the organization's strategy, affects the organization's productivity, allows the organization to gain advantages over its competitors, and therefore contributes to the organization's overall performance.

MAH

CCM

AJC

1 Hitt, M.A., Haynes, K.T., & Serpa, R. 2010. Strategic leadership for the twenty-first century. *Business Horizons*, in press.

2 Krishnan, H., Hitt, M.A., & Park, D. 2007. Acquisition premiums, subsequent workplace reductions and post-acquisition performance. *Journal of Management Studies*, 44: 709–732; Nixon, R.D., Hitt, M.A., Lee, H. & Jeong, E. 2004. Market reactions to announcements of corporate downsizing actions and implementation strategies. *Strategic Management Journal*, 25: 1121–1129.

3 Greer, C.R., & Ireland, T.C. 1992. Organizational and financial correlates of a 'contrarian' human resource investment strategy. *Academy of Management Journal*, 35: 956–984.

FOCUS AND PEDAGOGY

The book explains and covers all organizational behavior topics, based on the most current research available. Unlike other OB texts, it uses the lens of an organization's strategy as a guide. Elements of the book through which we apply this lens include:

Exploring Behavior in Action

Each chapter opens with a case, grounding the chapter in a real-world context. Some of the companies featured include Men's Wearhouse, McDonalds, W. L. Gore & Associates, Starbucks, and FedEx.

exploring behavior in action

Diversity in the Los Angeles Fire Department

Melissa Kelley had a rich background in firefighting. Early in life, she learned from her grandfather, who worked as a firefighter. In college, she learned through coursework as a fire-science major. After college, she spent five years learning and honing her skills as a firefighter with the California Department of Forestry.

Armed with her experiences and passion for the work, she joined the Los Angeles Fire Department in 2001. Although aware of possible discrimination and harassment against women in the department, she did not hesitate to join when presented with the opportunity. In her words, "I was willing to overlook … the dirty jokes, the porn, the … mentality. … I just wanted to be part of the team." To her, only two simple rules applied: "Do not touch me. Do not hurt me on purpose."

The Strategic Importance of ...

Links the issues in the opening case to the organizational behavior topic of the chapter. The issues are discussed in light of their importance to organization strategy and ultimately how they affect the organization's performance.

"The Strategic Importance of ... and The Strategic Lens are appropriate 'bookends' for the chapter; they set up how decision making is strategic and reinforce that at the end of the chapter."

(Pam Roffol-Dobies,
University of Missouri Kansas City)

the strategic importance of Organizational Diversity

As the LAFD case shows, negative reactions to diversity can have harmful effects on an organization. These reactions, including discrimination and harassment of various forms, often lead to lawsuits, turnover, reduced satisfaction, and performance issues. In the most effective organizations, associates and managers understand the value of diversity and capitalize on it to improve performance. Moreover, associates and managers cannot escape diverse workgroups and organizations. Differences in gender, race, functional background, and so on are all around us. The United States is a particularly diverse country with respect to race and ethnicity, and current demographic trends indicate that its population will become even more diverse.

LAFD's legal troubles, financial settlement costs, and public embarrassment have led to renewed efforts to change the culture. The changing nature of the firefighter's job, where 80 percent of fire calls no longer involve structural or brush fires, probably has helped in this process.[1] Many organizations, however, have not needed public embarrassment or changing jobs to motivate diversity efforts. Many organizations, particularly large ones, have voluntarily adopted diversity manage-

with fewer than 100 workers. Over 79 percent of human resource managers at *Fortune* 1000 companies said they believed that successfully managing diversity improves their organizations.[3]

Diversity, if properly managed, can help a business build competitive advantage. For example, hiring and retaining managers and associates from various ethnicities can help an organization better understand and serve an existing diverse customer base. Diversity among associates also might help the organization attract additional customers from various ethnic groups. Diverse backgrounds and experiences incorporated into a work team or task force can help the organization more effectively handle an array of complex and challenging problems. Kevin Johnson, Co-President of Platforms and Services at Microsoft, puts it this way: "[W]e must recognize, respect, and leverage the different perspectives our employees bring to the marketplace as strengths. Doing so will ensure that we will be more competitive in the global marketplace, will be seen as an employer of choice, and will be more creative and innovative ...."[4]

In the case of nonprofit organizations or governmental units such as the Los Angeles Fire Department, diversity

withheld from donation. In the case of the Los Angeles Fire Department, diverse captains, firefighters, and paramedics could better communicate with and predict the behavior of the diverse citizenry of Los Angeles. This would enable the department to better serve the city. It also would position it to receive more resources from the city and state and would increase its likelihood of being chosen over other organizations for additional duties in the Los Angeles area.

Many individuals feel most comfortable interacting and working with people who are similar to them on a variety of dimensions (such as age, race, ethnic background, education, functional area, values, and personality).[5] They must, however, learn to work with all others in an organization to achieve common goals. In a truly inclusive workplace, everyone feels valued and all associates are motivated and committed to the mission of the organization. Such outcomes are consistent with a high-involvement work environment and can help organizations achieve competitive advantage.

We begin this chapter by defining organizational diversity and distinguishing it from other concepts, such as affirmative action. Next, we describe

Experiencing Organizational Behavior

These two Exploring Organizational Behavior sections in each chapter apply the key concepts of the chapter. Real-world case situations are used including such topics as women, work, and stereotypes; Google and high-quality associates; Coca-Cola's new fizz; extreme jobs; and communication at J. Crew. Each discussion highlights the connection between an OB concept and the organization's strategy and performance.

"The Experiencing OB section is also useful since it provides a conceptual view of the changing approach to OB. I like the idea that it walks the students through a situation and then summarizes the prospects for acting successfully."

(Marian Schultz, University of West Florida)

"After reading the Experiencing OB section on the football league, I also found that the example was an excellent choice. My classroom includes both traditional and nontraditional students, ranging in age from 20–72 and I think it is important to provide a variety of examples that everyone can relate to in the course."

(Marilyn Wesner,
George Washington University)

EXPERIENCING ORGANIZATIONAL BEHAVIOR

Diversity at the Top

On November 4, 2008, the United States elected Barack Obama as president. President Obama personifies the concept of diversity in terms of race, ethnicity, and geography. His black father was from a small town in Kenya and his white mother was from Kansas. His parents met in Hawaii, where he was born. President Obama's parents were divorced when he was 2 years old. When he was six years old, his mother remarried a man from Indonesia, and the family moved there. At the age of ten, Barack Obama returned to Hawaii to live with his maternal grandparents. He has a half-sister who is part Indonesian and is married to a man who is Chinese Canadian. President Obama's wife, Michelle Obama, is African American. In an interview with Oprah Winfrey, President Obama described his family get-togethers as "mini United Nations meetings." He said he had some relatives that looked like Bernie Mac and some that looked like Margaret Thatcher. The Obama family clearly exemplifies the diversity inherent in the United States.

President Obama's intrapersonal diversity and strong beliefs that diversity in governance is necessary is reflected in the diversity of his cabinet. Thirty-four percent of his officials are female, 11 percent are black, 8 percent are Hispanic, and 4 percent are Asian. While these do not seem like large numbers, they reflect more diversity than was present in past administrations' cabinets. This diversity is expected to increase as President

©MANDEL NGAN/Getty Images, Inc.

Obama's tenure in office lengthens and he brings in new officials.

The presidency of Barack Obama brings up the question of whether the United States has overcome problems with racial, ethnic, and gender discrimination. Is the leadership in this country finally reflective of the population? Unfortunately, this is still not the case, as evidenced by the demography of corporate leaders. At the end of 2008, there were 5 black, 7 Latino, 7 Asian, and 13 female (2 of whom are Asian) CEOs of *Fortune* 500 companies. This means that 94 percent of *Fortune* 500 CEOs were white, non-Hispanic males. Examining the composition of boards of directors reveals the same lack of diversity. A Catalyst 2009 study of *Fortune* 500 companies revealed that women held 15.2 percent of board seats and women of color held 3.1 percent of all board director positions. Women held only 2 percent of board chair positions. These numbers have remained relatively consistent over the past five years. A study on African American representation on corporate boards found that representation had decreased from 8.1 percent in 2004 to 7.4 percent in 2008. In a recent study of *Fortune* 100 boards, the Alliance for Board Diversity (a

joint effort among organizations concerned with board diversity) concluded that:

- There is a severe underrepresentation of women and minorities on corporate boards when compared to general U.S. population demographics for race and gender.
- Particular areas of concern include the lack of representation of minority women and of Asian Americans and Hispanics.
- There is a recycling of the same minority individuals—especially African American men—as board members. Minority and female board members hold more seats per person than do white males.
- Very few boards have representation from all groups. Only four boards had representation by all four groups (women, African Americans, Asian Americans, and Hispanics).

Will the diversity evident in the Obama administration filter down to

Managerial Advice

These sections provide advice for future managers and make a connection to the organization's strategy and performance. Examples of Managerial Advice include multinational corporations and "glocalization", Phil Jackson's leadership success, surfing for applicants on MySpace and Facebook, managing virtual teams, finding a fit at Home Depot, and "green" policies and practices.

MANAGERIAL ADVICE

Promoting a Positive Diversity Environment

Robin Ely, Debra Meyerson, and Martin Davidson are professors at Harvard University, Stanford University, and the University of Virginia, respectively. In conjunction with the human development and organizational learning professionals at Learning as Leadership, they have developed several principles designed to ensure that members of various social identity groups do not become trapped in low-quality workplace relationships. These principles are designed to encourage engagement and learning. The principles are perhaps best applied in the context of individuals experiencing uncomfortable events that are open to interpretation, such as when the member of a minority group is told by someone from the majority that she is being too aggressive, or when a man is told by a woman that he is acting as his grandfather might have acted. The principles are listed below:

a. *Pause to short circuit the emotion and reflect.* Individuals who

©Tom Grill/Corbis

have experienced an uncomfortable event should take a few moments to identify their feelings and consider a range of responses.

b. *Connect with others in ways that affirm the importance of relationships.* Individuals who have experienced an uncomfortable event should reach out to those who have caused the difficulty, thereby valuing relationships.

c. *Question interpretations and explore blind spots.* Individuals who have experienced an uncomfortable event should engage in self-questioning as well as the questioning of others. They should be open to the interpretations that others have of the situation, while realizing that their own interpretations might be correct.

d. *Obtain genuine support that doesn't necessarily validate initial points of view but, rather, helps in gaining broader perspective.* Individuals who have experienced an uncomfortable event should seek input from those who will challenge their initial points of view on the situation.

e. *Shift the mindset.* Individuals who have experienced an uncomfortable event should be open to the idea that both parties might need to change to some degree.

Sources: R.J. Ely, D.E. Meyerson, and M.N. Davidson. 2006. "Rethinking Political Correctness," *Harvard Business Review,* 84 (September); Learning as Leadership, "Research," 2007, at http://www.learnaslead.com/index.php.

THE STRATEGIC LENS

Organizational diversity, when managed effectively, has many benefits for organizations. In general, effectively managed diversity programs contribute to an organization's ability to achieve and maintain a competitive advantage. Diversity in teams at all levels can be helpful in solving complex problems because heterogeneous teams integrate multiple perspectives. This benefit applies to the upper-echelon management team as well as to project teams, such as new-product-development teams, much lower in the organization. Not only can the diversity help resolve complex problems, but it also better mirrors U.S. society. Thus, it signals to potential associates and potential customers that the organization understands and effectively uses diversity. As a result, the organization has a larger pool of candidates for potential associates from which it can select the best. In addition, the organization is likely to have a larger potential market because of its understanding of the products and services desired by a diverse marketplace. Having a diverse organization that reflects the demographic composition of U.S. society is smart business.[106]

Critical Thinking Questions

1. How does organizational diversity contribute to an organization's competitive advantage?

2. What actions are required to create diversity in an organization, particularly in one that has homogeneous membership at present?

3. How does diversity in an organization affect its strategy?

The Strategic Lens

The Strategic Lens section concludes each chapter. The section explains the topic of the chapter through the lens of organizational strategy. Highlighted is the critical contribution of the chapter's concepts to the organization's achievement of its goals. The Strategic Lens concludes with *Critical Thinking Questions* that are designed to emphasize the student's knowledge of the OB topic, its effects on the organization's strategy, and its effects on organizational functioning.

Building Your Human Capital

To help students better know themselves and develop needed skills in organizational behavior, a personal assessment instrument is included in each chapter. This includes information on scoring and interpreting the results. Assessments, for example, are focused on approaches to difficult learning situations, the propensity to be creative, skill at managing with power, and the ability to tolerate change.

"The Building Your Human Capital segment is unique. Students need to recognize the importance of the topics for developing their personal skills. This section does a good job in forwarding that idea."

(CEASAR DOUGLAS, FLORIDA STATE UNIVERSITY)

building your human capital
What's Your DQ (Diversity Quotient)?

How well do you handle diversity? Your ability to be flexible, work with many different types of people, and deal with ambiguous situations will be crucial to a successful career in the twenty-first century. The following assessment will allow you to determine whether you have had the experience necessary to help in successfully navigating a diverse work environment.

Use the following scale to answer the questions below:

1 point = never	3 points = three or four times
2 points = once or twice	4 points = four or more times

In the last month, how often did you ...?

1. See a foreign movie.
2. Speak a language other than your first language.
3. Visit an art or history museum.
4. Have a conversation with someone who was of a different race.
5. Have a conversation with someone who was from a different country.
6. Attend a social event where at least half of the people differed from you in race or ethnic background.
7. Visit a church that was of a religion different from yours.

An Organizational Behavior Moment

The applied, hypothetical case at the end of each chapter gives students an opportunity to apply the knowledge they have gained throughout the chapter. Each case concludes with questions. Teaching suggestions are included in the instructor's resources.

"The case was a good illustration of what life as a manger is like and it lends itself to a discussion of what might keep a manager from being highly involved."

(DEBORAH BUTLER, GEORGIA STATE UNIVERSITY)

an organizational behavior moment
Project "Blow Up"

Big State University (BSU) is proud of the success of its international executive MBA (EMBA) program. The program is designed to bring together promising middle- and higher-level managers from around the globe for an exceptional learning experience. BSU's EMBA program has been ranked very highly by the business press. Alumni praise the program for its excellent faculty, networking opportunities, and exposure to colleagues from around the world. Students in the program can either attend weekend classes on BSU's campus or participate through distance-learning technology from campuses around the world.

One of the defining features of the program is the first-year team project. Students are randomly assigned to five-member teams. Each team has a faculty advisor, and each must develop a business plan for a startup company. A major part of the business plan involves developing a marketing strategy. The teams begin the project during orientation week and finish at the end of the next summer. Each team must turn in a written report and a business plan and make an hour-long presentation to the other students and faculty as well as several executives from well-respected multinational companies. Students must earn a passing grade on

Team Exercise

These experiential exercises expand the student's learning through activities and engage students in team building skills. Teaching suggestions are included in the instructor's resources.

"The Exercise at the end of the chapter seemed like a great way to get students involved and to help them understand the material."

(SHARON PURKISS, CALIFORNIA STATE UNIVERSITY AT FULLERTON)

team exercise
What Is It Like to Be Different?

One reason people have a difficult time dealing with diversity in others or understanding why it is important to value and respect diversity is that most people spend most of their lives in environments where everyone is similar to them on important dimensions. Many people have seldom been in a situation in which they felt they didn't belong or didn't know the "rules." The purpose of this exercise is to have you experience such a situation and open up a dialogue with others about what it feels like to be different and what you can personally learn from this experience to become better at managing diversity in the future.

STEP 1: Choose an event that you would not normally attend and at which you will likely be in the minority on some important dimension. Attend the event.

- You can go with a friend who would normally attend the event, but not one who will also be in a minority.
- Make sure you pick a place where you will be safe and where you are sure you will be welcomed, or at least tolerated. You may want to check with your instructor about your choice.
- Do not call particular attention to yourself. Just observe what is going on and how you feel.

Some of you may find it easy to have a minority experience, since you are a minority group member in your everyday life. Others may have a more difficult time. Here are some examples of events to consider attending:

- A religious service for a religion totally different from your own.
- A sorority or fraternity party where the race of members is mostly different from your own.
- A political rally where the politics are different from your own.

SUPPLEMENTS

Companion Website

The text's website at www.wiley.com/go/global/hitt contains myriad resources and links to aid both teaching and learning, including the web quizzes described above.

Instructor's Resource Guide

The Instructor's Resource Guide includes an Introduction with sample syllabi, Chapter Outlines, Chapter Objectives, Teaching Notes on how to integrate and assign special features within the text, and suggested answers for all quiz and test questions found in the text. The Instructor's Resource Guide also includes additional discussion questions and assignments that relate specifically to the cases, as well as case notes, self-assessments, and team exercises.

Test Bank

This robust Test Bank consists of true/false (approximately 60 per chapter), multiple choice (approximately 60 per chapter), short-answer (approximately 25 per chapter), and essay questions (approximately 5 per chapter). Further, it is specifically designed so that questions will vary in degree of difficulty, ranging from straightforward recall to more challenging application questions to ensure student mastery of all key concepts and topics. The organization of test questions also offers instructors the most flexibility when designing their exams. A **Computerized Test Bank** provides even more flexibility and customization options to instructors. The Computerized Test Bank requires a PC running Windows. This electronic version of the Test Bank includes all the questions from the Test Bank within a test-generating program that allows instructors to customize their exams and also to add their own test questions in addition to what is already available.

Power Point Presentations

These PowerPoint Presentations provide another visual enhancement and learning aid for students, as well as additional talking points for instructors. Each chapter's set of interactive PowerPoint slides includes lecture notes to accompany each slide. Each presentation includes roughly 30 slides with illustrations, animations, and related web links interspersed appropriately.

Lecture Notes

Lecture Notes provide an outline of the chapter and knowledge objectives, highlighting the key topics/concepts presented within each chapter. Power-Point slides have been integrated, where relevant, and the lecture notes suggest to instructors when it's best to show the class each slide within a particular chapter's PowerPoint Presentation.

Web Quizzes

Online quizzes with questions varying in level of difficulty have been designed to help students evaluate their individual comprehension of the key concepts and topics presented within each chapter. Each chapter's quiz includes 10 questions, including true/false and multiple choice questions. These review questions, developed by the Test Bank author, Melinda Blackman, have been created to provide the most effective and efficient testing system for students as they prepare for more formal quizzes and exams. Within this system, students have the opportunity to "practice" responding to the types of questions they'll be expected to address on a quiz or exam.

Prelecture and Postlecture Quizzes

The Prelecture and Postlecture Quizzes can be found exclusively in *WileyPLUS*. These quizzes consist of multiple-choice and true/false questions which vary in level of detail and difficulty while focusing on a particular chapter's key terms and concepts. This resource allows instructors to quickly and easily evaluate their students' progress by monitoring their comprehension of the material both before and after each lecture.

The prelecture quiz questions enable instructors to gauge their students' comprehension of a particular chapter's content so they can best determine what to focus on in their lecture.

The postlecture quiz questions are intended to be homework or review questions that instructors can assign to students after covering a particular chapter. The questions typically provide hints, solutions or explanations to the students, as well as page references.

Organizational Behavior Lecture Launcher Video

Video clips from the BBC and CBS News, ranging from 2 to 10 minutes in length tied to the current news topics in organizational behavior are available on DVD. These video clips provide an excellent starting point for lectures. An instructor's manual for using the lecture launcher is available on the Instructor's portion of the Hitt website. For more information on the OB Lecture Launcher, please contact your local Wiley sales representative.

ACKNOWLEDGMENTS

We thank the many people who helped us develop this book. We owe a debt of gratitude to the following people who reviewed this book through its development and revision, providing us with helpful feedback. Thanks to those professors who provided valuable feedback for the third edition: Lon Doty, San Jose State University; Don Gibson, Fairfield University; Richard J. Gibson, Embry-Riddle Aeronautical University; Aden Heuser, Ohio State University; Arlene Kreinik, Western Connecticut State University; Lorianne D. Mitchell, East Tennessee State University; Wendy Smith, University of Delaware; and Hamid Yeganeh, Winona State University. Also, thanks to those professors who reviewed the book in its prior editions and helped us hone its approach and focus: Syed Ahmed, Florida International University; Johnny Austin, Chapman University; Rick Bartlet, Columbus State Community College; Melinda Blackman, California State University–Fullerton; Fred Blass, Florida State University; H. Michael Boyd, Bentley College; Regina Bento, University of Baltimore; Ralph Brathwaite, University of Hartford; David Bush, Villanova University; Mark Butler, San Diego State University; Steve Buuck, Concordia University; Jay Caulfield, Marquette University; William Clark, Leeward Community College; Marie Dasborough, University of Miami; Michelle Duffy, University of Kentucky; Michael Ensby, Clarkson University; Cassandra Fenyk, Centenary College; Meltem Ferendeci-Ozgodek, Bilkent University; Dean Frear, Wilkes University; Sharon Gardner, College of New Jersey; James Gelatt, University of Maryland–University College; John George, Liberty University; Lucy Gilson, University of Connecticut-Storrs; Mary Giovannini, Truman State University; Yezdi Godiwalla, University of Wisconsin–Whitewater; Elaine Guertler, Lees-McRae College; Carol Harvey, Assumption College; David Hennessy, Mt. Mercy College; Kenny Holt, Union University; Janice Jackson, Western New England College; Paul Jacques, Western Carolina University; William Judge, University of Tennessee–Knoxville; Barbara Kelley, St. Joseph's University; Molly Kern, Baruch College; Robert Ledman, Morehouse College; James Maddox, Friends University; Bill Mellan, Florida Sothern College; Lorianne Mitchell, East Tennessee State University; Edward Miles, Georgia State University; Atul Mitra, University of Northern Iowa; Christine O'Connor, University of Ballarad; Regina O'Neill, Suffolk University; Laura Paglis, University of Evansville; Ron Piccolo, University of Central Florida; Chris Poulson, California State Polytechinal University–Pomana; Sharon Purkiss, California State University-Fullerton; David Radosevich, Montclair State University; William Reisel, St. John's University; Joe Rode, Miami University of Ohio; Pam Roffol-Dobies, University of Missouri–Kansas City; Sammie Robinson, Illinoise Wesleyan University; Bob Roller, Letourneau University; Sophie Romack, John Carroll University; William Rudd, Boise State College; Joel Rudin, Rowan University; Jane Schmidt-Wilk, Maharishi University of Management; Mel Schnake, Valdosta State University; Holly Schroth, University of California–Berkeley; Daniel Sherman, University of Alabama–Huntsville; Randy Sleeth, Virginia Commonwealth University; Shane Spiller, Morehead State University; John Stark, California State University–Bakersfield; Robert Steel, University of Michigan–Dearborn; David Tansik, University of Arizona; Tom Thompson, University of Maryland–University; Edward Tomlinson, John Carroll University; Tony Urban, Rutgers University–Camden; Fred Ware, Valdosta State University College; and Joseph Wright, Portland Community College. We also greatly appreciate the guidance and support we received from the excellent Wiley team consisting of George Hoffman, Lise Johnson, Karolina Zarychta, Sarah Vernon, and Sandra Dumas. We also acknowledge and thank former members of the editorial team who made contributions to this edition: Jayme Heffler, Kim Mortimer, and Jennifer Conklin. Our colleagues at Texas A&M University, University of Houston, and Tulane University have also provided valuable support by providing intellectual input through discussions and debates. There are many people over the years that have contributed to our own intellectual growth and development and led us to write this book. For all of your help and support, we thank you. Finally, we owe a debt of gratitude to our many students from whom we have learned and to the students who have used this text and provided feedback directly to us and through their instructors. Thank you.

MAH
CCM
AC

WHOLE FOODS,
whole people

Whole Foods Market is the largest natural food retailer in the world. With operations located primarily in the United States and also in Canada and the United Kingdom, Whole Foods sells natural and organic food products that include produce, meat, poultry, seafood, grocery products, baked and prepared goods, many drinks such as beer and wine, cheese, floral products, and pet products. The origin of the company dates to 1978 when John Mackey and his girlfriend used $45,000 in borrowed funds to start a small natural food store then named SaferWay. The store was located in Austin, Texas. John and his girlfriend lived in the space over the store (without a shower) because they were "kicked out" of their apartment for storing food products in it.

and its equipment was damaged. The total losses were approximately $400,000, and the company had no insurance. Interestingly, customers and neighbors helped the staff of the store to repair and clean up the damage. Creditors, vendors, and investors all partnered to help the store reopen only 28 days after the flood. With their assistance, Whole Foods survived this devastating natural disaster.

Whole Foods started to expand in 1984 when it opened its first store outside of Austin. The new store was located in Houston, followed by another store in Dallas and one in New Orleans. It also began acquiring other companies that sold natural foods, which helped to increase its expansion into new areas of the United States. In 2007, it expanded into international markets by opening its first Whole Foods branded store

In 1980, Mackey developed a partnership with Craig Weller and Mark Skiles, merging SaferWay with Weller's and Skiles's Clarksville Natural Grocer to create the Whole Foods Market. Its first store opened in 1980 with 12,500 square feet and 19 employees. This was a very large health food store relative to others at that time. There was a devastating flood in Austin within a year of its opening and the store was heavily damaged. Much of its inventory was ruined

in London, England. (In 2004, it acquired a small natural foods company in the United Kingdom, Fresh & Wild, but did not use the Whole Foods brand until opening its new store in London.) It also acquired one of its major U.S. competitors, Wild Oats, in 2007. It now has more than 54,000 employees in about 280 stores with annual sales of $7.95 billion. Thus, Whole Foods has become a major business enterprise and the most successful natural and organic food retailer in the world.

MANAGING HUMAN CAPITAL

Whole Foods Market has done a number of things right, thereby achieving considerable success. Yet, many people believe that one of the best things it has done is to implement an effective people-management system. Each Whole Foods store employs approximately 40 to as many as 650 associates. All of the associates are organized into self-directed teams; associates are referred to as team members. Each of the teams is responsible for a specific product or service area (e.g., prepared foods, meats and poultry, customer service). Team members report to a team leader, who then works with store management, referred to as store team leaders. The team members are a critically important part of the Whole Foods operation. Individuals are carefully selected and trained to be highly knowledgeable in their product areas, to offer friendly service, and to make critical decisions related to the types and quality of products offered to the public. Thus, they operate much differently than most "employees" in retail grocery

outlets. These team members work together with their team leader to make a number of decisions with regard to their specific areas, and they contribute to store level decisions as well. Some observers have referred to this approach as "workplace democracy." In fact, many of the team members are attracted to Whole Foods because of the discretion they have in making decisions regarding product lines and so on. Of course, there are other attractions such as the compensation. For example, the company's stock option program involves employees at all levels. In fact, 94 percent of the stock options offered by the company have been presented to nonexecutive members, including front-line team members. The company pays competitive wages and pays 100 percent of the health insurance premium for all associates working at least 30 hours per week, which includes 89 percent of its workforce. Although the annual deductible is high ($2,500), each associate receives a grant of up to $1,800 annually in a Personal Wellness Account to be used for health care out-of-pocket costs. All of the benefit options are voted on by the associates in the company. Current programs include options for dental, vision, disability, and life insurance in addition to the full medical coverage for full-time associates.

Whole Foods follows a democratic model in the selection of new associates. For example, potential new team members can apply for any one of the 13 teams that operate in most Whole Foods Markets. Current team members participate in the interview process and actually

vote on whether to offer a job to prospective colleagues. A candidate is generally given a four-week trial period to determine whether he or she has potential. At the end of that trial period, team members vote on whether to offer a permanent job to the candidate. The candidate must receive a two-thirds majority positive vote from the unit team members in order to be hired.

Teams also receive bonuses if they perform exceptionally well. They set goals relative to prior performance and must achieve those goals to attain a bonus. Exceptionally high-performing teams may earn up to $2 an hour more than their current wage base.

The top management of Whole Foods believes that the best philosophy is to build a shared identity with all team members. They do so by involving them in decisions and encouraging their participation at all levels in the business. They empower employees to make decisions and even allow them to participate in the decision regarding the benefit options, as noted above. All team members have access to full information on the company. It is referred to as Whole Foods' open-book policy. In this open-book policy, team members have access to the firm's financial records, which include compensation information for all associates and even the top management team and the CEO. Therefore, the firm operates with full transparency regarding its associates. This approach emphasizes the company's core values of collaboration and decentralization. The company attracts people who share those core values and tries to reward a highly engaged and productive workforce.

The company also limits the pay of top executives to no more than 19 times the lowest paid associate in the firm. While this amount has been increased over time in order to maintain competitive compensation for managers, it is still well below industry averages for top management team members. And, in recent times, John Mackey, the CEO, announced that he no longer will accept a salary above $1 annually or the stock options provided to him. Thus, his salary was reduced from $1 million to $1 per year. The money saved from his salary is donated to a fund to help needy associates.

The outcomes of this unique system for managing human capital have been impressive. For example, Whole Foods' voluntary turnover is much lower than the industry average. The industry average is almost 90 percent annually, but Whole Foods' data show that it has a voluntary turnover rate of approximately 26 percent. In addition, Whole Foods was ranked number 22 in the top 100 best companies to work for by *Fortune* magazine in 2009. It has been on the top 100 best companies to work for list for the past 12 years, and its ranking has been as high as number 5 (in 2007) but has always been among the best in the top 100.

In addition to its flat organization structure (few layers of management between associates and top managers) and decentralized decision making (e.g., selection of new associates), the company believes that each employee should feel a stake in the success of the company. In fact, this

TABLE 1   Whole Foods' Declaration of Interdependence (Five Core Values)

1. Selling the highest-quality natural and organic food products available.
2. Satisfying and delighting customers.
3. Supporting team member excellence and happiness.
4. Creating wealth through profits and growth.
5. Caring about communities and the environment.

is communicated in its "Declaration of Interdependence." The Declaration of Interdependence suggests that the company has five core values. They are listed in Table 1.

The company attempts to support team member excellence and happiness through its empowering work environment in which team members work together to create the results. In such an environment, they try to create a motivated work team that achieves the highest possible productivity. There is an emphasis on individuals taking responsibility for their success and failure and seeing both as opportunities for personal and organizational growth.

The company develops self-directed work teams and gives them significant decision-making authority to resolve problems and build a department and product line to satisfy and delight the customers. The company believes in providing open and timely information and in being highly transparent in all of its operations. It also focuses on achieving progress by continuously allowing associates to apply their collective creativity and intellectual capabilities to build a highly competitive and successful organization. Finally, the company emphasizes a shared fate

among all stakeholders. This is why there are no special privileges given to anyone, not even to top managers. It is assumed that everybody works together to achieve success.

SOCIAL AND COMMUNITY RESPONSIBILITIES

Whole Foods Market takes pride in being a responsible member of its community and of society. For example, it emphasizes the importance of sustainable agriculture. In particular, the firm tries to support organic farmers, growers, and the environment by a commitment to using sustainable agriculture and expanding the market for organic products. In this regard, the Whole Foods Market launched a program to loan approximately $10 million annually to help independent local producers around the country to expand. It holds seminars and teaches producers how to move their products onto grocery shelves and how to command and receive premium prices for their products. These seminars and related activities have been quite popular. As an example, its first seminar held in Colorado a few years ago attracted 130 growers, which was almost twice as many as expected. Overall, the Whole Foods Market does business with more than 2,400 independent growers.

Whole Foods Market also supports its local communities in other ways. For example, the company promotes active involvement in local communities by giving a minimum of 5 percent of its profits each year to a variety of community and nonprofit organizations. These actions encourage philanthropy and outreach in the communities that Whole Foods serves.

Whole Foods Market also tries to promote positive environmental practices. The company emphasizes the importance of recycling and reusing products and reducing waste wherever possible. Furthermore, Whole Foods was the first retailer to build a supermarket that met environmental standards of the Leadership in Energy and Environmental Design Green Building Rating System (LEED). It was the largest corporate purchaser of wind credits in the history of the United States when it purchased enough to offset 100 percent of its total electricity use in 2006. Finally, Whole Foods announced a new initiative a few years ago to create an animal compassion standard that emphasizes the firm's belief in the needs of animals. The company developed standards for each of the species that are used for foods and sold through their supermarkets.

Whole Foods launched a program to encourage higher wages and prices paid to farmers in poor countries, while simultaneously promoting environmentally safe practices. In fact, the company donates a portion of its proceeds to its Whole Planet Foundation, which in turn provides microloans to entrepreneurs in developing countries.

Very few, if any, major corporations, including competing supermarket chains, have established programs that rival those of the Whole Foods Market to meet social and community responsibilities.

SOME BUMPS IN THE ROAD

While the Whole Foods Market has been a highly successful company, it still has experienced some problems along the way. Obviously, it has produced a concept that has been imitated by other natural foods companies and a number of competing supermarkets as well. Yet, in general, Whole Foods has been able to maintain its competitive advantage and market leadership, partly by being the first to the market and partly because of its practices, which continue to generate a strong reputation and a positive company image. Yet, a number of firms have developed competing products and are making headway in selling organic foods, including some regular large supermarket chains. Even Wal-Mart has begun to offer organic foods in its grocery operations. In order to maintain its leadership and to continue to command a premium price, Whole Foods Market must continuously differentiate its products and its image so that people will buy from it rather than from competitors.

The top management of the Whole Foods Market has been strongly opposed to unionization. The belief is that the company pays workers well and treats them with dignity and respect and that a union is likely to interfere in its relationships with associates. Mackey, the CEO of the company, suggests that it is a campaign to "love the worker, not a union." Yet, the first union for Whole Foods was voted in at its Madison, Wisconsin, store. The vote by the Madison associates was 65 to 54 in favor of organizing a union. When this vote was announced, Mackey referred to it as a sad day in the history of the company. He suggested that the associates had made a mistake and believed that they would eventually realize the error of their ways. However, the Whole Foods Market executives have been able to fend off union efforts at other stores, including a campaign launched in 2009 that the company referred to as "union awareness training."

Another problem became evident in 2007, when it was announced that Mackey had, for a few years, posted on a Yahoo! financial message board anonymous online critiques of competitors and self-congratulating statements about the Whole Foods Market. These comments were made using a pseudonym so no one knew that he was the CEO of Whole Foods. This action was strongly criticized by analysts and others, and several questioned the ethics of his actions. Given that Whole Foods has emphasized its ethical approach to business and suggested that it conducts fair and open operations, such actions could be potentially harmful to the Whole Foods Market image and reputation. In fact, the company launched an investigation of his actions. In addition, the Securities and Exchange Commission (SEC) investigated some of the postings to Internet chat rooms by Mackey in which he used a pseudonym. The concern was that he may have released information that should not have been provided to the market. The Whole Foods' Board completed its investigation and reaffirmed its support for Mackey. In addition, the SEC investigated the incident but concluded that no enforcement action would be taken against the company or the CEO.

FIRM PERFORMANCE AND THE FUTURE

Whole Foods Market has performed well over the past several years, sustaining significant growth in sales and profits. Its stock price has also generally performed well. However, during the period 2005–2008, some analysts argued that the stock was overvalued, partly because they did not believe that Whole Foods' growth rate and returns could be sustained.

Undoubtedly, being able to maintain the growth rate will be difficult as the competition in its natural and organic foods grows and as the number of markets and opportunities narrows, particularly in the United States. This is especially of concern given the changed behaviors caused by the recent economic recession. Yet, some analysts are bullish on Whole Foods' stock. The price of its stock doubled early in 2009; according to some analysts, these outcomes portend the future because Whole Foods' business model seems to be strong in the face of a challenging economic environment. The company is highly profitable and continues to outperform its direct competitors.

Mackey has stated on several occasions that he does not make decisions on the basis of Wall Street's reactions. He argues that investors should not invest in his stock for the short term. Rather, they should look

for long-term value increases because he will make decisions in the best interest of the shareholders for the long term. Perhaps this approach will provide better returns over time, but only time will tell. Clearly, Whole Foods Market has been a very positive force in dealing with its associates through its highly unique means of managing human capital. It also has built a strong positive reputation and differentiated its products in the eyes of consumers. Yet, there are some challenges with which the firm must deal, such as growing competition and potential unionization. While the future likely remains bright, further evaluation will be needed to determine whether there will be continued growth and positive returns for all stakeholders of the Whole Foods Market.

Source: Whole Foods Market logo used with permission.

REFERENCES

1. 100 best companies to work for: Whole Foods Market 2009. *Fortune,* at http://money.cnn.com. accessed on June 15.
2. S. Cendrowski. 2009. What about Whole Foods? *Fortune,* July 20: 26.
3. Declaration of interdependence. 2007. Whole Foods Market website, at http://www.wholefoodsmarket.com, April 29.
4. C. Dillow. Innovating toward health care reform, the Whole Foods way. 2009. *Fast Company.com, at* http://fastcompany.com, August 12.
5. P.J. Erickson & L. Gratton. 2007. What it means to work here. *Harvard Business Review,* March: 85 (3): 104–112.
6. J.P. Fried. 2007. At Whole Foods, a welcome sign for immigrants seeking jobs. *New York Times,* at http://www.nytimes.com, April 29.
7. S. Hammer & T. McNicol. 2007. Low-cow compensation. *Business* 2.0, May: 62.
8. M. Hogan. 2007. Whole Foods: A little too rich? *BusinessWeek,* at http://www.businessweek.com, July 21.
9. P. Huetlin. 2007. Flagship Whole Foods opens in London. *BusinessWeek,* at http://www.businessweek.com, July 5.
10. L. Hunt. 2005. Whole Foods Market, Inc. At http://www.marketbusting.comlcasestudies, March 30.
11. D. Kesmodel & J. Eig. 2007. Unraveling rahodeb: A grocer's brash style takes unhealthy turn. *Wall Street Journal Online,* at http://oniine.wsj.com, July 30.
12. N.S. Koehn & K. Miller. 2007. John Mackey and Whole Foods Market. *Harvard Business School Case #9-807-111,* May 14.
13. J. Mackey. 2007. I no longer want to work for money. *Fast Company,* at http://www.fastcompany.com, February.
14. A. Nathans. 2003. Love the worker, not the union, a store says as some organize. *New York Times,* at http://www.nytimes.com, May 24.
15. Our core values. 2009. Whole Foods Market website, at http://www.wholefoodsmarket.com, April 29.
16. K. Richardson & D. Kesmodel. 2007. Why Whole Foods investors may want to shop around. *Wall Street Journal Online,* at http://online.wsj.com, November 23.
17. C. Rohwedder. 2007. Whole Foods opens new front. *Wall Street Journal Online,* at http://online.wsj.com, June 6.
18. S. Smith. 2009. Something stinks at Whole Foods. *Counterpunch,* at http://www.counterpunch.org, May 8–10.
19. J. Sonnenfeld. 2007. What's rotten at Whole Foods. *Business Week,* at http://www.businessweek.com, July 17.

20. B. Steverman. 2009. Wal-Mart vs. Whole foods. *Business-Week*, at http://www.businessweek.com, May 14.
21. S. Taub. 2008. Whole Foods "blogging" probe dropped by SEC. *CFO*, at http://www.cfo.com, April 28.
22. S. Thurm. 2007. Whole Foods CEO serves up heated word for FTC. *Wall Street Journal Online*, at http://online.swj.com, June 27.
23. Welcome to Whole Foods Market. 2009. Whole Foods Market website, http://www.wholefoodsmarket.com, August 30.
24. J.E. Wells & T. Haglock. 2005. Whole Foods Market, Inc. *Harvard Business School Case #9-705-476*, June 9.
25. Whole Foods closes buyout of Wild Oats. 2007. *New York Times*, at http://www.nytimes.com, August 29.
26. Whole Foods Market soars to #5 spot on *Fortune's "100 Best Companies to Work For"* list. Whole Foods Market website, at http://www.wholefoodsmarket.com, January 9.
27. Whole Foods Market. 2007. Wikipedia, at http://www.wikipedia.com, September 2.
28. Whole Foods promotes local buying. 2007. *New York Times*, at http://www.nytimes.com, April 29.

WHOLE FOODS CASE DISCUSSION QUESTIONS

Chapter 1
1. Describe how Whole Foods uses human capital as a source of competitive advantage.
2. Identify the aspects of high-involvement management contained in Whole Foods' approach to managing its associates.

Chapter 2
1. Compared to other companies in the service sector, is Whole Foods more or less likely to experience discrimination problems? Explain your answer.
2. How could Whole Foods' democratic model of selection interfere with the development or continuance of a diverse workforce? What should it do to prevent difficulties?

Chapter 3
1. How do you think that globalization will affect Whole Foods over time? Please explain several ways it could affect the company operations.
2. In what ways can national culture affect the management of human capital? Will Whole Foods have to adapt its democratic approach to selecting new team members or the benefits it provides to its associates as it expands further into international markets?

Chapter 4
1. To what extent do you think that training and associate learning would be more important for Whole Foods than for other grocery stores?
2. What type of perceptual problems on the part of associates and the public may have resulted from the scandal regarding John Mackey's blog activities?

Chapter 5
1. Given the nature of Whole Foods' jobs and the way in which associates are selected, what type of personality traits are important for Whole Foods' associates to possess?
2. Compared to the industry average, Whole Foods has a low turnover rate and is consistently ranked as a great place to work. Why do you think Whole Foods' associates are so satisfied and committed to the organization?

Chapter 6
1. Are Whole Foods' team members likely to experience problems with procedural and/or distributive justice? Explain.
2. Which of the major motivational practices are emphasized by Whole Foods in its management system? For example, do they include meaningful rewards, tying rewards to performance, designing enriched jobs, providing feedback, or clarifying expectations and goals?

Chapter 7
1. Based on the demand–control and effort–reward models of stress, are Whole Foods' team members likely to experience a great deal of stress? What about its executives?
2. Does Whole Foods need a wellness program? Why or why not?

Chapter 8
1. Is John Mackey a transformational leader? Why or why not?
2. Based on contingency theories of leadership, what approach to leadership should be used by Whole Foods' team leaders?

Chapter 9
1. Whole Foods' open-book policy allows all associates to have full access to all information about the company and its executives. Would this degree of open communication work as well in other companies? Why or why not? What impact do you think this degree of transparency has on the attitudes and behavior of Whole Foods' associates?

2. What ethical issues arise from John Mackey's use of a pseudonym to post opinions, information, and critiques on blog sites?

Chapter 10

1. What decision styles does John Mackey appear to use? Do these fit his situation?
2. Which group decision-making pitfalls appear most likely within Whole Foods' teams, and which decision-making techniques would you recommend to counter those pitfalls?

Chapter 11

1. What policies and procedures does Whole Foods enact that allow it to develop successful associate teams?
2. What impact do you think that the process of allowing team members to vote on hiring new members has on the dynamics and performance of the Whole Foods teams?

Chapter 12

1. Whole Foods' "Declaration of Interdependence" states that two of the company's core values are "creating wealth through profits and growth" and "caring about our communities and the environment." Often, these two values are in conflict for many companies. How does Whole Foods resolve this conflict?

2. Whole Foods has been opposed to the unionization of its associates. However, associates in a Madison, Wisconsin, store voted to become unionized. What type of conflicts or power struggles may have caused this to occur?

Chapter 13

1. Analyze the effects of the democratic approach to store operations and hiring new associates on store performance.
2. What does the transparency about company financial data and associate and managers' compensation communicate about Whole Foods' culture? How does the Declaration of Interdependence reflect aspects of Whole Foods' culture?

Chapter 14

1. Analyze how Whole Foods has managed change over the years since it started.
2. Whole Foods now faces a significant amount of competition. How should it respond to the changes in the competitive landscape of its industry? What future challenges do you envision for Whole Foods' market?

THE STRATEGIC LENS

| ORGANIZATIONAL BEHAVIOR | ORGANIZATIONAL DIVERSITY | ORGANIZATIONAL BEHAVIOR |
| A STRATEGIC APPROACH | | A GLOBAL CONTEXT |

INDIVIDUAL PROCESSES
LEARNING AND PERCEPTION
PERSONALITY, INTELLIGENCE, ATTITUDES, AND EMOTIONS
WORK MOTIVATION
STRESS AND WELL-BEING

GROUPS, TEAMS, AND SOCIAL PROCESSES
LEADERSHIP
COMMUNICATION
DECISION MAKING BY INDIVIDUALS AND GROUPS
GROUPS AND TEAMS
CONFLICT, NEGOTIATION, POWER, AND POLITICS

THE ORGANIZATIONAL CONTEXT
ORGANIZATIONAL STRUCTURE AND CULTURE
ORGANIZATIONAL CHANGE AND DEVELOPMENT

PART 1

the strategic lens

This book describes the rich and important concepts that make up the field of organizational behavior. We have based the book on cutting-edge research as well as current practices in organizations. Beyond this, the book is unique in presenting these concepts through a strategic lens. That is, in each chapter, we explain the strategic importance of the primary concepts presented in the chapter. Our discussions emphasize how managers can use knowledge of these concepts to improve organizational performance.

In Part I, we develop and explain the strategic lens for organizational behavior. To begin, we describe in **Chapter 1** the concept of competitive advantage and how behavior in an organization affects the organization's ability to gain and maintain an advantage over its competitors. Gaining and maintaining a competitive advantage is critical for organizations to perform at high levels and provide returns to their stakeholders (including owners). We emphasize the importance and management of human capital for high performance and describe the high-involvement organization and how to manage associates to achieve it.

Chapter 2 examines the critical topic of organizational diversity. Given the demographic diversity in the United States, all organizations' workforces are likely to become increasingly diverse. Thus, it is important to understand diversity and how to manage it effectively in order to gain a competitive advantage. This chapter explains how these outcomes can be achieved.

Chapter 3 discusses managing organizations in a global environment. International markets offer more opportunities but also are likely to present greater challenges than domestic markets. Understanding the complexities of managing in international markets is a necessity. It is especially important to understand how to manage diverse cultures and operations in varying types of institutional environments.

The three chapters of Part I provide the setting for exploring the topics covered in the chapters that follow.

a strategic approach to organizational behavior

exploring behavior in action

Strategic Use of Human Capital: A Key Element of Organizational Success

In their book, *The New American Workplace,* James O'Toole and Edward Lawler described the existence of high-involvement, high-performance companies that spanned many industries. Examples of such companies are Nucor, W.L. Gore & Associates, Proctor & Gamble, and the Men's Wearhouse, among others. For example, Proctor & Gamble adopted high-involvement work practices at some of its manufacturing facilities, including empowerment of work teams to allocate the tasks among their members, establish their own work schedules, recruit new members to their team and even to select the methods used to accomplish their tasks. In addition, P&G invests in building human capital, and much

of the training is done by P&G managers instead of human resource management or training specialists. In fact, P&G views work life as a career-long learning and development process. P&G has a different "college" for educating its workforce in the knowledge and skills needed for their current and future jobs. The company also carefully screens all candidates in the hiring process. The company received approximately 400,000 applications in 2009 for entry-level management positions and hired fewer than 2,000 (less than one-half of one percent).

The Men's Wearhouse is another company benefiting from high-involvement work practices. George Zimmer, founder and chief executive officer (CEO) of the Men's Wearhouse, described his company's approach in managing the people who carry out day-to-day work:

> We give people the space they need to be creative, set goals, define strategies, and implement a game plan. We call it "painting our own canvas." Our people like that freedom and the underlying trust behind it.

knowledge objectives

After reading this chapter, you should be able to:

1. Define organizational behavior and explain the strategic approach to OB.
2. Provide a formal definition of *organization*.
3. Describe the nature of human capital.
4. Discuss the conditions under which human capital is a source of competitive advantage for an organization.
5. Describe positive organizational behavior and explain how it can contribute to associates' productivity.
6. Explain the five characteristics of high-involvement management and the importance of this approach to management.

Under this philosophy, individuals are given substantial discretion in choosing work methods and goals. Training is both quantitatively and qualitatively greater at the Men's Wearhouse than at the vast majority of retailers. Such training provides the base for effective use of discretion by individuals.

Reward systems that value individual and team productivity help to encourage the type of behavior that is desired. Responsibility and accountability complement the system.

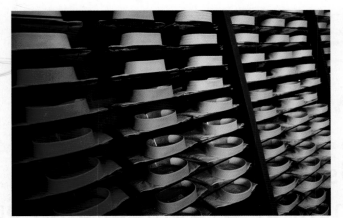

©iStockphoto

The base for the system of discretion and accountability is a core set of workplace beliefs, including the following:

1. Work should be fulfilling.

2. Workplaces should be fearless and energized.

3. Work and family life should be balanced.

4. Leaders should serve followers.

5. Employees should be treated like customers.

6. People should not be afraid to make mistakes.

The success of the Men's Wearhouse should promote frequent attempts to imitate its practices, but this has not been the case. Instead, confronted with difficult industry conditions, managers in many retailing firms have attempted to minimize costs through low compensation and little training. They have implemented supervision and surveillance systems designed to tightly control employees. Many companies make assumptions about their workforce, but their actions do not allow the human potential existing in their workforce.

Yet, some of the highest-performing companies treat their associates in a different way. The leadership of these 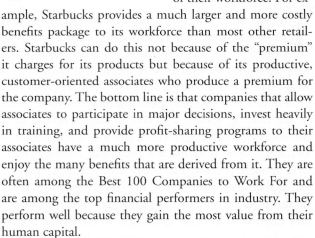 companies believe that valuing people is crucial for business success. They believe they get more out of their employees by providing them power and autonomy, and the results support this belief. These companies continue to grow, have low labor costs and achieve high profits while paying high compensation because of the productivity of their workforce. For example, Starbucks provides a much larger and more costly benefits package to its workforce than most other retailers. Starbucks can do this not because of the "premium" it charges for its products but because of its productive, customer-oriented associates who produce a premium for the company. The bottom line is that companies that allow associates to participate in major decisions, invest heavily in training, and provide profit-sharing programs to their associates have a much more productive workforce and enjoy the many benefits that are derived from it. They are often among the Best 100 Companies to Work For and are among the top financial performers in industry. They perform well because they gain the most value from their human capital.

Sources: "Fulfillment at Work," *Men's Wearhouse*, September 27, 2009, at http://www.menswearhouse.com; R. Crockett. 2009. "How P&G Finds and Keeps a Prized Workforce," *BusinessWeek*, Apr. 9, at http://www.businessweek.com; "Fortune 100 Best Companies to Work For 2009," *CNNMoney*, Feb. 2, 2009, at http://www.money.cnn.com; J. O'Toole and E. E. Lawler, III. 2007. "A Piece of Work," *Fast Company*, Dec. 19, at http://www.fastcompany.com; M. Cianciolo. 2007. "Tailoring Growth at Men's Wearhouse: Fool by the Numbers," *The Motley Fool*, May 23 at http://www.fool.com; C.A. O'Reilly and J. Pfeffer. 2000. *Hidden Value: How Great Companies Achieve Extraordinary Results with Ordinary People* (Boston: Harvard Business School Press); G. Zimmer. 2005. "Building Community through Shared Values, Goals, and Experiences," at http://www.menswearhouse.com/home_page/common_threads; G. Zimmer. 2005. "Our Philosophy," at http://www.menswearhouse.com/home_page/common_threads.

the strategic importance of *Organizational Behavior*

The examples of Men's Wearhouse, Procter & Gamble, and Starbucks show the powerful difference that a firm's human capital can make. Faced with less-than-favorable industry characteristics and a labor pool that many find unattractive in the retail field, Men's Wearhouse and Starbucks have succeeded in part by paying careful attention to human behavior. Any firm can sell men's clothing and coffee, but it requires special management to effectively embrace and use to advantage the complexities and subtleties of human behavior. From the motivational and leadership practices of managers to the internal dynamics of employee-based teams to the values that provide the base for the organization's culture, successful firms develop approaches that unleash the potential of their people (human capital).

In the current highly competitive landscape, the ability to understand, appreciate, and effectively leverage human capital is critical in all industries. A strategic approach to organizational behavior is focused on these issues. In this chapter, we introduce the concept of organizational behavior and explain how to view it through a strategic lens in order to enhance organizational performance.

To introduce the strategic approach to organizational behavior, or OB, we address several issues. First, we define organizational behavior and discuss its strategic importance for organizational performance. Next, we explore the concept of human capital and its role in organizations. We then discuss how human capital most likely contributes to a competitive advantage for an organization. An explanation of high-involvement management follows. This form of management is helpful in developing and using human capital and is becoming increasingly important as firms search for ways to maximize the potential of all of their people (managers and nonmanagers). In the final section of the chapter, we describe the model and plan for the concepts explained in this book.

Basic Elements of Organizational Behavior

Important resources for businesses and other types of organizations include technologies, distribution systems, financial assets, patents, and the knowledge and skills of people. **Organizational behavior** involves the actions of individuals and groups in an organizational context. **Managing organizational behavior** focuses on acquiring, developing, and applying the knowledge and skills of people. The **strategic OB approach** rests on the premise that people are the foundation of an organization's competitive advantages.[1] An organization might have exceptionally high-quality products and services, excellent customer service, best-in-class cost structure, or some other advantage, but all of these are outcomes of the capabilities of the organization's people—its human capital. If organized and managed effectively, the knowledge and skills of the people in the organization drive sustainable competitive advantage and long-term financial performance.[2] Thus, the strategic approach to OB involves organizing and managing the people's knowledge and skills effectively to implement the organization's strategy and gain a competitive advantage.

Individual, interpersonal, and organizational factors determine the behavior and the ultimate value of people in an organization; these factors are shown in Exhibit 1-1. For individuals, factors such as the ability to learn, the ability to be self-managing, technical skills, personality characteristics, and personal values are important. These elements represent or are related to important capabilities. At the interpersonal level, factors such

organizational behavior
The actions of individuals and groups in an organizational context.

managing organizational behavior
Actions focused on acquiring, developing, and applying the knowledge and skills of people.

strategic OB approach
An approach that involves organizing and managing people's knowledge and skills effectively to implement the organization's strategy and gain a competitive advantage.

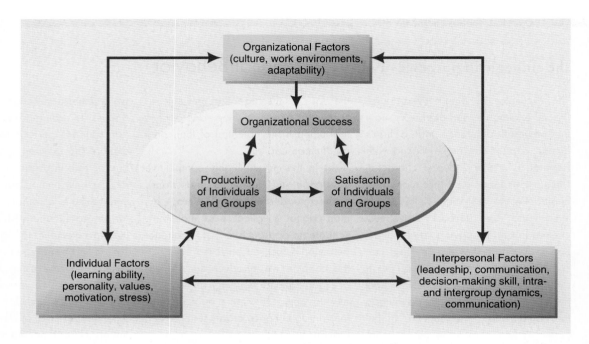

Exhibit 1-1 Factors and Outcomes of a Strategic Approach to Organizational Behavior

as quality of leadership, communication within and between groups, and conflict within and between groups are noteworthy. These elements influence the degree to which the capabilities of individuals are unleashed and fully utilized within an organization. Finally, at the organizational level, the culture and policies of the organization are among the most important factors, as they influence whether the talents and positive attitudes of individuals are effectively leveraged to create positive outcomes.

The factors discussed above interact to produce the outcomes of productivity, satisfaction, and organizational success. *Productivity* refers to the output of individuals and groups, whereas *satisfaction* relates to the feelings that individuals and groups have about their work and the workplace. *Organizational success* is defined in terms of competitive advantage and ultimately financial performance. In essence, then, a strategic approach to organizational behavior requires understanding how individual, interpersonal, and organizational factors influence the behavior and value of the people in an organization, where value is reflected in productivity, satisfaction, and ultimately the organization's competitive advantages and financial success.

The Importance of Using a Strategic Lens

Studying organizational behavior with a strategic lens is valuable for managers and aspiring managers at all levels of the organization, as well as for the workers who complete the basic tasks. For example, effective senior managers spend much of their time talking with insiders and outsiders about vision, strategy, and other major issues crucial to the direction of the organization.[3] Senior leaders make the strategic decisions for the firm.[4] Skills in conceptualizing, communicating, and understanding the perspectives of others are critical for these discussions, and these skills are addressed by strategic OB. Senior managers also spend time helping middle managers to define and redefine their roles and to manage conflict, because middle managers are often central to the organization's communication networks.[5] Skills in listening, conflict management, negotiating, and motivating are crucial for these activities. Finally, senior managers invest effort in shaping the internal norms and informal practices of the organization (that is, creating and maintaining the culture). Skill in interpersonal influence is an important part of this work. The strategic approach to OB addresses each of these issues.

In recent times, senior managers have commonly been referred to as *strategic leaders*.[6] However, exercising strategic leadership is not a function of one's level in the organization; rather, it is a matter of focus and behavior. Strategic leaders think and act strategically, and they use the skills noted above to motivate people and build trusting relationships to help implement the organization's strategy. Although their primary tasks differ from senior managers, middle and lower-level managers also can act as strategic leaders in the accomplishment of their tasks.[7]

Effective middle managers spend much of their time championing strategic ideas with senior managers and helping the firm to remain adaptive.[8] They also play an important role in implementing the organization's strategy. They serve as champions of the strategy and work with other middle managers and lower-level managers to build the processes and set them in motion to implement the strategy. Skills in networking, communicating, and influencing are important for these aspects of their work. Middle managers also spend time processing data and information for use by individuals at all levels of the firm, requiring skills in analysis and communication. When delivering the strategic initiatives to lower-level managers, skills in communicating, motivating, understanding values, and managing stress are among the most important. A strategic approach to OB addresses each of these aspects of managerial work.

Effective lower-level managers spend a great deal of their time coaching the firm's **associates**—our term for the workers who carry out the basic tasks.[9] Skills in teaching, listening, understanding personalities, and managing stress are among the most important for performing these activities. Lower-level managers also remove obstacles for associates and deal with personal problems that affect their work. Skills in negotiating and influencing others are critical for removing obstacles, whereas skills in counseling and understanding personalities are important for dealing with personal problems. Finally, lower-level managers expend effort to design jobs, team structures, and reward systems. Skills in analysis, negotiating, and group dynamics are among the most important for these activities. The strategic approach to OB addresses each of these aspects of managerial work.

Lower-level managers will be more effective when they understand the organization's strategy and how their work and that of their associates fit into the strategy. Much of what they do is required to implement the strategy. It is also helpful for these managers to take a longer-term view. If they do not take a strategic approach, many of these managers are likely to focus on short-term problems. In fact, they may emphasize resolving problems without examining how they can prevent them in the future. Taking a strategic approach enables them to use their skills to prevent problems, implement the strategy effectively, and complete their current tasks efficiently while remaining focused on the future.

associates
The workers who carry out the basic tasks.

Despite the relevance of formal study in OB, some people believe that managers can be successful solely on the basis of common sense. If this were true, fewer organizations would have difficulty unleashing the potential of people, and there would be less dissatisfaction and unhappiness with jobs. Also, if this were true, absenteeism and turnover rates would be lower. The truth is that fully leveraging the capabilities of people involves subtleties that are complex and difficult to manage. Common sense cannot be the only basis of action for managers. Effective managers deeply understand that knowledge about people and organizations is the true source of their success.

Without meaningful working knowledge of OB, managers' efforts to be successful resemble those of the drunkard and his keys. According to this classic story, the drunkard dropped his keys by the car but could not find them because it was very dark there. So, instead of bringing light to the appropriate area, he looked under a nearby streetlight where he could see better![10]

Managers in today's fast-paced organizations cannot afford to adopt the drunkard's approach when working with associates and each other, especially not in a challenging economic environment with significant competition. They must avoid looking for answers where it is easiest to see. Managers are often unsuccessful when they fail to develop the insights and skills necessary for working with others effectively.

In closing our discussion regarding the importance of understanding organizational behavior, we focus on the findings of two research studies. In both studies, the investigators examined the impact of formal business education on skills in information gathering, quantitative analysis, and dealing with people.[11] Significantly, they found that business education had positive effects on these important skills, including the interpersonal skills of leadership and helping others to grow. These findings suggest that understanding a strategic approach to OB can add value to our managerial knowledge and skills. There is no substitute for experience, but formal study can be very helpful in providing important insights and guidance.

Foundations of a Strategic Approach to Organizational Behavior

Insights from several disciplines inform our understanding of OB. The field builds on behavioral science disciplines, including psychology, social psychology, sociology, economics, and cultural anthropology. A strategic approach to OB, however, differs from these disciplines in two important ways. First, it integrates knowledge from all of these areas to understand behavior in organizations. It does not address organizational phenomena from the limited perspective of any one discipline. Second, it focuses on behaviors and processes that help to create competitive advantages and financial success. Unlike basic social science disciplines, where the goal is often to understand human and group behavior, the goal of the strategic OB approach is to improve the performance of organizations.

One might ask the following questions: Can taking courses in psychology, social psychology, sociology, economics, and cultural anthropology provide the knowledge needed to be an effective manager or to successfully accept the responsibility of working as a key member of an organization? Is it necessary to take a course in organizational behavior?

Acquiring knowledge directly from other disciplines can inform the study of organizational behavior. Knowledge from other disciplines, however, is not a substitute for the unique understanding and insights that can be gained from studying OB from a strategic perspective. As noted earlier, a strategic approach to OB integrates useful concepts from other disciplines while emphasizing their application in organizations.

Gaining an effective working knowledge of organizational behavior helps those who want to become successful managers. The following points summarize this important field of study:

1. There are complexities and subtleties involved in fully leveraging the capabilities of people. Common sense alone does not equip the manager with sufficient understanding of how to leverage human capabilities.

2. Managers must avoid the allure of seeking simple answers to resolve organizational issues. A working knowledge of OB helps managers gain the confidence required to empower associates and work with them to find creative solutions to problems that arise. The complexity of organizational life requires that managers and associates perform at high levels to contribute to organizational success and to achieve personal growth.

3. The strategic approach to OB integrates important behavioral science knowledge within an organizational setting and emphasizes application. This knowledge cannot be obtained from information derived independently from other specialized fields (psychology, economics, and the like).

Definition of an Organization

As we have already emphasized, OB is focused on organizations and what happens inside them. This is important, because organizations play an important role in modern society. Several commentators from Harvard University expressed it this way: "Modern societies are not market economies; they are organizational economies in which companies are the chief actors in creating value and advancing economic progress."[12] But what is an organization? Below we provide a formal definition of this term.

Although it is sometimes difficult to define the term *organization* precisely, most people agree that an organization is characterized by these features:[13]

- Network of individuals
- System
- Coordinated activities
- Division of labor
- Goal orientation
- Continuity over time, regardless of change in individual membership

Thus, we define an **organization** as a collection of individuals, whose members may change over time, forming a coordinated system of specialized activities for the purpose of achieving specific goals over an extended period of time.

A prominent type of organization is the business organization, such as Intel, Microsoft, or Procter & Gamble. There are other important types of organizations as well. Public-sector organizations (e.g., government organizations), for example, have a major

organization
A collection of individuals forming a coordinated system of specialized activities for the purpose of achieving certain goals over an extended period of time.

Creating Innovation: Leading and Managing the Human Capital at Apple

BusinessWeek has ranked Apple as the most innovative company for the past several years (2007–2009). And, largely because of Apple's successful innovations, Steve Jobs has been chosen by *Fortune* as the CEO of the decade (2000–2009). How has Apple achieved this lofty status? The following statement by Apple CEO, Steve Jobs explains, "Innovation has nothing to do with how many R&D dollars you have. When Apple came up with the Mac, IBM was spending at least 100 times more on R&D. It's not about money. It's about the people you have, how they're led, and how much you get it." In the early 1990s, Apple redesigned its workplace for the R&D associates, providing them both with private offices and also common areas where they could gather and share ideas, engage in teamwork, and generally discuss their research. A former manager at Apple notes that Apple's success is based on empowering its associates, delegating authority and responsibility down in the organization, and allowing the people a lot of freedom.

The results are obvious. *BusinessWeek* describes Apple as the creative king. For example, to launch the iPod, Apple's immensely successful portable music player, it integrated seven different innovations. It was able to create these innovations because of the innovation culture created at Apple and the high-quality scientists and engineers it has attracted to the company. Apple managers encourage and nurture a sense of community in which a passion for creative designs and innovation exists. Apple's designs have been described as more elegant, functional for customers, and effective than those developed by competitors. In short, Apple sets the standard in design. Apple and other innovative companies are the stars today and in the future. For example, Apple's iPhone has changed the standard in the wireless communications industry.

Apple is very careful in the hiring process by recruiting people who share its values and are passionate about what they do. In addition, they provide substantial training to build their skills and to emphasize the importance of working as a team. Yet, associates are valued as individuals;

© Justin Sullivan/Getty Images, Inc.

for example, staff associates in the Apple retail stores have personal business cards. This approach also suggests caring and quality to customers, not typical of most retail organizations.

Steve Jobs is a critical component of Apple's success, as suggested by his selection as the CEO of the decade. His vision and ability to see opportunities in future markets where others see only challenges has helped Apple rise above competitors and perform better than most other businesses in the world. Yet, his vision is only as good as the creativity and productivity of Apple's managers and associates. Warren Bennis states it this way, "The real test of exemplary leadership … [is in] developing a deep, talented bench who … can unite a company and unleash creativity in their own way." Michael Hawley, professional pianist and computer scientist, says that he thinks "of Apple as a great jazz orchestra." Hawley suggested that Apple has a talented staff and that the conductor's job is largely nominal at this stage.

© Justin Sullivan/Getty Images, Inc.

It involves continuing to attract highly talented members and adding energy in places where they are needed.

Apple's performance in the first decade of the 21st century has been exceptional. Sales of each of its major products have increased dramatically (several of those products were developed and introduced to the market in this decade). And the market value of the company increased by over $250 billion during the decade. Thus, Apple's passion for innovation and the power of its human capital portends a very bright future for the company.

Sources: A. Lashinsky. 2009. "The Decade of Steve: How Apple's Imperious, Brilliant CEO Transformed American Business," *Fortune*, Nov. 23, pp. 93–100; "The 50 Most Innovative Companies," *BusinessWeek*, at http://bwnt.businessweek.com/interactive_reports/innovative_50_2009, Nov. 16, 2009; S. Lohr. 2009. "One Day You're Indispensible, the Next Day …," *New York Times*, at http://www.nytimes.com, Jan. 18; A. Frankel. 2007. "Magic Shop," *Fast Company*, at http://www.fastcompany.com, Dec. 19; J. Scanton. 2007. "Apple Sets the Design Standard," *BusinessWeek.com*, at http://www.businessweek.com, Jan. 8; B. Helm. 2005. "Apple's Other Legacy: Top Designers," BusinessWeek.com, www.businessweek.com, Sept. 6; R. Enderle. 2004. "Apple's Competitive Advantage," *TechNewsWorld*, at http://www.technewsworld.com/story, Mar. 8.

presence in most countries. Although we focus primarily on business firms in this book, the strategic approach to OB applies to the public sector as well as the not-for-profit sector. For example, we can discuss motivating associates in the context of business firms, but motivating people is important in all types of organizations. Some organizations may have more motivational problems than others, but the knowledge of how to motivate workers is critical for managers in all types of situations.

As explained in the *Experiencing Organizational Behavior* feature, Apple has achieved significant success because of its innovations. In turn, Apple's innovations are due to the quality associates working in design, its innovation culture, and the way managers lead by empowering the associates to be creative and develop innovations. Apple's strategic leaders (exemplified by its CEO, Steve Jobs) are willing to take risks, and they nurture the innovation culture. But it also requires strategic leadership to implement Apple's innovation strategy throughout the company. As noted in the quote by Apple CEO Steve Jobs, the basic component of Apple's innovation is its human capital. Thus, Apple invests significant resources and energy into attracting, holding, and leading effectively high-quality human capital.

The Role of Human Capital in Creating Competitive Advantage

We have already noted the importance of human capital and competitive advantage to strategic OB. We now examine these concepts more closely.

The Nature of Human Capital

An organization's resource base includes both tangible and intangible resources. Property, factories, equipment, and inventory are examples of tangible resources. Historically, these types of resources have been the primary means of production and competition.[14] This is less true today because intangible resources have become critically important for organizations to successfully compete in the global economy. Intangible resources, including the reputation of the organization, trust between managers and associates, knowledge and skills of associates, organizational culture, brand name, and relationships with customers and suppliers, are the organization's nonphysical economic assets that provide value.[15] Such assets are often deeply rooted in a company's history and experiences, for they tend to develop through day-to-day actions and accumulate over time.[16] On a comparative basis, it is more difficult to quantify the value of intangible resources than that of tangible resources, but the importance of intangible resources continues to increase nonetheless.

human capital
The sum of the skills, knowledge, and general attributes of the people in an organization.

Human capital is a critical intangible resource. As a successful business executive recently stated, "Burn down my buildings and give me my people, and we will rebuild the company in a year. But leave my buildings and take away my people ... and I'll have a real problem."[17] As we highlighted in the opening case, **human capital** is the sum of the skills, knowledge, and general attributes of the people in an organization.[18] It represents capacity for today's work and the potential to exploit tomorrow's opportunities. Human capital encompasses not only easily observed skills, such as those associated with operating machinery or selling products, but also the skills, knowledge, and capabilities of managers and associates for learning, communicating, motivating, building trust, and effectively working on teams. It also includes basic values, beliefs, and attitudes.

Human capital does not depreciate in value as it is used, but rather, it is commonly enhanced through use. Contrast this with tangible resources—for example, manufacturing equipment—whose productive capacity or value declines with use. In economic terms, we can say that human capital does not suffer from the law of diminishing returns. In fact, increasing returns are associated with applications of knowledge because knowledge tends to expand with use.[19] In other words, we learn more as we apply knowledge. Knowledge, then, is "infinitely expansible" and grows more valuable as it is shared and used over time.[20]

Knowledge has become a critical resource for many firms.[21] Knowledge plays a key role in gaining and sustaining an advantage over competitors. Firms that have greater knowledge about their customers, markets, technologies, competitors, and themselves can use this knowledge to gain a competitive advantage. Because most knowledge in organizations is held by the managers and associates, it is important to acquire and hold a highly knowledgeable workforce to perform well.[22] Because of the importance of knowledge and human capital, firms need to invest in continuous development of their human capital. The goal is to enhance organizational learning and build the knowledge and skills in the firm. In short, firms try to acquire and enrich their human capital.[23]

The importance of human capital and knowledge is explained in the *Experiencing Organizational Behavior* on innovation. Apple is able to be a leader in innovation largely because of its high-quality human capital and the manner in which it empowers its associates working in design. These associates developed and designed the highly successful iPod and iPhone, for which major sales have been achieved.

competitive advantage
An advantage enjoyed by an organization that can perform some aspect of its work better than competitors can or in a way that competitors cannot duplicate, such that it offers products/services that are more valuable to customers.

The Concept of Competitive Advantage

A **competitive advantage** results when an organization can perform some aspect of its work better than competitors can or when it can perform the work in a way that competitors cannot duplicate.[24] By performing the work differently from and better than competitors, the organization offers products/services that are more valuable for the customers.[25] For example, Apple developed and marketed the iPod, which took significant market share from Sony's previously highly successful Walkman MP3 players. Its iPhone did the same in the wireless communications market. As noted by the statement by Steve Jobs, Apple's CEO, the primary difference in Apple's ability to create innovation is its people and how they are led.

Human Capital as a Source of Competitive Advantage

Although human capital is crucial for competitive advantage, not all organizations have the human resources needed for success. The degree to which human capital is useful for creating true competitive advantage is determined by its value, rareness, and difficulty to imitate.[26]

Value

In a general sense, the value of human capital can be defined as the extent to which individuals are capable of handling the basic work of an organization. Lawyers with poor legal training do not add value to a law firm because they cannot provide high-quality legal services. Similarly, individuals with poor skills in painting and caulking do not add value to a house-painting company.

More directly, **human capital value** can be defined as the extent to which individuals are capable of producing work that supports an organization's strategy for competing in the marketplace.[27] In general, business firms emphasize one of two basic strategies. The first involves creating low-cost products or services for the customer while maintaining acceptable or good quality.[28] Buyers at the Closeout Division of Consolidated Stores, Inc., for example, scour the country to purchase low-cost goods. Their ability to find such goods through manufacturers' overruns and discontinued styles is crucial to the success of Closeout, the largest U.S. retailer of closeout merchandise. The buyers' skills allow the division to sell goods at below-discount prices.[29] The second strategy involves differentiating products or services from those of competitors on the basis of special features or superior quality and charging higher prices for the higher-value goods.[30] Ralph Lauren designers, for example, create special features for which customers are willing to pay a premium.[31]

Human capital plays an important role in the development and implementation of these strategies. For example, top managers are generally highly valuable resources for the firm. Their human capital as perceived by investors coupled with the strategic decisions that they make affect the investors' decisions about whether to invest in the firm.[32] Yet, most senior managers' knowledge and skills become obsolete very quickly because of the rapidly changing competitive landscape. Thus, these managers must invest time and effort to continuously enrich their capabilities in order to maintain their value to the firm.[33] Overall, managers must expend considerable effort to acquire quality human capital and demonstrate to the firm's external constituencies its value.[34]

Rareness

Human capital rareness is the extent to which the skills and talents of an organization's people are unique in the industry.[35] In some cases, individuals with rare skills are

human capital value
The extent to which individuals are capable of producing work that supports an organization's strategy for competing in the marketplace.

human capital rareness
The extent to which the skills and talents of an organization's people are unique in the industry.

hired into the organization. Corporate lawyers with relatively rare abilities to reduce the tensions of disgruntled consumers, programmers with the unusual ability to produce thousands of lines of code per day with few errors, and house painters who are exceptionally gifted can be hired from the outside. In other cases, individuals develop rare skills inside the organization.[36] Training and mentoring programs assist in these efforts.

Sales associates at Nordstrom, an upscale retailer, have several qualities that are relatively rare in the retailing industry. First, they tend to be highly educated. Nordstrom explicitly targets college graduates for its entry-level positions. College graduates are willing to accept these positions because of their interest in retailing as a career, because managers are commonly drawn from the ranks of successful salespeople, and because Nordstrom's strong incentive-based compensation system provides financial rewards that are much higher than the industry average. Second, sales associates at Nordstrom have both the willingness and the ability to provide "heroic service." This type of service at times extends to delivering merchandise to the homes of customers, changing customers' flat tires, and paying for customers' parking. Nordstrom's culture, which is based on shared values that support exceptional customer service, is an important driver of heroic service. Some believe that Nordstrom's culture is more important to the company's performance than are its strategy and structure and even its compensation system.[37]

Imitability

human capital imitability
The extent to which the skills and talents of an organization's people can be copied by other organizations.

Human capital imitability is the extent to which the skills and talents of an organization's people can be copied by other organizations.[38] A competing retailer, for example, could target college graduates and use a promotion and compensation system similar to Nordstrom's. If many retailers followed this approach, some of the skills and talents at Nordstrom would be attracted to its competitors in the industry.

The skills and talents most difficult to imitate are usually those that are complex and learned inside a particular organization. Typically, these skills involve *tacit knowledge,*[39] a type of knowledge that people have but cannot articulate. Automobile designers at BMW, the German car manufacturer, cannot tell us exactly how they develop and decide on effective body designs. They can describe the basic process of styling with clay models and with CAS (computer-aided styling), but they cannot fully explain why some curves added to the auto body are positive while others are not. They just know. They have a feel for what is right.[40] As a result, those firms that manage their knowledge effectively can make their skills and capabilities difficult to imitate by competitors.[41]

The culture of an organization represents shared values, which in turn partially determine the skills and behaviors that associates and managers are expected to have.[42] In some cases, organizational culture promotes the development and use of difficult-to-imitate skills and behavior. Southwest Airlines, for example, is thought to have a culture that encourages people to display spirit and positive attitudes that are valuable, rare, and difficult to duplicate at other airlines. Spirit and attitude result from complex interactions among people that are challenging to observe and virtually impossible to precisely describe. Associates and managers know the spirit and attitude are there. They cannot, however, fully explain how they work to create value for customers.[43]

Overall Potential for Competitive Advantage

For human capital to be the basis for sustainable competitive advantage, it must satisfy all three conditions discussed earlier: it must be valuable for executing an organization's strategy, it must be rare in the industry, and it must be difficult to imitate. An organization that hires individuals with valuable but common skills does not have a basis for competitive advantage, because any organization can easily acquire those same skills. As shown in Exhibit 1-2, the human capital in such an organization can contribute only to competitive parity; that is, it can make the organization only as good as other organizations but not better. An organization that hires individuals with valuable and rare skills, or an organization that hires individuals with valuable skills and then helps them to develop additional rare skills, has the foundation for competitive advantage, but perhaps only in the short run. The organization may not have the foundation for long-term competitive advantage because other organizations may be able to copy what the organization has done. For long-term advantage through people, an organization needs human capital that is valuable, rare, and difficult to imitate.[44]

Although the value, rareness, and low imitability of skills and talents are crucial for competitive advantage, alone they are not enough. These three factors determine the potential of human capital. To translate that potential into actual advantage, an organization must leverage its human capital effectively.[45] An organization may have highly talented, uniquely skilled associates and managers, but if these individuals are not motivated or are not given proper support resources, they will not make a positive contribution. Thus, sustainable competitive advantage through people depends not only on the skills and talents of those people, but also on how they are treated and deployed.[46] In the next section, we discuss a general approach for effectively developing and leveraging

Are human resources in the firm . . .

Valuable?	Rare?	Difficult to Imitate?	Supported by Effective Management?	Competitive Implications	Performance
No	—	—		Competitive Disadvantage	Below normal
Yes	No	—		Competitive Parity	Normal
Yes	Yes	No		Temporary Competitive Advantage	Above normal
Yes	Yes	Yes		Sustained Competitive Advantage	Above normal

Exhibit 1-2   Human Capital and Competitive Advantage

Source: Adapted from J. Barney and P. Wright. 1999. "On Becoming a Strategic Partner," *Human Resource Management*, 37: 31–46.

MANAGERIAL ADVICE

Leveraging Human Capital with Twitter and Other Social Networking Tools: Managing the Tweets

Originally, businesses were concerned with the explosion in social networking tools used by people inside their organization (and externally as well). The concerns focused on staff members spending time on personal networking to the exclusion of completing tasks on their jobs. Thus, managers feared the loss of productivity. Yet, they began to realize the potential for the social networking tools such as Twitter and others. Some of the social networking tools are more personalized (i.e., Facebook is better suited to individualized interests, perhaps). But,

©AP/Wide World Photos

Twitter holds special promise to further business-related goals.

Twitter has been promoted to build brand names, enhance internal relationships among those who need to coordinate their tasks, and in building a broad sense of community within the organization. Twitter can help managers to obtain broad inputs for making decisions and to gain associates' commitment to decisions made. It can also be used to support or even change the organization's culture. Twitter (and other social networking tools) is also useful to build and maintain relationships with customers/clients. It may even be useful in attracting new customers for the organizations' products and services. Managers and associates can use Twitter to serve as brand ambassadors. Companies such as Dell, Whole Foods, JetBlue, Starbucks, Popeyes, and Home Depot use Twitter to further business goals. For example, JetBlue offers Twitter-based customer service. Whole Foods uses Twitter to communicate with customers, learning more about their tastes and interests, posting news about new food podcasts and inviting them to upcoming company events. Many of

these companies monitor what is said about them on Twitter. It is a way of monitoring their brand equity with the public and especially with customers.

The social networking sites are popular means of accessing the Internet. For example, more than 150 million people use Facebook and about 50 percent of them use it daily. Facebook achieved more than 1 billion visits monthly in 2009. Facebook is used in more than 170 countries, suggesting that social networking is cross cultural and is a global phenomenon. Recent research by Nielsen shows that Facebook is more popular than e-mail as a communications tool. Social networking now accounts for approximately 10 percent of all time spent on the Internet. Twitter use in 2009 was more than 1,000 percent higher than in 2008. The top three social networking tools are Facebook, MySpace, and Twitter.

Thus, companies are trying to harness the power of social networking to facilitate the productivity of managers and associates and to promote their business brands and goods and services in the marketplace. Social networking tools can help to enhance the capabilities of their human capital.

Sources: L. Safko. 2009. "The twitter about twitter." *Fast Company*, June 13, at http://www.fastcompany.com; M. Colin & D. MacMillan. 2009. "Managing the tweets," *BusinessWeek*, June 1, pp 20–21; A. Yee. 2009. "Social network rankings—Who's hot and who's not," *Ebizq*, April 13, at http://www.ebizq.net; C.D. Marcan. 2009. "10 Twitter tips for the workplace," *PCWorld*, April 12, at http://www.pcworld.com; L. King. 2009. "Put twitter to work," *PCWorld*, March 29, at http://www.pcworld.com; M. Gotta. 2009. "Twitter in the workplace," March 6, at http://mikeg.typepad.com; J.F. Rayport. 2009. "Social networks are the new web portals," *BusinessWeek*, January 21, at http://www.businessweek.com; J. Owyang. 2009. "A collection of social network stats for 2009," January 11, at http://www.web-strategist.com; L. Watrous. 2008. "The role of twitter in business," November 19, at http://www.brighthub.com; A. Smarty. 2008. "16 Examples of huge brands using twitter for business," October 7, at http://www.searchenginejournal.com; R. King. 2008. "How companies use twitter to bolster their brands," *BusinessWeek*, September 6, at http://www.businessweek.com.

human capital. As a prelude, we explore a unique new tool that can be used for leveraging human capital in the workplace, microblogging as a social networking tool in the *Managerial Advice* feature.

As suggested in the *Managerial Advice,* companies are trying to harness the potential power of social networking tools to facilitate the human capital in the organization and to increase its productivity. Because of the critical nature of human capital to gaining and maintaining competitive advantages, the countries and companies operating in them must invest heavily in attracting the best available talent and in developing managers' and associates' capabilities. It is also critical that their capabilities be fully used. Thus, social networking tools can help to use the skills and capabilities of the organization's human capital.

The previous arguments and research underscore the strategic value of human capital.[47] Because of the potential value of human capital to an organization, the way it is managed is critical. We next discuss *positive organizational behavior.*

Positive Organizational Behavior

Positive organizational behavior grew out of positive organizational psychology, which developed to avoid focusing on trying to "fix" what was wrong with people. Rather, **positive organizational behavior** focuses on nurturing individuals' greatest strengths and helping people use them to their and the organization's advantage.[48] Positive OB suggests that people will likely perform best when they have self-confidence, are optimistic (hope), and are resilient.[49]

People are healthier and more productive if they have a strong self-efficacy with regard to the work that they are doing. Thus, managers should try to build associates' self-efficacy for the tasks assigned to them. Yet, we know from research that the effects of self-efficacy are perhaps more important on average in the United States than in many other countries.[50] In addition to the self-efficacy of individual associates, recent research suggests the importance of the efficacy of teams' performance. To the extent that a team believes that it can accomplish its assigned tasks, the team's performance is likely to be higher.[51]

Leaders who practice positive organizational behavior build stronger ties with their associates and peers.[52] Research suggests that more than 25 percent of associates express distrust in their leaders.[53] Rebuilding trust after it has dissolved represents a significant challenge.[54] Alternatively, leaders are able to rebuild trust by developing positive psychological capital among their associates. And when positive psychological capital exists within units and organizations, individuals tend to be more highly motivated and persist longer in trying to achieve goals. Therefore, such units perform at higher levels.[55]

Individuals who are managed in a positive manner and who take a personally positive approach to outperform the other candidates often are healthier mentally and physically. These people are likely to have a positive self-concept, lead life with a purpose, and have quality relationships with other people. Such people tend to be healthier, happier, and more productive and thus usually experience less stress on the job.[56] As such, managers should help their associates to develop positive emotions in themselves and others. It helps them to develop the means and implement them so as to achieve success within the organization.[57]

positive organizational behavior
An approach to managing people that nurtures each individual's greatest strengths and helps people use them to their and the organization's advantage.

Providing leadership that encourages and nurtures positive emotions often requires the application of *emotional intelligence (EI)*. Persons with strong EI have self-awareness, possess good social skills, display empathy, have strong motivation, and regulate their own behavior without the oversight of others (discussed in more depth in Chapter 5).[58] Leaders using EI build trusting relationships with their associates, exhibit optimism, and build associates' efficacy by providing the training needed and empowering them to complete the task without direct oversight.[59] The leadership approach using positive OB resembles *high-involvement management,* which we discuss next.

High-Involvement Management

high-involvement management
Involves carefully selecting and training associates and giving them significant decision-making power, information, and incentive compensation.

High-involvement management requires that senior, middle, and lower-level managers all recognize human capital as the organization's most important resource. Sometimes referred to as "high-performance management" or "high-commitment management," the **high-involvement management** approach involves carefully selecting and training associates and giving them significant decision-making power, information, and incentive compensation.[60] Combining decision power with important tactical and strategic information provides associates with the ability to make or influence decisions about how to complete tasks in ways that create value for the organization. Associates are closer to the day-to-day activities than are others in the organization, and empowering them through high-involvement management allows them to use their unique knowledge and skills.[61] In general, empowerment can increase the likelihood that associates will provide maximum effort in their work, including a willingness to: (1) work hard to serve the organization's best interests, (2) take on different tasks and gain skills needed to work in multiple capacities, and (3) work using their intellect as well as their hands.[62]

Key Characteristics of High-Involvement Management

Five key characteristics of high-involvement management have been identified. We summarize these characteristics in Exhibit 1-3 and examine them further in the following discussion.

Selective Hiring

Sound selection systems are the first crucial characteristic of the high-involvement approach. An organization must select the right people if managers are to delegate authority and information to associates. Efforts to generate a large pool of applicants and to assess applicants through rigorous evaluations, including multiple rounds of interviews with managers and peers, are important in the selection process.[63] These efforts help to identify the most promising candidates while promoting the development of commitment on the part of the individuals chosen. Individuals selected in the course of thorough processes often respect the integrity of the organization.

Another important part of the selection process involves examining applicants' fit with the organization's culture and mission; selecting new hires solely on the basis of technical skills is a mistake. In situations where most or all of the required technical skills can be taught by the organization, it is quite acceptable to pay less attention to existing skills and more attention to cultural fit (along with the person's ability to learn the needed

> **EXHIBIT 1-3** Dimensions of High-Involvement Management
>
> | Aspect | Description |
> |---|---|
> | **Selective Hiring** | Large pools of applicants are built through advertising, word of mouth, and internal recommendations. Applicants are evaluated rigorously using multiple interviews, tests, and other selection tools. Applicants are selected on the basis not only of skills but also of fit with culture and mission. |
> | **Extensive Training** | New associates and managers are thoroughly trained for job skills through dedicated training exercises as well as on-the-job training. They also participate in structured discussions of culture and mission. Existing associates and managers are expected or required to enhance their skills each year through in-house or outside training and development. Often, existing associates and managers are rotated into different jobs for the purpose of acquiring additional skills. |
> | **Decision Power** | Associates are given authority to make decisions affecting their work and performance. Associates handle only those issues about which they have proper knowledge. Lower-level managers shift from closely supervising work to coaching associates. In addition to having authority to make certain decisions, associates participate in decisions made by lower-level and even middle managers. |
> | **Information Sharing** | Associates are given information concerning a broad variety of operational and strategic issues. Information is provided through bulletin boards, company intranets, meetings, posted performance displays, and newsletters. |
> | **Incentive Compensation** | Associates are compensated partly on the basis of performance. Individual performance, team performance, and business performance all may be considered. |

skills).[64] This is the approach taken by the Men's Wearhouse. A number of studies show the impact of cultural fit on satisfaction, intent to leave the organization, and job performance.[65] For example, a study of newly hired auditors in the largest accounting firms in the United States found that lack of fit with the organizational culture caused dissatisfaction and lower commitment among these auditors.[66] Furthermore, work context can affect the creative output of individuals so that individuals wishing to use their creative capabilities are attracted to organizations with cultures that promote the expression of creativity in work.[67] Finally, research suggests that careful selection of new associates leads to the provision of better customer service that in turn produces higher financial performance for the firm.[68]

Extensive Training

Training is the second vital component of high-involvement management. Without proper education and training, new hires cannot be expected to perform adequately.[69] And even when new hires are well trained for a position, it is important to help them build skills and capabilities beyond those needed in their present position. Furthermore, socialization into the norms of the organization is an important part of initial training. For existing associates, ongoing training in the latest tools and techniques is crucial.

Although valid calculations of return on investment for training are difficult to make, several studies reinforce the value of training. One study involving 143 *Fortune* 1000 companies reported that training significantly affected productivity, competitiveness, and employee satisfaction. (Training included job skills, social skills, quality/statistical analysis, and cross-training in different jobs.)[70]

Decision Power

The third key dimension of high-involvement management is decision-making power—providing associates with the authority to make some important decisions while inviting them to influence other decisions. For example, in a mass-production firm, such as Dell Computer, a single associate might have the authority to stop an entire production line to diagnose and address a quality problem. The associate might also have the authority, in conjunction with co-workers, to contact a supplier about quality problems, to schedule vacation time, and to discipline co-workers behaving in inappropriate ways. Beyond this decision-making authority, an associate might have significant input to capital expenditure decisions, such as a decision to replace an aging piece of equipment.

In many cases, decision power is given to teams of associates. In fact, self-managed or self-directed teams are a central part of most high-involvement systems.[71] With regard to our mass-production example, such a team might include the individuals working on a particular production line, or it might include individuals who complete similar tasks in one part of a production line. The tellers in a particular branch bank can operate as a team, the nurses in a particular hospital unit on a particular shift could be a team, and junior brokers in an investment banking firm might act as a formal team in a particular area. Teams working in high-involvement contexts often achieve the outcomes desired by the organization.[72]

Many studies of decision-making power have been conducted over the years. In general, these studies support giving associates bounded authority and influence. The study of *Fortune* 1000 firms discussed earlier assessed the impact of associates' holding significant decision power. As with training, the executives in the 143 firms reported a positive effect on productivity, competitiveness, and employee satisfaction.[73] Another recent study of empowering associates found that it enhanced knowledge sharing within and the efficacy of teams that in turn increased performance.[74]

Information Sharing

The fourth characteristic of high-involvement management is information sharing. In order for associates to make effective decisions and provide useful inputs to decisions made by managers, they must be properly informed. Furthermore, sharing information among team members promotes collaboration, coordination and high team performance.[75] Examples of information that could be shared include the firm's operating results and business plan, costs of materials, costs of turnover and absenteeism, potential technologies for implementation, competitors' initiatives, and results and roadblocks in supplier negotiations. At AES, a Virginia-based power company, so much information had been shared with associates that the Securities and Exchange Commission (SEC) identified every employee of the firm as an insider for stock-trading purposes. This was unusual; typically, only those at the top of a firm have enough information to be considered insiders by the SEC.

Incentive Compensation

The fifth and final dimension of high-involvement management is incentive compensation. This type of compensation can take many forms, including the following:

- Individual piece-rate systems, where associates are compensated based on the amount produced or sold
- Individual incentive systems, where associates receive bonuses based on short- or long-term performance
- Knowledge or skill-based pay, where associates are paid based on the amount of knowledge or number of skills they acquire
- Profit sharing, where associates earn bonuses based on company profits
- Gain sharing, where associates share in a portion of savings generated from employee suggestions for improvement

In the study of *Fortune* 1000 firms mentioned earlier, executives indicated that incentive pay positively affected productivity and competitiveness.[76]

Evidence for the Effectiveness of High-Involvement Management

Considering the five aspects of high-involvement management as a coherent system, research evidence supports the effectiveness of the approach. One study, for example, found this approach to have a positive effect on the performance of steel mini-mills.[77] In this study, 30 U.S. mini-mills were classified as having a control orientation or a commitment orientation. Under the control orientation, employees were forced to comply with detailed rules, had little decision-making authority or influence, received limited training and information, and had no incentive compensation. Under the commitment orientation, which closely resembled the high-involvement approach described above, employees had strong training; information on quality, costs, productivity, and usage rates of materials; incentive pay; the authority to make decisions regarding workflow scheduling and new equipment; and input into strategic decisions. The mills with commitment systems had lower rates of unused materials, higher productivity, and lower associate turnover.

In another study, 62 automobile plants around the world were classified as using traditional mass production or flexible production.[78] Under the traditional mass-production system, employees did not participate in empowered teams, whereas employees under the flexible approach participated in such teams. Companies that used the flexible system also offered employees more cross-training in different jobs and opportunities for incentive compensation. Furthermore, these companies displayed fewer symbols of higher status for managers (no reserved parking, no separate eating areas, and so on). The plants with flexible production had 47.4 percent fewer defects and 42.9 percent greater productivity than those with traditional production systems.

In a third study, firms were drawn from many different industries, ranging from biotechnology to business services.[79] Firms placing strong value on their people had a 79 percent probability of surviving for five years after the initial public offering (IPO), whereas firms placing low value on their people had a 60 percent probability of surviving five years.

©iStockphoto

Other studies have shown that high-involvement systems promote stronger relationships in the workplace and provide environments where associates and managers feel empowered. As such, they have higher job satisfaction and productivity. In turn, they service the organization's customers effectively to promote high customer satisfaction.[80]

Demands on Managers

When a high-involvement approach has all of the characteristics identified above, associates are fully and properly empowered. High-involvement managers place significant value on empowerment because empowered associates have the tools and support required to create value for the organization. But managers implementing high-involvement approaches must take specific and calculated actions to promote empowerment. We turn now to a discussion of the demands a high-involvement approach places on managers.

Because they believe strongly in empowering associates, high-involvement managers constantly seek to identify situations in which responsibility can be delegated. The intent is to move decision making to the lowest organization level at which associates have the information and knowledge required to make an effective decision. Managing through encouragement and commitment rather than fear and threats, high-involvement managers respect and value each associate's skills and knowledge. In addition, effective managers understand that cultural differences in a diverse workforce challenge them to empower people in ways that are consistent with their uniqueness as individuals.[81] Listening carefully to associates and asking questions of them in a genuine attempt to understand their perspectives demonstrates managerial respect and facilitates attempts to be culturally sensitive. People who feel respected for their values as well as for their skills and knowledge are motivated to act in a prudent and forthright manner in completing their assigned work. Over time, empowered, respected associates increase their confidence in their ability to help create value for the organization.

Trust between managers and associates is critical in a high-involvement organization. Managers must trust associates not to abuse their decision power. For their part, associates must trust managers not to punish them for mistakes when they are trying to do the right thing for the organization. Furthermore, research has shown that trust between associates and those formally responsible for their behavior has a positive effect on the organization's financial performance. Thus, effective managers invest effort in building and maintaining trust. In so doing, they dramatically increase their credibility with associates.[82] Confident in their abilities as well as their associates' abilities, high-involvement managers recognize that they don't have all the knowledge necessary for the organization to be successful. As a result, they work with their peers and associates to find solutions when problems arise.[83] Managers employing a high-involvement approach to management of their associates exhibit many of the characteristics of a transformational leader (this leadership approach is discussed in more depth in Chapter 8).[84]

High-involvement managers think continuously about how human capital can be used as the foundation for competitive advantage. Is there another way to use our people's skills and knowledge to further reduce costs or to more crisply differentiate the products we produce? How can the creativity of our empowered associates be used to create more value for the organization? How can we use information our associates gather through their work with people outside our organization (such as customers and suppliers) to make certain we are currently doing things that will allow us to shape the competitive advantages needed to be successful tomorrow? Finding answers to these questions and others that are unique to a particular organization can lead to long-term success.

As suggested in the *Experiencing Organizational Behavior* feature, firms use their core strengths to provide value to customers. And core strengths are commonly based on human capital, which is clearly the case with Pixar. Pixar's managers and associates have been critical to the production of ten major animated film successes. Pixar largely exhibits the characteristics of a high-involvement organization. It empowers its associates with considerable authority to determine their work projects, schedule, and how they will complete most of their work. Pixar hires top talent and gains the most from their capabilities. The freedom it provides its associates, the development of their skills and the culture promoting a happy, trusting and collaborative atmosphere retain their services for Pixar over the long term. It has been described as the "corporation of the future."[85] Pixar's success suggests why there is now global competition for the best human capital.[86] The Pixar experience suggests the importance of human capital for all organizations in order to compete effectively in the highly complex and challenging global economy they face in the current environment.

Organization of the Book

Our objective in this book is to provide managers, aspiring managers, and even individual contributors with the knowledge they need to perform effectively in organizations, especially in today's high-involvement organizations. Essentially, the book offers readers a working knowledge of OB and its strategic importance. The book has 14 chapters divided into four parts. The titles of the parts and the topics of the chapters are presented in Exhibit 1-4, which graphically depicts the model for the book.

As suggested in the exhibit, the strategic approach to OB emphasizes how to manage behavior in organizations to achieve a competitive advantage. The book unfolds in a logical sequence. In Part I, The Strategic Lens, we explain the strategic approach to OB (Chapter 1) and then discuss the importance of managing diversity in organizations (Chapter 2) and describe how organizations must operate in a global context (Chapter 3). In Part II, Individual Processes, we focus on the individual as the foundation of an organization's human capital, emphasizing the development of a sound understanding of individuals and how they affect each other and the organization's success. Topics considered include learning and perception (Chapter 4), personality (Chapter 5), motivation (Chapter 6), and stress (Chapter 7). In Part III, Groups, Teams, and Social Processes, we examine the effects of interpersonal processes on individual and organizational outcomes. Specific interpersonal processes include leadership (Chapter 8), communication (Chapter 9), decision making (Chapter 10), group dynamics (Chapter 11), and conflict (Chapter 12). Finally, in Part IV, The Organizational Context, we examine several organization-level processes and phenomena. Using insights from the book's first three parts, we study organizational design and culture (Chapter 13) and organizational change (Chapter 14). Overall, the book takes you on an exciting journey through managerial opportunities and problems related to behavior in organizations.

Pixar: An Organization of Happy, Innovative People

Pixar is one of the most successful and unique organizations in its industry and perhaps anywhere. It has produced ten major movie hits, and they are all highly creative and computer animated. The highly acclaimed movies include *Toy Story, A Bug's Life, Monsters Inc, Finding Nemo, The Incredibles, Cars,* and *Wall·E,* among others. In fact, all of Pixar's movies have been successful, which is an incredible feat. And they developed these movies in a highly unique way, not in the tradition of Hollywood. A typical movie involves a number of free agents in key positions brought together for a single, albeit major, movie project. Yet, all of Pixar's movies are developed and produced totally by its in-house staff.

Pixar's success is due to the incredible talent of its managers and associates and how it manages its human capital. It begins with a thorough recruiting and careful selection

© CARS (2006) Directed by John Lasseter, Photo provided by Buena VistaPictures/Photofest

process. The firm searches for people who are innovative with good communication skills. In fact, the people in charge of hiring like to find people who have failed but overcame the failure. Randy Nelson, the person in charge of recruiting, explains the reason why these people are attractive to Pixar, "the core skill of innovators is error recovery not failure avoidance." But identifying and hiring top human capital is only the first step on the road to success. Managing this talent in ways that allow the people to reach their potential and to be highly productive in their tasks is highly critical to Pixar's success.

Pixar leaders build teams of people and expect them to work together to produce their end product. Everyone is expected to participate. When they have problems to solve, they do it as a team. In fact, all 200 to 250 members of a production group are encouraged and expected to offer their ideas. Essentially, the company produces team innovations. Pixar University was created, and all members of the organization (artists, software programmers, accountants, security guards) are encouraged to take courses up to four hours per week. PU

offers 110 different courses, essentially a complete curriculum on making films. In these courses, they also learn to collaborate and to trust each other. In addition, they build new capabilities and sometimes discover new passions.

The culture of Pixar emphasizes teamwork, honesty, communication, collaboration in an environment where people can have fun and pursue their passions. Interdisciplinary learning is encouraged, creativity is rewarded, and intensity is prized. Taking risks is valued. One analyst claimed that Pixar's culture "out-Googled Google." The end results of the top human capital and effective management of it has been a string of hit movies. And the success has been aided by the ability of Pixar not only to attract and develop highly talented staff but also to keep it. Turnover at Pixar is less than five percent annually.

George Lucas, the legendary filmmaker (creator of *Star Wars*) founded Pixar in the 1970s. He sold it to Steve Jobs in the late 1980s for $10 million. Jobs sold Pixar to Walt Disney in 2006 for $7.4 billion. When one considers that the major assets of this company are a building, some computer equipment, and about 400 people, one can understand the potential value of excellent human capital and managing that talent to gain the most from it.

Sources: G. Adams. 2009. "Pixar: The real toon army," *The Independent,* September 23, at http://license.icopyright.net; C. Kuang. 2009. "Pixar's approach to HR," *Fast Company,* February 8, at http://www.fastcompany.com; E. Catmull. 2008. "How Pixar fosters collective creativity," *Harvard Business Review,* September, at http://hbr.harvardbusiness.org; W.C. Taylor. 2008 "Bill Taylor: Pixar's blockbuster secrets," *BusinessWeek,* July 8, at http://www.businessweek.com; C. Hawn. 2008. "Pixar's Brad Bird on fostering innovation," *The GigaOM Network,* April 17, at http://www.gigaom.com; T. Balf. 2007. "Out of juice? Recharge!" *Fast Company,* December 18, at http://www.fastcompany.com; M. Greer. 2006. "Pixar U and whistling while you work," *The Motley Fool,* November 16, at http://www.fool.com.

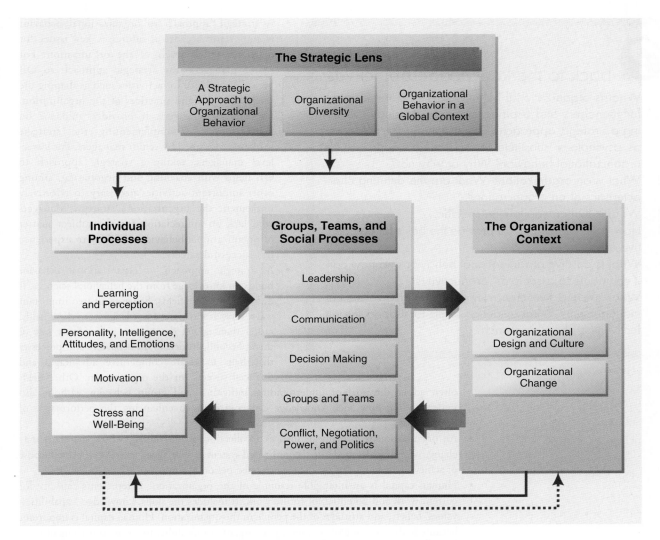

Exhibit 1-4   Managing Organizational Behavior for Competitive Advantage

What This Chapter Adds to Your Knowledge Portfolio

In this chapter, we have examined the strategic importance of organizational behavior to the success of individuals and organizations. In addition, we have discussed the nature of human capital and the circumstances under which it can be the source of competitive advantage for an organization. Finally, we have explored the high-involvement approach to management. To summarize, we have covered the following points:

- The strategic approach to organizational behavior involves knowledge and application of how individual, interpersonal, and organizational factors influence the behavior and value of an organization's people, where value is represented by productivity, satisfaction, and ultimately the organization's competitive advantages and financial success.

back to the knowledge objectives

1. What is organizational behavior? Why is it important for managers and aspiring managers to study OB using a strategic approach? Can the study of a field such as psychology substitute for a strategic approach to organizational behavior? Why or why not?
2. What is an organization? What are the defining characteristics of an organization?
3. What is human capital? Be specific.
4. How does human capital provide the basis for competitive advantage?
5. What is positive organizational behavior and how can it contribute to associates' productivity?
6. What are the five characteristics of high-involvement management? What evidence exists to support the effectiveness of this approach?

- A strategic approach to organizational behavior is important because it addresses key issues for managers at all levels of the organization. For senior managers, the strategic approach to OB provides guidance for activities such as shaping the internal norms and practices of the organization. For middle managers, it provides guidance on matters such as implementing the strategic initiatives designed by senior managers. For lower-level managers, taking a strategic approach to OB helps with coaching and negotiating, among other important activities necessary to effectively implement the organization's strategy. Managers who lack an appreciation for the subject matter of organizational behavior are likely to experience less-successful careers.

- A strategic approach to organizational behavior builds on knowledge from the behavioral sciences. It differs from these fields, however, in two important ways. First, it integrates knowledge from these fields, rather than taking the narrow view of any one of them. Second, it focuses on behaviors and processes that help to create competitive advantages and financial success for the organization. Other fields often adopt the goal of understanding individual and group behavior without also understanding how such knowledge can contribute to enhancing the performance of organizations.

- An organization is formally defined as a collection of individuals, whose members may change over time, formed into a coordinated system of specialized activities for the purpose of achieving certain goals over some extended period of time.

- Human capital is an intangible resource of the organization. It represents capacity for current work and potential for future work. It includes the skills, knowledge, capabilities, values, beliefs, and attitudes of the people in the organization. Human capital is important because in the current global economy, an organization's ability to create something of value for customers comes largely from the know-how and intellect embodied in its people rather than from machinery and other tangible assets.

- Human capital can be a source of competitive advantage for an organization when it has *value* (it is relevant for the organization's strategy), is *rare* (skills and knowledge are possessed by relatively few outside the organization), and has *low imitability* (other organizations cannot easily duplicate the skills and knowledge). These three characteristics set the stage for gaining an advantage. For human capital to be a source of competitive advantage, it must be managed effectively.

- Positive organizational behavior focuses on nurturing individuals' greatest strengths and helping people use them to their and the organization's advantage. Positive OB suggests that people will likely perform best when they have self-confidence, are optimistic (hope), and are resilient. People are healthier and more productive if they have a strong self-efficacy with regard to the work that they are doing. Individuals who are managed in a positive manner and who take a personally positive approach to outperform the other candidates often are healthier mentally and physically.

- High-involvement management is an important method for developing and leveraging human capital. This approach has five key components: (1) selective hiring, (2) extensive training, (3) decision power, (4) information sharing, and (5) incentive compensation. Collectively, these five aspects of high-involvement management yield empowered workers.

- The effectiveness of high-involvement management is supported by strong evidence. In studies of many industries, high-involvement management has been found to lead to high productivity, satisfaction, financial success, and competitiveness.

Key Terms

organizational behavior, p. 13

managing organizational behavior, p. 13

strategic OB approach, p. 13

associates, p. 15

organization, p. 17

human capital, p. 20

competitive advantage, p. 20

human capital value, p. 21

human capital rareness, p. 21

human capital imitability, p. 22

positive organizational behavior, p. 25

high-involvement management, p. 26

building your human capital

Career Style Inventory

Different people approach their careers in different ways. Some, for example, attempt to obtain as much power as possible in order to control personal and organizational outcomes. Others emphasize hard work and cooperative attitudes. The questionnaire that follows is designed to assess your tendencies, as well as your beliefs about the approaches of most managers. Following the questionnaire, we describe four distinct approaches to careers, some of which are more useful in high-involvement organizations than others.

Instructions

A number of descriptive paragraphs appear below. They describe sets of beliefs or perceptions that vary among individuals. The paragraphs are divided into four sections: Life Goals, Motivation, Self-Image, and Relations with Others. Please evaluate each paragraph as follows:

1. Read the paragraph. Taking the paragraph as a whole (using all of the information in the paragraph, not just one or two sentences), rate the paragraph on a scale from "not characteristic of me" (1) to "highly characteristic of me" (7). If you are currently a full-time student, rate each paragraph on the basis of how you believe you would feel if you were working full-time in an organization. If you are a part-time student with a career, rate each paragraph on the basis of how you actually feel.

1	2	3	4	5	6	7
Not characteristic of me		Somewhat characteristic of me		Generally characteristic of me		Highly characteristic of me

2. In addition, rate each paragraph in terms of the way you would *like* to be, regardless of how you are now. Rate each on a scale from "would not like to be like this" (1) to "would very strongly like to be like this" (7).

1	2	3	4	5	6	7
I would not like to be like this		I would somewhat like to be like this		I would generally like to be like this		I would very strongly like to be like this

3. Finally, rate each paragraph in terms of how descriptive it is of most managers, from "not at all characteristic of most managers" (1) to "very characteristic of most managers" (7). In providing this assessment, think about managers with whom you have worked, managers you have read about or heard about, and managers you have seen in videos.

1	2	3	4	5	6	7
Not at all characteristic of most managers		Somewhat characteristic of most managers		Generally characteristic of most managers		Very characteristic of most managers

Questionnaire

Please be as honest, realistic, and candid as possible in your self-evaluations. Try to accurately describe yourself, not represent what you think others might want you to say or believe. In general, individuals do not have high scores on every question.

A. Life Goals

1. I equate my personal success in life with the development and success of the organization for which I work. I enjoy a sense of belonging, responsibility, and loyalty to an organization. If it were best for my organization, I would be satisfied with my career if I progressed no higher than a junior- or middle-management level.

   How characteristic is this of you (1–7)?_____
   How much would you like to be like this (1–7)?_____
   How characteristic is this of most managers (1–7)?_____

2. I have two major goals in life: to do my job well and to be committed to my family. I believe strongly in the work ethic and want to succeed by skillfully and creatively accomplishing goals and tasks. I also want to be a good family person. Work and family are equally important.

   How characteristic is this of you (1–7)?_____
   How much would you like to be like this (1–7)?_____
   How characteristic is this of most managers (1–7)?_____

3. My goal in life is to acquire power and prestige; success for me means being involved in a number of successful, diverse enterprises. I generally experience life and work as a jungle; like it or not, it's a dog-eat-dog world, and there will always be winners and losers. I want to be one of the winners.

   How characteristic is this of you (1–7)?_____
   How much would you like to be like this (1–7)?_____
   How characteristic is this of most managers (1–7)?_____

4. I tend to view life and work as an important game. I see my work, my relations with others, and my career in terms of options and possibilities as if they were part of a strategic game that I am playing. My main goal in life is to be a winner at this game while helping others to succeed as well.

   How characteristic is this of you (1–7)?_____
   How much would you like to be like this (1–7)?_____
   How characteristic is this of most managers (1–7)?_____

B. Motivation

1. My interest in work is in the process of building something. I am motivated by problems that need to be solved; the challenge of work itself or the creation of a quality product gets me excited. I would prefer to miss a deadline rather than do something halfway—quality is more important to me than quantity.

   How characteristic is this of you (1–7)?_____

   How much would you like to be like this (1–7)?_____

   How characteristic is this of most managers (1–7)?_____

2. I like to take risks and am fascinated by new methods, techniques, and approaches. I want to motivate myself and others by pushing everyone to the limit. My interest is in challenge, or competitive activity, where I can prove myself to be a winner. The greatest sense of exhilaration for me comes from managing a team of people and gaining victories. When work is no longer challenging, I feel bored and slightly depressed.

   How characteristic is this of you (1–7)?_____

   How much would you like to be like this (1–7)?_____

   How characteristic is this of most managers (1–7)?_____

3. I like to control things and to acquire power. I want to succeed by climbing the corporate ladder, acquiring positions of greater power and responsibility. I want to use this power to gain prestige, visibility, and financial success and to be able to make decisions that affect many other people. Being good at "politics" is essential to this success.

   How characteristic is this of you (1–7)?_____

   How much would you like to be like this (1–7)?_____

   How characteristic is this of most managers (1–7)?_____

4. My interest in work is to derive a sense of belonging from organizational membership and to have good relations with others. I am concerned about the feelings of people with whom I work, and I am committed to maintaining the integrity of my organization. As long as the organization rewards my efforts, I am willing to let my commitment to my organization take precedence over my own narrow self-interest.

   How characteristic is this of you (1–7)?_____

   How much would you like to be like this (1–7)?_____

   How characteristic is this of most managers (1–7)?_____

C. Self-Image

1. I am competitive and innovative. My speech and my thinking are dynamic and come in quick flashes. I like to emphasize my strengths and don't like to feel out of control. I have trouble realizing and living within my limitations. I pride myself on being fair with others; I have very few prejudices. I like to have limitless options to succeed; my biggest fears are being trapped or being labeled as a loser.

   How characteristic is this of you (1–7)?_____

   How much would you like to be like this (1–7)?_____

   How characteristic is this of most managers (1–7)?_____

2. My identity depends on being part of a stable, noteworthy organization. I see myself as a trustworthy, responsible, and reasonable person who can get along with almost anyone. I'm concerned about making a good impression on others and representing the organization well. I may not have as much toughness, aggressiveness, and risk-taking skills as some, but I make substantial contributions to my organization.

   How characteristic is this of you (1–7)?_____

   How much would you like to be like this (1–7)?_____

   How characteristic is this of most managers (1–7)?_____

3. My sense of self-worth is based on my assessment of my skills, abilities, self-discipline, and self-reliance. I tend to be quiet, sincere, and practical. I like to stay with a project from conception to completion.

    How characteristic is this of you (1–7)?_____

    How much would you like to be like this (1–7)?_____

    How characteristic is this of most managers (1–7)?_____

4. I tend to be brighter, more courageous, and stronger than most of the people with whom I work. I see myself as bold, innovative, and entrepreneurial. I can be exceptionally creative at times, particularly in seeing entrepreneurial possibilities and opportunities. I am willing to take major risks in order to succeed and willing to be secretive if it will further my own goals.

    How characteristic is this of you (1–7)?_____

    How much would you like to be like this (1–7)?_____

    How characteristic is this of most managers (1–7)?_____

D. Relations with Others

1. I tend to dominate other people because my ideas are better. I generally don't like to work closely and cooperate with others, I would rather have other people working for me, following my directions. I don't think anyone has ever really helped me freely; either I controlled and directed them, or they were expecting me to do something for them in return.

    How characteristic is this of you (1–7)?_____

    How much would you like to be like this (1–7)?_____

    How characteristic is this of most managers (1–7)?_____

2. My relations with others are generally good. I value highly those people who are trustworthy, who are committed to this organization, and who act with integrity in the things that they do. In my part of the organization, I attempt to sustain an atmosphere of cooperation, mild excitement, and mutuality. I get "turned off" by others in the organization who are out for themselves, who show no respect for others, or who get so involved with their own little problems that they lose sight of the "big picture."

    How characteristic is this of you (1–7)?_____

    How much would you like to be like this (1–7)?_____

    How characteristic is this of most managers (1–7)?_____

3. At times, I am tough and dominating, but I don't think I am destructive. I tend to classify other people as winners and losers. I evaluate almost everyone in terms of what they can do for the team. I encourage people to share their knowledge with others, trying to get a work atmosphere that is both exciting and productive. I am impatient with those who are slower and more cautious, and I don't like to see weakness in others.

    How characteristic is this of you (1–7)?_____

    How much would you like to be like this (1–7)?_____

    How characteristic is this of most managers (1–7)?_____

4. My relations with others are generally determined by the work that we do. I feel more comfortable working in a small group or on a project with a defined and understandable structure. I tend to evaluate others (both peers and managers) in terms of whether they help or hinder me in doing a craftsman-like job. I do not compete against other people as I do against my own standards of quality.

    How characteristic is this of you (1–7)?_____

    How much would you like to be like this (1–7)?_____

    How characteristic is this of most managers (1–7)?_____

When you have evaluated each paragraph, follow the instructions below and "score" the questionnaire.

Scoring Key for Career Style Inventory

To calculate scores for each of the four primary career orientations, add up your scores for individual paragraphs as shown below. For example, to obtain your "characteristic of me" score for the orientation known as "craftsperson," add your "characteristic of me" scores for paragraph 2 under Life Goals, paragraph 1 under Motivation, paragraph 3 under Self-Image, and paragraph 4 under Relations with Others.

Scores can range from 4 to 28. A score of 23 or higher can be considered high. A score of 9 or lower can be considered low.

	Characteristic of me	Would like to be like this	Characteristic of most managers
Craftsperson Orientation			
Life Goals—Paragraph 2	_____	_____	_____
Motivation—Paragraph 1	_____	_____	_____
Self-Image—Paragraph 3	_____	_____	_____
Relations with Others—Paragraph 4	_____	_____	_____
TOTAL scores for Craftsperson	_____	_____	_____
Company Orientation			
Life Goals—Paragraph 1	_____	_____	_____
Motivation—Paragraph 4	_____	_____	_____
Self-Image—Paragraph 2	_____	_____	_____
Relations with Others—Paragraph 2	_____	_____	_____
TOTAL scores for Company Man/Woman	_____	_____	_____
Jungle Fighter Orientation			
Life Goals—Paragraph 3	_____	_____	_____
Motivation—Paragraph 3	_____	_____	_____
Self-Image—Paragraph 4	_____	_____	_____
Relations with Others—Paragraph 1	_____	_____	_____
TOTAL scores for Jungle Fighter	_____	_____	_____
Strategic Game Orientation			
Life Goals—Paragraph 4	_____	_____	_____
Motivation—Paragraph 2	_____	_____	_____
Self-Image—Paragraph 1	_____	_____	_____
Relations with Others—Paragraph 3	_____	_____	_____
TOTAL scores for Gamesman/ Gameswoman	_____	_____	_____

Descriptions of the Four Primary Career Orientations

- The *Craftsperson,* as the name implies, holds traditional values, including a strong work ethic, respect for people, concern for quality, and thrift. When talking about work, such a person tends to show an interest in specific projects that have a defined structure. He or she sees others, peers as well as managers, in terms of whether they help or hinder the completion of work in a craftsman-like way.

  The virtues of craftspersons are admired by almost everyone. In high-involvement organizations, craftspersons are valuable because they respect people and work hard and smart. On the downside, they can become overly absorbed in perfecting their projects, which can slow them down and harm their leadership on a broader stage.

- *The Jungle Fighter* lusts for power. He or she experiences life and work as a jungle where "eat or be eaten" is the rule and the winners destroy the losers. A major part of his or her psychic resources is budgeted for a personal department of defense. Jungle fighters tend to see their peers as either accomplices or enemies and their associates as objects to be used.

  There are two types of jungle fighters: lions and foxes. The lions are the conquerors who, when successful, may build an empire. The foxes make their nests in the corporate hierarchy and move ahead by stealth and politicking. The most gifted foxes rise rapidly by making use of their entrepreneurial skills. In high-involvement organizations, jungle fighters can cause many problems. They tend not to value people. Leveraging human capital may take place, but only in limited ways for the purpose of self-gain.

- *The Company Man or Woman* bases personal identity on being part of a protective organization. He or she can be fearful and submissive, seeking security even more than success. These are not positive attributes for high-involvement organizations. On the other hand, the company man or woman is concerned with the human side of the company, interested in the feelings of people, and committed to maintaining corporate integrity. The most creative company men and women sustain an atmosphere of cooperation and stimulation, but they tend to lack the daring to lead in competitive and innovative organizations.

- The *Strategic Gamesman or Gameswoman* sees business life in general, and his or her career in particular, in terms of options and possibilities, as if he or she were playing a game. Such a person likes to take calculated risks and is drawn to new techniques and methods. The contest is invigorating, and he or she communicates enthusiasm, energizing peers and associates like the quarterback on a football team. Unlike the jungle fighter, the gamesman or gameswoman competes not to build an empire or to pile up riches, but to gain the exhilaration of victory. The main goal is to be known as a winner, along with the rest of the team.

  The character of a strategic gamesman or gameswoman, which might seem to be a collection of near paradoxes, is very useful in a high-involvement organization. Such a person is cooperative but competitive, detached and playful but compulsively driven to succeed, a team player but a would-be superstar, a team leader but often a rebel against bureaucratic hierarchy, fair and unprejudiced but contemptuous of weakness, tough and dominating but not destructive. Balancing these issues is important in a team-oriented organization, where associates and managers at all levels are expected to work together for personal and organizational success.

Source: Adapted from *Experiences in Management and Organizational Behavior*, 4th ed. (New York: John Wiley & Sons, 1996). Original instrument developed by Roy J. Lewicki.

---

an organizational behavior moment
All in a Day's Work

After earning a business degree with a major in marketing, Ann Wood went to work for Norwich Enterprises as a research analyst in the Consumer Products Division. While working, she also attended graduate school at night, receiving her MBA in three years. Within a year of reaching that milestone, Ann was promoted to manager of market research. Ann became assistant director of marketing after another three years. After a stay of slightly less than 24 months in that position, Ann was appointed director of marketing for the Consumer Products Division. In this new role, she leads many more people than in her previous roles—85 in total across three different groups: market research, marketing strategy and administration, and advertising and public relations.

Ann felt good this morning, ready to continue working on several important projects that Anil Mathur, Norwich's executive vice president for marketing, had assigned to her. Ann felt that she was on a fast track to further career success and wanted to continue performing well. With continuing success, she expected an appointment in Norwich's international business operations in the near future. Ann was pleased about this prospect, as international experience was becoming a prerequisite at Norwich for senior-level managerial positions—her ultimate goal. Several problems, however, were brought to her attention on what she thought was going to be a good day at the office.

As Ann was entering the building, Joe Jackson, the current manager of the market research group, stopped her in the hall and complained that the company's intranet had been down about half of the night. This technical problem had prevented timely access to data from a central server, resulting in a delay in the completion of an important market analysis. Ann thought that immediately jumping in to help with the analysis would be useful in dealing with this matter. She had promised Anil that the analysis would be available to him and other upper-level managers this morning. Now it would have to be finished on a special priority basis, delaying work on other important projects.

Joe also told Ann that two of his analysts had submitted their resignations over the last 24 hours. Ann asked, "Why are we having so much trouble with turnover?" The manager responded, "The market is tight for smart analysts who understand our product lines. We've been having problems hiring anyone with the skills we need, much less people who have any loyalty. Maybe we should offer higher starting salaries and more attractive stock options if we expect to have much hope of keeping the people we need." Ann asked Joe to develop a concrete proposal about what could be done to reduce turnover, promising to work with him to resolve the issue.

Just as she reached her office, Ann's phone rang. It was Brooke Carpenter, the manager of market strategy and administration. "I'm glad you're here, Ann. I need to talk to you now. I'm on my way." As Brooke came through the door, Ann could tell that he was quite upset. He explained that two of his people had discovered through searches on the Internet that the average pay for their type of work was 7 percent higher than what they were currently earning. Sharing this information with co-workers had created an unpleasant environment in which people were concentrating on pay instead of focusing on tasks to be completed. Ann had a conference call coming in a few minutes, stopping her from dealing with the matter further, but she asked Brooke to set up a time when the two of them could meet with his people to talk about their concerns.

After her conference call, Ann spent the rest of her morning dealing with e-mails that were primarily related to dissatisfaction with her department's work. Most of these concerned the delays that other Norwich units were experiencing in receiving outputs from her department. The problem was complicated by the inability to retain workers.

Ann had just returned from lunch when her phone rang. "Ann, it's Brooke. Can you meet with us at 2:30 this afternoon? I know that this is short notice, but we really do need to talk with my people." Although the time was inconvenient, given that Anil expected his analysis today, Ann knew that dealing with issues concerning Brooke's associates was also important. Plus, she believed that Anil's report was about to be finished by the research group, taking that immediate problem off her plate.

The meeting with Brooke and his people lasted almost an hour. Not surprisingly, other concerns surfaced during the conversation. Ann thought to herself that this was to be expected. Her managerial experience indicated that complaints about pay often masked concerns about other issues. She learned that people weren't satisfied with the technology made available to them to do their work or Norwich's commitment to training and development. Young and eager to advance, Brooke's associates wanted assurances from Ann that Norwich would spend more money and time to develop their skills. Ann agreed to the importance of skill development—both for associates and for Norwich. She said that she would examine the matter and provide feedback to them. "It may take some time, but my commitment to you is that I'll work hard to make this happen. While I can't promise much about the pay structure overnight, I'll also investigate this matter to become more informed. Brooke and I will work on this together so you can have direct access to what is going on." Ann wanted to deal with these issues, knowing that their resolution had the potential to help both associates and the company reach their goals.

Ann then spent a couple of hours dealing with still more e-mail messages, a few phone calls, and other requests that reached her desk during the day. Anil received the report he needed and seemed to be satisfied. Although she had been busy, Ann felt good as she left for home around 8:30 that night. Nothing came easily, she thought.

Discussion Questions

1. Describe the people-related problems or issues Ann Wood faced during the day. Did she handle these effectively? If not, what do you believe she should have done?
2. Is Ann Wood a high-involvement manager? If so, provide evidence. If not, how well do you think she'll perform in her new job as head of marketing?
3. Assume that Ann Wood wants her managers and associates to be the foundation for her department's competitive advantages. Use the framework summarized in Exhibit 1-2 (in the chapter text) to assess the degree to which Ann's people are a source of competitive advantage at this point in time.

team exercise

McDonald's: A High-Involvement Organization?

One experience most people in North America and Europe have shared is that of dining in the hamburger establishment known as McDonald's. In fact, someone has claimed that thirtieth-century archeologists may dig into the ruins of our present civilization and conclude that twenty-first-century religion was devoted to the worship of golden arches.

Your group, Fastalk Consultants, is known as the shrewdest, most insightful, and most overpaid management consulting firm in the country. You have been hired by the president of McDonald's to make recommendations for improving the motivation and performance of personnel in their franchise operations. Some of the key activities in franchise operations are food preparation, order-taking and dealing with customers, and routine clean-up operations.

The president of McDonald's must always be concerned that his company's competitors, such as Burger King, Wendy's, Jack in the Box, Dunkin' Donuts, various pizza establishments, and others, have the potential to make heavy inroads into McDonald's market. Thus, he hired a separate market research firm to investigate and compare the relative merits of the sandwiches, french fries, and drinks served by McDonald's and the competitors and asked the market research firm to assess the advertising campaigns of the competitors. Hence, you will not be concerned with marketing issues, except as they may affect employee behavior. The president wants you to evaluate the organization's franchises to determine their strengths and weaknesses of how they manage their associates hoping their work will be productive. He is very interested in how the restaurants' management approach compares to high-involvement management and the impact on their approach on McDonald's.

The president has established an unusual contract with you. He wants you and your colleagues in the firm to make recommendations based on your observations as customers. He does not want you to do a complete analysis with interviews, surveys, or behind-the-scenes observations.

STEPS

1. Assemble into groups of four to five. Each group will act as a separate Fastalk consulting team.
2. Think about your past visits to McDonald's. What did you see and experience? How was the food prepared and served? What was the process? Did the employees seem to be happy with their work? Did they seem to be well trained and well suited for the work? Did the supervisor act as a coach or a superior? Your instructor may ask you to visit a McDonald's in preparation for this exercise and/or to research the organization via the Internet or school library.
3. Assess McDonald's on each dimension of high-involvement management.
4. Develop recommendations for the president of McDonald's.
5. Reassemble as a class. Discuss your group's assessments and recommendations with the rest of the class, and listen to other groups' assessments. Do you still assess McDonald's in the same way after hearing from your colleagues in the class?
6. The instructor will present additional points for consideration.

Source: Adapted from *Experiences in Management and Organizational Behavior*, 4th ed. (New York: John Wiley & Sons, 1996). Original version developed by D.T. Hall and F.S. Hall.

Endnotes

1. Wang, H.C., He, J. & Mahoney, J.T. 2009. Firm-specific knowledge resources and competitive advantage: The roles of economic- and relationship-based employee governance mechanisms. *Strategic Management Journal*, 30: 1265–1285.

2. Holcomb, T.R., Holmes, R.M. & Connelly, B.L., 2009. Making the most of what you have: Managerial ability as a source of resource value creation. *Strategic Management Journal*, 30: 457–485; Athey, R. 2008. It's 2008: Do you know where your talent is?

Connecting people to what matters. *Journal of Business Strategy*, 29 (4): 4–14; ; Barney, J.B. 1991. Firm resources and sustained competitive advantage. *Journal of Management*, 17: 99–120; Hitt, M.A., & Ireland, R.D. 2002. The essence of strategic leadership: Managing human and social capital. *Journal of Leadership and Organizational Studies*, 9: 3–14.

3. Ling, Y., Simsek, Z., Lubatkin, M.H. & Veiga. J.F. 2008. Transformational leadership's role in promoting corporate entrepreneurship: Examining the CEO=TMT interface, *Academy of Management Journal*, 51: 557–576; Kor, Y.Y. 2006. Direct and interaction effects of top management team and board compositions on R&D investment strategy. *Strategic Management Journal*, 27: 1081–1099; Heifetz, R.A., & Laurie, D.L. 1997. The work of the leader. *Harvard Business Review*, 75(1): 124–134; Ireland, R.D., & Hitt, M.A. 1999. Achieving and maintaining strategic competitiveness in the 21st century: The role of strategic leadership. *Academy of Management Executives*, 13(1): 43–57.

4. Adegbesan, J.A. 2009. On the origins of competitive advantage: Strategic factor markets and heterogeneous resource complementarity. *Academy of Management Review*, 34: 463–475; Elbanna, S., & Child, J. 2007. Influences on strategic decision effectiveness: Development and test of an integrative model. *Strategic Management Journal*, 28: 431–453.

5. Cocks, G. 2009. High performers down under: Lessons from Australia's winning companies. *Journal of Business Strategy*, 30 (4): 17–22; Pappas, J.M., & Woolridge, B. 2007. Middle managers divergent strategic activity: An investigation of multiple measures of network centrality. *Journal of Management Studies*, 44: 323–341.

6. Finklestein, S., Hambrick, D.C., & Cannella, A.A. 2008. *Strategic leadership: Top executives and their effects on organizations*. New York: Oxford University Press.

7. Hitt, M.A., Black, S., & Porter, L. 2008. *Management*. Upper Saddle River, NJ: Prentice Hall.

8. Pappas & Woolridge. Middle managers divergent strategic activity; Huy, Q.N. 2001. In praise of middle managers. *Harvard Business Review*, 76(8): 73–79; Sethi, D. 1999. Leading from the middle. *Human Resource Planning*, 22(3): 9–10.

9. Manz, C., & Neck, C.P. 2007. *Mastering self leadership*. Upper Saddle River, NJ: Prentice Hall.

10. Faris, G.F. 1969. The drunkard's search in behavioral science. *Personnel Administration*, 32(1): 11–18.

11. Boyatzis, R.E., Baker, A., Leonard, L., Rhee, K., & Thompson, L. 1995. Will it make a difference? Assessing a value-added, outcome-oriented, competency-based professional program. In R.E. Boyatzis, S.S. Cowan, & D.A. Kolb (Eds.), *Innovation in professional education: Steps on a journey from teaching to learning*. San Francisco: Jossey-Bass; Kretovics, M.A. 1999. Assessing the MBA: What do our students learn? *The Journal of Management Development*, 18: 125–136.

12. Ghoshal, S., Bartlett, C.A., & Moran, P. 1999. A new manifesto for management. *Sloan Management Review*, 40(3): 9–20.

13. Etzioni, A. 1964. *Modern organizations*. Englewood Cliffs, NJ: Prentice Hall.

14. Dess, G.G., & Picken, J.C. 1999. *Beyond productivity: How leading companies achieve superior performance by leveraging their human capital*. New York: AMACOM.

15. Sirmon, D.G., & Hitt, M.A. 2009. Contingencies within dynamic managerial capabilities: Interdependent effects of resource investment and deployment on firm performance. *Strategic Management Journal*, 30: 1375–1394; Six, F., & Sorge, A. 2008. Creating a high-trust organization: An exploration into organizational policies that stimulate interpersonal trust building. *Journal of Management Studies*, 45: 857–884; Dickson, G.W., & DeSanctis, G. 2001. *Information technology and the future enterprise*. Upper Saddle River, NJ: Prentice Hall.

16. Hitt, M.A., Ireland, R.D., & Hoskisson, R.E. 2011. *Strategic management: Competitiveness and globalization*. Mason, OH: South-Western Cengage Learning.

17. Nelson, M.C. 2000. Facing the future: Intellectual capital of our workforce. *Vital Speeches of the Day*, December 15: 138–143.

18. Dess & Picken, *Beyond productivity*; Hitt, Ireland, & Hoskisson, *Strategic management*.

19. Day, J.D., & Wendler, J.C. 1998. The new economics of the organization. *The McKinsey Quarterly*, 1998 (1): 4–17.

20. Dess & Picken, *Beyond productivity*.

21. McGee, J., & Thomas, H. 2007, Knowledge as a lens on the jigsaw puzzle of strategy. *Management Decision*, 45: 539–563.

22. Dragoni. L., Tesluk, P.E., Russell, J.A. & Oh, I.-S. 2009. Understanding managerial development: Integrating developmental assignments, learning orientation, and access to developmental opportunities in predicting managerial competencies, *Academy of Management Journal*, 52: 731–743; McGee, J., & Thomas, H. 2007, Knowledge as a lens on the jigsaw puzzle of strategy. *Management Decision*, 45: 539–563.

23. Salk, J., & Lyles, M.A. 2007. Gratitude, nostalgia and what now? Knowledge acquisition and learning a decade later. *Journal of International Business Studies*, 38: 19–26; Gupta, A.K., Smith, K.G., & Shalley, C.E. 2006. The interplay between exploration and exploitation. *Academy of Management Journal*, 49: 693–706.

24. Porter, M.E. 1980. *Competitive strategy*. New York: Free Press; Porter, M.E. 1985. *Competitive advantage*. New York: Free Press.

25. Sirmon, D.G., Hitt, M.A., & Ireland, R.D. 2007. Managing firm resources in dynamic environments to create value: Looking inside the black box. *Academy of Management Review*, 32: 273–292.

26. Our discussion of the value, rare, and nonimitable terms draws significantly from: Barney, J.B., & Wright, P.M. 1998. On becoming a strategic partner: The role of human resources in gaining competitive advantage. *Human Resource Management*, 37: 31–46.

27. Barney, J.B., & Clark, D.N. 2007. *Resource-based theory: Creating and sustaining competitive advantage*. New York: Oxford University Press; Barney, Firm resources and sustained competitive advantage; Barney & Wright, On becoming a strategic partner; Lepak, D.P., & Snell, S.A. 1999. The human resource architecture: Toward a theory of human capital allocation and development. *Academy of Management Review*, 24: 31–48.

28. Porter, *Competitive strategy*.

29. Hitt, Ireland, & Hoskisson, *Strategic management*.

30. Porter, *Competitive strategy*.

31. Hitt, Ireland, & Hoskisson, *Strategic management*.

32. Smith, W.S. 2009. Vitality in business: Executing a new strategy at Unilever. *Journal of Business Strategy*, 30 (4): 31–41; Higgins,

M.C., & Gulati, R. 2006. Stacking the deck: The effects of top management backgrounds on investor decisions. *Strategic Management Journal*, 27: 1–25.

33. Henderson, A.D., Miller, D., & Hambrick, D.C. 2006. How quickly do CEOs become obsolete? Industry dynamism, CEO tenure, and company performance. *Strategic Management Journal*, 27: 447–460.

34. Ployhart, R.E. 2006. Staffing in the 21st century: New challenges and strategic opportunities. *Journal of Management*, 32: 868–897.

35. Newbert, S.L. 2007. Empirical assessments of the resource-based view of the firm: An assessment and suggestions for future research. *Strategic Management Journal*, 28: 121–146; Barney & Wright, On becoming a strategic partner; Lepak & Snell, The human resource architecture.

36. Laamanen, T. & Wallin, J. 2009. Cognitive dynamics of capability development paths. *Journal of Management Studies*, 46: 950–981.

37. Pfeffer, J. 1994. *Competitive advantage through people: Unleashing the power of the work force*. Boston: Harvard Business School Press.

38. Barney & Wright, On becoming a strategic partner.

39. Ibid.

40. Bangle, C. 2001. The ultimate creativity machine: How BMW turns art into profit. *Harvard Business Review*, 79(1): 47–55.

41. Bogner, W.C., & Bansal, P. 2007. Knowledge management as the basis of sustained high performance. *Journal of Management Studies*, 44: 165–188.

42. Tsui, A.S., Wang, H., & Xin, K.R. 2006. Organizational culture in China: An analysis of culture dimensions and culture types. *Management and Organization Review*, 2: 345–376.

43. Pfeffer, *Competitive advantage*.

44. Barney & Wright, On becoming a strategic partner.

45. Sirmon, D.G., Gove, S. & Hitt, M.A. 2008. Resource management in dyadic competitive rivalry: The effects of resource bundling and deployment. *Academy of Management Journal*, 51: 918–935; Sirmon, Hitt, & Ireland, Managing firm resources in dynamic environments to create value.

46. Sirmon & Hitt, Contingencies within dynamic managerial capabilities; Bowman, C., & Swart, J. 2007. Whose human capital? The challenge of value capture when capital is embedded. *Journal of Management Studies*, 44: 488–505.

47. Collins, C.J., & Smith, K.G. 2006. Knowledge exchange and combination: The role of human resource practices in the performance of high-technology firms. *Academy of Management Journal*, 49: 544–560; Reed, K.K., Lubatkin, M., & Srinivasan, N. 2006. Proposing and testing an intellectual capital-based view of the firm. *Journal of Management Studies*, 43: 867–893.

48. West, B.J., Patera, J.L. & Carsten, M.K. 2009. Team-level positivity: Investigating positive psychological capacities and team level outcomes. *Journal of Organizational Behavior*, 30: 249–267; Luthans, F. 2002. The need for and meaning of positive organizational behavior. *Journal of Organizational Behavior*, 23: 695–706.

49. Avey, J.B. Luthans, F. & Smith, R.M. 2010. Impact of psychological capital on employee well-being over time. *Journal of Occupational Health Psychology*, 15: 17–28.

50. Luthans, F. 2006. The impact of efficacy on work attitudes across cultures. *Journal of World Business*, 41: 121–132.

51. Gibson, C.B., & Earley, P.C. 2007. Collective cognition in action: Accumulation, interaction, examination, and accommodation in the development and operation of group efficacy beliefs in the workplaces. *Academy of Management Review*, 32: 438–458.

52. Walumbwa, F.O., Luthans, F, Avey, J.B. & Oke, A. 2009. Authentically leading groups: The mediating role of collective psychological capital and trust. *Journal of Organizational Behavior*, 30: 1–21.

53. Keyton, J. & Smith, F.L. 2009. Distrust in leaders: Dimensions, patterns and emotional intensity. *Journal of Leadership and Organizational Studies*, 16: 6–18; Luthans, F. & Avolio, B.J. 2009. The point of positive organizational behavior. *Journal of Organizational Behavior*, 30: 291–307.

54. Gillespie, N., & Dietz, G. 2009. Trust repair after an organization-level failure. *Academy of Management Review*, 34: 127–145.

55. Gooty, J., Gavin, M. Johnson, P.D., Frazier, M.L., & Snow, D.B. 2009. In the eyes of the beholder: Transformational leadership, positive psychological capital and performance. *Journal of Leadership and Organizational Studies*, 15: 353–367.

56. Cooper, C.L., Quick, J.C. & Schabracq, M.J. 2010. Epilogue. In C.L. Cooper, J.C. Quick & M.J. Schabracq (Eds.), *Work and health psychology: The handbook*. Hoboken, NJ: John Wiley & Sons; Quick, J.C., Macik-Frey, M., & Cooper, C.L. 2007. Managerial dimensions of organizational slack. *Journal of Management Studies*, 44: 189–205.

57. Fineman, S. 2006. On being positive: Concerns and counterpoints. *Academy of Management Review*, 31: 270–291.

58. Goleman, D. 2004. What makes a leader? *Harvard Business Review*, 82 (January): 82–91.

59. McKee, A., & Massimillian, D. 2006. Resonant leadership: A new kind of leadership for the digital age. *Journal of Business Strategy*, 27(5): 45–49.

60. The five aspects of high-commitment management that are used in this book are the most commonly mentioned aspects. See, for example, the following: Arthur, J.B. 1994. Effects of human resource systems on manufacturing performance and turnover. *Academy of Management Journal*, 37: 670–687; Becker, B., & Gerhart, B. 1996. The impact of human resource management on organizational performance: Progress and prospects. *Academy of Management Journal*, 39: 779–801; Guthrie, J.P. 2001. High-involvement work practices, turnover, and productivity: Evidence from New Zealand. *Academy of Management Journal*, 44: 180–190; MacDuffie, J.P. 1995. Human resource bundles and manufacturing performance: Organizational logic and flexible production systems in the world auto industry. *Industrial and Labor Relations Review*, 48: 197–221; Pfeffer, The human equation; Pfeffer, J., & Veiga, J.F. 1999. Putting people first for organizational success. *Academy of Management Executive*, 13(2): 37–48.

61. Zatzick, C.D., & Iverson, R.D. 2006. High-involvement management and workforce reduction: Competitive advantage or disadvantage. *Academy of Management Journal*, 49: 999–1015.

62. Takeuchi, R, Chen, G. & Lepak, D.P., 2009. Through the looking glass of a social system: Cross-level effects of high-performance

work systems on employees' attitudes. *Personnel Psychology*, 62: 1–29; Baron, J.N., & Kreps, D.M. 1999. *Strategic human resources: Frameworks for general managers.* New York: John Wiley & Sons.

63. Ployhart, Staffing in the 21st century; Pfeffer, *The human equation*; Pfeffer & Veiga, Putting people first for organizational success.

64. Ibid.

65. For example, see Erdogan, B., Liden, R.C., & Kraimer, M.L. 2006. Justice and leader-member exchange: The moderating role of organizational culture, *Academy of Management Journal*, 49: 395–406.

66. O'Reilly, C.A., Chatman, J., & Caldwell, D.F. 1991. People and organizational culture: A profile comparison approach to assessing person-organization fit. *Academy of Management Journal*, 34: 487–516.

67. Perry-Smith, J.E. 2006. Social yet creative: The role of social relationships in facilitating individual creativity. *Academy of Management Journal*, 49: 85–101.

68. Van Iddekinge, C.H., Ferris, G., Perrewe, P., Perryman, A., Blass, F.R. & Thomas, D. 2009. Effects of selection and training on unit-level performance over time: A latent growth modelling approach. *Journal of Applied Psychology*, 94: 829–843.

69. Ng, T.W.H., & Feldman, D.C. 2009. How broadly does education contribute to job performance? *Personnel Psychology*, 62: 89–134.

70. Lawler, E.E., Mohrman, S.A., & Benson, G. 2001. *Organizing for high performance: Employee involvement, TQM, reengineering, and knowledge management in the Fortune 1000.* San Francisco: Jossey-Bass.

71. Manz & Neck, *Mastering self leadership*; Pfeffer, *The human equation*; Pfeffer & Veiga, Putting people first for organizational success.

72. Hulsheger, U.R., Anderson, N. & Salgado, J.F. 2009. Team-level predictors of innovation at work: A comprehensive meta-analysis spanning three decades of research. *Journal of Applied Psychology*, 94: 1126–1145.

73. Lawler, Mohrman, & Benson, *Organizing for high performance.*

74. Srivastava, A., Bartol, K.M., & Locke, E.A., 2006. Empowering leadership in management teams: Effects on knowledge sharing, efficacy and performance. *Academy of Management Journal*, 49: 1239–1251.

75. Mesmer-Mangus, J.R. & DeChurch, L.A. 2009. Information sharing and team performance: A meta-analysis, *Journal of Applied Psychology*, 94: 535–546.

76. Lawler, Mohrman, & Benson, *Organizing for high performance.*

77. Arthur, Effects of human resource systems on manufacturing performance and turnover.

78. MacDuffie, Human resource bundles and manufacturing performance.

79. Welbourne, T.M., & Andrews, A.O. 1996. Predicting the performance of initial public offerings: Should human resource management be in the equation? *Academy of Management Journal*, 39: 891–919.

80. Gittell, J.H., Seidner, R., & Wimbush, J. 2010. A relational model of how high-performance work systems work. *Organization Science*, 21: 490–506; Liao, H., Toya, K., Lepak, D.P. & Hong, Y. 2009. Do they see eye to eye? Management and employee perspectives of high-performance work systems and influence processes on service quality. *Journal of Applied Psychology*, 94: 371–391.

81. Kirkman, B.L., Chen, G., Farh, J.-L., Chen, Z.X., & Lowe, K.B. 2009. Individual power distance orientation and follower reactions to transformational leaders: A cross-level, cross-cultural examination. *Academy of Management Journal*, 52: 744–764.

82. Davis, J.H., Schoorman, F.D., Mayer, R.C., & Tan, H.H. 2000. The trusted general manager and business unit performance: Empirical evidence of a competitive advantage. *Strategic Management Journal*, 21: 563–576; Mayer, R.C., Davis, J.H., & Schoorman, F.D. 1995. An integrative model of organizational trust. *Academy of Management Review*, 20: 709–734.

83. Guaspari, J. 2001. How to? Who cares! *Across the Board*, May/June: 75–76.

84. Gong, Y., Huang, J.-C. & Farh, J.-L. 2009. Employee learning orientation, transformational leadership, and employee creativity: The mediating role of employee creative self-efficacy. *Academy of Management Journal*, 52: 765–778.

85 Taylor, W.C., 2008. Bill Taylor: Pixar's blockbuster secrets. *BusinessWeek*, at http://www.businessweek.com, July 10.

86 Lewin, A.Y., Massini, S. & Peeters, C. 2009. Why are companies offshoring innovation? The emerging global race for talent. *Journal of International Business Studies*, 40: 901–925.

organizational diversity

exploring behavior in action

Diversity in the Los Angeles Fire Department

Melissa Kelley had a rich background in firefighting. Early in life, she learned from her grandfather, who worked as a firefighter. In college, she learned through coursework as a fire-science major. After college, she spent five years learning and honing her skills as a firefighter with the California Department of Forestry.

knowledge objectives

After reading this chapter, you should be able to:

1. Define organizational diversity and distinguish between affirmative action and diversity management.

2. Distinguish among multicultural, plural, and monolithic organizations.

3. Describe the demographic characteristics of the U.S. population and explain their implications for the composition of the workplace.

4. Discuss general changes occurring in the United States that are increasing the importance of managing diversity effectively.

5. Understand why successfully managing diversity is extremely important for high-involvement work organizations.

6. Discuss the various roadblocks to effectively managing a diverse workforce.

7. Describe how organizations can successfully manage diversity.

Armed with her experiences and passion for the work, she joined the Los Angeles Fire Department in 2001. Although aware of possible discrimination and harassment against women in the department, she did not hesitate to join when presented with the opportunity. In her words, "I was willing to overlook … the dirty jokes, the porn, the … mentality. … I just wanted to be part of the team." To her, only two simple rules applied: "Do not touch me. Do not hurt me on purpose."

According to media accounts, the first of her rules was violated early in her career with the LAFD. Soon after joining the department, a male colleague entered her bed at the firehouse. He then attempted to kiss and touch her. She resisted and the colleague left, but for several weeks following the incident he clucked like a chicken whenever she was present.

During a routine training exercise later in her career, the second rule came into sharp focus. While the rule probably was not violated explicitly, it is relevant nonetheless to the events that occurred. Following a fire call, Ms. Kelley engaged in the "Humiliator" drill, a drill that involves lifting and positioning a heavy ladder, climbing the ladder with a large saw, and using the saw to cut through metal bars in a window. Although she had previously demonstrated the abilities needed for the drill, on that particular day she dropped the ladder onto her head, resulting in her helmet becoming stuck between two of its rungs. She immediately felt pain and could not lift her arm to free herself, saying in a later interview: "In my head I'm thinking, I'm dying. My arm is messed up. My back is hurting. My legs are going to give out if I don't get this ladder off me." She continued to struggle with the ladder while showing obvious signs of pain. One colleague apparently tried to help but was stopped. Others reportedly cursed at the struggling firefighter. In the end, Ms. Kelley was taken to a local hospital where multiple injuries were discovered. She subsequently had to be reassigned as a dispatcher. In reflecting on the events of that day, she summed up the situation this way: "Those were my teammates. They would help a dog pinned under a ladder. But they wouldn't help me."

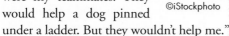

©iStockphoto

Ms. Kelley's experiences are not unique. Alicia Mathis, a captain who joined the LAFD in 1989, also reports being approached in bed at a firehouse. She filed a complaint with the California Department of Fair Employment and Housing. Ruthie Bernal settled a lawsuit related to sexual advances that were followed by harsh treatment when the advances were rejected. Interestingly, Ms. Bernal reports that such advances and subsequent harsh treatment occurred in three different situations involving three different firefighters. Beyond sexual advances, other inappropriate acts have been reported, including mouthwash bottles being filled with inappropriate substances, unflattering female training experiences being captured on video and circulated among male colleagues, sexual materials being delivered, and disproportionately difficult training/testing being applied. In a survey released by the City Controller, 80 percent of women reported discrimination as an issue.

Beyond gender-based problems, race also has played a role in the Los Angeles Fire Department. In a racially charged incident that took place a few years ago, an African American firefighter ate dog food that had been put into his spaghetti at a firehouse. The nature of this incident remains a matter of controversy, as some claim it was harmless horseplay. Even so, because of a history of racial discrimination and harassment, it sparked outrage and a lawsuit. In the survey just mentioned, 87 percent of African Americans reported discrimination as an issue. Hispanics have also reported problems.

The overall effects of these gender and racial issues have been significant. Beyond the loss of talented individuals and the reduced opportunity to attract talented women and minorities, the LAFD has had to pay millions of dollars to settle lawsuits. For example, Brenda Lee was recently awarded more than $6.2 million in a discrimination, harassment, and retaliation case against the LAFD and her former supervisor for being harassed because she is African American, female, and gay.

Job satisfaction also has been affected for some individuals of both genders and all races. In addition, turmoil at the top of the organization has been significant, as multiple fire chiefs have been fired because of the discrimination and harassment. Has the ultimate mission of the organization been compromised? The mission is to "preserve life and property, promote public safety and foster economic growth. ..." Given the loss of talent, reduced satisfaction for some, and turmoil at the top, the effective pursuit of the mission has not been helped.

The news is not all bad, however. City and fire department officials have taken steps to remedy the situation. Surveys designed to stay abreast of the problems have been conducted, as noted earlier. Events such as "Black History Month Recruitment Exposition and Family Carnival" have been held. A new fire chief committed to a positive culture has been hired. The first female African American fire captain has been installed.

Sources: S. Banks. 2006. "Firehouse Culture an Ordeal for Women," *Los Angeles Times*, Dec. 3, p. A.1; S. Glover. 2007. "Rising Star Caught in Turmoil at the LAFD," *Los Angeles Times*, Feb. 12, B.1; D. Hernandez. 2006. "Bringing Diversity to the Force," *Los Angeles Times*, Feb. 6, B.4; J. Kandel. 2006. "Hostile Acts," *The IRE Journal* 29, no. 4: 22; LAFD, "Core Values," 2007, at http://www.joinlafd.org/CoreValues.htm; L. Richardson. 2006. "Audit Faults Fire Dept.," *Los Angeles Times*, Jan. 27, p. B.4; L. Richardson. 2006. "L.A. Fire Captain Alleges Gender Bias," *Los Angeles Times*, Sept. 28, p. B.4. "Lesbian firefighter in L.A. wins $6.2 mil. in discrimination case." *Jet*, July 30, 2007, at FindArticles.com. http://findarticles.com/p/articles/mi_m1355/is_4_112/ai_n27328045.

the strategic importance of Organizational Diversity

As the LAFD case shows, negative reactions to diversity can have harmful effects on an organization. These reactions, including discrimination and harassment of various forms, often lead to lawsuits, turnover, reduced satisfaction, and performance issues. In the most effective organizations, associates and managers understand the value of diversity and capitalize on it to improve performance. Moreover, associates and managers cannot escape diverse workgroups and organizations. Differences in gender, race, functional background, and so on are all around us. The United States is a particularly diverse country with respect to race and ethnicity, and current demographic trends indicate that its population will become even more diverse.

LAFD's legal troubles, financial settlement costs, and public embarrassment have led to renewed efforts to change the culture. The changing nature of the firefighter's job, where 80 percent of fire calls no longer involve structural or brush fires, probably has helped in this process.[1] Many organizations, however, have not needed public embarrassment or changing jobs to motivate diversity efforts. Many organizations, particularly large ones, have voluntarily adopted diversity management programs aimed at recruiting, retaining, and motivating high-quality associates from all demographic backgrounds. Most *Fortune* 500 companies, for example, have diversity management programs.[2] A full 78 percent of organizations with 10,000 or more employees report having a diversity strategy, as compared with 44 percent of companies with 100 to 999 employees and 31 percent in companies

with fewer than 100 workers. Over 79 percent of human resource managers at *Fortune* 1000 companies said they believed that successfully managing diversity improves their organizations.[3]

Diversity, if properly managed, can help a business build competitive advantage. For example, hiring and retaining managers and associates from various ethnicities can help an organization better understand and serve an existing diverse customer base. Diversity among associates also might help the organization attract additional customers from various ethnic groups. Diverse backgrounds and experiences incorporated into a work team or task force can help the organization more effectively handle an array of complex and challenging problems. Kevin Johnson, Co-President of Platforms and Services at Microsoft, puts it this way: "[W]e must recognize, respect, and leverage the different perspectives our employees bring to the marketplace as strengths. Doing so will ensure that we will be more competitive in the global marketplace, will be seen as an employer of choice, and will be more creative and innovative ...."[4]

In the case of nonprofit organizations or governmental units such as the Los Angeles Fire Department, diversity can help build a form of competitive advantage. For instance, hiring and retaining managers and associates from both genders and multiple ethnic groups could help a nonprofit organization better understand its actual and potential client base as well as its actual and potential donors. Thus, the organization might be able to attract resources that would have gone to another nonprofit organization or that would have been

withheld from donation. In the case of the Los Angeles Fire Department, diverse captains, firefighters, and paramedics could better communicate with and predict the behavior of the diverse citizenry of Los Angeles. This would enable the department to better serve the city. It also would position it to receive more resources from the city and state and would increase its likelihood of being chosen over other organizations for additional duties in the Los Angeles area.

Many individuals feel most comfortable interacting and working with people who are similar to them on a variety of dimensions (such as age, race, ethnic background, education, functional area, values, and personality).[5] They must, however, learn to work with all others in an organization to achieve common goals. In a truly inclusive workplace, everyone feels valued and all associates are motivated and committed to the mission of the organization. Such outcomes are consistent with a high-involvement work environment and can help organizations achieve competitive advantage.

We begin this chapter by defining organizational diversity and distinguishing it from other concepts, such as affirmative action. Next, we describe the forces in a changing world that have made diversity such a crucial concern. We then discuss possible benefits of effective diversity management, followed by roadblocks to such management and to the development of an inclusive workplace. We conclude the chapter with a discussion of what can be done to successfully manage a diverse organization.

Diversity Defined

Diversity can be defined as a characteristic of a group of people where differences exist on one or more relevant dimensions such as gender.[6] Notice that diversity is a *group* characteristic, not an individual characteristic. Thus, it is inappropriate to refer to an individual as "diverse." If the group is predominantly male, the presence of a woman will make the group more diverse. However, if the group is predominantly female, the presence of a particular woman will make the group more homogeneous and less diverse.

In practice, diversity is often defined in terms of particular dimensions, most commonly gender, race, and ethnicity. Other important dimensions also exist.[7] These include age, religion, social class, sexual orientation, personality, functional experience (e.g., finance, marketing, accounting), and geographical background (e.g., background in the Canadian province of Ontario versus the province of Saskatchewan).[8] Any characteristic that would influence a person's identity or the way he or she approaches problems and views the world can be important to consider when defining diversity.[9] Two diversity scholars put it this way: "the effects of diversity can result from any attribute that people use to tell themselves that another person is different."[10] Visible attributes (e.g., race, gender, ethnicity),[11] attributes directly related to job performance (e.g., education and functional experience),[12] and rare attributes[13] are the most likely to be seen as important. Examples of how some large organizations define diversity appear below:

> **Texas Instruments:** "Diversity refers to the ways in which people differ. This includes obvious differences such as race and gender, and more subtle differences in religion and culture, as well as variations in work styles, thoughts and ideas."[14]
>
> **Microsoft:** "[Diversity] means not only having a workforce balanced by race, ethnic origin, gender, sexual orientation, and gender identity and expression, but also having a workforce that embraces differences in approaches, insights, ability, and experience."[15]
>
> **Bank of America:** "Our commitment to diversity is … about creating an environment in which all associates can fulfill their potential without artificial barriers, and in which the team is made stronger by the diverse backgrounds, experiences and perspectives of individuals."[16]

Affirmative action programs (AAPs) differ from diversity management programs. This important distinction should be noted before proceeding. AAPs are specific measures an organization takes to remedy and/or prevent discrimination. The key idea is to ensure fair representation of women and racial and ethnic minorities in the workplace. In the United States, federal contractors (with 50 or more employees or government contracts over $50,000) are required to have AAPs. Other organizations may voluntarily adopt an AAP or may be court-ordered to adopt a program to remedy discriminatory practices. Central features of AAPs include a utilization analysis, which indicates the proportion of women and minorities hired and occupying various positions; goals and timetables for remedying underutilization of women and minorities; specific recruiting practices aimed at recruiting women and minorities (for example, recruiting at traditionally African American universities); and provision of developmental opportunities.[17] AAPs do not require that specific hiring quotas be implemented (which may be illegal) or that standards for selection and promotion be lowered. Also, AAPs usually provide temporary action; once women and minorities are appropriately represented in an organization, the AAP (with the exception of monitoring) is no longer necessary.

diversity
A characteristic of a group of people where differences exist on one or more relevant dimensions such as gender.

EXHIBIT 2-1 Differences between Affirmative Action Programs and Diversity Management Programs

	Affirmative Action	Diversity Management
Purpose	To prevent and/or remedy discrimination	To create an inclusive work environment where all associates are empowered to perform their best
Assimilation	Assumes individuals will individually assimilate into the organization; individuals will adapt	Assumes that managers and the organizations will change (i.e., culture policies, and systems foster an all-inclusive work environment)
Focus	Recruitment, mobility, and retention	Creating an environment that allows all associates to reach their full potential
Cause of Diversity Problems	Does not address the cause of problems	Attempts to uncover the root causes of diversity problems
Target	Individuals identified as disadvantaged (usually racial and ethnic minorities, women, people with disabilities)	All associates
Time Frame	Temporary, until there is appropriate representation of disadvantaged groups	Ongoing, permanent changes

Sources: Adapted from R.R. Thomas, Jr. 1992. "Managing Diversity: A Conceptual Framework," in S.E. Jackson et al. (Eds.), *Diversity in the Workplace* (New York: Guilford Press), pp. 306–317. Society for Human Resource Management, "How Is a Diversity Initiative Different from My Affirmative Action Plan?," 2004, at http://www.shrm.org/diversity.

In contrast, diversity management programs are put in place to improve organizational performance. Because of their different goals, these programs differ from AAPs in several ways,[18] as summarized in Exhibit 2-1. Diversity management programs address diversity on many dimensions. They are often meant to change the organizational culture to be more inclusive and to enable and empower all associates. In addition, they focus on developing people's ability to work together.

When diversity is managed successfully, a multicultural organization is the result.[19] A **multicultural organization** is one in which the organizational culture fosters and values differences. As Google, a company often praised for their diversity initiatives, states on their website "At Google, we don't just accept difference—we thrive on it. We celebrate it. And we support it, for the benefit of our employees, our products and our community." People of any gender, ethnic, racial, and cultural backgrounds are integrated and represented at all levels and positions in the organization. Because of the effective management of diversity, there is little intergroup conflict. Very few organizations in the United States or elsewhere are truly multicultural organizations; most organizations are either plural or monolithic.

Plural organizations have diverse workforces and take steps to be inclusive and respectful of people from different backgrounds. However, diversity is tolerated rather than valued and fostered. Whereas multicultural organizations take special actions to make the environment inclusive and to ensure that all members feel valued, plural organizations focus on the law and on avoiding blatant discrimination.[20] Furthermore, people of various backgrounds may not be integrated throughout the levels and jobs of the organization, as they are in multicultural organizations. For example, even though a company may

multicultural organization
An organization in which the organizational culture values differences.

plural organization
An organization that has a diverse workforce and takes steps to be inclusive and respectful of differences, but where diversity is tolerated rather than truly valued.

employ a large number of women, most of them may be in secretarial jobs. Plural organizations may also have human resource management policies and business practices that exclude minority members, often unintentionally. For example, many companies reward people for being self-promoters; that is, people who brag about themselves and make their achievements known are noticed and promoted, even though their achievements may not be as strong as those who do not self-promote. However, self-promoting behavior may be quite unnatural for people from cultural backgrounds where modesty and concern for the group are dominant values, such as the Japanese and Chinese cultures.[21] Finally, we would expect more intergroup conflict in plural organizations than in multicultural organizations because diversity is not proactively managed.

Finally, **monolithic organizations** are homogeneous. These organizations tend to have extreme occupational segregation, with minority group members holding low-status jobs. Monolithic organizations actively discourage diversity; thus, anyone who is different from the majority receives heavy pressure to conform. Most U.S. organizations have moved away from a monolithic model because changes in the external environment and the workforce have required them to do so.[22] In the next section, we describe what these changes have been.

monolithic organization
An organization that is homogeneous.

Forces of Change

Over the past 20 years, several important changes in the United States and in many other countries have focused more attention on diversity, and these trends are expected to continue. The most important changes are: (1) shifts in population demographics, (2) increasing importance of the service economy, (3) the globalization of business, and (4) new management methods that require teamwork.

Changing Population Demographics

Over the past ten years, more than one-third of people entering the U.S. workforce have been members of racial or ethnic minority groups.[23] Moreover, the proportion of racial and ethnic minorities in the workforce is expected to increase indefinitely. The situation is similar in some European countries.[24]

Exhibit 2-2 provides data on trends that affect the workforce in the United States. It shows, for example, that non-Hispanic white people are expected to decrease as a percentage of the overall population, moving from almost 65 percent to less than 50 percent by 2050 (note that most Hispanics are racially white). The percentage of the population from Hispanic origins (any race) is expected to almost double, from just under 16 percent to almost 30 percent. The Asian American population is also expected to grow, from approximately 5 percent to 9 percent of the overall population. The expansion of the Hispanic American and Asian American populations is due in part to immigration. The percentage of black Americans (some of whom are of Hispanic origin) is expected to remain stable at around 13 percent.

Exhibit 2-2 also shows a trend related to the continued aging of the U.S. population. The decade between 2000 and 2010 saw a growth spurt in the group made up of people aged 45 through 64. This spurt reflects the aging of the post–World War II baby boom generation—people born between 1946 and 1964. A major U.S. labor shortage is expected between 2015 and 2025 as members of the baby boom generation retire.[25] Thus,

EXHIBIT 2-2 Projected U.S. Population Demographics

Percentage by Race or Hispanic Origin	2010	2030	2050
White, alone	79.5	76.6	74.0
Black, alone	12.9	13.1	13.0
Asian, alone	5.3	7.3	9.2
More than one	1.8	2.6	3.7
Hispanic origin (all races)	15.8	22.6	29.6
White (not Hispanic origin)	64.7	55.5	46.3

Percentage by Age	2010	2030	2050
0–4	6.8	6.5	6.4
5–17	17.4	17.0	16.7
18–24	9.9	9.1	9.0
25–44	26.8	25.5	25.2
45–64	26.1	22.6	22.4
65+	12.5	19.3	20.2

Percentage by Sex	2010	2030	2050
Male	49.1	49.1	49.2
Female	50.9	50.9	50.8

Source: U.S. Census Bureau, "U.S. Population Projections," 2009. At http://www.census.gov/population/www/projections/summarytables.html.

it will be even more important for organizations to be able to attract and retain talented associates. Another aspect of the aging population also will likely influence the composition of the labor force. As can be seen in the exhibit, the population over 65 years old will continue to grow. In 2050, it is expected that one in five Americans will be 65 years old or older. If people work beyond the traditional retirement age of 65 due to improved health and the Age Discrimination Act (which protects people 40 and older from discrimination such as being forced to retire), the workforce will continue to age.

Finally, Exhibit 2-2 indicates that the proportion of men and women in the population is likely to remain stable. While women make up 50.9 percent of the population, approximately 48 percent of the labor force is female.[26] This number has grown from 40 percent in 1975 and is expected to increase slightly over the next decade,[27] indicating that proportionally more women than men will be entering the workforce. About 73 percent of mothers work, and about 60 percent of mothers who work have children under the age of three.[28] In contrast, less than 50 percent of mothers worked in 1975. The number of combined hours per week that married couples with children work increased from 55 in 1969 to 66 in 2000.[29] These trends create a need for policies that take family issues into consideration and that deal with the differing issues of workers who have children versus those who do not have children.

Increase in the Service Economy

The U.S. Bureau of Labor Statistics has predicted that the number of service-producing jobs (including those in transportation, utility, communications, wholesale and retail

trade, finance, insurance, real estate, and government) will grow by approximately 17 percent between 2004 and 2014.[30] Service jobs are projected
to make up more than 78 percent of all jobs in the
United States by 2014.[31] Importantly, a service-
based economy depends on high-quality interactions between people, whether between beauticians
and their clients, home health-care workers and their
patients, or human resource managers and their
corporate associates. Because diversity within these
and other customer groups is increasing, the service
economy demands greater understanding and appreciation of diversity.[32]

©AP/Wide World Photos

The Global Economy

Globalization of the business world is an accelerating trend, gaining momentum from the
increasing ease of communication, the opening of new markets, and growth in the number of multinational firms. In 2006, the United States exported $1,437 billion in goods
and services and imported $2,202 billion in goods and services.[33] Since 2003, the export
figure has increased by more than 40 percent in nominal dollars, while the import figure
has increased by 45 percent.[34] Most of the largest companies in the world (for example,
GE, Exxon, and Toyota) are the largest owners, worldwide, of foreign assets.[35] These same
companies employ millions of workers outside of their home countries. Also, many of
these companies require workers in their home countries to work with people from other
parts of the world. Finally, many companies now conduct worldwide searches for managers and executives, so that the world serves as the labor market.

    The continuing growth of globalization indicates that people will be working with
others from different countries and cultures at an ever-increasing rate. Furthermore, many
U.S. associates will work outside the United States with people who speak different languages, are accustomed to different business practices, and have different worldviews. As
globalization increases, the need for successful diversity management also increases. You
will read more about global issues in Chapter 3.

Requirements for Teamwork

Organizations that wish to succeed must respond to increasing globalization, rapidly
changing technology and knowledge, and increasing demands for meaningfulness of associates' work. Teamwork is one way to provide better-quality goods and services, because
people are more likely to become engaged and committed to the goals of the organization
when they are members of strong teams. Whole Foods Market provides an example. At
this very successful U.S.-based international provider of organic foods, everyone is assigned to a small, self-directed team.[36]

    Teamwork requires that individuals work well together. Having diverse teams may
allow for synergistic effects, where the variety of team experiences, attitudes, and viewpoints leads to better team performance.[37] However, to realize these positive effects, diversity must be managed effectively. Teams are discussed in more detail in Chapter 11.

Diversity Management and High-Involvement Organizations

High-involvement organizations expect their associates to respect, learn from, and help one another. They also recognize that associates must be committed to the organization in order to use training, information, and decision power in appropriate ways. Managing diversity effectively is important in the achievement of these aims. Individuals, groups, organizations, and even society as a whole can benefit.

Individual Outcomes

Associates' perceptions of the extent to which they are valued and supported by their organization have a strong effect on their commitment to the organization and their job involvement and satisfaction.[38] In the case of associates who are different from those around them, a positive, inclusive climate for diversity is necessary for full engagement in the work.[39] Research has found that women, racial and ethnic minority group members, and people with disabilities have less positive attitudes toward their organizations, jobs, and careers when they feel that their organizations have poor climates for diversity.[40] In addition, when an organization encourages and supports diversity, individuals are less likely to feel discriminated against and to be treated unfairly. When people feel they have been treated unfairly, they react negatively by withdrawing, performing poorly, retaliating, or filing lawsuits.[41]

Consider the case of a person whose religion forbids alcohol use, requires prayer at certain times of the day, and considers sexual jokes and materials offensive. This person, though, works in an environment where many deals are made over drinks in the local bar, where co-workers tease him because of his daily prayers, and where office walls are covered with risqué pictures. It is likely that this person feels uncomfortable in the office and devalued by his co-workers, leading to dissatisfaction and low commitment to his associates and the organization. Furthermore, he may avoid uncomfortable social activities where important information is exchanged and work accomplished, thus hurting his job performance. A work environment and culture that are sensitive, respectful, and accepting of this person's beliefs would likely result in a more committed, satisfied, and higher-performing associate.

With respect to individuals who are in the majority, diversity management programs must be sensitive to their needs as well. Otherwise, the ideals of diversity management will not be met and outcomes for some individuals will be less positive than they should be. In the United States, white men are often in the majority in a given organizational situation. For them, diversity management can be threatening. One study showed that white men placed less value on efforts to promote diversity.[42] Another study showed that white men perceived injustice when laid off in disproportionate numbers in the face of active diversity management, but did not perceive injustice in the face of disproportionate layoffs in situations without active diversity management.[43] To ensure commitment, satisfaction, and strong performance among those in a majority group, organizational leaders must: (1) carefully build and communicate the case for diversity by citing the forces of change discussed earlier and (2) ensure fair decision processes and fair outcomes for all.

Organizations that create, encourage, and support diversity make all associates feel valued and provide them with opportunities to reach their full potential and be truly engaged in their work. This is a necessary condition of high-involvement work environments.

To put it another way, creating and successfully managing diversity is a necessary condition for achieving a high-involvement work environment.

Group Outcomes

Diversity should have positive effects on the outcomes of organizational groups, particularly on decision-making, creative, or complex tasks.[44] This is because individual group members have different ideas, viewpoints, and knowledge to contribute, resulting in a wider variety of ideas and alternatives being considered.[45] Individuals who are different in terms of age, gender, race, ethnicity, functional background, and education often think about issues differently.[46]

For example, have you ever wondered why phones have rounded edges instead of sharp corners and why there is often a raised dot on the "5" key? One reason is that design groups at AT&T include people who have disabilities, including visual impairments. Rounded corners are less dangerous for people who cannot see the phone, and a raised dot on the "5" key allows people who cannot see to orient their fingers on the keypad. Ohmny Romero, who has worked as a manager in AT&T's technical division and is visually impaired, stated that AT&T associates with disabilities become involved in developing new technologies because they want to "give back" to their community.[47] As a result, everyone has less dangerous phones and keypads that can be used when it is difficult to see. These innovations might never have come about if AT&T design teams had not included members with disabilities and respected their inputs.

In spite of its potential benefits, diversity has been described as a "mixed blessing" in terms of outcomes for organizational groups.[48] Indeed, research has produced mixed results, with some studies showing positive effects but other studies failing to show such effects.[49] There are two issues to consider in interpreting these research outcomes. First, fault lines can be present in situations characterized by diversity. *Fault lines* occur when two or more dimensions of diversity are correlated. For example, if all/most of the young people on a cross-functional task force represent marketing while all/most of the older individuals represent product engineering, then a fault line is said to exist. Fault lines merge multiple identities (e.g., young and marketing focused) to produce barriers to effective collaboration within a group. Research on this phenomenon is relatively new, but has produced findings suggesting poor group outcomes.[50]

Second, problems can develop in all situations characterized by some level of diversity. People often label group members who are different from themselves as "out-group members" and like them less,[51] leading to difficulties in group problem solving and decision making. Diverse organizational groups are more likely to experience personal conflict, problems in communication, and conflict among subgroups.[52]

In light of the above issues, the goal becomes one of facilitating the positive effects of diversity while eradicating the potentially negative effects. One way of harnessing the positive potential of group diversity, while avoiding the negative, is to establish a common identity for the group and to focus on common goals.[53] Richard Hackman, a leading researcher and consultant in the area of teams, has pointed out the importance of common goals for a team, as well as the importance of coaching for team problems.[54] Furthermore, when a company has a positive diversity culture, the problems associated with group diversity are much less likely to occur.[55] An organization that implements effective diversity programs, philosophies, and practices tends to avoid the problems associated with diversity, allowing it to yield the benefits that can be so important.[56] We develop these ideas later in this chapter.

Organizational Outcomes

As discussed above, diversity can lead to more satisfied, motivated, and committed associates who perform more effectively at their individual tasks. Properly managed, diversity can also lead to better-performing and more innovative groups. Therefore, diversity, through its effects on individual and group outcomes, is likely to affect the bottom-line performance of the organization.[57]

Despite the importance of the issue, little systematic research has been conducted that explicitly examines whether the diversity of an organization's workforce is tied to bottom-line performance. One exception is a study that examined the effect of racial and ethnic diversity in the banking industry. Diversity was positively related to the productivity, return on equity, and market performance of banks, but only when the bank had a corporate strategy that reflected growth. The positive relationship between diversity and firm performance was not found in banks that were pursuing a downsizing strategy. In these banks, greater diversity tended to result in poorer performance.[58] Another exception is a large-scale study commissioned by business executives and conducted by researchers at MIT's Sloan School of Management, Harvard Business School, the Wharton School, Rutgers University, the University of Illinois, and the University of California at Berkeley.[59] This research examined the impact of demographic diversity on various aspects of firm performance in several *Fortune* 500 companies. Diversity was found to have no straightforward effects on performance. The researchers concluded that organizations need to manage diversity more effectively, especially because of the potential benefits that diversity offers. That is, diversity alone does not guarantee good corporate performance. It's what the company does with diversity that matters!

In addition to diversity in the workforce, diversity among those leading an organization might have effects. During the past decade or so, the business press has called for an increase in the demographic diversity of boards of directors and upper-echelon management teams.[60] Indeed, the number of women and racial/ethnic minority group members on corporate boards and in top executive positions has been consistently increasing.[61]

This trend appears to make good sense. A recent study of *Fortune* 500 firms found that the companies with the highest representation of women in top positions strongly outperformed those with the poorest representation of women in terms of return on equity and return to shareholders.[62] Other studies have found that the demographic diversity of boards of directors (in terms of race, gender, and age) is positively related to firm performance.[63] Thus, demographic diversity on boards can have a direct positive impact on the organization. One reason for this effect is that women and minorities who actually make it to the top may be better performers and better connected than typical board members.[64] Thus, including them on boards of directors usually increases the quality and talent of the board; the same is usually true for the upper-echelon management team. Another reason for positive outcomes is that by having demographically diverse boards and management teams, companies are sending positive social signals that attract both associates and potential shareholders.[65]

Other types of diversity on boards of directors and upper-echelon management teams also might be beneficial to the firm's bottom-line performance. Research suggests that diversity in functional areas, educational background, social/professional networks, and length of service can have positive effects on firm performance through better decision making.[66] Again, the diversity must be managed properly for benefits to appear.

Societal and Moral Outcomes

In order to have a society based on fairness and justice, U.S. federal laws prohibit employers from discriminating against applicants or employees on the basis of age, gender, race, color, national origin, religion, or disability. Discrimination is an expensive proposition for companies. Some recent awards to plaintiffs resulting from either out-of-court settlements or court cases include the following:

- Ford Motor Company paid out $10.5 million for age discrimination and $8 million for sex discrimination.
- Coca-Cola paid out $192.5 million for race discrimination.
- Texaco paid out $176 million for race discrimination.
- CalPERS paid out $250 million for age discrimination.
- Shoneys paid out $132.5 million for race discrimination.
- Rent-A-Center paid out $47 million for sex discrimination.
- Information Agency and Voice of America paid out $508 million for sex discrimination.
- Wal-Mart recently paid $17.5 million to settle a class action lawsuit regarding discrimination against African Americans in recruitment and hiring of truck drivers for its private fleet. The company is currently dealing with the largest discrimination lawsuit in history. There is an unresolved class action suit filed by two million current and former female employees for sex discrimination.

Apart from these direct costs, firms suffer other losses when suits are filed against them, including legal costs, bad publicity, possible boycotts, and a reduction in the number of job applicants. One study found that stock prices increased for companies that won awards for affirmative action and diversity initiatives, whereas they fell for companies that experienced negative publicity because of discrimination cases.[67] Exhibit 2-3 summarizes applicable federal laws. Individual states may also have laws that protect people from discrimination based on additional characteristics, such as sexual orientation and marital status.

EXHIBIT 2-3 Federal Laws Preventing Employment Discrimination

Law	Employers Covered	Who Is Protected
Title VII of the 1964 Civil Rights Act, Civil Rights Act of 1991	Private employers, state and local governments, education institutions, employment agencies, and labor unions with 15 or more individuals	Everyone based on race, color religion, sex, or national origin
Equal Pay Act of 1963	Virtually all employers	Men and women who perform substantially equal work
Age Discrimination in Employment Act of 1967	Private employers, state and local governments, education institutions, employment agencies, and labor unions with 20 or more individuals	Individuals who are 40 years old or older
Title I of the Americans with Disabilities Act of 1990	Private employers, state and local governments, education institutions, employment agencies, and labor unions with 15 or more individuals	Individuals who are qualified and have a disability

Source: U.S. Equal Employment Opportunity Commission, 2002, http://www.eeoc.gov/facts/qanda.html.

EXPERIENCING ORGANIZATIONAL BEHAVIOR

Diversity at the Top

On November 4, 2008, the United States elected Barack Obama as president. President Obama personifies the concept of diversity in terms of race, ethnicity, and geography. His black father was from a small town in Kenya and his white mother was from Kansas. His parents met in Hawaii, where he was born. President Obama's parents were divorced when he was 2 years old. When he was six years old, his mother remarried a man from Indonesia, and the family moved there. At the age of ten, Barack Obama returned to Hawaii to live with his maternal grandparents. He has a half-sister who is part Indonesian and is married to a man who is Chinese Canadian. President Obama's wife, Michelle Obama, is African American. In an interview with Oprah Winfrey, President Obama described his family get-togethers as "mini United Nations meetings." He said he had some relatives that looked like Bernie Mac and some that looked like Margaret Thatcher. The Obama family clearly exemplifies the diversity inherent in the United States.

President Obama's intrapersonal diversity and strong beliefs that diversity in governance is necessary is reflected in the diversity of his cabinet. Thirty-four percent of his officials are female, 11 percent are black, 8 percent are Hispanic, and 4 percent are Asian. While these do not seem like large numbers, they reflect more diversity than was present in past administrations' cabinets. This diversity is expected to increase as President Obama's tenure in office lengthens and he brings in new officials.

The presidency of Barack Obama brings up the question of whether the United States has overcome problems with racial, ethnic, and gender discrimination. Is the leadership in this country finally reflective of the population? Unfortunately, this is still not the case, as evidenced by the demography of corporate leaders. At the end of 2008, there were 5 black, 7 Latino, 7 Asian, and 13 female (2 of whom are Asian) CEOs of *Fortune* 500 companies. This means that 94 percent of *Fortune* 500 CEOs were white, non-Hispanic males. Examining the composition of boards of directors reveals the same lack of diversity. A Catalyst 2009 study of *Fortune* 500 companies revealed that women held 15.2 percent of board seats and women of color held 3.1 percent of all board director positions. Women held only 2 percent of board chair positions. These numbers have remained relatively consistent over the past five years. A study on African American representation on corporate boards found that representation had decreased from 8.1 percent in 2004 to 7.4 percent in 2008. In a recent study of *Fortune* 100 boards, the Alliance for Board Diversity (a

©MANDEL NGAN/Getty Images, Inc.

joint effort among organizations concerned with board diversity) concluded that:

- There is a severe underrepresentation of women and minorities on corporate boards when compared to general U.S. population demographics for race and gender.

- Particular areas of concern include the lack of representation of minority women and of Asian Americans and Hispanics.

- There is a recycling of the same minority individuals—especially African American men—as board members. Minority and female board members hold more seats per person than do white males.

- Very few boards have representation from all groups. Only four boards had representation by all four groups (women, African Americans, Asian Americans, and Hispanics).

Will the diversity evident in the Obama administration filter down to corporate America? Gloria Castillo, president of Chicago United (an organization that advocates for diversity in business) suggests that the Obama administration will help change things. She states "The Obama lesson for corporate directors and C.E.O.'s is that they must accept accountability for proactively seeking out executives of difference to unleash even greater innovation in their enterprises. ... [O]nce they institute true diversity and inclusion in their businesses, other leaders throughout the organizations must follow that lead and actively create an environment that fully engages the best qualified stakeholders ... regardless of ethnicity." In the next Experiencing Organizational Behavioral section "Women, Work, and Stereotypes" we indicate that women are advancing into management positions. Will women and minorities continue their integration into the very top positions, as evidenced in the White House? Only time will tell.

Sources: E.J. Cepeda. November 11, 2008. At "More Diversity in Workplace? Black Man in White House No Silver Bullet, But a Start". At http://www.huffingtonpost.com/esther-j-cepeda/more-diversity-in-workpla_b_142938.html; Oprah Winfrey Interview with Barack Obama, January 11, 2009. At http://www.oprah.com/media/20090112_inaug_diversity.; " Meet Barack." At http://www.barackobama.com/about/; J.A Barnes. June 20, 2009. Obama's Team: The Face Of Diversity. National *Journal Magazine*. At http://www.nationaljournal.com/njmagazine/nj_20090620_3869.php; "Fortune 500 Black, Latino, and Asian CEOs." July 22, 2009. Diversity Inc. At http://www.diversityinc.com/content/1757/article/3895/?Fortune_500_Black_Latino_Asian_CEOs; D. Jones. January 2, 2009. "Women CEOs slowly gain on Corporate America". At http://www.usatoday.com/money/companies/management/2009-01-01-women-ceos-increase_N.htm.; "2009 Catalyst Census of the Fortune 500 Reveals Women Missing From Critical Business Leadership' December 9, 2009. At http://www.catalyst.org/press-release/161/2009-catalyst-census-of-the-fortune-500-reveals-women-missing-from-critical-business-leadership; "African Americans Lost Ground on Fortune 500 Boards" July 21, 2009. At http://urbanmecca.net/news/?p=7649; "Alliance for Board Diversity: Fact Sheet" December 2009. Catalyst. At http://www.catalyst.org/press-release/117/alliance-for-board-diversity-fact-sheet.

Companies that manage diversity well do not discriminate, and their associates are less likely to sue for discrimination. Managing diversity means more than just avoiding discrimination, however. In addition to legal reasons for diversity, there are also moral reasons.

The goal of most diversity programs is to foster a sense of inclusiveness and provide all individuals with equal opportunity—an important cultural value in the United States and in many other countries. Although many countries pride themselves on equality and inclusiveness, they take very different approaches to encourage these ideals. For example, in the United States, differences across groups are highlighted and even celebrated, and laws are used to help in the advancement of minority and disadvantaged groups. In France, differences are downplayed as unimportant and there is limited affirmative action to promote the advancement of minority groups. Britain takes the middle road by recognizing differences but with limited affirmative action to promote fair outcomes in society.[68]

Roadblocks to Diversity

In the preceding section, we focused on the potential benefits of creating and managing diversity in organizations. Organizations working to institute effective diversity management programs face a number of obstacles, however. In this section, we consider the roadblocks to creating an inclusive workplace.

Prejudice and Discrimination

prejudice
Unfair negative attitudes we hold about people who belong to social or cultural groups other than our own.

discrimination
Behavior that results in unequal treatment of individuals based on group membership.

modern racism
Subtle forms of discrimination that occur despite people knowing it is wrong to be prejudiced against other racial groups and despite believing they are not racist.

Prejudice refers to unfair negative attitudes we hold about people who belong to social or cultural groups other than our own. Racism, sexism, and homophobia are all examples of prejudice. Prejudice influences how we evaluate other groups ("Arabs are bad," "People with disabilities are to be pitied") and can also lead to emotional reactions, such as hate, fear, disgust, contempt, and anxiety. Unfair **discrimination** is behavior that results in unequal treatment of individuals based on group membership. Examples of discrimination include paying a woman less than a man to do the same work, assigning people with disabilities easier jobs than others, and not promoting Asian Americans to leadership positions.

Prejudice and discrimination do not have to be overt or obvious. Consider racism as an example. Overt prejudice and discrimination toward racial minorities have been on the decline in the United States since passage of the 1964 Civil Rights Act.[69] Whites have become more accepting of residential integration and interracial marriage over the past several decades, for example. However, prejudice and discrimination still exist in more subtle forms, a phenomenon often referred to as "modern racism."[70] In general, **modern racism** occurs when people know that it is wrong to be prejudiced against other racial groups and believe themselves not to be racists. However, deep-seated, perhaps unconscious, prejudice still exists in these people, conflicting with their belief that racism is wrong.

People who are modern racists do not make racial slurs or openly treat someone of another race poorly. However, they may discriminate when they have an opportunity to do so, and then attribute their discriminatory behavior to another cause (such as poor performance) or hide their discriminatory behavior. In some cases, the discrimination is unintentional.

A recent study demonstrates modern racism in action.[71] Participants were asked to evaluate candidates for a university peer counseling position. White participants evaluated either a black or a white candidate. The qualifications of the candidates were varied, so that sometimes the candidates had very good qualifications, sometimes they had very bad qualifications, and sometimes qualifications were ambiguous and less obviously good or bad. The white evaluators showed no discriminatory behavior toward black candidates who had either very good or very bad qualifications. These candidates were chosen (or rejected) as frequently as white candidates with similar credentials. However, when qualifications were ambiguous and it was not obvious what hiring decision was appropriate, the evaluators discriminated a great deal against black candidates. When qualifications were ambiguous, black candidates were chosen only 45 percent of the time, whereas white candidates with ambiguous qualifications were chosen 76 percent of the time.

Most research and discussion concerning modern racism has focused on whites' attitudes toward and treatment of blacks. However, evidence reveals that the same dynamics occur with non-Hispanic white behavior toward Hispanics, men's behavior toward women, nondisabled individuals' behavior toward people with disabilities, and heterosexuals' behavior toward homosexuals.[72] Further, minority group members may hold negative attitudes toward majority group members, and one minority group may hold

©Tyler Edwards/Photodisc/Getty Images, Inc.

negative attitudes toward another. Regardless of the source, prejudice and discrimination can prevent people from working effectively, getting along with one another, and reaping the benefits that can be derived from a diverse workforce.

Prejudice and discrimination can serve as barriers to effectively managing diversity, leading to stress, poor performance, feelings of injustice, and poor organizational commitment on the part of its victims.[73] In addition to preventing an organization from becoming a high-involvement workplace, prejudice and discrimination, as discussed above, can also be costly in terms of lawsuits and poor public relations. The Los Angeles Fire Department has experienced this firsthand. Thus, diversity management programs must eliminate prejudice and discrimination before they can be effective and foster a high-involvement work environment.

Stereotyping

A **stereotype** is a generalized set of beliefs about the characteristics of a group of individuals. Stereotypes are unrealistically rigid, often negative, and frequently based on factual errors.[74] When individuals engage in stereotyping, they believe that all or most members of a group have certain characteristics or traits. Thus, when we meet a member of that group, we assume that the person possesses those traits.

The problem with stereotypes is, of course, that they ignore the fact that the individuals within any group vary significantly. We can always find examples of someone who fits our stereotype; alternatively, we can just as easily find examples of people who do not fit the stereotype. For example, a common stereotype is that black people are poor.[75] However, the overwhelming majority of black people are middle class (just as are the majority of white people). It is statistically easier to find a middle-class black person than a poor one—and yet the stereotype persists.

Stereotyping is particularly difficult to stop for several reasons. First, stereotypes are very difficult to dispel. When we meet someone who has characteristics that are incongruent with our stereotypes (a smart athlete, a rich black person, a socially skilled accountant, or a sensitive white male), we ignore the discrepancy, distort the disconfirming information, see the individual as an exception to the rule, or simply forget the disconfirming information.[76] Thus, disconfirming information is not as likely as it should be to change stereotypes.

Second, stereotypes guide what information we look for, process, and remember.[77] For example, suppose I believe that all accountants are socially inept. When I meet an accountant, I will look for information that confirms my stereotype. If the accountant is alone at a party, I will assume he or she is antisocial. I will remember instances of when the accountant was quiet and nervous around people. I may also actually "remember" seeing the accountant acting like a nerd, even if I actually did not. Thus, my stereotype is guiding how I process all information about this person based on his or her membership in the accountant group.

Third, stereotypes seem to be an enduring human quality; we all hold stereotypes. Stereotyping is so prevalent in part because it allows us to simplify the information that we deal with on a day-to-day basis.[78] Another reason is that it allows us to have a sense of predictability. That is, if we know a person's group membership (such as race, occupation, or gender), we also believe we have additional information about that person based on our stereotype for that group. Thus, the stereotype provides us with information about other

stereotype
A generalized set of beliefs about the characteristics of a group of individuals.

people that enables us to predict their behavior and know how to respond to them. The comedian Dave Chappelle provides an amusing example of this in a skit in which he plays a fortuneteller. Instead of relying on mystic powers, he relies on his stereotypes. Given the race and gender of a phone-in caller, fortuneteller Chappelle can identify all sorts of information about the person's life (like whether the person is calling from prison or is on drugs).

Because stereotypes can drive behavior and lead to unrealistic or false assumptions about members of other groups, they can have very detrimental effects on interpersonal relations. Stereotypes can also have direct effects on individuals' careers by causing unfair treatment. In essence, when we rely on stereotypes to make judgments about an individual, rather than obtaining factual information, we are engaging in faulty decision making that causes harm. Exhibit 2-4 lists some common stereotypes for select groups.

The *Experiencing Organizational Behavior* feature shows that many individuals continue to stereotype women, and to harm their outcomes. Over time, changes in how women are viewed might be aided by examples of success and ambition among women

---

EXHIBIT 2-4 Common Stereotypes Applied to Various Groups of People

Women	People with Disabilities	White Men
Dependent	Quiet	Responsible for society's problems
Passive	Helpless	Competitive
Uncompetitive	Hypersensitive	Intelligent
Unconfident	Bitter	Aggressive
Unambitious	Benevolent	Ignorant
Warm	Inferior	Racist
Expressive	Depressed	Arrogant

Black People	Japanese Men	Jewish People
Athletes	Meticulous	Rich
Underqualified	Studious	Miserly
Poor	Workaholics	Well-educated
Good dancers	Racist	Family-oriented
Unmotivated	Unemotional	Cliquish
Violent	Defer to authority	Status conscious
Funny	Unaggressive	Good at business

Athletes	Accountants	Arab People
Dumb	Smart	Terrorists
Strong	Nerdy	Extremely religious
Sexist	Unsociable	Extremely sexist
Macho	Good at math	Rich
Male	Bad dressers	Hate Americans
Uneducated	Quiet	Jealous of Americans
Greedy	Dishonest	Don't value human life

Sources: M.E. Heilman. 1983. "Sex Bias in Work Settings: The Lack of Fit Model," in B.M. Staw and L.L. Cummings (Eds.), *Research in Organizational Behavior, Vol. 5* (Greenwich, CT: JAI Press), pp. 269–298; C.S. Fichten and R. Amsel. 1986. "Trait Attributions about College Students with a Physical Disability: Circumplex Analysis and Methodological Issues," *Journal of Applied Social Psychology*, 16: 410–427; Reprinted with permission of the publisher. From *Cultural Diversity in Organizations: Theory, Research and Practice,* © 1993 by T.H. Cox, Jr., Berrett-Koehler Publishers, Inc., San Francisco, CA. All rights reserved. www.bkconnection.com.

EXPERIENCING ORGANIZATIONAL BEHAVIOR

Women, Work, and Stereotypes

Over the past three decades, women in Western, industrialized nations have achieved a great deal in workplace acceptance, respect, and advancement. In fields as diverse as accounting, risk management, general management, and police work, women have made substantial progress. For example, chief financial officers, polled a few years ago by America's Community Bankers, reported substantial increases in the number of women managers in their banks. *Women in Business* recently reported that the percentage of women holding supervisory roles had increased from 20 percent to almost 50 percent in a recent 30-year period. *Fortune 500* firms reported a few years ago that women in officer positions had increased from 2 percent to more than 10 percent.

With this advancement, it would seem that stereotypes characterizing women as submissive, frivolous, indecisive, and uncommitted to the workplace have been eliminated. Even though one study found that stereotypes of women were becoming more compatible with beliefs about what it takes to be a good manager, problems still exist. Consider the language used in major media outlets to describe some businesswomen.

Carly Fiorina, former chief executive officer of Hewlett-Packard, has been characterized as being "as comfortable with power as any woman could be." A former chief executive at Mattel, Jill Barad—who admittedly had some problems—was slighted with the following dismissive statement: "She should have stuck to marketing, rather than worrying her pretty little head about running the company." Darla Moore, who contributed $25 million to the University of South Carolina School of Business, was characterized as a "babe in business." This type of language may help to keep gender stereotypes alive. Stereotypical language and images routinely found in such places as television commercials, radio ads, and travel brochures may also contribute.

Further evidence that gender stereotypes are not dead comes from the financial sector. According to Sheila McFinney, an organizational psychologist familiar with Wall Street, "Stereotypes about women's abilities run rampant in the financial industry. A lot of men in management feel that women don't have the stomach for selling on Wall Street." In support of this statement, a number of Wall Street firms have been forced to settle major harassment and discrimination claims with thousands of current and former women associates. Interestingly, women are more prevalent in finance than in many other functional areas.

Finally, evidence that suggests ongoing stereotypes comes from a 2007 survey conducted by *Elle* magazine in conjunction with MSNBC .com. Sixty-thousand respondents from a variety of occupations and industries answered questions about women and men as leaders. Approximately half of them indicated that women and men have differing abilities, with women being less able than men. Women, however, were given high marks for supportive environments.

© Steve Hix/Somos Images/Corbis

Sources: "Women Accountants Advance in Management Ranks," *Community Banker*, 10, no. 4 (2001): 52; J. Anderson. 2006. "Six Women at Dresdner File Bias Suit," *New York Times*, Jan. 10, C.1; C. Daily and D.R. Dalton. 2000. "Coverage of Women at the Top: The Press Has a Long Way to Go," *Columbia Journalism Review*, 39, no. 2: 58–59; M.K. Haben. 2001. "Shattering the Glass Ceiling," *Executive Speeches*, 15, no. 5: 4–10; M.-L. Kamberg. 2005. "A Woman's Touch," *Women in Business*, 57, no. 4: 14–17; M. Ligos. 2000. "Nightmare on Wall Street," *Sales and Marketing Management*, 152, no. 2: 66–76; E. Tahmincioglu. 2007. "Men Rule—At Least in Workplace Attitudes," at http://www.msnbc.msn.com/id/17345308; E. E. Duehr, & J.E. Bono. 2006. Men, women, and managers: Are stereotypes finally changing? *Personnel Psychology*, 59: 815–846.

leaders. Anne Mulcahy, CEO of Xerox, and Meg Whitman, former CEO of eBay, are examples. Mulcahy has been instrumental in turning around a company that was near death only a few years ago.[79] Whitman helped to build eBay from a very small company to one in which millions of people do more than $50 billion in business annually. Her vision for eBay was ambitious and included changing consumers' current emphasis on buying at retail stores. Although competition and market dynamics have cooled the company's growth to some degree, eBay continues to be strong.[80]

Differences in Social Identity

social identity
A person's knowledge that he or she belongs to certain social groups, where belonging to those groups has emotional significance.

Everyone's personal self-identity is based in part on his or her membership in various social groups.[81] This aspect of self-identity is referred to as "social identity." **Social identity** is defined as a person's knowledge that he or she belongs to certain social groups, where belonging to those groups has emotional significance.[82] In describing yourself, you might respond with a statement such as "I am a Catholic," "I am Jewish," "I am a member of my sorority," "I am of Puerto Rican descent," "I am an African American," or "I am a Republican." Such a statement describes an aspect of your social identity structure. Exhibit 2-5 provides examples of overall structures.

Having a social identity different from that of the majority can be very difficult, for several reasons. First, a person's social identity becomes more salient, or noticeable, when the person is in the minority on an important dimension. Accordingly, racial and ethnic minorities are much more likely to state that their membership in a racial or ethnic group is an important part of their self-concept.[83] For example, in one study, researchers said to people, "Tell me about yourself."[84] Only one out of every 100 white people mentioned

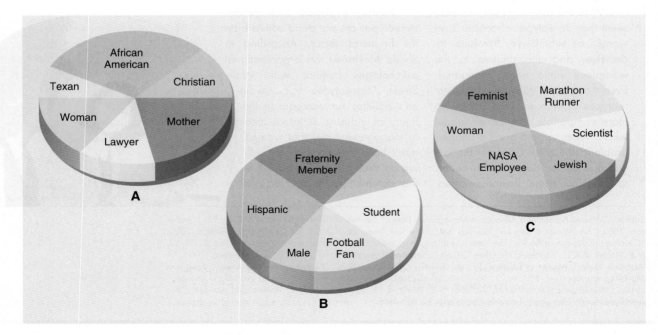

Exhibit 2-5 Sample Social-Identity Structures

that she was white. However, one in six black respondents mentioned his race, and one in seven Hispanic respondents mentioned ethnicity. Also, many women remark that they are more conscious of being female when they are in a work environment that is all male than when they are in a mixed-gender group. When a person's minority social identity becomes salient, the person is made more aware that he or she is different from the majority of people in the situation.

Second, having a social identity different from that of the majority may make people feel they have to behave in ways that are unnatural for them in certain contexts. Feeling that they are acting out a false role will in turn lead to stress and dissatisfaction.[85] For example, women operating in an all-male environment may try to act more like men in order to fit in and meet others' expectations.[86] In discussing being an African American in a predominantly white business world, Kenneth I. Chenault, CEO of American Express, says that he had to learn how to become comfortable dealing with multiple cultures with different expectations. He states, "I learned very early on how to move between both worlds and develop a level of comfort and confidence no matter what world I'm operating in."[87] Clearly, if you belong to the majority group, you do not have to learn how to act in different worlds.

A third issue resulting from differences in social identities is that often minority group members fear losing this social identity.[88] Social identity is often a source of pride and honor.[89] Thus, being forced to "check their identity at the gate" creates a sense of loss and discomfort for many people.

A final issue related to differences in social identities concerns the fact that people often evaluate others based on their membership in social groups. People tend to favor members of their own groups because their group membership is often tied to feelings of high self-esteem.[90] We think people who belong to our own group must somehow be better than those who do not belong. In other words, we tend to categorize people according to in-group and out-group membership,[91] and we tend to favor members of our own group—the in-group—and disfavor those whom we have categorized as belonging to an out-group. We often exaggerate the positive attributes of our own group and the negative aspects of the out-group. Furthermore, we are more likely to have stereotypes regarding out-group members and to ignore differences among out-group members.[92] So, for example, members of the legal department, who have strong identities as lawyers, may view other associates who are not lawyers as being similar, less savvy, and peripheral to the success of the company. In contrast, the lawyers are more likely to see other lawyers as individuals, and think they are smarter and are central to the company's success. In conclusion, social identity dynamics can be a roadblock to successful diversity management because they foster forming in-groups and out-groups and can lead to stress and dissatisfaction among those with minority identities.

Power Differentials

Power is not equally distributed among the individuals and groups in an organization. Individuals gain power in many ways—by having expert knowledge or a powerful formal position, by controlling valuable rewards or important resources, or by being irreplaceable, for example.[93] In some organizations that rely on selling, the individuals in the sales and marketing departments have most of the power, whereas the individuals in the human resources and accounting departments have less power. An executive secretary controlling those who are allowed to meet with and speak to the CEO also has power. In essence, this secretary controls everyone's communication with top management.

On the other hand, people are also awarded or deprived of power and status for reasons that have nothing to do with work life. On a societal level, groups of people have what is called *ascribed* status and power. **Ascribed status** is status and power that is assigned by cultural norms and depends on group membership.[94] In other words, societal culture defines who has power and who does not. In North America, women, racial and ethnic minorities, and people with disabilities, among other groups, are traditionally perceived to be of lower status than white men.[95] Thus, members of these groups have traditionally had less power in the workplace than white men. When such power differentials exist, they can prevent an organization from developing an inclusive workplace for at least two reasons.

First, research has shown that high-status individuals speak more and use stronger influence tactics than members of low-status groups.[96] Thus, low-status individuals may not have a chance to contribute as much to group problem-solving tasks. When people do not feel free to speak up, a major benefit of diversity is lost because different ideas and viewpoints are not presented. This phenomenon also causes problems because it perpetuates status differentials and may lead to frustration and dissatisfaction among people who do not feel free to speak up.

Second, people belonging to groups with different amounts of power and status may avoid interacting with one another and may form cliques with members of their own groups.[97] High-status groups may downgrade, ignore, or harass members of low-status groups. Associates in low-status groups may stay away from high-status associates in order to avoid rejection or humiliation. This tendency to form cliques undermines diversity efforts by setting the stage for increased conflict among groups.

Poor Structural Integration

You may have heard phrases such as "pink-collar ghetto" and "glass ceiling." These phrases refer to the tendency for women and members of racial and ethnic minority groups to be "stuck" in certain occupations or at certain levels in an organization. Recall from the earlier part of this chapter that one criterion for having a truly multicultural organization is that people from traditionally underrepresented groups appear at all levels and in all occupations. Exhibit 2-6 illustrates a well-integrated organization and a poorly integrated organization.

Note in the figure that 35 percent of the employees in both Company A and Company B are either female and/or a member of a racial minority group. So if we look only at the total number of employees, then we might conclude that both companies are equally well integrated. Such a conclusion would be erroneous, however.

In Company A, on average across functional areas, only .5 percent of top management jobs are held by women or minorities. At the same time, on average across functional areas, 70 percent of the lowest-level jobs are held by women and minorities. These figures indicate that women and minorities are extremely underrepresented in high-level positions and overrepresented in low-level (low-status, low-power, and low-pay) positions. Furthermore, in Company A, women and racial minorities are severely underrepresented in the areas of finance, marketing, and sales. Coca-Cola was sued by African Americans because it resembled Company A (to some degree) despite having talented people in the minority group. The company settled in 2000 for $192.5 million.[98]

ascribed status
Status and power that is assigned by cultural norms and depends on group membership.

Company A
Poorly Integrated

Functional Area

Level	Finance	Marketing	HR	Sales	Average across functions
Top Management	0%	0%	2%	0%	.5%
Mid Management	0%	1%	10%	2%	3.25%
Supervisor	0%	5%	15%	5%	6.25%
Staff	25%	25%	40%	26%	29%
Line Worker	60%	65%	80%	75%	70%

Company B
Well Integrated

Functional Area

Level	Finance	Marketing	HR	Sales	Average across functions
Top Management	35%	35%	35%	35%	35%
Mid Management	35%	35%	35%	35%	35%
Supervisor	35%	35%	35%	35%	35%
Staff	35%	35%	35%	35%	35%
Line Worker	35%	35%	35%	35%	35%

The numbers in each cell represent the percentage of people in each job level and functional area who are female and/or racial and ethnic minority group members.

The total percentage of employees for both companies who are female and/or a racial ethnic minority is 35%.

Exhibit 2-6 Examples of Poorly Integrated and Well-Integrated Organizations

Contrast these patterns with those in Company B. In that company, women and minorities are represented in all areas in proportion to their total representation in the company. Company B illustrates the ideal distribution for an inclusive organization—which occurs infrequently.

Data compiled in 2003 by the Equal Employment Opportunity Commission suggest that U.S. companies look more like Company A than Company B.[99] White males made up about 37 percent of the workforce in private industry but held about 56 percent of the executive and managerial jobs. In contrast, they only held about 13 percent of lower-level clerical jobs and 21 percent of service jobs. White women, who made up almost 33 percent of the workforce, held almost 55 percent of clerical jobs. Black people (both men and women) made up almost 14 percent of the workforce but held less than 7 percent of executive and managerial jobs. Black women were overrepresented in clerical and service jobs, and black men were overrepresented in operations and laborer jobs. This pattern held true for most other minority groups as well.

Why are social groups so unequally distributed across occupations and job levels? Many explanations have been offered, with discrimination being a common one. Lack of skills on the part of groups holding lower-level positions is also cited frequently. Whatever the reason, poor integration of women and minorities in organizations can present several roadblocks to creating a multicultural environment.

- Poor integration creates power and status differentials, which then become associated with gender or race.
- Poor integration fosters negative stereotypes.

- Where integration is poor overall, women and minorities who do reach higher levels may have token status. That is, since they may be the only persons of their race or gender in that type of job, they will be considered an exception.[100]
- Where integration is poor, most women and minorities may feel that it is impossible for them to rise to the top.

Communication Problems

Communication can be a roadblock to establishing an effective diversity environment. One potential communication problem arises when not everyone speaks the same language fluently. Associates who are less fluent in the dominant language may refrain from contributing to conversations. Furthermore, groups may form among those who speak the same language, excluding those who do not speak that language. Finally, many misunderstandings may occur because of language differences. For example, U.S. college students often complain that having teachers who are not fluent in English makes it difficult for them to understand class lectures.

Another communication problem arises because different cultures have different norms about what is appropriate. For example, African Americans, Hispanics, and Asians are less likely than Anglo Americans to feel they can speak freely during meetings.[101] Common areas of communication disagreement among cultures include the following:

- Willingness to openly disagree
- The importance of maintaining "face," or dignity
- The way agreement is defined
- The amount of time devoted to establishing personal relationships
- Willingness to speak assertively
- Mode of communication (written, verbal)
- Personal space and nonverbal communication

While communication differences exist for people from different backgrounds, it is important not to stereotype. Some individuals from a particular background will not share the communication preferences often associated with that background.

Effectively Creating and Managing Diversity

Organizations face many roadblocks to creating multicultural environments, but these roadblocks are not insurmountable. In this section, we discuss some strategies for effectively creating and managing diversity.

Most large companies and many small companies have in recent years instituted some type of diversity management plan. These plans have varied in effectiveness, from being very successful at creating a diverse, inclusive, and productive workplace to having no effect or to actually having negative effects. Because so many diversity programs have been instituted, there is substantial knowledge about what works and what does not work. The U.S. Department of Commerce studied 600 firms that had been cited for having excellent diversity climates.[102] The study revealed several criteria for success, including commitment by the organization's leaders, integration of the program with the organization's strategic plan, and involvement of all associates.

Commitment of the Organization's Leaders

The first criterion for having an effective diversity program is genuine commitment from the organization's upper-level leadership. Insincere support of diversity is damaging. Leaders must take ownership of diversity initiatives and effectively communicate the vision that inclusiveness is important. Actions that corporate leaders have initiated to ensure that the message comes across include the following:

- High-ranking leaders send relevant communications through multiple channels, such as intranet postings, policy statements, formal newsletters, meetings, speeches, and training programs.
- One high-ranking leader personally leads all diversity efforts. He holds town meetings and eats lunch in the cafeteria to talk about diversity.
- Multiple high-ranking executives sponsor employee councils devoted to fostering cross-cultural communication. The councils are all-inclusive—anyone who wants to join can do so. Therefore, anyone can "have the ears" of executives on diversity issues.
- Managers at all levels are held accountable for advancing diversity initiatives.

The *Managerial Advice* feature focuses on ideas that managers can use to promote positive work environments. The actions recommended are valuable for associates but are most important for managers because they have the strongest effects on the organization's culture.

Integration with the Strategic Plan

The second criterion for effective diversity management requires that diversity be linked to the organization's strategic plan. That is, it is necessary to be clear about the ways in which diversity can contribute to the strategic goals, directions, and plans of the organization. The organization must develop ways of defining and measuring diversity effectiveness and then use these measures in the strategic planning process. Common measures of diversity effectiveness focus on:

- Increased market share and new customer bases
- External awards for diversity efforts
- Associates' attrition rate
- Associates' work satisfaction
- Associates' and managers' satisfaction with the workplace climate

Another tactic for elevating diversity to the strategic level involves making it a core value and part of the formal mission statement of the organization. Many organizations that truly value diversity express this as a core value and include their beliefs in a mission statement. These statements go beyond the common catchphrase that "We are an affirmative action employer." For example, one of six principles in Starbucks' mission statement is: "Embrace diversity as an essential component in the way we do business." Another is: "Provide a great work environment and treat each other with respect and dignity."[103]

Associate Involvement

The third criterion for effective diversity management calls for the involvement of all associates. Diversity programs can produce suspicion or feelings of unfairness in some associates, particularly if they misinterpret the program's purpose. Some individuals may feel they are excluded from the program, whereas others may feel that it infringes on benefits

MANAGERIAL ADVICE

Promoting a Positive Diversity Environment

Robin Ely, Debra Meyerson, and Martin Davidson are professors at Harvard University, Stanford University, and the University of Virginia, respectively. In conjunction with the human development and organizational learning professionals at Learning as Leadership, they have developed several principles designed to ensure that members of various social identity groups do not become trapped in low-quality workplace relationships. These principles are designed to encourage engagement and learning. The principles are perhaps best applied in the context of individuals experiencing uncomfortable events that are open to interpretation, such as when the member of a minority group is told by someone from the majority that she is being too aggressive, or when a man is told by a woman that he is acting as his grandfather might have acted. The principles are listed below:

a. *Pause to short circuit the emotion and reflect.* Individuals who have experienced an uncomfortable event should take a few moments to identify their feelings and consider a range of responses.

b. *Connect with others in ways that affirm the importance of relationships.* Individuals who have experienced an uncomfortable event should reach out to those who have caused the difficulty, thereby valuing relationships.

c. *Question interpretations and explore blind spots.* Individuals who have experienced an uncomfortable event should engage in self-questioning as well as the questioning of others. They should be open to the interpretations that others have of the situation, while realizing that their own interpretations might be correct.

©Tom Grill/Corbis

d. *Obtain genuine support that doesn't necessarily validate initial points of view but, rather, helps in gaining broader perspective.* Individuals who have experienced an uncomfortable event should seek input from those who will challenge their initial points of view on the situation.

e. *Shift the mindset.* Individuals who have experienced an uncomfortable event should be open to the idea that both parties might need to change to some degree.

Sources: R.J. Ely, D.E. Meyerson, and M.N. Davidson. 2006. "Rethinking Political Correctness," *Harvard Business Review*, 84 (September); Learning as Leadership, "Research," 2007, at http://www.learnaslead.com/index.php.

they are currently enjoying. It is important for diversity programs to address the needs of both majority group members and minority group members. Organizations can use many methods to obtain input from associates. Some of these include:

- Discussion groups made up of all types of associates who help in developing, implementing, and evaluating the program
- Employee satisfaction surveys
- Cultural diversity audits, which help the company studying the diversity culture and environment of the organization
- Informal employee feedback hotlines where associates can provide unsolicited feedback

Another common way of involving associates in diversity programs is to develop and support *affinity groups*—groups that share common interests and serve as a mechanism for the ideas and concerns of associates to be heard by managers. Affinity groups are also good sources of feedback about the effectiveness of diversity initiatives. Finally, these groups can provide networking opportunities, career support, and emotional support to their members. Ford Motor Company has the following affinity groups: Ford-Employee African American Ancestry Network; Ford Asian Indian Association; Ford Chinese Association; Ford Finance Network; Ford Gay, Lesbian, or Bisexual Employees; Ford Hispanic Network Group; Professional Women's Network; Ford's Parenting Network; Women in Finance; Ford Interfaith Network; Middle Eastern Community @ Ford Motor Company; and Ford Employees Dealing with Disabilities.[104]

Finally, another way of involving all associates is through training. Training programs often include an explanation of the business necessity for effectively managing diversity, along with empathy training, cross-cultural knowledge instruction, and exercises to help associates avoid stereotyping and engaging in offensive or prejudicial treatment of others. To create a truly inclusive environment, diversity programs also need to teach people how to value and respect diversity rather than just tolerate it.

Denny's, the U.S. restaurant chain, is an example of a company that has implemented the three aspects of diversity management discussed here. Following lawsuits and settlements in the 1990s, Jim Anderson became the CEO in 1996 and drove true commitment to diversity. Anderson himself was committed to building what Roosevelt Thomas, an expert on corporate diversity, terms a *diversity-mature* organization, in which the mission and vision of the company includes a diversity management component.

To fully integrate the management of diversity into its mission, Denny's requires all managers and associates to participate in diversity training sessions. In addition, they are held accountable for their behavior. Associates who engage in inappropriate behavior are

THE STRATEGIC LENS

Organizational diversity, when managed effectively, has many benefits for organizations. In general, effectively managed diversity programs contribute to an organization's ability to achieve and maintain a competitive advantage. Diversity in teams at all levels can be helpful in solving complex problems because heterogeneous teams integrate multiple perspectives. This benefit applies to the upper-echelon management team as well as to project teams, such as new-product-development teams, much lower in the organization. Not only can the diversity help resolve complex problems, but it also better mirrors U.S. society. Thus, it signals to potential associates and potential customers that the organization understands and effectively uses diversity. As a result, the organization has a larger pool of candidates for potential associates from which it can select the best. In addition, the organization is likely to have a larger potential market because of its understanding of the products and services desired by a diverse marketplace. Having a diverse organization that reflects the demographic composition of U.S. society is smart business.[106]

Critical Thinking Questions

1. How does organizational diversity contribute to an organization's competitive advantage?

2. What actions are required to create diversity in an organization, particularly in one that has homogeneous membership at present?

3. How does diversity in an organization affect its strategy?

put on notice and must indicate how they will change their behavior in the future. Those who do not change their behavior are terminated. More blatant transgressions, such as racial slurs, result in immediate termination.

Overall, companies such as Denny's use diversity initiatives in at least seven different areas:[105]

1. Recruiting (e.g., diverse recruiting teams, minority job fairs)
2. Retention (e.g., affinity groups, on-site child care)
3. Development (e.g., mentoring programs, leadership development programs)
4. External partnerships (e.g., minority supplier programs, community outreach)
5. Communication (e.g., addresses by high-ranking leaders, newsletters)
6. Training (e.g., awareness training, team building)
7. Staffing and infrastructure (e.g., dedicated diversity staffs, executive diversity councils).

back to the knowledge objectives

1. What is organizational diversity, and how does diversity management differ from affirmative action? Do these kinds of programs have anything in common?

2. Distinguish between multicultural, plural, and monolithic organizations. How might these organizations differ in the types of policies they use? For example, how would they differ in terms of staffing practices?

3. What trends can be seen in the demographic characteristics of the U.S. population? What are the implications of these trends for organizational diversity?

4. What other changes are occurring in the environment that contribute to the importance of managing diversity effectively? Why do these changes have this effect?

5. Why is successfully managing diversity important to high-involvement work organizations? Give specific examples.

6. What problems do discrimination, prejudice, and stereotyping create in an organization attempting to manage a diverse workforce?

7. How do social identities, power differentials, and poor structural integration affect the successful management of diversity?

8. What does a diversity program need in order to be effective? How would you determine whether your diversity program was effective?

What This Chapter Adds to Your Knowledge Portfolio

In this chapter we discussed the importance of diversity to organizations and the need to effectively manage diversity. We also discussed the forces of change that have made diversity a primary concern of many organizations, and we described some of the more common roadblocks to successfully managing diversity. Finally, we discussed the essential components of an effective diversity program. To summarize, we made the following points:

- *Organizational diversity* refers to differences among the individuals in an organization. Important differences are those that are personally important to people and affect the way in which they perceive the world. Common dimensions of diversity include race, ethnicity, gender, disability, functional area, sexual orientation, and parenthood.

- Diversity programs are aimed at developing inclusive work cultures, which are important in high-involvement work environments. Affirmative action programs are aimed at making sure there is fair representation or numbers of various groups within jobs and organizations. Affirmative action programs can be legally mandated or voluntarily adopted.

- Multicultural organizations have diverse associates and are inclusive of all associates. Plural organizations have reasonably diverse associates and tolerate diversity. Monolithic organizations are homogeneous and do not tolerate diversity.
- The U.S. population is getting older and more diverse in terms of race and ethnicity. Other changes that are occurring in the environment include an increasing service economy, increasing globalization, and increasing need for teamwork. These changes make management of diversity more important today than ever.
- Successfully managing diversity is important because it can lead to more committed, better satisfied, better-performing employees, attraction of the best talent, better group decision making, and potentially better financial performance for the organization. Effectively managing diversity also ensures that the moral principle that everyone be treated fairly will be upheld. Furthermore, effective diversity management can result in fewer lawsuits for discrimination.
- Discrimination, prejudice, stereotyping, differing social identities, power differentials, poor structural integration, and communication concerns have a negative impact on managing a diverse workforce.
- Organizations that successfully manage diversity have senior managers who fully support diversity initiatives, tie their diversity plans to the overall strategic goals of the organization, and ensure involvement from all associates through a variety of mechanisms.

Key Terms

diversity, p. 49

multicultural
    organization, p. 50

plural organization, p. 50

monolithic
    organization, p. 51

prejudice, p. 60

discrimination, p. 60

modern racism, p. 60

stereotype, p. 61

social identity, p. 64

ascribed status, p. 66

---

building your human capital

What's Your DQ (Diversity Quotient)?

How well do you handle diversity? Your ability to be flexible, work with many different types of people, and deal with ambiguous situations will be crucial to a successful career in the twenty-first century. The following assessment will allow you to determine whether you have had the experience necessary to help in successfully navigating a diverse work environment.

Use the following scale to answer the questions below:

1 point = never	3 points = three or four times
2 points = once or twice	4 points = four or more times

In the last month, how often did you ...?

1. See a foreign movie.
2. Speak a language other than your first language.
3. Visit an art or history museum.
4. Have a conversation with someone who was of a different race.
5. Have a conversation with someone who was from a different country.

6. Attend a social event where at least half of the people differed from you in race or ethnic background.
7. Visit a church that was of a religion different from yours.
8. Visit a place where people spoke a language different from your first language.
9. Do something you've never done before.
10. Attend a cultural event (art show, concert).
11. Eat ethnic food.
12. Visit a foreign country.
13. Watch a program about world (non-U.S.) history.
14. Read a book about another culture.
15. Watch a movie or TV show about another culture.
16. Attend a social event where you didn't know anyone.
17. Read a book written by a foreign author.
18. Listen to music from a different culture.
19. Attend an event where you were in a minority based on any demographic characteristic (age, gender, race, ethnicity, religion, sexual orientation).
20. Learn something new about a country or culture other than your own.
21. Study a different language.
22. Attend an event about a different culture (an ethnic festival, a concert by musicians from a different culture, a student meeting of an ethnic group).
23. Have a conversation with someone from a different social class.
24. Develop a friendship with someone from a different background.
25. Discuss world affairs with someone who disagreed with you.

Scoring: Add up your total points for the 25 questions.
Scoring can range from 25 to 100

25–39: Your current environment is rather homogeneous. You can increase your DQ by making a concerted effort to reach out to people who are different from you, attend events that expose you to different cultures, and learn about people and cultures that differ from yours. Your score may be low because you live in an area where there is little diversity in people or cultural events. You will need to go out of your way to gain exposure to different cultures.

40–59: Your current environment could be more diverse than it currently is. You can increase your DQ by making a concerted effort to reach out to people who are different from you, attend events that expose you to different cultures, and learn about people and cultures that differ from yours.

60–79: Your environment is fairly culturally diverse. Look more closely at your scores for each question and determine whether there are any areas in which you can broaden your horizons even further. Perhaps, for example, you read and watch materials that expose you to different cultures but do not personally interact frequently with people who are different from you. If that is the case, join a club where you are likely to meet people different from yourself.

80–100: Your environment is quite culturally diverse. You experience a great deal of cultural variety, which should help prepare you for working in a culturally diverse work environment.

an organizational behavior moment
Project "Blow Up"

Big State University (BSU) is proud of the success of its international executive MBA (EMBA) program. The program is designed to bring together promising middle- and higher-level managers from around the globe for an exceptional learning experience. BSU's EMBA program has been ranked very highly by the business press. Alumni praise the program for its excellent faculty, networking opportunities, and exposure to colleagues from around the world. Students in the program can either attend weekend classes on BSU's campus or participate through distance-learning technology from campuses around the world.

One of the defining features of the program is the first-year team project. Students are randomly assigned to five-member teams. Each team has a faculty advisor, and each must develop a business plan for a startup company. A major part of the business plan involves developing a marketing strategy. The teams begin the project during orientation week and finish at the end of the next summer. Each team must turn in a written report and a business plan and make an hour-long presentation to the other students and faculty as well as several executives from well-respected multinational companies. Students must earn a passing grade on the project to graduate from the program. The project is also a good way of meeting and impressing important executives in the business community.

The A-Team consists of five people, who did not know each other before the project began. They are:

- **Rebecca**—A 27-year-old marketing manager for a large, high-end Italian fashion company. Rebecca is a white female of Italian descent who was born and raised in New York City. Rebecca earned her bachelor's degree in business at the University of Virginia's McIntire Business School when she was 22. She speaks English, Italian, and Spanish fluently. She speaks a little German and Japanese as well. Rebecca is single. Her job involves analyzing worldwide markets and traveling to the 136 stores around the world that carry her company's clothes. She hopes the EMBA from BSU will help her to be promoted to an executive position.

- **Aran**—The 52-year-old founder and CEO of an Egyptian management consulting firm. His firm employs 12 people who consult with local companies on issues involving information systems. Aran is an Egyptian male who is a fairly devout Muslim. He earned his business degree 25 years ago at the American University in Cairo. He speaks English and Arabic fluently. Aran is married with two adult children. He is attending BSU's program because he wants to retire from his consulting firm and become an in-house information systems consultant to a large multinational firm.

- **Katie**—A 30-year-old financial analyst at a large Wall Street firm. At present, Katie's job requires little travel, but she works long hours as a financial analyst. Katie is an American female who does not consider herself to have any strong ethnic roots. She earned her business degree two years ago from New York University. Before going to college, she worked as a bank teller on Long Island. She was concerned about her lack of progress and went back to college to get

a degree. She now wants to further her education to open up even more opportunities. Katie speaks only English. She is married but has no children. However, she cares for her elderly mother, who lives nearby in New Jersey.

- **Cameron**—A 23-year-old Internet entrepreneur who heads his own small but successful company. He is the youngest student BSU has ever accepted. He was something of a child prodigy, graduating from Georgia Tech at the age of 19 with a degree in computer science. Cameron is a single, African American male who has lived all over the United States. His company is based in Austin, Texas. He speaks only English. He is attending BSU's program because, though confident of his technical expertise, he would like to learn more about business, since he is planning to expand his company.

- **Pranarisha**—A 31-year-old manager for a nongovernmental organization (NGO) that provides support to poverty-stricken areas of Thailand. Pranarisha's job is to coordinate efforts from a variety of worldwide charitable organizations. She speaks four languages fluently; however, she is not fluent in English. She graduated from the most prestigious university in Thailand. She is married with a four-year-old son and is a devout Buddhist. She is attending BSU's program at the request of her organization, so she can help to make the organization more efficient.

The A-Team was doomed almost as soon as the project began. The team's first task was to decide how roles would be allocated to individuals on the team.

Aran: Before we begin, we need to decide what everyone will be doing on this project, how we will divide and coordinate the work. Since I have the most experience, I should serve in the executive function. I'll assign and oversee everyone's work. I will also give the presentation at the end of the project, since I know how to talk to important people. Cameron will be in charge of analyzing the financial feasibility of our project, developing the marketing plan, and evaluating the technical operations. The girls will assist him in …

Rebecca (Interrupting): Hold on a minute! First, we are not girls! Second, Cameron, Katie, and I decided last night over beers at happy hour that I should handle the marketing plan, Cameron the technical aspects, and Katie the financial aspects. You can serve as the coordinator, since you're not going to be attending class on campus—you can keep track of everything when we submit electronic reports.

Cameron: Yeah—your role would be to just make sure everyone is on the same page, but we'd individually decide how to conduct our own projects.

Aran: This team needs a leader and I …

Cameron and Katie (in unison): Who says?

Rebecca: We're all responsible adults, and since the three of us are most accustomed to the Western way of doing business—which as we all know focuses on *individual empowerment*—then we'll get the most out of the project doing it our way.

Aran: You are all young and inexperienced. What do you know about the business world?

Katie: I know a lot more about finance than you.

Rebecca: Get with the twenty-first century. Just because we're women doesn't mean …

Cameron: He isn't just ragging on women. He's ragging on me, too.

Katie: Yeah, but at least he gave you a real job. You're a guy—"Boy Wonder."

Cameron: What kind of crack was that? After all, you two didn't start your own company. You're a number cruncher, and Rebecca sells dresses, and …

Rebecca: I think we need to stop this right now, and the four of us need to decide once and for all who is doing what!

Katie: Four of us? Wasn't our team supposed to have five people? Where's that other woman? The one from Vietnam? Parisa? Prana? Whatever her name is?

At this point, Professor Bowell, the group's advisor, walks in and tells them that the team is to be disbanded. Pranarisha had walked out of the group meeting (without anyone noticing) and informed Dr. Bowell that she just couldn't take it any longer. She had come here to learn how to run an organization more efficiently and how to work with businesspeople. However, she was so disheartened by the way the group was acting, she was going to quit the program. This was the first time in over 10 years that Dr. Bowell had heard of anyone quitting the program in the first week because of the behavior of the members of her team. The advisor just didn't see any way that this group of individuals could get their act together to become a functioning team.

Discussion Questions

1. What happened with the A-Team? Why did the group process break down? What dimensions of diversity were responsible for the conflict?
2. Describe which barriers to effectively managing diversity were present in this situation.
3. What could have been done to manage the group process better?

team exercise

What Is It Like to Be Different?

One reason people have a difficult time dealing with diversity in others or understanding why it is important to value and respect diversity is that most people spend most of their lives in environments where everyone is similar to them on important dimensions. Many people have seldom been in a situation in which they felt they didn't belong or didn't know the "rules." The purpose of this exercise is to have you experience such a situation and open up a dialogue with others about what it feels like to be different and what you can personally learn from this experience to become better at managing diversity in the future.

STEP 1: Choose an event that you would not normally attend and at which you will likely be in the minority on some important dimension. Attend the event.

- You can go with a friend who would normally attend the event, but not one who will also be in a minority.
- Make sure you pick a place where you will be safe and where you are sure you will be welcomed, or at least tolerated. You may want to check with your instructor about your choice.
- Do not call particular attention to yourself. Just observe what is going on and how you feel.

Some of you may find it easy to have a minority experience, since you are a minority group member in your everyday life. Others may have a more difficult time. Here are some examples of events to consider attending:

- A religious service for a religion totally different from your own.
- A sorority or fraternity party where the race of members is mostly different from your own.
- A political rally where the politics are different from your own.

STEP 2: After attending the event, write down your answers to the following questions:

1. How did you feel being in a minority situation? Did different aspects of your self-identity become salient? Do you think others who are in minority situations feel as you did?
2. What did you learn about the group you visited? Do you feel differently about this group now?
3. What did people do that made you feel welcome? What did people do that made you feel self-conscious?
4. Could you be an effective team member in this group? How would your differences with group members impact on your ability to function in this group?
5. What did you learn about managing diversity from this exercise?

STEP 3: Discuss the results of the exercise in a group as assigned by the instructor.

Endnotes

1. Bamattre, W. (former LAFD Fire Chief), as reported in Richardson, L. 2006. Audit faults fire department. *Los Angeles Times*, January 27, B.4.
2. See, for example, Ball, P., Monaco, G., Schmeling, J., Schartz, H., Blanck, P. 2005. Disability as diversity in *Fortune* 100 companies. *Behavioral Sciences and Law*, 23: 97–121; Jolna, K.A. 2003. Beyond race and gender? Doctoral Dissertation. Atlanta, GA: Emory University; Society of Human Resources Management. 1997. *SHRM survey of diversity of programs*. Alexandria, VA: Society for Human Resources Management.
3. Samdahl, E. November 6, 2009. "Most Companies Don't Measure the Bottom-Line Impact of Diversity Programs," at http://hrmtoday.com.; Campbell, T. 2003. Diversity in depth. *HRMagazine*, 48(3): 152.
4. Johnson, K. 2007. Kevin Johnson, Diversity Executive Workgroup Sponsor, on executive commitment. At http://www.microsoft.com/about/diversity/exec.mspx.
5. Schneider, B., Goldstein, H.W., & Smith, D.B. 1995. The ASA framework: An update. *Personnel Psychology*, 48: 747–773.
6. Ely, R.J., & Thomas, D.A. 2001. Cultural diversity at work: The effects of diversity perspectives on work group processes and outcomes. *Administrative Science Quarterly*, 46: 229–274.
7. See, for example, Kochan, T., Bezrukova, K., Ely, R., Jackson, S., Joshi, S., Jehn, K., Leonard, J., Levine, D., & Thomas, D. 2003. The effects of diversity on business performance: Report of the diversity research network. *Human Resource Management*, 42: 3–21.
8. For additional commentary on the various dimensions, see the following: Ball, C., & Haque, A. 2003. Diversity in religious practice: Implications of Islamic values in the public workplace. *Public Personnel Management*, 32: 315–328; Bantel, K.A., & Jackson, S.E. 1989. Top management and innovations in banking: Does the composition of the top team make a difference? *Strategic Management Journal*, 10: 107–124; Barsade, S.G., Ward, A.J., Turner, J.D.F., & Sonnenfeld, J.A. 2000. To your heart's content: A model of affective diversity in top management teams. *Administrative Science Quarterly*, 45: 802–837; Cummings, J.N. 2004. Work groups, structural diversity, and knowledge sharing in a global organization. *Management Science*, 50: 352–365; Ely, R.J., & Thomas, D.A. 2001. Cultural diversity at work: The effects of diversity perspectives on work group processes and outcomes.

Administrative Science Quarterly, 46: 229–274; Kochan et al., The effects of diversity on business performance; Richard, O.C., Ford, D., & Ismail, K. 2006. Exploring the performance effects of visible attribute diversity: The moderating role of span of control and organizational life cycle. *International Journal of Human Resource Management*, 17: 2091–2109.
9. Konrad, A.M. 2003. Special issue introduction: Defining the domain of workplace diversity scholarship. *Group and Organization Management*, 28: 4–18.
10. Williams, K.Y., & O'Reilly, C.A. 1998. Demography and diversity in organizations: A review of 40 years of research. In L.L. Cummings & B.M. Staw (Eds.), *Research in Organizational Behavior*, 20: 77–140. Greenwich, CT: JAI Press, p. 81.
11. Ibid.
12. See, for example, Jehn, K.A., Northcraft, G.B., & Neale, M.A. 1999. Why differences make a difference: A field study of diversity, conflict, and performance in groups. *Administrative Science Quarterly*, 44: 741–763.
13. Kanter, R.M. 1977. *Men and women of the corporation*. New York: Basic Books.
14. Texas Instruments. 2009. Diversity and inclusion. At http://www.ti.com/corp/docs/csr/empwellbeing/diversity.
15. Microsoft. 2007. Message from Claudette Whiting. At http://www.microsoft.com/about/diversity/fromoffice.mspx?pf=true.
16. Bank of America. 2007. Fact sheets. At http://careers.bankofamerica.com/learnmore/factsheets.asp.
17. U.S. Department of Labor. 2002. Facts on Executive Order 11246—Affirmative Action. At www.dol.gov/esa/regs/compliance/ofccp/aa.htm.
18. Thomas, R.R., Jr. 1992. Managing diversity: A conceptual framework. In S.E. Jackson & Associates (Eds.), *Diversity in the workplace*. New York: Guilford Press, pp. 306–317.
19. Cox, T.H., Jr. 1993. *Cultural diversity in organizations: Theory, research, and practice*. San Francisco, CA: Berrett-Koehler Publishers.
20. Gilbert, J.A., & Ivancevich, J.M. 2000. Valuing diversity: A tale of two organizations. *Academy of Management Review*, 14: 93–106.
21. Farh, J.L., Dobbins, G.H., & Cheng, B. 1991. Cultural relativity in action: A comparison of self-ratings made by Chinese and U.S. workers. *Personnel Psychology*, 44: 129–147.
22. Cox, *Cultural diversity in organizations*.

23. See, for example, Campbell, T. 2003. Diversity in depth. *HR-Magazine, 48*(3): 152.

24. Farouky, J. 2007. The many faces of Europe. *Time International,* 169 (9): 16–20.

25. U.S. Department of Labor. 2000. Working in the 21st century. At http://www.bls.gov/opub/home.htm.

26. U.S. Equal Employment Opportunity Commission. 2003. Occupational employment in private industry by race/ethnic group/sex, and by industry. At http://www.eeoc. gov/stats/jobpat/2003/national.html.

27. U.S. Department of Labor, Working in the 21st century.

28. Ibid.

29. Ibid.

30. Bureau of Labor Statistics. 2005. Economic and employment projections. At http://www.bls.gov/news.release/ecopro.toc.htm.

31. Ibid.

32. See, for example, Jackson, S.E., & Alvarez, E.B. 1992. Working through diversity as a strategic imperative. In S.E. Jackson & Associates (Eds.), *Diversity in the workplace,* pp. 13–29.

33. U.S. Department of Commerce. 2007. FT900: U.S. International trade in goods and services. At http://www.census.gov/foreign-trade/Press-Release/current_press_release/press.html#current.

34. Ibid.

35. Hitt, M.A., Ireland, D.I., & Hoskisson. 2007. *Strategic management: Competitiveness and globalization* (7th ed.). Stamford, CT: Thompson Learning.

36. Whole Foods Market. 2007. Our core values. At http://www.wholefoodsmarket.com/company/corevalues.html.

37. Cox, T.H., & Blake, S. 1991. Managing cultural diversity: Implications for organizational competitiveness. *Academy of Management Executive,* 5(3) 45–56; Jackson & Alvarez, Working through diversity as a strategic imperative.

38. Eisenberger, R., Huntington, R., Hutchison, S., & Sowa, D. 1986. Perceived organizational support. *Journal of Applied Psychology,* 71: 500–507; Eisenberger, R., Fasolo, P., & Davis-LaMastro, V. 1990. Perceived organizational support and employee diligence, commitment, and innovation. *Journal of Applied Psychology,* 75: 51–59.

39. Cox, *Cultural diversity in organizations;* McKay, P.F., Avery, D.R., & Morris, M.A. 2008. Mean racial differences in employee sales performance: The moderating role of diversity climate. *Personnel Psychology,* 61:349–374.

40. Hicks-Clarke, D., & Iles, P. 2000. Climate for diversity and its effects on career and organizational perceptions. *Personnel Review,* 29: 324–347.

41. For research on these outcomes, see: Colquitt, J.A., Conlon, D.E., Wesson, M.J., Porter, C.O.L.H., & Ng, K.Y. 2001. Justice at the millennium: A meta-analytic review of 25 years of organizational justice research. *Journal of Applied Psychology,* 86: 425–445; Goldman, B.M. 2001. Toward an understanding of employment discrimination claiming by terminated workers: Integration of organizational justice and social information processing theories. *Personnel Psychology,* 54: 361–386; Goldman, B.M. 2003. The application of referent cognitions theory to legal-claiming by terminated workers: The role of organizational justice and anger. *Journal of Management,* 29: 705–728; Skarlicki, D.P., & Folger,

R. 2003. Broadening our understanding of organizational retaliatory behavior. In R.W. Griffin & A.M. O'Leary-Kelly (Eds.), The *darkside of organizational behavior.* San Francisco, CA: Jossey-Bass, pp. 373–402.

42. Kossek, E.E., & Zonia, S.C. 1993. Assessing diversity climate: A field-study of reactions to employer efforts to promote diversity. *Journal of Organizational Behavior,* 14: 61–81.

43. Mollica, K.A. 2003. The influence of diversity context on white men's and racial minorities' reactions to disproportionate group harm. *Journal of Social Psychology,* 143: 415–431. Jehn, Northcraft, & Neale, Why differences make a difference.

44. Bantel, K.A., & Jackson, S.E. 1989. Top management and innovations in banking: Does the composition of the top team make a difference? *Strategic Management Journal,* 10: 107–124; Jackson, S.E. 1992. Consequences of group composition for the interpersonal dynamics of strategic issue processing. *Advances in Strategic Management,* 8: 345–382.

45. For research related to these dimensions, see: Hambrick, D.C., Cho, S.T., & Chen, M.J. 1996. The influence of top management team heterogeneity on firm's competitive moves. *Administrative Science Quarterly,* 41: 659–684; Jackson, S.E., May, K., & Whitney, K. 1995. Diversity in decision making teams. In R.A. Guzzo & E. Salas (Eds.), *Team effectiveness and decision making in organizations.* San Francisco, CA: Jossey-Bass, pp. 204–261; Jehn, Northcraft, & Neale, Why differences make a difference; Wood, W. 1987. Meta-analysis of sex differences in group performance. *Psychological Bulletin,* 102: 53–71; Zajac, E.J., Golden, B.R., & Shortell, S.M. 1991. New organizational forms for enhancing innovation: The case of internal corporate joint ventures. *Management Science,* 37: 170–184.

46. Grensing-Phophal, L. 2002. Reaching for diversity: What minority workers hope to get from diversity programs is what all employees want in the workplace. *HRMagazine,* 47 (5): 52–56.

47. Williams & O'Reilly, Demography and diversity in organizations.

48. Van Knippenberg, D., & Schippers, M.C. 2007. Work group diversity. *Annual Review of Psychology,* 58: 515–541.

49. See, for example, Li, J.T., & Hambrick, D.C. 2005. Factional groups: A new vantage on demographic faultlines, conflict, and disintegration in work teams. *Academy of Management Journal,* 48: 794–813; Molleman, E. 2005. Diversity in demographic characteristics, abilities and personality traits: Do faultlines affect team functioning? *Group Decision and Negotiation,* 14: 173–193; Rico, R., Molleman, E., Sanchez-Manzanares, M., & Van der Vegt, G.S. 2007. The effects of diversity faultlines and team task autonomy on decision quality and social integration. *Journal of Management,* 33: 111–132; Sawyer, J.E., Houlette, M.A., & Yeagley, E.L. 2006. Decision performance and diversity structure: Comparing faultlines in convergent, crosscut, and racially homogeneous groups. *Organizational Behavior and Human Decision Processes,* 99: 1–15.

50. Williams & O'Reilly, Demography and diversity in organizations.

51. See, for example, Richard, O.C., Kochan, T.A., & McMillan-Capehart. 2002. The impact of visible diversity on organizational effectiveness: Disclosing the contents in Pandora's black box. *Journal of Business and Management,* 8: 265–291; Pelled, L.H. 1996. Demographic diversity, conflict, and work group outcomes: An intervening process theory. *Organization Science,* 7: 615–631.

52. Williams & O'Reilly, Demography and diversity in organizations.

53. Hackman, J.R. 2002. *Leading teams: Setting the stage for great performances.* Boston, MA: Harvard Business School Press.

54. Richard, Kochan, & McMillan-Capehart, The impact of visible diversity on organizational effectiveness.

55. Ibid.

56. Cox, *Cultural diversity in organizations;* Cox & Blake, Managing cultural diversity.

57. Richard, O.C. 2000. Racial diversity, business strategy, and firm performance: A resource based view. *Academy of Management Journal,* 43: 164–177.

58. Kochan, T., Bezrukova, K., Ely, R., Jackson, S., Joshi, A., Jehn, K. Leonard, J., Levine, D., & Thomas, D. 2003. The effects of diversity on business performance: Report of the Diversity Research Network. *Human Resource Management,* 42: 3–21.

59. See, for example, Fletcher, A.A. 2000. Business and race: Only halfway there. *Fortune,* 141 (5): 76–77.

60. See, for example, Westphal, J., & Zajac, E. 1997. Defections from the inner circle: Social exchange, reciprocity and the diffusion of board independence in U.S. corporations. *Administrative Science Quarterly,* 42: 161–183.

61. Sellers, P. 2004. By the numbers: Women and profits. *Fortune,* at http://www.fortune.com/fortune/subs/article/0,15114,582783, 00.html.

62. Siciliano, J.I. 1996. The relationship of board member diversity to organizational performance. *Journal of Business Ethics,* 15: 1313–1320.

63. Hillman, A.J., Cannella, A.A., Jr., & Harris, I.C. 2002. Women and racial minorities in the boardroom: How do directors differ? *Journal of Management,* 28: 747–763.

64. Ibid.

65. Bantel, & Jackson, Top management and innovations in banking; Hambrick, Cho, & Chen, The influence of top management team heterogeneity on firm's competitive moves.

66. Wright, P., Ferris, S.P., & Kroll, M. 1995. Competitiveness through management of diversity: Effects on stock price evaluation. *Academy of Management Journal,* 38: 272–287.

67. Cowell, A. 2005. What Britain can tell France about rioters. *The New York Times,* November 20, 4.4.

68. Dovidio, J.F., Gaertner, S.L., Kawakami, K., & Hodson, G. 2002. Why can't we just get along? Interpersonal biases and interracial distrust. *Cultural Diversity and Ethnic Minority Psychology,* 8: 88–102.

69. Bobo, L.D. 2001. Racial attitudes and relations at the close of the twentieth century. In N.J. Smelser, W.J. Wilson, & F. Mitchell (Eds.), *Racial trends and their consequences (Vol. 1).* Washington, DC: National Academic Press, pp. 264–301.

70. McConahay, J.B. 1986. Modern racism, ambivalence, and the modern racism scale. In J.F. Dovidio & S.L. Gaertner (Eds.), *Prejudice, discrimination, and racism.* Orlando, FL: Academic Press, pp. 91–125.

71. Dovidio, J.F., & Gaertner, S.L. 2000. Aversive racism and selection decisions: 1989 and 1999. *Psychological Science,* 11: 319–323.

72. For example research, see: Cleveland, J.N., Vescio, T.K., & Barnes-Farrell, J.L. 2005. Gender discrimination in organizations. In R.L. Dipboye, & A. Colella (Eds.), *Discrimination at work: The psychological and organizational bases.* Mahwah, NJ:

Lawrence Erlbaum; Colella, A., & Varma, A. 2001. The impact of subordinate disability on leader-member exchange dynamics. *Academy of Management Journal,* 44: 304–315; Dovidio, J.F., Gaertner, S.L., Anastasio, P.A., & Sanitaso, R. 1992. Cognitive and motivational bases of bias: The implications of aversive racism for attitudes towards Hispanics. In S. Knouse, P. Rosenfeld, & A. Culbertson (Eds.). *Hispanics in the workplace.* Newbury Park, CA: Sage, pp. 75–106; Hebl, M.R., Bigazzi Foster, J., & Dovidio, J.F. 2002. Formal and interpersonal discrimination: A field study of bias toward homosexual applicants. *Personality and Social Psychology Bulletin,* 28: 815–825.

73. Dipboye, R.L. & Colella, A. 2005. The dilemmas of workplace discrimination. In R.L. Dipboye & A. Colella (Eds.), *Discrimination at work: The psychological and organizational bases.* Mahwah, NJ: Lawrence Erlbaum. pp. 425–462.

74. Cox, *Cultural diversity in organizations.*

75. Crocker, J., Fiske, S.T., & Taylor, S.E. 1984. Schematic bases of belief change. In J.R. Eiser (Ed.), *Attitudinal judgment.* New York: Springer-Verlag, pp. 197–226; Weber, R., & Crocker, J. 1983. Cognitive processes in the revision of stereotypic beliefs. *Journal of Personality and Social Psychology,* 45: 961–977.

76. von Heppel, W., Sekaquaptewa, D., & Vargas, P. 1995. On the role of encoding processes in stereotype maintenance. In M.P. Zanna (Ed.), *Advances in experimental social psychology, Vol. 27.* San Diego, CA: Academic Press, pp. 177–254.

77. Fiske, S.T. 1998. Stereotyping, prejudice, and discrimination. In D.T. Gilbert, S.T. Fiske, & G. Lindzey (Eds.), *The handbook of social psychology, Vol. 2* (4th ed.). New York: McGraw-Hill, pp. 357–411.

78. Cox, *Cultural diversity in organizations.*

79. Helft, M. 2007. Xerox's strategy pays off with a new search venture. *The New York Times,* February 9, C.3; Maney, K. 2006. Mulcahy traces steps of Xerox's comeback. *USA Today,* September 21, 4B.

80. Ireland, R.D., Hoskisson, R.E., & Hitt, M.A. 2006. *Understanding business strategy.* Mason, OH: South-western Publishing; Stone, B. 2007. eBay beats the estimates for 4th-quarter earnings. *New York Times,* January 25, C.3; Vara, V. 2007. eBay's strong earnings, outlook help to quiet critics, for now. *Wall Street Journal,* January 25, A.3.

81. Brewer, M.B., & Miller, N. 1984. Beyond the contact hypothesis: Theoretical perspectives on desegregation. In N. Miller & M.B. Brewer (Eds.), *Groups in contact.* San Diego, CA: Academic Press, pp. 281–302; Tajfel, H. 1978. *Differentiation between social groups: Studies in the social psychology of intergroup relations.* San Diego, CA: Academic Press; Ashforth, B., & Mael, F. 1989. Social identity theory and the organization. *Academy of Management Review,* 14: 20–39.

82. Abrams, D., & Hogg, M.A. 1990. An introduction to the social identity approach. In D. Abrams & M.A. Hogg (Eds.), *Social identity theory: Constructive and critical advances.* New York: Springer-Verlag, pp. 1–9.

83. Cox, *Cultural diversity in organizations.*

84. McGuire, W.J., McGuire, C.V., Child, P., & Fujioka, T. 1978. Salience of ethnicity in the spontaneous self-concept as a function of one's ethnic distinctiveness in the social environment. *Journal of Personality and Social Psychology,* 36: 511–520.

85. Cox, *Cultural diversity in organizations.*

86. Ely, R.J. 1994. The effects of organizational demographics and social identity on relationships among professional women. *Administrative Science Quarterly,* 39: 203–239.

87. Cited in Slay, H.S. 2003. Spanning two worlds: Social identity and emergent African American leaders. *Journal of Leadership and Organizational Studies,* 9: 56–66.

88. Cox, *Cultural diversity in organizations.*

89. Abrams & Hogg, An introduction to the social identity approach.

90. Turner, J.C. 1975. Social comparison and social identity: Some prospects for intergroup behavior. *European Journal of Social Psychology,* 5: 5–34.

91. Hogg, M.A., & Terry, D.J. 2000. Social identity and self-categorization processes in organizational contexts. *Academy of Management Review,* 25: 121–140.

92. Ibid.

93. French, J.R.P., & Raven, B. 1959. The bases of social power. In D. Cartwright (Ed.), *Social power.* Ann Arbor: University of Michigan, Institute for Social Research, pp. 150–167; Pfeffer, J., & Salancik, G.R. 1978. *The external control of organizations: A resource dependence view.* New York: Harper and Row.

94. Sidananius, J., & Pratto, F. 1999. *Social dominance.* Cambridge, UK: Cambridge University Press.

95. Ibid.

96. Kalkhoff, W., & Barnum, C. 2000. The effects of status-organizing and social identity processes on patterns of social influence. *Social Psychology Quarterly,* 63: 95–115.

97. Konrad, A.M. 2003. Special issue introduction: Defining the domain of workplace diversity scholarship. *Group and Organizational Management,* 28: 4–18.

98. For additional details, see Deogun, N. Coke was told in '95 of need for diversity. *Wall Street Journal,* May 20, A.3; McKay, B. 2000. Coke settles bias suit for $192.5 million. *Wall Street Journal,* November 17, A.3.

99. U.S. Equal Employment Opportunity Commission. 2005. Occupational employment in private industry by race/ethnic group/sex, and by industry. At http://archive.eeoc.gov/stats/jobpat/2005/national.html.

100. Kanter, *Men and women of the corporation.*

101. Winters, M.F. 2003. Globalization presents both opportunities and challenges for diversity. At http://search.shrm.org/search?q=cache:8b6YiQjDjFoJ:www.shrm.org/diversity/library_published/nonIC/CMS_012382.asp+++globalization1challenges1diversity&access=p&output=xml_no_dtd&ie=UTF-8&lr=&client=shrm_frontend&num=10&site=&proxystylesheet=shrm_frontend&oe=ISO-8859-1.

102. U.S. Department of Commerce and Vice President Al Gore's National Partnership for Reinventing Government Benchmarking Study. 1998. Best practices in achieving workplace diversity. Washington, DC: U.S. Department of Commerce.

103. Starbucks. 2007. Starbucks mission statement. At http://www.starbucks.com/aboutus/environment.asp.

104. Ford Motor Company. 2007. Valuing diversity. At http://www.mycareer.ford.com/ONTHETEAM.ASP?CID=15.

105. Jayne, M.E.A., & Dipboye, R.L. 2004. Leveraging diversity to improve business performance: Research findings and recommendations for organizations. *Human Resource Management,* 43: 409–424.

106. Cox, T.H. 2001. *Creating the multicultural organization: A strategy for capturing the power of diversity.* San Francisco: Jossey-Bass.

organizational behavior in a global context

exploring behavior in action
McDonald's Thinks Globally and Acts Locally

In 1948, brothers Richard and Maurice McDonald opened the first McDonald's restaurant in San Bernardino, California. Over the next decade, hundreds of McDonald's restaurants were built alongside the new interstate highway systems in the United States. McDonald's was one of the first restaurants to make fast food available to the newly mobile American population. In 1967, McDonald's decided to go international and opened its first restaurant outside the United States in Richmond, British Columbia. Today there are over 32,000 McDonald's restaurants in 122 countries. And, its international operations have become highly important to McDonald's financial performance. For example, its restaurants in Europe now produce more revenues than its restaurants in the United States, despite the fact that McDonald's has more units in the United States. McDonald's success in international operations is partially because it has adapted to the cultural differences in the various foreign locations of its restaurants.

Trying to maintain a global brand is difficult because of the different cultural expectations experienced across different countries. It is important to ensure a positive reputation for the company and also maintain the quality of its products. So, McDonald's had to build and sustain a reputation for quality products and efficient service globally while simultaneously meeting consumer expectations across different cultures. McDonald's developed a competitive advantage because the company has taken steps to know, understand, and service customers' needs without compromising its core strengths (fast, easy, clean meals for families to enjoy). An example of McDonald's adaptation to cultural differences is exhibited in how McDonald's dispenses its food products in order to respect and serve its Israeli customers. All meat served in McDonald's restaurants located in Israel is 100 percent kosher. McDonald's operates both kosher and nonkosher restaurants in Israel. The kosher restaurants are closed on Saturday and on religious holidays, while the nonkosher restaurants remain open for those customers who do not

knowledge objectives

After reading this chapter, you should be able to:

1. Define *globalization* and discuss the forces that influence this phenomenon.
2. Discuss three types of international involvement by associates and managers and describe problems that can arise with each.
3. Explain how international involvement by associates and managers varies across firms.
4. Describe high-involvement management in the international arena, emphasizing the adaptation of this management approach to different cultures.
5. Identify and explain the key ethical issues in international business.

strictly adhere to kosher law. In the kosher restaurant, the menu includes no dairy products and food is prepared in accordance with kosher law. In addition, McDonald's supports the local communities by obtaining many of its food products (e.g., beef, potatoes, lettuce, etc.) from local suppliers. In Israel, it obtains 80 percent of its food supplies within the country.

To display the efficiency and cleanliness of its restaurants in Egypt, McDonald's operates an open-door policy, in which customers are invited to visit their kitchens to view the preparation of the food. In this way, consumers can view how McDonald's restaurants prepare their food efficiently, maintaining quality and in ways that meet high health and safety standards. For example, employees must wash their hands with disin-

©ZAHID HUSSEIN/Reuters/Landov LLC

fectant soap every 30 minutes and continuously wash and disinfect utensils. The tours provided to customers fulfill a process of transparency and have elicited highly positive customer responses and expressions of appreciation.

Other examples of how McDonald's adapts to local culture and ways of life include vegetarian meals in India, with local creations such as the McPuff and the McVeggie. Today, 70 percent of the menu in India has been altered to meet the customers' needs and desires. In Europe, McDonald's introduced a menu featuring salads, fruit, and the option of substituting carrots in Happy Meals for French fries, a menu modification made to appeal to health-conscious consumers. These same menu items have been offered in the United States as well. So, while the menu may be different in some ways, the McDonald's experience around the world is consistent by offering quality, great service, cleanliness, and value. It is equally

important to develop a culturally appropriate strategy for a new international location. Innovation is successful when it is culturally appropriate. In Brazil, McDonald's promotes an afternoon meal rather than a lunch meal. This change was made because Brazilians prefer their main meal at midday, often eating at a leisurely pace with business associates.

There are many abroad who are concerned about having companies like McDonald's expand their restaurants globally, such as the concerns expressed about a McDonald's restaurant opening in the food court adjoining France's famous Louvre museum. Countering some of these concerns is McDonald's commitment to important local social concerns. For example, McDonald's supports Conservation International's efforts to protect wild pandas, a threatened species. Taking this further, McDonald's announced a local treasures program in China to encourage children to learn about their country's special environment and rare animals. Another example is McDonald's major donation to the Dubai Autism Center as a part of McDonald's World Children's Day campaign.

McDonald's is regularly adapting its restaurants and marketing tactics to reflect cultural, architectural, and regional differences within each country. Even in the United States, McDonald's adapts to local communities. In Maine, McDonald's offers lobster rolls. And in Michigan, customers can purchase Halal McNuggets, chicken that is processed under strict religious supervision in order to cater to the 150,000 Muslims who live in the Detroit area. Thus, McDonald's is a prime example of a company that thinks globally and acts locally.

Sources: "Welcome to McDonald's Israel", McDonald's, Nov. 22, 2009, www.mcdonalds.com; E. Ganley. 2009. "McDonald's to Become Mona Lisa's New Neighbor," *BusinessWeek*, Oct. 5, www.businessweek.com; S.E.D. Aloui & Y. Genena. 2009. "McDonald's Egypt continues the 'Open Door' program," AMEinfo, June 28, at http://www.ameinfo.com; N. El Ajou. 2008. "McDonald's UAE Concludes its 7th World Children's Day Campaign," AMEinfo, Dec. 24, 2008; K. Capell. 2008. "A Golden Recipe for McDonald's Europe," *BusinessWeek*, July 17; "McDonalds's and Conservation International Team Up to Protect China's Panda Habitats", McDonalds, June 10, 2008, at http://www.crmcdonalds.com; Nini Bhan and Brad Nemer. 2006. "Brand Magic in India," *BusinessWeek*, May 8, at http://www.businessweek.com; Beth Carney. 2005. "In Europe, the Fat Is in the Fire," *BusinessWeek*, Feb. 8, at http://www.businessweek.com; Conrad P. Kottak. 2003. McDonald's in Brazil: Culturally Appropriate Marketing, *Ethnographic Solutions*, at http://www.ethnographic-solutions.com.

the strategic importance of Organizational Behavior in a Global Context

The *Exploring Behavior in Action* discussion of McDonald's shows how one firm operates on the world stage and emphasizes the importance of cross-cultural knowledge and skills. Because of substantial competition and differing cultural expectations across the many countries in which McDonald's has restaurants, the company has strong needs for flexibility and for efficiency in resource use. McDonald's has developed a global reputation for providing clean restaurants and fast and easy meals for value-conscious families. From strategic locations, the firm develops, produces, sells, and supports its products for the world marketplace. To be successful, however, this firm must be especially attentive to local cultural values and desired foods. McDonald's always provides some consistent products on its menu regardless of location (e.g., the Big Mac) but it also provides menu items adapted to the local cultural tastes (such as vegetable meals in India and kosher foods in Israel). Obviously, McDonald's has trained its managers to be sensitive to local culture and yet to take advantage of global efficiencies. Actions such as those used by McDonald's to take advantage of the different international markets opened due to globalization have led to higher overall firm performance.[1]

To create cost advantages, to pursue growth, or to spread risk across different markets, many firms have adopted strategies that call for investment in foreign countries. Such involvement can take many forms, including the creation of company-owned manufacturing or back-office facilities, company-owned marketing and sales units, and/or alliances with companies based in a particular foreign country. In all cases, effectively handling cross-country cultural differences is crucial. Executing competitive strategies would be impossible without an understanding of how these differences affect day-to-day relationships among associates and managers, as well as relationships with external parties (such as suppliers and customers).[2]

One of the most famous examples of a corporate failure that emphasizes the importance of cultural differences is Walt Disney Company's attempt to execute a strategy involving efficient operations and exceptional customer service in its theme park located close to Paris.[3] American leaders of the Euro Disney project failed to understand some European workplace norms that produced a less friendly approach to guests in the park. Disney leaders also failed to anticipate the uproar over grooming and dress requirements for associates, including "appropriate undergarments," and they did not recognize the potential for conflict between individuals of different nationalities. One of the 1,000 associates and lower-level managers who departed in the first nine weeks of Euro Disney's operation commented, "I don't think [non-European supervisors] realized what Europeans were like." Concerning the park, a critic expressed the feelings of the French elite: "A horror made of cardboard, plastic, and appalling colors; a construction of hardened chewing gum and idiotic folklore taken straight out of comic books written for obese Americans."[4] Failure to fully appreciate and respond to cultural differences contributed to a disastrous early period for Euro Disney. Its performance suffered, but having learned several hard lessons, the company improved its practices in the park and increased its performance as well.

Because of the importance of globalization and the related diversity and ethical issues it poses, we present examples and applications involving firms operating in multiple countries throughout the book. In this chapter, we discuss these issues in depth. We open the chapter with a discussion of globalization, addressing the opportunities and challenges that globalization presents for nations and firms. Next, we discuss the ways in which associates and managers can deal with international problems and the pitfalls to avoid in their activities. A discussion of high-involvement management follows, with a focus on how this management approach can be tailored to different countries and regions of the world. Finally, we describe ethical issues frequently confronted by firms with substantial international involvement.

Forces of Globalization

In a global economy, products, services, people, technologies, and financial capital move relatively freely across national borders.[5] Tariffs, currency laws, travel restrictions, immigration restrictions, and other barriers to these international flows become less difficult to manage. Essentially, a global economy provides firms with a unified world market in which to sell products and services, as well as a unified world market for acquiring the resources needed to create those products and services.

globalization
The trend toward a unified global economy where national borders mean relatively little.

Globalization, the trend toward a more global economy, has increased substantially since 1980. Direct foreign investment by firms based in developed countries has increased. While several developed countries suffered a recession early in the twenty-first century, there were healthy increases in direct foreign investments made by them through 2007. In fact, such investments reached an all-time high in 2007. In this year, the total stock of direct foreign investments achieved $15 trillion in value.[6] However, the global economic recession led to a reduction in the total amount of direct foreign investments in 2008 and 2009. Yet, with the recovery, projections call for increases in direct foreign investment in 2010 and several years beyond.[7] These investments represent increased interest in producing goods and services in foreign countries. Exporting goods and services into other countries increased over the same time period. Exports have grown at a high rate in recent years except during the major global recession.[8] Interestingly, in recent years, significant amounts of foreign investment has been focused on emerging-economy countries such as China and India. Furthermore, these emerging economies have been making major foreign investments in other countries. Their growing economic power is evident in the projections that within the next few decades China and India are expected to have the largest and third largest economies, respectively, in the world.[9] The results of globalization are evident in the fact that major multinational firms obtain almost 55 percent of their sales from outside their home country and almost 50 percent of their assets and associates reside outside of their home country.[10] Clearly, goods and services flowed across borders in record amounts at the end of the twentieth century and early in the twenty-first century, with firms such as Toyota leading the way.

Many national leaders promote globalization as a means for economic growth inside their countries as well as in the world as a whole. Most economists agree that a highly global economy would be beneficial for most countries. Goods, services, and the resources needed to produce them freely flowing across borders likely reduce the costs of doing business, resulting in economic stimulation.[11] It has been estimated that genuine free trade (i.e., trade with no tariffs) in manufactured goods among the United States, Europe, and Japan would result in a 5 to 10 percent annual increase in the economic output of these three areas. Genuine free trade in services would increase economic output by an additional 15 to 20 percent.[12]

culture
Shared values and taken-for-granted assumptions that govern acceptable behavior and thought patterns in a country and give a country much of its uniqueness.

Despite the potential economic benefits, officials in a number of nations have expressed concerns about globalization's long-term effects on societal culture.[13] **Culture** involves shared values and taken-for-granted assumptions about how to act and think.[14] Many fear that unique cultures around the world will disappear over time if the world becomes one unified market for goods and services. They argue that cultural distinctiveness—indeed what makes a country special—will disappear as similar products and services are sold worldwide.[15] Individuals with these concerns took notice when a Taiwanese Little League baseball team playing in the United States was comforted by a McDonald's restaurant because it reminded them of home.[16] In developing nations, there are also concerns over labor exploitation and natural resource depletion. In wealthy nations, there are concerns over the export of jobs to low-wage countries and the possibility that wealthy nations ultimately will need to lower their wage structures in order to compete in a truly global economy.[17]

From the perspective of an individual company, there are many reasons to consider substantial international involvement (see Exhibit 3-1). First, a firm may want to expand sales efforts across borders in order to sustain growth. Opportunities for growth may have been exhausted in the home country (e.g., if the market is saturated), but owners, business analysts, and the media often demand continuing sales and profit growth.[18] Second, a firm may be able to reduce its business risk by selling its products and services in a number of different countries. By diversifying its sales across a number of regions of the world, a company may be able to offset bad economic times when they occur in one part of the world with good economic times in other parts of the world. Third, a firm may enjoy greater economies of scale by expanding its markets internationally. This applies most often to manufacturing firms. Hyundai, for example, could not develop operations with efficient scale by serving only the domestic South Korean automobile market.[19] To achieve a reasonable cost structure, the firm needed to build and sell more automobiles than the South Korean market could handle. The larger volume of automobiles manufactured and sold allows them to obtain quantity discounts on raw materials purchased and to spread their fixed costs across more autos, thereby reducing their cost per unit (increasing their profit margins). Fourth, when locating units internationally, a firm may enjoy location advantages such as low labor costs, specialized expertise, or other valuable resources.[20]

Clearly, globalization and the value to be gained from participating in international markets is changing the competitive landscape for many firms, regardless of their home base.[21] Even many smaller and younger firms are now participating in international markets. The openness of markets and advancing technology (and lower costs of this technology) provide opportunities for young and small firms as well as for older, larger, and established firms.[22] These opportunities in international markets have been prompted by changes in many countries' institutional environments. For example, several emerging-economy countries have reduced regulations to allow more foreign firms to enter their markets (e.g., China and India). In this way, their economies have grown larger and their firms have learned new capabilities, allowing them to compete more effectively in their home markets and abroad. Thus, the countries' institutional environments affect home and foreign country firms' strategies.[23] Institutional environments contribute to the opportunities and challenges depicted in Exhibit 3-1.

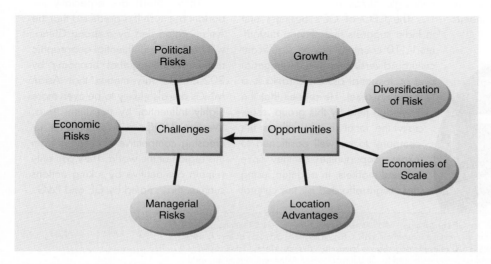

Exhibit 3-1 Opportunities and Challenges for Firms with International Involvement

MANAGERIAL ADVICE

Multinational Corporations Achieving Glocalization

Globalization has greatly increased the interactions among countries and cultures. The vast improvements in communication technologies (and transportation as well) have affected much of what we do across the world. The world's financial markets have become tightly integrated, as shown by the world recession in 2008–2009. The political actions of opening country markets and the entry into those markets by multinational corporations (MNCs) have jointly increased the amount and speed of globalization. MNCs sell more than $11 trillion in goods globally on an annual basis. And, although MNCs have been blamed for a number of ills (e.g., violation of workers' rights, harm to the natural environment, etc.), they have also enriched the fortunes of people in less-developed countries. MNCs have played a major role in the economic development in important regions of the world such as China, India, and even Latin America.

However, MNCs now face a number of challenges, including significant competition from major companies in emerging markets such as Tata, Cemex, and Lenova, among others. These companies are not only competing effectively in their home markets, but they are also developing capabilities (ability to successfully enter new foreign markets, building global resource bases) to become major forces in global markets. Thus, MNCs must not only develop major global capabilities but also must learn the local markets well and acquire knowledge from these countries/markets that can be diffused throughout the company to enhance their ability to compete in global markets. This is sometimes called glocalization.

The CEO of GE's business unit in India suggests that serving customers in 10 countries having significant cultural diversity in the managerial and professional associate ranks is a tremendous asset. He argues that the knowledge held by this group, especially the local insight, allows the company to be well positioned to exploit opportunities as they arise in local markets. In addition, using the insight afforded by the cultural diversity allows the management team to "see around the corner" regarding expectations for the future and thereby to stay ahead of the competition.

Procter & Gamble (P&G) has also learned to gain greater value from its international operations. Specifically, they design units and programs to help them acquire new knowledge available in certain countries and regions. They then use this knowledge to enrich their products, services, and processes in other regions of the world. In this way, they stay ahead of their global and local competitors. For example, in China, they have encouraged reluctant research and development (R&D) researchers to speak up and share their ideas with others. In so doing, they have enhanced their R&D output there and also added unique knowledge to their global R&D efforts.

These efforts are especially important because it is predicted that the Asian region, led by a strong China, will be the most influential geographic region for the global economy by 2020. And this means that Asian MNCs are also likely to be even more highly influential by this time. Thus, Western MNCs will experience increasing competitive challenges from this region of the world. They can only remain competitive by taking actions such as those noted by GE and P&G.

©Courtesy of Proctor & Gamble

Sources: "Earning staff's respect was pivotal for GE capital man," *Wall Street Journal,* Nov. 16, 2009, at http://www.wsj.com; V. Govindarajan. 2009. "The case for 'reverse innovation' now," *BusinessWeek,* Oct. 26, at http://www.businessweek.com; R.O. Crockett. 2009. "P&G gets reticent researchers to speak up," *BusinessWeek,* Oct. 2, at http://www.businessweek.com; "Asian multinational corporations poised for global success and Asian region may be world's most influential economy by 2020," *Fleishman-Hillard Point of View,* Sept. 10, 2009, at http://pov.fleishman.com; D. Patel. 2009. "Multinational corporations in an increasingly globalized world," *Prospect,* Feb. 3, at http://www.prospectjournal.ucsd.edu.

These powerful forces encourage many firms to expand into international markets, but there are substantial risks. These risks can be classified as political, economic, and managerial.[24]

- *Political risks* relate to instability in national governments, the threat of civil or international war, and the threat of state-sponsored terrorism. These risks create uncertainty, and they can result in the destruction of assets and disruption of resource flows.[25] One of the most difficult situations occurs when a government nationalizes an industry, meaning that it takes over the assets of private companies, often with little or no compensation provided to the firms.
- *Economic risks* relate to fluctuations in the value of foreign currencies and the possibility of sudden economic contraction in some countries.[26] When a foreign country's currency declines in value relative to the home country's currency, assets and earnings in that foreign country are worth less, and exporting to that country becomes more difficult, as exported goods cost more there.
- *Managerial risks* relate to the difficulties inherent in managing the complex resource flows required by most international firms.[27] Tariffs, logistics, and language issues can become a significant challenge as a firm does business in an increasing number of countries. Radically new marketing programs and distribution networks may be needed as firms enter new countries. Some executives and managers are better at managing these complexities than are others.

The *Managerial Advice* segment explains how managers develop their firm's capabilities to compete effectively in global markets. They must develop a global mindset but also understand local market requirements. The most effective firms such as GE and P&G enter markets with the intent to learn. Firms can gain valuable ideas in foreign markets that they can then use in business units competing in other regions of the world.[28] Multinational firms based in Western (developed) countries have a number of advantages. However, companies from Asia, particularly China and India, are building their resources and capabilities. They will be formidable competitors in the coming decade.

The Globalization Experience for Associates and Managers

For individual associates and managers, international exposure or experience can occur in several ways, which we discuss below. In each case, opportunities for personal learning, growth, and advancement are substantial. Several pitfalls, however, must be avoided.

Internationally Focused Jobs

An individual may work directly on international issues as part of her day-to-day job. Although dealing with finance issues, accounting concerns, information technology tasks, and so on can be challenging in a purely domestic context, adding an international dimension usually creates situations with significant complexity. Individuals who thrive on challenge are well suited to these environments. At Dow Chemical, for example, international finance activities are often demanding because of the firm's exposure to fluctuations in the value of many different countries' currencies. With manufacturing facilities in dozens of countries and sales in well over 100 countries, Dow faces substantial currency risk.

Associates and managers who hold internationally focused jobs are often members of geographically dispersed teams. Many of these teams complete work related to new marketing programs, new-product-development projects, and other nonroutine initiatives. Other teams focus on routine issues, such as product flow from central manufacturing facilities. In many cases, associates and managers working on geographically dispersed teams have different working and decision styles because of cultural differences. Some prefer starting meetings with social rather than business topics, others prefer an autocratic rather than an egalitarian team leader, and still others prefer indirect to direct confrontations. To facilitate their work, team members use a complex set of tools to communicate, including electronic mail, Internet chat rooms, company intranets, teleconferencing, videoconferencing, and perhaps occasional face-to-face meetings.[29] Individuals complete team-related tasks around the clock as they live and work in different time zones, creating additional coordination challenges.

Because international teams largely rely on electronically mediated communication to coordinate and accomplish their work, they are often referred to as **virtual electronic teams**.[30] Although virtual teams are efficient, a virtual world with little face-to-face communication combined with substantial cross-cultural differences sets the stage for misperceptions and misunderstandings. Small disagreements can escalate quickly, and trust can be strained. One study showed that virtual teams with substantial cross-cultural differences often exhibit lower trust than virtual teams with more cross-cultural similarities.[31] Low trust, suggesting little confidence that others will maintain their promises, be honest, and not engage in negative politics, is harmful to the team's efforts.[32] Researchers have discovered several potential negative outcomes for virtual teams with low trust, including unwillingness to cooperate, poor conflict resolution, few or no goals established, poor risk mitigation, and lack of adjustment to the virtual format for work.[33] Although trust is important for any group, it is particularly important for virtual teams because of the propensity for misunderstanding as well as the absence of traditional direct supervision.[34]

The initial communications of a virtual cross-cultural team may be particularly important in the development of trust. When early communication is task-focused, positive, and reciprocated (i.e., questions and inputs do not go unanswered), a phenomenon known as **swift trust** can occur.[35] Swift trust occurs when individuals who have little or no history of working together, but who have a clear task to accomplish, quickly develop trust in one another based on interpersonal communication. Although social communication (i.e., friendly, non-task-related) can help to maintain this trust, task-related exchanges that facilitate the team's progress are critical.[36]

In the face of possible trust issues, it is important for managers to help team members identify with the team. According to identity theory, when an individual identifies with a team, he feels connected to it, and he takes very seriously his role as a team member. Failure to identify with the team often results in withholding of effort on team projects, a common problem.[37] Steps can be taken to increase the chances that an individual will identify with the international team. First, it is important to provide training in international negotiating and conflict resolution.[38] Techniques that are sensitive to cultural differences and focused on collaborative outcomes work best. Exhibit 3-2 provides specific ideas on how managers can be sensitive to cultural differences. Second, it is important to have team members jointly develop a unified vision.[39] The shared experience of discussing the future of the team, its goals and aspirations, can draw people together. Finally, it is helpful for team members to spend some time in face-to-face meetings, especially early in a team's life.[40] Face-to-face meetings increase the chances that team members will identify personal

virtual electronic teams
Teams that rely heavily on electronically mediated communication rather than face-to-face meetings as the means to coordinate work.

swift trust
A phenomenon where trust develops rapidly based on positive, reciprocated task-related communications.

> **EXHIBIT 3-2** Learning about a Counterpart's Culture
>
> - Don't attempt to identify another's culture too quickly. Common cues (name, physical appearance, language, accent, and location) may be unreliable. In a global economy and multicultural societies, some people are shaped by more than one culture.
>
> - Beware of the Western bias toward taking actions. In some cultures, thinking and talking affect relationships more than actions do.
>
> - Try to avoid the tendency to formulate simple perceptions of others' cultural values. Most cultures are highly complex, involving many dimensions.
>
> - Don't assume that your values are the best for the organization. For example, U.S. culture is individualistic, and this is often assumed to be productive. While individual competition and pride can be positive to some degree, cultural values in India and China emphasize the importance of family, friends, and social relationships, making associates in these countries highly loyal to the organizations for which they work, and this is positive as well. Loyalty to the organization is less common among U.S. associates.
>
> - Recognize that norms for interactions involving outsiders may differ from those for interactions between compatriots. Trust is especially important in some cultures and greatly affects interactions with others.
>
> - Be careful about making assumptions regarding cultural values and expected behaviors based on the published dimensions of a person's national culture. Different ages, genders, and even geographic regions may cause differences within a country.
>
> Source: Based on work in M. Javidan & R.J. House. 2001. Cultural acumen for the global manager. *Organizational Dynamics*, 29(4): 289–305; C.J. Robertson, J.A. Al-Khatib, M. Al-Habib, & D. Lanoue. 2001. Beliefs about work in the Middle East and the convergence versus divergence of values. *Journal of World Business*, 36(3): 223–244; S.E. Weiss. 1994. Negotiating with "Romans"—Part 2. *MIT Sloan Management Review*, 35 (3): 85–99.

similarities, and these similarities contribute to understanding and cooperation.[41] Absent face-to-face interactions, videoconferencing provides richer communication than Internet chat rooms and teleconferencing because of the value of seeing each other. In one study, members of international teams reported that it was even helpful to have photographs of teammates posted in the workplace.[42]

Although research on the role of personal characteristics is not conclusive, several characteristics appear to play important roles in the success of cross-cultural virtual teams.[43] Individuals who value diversity, flexibility, and autonomy may offer more positive contributions to both the task and social aspects of the team. A general disposition to trust, a significant degree of trustworthiness, relational skills (involving the ability to work with others who possess different knowledge), and skills for communicating through electronic means are also important to success in virtual teams.

Foreign Job Assignments

Individuals may accept foreign job assignments that entail dealing directly with the complexities of operating in a foreign culture. These people are referred to as **expatriates**, or "expats" for short.[44] Foreign experience can be exciting because of the new and different work situations that are encountered. The opportunity outside of work to learn about and

expatriate
An individual who leaves his or her home country to live and work in a foreign land.

live in a different culture can also be valuable. Many companies indicate that international experience results in faster promotions and makes associates more attractive to other companies because of the enhanced knowledge and capabilities they develop. In addition to the knowledge gained by expatriates, they also provide a means of transferring knowledge from the home company to foreign subsidiaries. In other words, expatriates carry with them the knowledge of the industry, technology, and firm.[45] Using expatriate managers also can facilitate coordination between the home office and foreign subsidiaries.[46]

Petroleum engineers, management consultants, operations managers, sales managers, and information technology project managers are among the common candidates for international assignments. According to recent relocation trends, international assignments are commonly made to fill skill gaps in foreign units, to launch new units, to facilitate technology transfer to another country, and to help build management expertise in a foreign unit.[47]

International assignments, however, should be treated with caution. Many things can go wrong, resulting in poor job performance and an early return to the home country.[48] **Culture shock** is a key factor in failure. This stress reaction can affect an individual who faces changes in and uncertainty over what is acceptable behavior.[49] Some behaviors that are acceptable in the home country may not be acceptable in the new country, and vice versa. For example, in many cultures, one of the hands (either the left or the right, depending on the culture) is considered dirty and should not be used in certain situations. This can be difficult for an American or European to remember. In addition, simple limitations such as an inability to acquire favorite foods, read road signs, and communicate easily often cause stress.

culture shock
A stress reaction involving difficulties coping with the requirements of life in a new country.

©Hans Neleman/Photonica/Getty Images, Inc.

Beyond the associate's or manager's experience of culture shock, a spouse may also experience stress. Research suggests that spousal inability to adjust to the new setting is a significant cause of premature departure from a foreign assignment.[50] One study suggested that spousal adjustment occurs on three dimensions: (1) effectiveness in building relationships with individuals from the host country, (2) effectiveness in adjusting to local culture in general, and (3) effectiveness in developing a feeling of being at home in the foreign country.[51] This same study showed that spouses who spoke the language of the host country adjusted much more effectively. Spouses with very young children also fared better because that spouse will likely spend a great deal of time engaged in the same activities as before the move—child care in the home. Familiar activities make the adjustment easier. In short, the family plays an important role in the ability of the associate or manager to adjust to and be effective in foreign assignments.[52]

ethnocentrism
The belief that one's culture is better than others.

Individuals exposed to **ethnocentrism** in foreign assignments can also experience stress. Ethnocentrism is the belief that one's culture is superior to others, and it can lead to discrimination and even hostility.[53] In some cases, discrimination is subtle and even unintentional. It nonetheless can harm an expatriate's ability to adjust.

A number of remedies have been proposed to reduce or eliminate expatriate stress. In most cases, these remedies include screening and training before departure, training and social support after arrival in the country, and support for the individual returning to the home country.

Predeparture activities set the stage for success. Such activities include favoring for selection those individuals who have personal characteristics associated with success in foreign assignments. Although there are no simple relationships between personal characteristics and success in foreign posts, associates and managers who possess strong interpersonal skills, are flexible, and are emotionally stable often adapt effectively as expatriates.[54] Even so, predeparture training often plays a more important role than do personal characteristics.

Training can take many forms; a firm may provide books and CDs or arrange for role playing and language training, for example.[55] An expert on training for expatriates has offered the following advice.[56]

- *Train the entire family, if there is one.* If the spouse or children are unhappy, the expatriate assignment is more likely to be unsuccessful.
- *Conduct the predeparture orientation one to two months prior to departure.* The associate or manager and the family can forget information provided earlier than that, and if the orientation occurs too close to departure, the individuals may be too preoccupied to retain training information. Activities such as packing and closing up a home must be handled and will occupy family members in the days immediately prior to moving.
- *Include in the training key cultural information.* The Aperian Global consulting firm provides training for associates selected for expatriate assignments. The firm recommends providing side-by-side cultural comparisons of the home and host cultures, an explanation of the challenges that will likely be faced and when, lifestyle information related to areas such as tipping and gift-giving, and personal job plans for the jobholder, with an emphasis on cultural issues that help the expatriate to thrive in the new environment.[57]
- *Concentrate on conversational language training.* The ability to converse with individuals is more important than the ability to fully understand grammar or to write the foreign language.
- *Be prepared to convince busy families of the need for training.* Families with little foreign experience may not recognize the value of predeparture training.

After arrival, additional training may be useful, especially if little training was provided before departure. Language training may continue, and initial cultural exposure may bring new questions and issues. Host-country social support is also important, particularly in the early months. Individuals familiar with the country may assist in showing newcomers the area, running errands, identifying appropriate schools, and establishing local bank accounts.[58]

Finally, reintegration into the home country should be carefully managed following an international assignment. And companies should be especially mindful to take advantage of the knowledge these individuals have gained through the expatriate assignment. In fact, if managed effectively, the learning by associates and managers can provide them with additional capabilities and thereby increase their motivation and job performance after they return.[59] Such actions by the firm are even more important because research suggests that many associates and managers returning from foreign assignments leave their companies in the first year or two.[60] Old social and political networks may not be intact; information technology may have changed; and key leaders with whom important relationships existed may have departed. Each of these factors can influence the decision to leave. Career planning and sponsors inside the company can help in understanding the new landscape.

The Glass Ceiling, the Glass Floor, and the Glass Border: The Global Business Environment for Women

There are many women who experience barriers preventing them from reaching career aspirations. For international women, these barriers may be even stronger. For example, women in Asian and Middle Eastern countries often experience these barriers because of cultural values and traditions. For many women, marriage and male chauvinism are primary reasons they are unable to reach their career potential. All countries should be concerned about this problem because of the need for more human capital, which is especially troubling when they are not fully utilizing the human capital available.

With the population rapidly aging and most able-bodied men already employed in many economies (especially in strong economies such as China), companies throughout the world need more women associates. They will need to develop and effectively utilize all of the organization's human capital. The current situation has led Korean companies to adopt global business practices that include rewarding performance regardless of seniority or gender.

Interestingly, this is a global phenomenon. While there are some high-profile women executives in the United States, such as Indra Nooyi (CEO of Pepsico), Ursula Burns (CEO of Xerox) and Irene Rosenfeld (CEO of Kraft), the percentage of women in top executive positions has not

increased in recent years. For example, one survey showed that only about 10 percent of the executives and board members were women

©Image Source/Getty Images, Inc.

at the 400 largest publicly traded companies in California. In addition, a study of the top 100 companies based in Massachusetts showed that only 8.6 of their executives were women. A global study by Grant Thornton International found that only 24 percent of senior executive positions in privately held companies were held by women. In fact, 34 percent of the companies had no women executives. There were a few bright spots, however. In the Philippines, 47

percent of the senior management positions were held by women and 42 percent were held by women in Russia. In total, these data suggest that the glass ceiling continues to exist in most countries.

One prominent analyst of the general treatment of women, Shere Hite, argues that they also experience a glass floor. The glass floor hinders even lateral movement into other positions at the basic level. The glass floor barriers include short-term job contracts, child-care tasks, labor markets divided along gender lines, caring for elderly family members, etc. Many of these are the result of culture- and gender-based biases.

The third concern is the glass border. For example, it remains problematic in many Asian cultures to have a woman in charge. Even though women have been a part of the workforce for a long time, for the most part their roles have been limited to staff entry-level positions and lower-level positions in manufacturing; rarely are they found in managerial or executive positions. A glass border (which is an unseen and strong discriminatory barrier) exists, blocking women from accessing many managerial and executive-level positions. It is important to note that many Asian companies are still family-owned, with the men in the family in higher-level positions than the women. In addition, Asian companies often are unwilling to support having the female as the expatriate while her husband remains at his job in the home country. In addition, in some Asian cultures, men rarely help to care for the children, thereby requiring women who work outside the home to rely on female relatives for babysitting. Finally, patriarchal attitudes are difficult to change, especially at the office. Many clients still ask to replace women consultants with men and some bankers continue to require female CEOs to obtain loan guarantees from their husbands.

There is some light beginning to shine in some parts of the world. For example, in 2009 the first two female Islamic judges were appointed in the Palestinian territories. In the Arab countries, these are the first women judges outside of Sudan. In addition, the Saudi king appointed the first women to his council of ministers. While these represent a minor crack in the glass ceiling, these are positive steps for women.

Even though there is an increase in the number of female nonexecutives and a few positive appointments of women to leadership positions, the change in the number becoming executives and directors has been small. To overcome this problem, companies must promote on the basis of merit and ignore gender in the workplace. Women must continue to work hard to break these barriers and overcome the glass ceilings, floors, and borders. Given the demographics around the world, the most successful companies will have a healthy number of women leaders. They will be successful because they are taking advantage of the total human capital available.

Sources: "Women still hold less than a quarter of senior management positions in privately held businesses," *Grant Thornton International,* Nov. 21, 2009, at http://www.internationalbusinessreport.com; Amy Laskowsky. 2009. "The Glass Ceiling Remains Strong," Nov. 20, www.bu.edu; Don Thompson. 2009. "Study finds women still face difficult time breaking through glass ceiling at Calf. Companies," Nov. 19, at http://www.baltimoresun.com; Steve Tobak. 2009. "Is there still a glass ceiling for women in business?" Aug. 24, at http://www.blogs.bnet.com; Diane Tucker. 2009. "Arab women beginning to crack the glass ceiling," March 18, at http://www.huffingtonpost.com; Nasser Shiyoukhi. 2009. "2 Palestinian women crack the glass ceiling in court," Feb. 24, at http://www.abcnews.go.com; Hiroko Tashiro & Ian Rowley. 2005. "Japan: The Glass Ceiling Stays Put," *BusinessWeek,* May 2, at http://www.businessweek.com.

Although participation by women appears to be increasing,[61] women historically have not had as many opportunities for expatriate assignments as men. Managers must be sensitive to this deficit because they need to develop and effectively utilize all of the organization's human capital. As explained in the *Experiencing Organizational Behavior* feature, there are several reasons for the development of this **glass border**. By not providing women with international assignments, they are failing to develop women's knowledge and capabilities for higher-level jobs. As a result, these organizations may not be able to exploit strategic opportunities in international markets because of a shortage of human capital. And interestingly, some research suggests that women are often more effective in expatriate roles because they tend to be flexible and develop a more empowering identity in order to be effective in a variety of situations.[62] The plight of women executives is largely a global phenomenon, as the segment suggests. Women professionals in many countries must contend with glass ceilings, glass borders, and even glass floors. The human capital represented by these women presents a significant opportunity for businesses. Companies that utilize all of their human capital effectively are more likely to gain a competitive advantage.

glass border
The unseen but strong discriminatory barrier that blocks many women from opportunities for international assignments.

Foreign Nationals as Colleagues

Beyond gaining international exposure and experience through a job focused on international work or through a foreign assignment, an associate or manager can gain international experience in other ways. For example, associates and managers may work in a domestic unit with people from other countries or may report to a manager/executive who has relocated from another country. In the United States, H-1B visas allow skilled foreign professionals to live and work in the country for up to six years. L1 visas allow workers in foreign-based multinational companies to be transferred to the United States. Finally, J1 visas allow foreign students to fill seasonal jobs in U.S. resort areas, including jobs as waiters, lifeguards, fast-food cooks, and supermarket clerks. In fact, in recent years the demand for foreign skilled workers has been growing in many countries, including the United States.[63]

With hundreds of thousands of visas approved each year, an individual born in the United States and working in a domestic company may therefore work alongside a foreign national. U.S.-based associates and managers at Microsoft, for example, often work with foreign nationals. An associate there observed, "I am surrounded every day by people from many diverse cultural and ethnic backgrounds, each contributing their unique ideas and talents so that people around the world can realize their full potential."[64] True to its multicultural profile, Microsoft supports a number of international worker groups, including Brazilian, Chinese, Filipino, Hellenic, Indian, Korean, Malaysian, Pakistani, Singaporean, and Taiwanese groups.[65]

Working side by side with individuals from other countries can indeed be a rich and rewarding experience, but problems sometimes develop. As already noted, individuals from different countries often have different values and different ways of thinking—and even different norms for behavior in business meetings.[66] Although differences in values and thought patterns can be a source of creativity and insight, they also can create friction. Preferences for different working styles and decision styles can be particularly troublesome.[67]

A key aspect of the cultural effects on international working relationships is high versus low context cultural values.[68] In **high-context cultures**, such as Japan and South Korea, individuals value personal relationships, prefer to develop agreements on the basis of trust, and prefer slow, ritualistic negotiations.[69] Understanding others and understanding particular messages depend in large part on contextual cues, such as the other person's job, schooling, and nationality. Being familiar with a person's background and current station in life is crucial, and likely important in establishing trust-based relationships in international exchange relationships.[70] In **low-context cultures**, such as the United States and Germany, individuals value performance and expertise, prefer to develop agreements that are formal and perhaps legalistic, and engage in efficient negotiations.[71] Understanding others in general and understanding particular messages depend on targeted questioning. Written and spoken words are crucial; contextual cues tend to carry less meaning.

A related aspect of culture is monochronic versus polychronic time.[72] Individuals with a **monochronic time orientation** prefer to do one task or activity in a given time period. They dislike multitasking; they prefer not to divert attention from a planned task because of an interruption; and they usually are prompt, schedule-driven, and time-focused.[73] North Americans and Northern Europeans are usually viewed as relatively monochronic. In contrast, individuals with a **polychronic time orientation** are comfortable engaging in more than one task at a time and are not troubled by interruptions.[74] For these individuals, time is less of a guiding force, and plans are flexible. Latin Americans and Southern Europeans are often polychronic. Individuals from the Southern region of Asia are also largely polychronic, but many Japanese do not fit this pattern.

Understandably, individuals from high-context cultures can have difficulty working with people from low-context cultures. A high-context individual may not understand or appreciate the direct questioning and task orientation of a low-context individual. As a result, the high-context individual can experience hurt feelings, causing him or her discomfort in a low-context culture. In the same way, a low-context person can be frustrated

high-context cultures
A type of culture where individuals use contextual cues to understand people and their communications and where individuals value trust and personal relationships.

low-context cultures
A type of culture where individuals rely on direct questioning to understand people and their communications and where individuals value efficiency and performance.

monochronic time orientation
A preference for focusing on one task per unit of time and completing that task in a timely fashion.

polychronic time orientation
A willingness to juggle multiple tasks per unit of time and to have interruptions, and an unwillingness to be driven by time.

with the pace and focus of a high-context culture. In addition, monochronic individuals may experience conflict with people who are more polychronic. People who are driven by schedules and who do not appreciate interruptions often are frustrated by the more relaxed view of time held by polychronic people. To alleviate these cross-cultural difficulties, training in cultural differences is crucial in order to build managers' cultural intelligence. **Cultural intelligence** helps people understand others' behavior, with the ability to separate those aspects that are universally human from those that are unique to the person and those that are based in culture. It allows managers to understand and respond effectively to people from different cultures.[75] Cultural intelligence is important for managers, as they need to be sensitive to these differences when they evaluate the performance of associates and assign rewards based on these evaluations.[76]

cultural intelligence
The ability to separate the aspects of behavior that are based in culture from those unique to the individual or all humans in general.

Opportunities for International Participation

Associates' and managers' opportunities for international experiences differ across firms. Purely domestic firms offer few opportunities beyond perhaps working with foreign nationals who have been hired or trying to compete with foreign firms operating in the local markets where they sell their goods. Firms that export their goods into foreign markets offer more opportunities, because some individuals are needed for internationally focused work, such as international accounting, and a few are needed to staff foreign sales offices. Firms that have more substantial commitments to foreign operations usually provide even greater opportunities for international work, but the amount and type of opportunities vary with the type of strategy. Furthermore, the different approaches to markets in separate countries used by firms affect associates' and managers' behavior and job satisfaction.[77] As shown in Exhibit 3-3, we can classify firms with substantial commitments to foreign operations as multidomestic, global, or transnational.

EXHIBIT 3-3 International Approaches and Related Organizational Characteristics

	Multidomestic	Global	Transnational
Local responsiveness			
Local production	High	Low	Medium
Local R&D	High	Low	Medium
Local product modification	High	Low	Medium/High
Local adaptation of marketing	High	Low/Medium	Medium/High
Organizational design			
Delegation of power to local units	High	Low	Medium/Low
Interunit resource flows between and among local units	Low	Low/Medium	High
International resource flows from and/or controlled by corporate headquarters	Low	High	Low/Medium
International participation			
Opportunities for associates and managers	Low	High	High

Source: Information in this exhibit is based on A.-W. Harzing. 2000. "An Empirical Analysis and Extension of the Bartlett and Ghoshal Typology of Multinational Companies," *Journal of International Business Studies*, 31: 101–120.

Multidomestic Firms

multidomestic strategy
A strategy by which a firm tailors its products and services to the needs of each country or region in which it operates and gives a great deal of power to the managers and associates in those countries or regions.

Firms that use a **multidomestic strategy** tailor their products and services for various countries or regions of the world.[78] When customer tastes and requirements vary substantially across countries, a firm must be responsive to these differences. Tastes often vary, for example, in consumer packaged goods. Unilever, the British/Dutch provider of detergents, soaps, shampoos, and other consumer products, is a prime example by offering different versions of its products in various parts of the world.[79] It produces, for example, approximately 20 brands of black tea in order to meet the unique tastes of individuals in different countries.

Firms such as Unilever often transfer power from the corporate headquarters to units based in various countries or homogeneous regions of the world (i.e., local units).[80] These units typically are self-contained—they conduct their own research and development, produce their own products and services, and individually market and distribute their goods. This approach is expensive because geographically based units do not share resources or help one another as much as in firms using other international strategies. Yet, it may be important to allow autonomy when the subsidiary is a long distance from the home office, especially when that distance entails major differences in culture and institutional environments. In these cases, the subsidiary needs to develop a strategy that fits its competitive environment, and the home office is less likely to be of help in doing so.[81]

Among firms with substantial foreign commitments, multidomestic firms provide fewer opportunities for associates, lower-level managers, and midlevel managers to participate in international activities. Individuals tend to work within their home countries and have little interaction with people located in other geographical locations. Individuals in each unit are focused on their unit's country or homogeneous set of countries (region). Interunit learning, interunit transfers of people, and interunit coordination are rare in firms using a multidomestic strategy.

Global Firms

global strategy
A strategy by which a firm provides standard products and services to all parts of the world while maintaining a strong degree of central control in the home country.

Firms following a **global strategy** offer standardized products and services in the countries in which they are active.[82] When cost pressures demand efficient use of resources and when tailoring to local tastes is not necessary, a firm must do all it can to manage its resources efficiently. It is costly to develop, produce, and market substantially different versions of the same basic product or service across different countries. For example, Microsoft does not significantly tailor the functionality of Windows for different countries. Nor does Cemex, the world's third largest cement company, tailor its cement for different countries. While the firm sells almost 240 million metric tons of cement annually across four major regions of the world, the firm provides the same product in all countries where it operates.

Cemex exhibits many features typical of global firms.[83] First, key decisions related to: (1) products and services, (2) research and development, and (3) methods for serving each country are often made at corporate headquarters in Monterrey, Mexico. (In contrast, firms using the multidomestic strategy make key decisions locally.) Second, country- and region-based units do not have a full complement of resources covering all of the major functions (production, marketing, sales, finance, research and development, human resources). For example, Cemex has operations in more than 50 countries but only has manufacturing operations in select parts of the world. A great deal of manufacturing also takes place in the home country of Mexico, and the product is then exported to other countries. By not having manufacturing plants located in and dedicated to each country or even each region, and by having large-scale manufacturing facilities in select locations, Cemex efficiently uses its resources. Cemex also focuses significant attention on global coordination. With units depending on decisions and resources controlled by the home country as well as resources from other countries, coordinating a global flow of information and resources is crucial. One means of growth for Cemex has been by acquisition. Fortunately, the strong global coordination used by the firm helps to rapidly integrate major acquisitions.

Compared with firms following a multidomestic strategy, firms using the global strategy provide more opportunities for associates and managers to participate in international activities. For example, many individuals in the home country and in foreign units must coordinate effectively to ensure a smooth flow of worldwide resources. Thus, many jobs are internationally oriented. In addition, there are often a large number of expatriate assignments. Global firms treat the world as a unified market and frequently transfer people across borders. Thus, in any given unit, there may be a significant number of foreign nationals. As noted earlier, expatriates learn and transfer knowledge across borders. Yet, to achieve the most learning at the team level requires the firm to consciously manage the flow of knowledge across the organization.[84]

Transnational Firms

Firms using a **transnational strategy** attempt to achieve both local responsiveness and global efficiency.[85] In industries where both of these criteria are important for success, a careful integration of multidomestic and global approaches is necessary. Thus, a transnational strategy calls for more tailoring to individual countries than is typically found in global firms but generally less tailoring than in multidomestic firms.

Such an approach also requires the deployment of more resources in a given country than is typical in the global firm but fewer resources in each country than is typical in the multidomestic firm. Finally, the approach calls for less central direction from the corporate headquarters than the global strategy but more central coordination than the multidomestic strategy. In a transnational firm, interdependent geographical units must work closely together to facilitate interunit resource flows and learning. In the multidomestic firm, these flows are trivial. In the global firm, they are largely controlled by corporate headquarters.

Ogilvy & Mather Worldwide, a U.S.-based advertising subsidiary of WPP, a worldwide marketing communications group, uses a transnational strategy.[86] At one time, the firm used a strategy that most closely resembled a multidomestic approach. Ogilvy & Mather tailored the advertising it produced to different areas of the world based on local customs, expressions, sensibilities, and norms for humor. To support this strategy, it had strong, self-contained local units. Clients, however, began to object to costs, and because many of these clients were becoming global firms, they wanted a more unified message spread around the world through advertising. Ogilvy & Mather began to pursue global efficiency and local responsiveness simultaneously. It refers to itself as "the most local of internationals and the most international of the locals." It has more than 450 offices in 120 countries across the globe.[87]

To prevent local units from reinventing largely the same advertising campaign (in other words, unnecessarily tailoring campaigns to the local market), Ogilvy & Mather implemented international teams that were assigned to service major accounts.[88] These teams create ad campaigns and send them to local units for implementation. One team is called Ogilvy*Action*, designed to provide a full range of brand activation services to customers on a global basis.[89] Local units pursue local accounts and have complete control over them but are constrained in their ability to pursue and oversee international work.

Overall, individual associates and managers have many opportunities for international exposure and experiences in firms using a transnational approach. Geographically based units are highly interdependent because they must exchange resources, and they often must coordinate these resource exchanges for their benefit as well. Rich personal networks and formal coordination mechanisms such as international work teams are developed to handle the interdependence. International meetings and travel are very important, and foreign assignments are common. Interestingly, the location of the headquarters for these firms is less important and some move their headquarters unit from their traditional home country when they adopt the transnational strategy. Normally, these moves are designed to respond to external stakeholders such as shareholders and financial markets.[90]

High-Involvement Management in the International Context

High-involvement management provides associates with decision power and the information they need to use that power effectively. As discussed in Chapter 1, firms that adopt this approach often perform better than other firms. Although most evidence supporting the effectiveness of the high-involvement approach has been collected from domestic units of North American firms,[91] sound evidence has come from other countries as well. Studies, for example, have been conducted in automobile plants worldwide,[92] in a variety of firms in New Zealand,[93] and in firms in 11 different countries.[94] A study in China suggested that such practices enhanced short-term associates' feelings of competence and increased their commitment to the organization.[95]

Although available evidence is supportive of high-involvement management, care must be taken when implementing this approach in different cultures. Modifying the approach to fit local circumstances is crucial.[96] In this section, we discuss several dimensions of national culture that should be considered. The dimensions are drawn from the GLOBE (Global Leadership and Organizational Behavior Effectiveness) research program, in which a number of researchers studied issues regarding organizational behavior in 61 countries.[97]

Dimensions of National Culture

As shown in Exhibit 3-4, the GLOBE project uses nine dimensions of national culture. Four of these dimensions have been used by many other researchers over the years. These four dimensions were originally developed by the Dutch social scientist Geert Hofstede[98] and they are listed first.

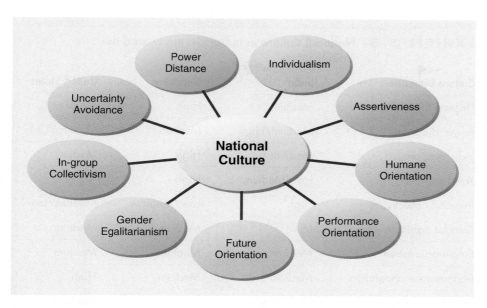

Exhibit 3-4   Dimensions of National Culture

1. *Uncertainty avoidance* is the degree to which members of a society wish to avoid unpredictable lives. It is focused on a society's desire for orderliness through formal procedures and rules as well as through strong norms that govern behavior. Countries with high scores do not value free spirits. Such countries include Austria and Germany. Countries with lower scores include Russia and Hungary. The United States has a midrange score.

2. *Power distance* is the degree to which members of a society expect power to be unequally distributed. This dimension corresponds to expectations for strong autocratic leadership rather than more egalitarian leadership. Strong central governments and centralized decision structures in work organizations are frequently found in countries with high scores. For example, Russia scores high on this dimension. Alternatively, Denmark and the Netherlands have low scores on power distance.

3. *Individualism* is the degree to which members of society are comfortable focusing on personal goals and being rewarded for personal efforts and outcomes. In individualistic cultures, personal outcomes are valued. Countries scoring high on individualism include Italy and Germany. Countries scoring low on this dimension include Japan, Singapore, and South Korea.[99]

4. *Assertiveness* is the degree to which members of society are aggressive and confrontational. In his original work, Hofstede labeled this aspect of culture "masculinity." Examples of countries with high scores on this dimension are the United States, Austria, and Germany. Examples of countries with low scores are Sweden and Kuwait.

5. *In-group collectivism* indicates how much members of society take pride in the groups and organizations to which they belong, including the family. China and India have high scores on this dimension in the GLOBE research.

EXHIBIT 3-5 National Culture in India, Germany, and the United States

Culture Dimension	India	Germany	United States
Uncertainty avoidance	Medium	High	Medium
Power distance	Medium/High	Medium	Medium/Low
Individualism	Medium	High	Medium
Assertiveness	Low/Medium	High	High
In-group collectivism	High	Low/Medium	Medium/Low
Gender egalitarianism	Low	Medium/Low	Medium
Future orientation	Medium	Medium	Medium
Performance orientation	Medium	Medium	High
Humane orientation	High/Medium	Low	Medium

Source: Based on the GLOBE Project.

6. *Gender egalitarianism* refers to equal opportunities for women and men. Sweden and Denmark score high on this dimension.

7. *Future orientation* is the degree to which members of the society value long-term planning and investing in the future. Denmark and the Netherlands are among those scoring high on this dimension.

8. *Performance orientation* is the degree to which members of society appreciate and reward improvement and excellence in schoolwork, athletics, and work life. The United States, Taiwan, Hong Kong, and Singapore have high performance orientations.

9. *Humane orientation* is the degree to which members of society value generous, caring, altruistic behavior. Countries scoring high on this dimension include the Philippines and Malaysia.

Exhibit 3-5 compares India, Germany, and the United States on all nine culture dimensions.

Research has shown that national culture affects major business practices.[100] For example, decisions to enter particular international markets are affected by the cultural dimensions of the targeted country.[101] In particular, the cultural distance between a firm's home country and the country targeted for entry has a major impact. *Cultural distance* refers to the extent of the differences in culture between countries.[102] Therefore, managers must pay careful attention to culture in designing and implementing management practices in each country.

In the *Experiencing Organizational Behavior* feature, we learn of the pioneering work of Geert Hofstede to identify the universal dimensions of national culture. He also discovered that national culture had a stronger effect on the behavior of managers and associates than did organizational culture. Hofstede's work suggested the need to understand and manage diverse cultures. This need is highlighted in the problems experienced in

Managing Diverse Cultures

Geert Hofstede pioneered the study of culture in the workplace and conducted research to examine global variations in the psychology of work and of organizations, which affected international human resource management. While working at IBM in 1968, he noticed that although the company had a strong company culture, there were variations in cultural values among the employees of IBM subsidiaries around the world. Between 1968 and 1972, he surveyed over 116,000 employees. His survey responses from over 40 countries showed general similarities within cultural groups, even when their social and economic histories were profoundly different. For example, Hong Kong and mainland China have more in common with each other but are quite different from Sweden and the United States. Hofstede found that values we observe in the workplace reflect much deeper cultural attributes, suggesting that the impact of national culture on the workplace is much greater than that of the organization's culture. His work has profound meaning for managers employed by multinational organizations.

Managers and top executives of companies seeking to expand globally need to recognize the complexities of cross-border collaboration. Difficulty in managing people is magnified when even small differences in perceptions and expectations occur, making collaboration difficult, as reflected in the cross-cultural problems that occurred in the merger between Daimler and Chrysler. Some experts believed that the merger had substantial potential because of the different but complementary capabilities possessed by the two firms. However, that potential was not realized partly because of national cultural differences between Germans and Americans. The Germans in Daimler disliked Chrysler managers' unstructured approach, while American Chrysler managers found the German Daimler managers too rigid and formal. The culture clash disallowed effective integration of the two firms and their respective associates. Many Chrysler managers left the organization, and the potential synergy between the two firms was never realized. Daimler eventually sold the Chrysler business at a tremendous loss over what it paid to acquire it.

Managers may need to utilize different concepts and methods for different times and places. Managers need to be aware of the local cultures' values, social ideals, and their workplace behavior and attitudes. Multinational companies engaging in cross-border mergers can be successful when they have managers who possess "cultural intelligence," the ability to understand and effectively manage different values and expectations existing in different parts of the world. Several firms have promoted diversity in their workforce as a means of managing and taking advantage of many cultures in the world. For example, Siemens believes that a diverse workforce can be a competitive advantage because it helps the company to understand and better serve its customers across

©Siemens AG

the world. Siemens currently employs more than 430,000 managers and associates representing 140 different nationalities in its top 10 markets. To encourage collaboration and communication among its workforce members, it has launched several networks such as the Global Leadership Organization of Women (GLOW Network) and the diversity ambassadors program. The diversity ambassadors are 100 specially selected managers and associates who are profiled and share their success stories while serving as role models and mentors for others in the company.

Other companies are also promoting diversity as a way to take advantage of culturally diverse knowledge and ways of thinking. For example, ABB has a highly diverse board of directors with members from Belgium, Finland, France, Germany, India, Scotland, Sweden, Switzerland, and the United States. Procter & Gamble (P&G) also promotes a diverse workforce. The firm does so to understand and maintain a good relationship with its customers around the world and its global suppliers as well. P&G's CEO stated that "Diverse organizations will out-think, out-innovate and out-perform a homogeneous organization. ..."

Sources: "Siemens AG—Diversity," Siemens, Nov. 22, 2009, at http://www.siemens.com; G. Schoech. 2009. "Diversity to strengthen Siemens leadership—catching up or taking the lead?" Gehson Lehrman Group, March 17, at http://www.glgroup.com; H. Brown. 2009. "Diversity does matter," Forbes, July 21, at http://www.forbes.com; "No. 14: Procter & Gamble," Diversity Inc., May, 2007, at http://www.diversityinc.com; Morgan Witzel. 2003. "Geert Hofstede: The Quantifier of Culture," Financial Times, Aug. 25, at http://www.ft.com; M.A. Hitt, R.S. Harrison, & R.D. Ireland. 2001. Mergers and Acquisitions: A Guide to Creating Value for Stakeholders, New York: Oxford University Press.

the merger between Daimler Benz and Chrysler, in which the managers of the respective firms were not understanding and tolerant of the cultural attributes that differed from their own. Yet, other companies recognize the value of diversity and have promoted it in various ways. For example, Siemens does so through its global networks to encourage collaboration across cultures and its diversity ambassadors program. ABB has a highly diverse board of directors, and P&G promotes diversity because it will provide the company with a competitive advantage. With increasing globalization, understanding and managing diverse cultures has become a critical managerial attribute for competitive success in international markets.

National Culture and High-Involvement Management

High-involvement management must be implemented in accordance with a country's cultural characteristics. Although not every individual from a country will possess all of the cultural characteristics associated with that country, many people will share these traits. In the next section, we discuss how information sharing and decision power can be adapted to different levels of power distance, uncertainty avoidance, individualism, and assertiveness.[103]

Information Sharing

A firm's leaders must share tactical and strategic information if empowered individuals and teams are to make high-quality decisions. In cultures high in uncertainty avoidance, associates must have information to clarify issues and provide basic direction. If they lack such information, anxiety and poor performance can result. Where uncertainty avoidance is low, associates need less information of this kind. Rather, increasing information that encourages new ideas and ways of thinking can be useful. In cultures where assertiveness is high, associates want information that clearly and directly informs them what is needed for effective performance. In addition, they desire continuous information on how well they are performing. In cultures with low assertiveness, associates do not want information that is exclusively focused on performance and bottom-line business goals. Instead, they desire information on improving soft processes such as teamwork. Similarly, associates in individualistic cultures desire information regarding their individual jobs and responsibilities; they are less interested in information on team, department, and company issues. Associates in collectivistic cultures tend to have the opposite needs. Finally, associates in high-power-distance cultures do not expect to receive a great deal of information and may not pay much attention to it if they receive it. For these individuals, careful training in information use is often required. In low-power-distance cultures, associates expect information and put it to use when it is received. Thus, cultural attributes affect the type and amount of information shared and the knowledge learned in organizations.[104]

Decision Power and Individual Autonomy

Some high-involvement systems give a great deal of decision power to individual associates rather than to teams. In cultures characterized by high uncertainty avoidance, such autonomy can cause stress because it is associated with less direction from above as well as less support from peers. To avoid stress, clear boundaries must be set for how the autonomy is used, and managers must be readily available to provide direction. In cultures with low uncertainty avoidance, associates do not need direction and are generally able to tolerate uncertainty regarding the boundaries to their authority. In high-assertiveness cultures, associates are likely to use autonomy creatively to achieve task success. In low-assertiveness cultures, associates may channel too much of their autonomy into work on soft issues such as relationships and social networks. Managers must guard against any such excesses. In countries characterized by an individualistic culture, associates appreciate autonomy provided to individuals rather than to teams, and emphasize individual goals. Because of this focus, managers may need to explicitly channel associates' attention to any required group or team tasks. In countries characterized by a collectivistic culture, associates are unlikely to be motivated by individual autonomy. Managers may wish to emphasize autonomy at the team level in such cultures. Finally, in cultures characterized by high power distance, autonomy may be difficult to implement. Associates expect a great deal of direction from managers. In this situation, managers may want to provide small increases in autonomy over time, allowing associates to become accustomed to having discretion. Managers may want to maintain a fairly strong role even in the long run. In cultures characterized by low power distance, associates welcome autonomy from managers and can channel their efforts to be more innovative.[105]

Decision Power and Self-Managing Teams

In cultures with high uncertainty avoidance, associates need clear boundaries for self-managing teams, and managers must be readily available for mentoring and coaching.[106] In cultures with low uncertainty avoidance, teams can define their own roles. In countries characterized by high assertiveness, teams often are task-focused. For low-assertiveness cultures, associates frequently devote a great deal of time to soft issues, such as team dynamics, requiring managers to monitor the time focused on such issues. In cultures characterized by individualism, managers must pay particular attention to team training for associates and to the design of team-based reward systems. Alternatively, in cultures characterized by collectivism, managers have a more favorable situation because associates prefer teamwork. Finally, in cultures characterized by high power distance, associates may have difficulties using their decision power if their manager is too visible. Managers must be less visible and resist the temptation to offer a great deal of assistance to the team. Where power distance is low, associates work comfortably with the manager as an equal or as a coach rather than a supervisor.

AES, a U.S.-based power-generation company, is known for its high-involvement management system. Associates enjoy tremendous freedom to make decisions individually and in teams. Firing vendors for safety violations, expending funds from capital budgets, and making key decisions about important day-to-day work are common for associates. With careful selection and training, and with access to key information, AES associates typically use their freedom wisely.

As AES began to grow and establish operations in several countries, many analysts and reporters questioned whether its high-involvement system and underlying values could be applied in an international context. Although AES leaders remained committed to the system, they realized that some modifications might be needed for a particular country. Therefore, while the core of the approach was preserved, some aspects were altered to fit each local culture.

When entering Nigeria, for example, AES responded appropriately to the prevailing culture. Norman Bell, the lead on the Nigerian project, and his AES colleagues encountered high power distance and high individualism among the associates in Nigeria. These prominent cultural values initially forced Bell to adopt a more autocratic management system. Bell needed time to delegate decision power to associates, and teams required training and team-based reward systems.

AES used the same basic approach in its operations across 29 countries and 25,000 managers and associates: high-involvement management built on the company's core values with sensitivity to local cultural differences.[107] Thus, executives and managers at AES effectively used the high-involvement approach on a global basis while modifying the approach to fit local cultures. The high-involvement approach facilitated the global strategy used by AES. Therefore, it helped top managers to implement the firm's strategy.

Ethics in the International Context

A critically important issue in globalization and international business is ethics. The *American Heritage Dictionary* defines ethics as "principle[s] of right or good conduct; a system of moral principles and values." Implicit in this definition is the idea that ethical conduct can be different in different cultures. What one society deems "appropriate conduct" may be unacceptable to another. For example, nepotism that is unacceptable in many Western cultures is often more acceptable in relationship-oriented cultures. Alternatively, the use of formal contracts and lawsuits are highly acceptable in many Western cultures but are perceived negatively in other cultures.[108] Thus, **international ethics** are complex.

international ethics
Principles of proper conduct focused on issues such as corruption, exploitation of labor, and environmental impact.

Corruption is often considered to be the misuse of power for private gain.[109] Three issues are prominent in discussions of proper conduct in developed nations: (1) corruption, (2) exploitation of labor, and (3) environmental impact.[110] For corruption, the chief issue involves bribing foreign public officials in order to win business. Asking for payment of bribes is based partially on culture and partly on economic needs and institutional weaknesses in a country.[111] Many developed nations have taken steps to fight corruption because it creates uncertainty and results in a reduction of merit-based decision making. The United States, for example, passed the Foreign Corrupt Practices Act in 1977 to prevent U.S. managers from bribing foreign officials. (See Exhibit 3-6 for a recent ranking of countries based on corruption.) Exploitation of labor involves the employment of children, the forced use of prison labor, unreasonably low wages, and poor working conditions. In one well-known example involving a line of clothing produced for Wal-Mart, Chinese women were working 84 hours per week in dangerous conditions while living in monitored dormitories with 12 persons to a room.[112] Americans and others expressed their strong unhappiness with this practice, and Wal-Mart discontinued it. Finally, environmental impact relates to pollution and overuse of scarce resources. From global warming to clear cutting of forests, the concerns are many. In the United States and globally, many people have become more sensitive to the environment because of the obvious effects of global warming.

The economic development of countries with higher levels of corruption tends to suffer. For example, countries with high corruption index scores as shown in Exhibit 3-6 often receive less direct investment from foreign firms. In addition, the foreign investment in these countries more commonly comes from firms based in other countries with greater corruption.[113] Thus, corruption harms the country and its citizens.

EXHIBIT 3-6   Absence of Corruption in Select Countries

Rank	Country	Rank	Country
1	New Zealand	158	Tajikistan
2	Denmark	162	Angola
3	Singapore	162	Congo Brazzaville
3	Sweden	162	Democratic Republic of Congo
5	Switzerland	162	Guinea-Bissau
6	Finland	162	Kyrgyzstan
6	Netherlands	162	Venezuela
8	Australia	168	Burundi
8	Canada	168	Equatorial Guinea
8	Iceland	168	Guinea
11	Norway	168	Haiti
12	Hong Kong	168	Iran
12	Luxembourg	168	Turkmenistan
14	Germany	174	Uzbekistan
14	Ireland	175	Chad
16	Austria	176	Iraq
17	Japan	176	Sudan
17	United Kingdom	178	Myanmar
19	United States	179	Afghanistan
20	Barbados	180	Somalia

Source: Rankings are drawn from Transparency International's Corruption Perception's Index 2009 for 180 countries (http://www.transparency.org). Scores are based on the perceptions of the degree of corruption as seen by businesspeople and country analysts. The score ranges from 10 (highly clean) to 0 (highly corrupt).

The United Nations, the World Bank, the International Labor Organization, the World Trade Organization, and the Organization for Economic Co-operation and Development are among many organizations that advocate a unified set of global ethical standards to govern labor practices and general issues related to international business. As shown in the Exhibit 3-7, business leaders from Japan, Europe, and North America in the Caux Round Table have developed a list of expectations for companies engaging in international business. These ethical standards are intended to govern what strategies managers select and how they implement those strategies in dealings with others, both within and outside their organizations.

EXHIBIT 3-7   Caux Round Table Principles for Business

Business leaders from Japan, Europe, and North America formed the Caux Round Table in 1986 to promote moral values in business. The principles they developed are based on two ideals: *kyosei* and human dignity. *Kyosei*, a Japanese concept, means "living and working together for the common good, enabling cooperation and mutual prosperity to exist with healthy and fair competition." The seven specific principles the executives promote are listed below:

1. *The Responsibilities of Business.* The value of a business to society is the wealth and employment it creates and the marketable products and services it provides to consumers at a reasonable price commensurate with quality. To create such value, a business must maintain its economic health and viability, but survival is not a sufficient goal. Businesses have a role to play in improving the lives of all of their customers, associates, and shareholders by sharing with them the wealth they have created. Suppliers and competitors as well should expect businesses to honor their obligations in a spirit of honesty and fairness. As responsible citizens of the local, national, regional, and global communities in which they operate, businesses have a part in shaping the future of those communities.

2. *The Economic and Social Impact of Business.* Businesses established in foreign countries to develop, produce, or sell should also contribute to the social advancement of those countries by creating productive employment and helping to raise the purchasing power of their citizens. Businesses also should contribute to human rights, education, welfare, and vitalization of the countries in which they operate.

    Businesses should contribute to economic and social development not only in the countries in which they operate, but also in the world community at large, through effective and prudent use of resources, free and fair competition, and emphasis upon innovation in technology, production methods, marketing, and communications.

3. *Business Behavior.* While accepting the legitimacy of trade secrets, businesses should recognize that sincerity, candor, truthfulness, the keeping of promises, and transparency contribute not only to their own credibility and stability but also to the smoothness and efficiency of business transactions, particularly on the international level.

4. *Respect for Rules.* To avoid trade frictions and to promote freer trade, equal conditions for competition, and fair and equitable treatment for all participants, businesses should respect international and domestic rules. In addition, they should recognize that some behavior, although legal, can still have adverse consequences.

5. *Support for Multilateral Trade.* Businesses should support the multilateral trade systems of the General Agreement in Tariffs and Trade (GATT) World Trade Organization (WTO), and similar international agreements. They should cooperate in efforts to promote the progressive and judicious liberalization of trade and to relax those domestic measures that unreasonably hinder global commerce, while giving respect to national policy objectives.

6. *Respect for the Environment.* A business should protect and, where possible, improve the environment, promote sustainable development, and prevent the wasteful use of natural resources.

7. *Avoidance of Illicit Operations.* A business should not participate in or condone bribery, money laundering, or other corrupt practices: indeed, it should seek cooperation with others to eliminate these practices. It should not trade in arms or other materials used for terrorist activities, drug traffic, or other organized crime.

Sources: Caux Round Table, "Principles for Business," 2007, at http://www.cauxroundtable.org; P. Carlson and M.S. Blodgett. 1997. "International Ethics Standards for Business: NAFTA, CAUX Principles and Corporate Code of Ethics," *Review of Business*, 18, no. 3: 20–23.

THE STRATEGIC LENS

Organizations large and small must develop strategies to compete in the global economy. For some organizations, strategies leading to direct investment in foreign operations are valuable for growth, lower costs, and better management of the organization's risk. For other organizations, only exporting goods and services for selling in other countries is sufficient to meet their goals. For still other firms, particularly small ones, participation in international markets may be limited, but competition from foreign firms in their local domestic markets may require that they respond with competitive actions. In all cases, understanding other cultures and effectively managing cross-cultural activities and contexts are crucial. Without insight and sensitivity to other cultures, senior managers are unlikely to formulate effective strategies. Without appreciation for other cultures, associates and midlevel and lower-level managers can also fail in their efforts to implement carefully developed strategic plans. Furthermore, managers must prepare associates to work in international environments. This preparation often requires training and international assignments. Managers must also develop all of the organization's human capital—including women, who often have not had as many opportunities for expatriate assignments as men—and must ensure that the organization has the capabilities to take advantage of and exploit opportunities in international markets when they are identified. Cultural diversity among the firm's human capital can be an advantage if managers use it effectively. Many organizations operate or sell their products in foreign markets. Thus, managers and associates must understand cultural diversity and use this knowledge to their advantage in managing it.

Critical Thinking Questions

1. Given the complexity and challenges in operating in foreign countries, why do organizations enter international markets?

2. How can understanding and managing cultural diversity among associates contribute positively to an organization's performance?

3. How can being knowledgeable of diverse cultures enhance an individual's professional career?

What This Chapter Adds to Your Knowledge Portfolio

In this chapter, we have defined globalization and discussed the forces that influence it. We have also discussed three types of international involvement on the part of associates and managers: internationally focused jobs, foreign job assignments, and working with foreign nationals in the home country. After describing differing opportunities for international involvement, we explored dimensions of culture from the GLOBE project and examined the implications of cultural differences for high-involvement management. Finally, we examined issues regarding ethics in international settings. More specifically, we covered the following points:

- Globalization is the trend toward a global economy whereby products, services, people, technologies, and financial capital move relatively freely across national borders. Globalization increased dramatically in the last 20 years of the twentieth century and in the first decade of the twenty-first century.

- Globalization presents opportunities and challenges for nations. The principal opportunity is for economic growth. Challenges include the possible loss of a nation's cultural uniqueness as uniform goods and services become commonplace throughout the world. For developing nations, additional challenges include the

? back to the knowledge objectives

1. What is globalization?
2. What are the three types of international involvement available to associates and managers? What problems can be encountered with each type?
3. How do opportunities for international involvement differ in firms emphasizing multidomestic, global, and transnational strategies? Which type of firm would you prefer to join and why?
4. What are the key dimensions of national culture that influence the success of high-involvement management? How should high-involvement management be adapted to differences in culture?
5. What are several international standards for ethical behavior by businesses (refer to the Caux Round Table Principles)? Briefly discuss each one.

protection of labor from exploitation and natural resources from depletion. For wealthy nations, additional challenges include prevention of job loss to lower-wage countries and preservation of high-level wage structures at home.

- Globalization presents opportunities and challenges for organizations. Opportunities include growth, risk reduction through diversification, greater economies of scale, and location advantages (e.g., moving into an area with a particularly talented labor pool). Challenges include political risk (instability of national governments, threat of war, and threat of state-sponsored terrorism), economic risk (fluctuation in the value of foreign currencies and the possibility of sudden economic contraction in some countries), and managerial risk (difficulties inherent in managing the complex resource flows required in a global or transnational firm).

- Individuals can be involved in the international domain through internationally focused jobs. Such individuals work from their home countries but focus on international issues as part of their day-to-day work. Membership in one or more virtual teams is often part of the job. Members of a virtual team coordinate their activities mainly through videoconferencing, teleconferencing, chat rooms, and e-mail. Having some face-to-face meetings and taking steps to ensure that individuals identify with the team facilitate team success.

- Individuals can also be involved in the international domain through foreign job assignments. These individuals are known as expatriates, and they often are on a fast track for advancement. In their new countries, expatriates may experience culture shock, a stress reaction caused by the foreign context. Failure of a spouse to adjust and strong ethnocentrism in the host country are two additional factors leading to stress for expats. Careful screening of candidates for foreign assignments and rich cultural training can reduce stress and improve chances for success.

- Individuals can be involved in the international domain by working alongside foreign nationals. This is often exciting and rewarding, but cultural differences must be appreciated and accommodated, particularly those differences related to low- versus high-context values and monochronic versus polychronic time values.

- Some executives and managers choose a multidomestic strategy for their firm's international activities. This strategy, involving tailoring products and services for different countries or regions, tends to be used when preferences vary substantially across local markets where the firm has subsidiary operations. Because country-based or regionally based units are focused on their own local domains, associates and managers have limited opportunities for international exposure and experience.

- Some executives and managers choose a global strategy for their firm's international activities. This strategy, involving standardized products and services for world markets, tends to be emphasized when needs for global efficiency are strong.

Country- or region-based units are not self-contained, independent, or exclusively focused on local markets. Instead, at a minimum, each unit interacts frequently and intensively with the home country, and probably with some units located in other countries. Global firms offer associates and managers many more opportunities for international involvement than do multidomestic firms.

- Some executives and managers choose a transnational strategy for their firm's international activities. This strategy balances needs for local responsiveness and global efficiency through a complex network of highly interdependent local units. Associates and managers enjoy many opportunities for international involvement in transnational firms.
- National cultures differ in many ways. Four dimensions have proven to be particularly useful in understanding these differences: uncertainty avoidance, power distance, individualism, and assertiveness. Organizational behavior researchers have proposed five other dimensions: in-group collectivism, gender egalitarianism, future orientation, performance orientation, and humane orientation.
- High-involvement management must be adapted to differences in national culture. Two aspects of this management approach, information sharing and decision power, are particularly important for adaptation.
- Many groups, including the World Trade Organization and the Caux Round Table, have developed guidelines for ethics in the international context. Key issues for developed countries include: (1) corruption, (2) exploitation of children, and (3) environmental impact.

Key Terms

globalization, p. 84
culture, p. 84
virtual electronic teams, p. 88
swift trust, p. 88
expatriate, p. 89
culture shock, p. 90
ethnocentrism, p. 90

glass border, p. 93
high-context cultures, p. 94
low-context cultures, p. 94
monochronic time
    orientation, p. 94
polychronic time
    orientation, p. 94

cultural intelligence, p. 95
multidomestic
    strategy, p. 96
global strategy, p. 96
transnational
    strategy, p. 97
international ethics, p. 104

building your human capital
Assessment of Openness for International Work

In this age of globalization, it is important to clearly understand your own feelings about international teams and assignments. In the following installment of *Building Your Human Capital,* we present an assessment of openness for international work. The assessment measures specific attitudes and behaviors thought to be associated with this type of openness.

Instructions

In the following assessment, you will read 24 statements. After carefully reading each statement, use the accompanying rating scale to indicate how the statement applies to you. Rate yourself as honestly as possible.

		Never				Often
1.	I eat at a variety of ethnic restaurants.	1	2	3	4	5
2.	I attend foreign films.	1	2	3	4	5
3.	I read magazines that address world events.	1	2	3	4	5
4.	I follow world news on television or the Internet.	1	2	3	4	5
5.	I attend ethnic festivals.	1	2	3	4	5
6.	I visit art galleries and/or museums.	1	2	3	4	5
7.	I attend the theater, concerts, ballet, etc.	1	2	3	4	5
8.	I travel widely within my own country.	1	2	3	4	5

		Strongly Disagree				Strongly Agree
9.	I would host a foreign exchange student.	1	2	3	4	5
10.	I have extensively studied a foreign language.	1	2	3	4	5
11.	I am fluent in another language.	1	2	3	4	5
12.	I have spent substantial time in another part of the world.					
13.	I visited another part of the world by the age of 18.	1	2	3	4	5
14.	My friends' career goals, interests, and education are diverse.	1	2	3	4	5
15.	My friends' ethnic backgrounds are diverse.	1	2	3	4	5
16.	My friends' religious affiliations are diverse.					
17.	My friends' first languages are diverse.	1	2	3	4	5
18.	I have moved or been relocated substantial distances.	1	2	3	4	5
19.	I hope the company I work for (or will work for) will send me on an assignment to another part of the world.	1	2	3	4	5
20.	Foreign-language skills should be taught in elementary school.	1	2	3	4	5
21.	Traveling the world is a priority in my life.	1	2	3	4	5
22.	A year-long assignment in another part of the world would be a fantastic opportunity for me and/or my family.	1	2	3	4	5
23.	Other cultures fascinate me.	1	2	3	4	5
24.	If I took a vacation in another part of the world, I would prefer to stay in a small, locally owned hotel rather than a global chain.	1	2	3	4	5

Scoring Key for Openness to International Work

Four aspects of openness to international work have been assessed. To create scores for each of the four, combine your responses as follows:

Extent of participation in cross-cultural activities: Item 1 + Item 2 + Item 3 + Item 4 + Item 5 + Item 6 + Item 7 + Item 8

Participation scores can range from 8 to 40. Scores of 32 and above may be considered high, while scores of 16 and below may be considered low.

Extent to which international attitudes are held: Item 9 + Item 19 + Item 20 + Item 21 + Item 22 + Item 23 + Item 24

Attitude scores can range from 7 to 35. Scores of 28 and above may be considered high, while scores of 14 and below may be considered low.

Extent of international activities: Item 10 + Item 11 + Item 12 + Item 13 + Item 18

Activity scores can range from 5 to 25. Scores of 20 and above may be considered high, while scores of 10 and below may be considered low.

Degree of comfort with cross-cultural diversity: Item 14 + Item 15 + Item 16 + Item 17

Diversity scores can range from 4 to 20. Scores of 16 and above may be considered high, while scores of 8 and below may be considered low.

High scores on two or more aspects of openness, with no low scores on any aspects, suggest strong interest in and aptitude for international work.

Source: Based on P.M. Caligiuri, R.R. Jacobs, & J.L. Farr. 2000. "The Attitudinal and Behavioral Openness Scale: Scale Development and Construct Validation," *International Journal of Intercultural Relations,* 24: 27–46.

---

an organizational behavior moment
Managing in a Foreign Land

Spumonti, Inc., is a small manufacturer of furniture. The company was founded in 1987 by Joe Spumonti, who had been employed as a cabinetmaker in a large firm before he decided to open his own shop in the town of Colorado Springs. He soon found that some of his customers were interested in special furniture that could be built to complement their cabinets. Joe found their requests easy to accommodate. In fact, it wasn't long before their requests for custom furniture increased to the point that Joe no longer had time to build cabinets.

Joe visited a banker, obtained a loan, and opened a larger shop. He hired several craftspeople, purchased more equipment, and obtained exclusive rights to manufacture a special line of furniture. By 1997, the business had grown considerably. He then expanded the shop by purchasing adjoining buildings and converting them into production facilities. Because of the high noise level, he also opened a sales and administrative office several blocks away, in the more exclusive downtown business district.

Morale was very good among all associates. The workers often commented on Joe Spumonti's dynamic enthusiasm, as he shared his dreams and aspirations with them and made them feel like members of a big but close-knit family. Associates viewed the future with optimism and anticipated the growth of the company along with associated growth in their own responsibilities. Although their pay was competitive with that provided by other local businesses, it was not exceptional. Still, associates and others in the community viewed jobs with Spumonti as prestigious and desirable. The training, open sharing of information, and individual autonomy were noteworthy.

By 2009, business volume had grown to the extent that Joe found it necessary to hire a chief operating officer (COO) and to incorporate the business. Although incorporation posed no problem, the COO did. Joe wanted someone well acquainted with modern management techniques who could monitor internal operations and help computerize many of the procedures. Although he preferred to promote one of his loyal associates, none of them seemed interested in management at that time. Ultimately, he hired Wolfgang Schmidt, a visa holder from Germany who had recently completed his MBA at a German university. Joe thought Wolfgang was the most qualified among the applicants, especially with his experience in his family's furniture company in Germany.

Almost immediately after Wolfgang was hired, Joe began to spend most of his time on strategic planning and building external relationships with key constituents. Joe had neglected these functions for a long time and felt they demanded his immediate attention. Wolfgang did not object to being left on his own because he was enthusiastic about his duties. It was his first leadership opportunity.

Wolfgang was more conservative in his approach than Joe had been. He did not like to leave things to chance or to the gut feel of the associates, so he tried to intervene in many decisions the associates previously had been making for themselves. It wasn't that Wolfgang didn't trust the associates; rather, he simply felt the need to be in control. Nonetheless, his approach was not popular.

Dissatisfaction soon spread to most associates in the shop, who began to complain about lack of opportunity, noise, and low pay. Morale was now poor, and productivity was low among all associates. Absenteeism increased, and several longtime associates expressed their intention to find other jobs. Wolfgang's approach had not been successful, but he attributed its failure to the lack of employee openness to new management methods. He suggested to Joe that they give a pay raise to all associates "across the board" to improve their morale and reestablish their commitment. The pay raise would cost the company $120,000 annually, but Joe approved it as a necessary expense.

Morale and satisfaction did not improve, however. Shortly after the pay raise was announced, two of Spumonti's senior associates accepted jobs at other companies and announced their resignations. Wolfgang was bewildered and was considering recommending a second pay increase.

Discussion Questions

1. What weaknesses do you see in Joe's handling of Wolfgang?
2. Could Joe have anticipated Wolfgang's approach?
3. Can Wolfgang's career at Spumonti be saved?

---

team exercise

International Etiquette

A business traveler or expatriate must be aware of local customs governing punctuality, greetings, introductions, gift-giving, dining behavior, and gestures. Customs vary dramatically around the world, and what is accepted or even valued in one culture may be highly insulting in another. Many business deals and relationships have been harmed by a lack of awareness. In the exercise that follows, your team will compete with other teams in a test of international etiquette.

STEP 1: As an individual, complete the following quiz by selecting T (True) or F (False) for each item.

a. In Japan, slurping soup is considered bad manners.	T	F
b. In Italy, giving chrysanthemums is appropriate for a festive event.	T	F
c. In Ecuador, it is generally acceptable to be a few minutes late for a business meeting.	T	F
d. In England, the "V" sign formed with two fingers means victory when the palm faces outward but is an ugly gesture if the palm is facing inward.	T	F
e. In China, a person's surname is often given or written first with the given name appearing after.	T	F
f. In Japan, shoes are generally not worn past the doorway of a home.	T	F
g. In Brazil, hugs among business associates are considered inappropriate.	T	F
h. In Germany, use of formal titles when addressing another person is very common.	T	F
i. In Saudi Arabia, crossing one's legs in the typical style of U.S. men may cause problems.	T	F
j. In China, green hats are a symbol of achievement for men.	T	F
k. In China, a gift wrapped in red paper or enclosed in a red box is appropriate for celebrating a successful negotiation.	T	F
l. In Kuwait, an invitation to a pig roast would be warmly received.	T	F
m. In India, a leather organizer would be warmly received as a gift.		
n. In Japan, it is most appropriate to give a gift with two hands.		
o. In Iraq, passing a bowl or plate with the left hand is appropriate.		
p. In Saudi Arabia, ignoring a woman encountered in a public place is insulting to the woman's family.		

STEP 2: Assemble into groups of four to five, using the assignments or guidelines provided by the instructor.

STEP 3: Discuss the quiz as a group, and develop a set of answers for the group as a whole.

STEP 4: Complete the scoring form that follows using the answer key provided by your instructor.

Number of answers that I had correct: _____

Average number of answers that individuals in the group had correct: _____

Number of answers that the group had correct following its discussion: _____

International mastery: 13–15 correct
International competence: 9–12 correct
International deficiency: 5–8 correct
International danger: 1–4 correct

STEP 5: Designate a spokesperson to report your group's overall score and to explain the logic or information used by the group in arriving at wrong answers.

Endnotes

1. Dastidar, P. 2009. International corporate diversification and performance: Does firm self-selection matter? *Journal of International Business Studies*, 40: 71–85; Gande, A., Schenzler, C. & Senbet, L.W. 2009. Valuation of global diversification. *Journal of International Business Studies*, 40: 1515–1532; Makino, S., Isobe, T., & Chan, C.M. 2005. Does country matter? *Strategic Management Journal*, 25: 1027–1043.

2. Bouquet, C, Morrison, A., & Birkinshaw, J. 2009. International attention and multinational enterprise performance. *Journal of International Business Studies*, 40: 108–131.

3. Loveman, G., Schlesinger, L., & Anthony, R. 1993. *Euro Disney: The first 100 days*. Boston: Harvard Business School Publishing.

4. Ibid.

5. Hitt, M.A., Ireland, R.D., & Hoskisson, R.E. 2011. *Strategic management: Competitiveness and globalization* (9th ed.). Mason, OH: South-Western Cengage Learning.

6. United Nations Conference on Trade and Development. 2008. *World Investment Report*, New York, U.S.A.; United Nations Conference on Trade and Development. 2009. *World Investment Report*, New York, U.S.A.

7. United Nations Conference on Trade and Development. 2010. *World Investment Report*, New York, U.S.A.

8. World Trade Organization. 2009. *World Trade Report* 2009. Geneva, Switzerland.

9. Hitt, M.A. & He, X. 2008. Firm strategies in a changing global competitive landscape. *Business Horizons*, 51: 363–369.

10. *World Investment Report*, 2005. Transnational corporations and the internationalization of R&D. Geneva, Switzerland: United Nations Conference on Trade and Development (UNTAD).

11. Wiersema, M.E. & Bowen, H.P. Corporate diversification: The impact of foreign competition, industry globalization and product diversification. *Strategic Management Journal*, 29: 115–132; Malik, O.R. & Kotabe, M. 2009. Dynamic capabilities, government policies and performance in firms from emerging economies: Evidence from India and Pakistan. *Journal of Management Studies*, 46:421–450.

12. Hitt, Ireland, & Hoskisson, *Strategic management*.

13. For a discussion of this issue, see Asgary, N., & Walle, A.H. 2002. The cultural impact of globalization: Economic activity and social change. *Cross Cultural Management*, 9(3): 58–75; Holton, R. 2000. Globalization's cultural consequences. *The Annals of the American Academy of Political and Social Science*, 570: 140–152; Zhelezniak, O. 2003. Japanese culture and globalization. *Far Eastern Affairs*, 31(2): 114–120.

14. Hall, P.A. & Soskice, D. 2001. An introduction to the varieties of capitalism. In P. A. Hall & D. Soskice (Eds.), *Varieties of capitalism: The institutional foundations of comparative advantage*. Oxford, UK: Oxford University Press, 1–68; Hall, E.T. 1976. *Beyond culture*. New York: Anchor Books–Doubleday.

15. Sheth, J.N. 2006. Clash of cultures or fusion of cultures? Implications for international business. *Journal of International Management*, 12: 218–221; Gong, W. 2009. National culture and global diffusion of business-to-consumer e-commerce. *Cross Cultural Management*, 16: 83–101.

16. Asgary & Walle, The cultural impact of globalization.

17. Friedman, T.L. 2005. *The world is flat*. New York: Farrar, Straus and Giroux.

18. Towsend, J.D., Yeniyurt, S., & Talay, M.B. 2009. Getting to global: An evolutionary perspective of brand expansion in international markets. *Journal of International Business Studies*, 40: 539–558.

19. Hitt, Ireland & Hoskisson, *Strategic management*.

20. Ibid.; Hitt, M.A., Tihanyi, L., Miller, T., & Connelly, B. 2006. International diversification: Antecedents, outcomes and moderators. *Journal of Management*, 32: 831–867; Bruton, G.D., Ahlstrom, D., & Puky, T. 2009. Institutional differences and the development of entrepreneurial ventures: A comparison of the venture capital industries in Latin America and Asia. *Journal of International Business Studies*, 40:762–778.

21. Meyer, K. 2006. Global focusing: From domestic conglomerates to global specialists. *Journal of Management Studies*, 43: 1109–1144.

22. Sapienza, H.J., Autio, E., George, G., & Zahra, S. 2006. A capabilities perspective on the effects of early internationalization on firm survival and growth. *Academy of Management Review*, 31: 914–933; Madhaven, R. & Iriyama, A. 2009. Understanding global flows of venture capital: Human networks as the carrier wave of globalization. *Journal of International Business Studies*, 40: 1241–1259.

23. Hitt, M.A., Franklin, V., & Zhu, H. 2006. Culture, institutions and international strategy. *Journal of International Management*, 12: 222–234

24. Hitt, Ireland, & Hoskisson, *Strategic management*

25. Xia, J., Boal, K., Delios, A. 2009. When experience meets national institutional environmental change: Foreign entry attempts of U.S. firms in the central and Eastern European region. *Strategic Management Journal*, 30: 1286–1309.

26. Lin, Z, Peng, M.W., Yang, H. & Sun, S.L. 2009. How do networks and learning drive M&As? An institutional comparison

between China and the United States. *Strategic Management Journal*, 30: 1113–1132.

27. Estrin, S., Baghdasaryan, D. & Meyer, K.E. 2009. The impact of institutional and human resource distance on international entry strategies. *Journal of Management Studies*, 461171–1196.

28. Chung, W. & Yeaple, S. 2008. International knowledge sourcing: Evidence from U.S. firms expanding abroad. *Strategic Management Journal*, 29: 1207–1224.

29. Shapiro, D.L., Furst, S.A., Spreitzer, G.M., & Von Glinow, M.A. 2002. Transnational teams in the electronic age: Are team identity and high performance at risk? *Journal of Organizational Behavior*, 23: 455–467.

30. Cohen, S.G., & Gibson, C.B. 2003. In the beginning: Introduction and framework. In C.B. Gibson & S.G. Cohen (Eds.), *Virtual teams that work: Creating conditions for virtual team effectiveness*. San Francisco: Jossey-Bass.

31. Gibson, C.B., & Manuel, J.A. 2003. Building trust: Effective multicultural communication processes in virtual teams. In Gibson & Cohen (Eds.), *Virtual teams that work*.

32. Kim, P.H., Dirks, K.T., & Cooper, C.D. 2009. The repair of trust: A dynamic bilateral perspective and multilevel conceptualization. *Academy of Management Review*, 34: 401–422.

33. Shin, Y. 2004. A person–environment fit model for virtual organizations. *Journal of Management*, 30: 725–743. Also see: Grabowski, M., & Roberts, K.H. 1999. Risk mitigation in virtual organizations. *Organization Science*, 10: 704–721; Jarven-paa, S.L., & Leidner, D.E. 1999. Communication and trust in global virtual teams. *Organization Science*, 10: 791–815; Kasper-Fuehrer, E.C., & Ashkanasy, N.M. 2001. Communicating trust-worthiness and building trust in interorganizational virtual organizations. *Journal of Management*, 27: 235–254; Raghuram, S., Garud, R., Wiesenfeld, B., & Gupta, V. 2001. Factors contributing to virtual work adjustment. *Journal of Management*, 27: 383–405.

34. Shin, A person–environment fit model for virtual organizations.

35. Jarvenpaa & Leidner, Communication and trust in global virtual teams.

36. Chua, R.Y.J., Morris, M.W., & Ingram, P. 2009. Guanxi vs networking: Distinctive configurations of affect- and cognition-based trust in the networks of Chinese vs American managers. *Journal of international Business Studies*, 40: 490–508.

37. Blackburn, R.S., Furst, S.A., & Rosen, B. 2003. Building a winning virtual team: KSAs, selection, training, and evaluation. In Gibson & Cohen (Eds.), *Virtual teams that work*; Shapiro, Furst, Spreitzer, & Von Glinow, Transnational teams in the electronic age.

38. Weiss, S.E. 1994. Negotiating with "Romans"—Part 2. *Sloan Management Review*, 35(3): 85–99.

39. Blackburn, Furst, & Rosen, Building a winning virtual team.

40. Shapiro, Furst, Spreitzer, & Von Glinow, Transnational teams in the electronic age.

41. Cramton, C.D., & Webber, S.S. 2002. *The impact of virtual design on the processes and effectiveness of information technology work teams*. Fairfax, VA: George Washington University.

42. Blackburn, Furst, & Rosen, Building a winning virtual team.

43. Shin, A person–environment fit model for virtual organizations.

44. Brock, D.M., Shenkar, O., Shoham, A., & Siscovick, I.C. National culture and expatriate deployment, *Journal of International Business Studies*, 39: 1293–1309.

45. Li, S. & Scullion, H. 2006. Bridging the distance: Managing cross-border knowledge holders. *Asia Pacific Journal of Management*, 23: 71–92; Nielsen, B.B. and Nelson, S. 2009. Learning and innovation in international strategic alliances: An empirical test of the role of trust and tacitness. *Journal of Management Studies*, 46: 1031–1056.

46. Reiche, B.S., Harzing, A.-W. & Kraimer, M.L. 2009. The role of international assignees' social capital in creating inter-unit intellectual capital: A cross-level model. *Journal of International Business Studies*, 40: 509–526.

47. Tan, D., & Mahoney, J. T. 2006. Why a multinational firm chooses expatriates: Integrating resource-based, agency and transaction costs perspectives. *Journal of Management Studies*, 43: 457–484; Brannen, M.Y., & Peterson, M.F. 2009. Merging without alienating: Interventions promoting cross-cultural organizational integration and their limitations. *Journal of International Business Studies*, 40: 468–489.

48. Andreason, A.W. 2003. Direct and indirect forms of in-country support for expatriates and their families as a means of reducing premature returns and improving job performance. *International Journal of Management*, 20: 548–555; McCall, M.W., & Hollenbeck, G.P. 2002. Global fatalities: When international executives derail. *Ivey Business Journal*, 66(5): 74–78.

49. Black, J.S., & Gregersen, H.B. 1991. The other half of the picture: Antecedents of spouse cross-cultural adjustment. *Journal of International Business Studies*, 3: 461–478; Sims, R.H., & Schraeder, M. 2004. An examination of salient factors affecting expatriate culture shock. *Journal of Business and Management*, 10: 73–87

50. See, for example: Andreason, Direct and indirect forms of in-country support for expatriates and their families as a means of reducing premature returns and improving job performance; Tung, R. 1982. Selection and training procedures of U.S., European, and Japanese multinationals. *California Management Review*, 25(1): 57–71.

51. Shaffer, M.A., & Harrison, D.A. 2001. Forgotten partners of international assignments: Development and test of a model of spouse adjustment. *Journal of Applied Psychology*, 86: 238–254.

52. Rothausen, T.J. 2009. Management work-family research and work-family fit. *Family Business Review*, 22: 220–234.

53. Gouttefarde, C. 1992. Host national culture shock: What management can do. *European Management Review*, 92(4): 1–3.

54. Andreason, Direct and indirect forms of in-country support for expatriates and their families as a means of reducing premature returns and improving job performance; Caligiuri, P.M. 2002. The big five personality characteristics as predictors of expatriate's desire to terminate the assignment and supervisor-rated performance. *Personnel Psychology*, 53: 67–98; McCall & Hollenbeck, Global fatalities; Sims & Schraeder, An examination of salient factors affecting expatriate culture shock.

55. For a recent information company training in cross-cultural environments see: Beck, N., Labst, R., & Walgenbach, P. 2009. The cultural dependence of vocational training. *Journal of International Business Studies*, 40: 1374–1395.

56. Frazee, V. 1999. Culture and language training: Send your expats prepared for success. *Workforce*, 4(2): 6–11.

57. Aperian Global, 2007. Global assignment services. At http://www.aperianglobal.com/practice_areas_global_assignment_services. asp.

58. Sims & Schraeder, An examination of salient factors affecting expatriate culture shock.

59. Furuya, N., Stevens, M.J., Bird, A., Oddou, G., & Mendenhall, M. 2009. Managing the learning and transfer of global management competence: Antecedents and outcomes of Japanese repatriation effectiveness. *Journal of International Business Studies*, 40: 200–215.

60. Oddou, G., Osland, J.S. & Blakeney, R.N. 2009. Repatriating knowledge: Variables influencing the "transfer" process. *Journal of International Business Studies*, 40: 181–199. Black, J.S., & Gregersen, H. 1999. The right way to manage expatriates. *Harvard Business Review*, 77(2): 52–63; Paik, Y., Segaud, B., & Malinowski, C. 2002. How to improve repatriation management: Are motivations and expectations congruent between the company and expatriates? *International Journal of Manpower*, 23: 635–648; Stroh, L., Gregersen, H., & Black, S. 1998. Closing the gap: Expectations versus reality among repatriates. *Journal of World Business*, 33: 111–124.

61. Fisher, C.M. 2002. Increase in female expatriates raises dual-career concerns. *Benefits & Compensation International*, 32(1): 73.

62. Janssens, M., Cappellen, T., & Zanoni, P. 2006. Successful female expatriates as agents: Positioning oneself through gender, hierarchy and culture. *Journal of World Business*, 41: 133–148.

63. Manning, S., Massini, S., & Lewin, A.Y. 2008. A dynamic perspective on next-generation offshoring: The global sourcing of science and engineering talent. *Academy of Management Perspectives*, 22(3): 35–54; Farrell, D., Laboissiere, M.A., & Rosenfeld, J. 2006. Sizing the emerging global labor market: Rational behavior from both companies and countries can help it work. *Academy of Management Perspectives*, 20 (4): 23–34.

64. Anonymous. 2003. College careers: Pride in diversity. At http://www.microsoft.com/college/diversity/jose.asp.

65. Microsoft Corporations. 2007. Pride in diversity: Diversity & employee groups. At http://members.microsoft.com/careers/mslife/diversepride/employeegroups.mspx.

66. Rothhausen, T.J., Gonzales, J.A., & Griffin, A.E.C. 2009. Are all the parts there everywhere? Facet job satisfaction in the United States and the Philippines. *Asia Pacific Journal of Management*, 26: 681–700.

67. Tomlinson, F., & Egan, S. 2002. Organizational sensemaking in a culturally diverse setting: Limits to the "valuing diversity" discourse. *Management Learning*, 33: 79–98.

68. Hall, *Beyond culture*.

69. Fitzgerald, M. 2007. Can you ace this test? A new exam forces managers to prove their mettle. *Fast Company*, February: 27.

70. Katsikeas, C.S., Skarmeas, D., & Bello, D.C. 2009. Developing successful trust-based international exchange relationships. *Journal of International Business Studies*, 40: 132–155.

71. Munter, M. 1993. Cross-cultural communication for managers. *Business Horizons*, 36(3): 69–78.

72. Hall, E.T. 1983. *The dance of life: The other dimension of time.* New York: Anchor Books.

73. Bluedorn, A.C., Felker, C., & Lane, P.M. 1992. How many things do you like to do at once? An introduction to monochronic and polychronic time. *Academy of Management Executive*, 6(4): 17–26; Wessel, R. 2003. Is there time to slow down? As the world speeds up, how cultures define the elastic nature of time may affect our environmental health. *Christian Science Monitor*, January 9: 13.

74. Bluedorn, Felker, & Lane. 1992. How many things do you like to do at once? Wessel, Is there time to slow down?

75. Earley, P.C., & Ang, S. 2003. *Cultural intelligence: Individual interactions across cultures.* Stanford, CA: Stanford University Press.

76. Williamson, I.O., Burnett, M.F. & Bartol, K.M. 2009. The interactive effect of collectivism and organizational rewards on affective organizational commitment. *Cross Cultural Management*, 16: 28–43.

77. Zhou, K.Z., Li, J.J., Zhou, N., & Su, C. 2008. Market orientation, job satisfaction, product quality and firm performance: Evidence from China. *Strategic Management Journal*, 29: 985–1000.

78. Bartlett, C.A., & Ghoshal, S. 1998. *Managing across borders: The transnational solution* (2nd ed.). Boston: Harvard Business School Press; Harzing, A.-W. 2000. An empirical analysis and extension of the Bartlett and Ghoshal typology of multinational companies. *Journal of International Business Studies*, 31: 101–120; Hitt, Ireland, & Hoskisson, *Strategic management*.

79. Unilever N.V./Unilever PLC. 2007. About Unilever. At http://www.unilever.com/ourcompany/aboutunilever/introducingunilever/asp.

80. Li, L. 2005. Is regional strategy more effective than global strategy in the U.S. service industries? *Management International Review*, 45: 37–57; Harzing, An empirical analysis and extension of the Bartlett and Ghoshal typology of multinational companies.

81. Harzing, A.-W., & Nooderhaven, N. 2006. Geographical distance and the role and management of subsidiaries: The case of subsidiaries down-under. *Asia Pacific Journal of Management*, 23: 167–185; Capron, L., & Guillen, M. 2009. National corporate governance institutions and post-acquisition target reorganization. *Strategic Management Journal*, 30: 803–833.

82. Bartlett & Ghoshal, Managing across borders: The transnational solution; Harzing, An empirical analysis and extension of the Bartlett and Ghoshal typology of multinational companies; Hitt, Ireland, & Hoskisson, *Strategic management*.

83. This is Cemex. 2009. Cemex web site. At http://www.cemex.com/tc/tc_lp.asp, December.

84. Zellmer-Bruhn, M., & Gibson, C. 2006. Multinational organization context: Implications for team learning and performance. *Academy of Management Journal*, 49: 501–518; Zhang, Y., Dolan, S., Lingham, T., & Altman, Y. 2009. International strategic human resource management: A comparative case analysis of Spanish firms in China. *Management and Organization Review*, 5: 195–222.

85. Bartlett & Ghoshal, Managing across borders: The transnational solution; Harzing, An empirical analysis and extension of the Bartlett and Ghoshal typology of multinational companies; Hitt, Ireland, & Hoskisson, *Strategic management*.

86. Ibarra, H., & Sackley, N. 1995. *Charlotte Beers at Ogilvy & Mather Worldwide.* Boston: Harvard Business School Publishing.

87. Ogilvy & Mather. 2009. Company information. At http://www.ogilvy.com/company.

88. Bentley, S. 1997. Big agencies profit from global tactics. *Marketing Week*, 19(43): 25–26.

89. Ogilvy & Mather. 2009. About Ogilvy*Action*. At http://www.ogilvy.com/#/About/Network/OgilvyAction.aspx, December.

90. Birkinshaw, J., Braunerhjelm, P., & Holm, U. 2006. Why some multinational corporations relocate their headquarters overseas. *Strategic Management Journal*, 27: 681–700.

91. See, for example, Zatzick, C.D., & Iverson, R.D. 2006. High-involvement and workforce reduction: Competitive advantage or disadvantage? *Academy of Management Journal*, 49: 999–1015.

92. MacDuffie, J.P. 1995. Human resource bundles and manufacturing performance: Organizational logic and flexible production systems. *Industrial and Labor Relations Review*, 48: 197–221.

93. Guthrie, J.P. 2001. High-involvement work practices, turnover, and productivity: Evidence from New Zealand. *Academy of Management Journal*, 44: 180–190.

94. Black, B. 1999. National culture and high commitment management. *Employee Management*, 21: 389–404.

95. Huang, X., Shi, K., Zhang, Z., & Cheung, Y.L. 2006. The impact of participative leadership behavior on psychological empowerment and organizational commitment in Chinese state-owned enterprises: The moderating role of organizational tenure. *Asia Pacific Journal of Management*, 23: 345–367.

96. Benito, G.R.G., Petersen, B., & Welch, L.S. 2009. Towards more realistic conceptualizations of foreign operation modes. *Journal of International Business Studies*, 40: 1455–1470.

97. House, R., Javidan, M., Hanges, P., & Dorfman, P. 2002. Understanding cultures and implicit leadership theories across the globe: An introduction to project GLOBE. *Journal of World Business*, 37: 3–10; Javidan, M., & House, R.J. 2001. Cultural acumen for the global manager: Lessons from Project GLOBE. *Organizational Dynamics*, 29: 289–305.

98. Hofstede, G. 1984. *Culture's consequences: International differences in work-related values (abridged edition).* Beverly Hills, CA: Sage Publications.

99. Witt, M.A., & Redding, G. 2009. Culture, meaning and institutions: Executive rationale in Germany and Japan. *Journal of International Business Studies*, 40: 859–885.

100. Leung. K., Bhagat, R.S., Buchan, N.R., Erez, M., & Gibson, C.B. 2005. Culture and international business: Recent advances and their implications for future research. *Journal of International Business Studies*, 36: 357–378.

101. Rothaermel, F.T., Kotha, S., & Steensma, H.K. 2006. International market entry by U.S. Internet firms: An empirical analysis of country risk, national culture and market size. *Journal of Management*, 32: 56–82; Bhaskaran, S., & Gligorovska, E. 2009. Influence of national culture on transnational alliance relationships. *Cross Cultural Management*, 16: 44–61.

102. Zaheer, S., & Zaheer, A. 2006. Trust across borders. *Journal of International Business Studies*, 37: 21–29.

103. Randolph, W.A., & Sashkin, M. 2002. Can organizational empowerment work in multinational settings? *Academy of Management Executive*, 16: 112–115.

104. Michailova, S., & Hutchings, K. 2006. National cultural influences on knowledge sharing: A comparison of China and Russia. *Journal of Management Studies*, 43: 383–405; Wong, A., & Tjosvold, D. 2006. Collectivist values for learning in organizational relationships in China: The role of trust and vertical coordination. *Asia Pacific Journal of Management*, 23: 299–317.

105. van der Vegt, G.S., van de Vliert, E., & Huang, X. 2005. Location-level links between diversity and innovative climate depend on national power distance. *Academy of Management Journal*, 48: 1171–1182.

106. Newburry, W., & Yakova, N. 2006. Standardization preferences: A function of national culture, work interdependence and local embeddedness. *Journal of International Business Studies*, 37: 44–60.

107. AES Company home page, 2009, at http://www.aes.com/aes/index?page=home, December; Hamilton, M.M. 2003. AES's new power structure: Struggling utility overhauls corporate (lack of) structure. *The Washington Post*, June 2, E1; McMillan, J., & Dosunmu, A. 2002. Nigeria. Palo Alto, CA: Stanford Graduate School of Business; O'Reilly, C.A., & Pfeffer, J. 2000. *Hidden value: How great companies achieve extraordinary results with ordinary people.* Boston: Harvard Business School Press.

108. Hooker, J. 2009. Corruption from a cross-cultural perspective. *Cross Cultural Management*, 16: 251–267.

109. Rodriguez, P., Siegel, D.S., Hillman, A., & Eden, L. 2006. Three lenses on the multinational enterprise: Politics, corruption, and corporate social responsibility. *Journal of International Business Studies*, 37: 733–746; Meschi, P.-X. 2009. Government corruption and foreign stakes in international joint ventures in emerging economies. *Asia Pacific Journal of Management*, 26: 241–261.

110. Davids, M. 1999. Global standards, local problems. *The Journal of Business Strategy*, 20: 38–43.

111. Sanyal, R. 2009. The propensity to bribe in international business: The relevance of cultural variables. *Cross Cultural Management*, 16: 287–300.

112. Davids, Global standards, local problems.

113. Cuervo-Cazurra, A. 2006. Who cares about corruption? *Journal of International Business Studies*, 37: 807–822; Ralston, D.A., Egri, C.P., Garcia Carranza, M.T., Ramburuth, P., et al., 2009. Ethical preferences for influencing superiors: A 41-society study. *Journal of International Business Studies*, 40: 1022–1045.

PART 2

individual processes

The chapters in Part I provided the strategic lens that is central to discussions throughout the book, and they explained how organizational diversity and the global environment affect all organizations. In Part II, we explore important concepts related to individual-level processes in organizations.

Chapter 4 explains the concepts of learning and perception. Through individual learning, associates gain the knowledge and skills they need to perform their jobs in organizations. Individual learning contributes to the value of an organization's human capital and provides the base for organizational learning, both of which are critical for organizations to capture a competitive advantage.

Chapter 5 focuses on personality, intelligence, attitudes, and emotions. Managers in organizations need to understand how each of these human characteristics affects individual behavior. Personality and intelligence are an important determinant of a person's behavior and performance and cannot be easily changed. Thus, organizations must learn how to select associates with desirable personalities and intelligence levels to maximize the value of their human capital. However, attitudes and emotions can and do vary. Attitudes and emotions affect behavior, and managers can have a significant effect on individuals' behavior by taking actions that affect their attitudes and emotions.

Chapter 6 examines a fundamental concept in organizational behavior: motivation. Individuals can be motivated in various ways and by various factors. Because individual motivation is highly critical to individual and organizational productivity, understanding how to motivate is vital to effective management.

Chapter 7 deals with stress and well-being, critical issues in today's workplace. While some stress can be functional, much of the stress individuals experience can have negative effects on their productivity and health. When managers understand the causes and consequences of stress, they can attempt to manage it to reduce dysfunctional outcomes.

learning and perception

exploring behavior in action

The Strategic Importance of Learning and Perception

VF Corporation, headquartered in Greensboro, North Carolina, is the world's largest apparel manufacturer, with revenues of $7 billion plus annually. Chances are that you have several items of their clothing in your closet. Their more than thirty brands include: Wrangler, Lee, Vans, The North Face, 7 for all mankind, and Jansport. In 2004, the VF Corporation launched a new growth plan, that has been incredibly successful. The goal of this plan was to transform the VF Corporation in a global lifestyle apparel company. At the center of the plan are six Growth Drivers, one of which is building new growth enablers. The company describes this goal as: "Taking our company to new heights requires new capabilities and skills, and we've invested in areas that are specifically designed to support our growth. … [W]e know that providing our leaders and associates with new tools and training that stretches their capabilities is crucial to our continued success." Thus, associate learning, development, and knowledge sharing has become one of the crucial drivers of the VF Corporation's new strategy. Tom Nelson, VF Corporation's manager of global sourcing states, "Learning and development makes a significant contribution to the company's ongoing success."

VF Asia Ltd., a subsidiary of VF Corporation located in Hong Kong, took this directive very seriously. This subsidiary totally reorganized its learning unit, which had previously been somewhat piecemeal, with a program here, a learning opportunity there. Tommy

knowledge objectives

After reading this chapter, you should be able to:

1. Describe the effects on learning of positive reinforcement, negative reinforcement, punishment, and extinction.
2. Discuss continuous and intermittent schedules of reinforcement.
3. Explain how principles of learning can be used to train newcomers as well as to modify the behavior of existing associates.
4. Describe the conditions under which adults learn, in addition to rewards and punishments.
5. Describe some specific methods that organizations use to train associates.
6. Discuss learning from failure.
7. Identify typical problems in accurately perceiving others and solutions to these problems.
8. Explain the complexities of causal attributions and task perception.

Lo, learning and development manager, guided the two-person regional training team by first creating a strategy. The company's 780 employees were grouped into one of four learning categories, determined by their level in the organization and the content that needed to be learned and skills developed. These categories are personal competencies, functional leadership, managerial leadership, and strategic leadership. Furthermore, all functions associated with training, performance review and development, feedback, and reward were grouped together in the same program. Thus, training and development is tied to on-the-job performance. A further part of the firm's learning and development strategy was to keep as many programs

©Martin Gerten/epa/Corbis

and initiatives as possible in-house rather than outsourcing them to vendors and contractors. Not only is this cost-effective, but it makes the most use out of in-house knowledge and talent. Finally, although VF Asia is across the world from its parent company, learning and development at the subsidiary is well integrated with that which takes place at headquarters. Tommy Lo belongs to the VF Global Learning Community, which shares new ideas and best practices through conference calls, and certain employees attend corporate learning programs such as the VF Leadership Institute.

There are many specific initiatives in place, all of which are tied to company core competencies. One concern was leadership development. To that end, Lo and his team developed a senior executive curriculum and middle-manager-level curriculum. Another concern was turnover.

Thus, they developed a program to improve managers' interviewing skills, so that they would be better at judging job candidates. Turnover decreased from 26.8 percent in 2007 to 19.3 percent in 2008. In order to improve associates' ability to deal with customers from diverse cultures, the SELF (Self Enhancement Learning Fundamentals) program was initiated. This is an online training program covering topics such as etiquette and negotiations. Associates can use this program at their own leisure. Overall, the 780 associates at VF Asia Ltd. underwent 14,200 hours of training in 2008.

The vast majority of organizations do not assess the effectiveness of their training programs beyond getting participants' reactions to the programs. Things are different at VF Asia Ltd. Learning goals are tied into individual performance evaluations and to the strategic goals of the organization. Monthly learning and development summaries are sent to executives. VF Asia Ltd. makes sure its training and development dollars are well spent. In 2009, this focus on learning was recognized with a BEST award by the American Society for Training and Development (ASTD). The criteria for this award are:

- learning has an enterprise-wide role
- learning has value in the organization's culture
- learning links to individual and organizational performance
- investment is made in learning and performance initiatives

Sources: ASTD BEST Awards. At http://www.astd.org/ASTD/aboutus/AwardsandBestPractices/bestAwards/; ASTD Learning Circuits, Nov. 17, 2009. At http://www.astd.org/LC/news.htm. J.J. Salopek, P. Harris, P. Ketter, M. Laff, & J. Llorens. 2009. "Success is in the details." *T + D*, Oct. 63, 10 ; pp. 36–38. VF Corporation. Dec. 2009. At http://www.vfc.com/about/our-strategy/growth-drivers.

The redevelopment of VF Asia Ltd.'s learning and development strategy illustrates the importance of learning to the overall strategic goals of the organization. The learning processes in this organization serve to develop current associates so that they have the knowledge, skills, and abilities to allow the organization to grow. Associates simply do not go through one-time training programs—what they learn in training is later assessed as part of their job performance and is thus tied to individual rewards. As we will soon discuss, rewards play an important role in the learning process.

At a second level, learning processes help VF Asia tie individual training, development, performance evaluation, and rewards to the overall strategic vision of the organization. The corporate strategy and goals determine what is to be learned, and the success of training and development initiatives are evaluated at the executive level by the degree to which they achieve the firm's strategic goals. Learning is fully integrated into the culture at VF Asia Ltd. and is therefore viewed as an important part of the organization's success by associates and leaders at all levels in the firm.

To be competitive in the dynamic twenty-first century, an organization must have associates and managers who can effectively learn and grow. Continuous learning based on trying new things plays a critical role in an organization's capability to gain and sustain a competitive advantage. Organizations can improve only when their human capital is enriched through learning. Their human capital must be better and produce more value for customers than their competitors to gain an advantage in the marketplace and to maintain that advantage.[1] Furthermore, providing developmental opportunities to associates helps organizations attract and retain the people most interested in personal growth and becoming better at their work. Thus, managers need to develop the means for associates and all managers to continuously improve their knowledge and skills.

To open this chapter, we explore the fundamentals of learning, including contingencies of reinforcement and various schedules of reinforcement. From there, we apply learning principles to the training of newcomers and the purposeful modification of existing associates' behavior. We focus on specific conditions helpful to learning, the use of behavior modification, simulations, and how people can learn from failure. Next, we move to a discussion of perception. Accurately perceiving characteristics of people, attributes of tasks, and the nature of cause-and-effect relationships is critical to properly assessing and learning from experiences. Several mental biases, however, can interfere with accurate perceptions.

Fundamental Learning Principles

When individuals first enter an organization, they bring with them their own unique experiences, perceptions, and ways of behaving. These patterns of behavior have developed because they have helped these individuals cope with the world around them. However, associates introduced to a new organization or to new tasks may need to learn new behaviors that will make them effective in the new situation. Associates and managers must therefore be acquainted with the principles and processes that govern learning.

In the field of organizational behavior, **learning** refers to relatively permanent changes in human capabilities that occur as a result of experience rather than a natural growth process.[2] These capabilities are related to specific learning outcomes, such as new behaviors, verbal information, intellectual skills, motor skills, attitudes, and cognitive strategies. Both parts of this definition are important. First, learning takes place only when changes in capabilities occur. Ultimately, these changes should result in changed behavior, since true learning represents adaptation to circumstances, and this must be reflected in behavior. Furthermore, this change should be relatively permanent until a new response is learned

learning
A process through which individuals change their relatively permanent behavior based on positive or negative experiences in a situation.

to the given situation. Second, learning is driven by experience with a particular situation. An associate may gain insights into a situation by thoughtfully trying different approaches to see what happens, by randomly trying different actions in a trial-and-error process, or by carefully observing others' actions. In all cases, however, the associate has gained experience in the situation—experience that affects behavior when the situation occurs again. Change in one's capabilities due to a natural growth process (e.g., gaining muscle strength) is not learning.

Operant Conditioning and Social Learning Theory

Most behavior exhibited by associates and managers is intentional in the sense that a given behavior is designed to bring about a positive consequence or avoid a negative consequence. Some associates shake hands when they see each other in the morning because it feels good and expresses respect or affection. Other associates apply the brakes on a forklift to avoid an accident. Managers may not develop close social relationships with their organization's associates in order to avoid the complications that can result. All of these behaviors have been learned.

Operant conditioning theory and social learning theory both can be used to explain learning. Both are reinforcement theories based on the idea that behavior is a function of its consequences.[3] **Operant conditioning theory** traces its roots at least back to a famous set of experiments involving cats, dogs, and other animals in the late 1800s.[4] The goal of the experiments was to show that animals learn from the consequences of their behavior in a very straightforward way—that presentation of a reward, such as food, conditions an animal to repeat the rewarded behavior in the same or similar situations. In later years, researchers such as B.F. Skinner emphasized this same conditioning in people.[5] These researchers, known as *behaviorists,* adopted the position that higher mental processes typically ascribed to human beings are irrelevant for behavior because all human learning is the result of simple conditioning, just as in cats, rats, dogs, and monkeys. In other words, people do not need to think to learn.

While operant conditioning explains a great deal of human learning, later scientists argued that people can learn in other ways. The most prominent of these theories is social learning theory. **Social learning theory**, developed by psychologist Albert Bandura, rejects the idea that higher mental processes are nonexistent or irrelevant in humans.[6] This theory emphasizes that humans can observe others in a situation and learn from what they see. Thus, humans do not need to directly experience a particular situation to develop some understanding of the behaviors that are rewarded in that situation.

operant conditioning theory
An explanation for consequence-based learning that assumes learning results from simple conditioning and that higher mental functioning is irrelevant.

social learning theory
An explanation for consequence-based learning that acknowledges the higher mental functioning of human beings and the role such functioning can play in learning.

Contingencies of Reinforcement

The basic elements of learning include:

- The situation (sometimes referred to as "the stimulus situation")
- The behavioral response of the associate or manager to the situation
- The consequence(s) of the response for the associate or manager

These elements interact to form contingencies of reinforcement. These contingencies, explained below, describe different types of consequences that can follow behavioral responses.

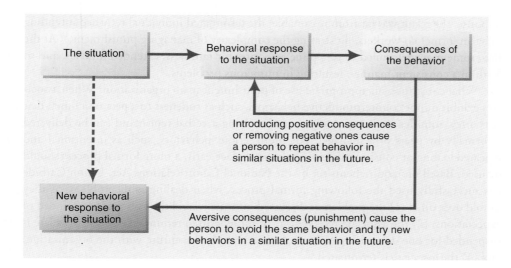

Exhibit 4-1 Effects of Reinforcing Consequences on Learning New Behaviors

Positive and Negative Reinforcement

As shown in Exhibit 4-1, when the consequences of a behavior are positive in a particular situation, individuals are likely to repeat that behavior when the situation occurs again. The introduction of positive consequences, such as peer approval for an associate's correction of quality problems, increases the likelihood of that behavior being repeated in similar settings. This is called **positive reinforcement**. Similarly, when a particular behavior in a given situation results in the removal of previous negative consequences, the likelihood of repeating the behavior in similar settings will probably increase. Thus, the removal of negative consequences is called **negative reinforcement**. If working harder and smarter removes the frown from a manager's face, an associate may attempt to work harder and smarter.

Punishment

When behavior results in the introduction of a negative consequence, individuals are less likely to repeat the behavior. This is called **punishment**. Punishment differs from negative reinforcement in that an undesirable consequence is introduced rather than removed. Punishment reduces the likelihood of a behavior, whereas negative reinforcement increases the likelihood. An associate who is reprimanded by peers for returning a few minutes late from lunch experiences punishment, as does an associate whose manager assigns him less preferred work hours in response to tardiness.

Punishment must be used judiciously in organizations because it can create a backlash both among those punished and among those who witness the punishment.[7] It is imperative when punishment is doled out that it be made contingent upon associates engaging in negative behavior.[8] Several examples illustrate this problem. At the *Providence Journal,* a newspaper organization in the northeastern United States, senior management reprimanded two individuals and suspended a third for an editorial cartoon that seemed to poke fun at the publisher. Union officials and many union members believed the punishments were too harsh, resulting in ill will at a time when relations were already strained.[9] At Fireman's Fund, the leadership of a Tampa office terminated an associate who had "dangerous and violent propensities." Although termination was probably a reasonable

positive reinforcement
A reinforcement contingency in which a behavior is followed by a positive consequence, thereby increasing the likelihood that the behavior will be repeated in the same or similar situations.

negative reinforcement
A reinforcement contingency in which a behavior is followed by the withdrawal of a previously encountered negative consequence, thereby increasing the likelihood that the behavior will be repeated in the same or similar situations.

punishment
A reinforcement contingency in which a behavior is followed by a negative consequence, thereby reducing the likelihood that the behavior will be repeated in the same or similar situations.

response, the result was far from reasonable; the terminated individual returned intending to harm former co-workers, illustrating the complexity of managing punishment.[10] At the IRS, some managers failed to discipline associates for tardiness, extended lunches, and so forth in a consistent manner, resulting in numerous problems.[11]

What constitutes an appropriate use of punishment in an organization? When associates exhibit minor counterproductive behaviors, such as rudeness to a peer or a lunch that lasts a few minutes too long, punishment involving a verbal reprimand can be delivered informally by peers or a manager. For more serious behaviors, such as intentional and repeated loafing or consistently leaving the workplace early, a more formal process should be used. Based on requirements set by the National Labor Relations Act, Union Carbide has successfully used the following formal process when dealing with problems as they unfold over time: (1) the problem is discussed informally, and the associate is reminded of expectations; (2) the associate receives one or more written reminders; (3) the associate is suspended for one day, with pay, and asked to consider his future with the organization; and (4) the associate is terminated.[12]

Whether they are imposing minor informal punishment or major formal punishment, associates and managers should follow several guidelines:

- Deliver the punishment as quickly as possible following the undesirable behavior.
- Direct the punishment at specific behaviors that have been made clear to the recipient.
- Deliver the punishment in an objective, impersonal fashion.
- Listen to the offending party's explanation before taking action.

The problems at Korean Air discussed in the *Managerial Advice* feature were caused at least in part by the overuse of punishment. Clearly, as the case illustrates, the use of punishment at this airline played a role in the crash. Being struck by a person above you in the organization is a particularly difficult situation, even for those in an authoritarian culture. Such an approach is inappropriate in a high-involvement organization. In complex situations, associates and managers need the input of others to avoid making possibly serious errors such as those leading to the Korean Air crash. The changes implemented by the new president of the airline and the director of flight operations have helped to resolve the problem. Because Korean culture respects traditional authority, changing the culture at this airline was difficult.[13] Yet the changes were important for the airline to compete in a global marketplace.

Extinction

Because punishment can be a difficult process to manage, organizations may instead desire to extinguish dysfunctional behavior by removing its reinforcing consequences. This procedure is called **extinction**. It is difficult to use extinction, however, unless a manager has full control over all reinforcing consequences. For instance, an associate may be consistently late to work because he prefers to avoid morning rush-hour traffic or likes to sleep late. Missing the rush hour and sleeping late are both activities that offer rewarding consequences for being late to work. Associates and managers desiring to extinguish this behavior are unlikely to be able to remove these reinforcing consequences.

The reinforcing consequences of some dysfunctional work behaviors, however, may be completely removable. For example, an associate may have developed a habit of regularly

extinction
A reinforcement contingency in which a behavior is followed by the absence of a previously encountered positive consequence, thereby reducing the likelihood that the behavior will be repeated in the same or similar situations.

MANAGERIAL ADVICE

Punishment Taken Too Far

At 1:00 A.M. on August 6, 1997, the pilots of a Korean Air 747 prepared to land at the Guam airport. Because the airport's glide slope guidance system had been turned off for maintenance and because the airport's radio beacon was located in a nonstandard position, the landing was more difficult than usual. A rainstorm further complicated the situation. Under these conditions, the captain needed frank and timely advice from a fully informed and empowered co-pilot and flight engineer. Sadly, no such advice was given by the intimidated subordinates. The resulting crash claimed 228 lives.

The suboptimal cockpit climate on board the aircraft that morning seems to have been caused in part by Korean Air's authoritarian culture, which included heavy-handed punishment delivered by captains for unwanted subordinate input and mistakes. Park Jae Hyun, a former captain with the airline and then a flight inspector with the Ministry of Transportation, believed that teamwork in the cockpit was nearly impossible in the existing "obey or else" environment, where co-pilots "couldn't express themselves if they found something wrong with the captain's piloting skills." This environment was perhaps most clearly evident during training. An American working as a pilot for the airline reported, "I've seen a captain punch a co-pilot ... for a mistake and the co-pilot just said, 'Oh, sorry, sorry.'" Another American reports being hit as well, but as an outsider he did not accept the abuse and said

©Charles Polidano/Touch the Skies/Alamy

to the captain, "Do it again and I'll break your arm."

Korean officials, American officials, and many others believed change was necessary to prevent additional accidents and to generally improve the organization. Following another crash and the forced resignations of key leaders in the late 1990s, new leaders inside Korean Air took actions to change the authoritarian, punishment-oriented culture. Yi Taek Shim, the new president, vowed that cultural and technological problems would be addressed whatever the cost. Koh Myung Joon, who became the new director of flight operations, sought captains for training duty who had "the right temperament," meaning they would not use inappropriate, heavy-handed punishment but rather would focus on positive reinforcement for desired behavior. These leaders clearly had useful insights. Korean Air has had an excellent safety record in the twenty-first century, and crucial relationships with partner airlines have been strengthened.

Consistent with actions and outcomes at Korean Air, Francis Friedman of Time & Place Strategies in New York has said that individuals in positions of authority should not "get into a kick-the-dog mentality." Even Simon Kukes, a Russian who achieved notoriety as CEO of Tyumen Oil, has suggested that managers should not "yell, scream, and try to find someone to punish." This is interesting advice, given the general authoritarian culture in Russia.

Sources: "Korean Air Is Restructuring Its Flight Operations Division," *Aviation Week & Space Technology,* 152, no. 21 (2000): 21; "Cargo Airline of the Year: Korean Air Cargo," *Air Transport World,* 40, no. 2 (2000): 30–31; W.M. Carley and A. Pasztor. 1999. "Pilot Error: Korean Air Confronts Dismal Safety Record Rooted in Its Culture," *Wall Street Journal,* July 7; Z. Coleman and M. Song. 2001. "Inquiry Blames Cockpit Crew for KAL Crash," *Wall Street Journal,* June 6, P.M. Perry. 2001. "Cage the Rage," *Warehousing Management,* 8, no. 2: 37–40; P. Starobin. 2001. "The Oilman as Teacher," *BusinessWeek,* June 25, G. Thomas. 2000. "Korean Air CEO Vows 'No More Excuses,'" *Aviation Week & Space Technology,* 153, no. 1: 48; G. Thomas. 2002. "The Yin and Yang of Korean Air," *Air Transport World,* 39, no. 10: 26–29.

visiting the manager's office to complain about her co-workers. Most of the complaints are trivial, and the manager wishes to extinguish this practice. However, the fact that the manager has appeared to be attentive and understanding is a positive, reinforcing consequence. The manager may therefore extinguish the behavior by refusing to listen whenever this associate complains about her co-workers. (During a useful conversation with the associate, the manager would, of course, be attentive; only the dysfunctional behavior should be extinguished.) To use extinction, then, managers must recognize the reinforcing consequences of a behavior, and these consequences must be controllable.

Extinction is supposedly used to eliminate dysfunctional behavior. However, this phenomenon can also result in unintended consequences by extinguishing desirable behavior. In a study of hospital employees, some researchers found that when managers failed to provide feedback for good performance (a reward), employees performed more poorly and became unsatisfied with their jobs.[14]

Schedules of Reinforcement

Positive and negative reinforcement are powerful tools in many situations. To fully leverage these two tools, it is important to understand schedules of reinforcement.[15] These schedules determine how often reinforcement is given for desired behavior. Reinforcement does not necessarily need to follow every instance of a positive behavior.

continuous reinforcement
A reinforcement schedule in which a reward occurs after each instance of a behavior or set of behaviors.

The simplest schedule is **continuous reinforcement**, whereby reward occurs after each instance of a particular behavior or set of behaviors. This schedule tends to produce reasonably high rates of the rewarded behavior because it is relatively easy for an individual to understand the connection between a behavior and its positive consequences.[16] Behavior in organizations, however, often is not reinforced on a continuous schedule, for several reasons. First, once initial learning has occurred through training and/or coaching, continuous reinforcement is not required to maintain learned behavior. Second, in today's organizations, both managers and associates are presumed to be self-managing, at least to some degree. Thus, they do not need continuous reinforcement of positive actions.

intermittent reinforcement
A reinforcement schedule in which a reward does not occur after each instance of a behavior or set of behaviors.

Intermittent reinforcement, then, is often used to maintain learned behavior. Schedules can vary by rewarding responses only after a specified number of correct behaviors have occurred or after a specified amount of time has passed. The four most common intermittent schedules found in organizations are as follows:

1. *Fixed interval.* With this schedule, a reinforcement becomes available only after a fixed period of time has passed since the previous reinforcement. For example, an associate at an airport car rental counter might receive a dollar and praise for saying "May I help you?" rather than using the grammatically incorrect "Can I help you?" Because the manager delivering the reinforcement has a limited amount of money and time to devote to this bonus plan, he might listen from his back office for the proper greeting only after two hours have passed since his last delivery of reinforcement. Upon hearing the greeting after the two-hour interval, the manager would provide the next reinforcement. A fixed-interval schedule like this one can make the desired behavior more resistant to extinction than the continuous schedule because the associate is not accustomed to being reinforced for every instance of the desired behavior. However, it can also yield lower probabilities of the desired behavior immediately after reinforcement has

occurred because the person may realize that no additional reinforcement is possible for a period of time. Moreover, it can yield generally low probabilities of the desired behavior if the fixed interval is too long for the situation.[17] Overall, this schedule of reinforcement tends to be the least effective.

2. *Variable interval.* With this second schedule, a reinforcement becomes available after a variable period of time has passed since the previous reinforcement. In our car rental example, the manager might listen for and reward the desired greeting one hour after the previous reinforcement and then again after one half hour, and then again after three hours. This schedule can produce a consistently high rate of the desired behavior because the associate does not know when reinforcement might be given next. If, however, the average time between reinforcements becomes too great, the variable-interval schedule can lose its effectiveness.[18]

3. *Fixed ratio.* With this third reinforcement schedule, a reinforcer is introduced after the desired behavior has occurred a fixed number of times. In our car rental example, the manager might listen closely to all of the greetings used by a given associate and reward the desired greeting every third time it is used. In industrial settings, managers may create piece-rate incentive systems whereby individual production workers are paid, for example, $5.00 after producing every fifth piece. Although the fixed-ratio schedule can produce a reasonably high rate of desired behavior, it can also result in a short period immediately following reinforcement when the desired behavior does not occur.[19] Such outcomes occur because associates and managers relax following reinforcement, knowing they are starting over.

4. *Variable ratio.* With our final schedule, a reinforcement is introduced after the desired behavior has occurred a variable number of times. The manager of our car rental counter may listen closely all day to the greetings but, because of money and time constraints, reward only the first desired greeting, the fifth, the eight, the fifteenth, the seventeenth, and so on. This schedule of reinforcement tends to produce consistently high rates of desired behavior and tends to make extinction less likely than under the other schedules.[20] The variable-ratio schedule is very common in many areas of life, including sports: baseball and softball players are reinforced on this schedule in their hitting, basketball players in their shot making, anglers in their fishing, and gamblers in their slot machine activities. In business organizations, salespersons are perhaps more subject to this schedule than others, with a variable number of sales contacts occurring between actual sales.

Exhibit 4-2 summarizes various schedules of reinforcement.

Social Learning Theory

Although the principles of operant conditioning explain a great deal of learning that takes place, people also learn in other ways. *Social learning theory*—and later, *social cognitive theory*—argues that in addition to learning through direct reinforcement, people can also learn by anticipating consequences of their behavior and by modeling others.[21] In other words, learning occurs through the mental processing of information.[22]

According to these approaches to learning, one way that associates can learn is through symbolization and forethought.[23] People have the ability to symbolize events and

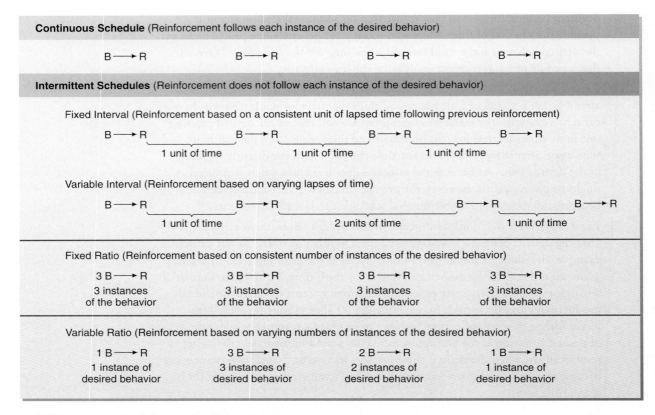

Exhibit 4-2   Schedules of Reinforcement

to anticipate consequences. This means that rather than having to directly experience possible consequences of one's behavior, a person can try out various scenarios in his or her mind to determine what potential consequences may result from a particular behavior. For example, if a manager has to make a decision about whether to open a new branch office, she can rely on past experience to come up with symbolic representation of the problem and then anticipate what outcomes may occur if she decides to open the new office.

According to social learning theory, people also learn by observing others. Rather than having to experience consequences first-hand, associates can observe the behavior of others and the results of that behavior.[24] When results are positive, then associates will model the behavior demonstrated by the other person. For example, if an associate is trying to learn how to give presentations, rather than try out many different presentation styles, he may observe his supervisor, who is a wonderful presenter, and then model the supervisor's presentation style. Associates are most likely to model the behavior of people they perceive to be competent, powerful, friendly, and of high status within the organization.[25]

Social learning theory also states that an individual's belief that he will be able to perform a specific task in a given situation is important to learning. This belief is referred to as one's **self-efficacy**.[26] When associates have high self-efficacy toward a particular task, they believe that they can perform that task well. People will not engage in behaviors or will perform poorly when they do not believe that they are able to accomplish the task at a satisfactory level. Athletes are often trained to visualize themselves performing extremely well

self-efficacy
An individual's belief that he or she will be able to perform a specific task in a given situation.

in order to increase their self-efficacy, and consequently their performance. A great deal of research has shown that self-efficacy increases performance and learning, beyond ability.[27] If there are two people with the same ability, the person with the higher self-efficacy will tend to perform better and learn more.

Other Conditions for Learning

In addition to learning through consequences and observing others, more recent research has noted that the following conditions help facilitate adult learning:[28]

- *Associates need to know why they are learning what they are learning.* People become more motivated to learn when they understand why what they are learning is important.[29] For example, in order for associates to successfully train to engage in safe behaviors, they must first understand what constitutes safe behavior and then understand the consequences of not engaging in these behaviors.[30] In order for associates to know why they are learning what they are learning, they must be provided with specific learning objectives.[31] Also, allowing associates to either directly or vicariously experience the negative effects of *not* learning may help them understand why learning the material is important.[32] We discuss learning from failure in more detail later in this chapter.
- *Associates need to use their own experiences as the basis for learning.* Many teaching and learning experts believe that people learn best when they can tie newly learned material to their past experiences, take an active role in their own learning, and are able to reflect on their learning experiences.[33] According to the experiential learning perspective, it is imperative for learning to include active experimentation and reflective observation.[34] This is why many MBA programs include team exercises to teach teamwork skills. Rather than just reading about the importance of teamwork and how to achieve it, students actually experience their lessons and later are asked to reflect upon what they have learned.
- *Associates need to practice what they have learned.* Practicing means repetitively demonstrating performance stated in the learning objectives. Overlearning due to constant practice improves the likelihood that associates will engage in newly learned behaviors once they leave the learning situation.[35] Overlearning means that performing the new behavior takes little conscious thought, so that the performance becomes automatic.
- *Associates need feedback.* A great deal of research has been conducted on the effects of feedback on learning.[36] Feedback can facilitate learning by providing associates with information about what they should be learning and it can also act as a reward. Feedback is most conducive to learning when associates are comfortably familiar with the material to be learned or when the material is relatively simple.[37]

Training and Enhancing the Performance of Associates

The learning concepts discussed thus far have been successfully used over the years to train newcomers as well as to improve the performance of existing associates. To achieve positive results when training a newcomer, managers often reinforce individuals as they move closer to the desired set of behaviors. The following steps capture the most important elements in the process:

1. Determine the new behaviors to be learned.
2. For more complex behavior, break the new behavior down into smaller, logically arranged segments.
3. Demonstrate desired behaviors to the trainee. Research indicates that modeling appropriate behaviors is very useful.[38] Research also indicates that unless the key behaviors are distinctive and meaningful, the trainee is not likely to remember them on the job.[39]
4. Have the trainee practice the new behaviors in the presence of the trainer.
5. Make reinforcement contingent on approximations of desired behavior. At the outset, mild reinforcement can be given for a good start. As the training continues, reinforcement should be given only as progress is made. Reinforcement should be immediate, and over time behavior should be reinforced only if it comes closer to the ultimate desired behavior.[40]

In newcomer training, managers in many organizations use this approach. Trilogy, a software firm based in Austin, Texas, uses positive reinforcement as new hires work through successively more difficult assignments in a boot camp that lasts several months.[41] E.L. Harvey & Sons, a refuse collector based in Westborough, Massachusetts, has used positive reinforcement as well as mild punishment in its training and orientation program for new drivers.[42] Dallas-based Greyhound Bus Company has used positive reinforcement and mild punishment as drivers master proper city, rural, and mountain driving techniques. As one recent trainee stated, "You're not going to be perfect the first time. Some things you'll get used to doing. I'll get better."[43]

Organizations use numerous methods to train employees.[44] On-the-job training methods include orientation programs, organizational socialization experiences, apprenticeship training, coaching, formal mentoring, job rotation, career development activities, and technology-based training. Off-site training methods include instructor-led classrooms, videoconferencing, corporate universities and institutes, and virtual-reality simulators. Learning can also take place informally through trial-and-error, informal mentoring relationships, interactions with co-workers, and from learning from one's mistakes. We highlight three learning methods below: OB Mod, simulation learning, and learning from failure.

OB Mod

OB Mod
A formal procedure focused on improving task performance through positive reinforcement of desired behaviors and extinction of undesired behaviors.

To improve the performance of existing associates on ongoing tasks, organizations must be concerned not only with developing good habits but also with breaking bad ones. As an aid in this process, a formal procedure known as *organizational behavior modification,* or **OB Mod**, is often used.[45] The basic goal of OB Mod, which some refer to as *performance management,* is to improve task performance through positive reinforcement of desirable behaviors and elimination of reinforcements that support undesirable behaviors.[46] Its value lies in the specific, detailed steps that it offers.

As shown in Exhibit 4-3, the OB Mod framework can be represented as a simple flowchart. In the initial steps, managers determine desirable and undesirable behaviors and assess the extent to which individuals are currently exhibiting those behaviors. Desirable

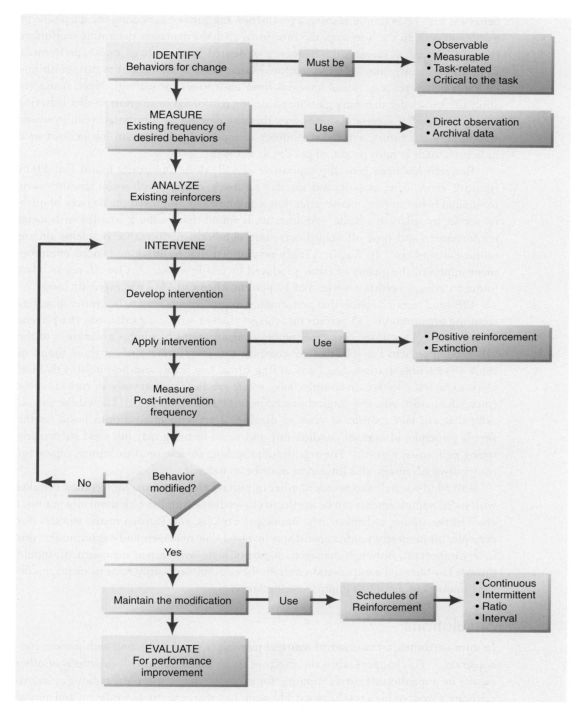

Exhibit 4-3   Shaping Behavior through OB Modification

Source: Adapted from Luthans, F., & Stajkovic, A.D. 1999. "Reinforce for Performance: The Need to Go Beyond Pay and Even Rewards," *Academy of Management Executive,* 13 (2): 49–57.

behaviors may be as simple as using a production machine or answering the telephone in a different way. In the next step, the functional analysis, managers determine reinforcers that can be used to increase the frequency of desired behavior (e.g., praise, preferential work arrangements, time off) and reinforcers that must be eliminated to extinguish undesirable behaviors (e.g., social approval from co-workers for loafing). Next, managers apply the knowledge they have gained concerning reinforcers in an effort to alter behavior in a fruitful way. If successful in this step, they can develop an appropriate reinforcement schedule for the future. Finally, the impact of modified behaviors on job performance indicators, such as units produced per day, is assessed.

Research has been generally supportive of OB Mod. One study found that PIGS (positive, immediate, graphic, and specific) feedback, coupled with social reinforcement for desired behavior (e.g., praise, attention, compliments), improved the delivery of quality service by tellers in a bank.[47] Another study found that feedback coupled with social reinforcement and time off helped overcome significant performance problems among municipal workers.[48] In Russia, a study determined that feedback and social reinforcement improved the quality of fabric produced by textile workers.[49] Overall, research has found an average performance gain of 17 percent when OB Mod was explicitly used.[50]

OB Mod research reveals that performance improvements tend to be greater in manufacturing organizations (33 percent on average) than in service organizations (13 percent on average).[51] This difference across types of organizations highlights a weakness of the OB Mod approach. For jobs that are complex and nonroutine, such as those found in some service organizations (e.g., accounting firms, law firms, and hospitals), OB Mod tends to be less effective. In complex jobs, where excellent performance in core job areas (successful audits, effective surgical procedures) is based on deep, rich knowledge and on skills that can take months or years to develop, short-term interventions based on the simple principles of operant conditioning and social learning may not yield particularly strong performance gains.[52] For organizations seeking to develop their human capital for competitive advantage, this limitation must be considered.

OB Mod research also reveals another important fact: performance feedback coupled with social reinforcements can be as effective as feedback coupled with monetary reinforcers.[53] In the studies of bank tellers, municipal workers, and Russian textile workers, for example, no monetary reinforcement was involved. For managers and organizations, this is very important. Although managers, as part of high-involvement management, should provide fair financial compensation overall, they do not necessarily need to spend significant amounts of money to improve performance.

Simulations

In some situations, an associate or manager may take a particular action with unclear consequences.[54] This happens when the effects of an action combine with the effects of other factors in unpredictable ways. Suppose, for example, that a team leader brings pizza to celebrate a week of high productivity. The team members express appreciation and appear generally pleased with the gesture, but the appreciation is not overwhelming. The team leader may conclude that having a pizza party is not worth the trouble. She may be correct, or she may be incorrect because other factors may have contributed to the situation. At the time of the pizza party, a key member of the team was out caring for a sick parent. In addition, rumors circulated among the team members that the new plant controller did

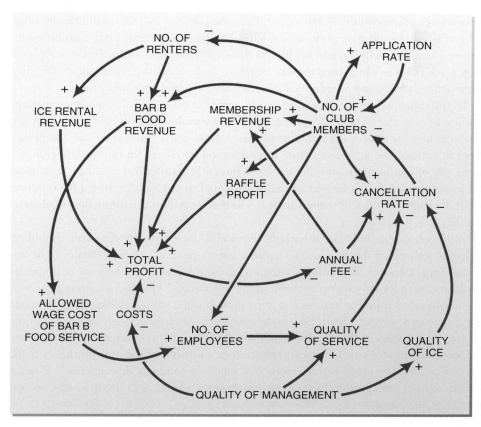

Exhibit 4-4   Causal Relationships at a Sports Club

Note: A "+" between two variables indicates a direct, noninverse relationship. When the variable at the start of an arrow exhibits an increase, there is upward pressure on the variable at the end of that arrow. When the variable at the start exhibits a decrease, there is downward pressure on the variable at the end. A "−" between two variables indicates an inverse relationship. When the variable at the start of an arrow exhibits an increase, there is downward pressure on the variable at the end of that arrow. When the variable at the start exhibits a decrease, there is upward pressure on the variable at the end.

Source: Reprinted by permission, R.D. Hall. 1983. "A Corporate System Model of a Sports Club: Using Simulation as an Aid to Policy Making in a Crisis," Management Science, 29 (1): 52–64, the Institute for Operations Research and the Management Sciences (INFORMS), 901 Elkridge Landing Road, Suite 400, Linthicum, Maryland 21090-2909 USA.

not embrace high-involvement management. Did these two factors affect the team's reaction to the pizza?

In this example, the team leader could discuss the situation with team members in order to better understand their reactions. Other situations may be so complex that discussions with team members may not be adequate. Consider the complex situation facing the general manager at a Canadian curling club. He plans to increase the annual membership fee to enhance profits. As shown in Exhibit 4-4, the annual fee does influence profits, but the effects are not clear. On the one hand, increasing the annual fee has a positive effect on revenue from membership fees because members who stay are paying more, and this in turn has a positive effect on profits. On the other hand, increasing the annual fee puts upward pressure on the cancellation rate among members and therefore downward pressure on the total number of club members. As the number of club members declines, revenue is lost, which reduces profits. What actual effect, then, will an increase in the membership fee have? Is the overall effect positive or negative? Perhaps an increase up to a point results in more revenue from the members who stay than is lost from the members who leave. But where is the point at which total revenue begins to decline? A further complication is that factors other than the membership fee influence revenues and costs and profits.

In situations where a complex system of variables exists and we have some understanding of how the variables affect one another, a **simulation** may be a useful tool for understanding the effects of a potential action. A simulation mimics the real system but allows us to take one action at a time to understand its effects. In our curling club example, the relationships among the variables shown in Exhibit 4-4 could be developed into a simulation. If the manager of the club wanted to change the annual fee to affect profits, he could implement various increases in this fee within the simulation to observe the effects.

Although simulations are important and useful, they typically represent simplified models of reality. For this reason, and because some situations are too complex to be accurately represented in simulations, some organizations prefer to substitute or augment simulations with formal experimentation in the real world.[55] The idea is to have associates and managers try different approaches, even though some will no doubt fail to discover which approach seems to work best under particular conditions. Such experimentation has often been used in the development of technology for new products,[56] and it has also been used in areas such as setting the strategic direction of the organization.[57] Bank of America is one of many organizations that regularly conducts experiments.[58] It has a number of branches specifically designated for testing new ideas in décor, kiosks, service procedures, and so on.

Learning from Failure

High-involvement firms often attempt to leverage their human capital in ways that will enhance innovation.[59] Accordingly, they often empower associates and managers to experiment. In addition to the formal experimentation discussed earlier, these organizations often promote informal and smaller-scale experimentation in almost all areas of organizational life, ranging from a manager trying a new leadership style to an associate on the assembly line trying a new method of machine setup. Such experimentation yields learning that otherwise would not occur. A manager's leadership style may have been working well, but trying a new style will provide him with information on the effectiveness of the new style.

Experimentation, however, does not always result in success; by its nature, it often produces failure. New approaches sometimes are less effective than old ways of doing things. New product ideas sometimes are not attractive in the marketplace. Gerber Singles (adult foods produced by the baby food company), Life-Savers Soda (carbonated beverages produced by the candy maker), and Ben-Gay Aspirin (pain relievers produced by the heating-rub company) are reasonable ideas that failed in the marketplace.[60]

The key is to learn from failure.[61] A failure that does not result in learning is a mistake; a failure that results in learning is an intelligent failure. Intelligent failures are the result of certain kinds of actions:[62]

- Actions are thoughtfully planned.
- Actions have a reasonable chance of producing a successful outcome.

simulation
A representation of a real system that allows associates and managers to try various actions and receive feedback on the consequences of those actions.

"We Are Ladies and Gentlemen Serving Ladies and Gentlemen"

This credo of the Ritz-Carlton Hotel Associates may seem simple. However, in order to enact it, associates must go through constant training of a quality that led *Training* magazine to name the Ritz-Carlton the number-one company for employee training and development in 2007. The Ritz-Carlton is known for its exemplary service, which has been recognized by two Malcolm Baldrige National Quality Awards and consistently high rankings in travel periodicals of the world's greatest hotels. The Ritz-Carlton has 78 hotels worldwide, with at least 14 other projects underway; 38,000 associates work for the company.

All Ritz-Carlton associates are expected to go for what the company calls the "wow" factor by not only meeting guests' needs but also anticipating them. If you order your favorite drink at a Ritz-Carlton in Hong Kong, the bartender at the Ritz-Carlton in New Orleans will know what you want when you sit down at his bar. Special room requests, such as M&Ms in the minibar, will be met each time someone visits a Ritz-Carlton without the guest ever having to ask for the favor. Special software makes such anticipatory service doable. However, this type of service could never be carried out without exceptional associate service performance.

In order to reach this performance level, all associates go through constant training throughout their careers with the Ritz-Carlton. It all begins with a two-day orientation session taught by master trainers. However, training does not stop there. New associates go through at least 310 hours of training in their first year, where they are personally paired with a departmental trainer. They receive a training certification, much like mastercraftsmen, when they can demonstrate mastery of their job. Reviews take place on days 21 and 365.

New employees are not the only associates who receive constant training. All Ritz-Carlton associates are trained continuously. Methods of training include:

- Daily meetings, where all employees give and receive feedback on what has been done right and what has been done wrong. Time is also spent discussing one of the Ritz-Carlton's 12 service values.

- On-the-job training by mentors and training directors.

- Classroom training delivery.

- Good performance is clearly rewarded either monetarily or by verbal praise. Ritz-Carlton Associates are almost twice as likely as other hotel associates to report

that they receive constructive feedback and are clearly rewarded.

Unlike many other companies, the Ritz-Carlton also devotes a great deal of time to evaluating their training programs, using knowledge tests, performance appraisals, associate and guest surveys, and quantitative service-quality measures. Their training programs are responsible for the fact that the Ritz-Carlton sets industry standards for the total revenue per hours worked, employee satisfaction, low turnover rates, and customer satisfaction. In fact, the Ritz-Carlton training methods are so successful that the company began the Leadership Center, which provides training to associates, mostly senior managers, from other companies.

©Keith Bedford/The New York Times/Redux Pictures

Sources: http://corporate.ritzcarlton.com. Anonymous, "Ritz-Carlton: Redefining Elegance (No. 1 of the Training Top 125)," *Training,* Mar. 1, 2007, at http://www.trainingmag.com; Lampton, B. 2003. "My Pleasure," *ExpertMagazine. com,* Dec. 1, at http://www.expertmagazine.com; The Ritz-Carlton Hotel Company, L.L.C., "Application Summary for the Malcolm Baldrige National Quality Award," 2000, at http://corporate.ritzcarlton.com.; Ritz-Carlton Press Release facts sheet. December, 2009, at http://corporate.ritzcarlton.com/en/Press/FactSheet.htm.

- Actions are typically modest in scale, to avoid putting the entire firm or substantial parts of it at risk.
- Actions are executed and evaluated in a speedy fashion, since delayed feedback makes learning more difficult.
- Actions are limited to domains that are familiar enough to allow proper understanding of the effects of the actions.

Firms serious about experimentation and intelligent failure create cultures that protect and nurture associates and managers willing to take calculated risks and to try new things.[63] Such cultures have visible examples of individuals who have been promoted even after having failed in trying a new approach. Such cultures also have stories of associates who have been rewarded for trying something new even though it did not work out. At IDEO, a product design firm based in Palo Alto, California, the culture is built on the idea that designers should "fail often to succeed sooner."[64] At 3-M, the global giant based in St. Paul, Minnesota, the culture is built on the idea that thoughtful failure should not be a source of shame.[65]

Learning from failure, OB Mod, and simulations are just three ways in which organizations can train associates. Many organizations, such as the Ritz-Carlton Hotel Company, use multiple methods as evidenced in the *Experiencing Organizational Behavior* feature. The Ritz-Carlton provides an excellent example of the strategic importance of training and continuous employee learning. Although the Ritz-Carlton Hotel Company spends much more on associate training than its competitors, the company sees payoff from its training on all important indicators. Customer satisfaction is higher and associates work harder and turn over less frequently at the Ritz-Carlton than they do at other hotels. This superb performance has led the Ritz-Carlton to win almost every prestigious business and training award, while making it an exceptionally successful company.

Perception

perception
A process that involves sensing various aspects of a person, task, or event and forming impressions based on selected inputs.

As we have shown in the preceding sections, associates and managers who can effectively learn from experience, and help others to do so, contribute positively to an organization's human capital and therefore contribute positively to its capacity to develop sustainable competitive advantage. To further develop the story of learning, we now turn to issues of **perception**. If an associate or manager does not perceive people, tasks, and events accurately, learning from experience is difficult. If an associate or manager does not perceive the world accurately, he will base his behavior on inaccurate perceptions of the world rather than on reality.

Associates and managers are constantly exposed to a variety of sensory inputs that influence their perceptions. Sensory inputs refer to things that are heard, seen, smelled, tasted, and touched. These inputs are processed in the mind and organized to form concepts pertaining to what has been sensed or experienced. For instance, an associate in a catering firm may sense a common item such as a loaf of bread. He touches it, squeezes it, smells it, looks at its shape and color, and tastes it. His mind processes all of the sensory inputs, and he forms ideas and attitudes about that loaf of bread and the bakery that produced it. He may determine that the bread is fresh or stale, good or bad, worth the price or not, and may subsequently decide whether products of this particular bakery are to be used. These are his perceptions of the bread and of the producer.

Perception comprises three basic stages:[66]

1. *Sensing various characteristics of a person, task, or event.* This stage consists of using the senses (touch, sight, smell, and so on) to obtain data. Some data in the environment, however, cannot be detected by the sensory organs. For example, operators of the Three Mile Island nuclear facility, which almost melted down in the 1970s, could not sense that a relief valve was stuck open in the nuclear core because they could not see it and the instrument panel indicated that it was closed.[67] Some data, though accessible, are not sensed. Engineers and managers with NASA and Morton Thiokol failed to sense certain features of their booster rockets when considering whether to launch the ill-fated *Challenger* shuttle in the 1980s.[68]

2. *Selecting from the data those facts that will be used to form the perception.* An individual does not necessarily use all of the data that she senses. At times, a person may be overloaded by information and unable to use all of it. For example, U.S. Defense Department officials dealt with overwhelming amounts of data from various sources with regard to the events of September 11 and the conflict in Iraq. At other times, a person may purposely exclude information that is inconsistent with her other existing perceptions. A manager who firmly believes an associate is a weak performer, for example, may discount and ultimately exclude information suggesting otherwise.[69] Accurate perception, however, requires the use of all relevant information.

3. *Organizing the selected data into useful concepts pertaining to the object or person.* An individual must order and sort data in a way that is useful in establishing approaches to dealing with the world. We now explore this aspect of perception in discussing perceptions of people.

©Ron Galella/WireImage/Getty Images, Inc.

©E.Neitzel/WireImage/Getty Images, Inc.

Perceptions of People

Shortcomings in the ability to sense the full range of data, to select appropriate data for further processing, and to organize the data into useful information can lead to inaccurate perceptions about people.[70] These erroneous perceptions in turn can interfere with learning how to best interact with a person and can lead to poor decisions about and actions toward the person. Effective associates and managers are able to develop complete and accurate perceptions of the various people with whom they interact—customers, sales representatives, peers, and so on. An effective manager, for example, knows when a sales representative is sincere, when an associate has truly achieved superior performance, and when another manager is dependable. These accurate perceptions are crucial to a firm's human capital that contributes to competitive advantage. Next, we discuss several factors that influence the process of perceiving other people. These factors are shown in Exhibit 4-5.

The Nature of the Perceiver

The perception process is influenced by several factors related to the nature of the perceiver. Impaired hearing or sight and temporary conditions such as those induced by alcohol or prescribed medications can, of course, affect perception. Beyond those challenges, the most important factors are the perceiver's familiarity with the other person, the perceiver's existing feelings about the other person, and the emotional state of the perceiver.

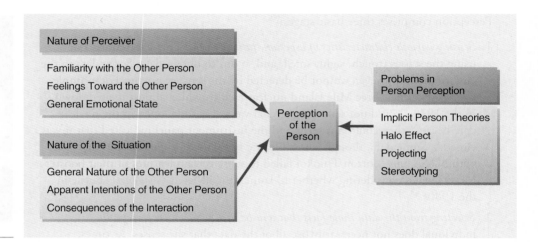

Exhibit 4-5 Person Perception

Familiarity with the person is important. On the one hand, an individual may have more accurate perceptions of people with whom she has had a substantial history. Over time, the individual has had many opportunities to observe those people. On the other hand, an individual may pay more attention to newcomers, making extra efforts to notice and process data about them.

If an individual has put a great deal of effort over time into properly understanding certain people, she probably has developed accurate perceptions of their characteristics and abilities. If, however, those characteristics and abilities change, or if the people act in ways that are not consistent with their longstanding characteristics and abilities, the perceiving individual may not accurately interpret the new characteristics or behaviors. In this case, the perceiver may be too focused on existing beliefs about the friends and associates to accurately interpret new characteristics or behaviors. A manager who has had an excellent, trusting relationship with an associate over many years may thus disregard evidence of lying or poor performance because it does not fit preexisting conceptions of the person.[71]

An individual's feelings about another person also may affect the perception process. If the individual generally has positive feelings toward a particular person, he may view the person's actions through a favorable lens and thus may interpret those actions more positively than is warranted. In contrast, if the individual generally has negative feelings toward a particular person, he may view the person's actions through an unfavorable lens and thus interpret those actions more negatively than is warranted.

Research conducted at a large multinational firm provides evidence for these commonsense effects. In this research, 344 middle managers were rated by 272 superiors, 470 peers, and 608 associates. The feelings of the 1,350 raters were assessed through measures of admiration, respect, and liking. Raters who had positive feelings toward a particular ratee consistently rated his or her performance more leniently than they should have. Raters who had negative feelings rated performance too severely.[72]

An individual's emotional state may also affect perceptions of others. If the individual is happy and excited, she may perceive others as more exuberant and cheerful than they really are. If the individual is sad and depressed, she may perceive others as more unhappy than they really are or even as more sinister than they really are. For example, in one study, several women judged photographs of faces after they had played a frightening game called "Murder." Those women perceived the faces to be more menacing than did women who had not played the game.[73]

The Nature of the Situation

Factors present in a situation can affect whether an associate or manager senses important information, and these factors can influence whether this information is used in perceptions. Relevant factors are numerous and varied. Three of them are discussed here: obvious characteristics of the other person, the other person's apparent intentions, and the consequences of interactions with the person.

As previously discussed, an individual's perceptions of another person can be influenced by his own internal states and emotions. In addition, the individual's perceptions of another person are affected by that person's most obvious characteristics (those that stand out). For instance, the perceiver is likely to notice things that are intense, bright, noisy, or in motion. He is also likely to notice highly attractive and highly unattractive people, people dressed in expensive clothes and those dressed in clothes reflecting poor taste, and bright, intelligent people or extremely dull-witted ones. He is less likely to notice normal or average people. This effect on perceptions has been demonstrated in research.[74]

In organizations, extremely good and bad performers may be noticed more than average associates. Managers must be aware of this tendency because most associates are average. Large numbers of associates may go unnoticed, unrewarded, and passed over for promotions, even though they have the potential to contribute to a firm's goals and to the achievement of competitive advantage.

An individual's perceptions may also be affected by the assumed intentions behind another person's actions. If, for example, assumed intentions are undesirable from the perceiver's point of view, the other person may be seen as threatening or hostile.[75]

Finally, an individual may be affected by the consequences of a single interaction with another person. If the consequences are basically positive, the individual is likely to perceive the other person favorably. If, however, the results of the interaction are negative, the individual is more likely to view the other person unfavorably.

©Tobi Corney/Getty Images, Inc.

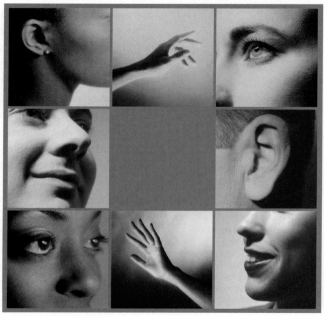

In one study, a researcher's accomplice was the only member of a work group to fail on the assigned task. The study included two conditions. In one condition, the accomplice's failure prevented the other members from receiving payment for the task. This accomplice was perceived unfavorably (as less competent, less dependable, and less likable). In a second condition, the other members received payment despite the accomplice's failure. This accomplice was seen as being more competent, dependable, and likable, even though the actual level of performance was the same as the first accomplice's.[76]

Problems in Person Perception

The preceding discussion shows that perceiving others accurately can be challenging. In fact, some of the most noteworthy conflicts in organizations have been the result of misperceiving others. In a well-known example involving Apple Computer, a midlevel manager in charge of distribution misperceived the character and motives of a manager in charge of one of the manufacturing operations, resulting in a battle that was unnecessarily protracted.[77] The distribution manager almost resigned her job with the organization before realizing the other manager was not committed to dismantling the existing distribution function. Because perceptions influence how associates and managers behave toward one another, it is important to strengthen our understanding of the perceptual process so that our perceptions of others reflect reality.

The perceptual process is influenced by factors associated with both the perceiver and the general situation. The problems that prevent the formation of accurate perceptions arise from factors that can be ordered into four general problem groups: implicit personality theories, halo effect, projecting, and stereotyping.

implicit person theories
Personal theories about what personality traits and abilities occur together and how these attributes are manifested in behavior.

People hold **implicit person theories**,[78] which are personal theories about what personality traits and abilities occur together and how these attributes are manifested in behavior. For example, if an associate notices that her colleague's office is brightly decorated and messy, she may infer that this associate will be very talkative and outgoing because her implicit personality theory states that messiness and extraversion go together.[79] One type of implicit personality theory that individuals hold concerns whether people believe that personality traits and abilities are fixed and unchangeable in people.[80] Those who believe that people cannot change are called *entity theorists,* while those who believe that people's attributes such as skills and abilities can change and develop are called *incremental theorists.* Research has shown that managers who hold an entity theorist perspective are less likely to help and coach their subordinates because they believe that their behavior is unchangeable.[81]

halo effect
A perception problem in which an individual assesses a person positively or negatively in all situations based on an existing general assessment of the person.

The **halo effect** occurs when a person makes a general assessment of another person (such as "good" or "bad"), and then uses this general impression to interpret everything that the person does, regardless of whether the general impression accurately portrays the behavior.[82] With regard to the halo effect, if a person is perceived as generally "good," a manager or associate will tend to view the person in a positive way in any circumstance or on any evaluative measure. Thus, if Marianne is perceived as being a generally "good" person, she may be seen as an active, positive force in the organization's culture even if she is actually neutral in promoting a positive culture. If Ted is perceived as being a "bad" person, he may be considered insolent and cunning even if he does not truly exhibit those particular negative traits. In the many studies of this phenomenon, halo error has been found in ratings given to job candidates, teachers, ice skaters, and others.[83]

projecting
A perception problem in which an individual assumes that others share his or her values and beliefs.

Assuming that most other people have the same values and beliefs as we do is known as **projecting**. For example, a production manager may think that lathe operators should always check with her on important decisions. The production manager may also believe that the lathe operators prefer this checking to making their own decisions. This may be an inaccurate perception, however, and the lathe operators may complain about the need to check with the manager. Obviously, falsely believing that other persons share our beliefs can lead to ineffective behavior. Specific problems include overestimating consensus, undervaluing objective assessments, and undervaluing those with opposing views.[84]

stereotyping
A perception problem in which an individual bases perceptions about members of a group on a generalized set of beliefs about the characteristics of a group of individuals.

As already noted in Chapter 2, when an individual has preconceived ideas or perceptions about a certain group of people, **stereotyping** can occur. When the individual meets someone who is obviously a member of a particular group, he may perceive that person as having the general characteristics attributed to the group rather than perceiving the person as an individual with a unique set of characteristics.[85] For example, a manager may perceive union members (a group) to be strong, assertive troublemakers. When she meets John, a union member, she perceives him to be a troublemaker simply because he is a union member. This type of perceptual problem is commonly found among managers who deal ineffectively with union leaders, associates who deal ineffectively with members of the other gender, and associates who deal ineffectively with members of other ethnic groups.

To fully leverage its human assets, an organization must have associates and managers who respect one other and appreciate the unique characteristics of each person. Stereotyping can interfere with these outcomes. Effective, productive interactions require accurate perceptions of people, and stereotypes are frequently incorrect, for two reasons. First, the stereotyped characteristics of a group may simply be wrong. Erroneous stereotypes may result from a number of factors, such as fear of a group and contact with only a select subset of a group. Obviously, when the stereotype itself is inaccurate, applying the stereotype to an individual can only result in error. Second, even if stereotyped characteristics of a group are generally correct, any given individual within the group is unlikely to have all, or even most, of the characteristics attributed to the group.

One basis for stereotyping individuals is their physical attractiveness. Elysa Yanowitz was fired by L'Oreal USA, Inc. for not firing a Macy's saleswoman who was "not good looking enough."[86] A company executive said, "Get me somebody hot" for the job. Annette McConnell, a sales company employee who weighed 300 pounds, was told by a manager that "they were going to lay me off because people don't like buying from fat people."[87] It is well documented that people associate those who are physically attractive with positive qualities and those who are unattractive with negative qualities.[88] Thus, perceptions of a person's attractiveness and/or weight can influence how they are evaluated on the job and even how much they get paid.[89] For example, overweight women were found to earn 7 to 30 percent less than normal-weight women performing at the same level in the same jobs.[90] Such bias, while usually not illegal, is strategically unsound for organizations. Bias of this type means that organizations are making less-than-optimal decisions about how to use their human capital.[91] Furthermore, such unfair treatment can be demoralizing and stressful and may lead associates to perform at less-than-optimal levels.[92] In some cases, such as the L'Oreal case, such treatment can lead to charges of sex discrimination when men and women are held to different attractiveness standards.[93] As discussed in Chapter 2, such cases are extremely costly for organizations, not to mention the individuals involved.

Self-Perception

It is widely recognized that perceptions of others have important consequences, but an individual's perception of self may have important consequences as well. Individuals who perceive themselves as highly competent are likely to try new approaches to tasks and perhaps be more productive than their peers. Self-confidence is a powerful force. In an examination of lower-level managers, self-perceptions of competence were found to play a significant role in task performance.[94]

Attributions of Causality

As individuals consider the behavior of others, they will perceive that actions have various causes. Different people, however, may see the same behavior as being caused by different

Great Bear Wilderness Crash

©AP/Wide World Photos

Flight SEA04GA192 took off from Glacier National Park airport on September 20, 2004. On board were five people, including pilot Jim Long, 60; Chief of Party, Ken Good, 58; and forestry scientists Davita Bryant, 32; Matthew Ramige, 29; and Jodee Hogg, 23. They were heading for Schafer Meadows, an airstrip in 1.5 million acres of Montana wilderness. They were heading out to collect forestry data for the U.S. Forest Service. The weather that day was horrible, with low clouds obscuring mountain peaks. Flight SEA04GA192 never reached her destination. Two days later, only two of the crew members barely survived, Matthew Ramige and Jodee Hogg. The rest of the crew lay dead at the site of the plane crash in the Great Bear Wilderness.

The weather, which had hampered visibility, led pilot Long to abandon the planned flight course. The plane flew into a boxed canyon with mountain walls on three sides and no way out. At the last minute, Long attempted to turn out of the canyon and crashed into the side of the mountain. Pilot Long and forestry scientist Bryant were killed at the time of the crash. Ken Good died at the crash site the following morning. The next day, Ramige and Hogg walked out of the canyon by themselves, without being rescued. They were found two days later when they reached civilization. Thus, apart from the disaster of the crash, there was also the failure of the search team to find the survivors.

While weather seems the most obvious cause of this problem, closer examination reveals that human error, based on a lack of learning and misguided perceptions, played a role in this disaster. Based on recollections of survivors Hogg and Ramige, there was confusion between pilot Long and Chief of Party Good when the plane ran into trouble. When trying to call in the plane's location, Good was unable to do so.

"Ken tried to radio in and Jim—I think Jim ended up actually making the radio because Ken didn't know the code word. ... [H]e looked at Jim and said, What's your number? ... He's like, Okay, How do you do it? And Jim's like, Here. Just let me do it. And Ken is like, I really want to do it, blah, blah, blah. ..."

Furthermore, while Good had superior knowledge of the area, Long failed to take his advice, possibly because he did not know how to

factors. For example, suppose two people observe someone busily working at a task. Both may conclude that he is being positively reinforced for the task, but they may disagree about the nature of the reinforcement. One of the observers may believe that the person is making diligent efforts "because the boss is looking and smiling," whereas the other observer may believe the efforts are caused by the satisfaction inherent in doing the task. As evidenced in the *Experiencing Organizational Behavior* section, Pilot Long inaccurately concluded that Ken Good's lack of knowledge about how to radio was due to a general lack of knowledge, and thus, later ignored his expert advice about their location. He could have concluded that Ken Good's lack of knowledge about the radio was simply due to his not knowing the correct password. The process of deciding what caused the behavior is known as *attribution*.[95]

Internal–External Attribution

A person's behavior is often interpreted as having been caused by either internal factors (such as personality, attitudes, and abilities) or external factors (such as organizational call in their location. Thus, he attributed Long's inability to use the radio as being due to his general lack of knowledge, and may have assumed he didn't know about anything. Indeed, right before the crash, pilot Long had radioed in a wrong position, after arguing with Good about it. Clearly, if these two men had been able to learn from each other, this disaster may have been avoided. Furthermore, Long was a retired chemist, who had very little experience flying in this type of terrain and certainly under these weather conditions. He just did not have the experience to handle the crisis situation.

A second tragic aspect of this disaster is that the search party arrived at the site of the accident the next day, September 21, after searching the wrong location. They surveyed the crash site and declared that there were no survivors, when in fact Hogg and Ramige had left the site after realizing that the search plane flying overhead had not seen them. Rather than looking for the survivors, it was just assumed that they were dead and that their bodies had been burned in the plane crash. Search efforts were canceled and the families were notified that their loved ones had perished. When asked to explain how they had made this mistake, the searchers blamed the survivors, rather than their own misreading of the scene. They stated, "There were no footprints leaving the site, no piled rocks, no written message—nothing indicating anyone had survived or left the area." Clearly, they had failed to learn from their error and engaged in making self-serving bias attributions for their failure to rescue the survivors.

In the end, learning, or lack of it, played a big role in this disaster. If Long and Good had been willing or able to learn from each other, the crash may have been avoided. If the search team were more accurate in their perceptions, Ken Good's life may have been saved and Jodee Hogg and Matthew Ramige would not have had to suffer for two days in the bitter cold wilderness while severely wounded.

Sources: W.S. Becker, & M.J. Burke. 2008. "Shared decision making in a wilderness aviation accident." In M. Burke (Chair), Shared Decision Making in Singular Events. Symposium at the 2008 Annual Meeting of the Academy of Management, Anaheim, California; W.S. Becker. 2007. "Missed Opportunities: The Great Bear Wilderness Disaster," *Organizational Dynamics, 36;* 363–376.; National Transportation Safety Board (NTSB. (2005). *Aircraft Accident Report: SEA04GA192, Essex, MT, September 20, 2004.* Washington, D.C. Probable Cause and Narrative Report; U.S. Department of Agriculture Forest Service (USFS) (2005). *Accident Investigation Factual Report.* Press Release FS-025A USDA Forest Service, 9/23/2004.

resources, luck, and uncontrollable influences). When making these internal–external attributions, we depend to a great extent on our perceptions of the consistency, consensus, and distinctiveness associated with the behavior.

- *Consistency* is the extent to which the same person behaves in the same manner in the same situation over time (he returns from lunch late every day).
- *Consensus* is the degree to which other people in the same situation behave in the same manner (everyone returns from lunch late).
- *Distinctiveness* is the degree to which the same person tends to behave differently in other situations (he returns from lunch late every day but does not come to work late in the morning or leave work early at night).[96]

As shown in Exhibit 4-6, when we see a person's behavior as high in consistency, low in consensus, and low in distinctiveness, we tend to attribute that behavior to internal factors. If the behavior is low in consistency, high in consensus, and high in distinctiveness, we tend to attribute the behavior to external factors. If the behavior is perceived as having

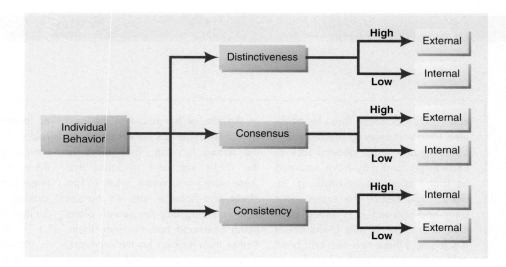

Exhibit 4-6
Attribution Theory

a mixed profile (such as high in consistency and high in distinctiveness with consensus being neutral), we often are biased toward internal attributions.

Studies have highlighted many situations in which internal and external attributions play major roles in attitudes and behavior. For example, one study suggests that unemployment counselors and their clients are influenced by these attributions in contrasting ways. On the one hand, unemployed persons are at the greatest risk for mental depression when they believe their situation is caused by uncontrollable external factors. The less control we perceive ourselves to have over events, the more likely we are to become despondent. On the other hand, a counselor is more likely to help an unemployed person if she sees that the unemployment is caused by uncontrollable external factors. If the counselor has attributed the cause of a client's unemployment to an internal factor (such as poor attitude or low motivation), she is less likely to be helpful.[97] Interestingly, researchers suggest that, in general, observers tend to overestimate the impact of internal causes on other people's behavior and underestimate the effect of external causes. This general tendency is called the **fundamental attribution error**.[98]

Attributions of Success and Failure

Monitoring and responding to poor performance are important tasks for managers and, in high-involvement organizations, for associates as well. To respond appropriately, managers must accurately assess the cause of any poor performance they observe. If they are unable to accurately identify the cause, individuals could suffer or benefit unjustly. Unfortunately, several troublesome attributional tendencies play a role.

First, the fundamental attribution error has an effect, although it may be minor. This error causes managers to attribute the behavior of others to internal factors. Thus, an individual's poor performance may have an external cause, but a manager may attribute it to an internal cause. For example, equity fund managers who perform poorly are often subjected to unfair criticism from those above them in the firm. Although skill is involved, fund-manager performance is often determined by uncontrollable factors.

Second, the **self-serving bias** plays a role, and it often has a significant effect on attributions. This bias works as follows. We have a strong tendency to attribute our own successes to internal factors (a high level of skill or hard work) and our own failures to

fundamental attribution error

A perception problem in which an individual is too likely to attribute the behavior of others to internal rather than external causes.

self-serving bias

A perception problem in which an individual is too likely to attribute the failure of others to internal causes and the successes of others to external causes, whereas the same individual will be too likely to attribute his own failure to external causes and his own successes to internal causes.

external causes (a difficult task or bad luck). Conversely, we tend to attribute someone else's success to external factors and someone else's failures to internal factors. We saw this bias at work when the rescue team in the Great Bear Wilderness case blamed the survivors for the team's failure to recognize that there had been survivors.

The fundamental attribution error and the self-serving bias work together to produce a significant bias toward assessments of internal causation for poor performance.[99] This bias means that managers and others make evaluation errors more often than they should. Was the Three Mile Island nuclear disaster in the late 1970s a function of several unforeseeable events coming together unexpectedly or a function of simple operator error? Operators received much of the blame, but it is not clear that they deserved it.[100] Are failures of new ventures typically a function of uncontrollable market developments or the missteps of entrepreneurs? Entrepreneurs receive much of the blame from venture capitalists,[101] but they may not deserve as much blame as they receive.

Task Perception

As we have described, perceptions of people and their behavior are created in subjective ways. Similarly, perceptions of tasks develop through subjective and sometimes idiosyncratic processes. Factors such as intelligence, age, and gender have been found to influence perceptions of tasks. One study, for example, found that individuals with higher levels of intelligence perceive more complexity in various tasks than individuals with lower levels of intelligence.[102] In addition, many studies have found that individuals with higher levels of satisfaction in the workplace perceive more autonomy and variety in their tasks than individuals with lower levels of satisfaction. In a study focused on

THE STRATEGIC LENS

Organizations compete on the basis of their resources. The strongest organizations usually win the competitive battles if their managers develop effective strategies and implement them well. To be competitive, managers use the organization's resources to create capabilities to act.[107] A critical component of these capabilities is knowledge. In fact, Bill Breen of *Fast Company* suggests that "Companies compete with their brains as well as their brawn. Organizations today must not only outgun and outhustle competitors, they must also outthink them. Companies win with ideas."[108]

Given the importance of knowledge in gaining a competitive advantage, learning is critical to organizational success. Managers and associates must continuously learn if they are to stay ahead of the competition. Perception is a key component of learning. It is particularly important to top executives, as they must carefully and thoroughly analyze their organization's external environment, with special emphasis on competitors. If they do not perceive their environment correctly, these executives may formulate ineffective strategies and cause the organization to lose its competitive advantage. Understanding the

concepts of learning and perception, then, is absolutely essential to the effective operation of an organization.

Critical Thinking Questions

1. How does the knowledge held by managers and associates affect the performance of an organization?

2. What are some important ways in which associates can learn and thereby enhance their stock of knowledge? What role does perception play in the learning process?

3. What are the connections between learning, perception, and organizational strategies?

past graduates of a Hong Kong university, satisfaction and job perceptions were assessed multiple times over a two-year period. Satisfaction was found to influence job perceptions to a greater extent than job perceptions were found to influence satisfaction.[103]

How managers and associates perceive their jobs has important implications for behavior and outcomes. Task perceptions have been linked to intrinsic motivation as well as job performance.[104] They have even been linked to mood.[105] One group of researchers proposed that employees first perceive their jobs at an information level, then perceive the tasks at an evaluative level, and thereafter react to their jobs behaviorally and emotionally.[106] The process of task perception and the resulting effects on behavior have important consequences for organizations. We explore these issues in greater depth in Chapter 6.

What This Chapter Adds to Your Knowledge Portfolio

In this chapter, we have discussed basic learning principles and described how they can be used in effectively training and developing associates and managers. We have discussed problems that can occur in complex learning situations and how these problems can be avoided. Finally, we have seen many problems associated with perception processes. For individuals to function as effectively as possible, these perception issues must be understood and managed. At a more detailed level, we have covered the following points:

- Learning is the process by which we acquire new, relatively permanent, behaviors from experience. Operant conditioning theory and social learning theory are important explanations for how learning from experience works in practice. Learning new behaviors involves three basic elements: the situation, the behavioral response to the situation, and the consequences of that response for the person.

- Positive reinforcement involves the presentation of positive consequences for a behavior, such as praise for working hard, which increases the probability of an individual repeating the behavior in similar settings. Negative reinforcement is the removal of a negative consequence following a behavior, such as taking an employee off probation, which also increases the probability of an individual repeating the behavior. Punishment involves the presentation of negative consequences, such as a reduction in pay, which reduces the probability of repeating a behavior. Extinction refers to the removal of all reinforcing consequences, which can be effective in eliminating undesired behaviors.

- Various schedules of reinforcement exist for learning, including continuous reinforcement and several types of intermittent schedules. Although continuous schedules are rare in organizational settings, several applications of intermittent schedules can be found. Strategic use of reinforcement schedules helps in effectively shaping the behavior of newcomers and modifying the behavior of current associates and managers.

- In addition to direct reinforcement or punishment, individuals also learn by anticipating potential outcomes associated with certain behaviors and by modeling similar or important others.

- Self-efficacy is an important condition for learning to occur. Other important conditions are that people know why they are learning what they are learning, that they can tie the material to be learned to their own previous experiences, that they have the opportunity to practice, and that they receive feedback.

- People learn through many formal and informal mechanisms in organizations. Three examples are OB Mod programs, simulations, and learning from failure.
- Perception refers to the way people view the world around them. It is the process of receiving sensory inputs and organizing these inputs into useful ideas and concepts. The process consists of three stages: sensing, selecting, and organizing.
- Person perception is influenced by several factors associated with the nature of the perceiver, including the perceiver's familiarity with the person, feelings toward the person, and general emotional state. Situational factors influencing person perception include the general nature of the other person, that person's apparent intentions, and the anticipated or actual consequences of the interaction between perceiver and perceived.

back to the knowledge objectives

1. Explain the difference between negative reinforcement and punishment. Give examples of how each process might be used by managers with their associates.
2. What are four intermittent schedules of reinforcement? Give an example of how each schedule might be used by managers with their associates.
3. Explain how an instructor might effectively apply OB Mod in the classroom.
4. What can an organization do to promote learning from failure?
5. What can organizations do to train people to deal with complex and novel problems?
6. What are implicit person theories and the halo effect? How can an individual overcome a tendency to make these mistakes?
7. Give an example of a situation in which you attributed someone's behavior to internal or external factors. What influenced the attribution?

- Four general perceptual problems are implicit person theories, halo effect, projecting, and stereotyping. Implicit person theories are individuals' beliefs about the nature of human personality and attributes that can influence how they perceive other people. Halo effect is similar but involves having a general impression of a person and allowing it to affect perceptions of all other aspects of the person. Projecting is the tendency to believe that other people have characteristics like our own. Stereotyping occurs when we have generalized perceptions about a group that we apply to an individual who belongs to that group.
- Attribution refers to the process by which individuals interpret the causes of behavior. Whether behavior is seen as resulting from internal or external forces is influenced by three factors: distinctiveness, consistency, and consensus. Beyond these factors, there is a general tendency to attribute someone else's failures to internal causes.

Key Terms

learning, p. 121
operant conditioning
   theory, p. 122
social learning theory, p. 122
positive reinforcement, p. 123
negative reinforcement, p. 123
punishment, p. 123

extinction, p. 124
continuous reinforcement, p. 126
intermittent reinforcement, p. 126
self-efficacy, p. 128
OB Mod, p. 130
simulation, p. 134
perception, p. 136

implicit person theories, p. 140
halo effect, p. 140
projecting, p. 140
stereotyping, p. 140
fundamental attribution
   error, p. 144
self-serving bias, p. 144

Assessment of Approaches Used to Handle Difficult Learning Situations

Associates and managers often face difficulties in learning from experience. When there is little opportunity to learn from experience and when experience is unclear, individuals at all levels in an organization may draw the wrong conclusions. Interestingly, individuals vary in how they handle these situations. Some are prone to contemplate major issues alone. Others tend to discuss major issues with others. Both approaches can be useful, but extremes in either direction may be risky. In this installment of *Building Your Human Capital*, we present an assessment tool focused on approaches to handling difficult learning situations.

Instructions

In this assessment, you will read 12 phrases that describe people. Use the rating scale below to indicate how accurately each phrase describes *you*. Rate yourself as you generally are now, not as you wish to be in the future, and rate yourself as you honestly see yourself. Keep in mind that very few people have extreme scores on all or even most of the items (a "1" or a "5" is an extreme score); most people have midrange scores for many of the items. Read each item carefully, and then circle the number that corresponds to your choice from the rating scale.

1	2	3	4	5
Not at all like me	Somewhat unlike me	Neither like nor unlike me	Somewhat like me	Very much like me

1. Spend time reflecting on things.	1	2	3	4	5
2. Enjoy spending time by myself.	1	2	3	4	5
3. Live in a world of my own.	1	2	3	4	5
4. Enjoy my privacy.	1	2	3	4	5
5. Don't mind eating alone.	1	2	3	4	5
6. Can't stand being alone.	1	2	3	4	5
7. Do things at my own pace.	1	2	3	4	5
8. Enjoy contemplation.	1	2	3	4	5
9. Prefer to be alone.	1	2	3	4	5
10. Have point of view all my own.	1	2	3	4	5
11. Don't like to ponder over things.	1	2	3	4	5
12. Want to be left alone.	1	2	3	4	5

Scoring Key for Approaches to Handling Difficult Learning Situations

To create your score, combine your responses to the items as follows:

Private reflection = (Item 1 + Item 2 + Item 3 + Item 4 + Item 5 + Item 7 + Item 8 + Item 9 + Item 10 + Item 12) + (12 − (Item 6 + Item 11))

Scores can range from 12 to 60. Scores of 50 and above may be considered high, while scores of 22 and below may be considered low. Other scores are moderate. High scores suggest that a person prefers to spend time alone considering major issues (high private reflection). Such a person spends quality quiet time considering the possibilities. Low scores suggest that a person prefers to talk through problems with others (low private reflection). This type of person spends time exchanging information and viewpoints with others.

Additional Task

Think of a time when you faced a major problem with no clear answer. Did you handle the situation mostly by thinking alone, mostly by consulting with others, or with a mix of these two approaches? How effective was your approach? Explain.

Source of the Assessment Tool: International Personality Item Pool (2001). A Scientific Collaboration for the Development of Advanced Measures of Personality Traits and Other Individual Differences, at http://ipip.ori.org.

an organizational behavior moment
It's Just a Matter of Timing

Teresa Alvarez ate dinner slowly and without enthusiasm. Mike, her husband of only a few months, had learned that Teresa's "blue funks" were usually caused by her job. He knew that it was best to let her work out the problem alone. He excused himself and went to watch TV. Teresa poked at her dinner, but the large knot in her stomach kept her from eating much.

She had been very excited when Vegas Brown had approached her about managing his small interior decorating firm. At the time, she was a loan officer for a local bank and knew Vegas through his financial dealings with the bank. As Vegas explained to her, his biggest problem was in managing the firm's financial assets, mostly because the firm was undercapitalized. It was not a severe problem, he assured her. "Mostly," he had said, "it's a cash flow problem. We have to be sure that the customers pay their accounts in time to pay our creditors. With your experience, you should be able to ensure a timely cash flow."

Teresa thought this was a good opportunity to build her managerial skills, since she had never had full responsibility for a company. It also meant a substantial raise in salary. After exploring the opportunity with Mike, she accepted the job.

During her first week with Vegas, she discovered that the financial problems were much more severe than he had led her to believe. The firm's checking account was overdrawn by about $40,000. There was a substantial list of creditors, mostly companies that sold furniture and carpeting to the firm on short-term credit. She was astonished that this financial position did not seem to bother Vegas.

"All you have to do, Teresa, is collect enough money each day to cover the checks we have written to our creditors. As you'll see, I'm the best sales rep in the business, so we have lots of money coming in. It's just a matter of timing. With you here, we should turn this problem around in short order."

Teresa, despite her misgivings, put substantial effort into the new job. She worked late almost every day and began to realize that it was more than simple cash-flow timing. For example, if the carpet layers made an error or if the furniture came in damaged, the customer would refuse to pay. This would mean that the

customer's complaint must be serviced. However, the carpet layers disliked correcting service complaints, and furniture reorders might take several weeks.

Thus, Teresa personally began to examine all customer orders at crucial points in the process. Eventually, this minimized problems with new orders, but there remained a large number of old orders still awaiting corrections.

Teresa also arranged a priority system for paying creditors that eased some financial pressures in the short run and that would allow old, noncritical debts to be repaid when old customer accounts were repaid. After six months, the day arrived when the checking account had a zero balance, which was substantial progress. A few weeks later, it actually had a $9,000 positive balance. During all this time Teresa had made a point of concealing the financial status from Vegas. But with the $9,000 positive balance, she felt elated and told Vegas.

Vegas was ecstatic, said she had done a remarkable job, and gave her an immediate raise. Then it was Teresa's turn to be ecstatic. She had turned a pressure-packed job into one of promise. The future looked exciting, and the financial pressures had developed into financial opportunities. But that was last week.

This morning Vegas came into Teresa's office and asked her to write him a check for $30,000. Vegas said everything was looking so good that he was buying a new home for his family ($30,000 was the down payment). Teresa objected violently. "But this will overdraw our account by $21,000 again. I just got us out of one hole, and you want to put us back in. Either you delay the home purchase or I quit. I'm not going to go through all the late nights and all the pressure again because of some stupid personal decision you make. Can't you see what it means for the business to have money in the bank?"

"No, I can't!" Vegas said sternly. "I don't want to have money in the bank. It doesn't do me any good there. I'll just go out and keep selling our services, and the money will come in like always. You've proved to me that it's just a matter of timing. Quit if you want, but I'm going to buy the house. It's still my company, and I'll do what I want."

Discussion Questions

1. What did Teresa learn?
2. Other than quitting, what can Teresa do to resolve the problem? What learning and perception factors should she consider as she analyzes the situation?

3. If you were an outside consultant to the firm, could you recommend solutions that might not occur to Teresa or Vegas? What would they be?

---

team exercise
Best Bet for Training

Management-development programs are expensive. When organizations are determining which of several managers to send to these programs, they must evaluate each person. Some of the criteria considered might be whether the manager has the ability to learn, whether the manager and the organization will benefit, and whether a manager is moving into or has recently moved into a new position. The purpose of this exercise is to evaluate three potential candidates for developmental training, thus gaining insight into the process.

The exercise should take about 20 minutes to complete and an additional 15 to 20 minutes to discuss. The steps are as follows.

1. Read the following case about *High Tech International*.
2. Assemble into groups of four.
3. List the criteria you should consider for determining which of the three managers to send to the training program.
4. Choose the manager to send using the criteria developed in step 3.
5. Reassemble. Discuss your group's choice with the rest of the class, and listen to other groups' choices and criteria. Do you still prefer your group's choice? Why or why not?
6. The instructor will present additional points for consideration.

High Tech International

High Tech International has reserved one training slot every other year in an off-site leadership-development program. The program emphasizes personal and professional assessment and requires six days of residency to complete. High Tech's vice president for human resources must choose the manager to attend the next available program, which is to be run in three months. The cost of the program is high, including a tuition fee of $7,500, round-trip airfare, and lodging. The challenge is to choose the individual who has the greatest capacity to learn from the assessment and apply that learning back in the organization. Because of prior commitments and ongoing projects, the list of nominees has been narrowed to three:

- Gerry is slated for a major promotion in four months from regional sales manager to vice president for marketing. Her division has run smoothly during the past three years. Anticipating the move upward, she has asked for training to increase her managerial skills. Gerry is to be married in two months.

- John was a supervisor over a portion of a production process for two years before being promoted one year ago to manager of the entire process. His unit has been under stress for the past eight months due to the implementation of new technology and a consequent decline in productivity and morale. No new technological changes are planned in John's unit for at least another year.

- Bill has been considered a "fast-tracker" by his colleagues in the organization. He came to the company four years ago, at the age of 37, as a vice president for foreign operations. Historically, this position has been the stepping stone for division president. In the past year, Bill has displayed less energy and enthusiasm for the work. Eight months ago Bill and his wife separated, and two months ago he was hospitalized temporarily with a mild heart problem. For one month twice a year Bill has to travel abroad. His next trip will be in four months.

Endnotes

1. Hitt, M.A., Bierman, L., Shimizu, K., & Kochhar, R. 2001. Direct and moderating effects of human capital on strategy and performance in professional service firms: A resource-based perspective. *Academy of Management Journal,* 44: 13–28; Sirmon, D.G., Hitt, M.A., & Ireland, R.D. 2007. Managing resources in dynamic environments to create value: Looking inside the black box. *Academy of Management Review,* 32, 273–292.

2. Gange, R.M., & Medsker, K.L. 1996. *The conditions of learning.* Fort Worth, TX: Harcourt-Brace.

3. Luthans, F., & Stajkovic, A.D. 1999. Reinforce for performance: The need to go beyond pay and even performance. *Academy of Management Executive,* 13(2): 49–57.

4. Thorndike, E.L. 1898. Animal intelligence. *Psychological Review,* 2: all of issue 8; Thorndike, E.L. 1911. *Animal intelligence: Experimental studies.* New York: Macmillan.

5. Hull, C.L. 1943. *Principles of behavior.* New York: D. Appleton Century; Skinner, B.F. 1969. *Contingencies of reinforcement: A theoretical analysis.* Englewood Cliffs, NJ: Prentice Hall.

6. Bandura, A. 1996. *Social foundations of thought and action: A social cognitive theory.* Englewood Cliffs, NJ: Prentice Hall; Kreitner, R., & Luthans, F. 1984. A social learning theory approach to behavioral management: Radical behaviorists "mellowing out." *Organizational Dynamics,* 13 (2): 47–65.

7. Podsakoff, P.M., Bommer, W.H., Podsakoff, N.P., & MacKenzie, S.B. 2006. Relationships between leader reward behavior and punishment behavior and subordinate attitudes, perceptions, and behaviors: A meta-analytic review of existing and new research. *Organizational Behavior and Human Decision Processes,* 99: 113–142.

8. Trevino, L.K., 1992. The social effects of punishment in organizations: A justice perspective. *Academy of Management Review,* 17: 647–676.

9. Strupp, J. 2000. No providence in Rhode Island. *Editor and Publisher,* 133 (11): 6–8.

10. Friedman, S. 1994. Allstate faces suit over Fireman's Fund Shooting. *National Underwriter,* 98 (39): 3.

11. Guffey, C.J., & Helms, M.M. 2001. Effective employee discipline: A case of the Internal Revenue Service. *Public Personnel Management,* 30: 111–127.

12. Ibid.

13. Hitt, M.A., Lee, H., & Yucel, E. 2002. The importance of social capital to the management of multinational enterprises: Relational networks among Asian and western firms. *Asia Pacific Journal of Management,* 19: 353–372.

14. Hinkin, T.R., & Schreisheim, C.A. 2004. "If you don't hear from me you know you are doing fine": The effects of management nonresponse to employee performance. *Cornell Hotel and Restaurant Administration Quarterly,* 45: 362–373.

15. Latham, G.P., & Huber, V. 1992. Schedules of reinforcement: Lessons from the past and issues for the future. *Journal of Organizational Behavior Management,* 12(1): 125–149.

16. Scott, W.E., & Podsakoff, P.M. 1985. *Behavioral principles in the practice of management.* New York: John Wiley & Sons.

17. Ibid.

18. Ibid.

19. Ibid.

20. Ibid.

21. Bandura, A. 1986. *Social foundations of thought and action.* Englewood Cliffs, NJ: Prentice Hall; Bandura, A. 2001. Social cognitive theory: An agentic perspective. *Annual Review of Psychology,* 52: 1–26.

22. Stajkovic, A.D., Luthans, F., & Slocum, J.W., Jr. 1998. Social cognitive theory and self-efficacy: Going beyond traditional motivational and behavioral approaches. *Organizational Dynamics,* 26: 62–74.

23. Ibid.

24. Bandura, *Social foundations of thought and action.*

25. Wexley, K.N, & Latham, G.P. 2002. *Developing and training human resources in organizations* (3rd ed.). Upper Saddle River, NJ: Prentice Hall.

26. Bandura, A. 1997. *Self-efficacy: The exercise of self-control.* New York: W.H. Freeman.

27. Judge, T.A., & Bono, J.E. 2001. Relationship of core self-evaluations traits, self-esteem, generalized self-efficacy, locus of control and emotional stability with job satisfaction and job performance: A meta-analysis. *Journal of Applied Psychology,* 86: 80–93; Judge, T.A., Jackson, C.L., Shaw, J.C., Scott, B.A., & Rich, B.L. 2007. Self-efficacy and work-related performance: The integral role of individual differences. *Journal of Applied Psychology,* 92: 107–127; Stajkovic, A.D., & Luthans, F. 1998. Social cognitive theory and work-related performance: A meta-analysis. *Psychological Bulletin,* 124: 240–261.

28. Noe, R.A. 1999. *Employee training and development.* Boston: Irwin McGraw-Hill.

29. Colquitt, J., Lepine, J., & Noe, R.A. 2000. Toward an integrative theory of training motivation: A meta-analytic pat analysis of 20 years of research. *Journal of Applied Psychology,* 85: 678–707.

30. Burke, M.J., Bradley, J., & Bowers, H.N. 2003. Health and safety programs. In J.E. Edwards, J. Scott, & N.S. Raju (Eds.), *The human resources-evaluation handbook.* Thousand Oaks, CA: Sage, pp. 429–446.

31. Noe, *Employee training and development.*

32. Burke, M.J., Holman, D., & Birdi, K. 2006. A walk on the safe side: The implications of learning theory for developing effective safety and health training. In G.P. Hodgkinson, & J.K. Ford (Eds.), *International review of industrial and organizational*

psychology, vol. 21. Hoboken, NJ: John Wiley & Sons, pp. 1–44.

33. Weill, S., & McGill, I. 1989. *Making sense of experiential learning.* Buckingham, UK: SRHE/OU Press.

34. Kolb, D.A. 1984. *Experiential learning: Experience as the source of learning and development.* Englewood Cliffs, NJ: Prentice Hall.

35. Ford, J.K., Smith, E.M., Weissbein, D.A., Gully, S.M., & Salas, E. 1998. Relationships of goal orientation, metacognitive memory, and practice strategies with learning outcomes and transfer. *Journal of Applied Psychology,* 83: 218–233.

36. Kluger, A.N., & DeNisi, A.S. 1996. The effects of feedback interventions on performance: Historical review, a meta-analysis and a preliminary feedback intervention theory. *Psychological Bulletin,* 119:254–284.

37. Ibid.

38. Bandura, A. 1977. *Social learning theory.* Englewood Cliffs, NJ: Prentice Hall.

39. Mann, R.B., & Decker, P.J. 1984. The effect of key behavior distinctiveness on generalization and recall in behavior modeling training. *Academy of Management Journal,* 27: 900–910.

40. Sidman, M. 1962. Operant techniques. In A.J. Bachrach (Ed.), *Experimental foundations of clinical psychology.* New York: Basic Books.

41. Tichy, N.M. 2001. No ordinary boot camp. *Harvard Business Review,* 79(4): 63–70.

42. Fickes, M. 2000. Taking driver training to new levels. *Waste Age,* 31 (4): 238–248.

43. Robertson, G. 2001. Steering true: Greyhound's training is weeding-out process. *Richmond Times-Dispatch,* May 14: B1, B3.

44. Wexley & Latham, *Developing and training human resources in organizations.*

45. Luthans, F., & Kreitner, R. 1975. *Organizational behavior modification.* Glenview, IL: Scott & Foresman; Luthans, F., & Kreitner, R. 1985. *Organizational behavior modification and beyond.* Glenview, IL: Scott & Foresman.

46. Frederiksen, L.W. 1982. *Handbook of organizational behavior management.* New York: John Wiley & Sons.

47. Luthans, F., & Davis, E. 1991. Improving the delivery of quality service: Behavioral management techniques. *Leadership and Organization Development Journal,* 12(2): 3–6.

48. Nordstrom, R., Hall, R.V., Lorenzi, P., & Delquadri, J. 1988. Organizational behavior modification in the public sector. *Journal of Organizational Behavior Management,* 9 (2): 91–112.

49. Welsh, D.H.B., Luthans, F., & Sommer, S.M. 1993. Managing Russian factory workers: The impact of U.S.-based behavioral and participatory techniques. *Academy of Management Journal,* 36: 58–79; Welsh, D.H.B., Luthans, F., & Sommer, S.M. 1993. Organizational behavior modification goes to Russia: Replicating an experimental analysis across cultures and tasks. *Journal of Organizational Behavior Management,* 13 (2): 15–35.

50. Stajkovic, A.D., & Luthans, F. 1997. A meta-analysis of the effects of organizational behavior modification on task performance, 1975–95. *Academy of Management Journal,* 5: 1122–1149.

51. Ibid.

52. Schneier, C.J. 1974. Behavior modification in management. *Academy of Management Journal,* 17: 528–548.

53. Stajkovic & Luthans, A meta-analysis of the effects of organizational behavior modification on task performance, 1975–95.

54. Levitt, B., & March, J.G. 1988. Organizational learning. *Annual Review of Sociology,* 14: 319–340.

55. Thomke, S. 2001. Enlightened experimentation: The new imperative for innovation. *Harvard Business Review,* 79 (2): 66–75.

56. Thomke, S.H. 1998. Managing experimentation in the design of new products. *Management Science,* 44: 743–762.

57. Nicholls-Nixon, C.L., Cooper, A.C., & Woo, C.Y. 2000. Strategic experimentation: Understanding change and performance in new ventures. *Journal of Business Venturing,* 15: 493–521.

58. Thomke, S. 2003. R&D comes to service: Bank of America's pathbreaking experiments. *Harvard Business Review,* 81(4): 70–79.

59. Pfeffer, J. 1998. *The human equation.* Boston: Harvard Business School Press.

60. Master, M. 2001. Spectacular failures. *Across the Board,* 38 (2): 20–26.

61. McGrath, G. 1999. Falling forward: Real options reasoning and entrepreneurial failure. *Academy of Management,* 24: 13–30; Sitkin, S.B. 1992. Learning through failure: The strategy of small losses. *Research in Organizational Behavior,* 14: 231–266.

62. Sitkin, Learning through failure.

63. Shimizu, K., & Hitt, M.A. 2004. Strategic flexibility: Managerial capability to reverse poor strategic decisions. *Academy of Management Executive,* 18, 44–59.

64. Thomke, Enlightened experimentation.

65. Ibid.

66. Robinson, H. 1994. *Perception.* New York: Routledge.

67. Perrow, C. 1984. *Normal accidents: Living with high-risk technologies.* New York: Basic Books.

68. Tufte, E.R. 1997. *Visual and statistical thinking: Displays of evidence for making decisions.* Cheshire, CT: Graphics Press.

69. Einhorn, H.J., & Hogarth, R.M. 1978. Confidence in judgment: Persistence in the illusion of validity. *Psychological Review,* 85: 395–416; Wason, P.C. 1960. On the failure to eliminate hypotheses in a conceptual task. *Quarterly Journal of Experimental Psychology,* 20: 273–283.

70. Bierhoff, H.-W. 1989. *Person perception.* New York: Springer-Verlag; Heil, J. 1983. *Perception and cognition.* Berkeley: University of California Press.

71. Jacobs, R., & Kozlowski, S.W.J. 1985. A closer look at halo error in performance ratings. *Academy of Management Journal,* 28: 201–212.

72. Tsui, A.S., & Barry, B. 1986. Interpersonal affect and rating errors. *Academy of Management Journal,* 29: 586–599.

73. Murray, H.A. 1933. The effects of fear upon estimates of the maliciousness of other personalities. *Journal of Social Psychology,* 4: 310–329.

74. See, for example, Assor, A., Aronoff, J., & Messe, L.A. 1986. An experimental test of defensive processes in impression formation. *Journal of Personality and Social Psychology,* 50: 644–650.

75. Berkowitz, L. 1960. Repeated frustrations and expectations in hostility arousal. *Journal of Abnormal and Social Psychology,* 60: 422–429.

76. Jones, E.E., & deCharms, R. 1957. Changes in social perception as a function of the personal relevance of behavior. *Sociometry,* 20: 75–85.

77. Jick, T., & Gentile, M. 1995. Donna Dubinsky and Apple Computer, Inc. (Part A). Boston: Harvard Business School Publishing.

78. Mehl, M.R., Gosling, S.D., & Pennebaker, J.W. 2006. Personality in its natural habitat: Manifestations and implicit folk theories of personality in daily life. *Journal of Personality and Social Psychology,* 90: 862–877.

79. Gosling, S.D., Ko, S.J., Mannarelli, T., & Morris, M.E. 2002. A room with a cue: Personality judgments based on offices and bedrooms. *Journal of Personality and Social Psychology,* 82: 379–398.

80. Dweck, C.S. 1999. *Self-theories: Their role in motivation, personality, and development.* Philadelphia, PA: Psychology Press.

81. Heslin, P.A., Vandewalle, D., & Latham, G.P. 2006. Keen to help: Managers' implicit person theories and their subsequent employee coaching. *Personnel Psychology,* 59: 871–902.

82. Guilford, J.P. 1954. *Psychometric methods.* New York: McGraw-Hill.

83. Becker, B.E., & Cardy, R.L. 1986. Influence of halo error on appraisal effectiveness: A conceptual and empirical reconsideration. *Journal of Applied Psychology,* 71: 662–671; Jacobs, R., & Kozlowski, S.W.J. 1985. A closer look at halo error in performance ratings. *Academy of Management Journal,* 28: 201–212; Nisbett, R.D., & Wilson, T.D. 1977. The halo effect: Evidence for unconscious alteration of judgments. *Journal of Personality and Social Psychology,* 35: 250–256; Solomon, A.L., & Lance, C.E. 1997. Examination of the relationship between true halo and halo error in performance ratings. *Journal of Applied Psychology,* 82: 665–674.

84. Gross, R.L., & Brodt, S.E. 2001. How assumptions of consensus undermine decision making. *Sloan Management Review,* 42(2): 86–94.

85. See, for example, Finkelstein, L.M., & Burke, M.J. 1998. Age stereotyping at work: The role of rater and contextual factors on evaluation of job applicants. *Journal of General Psychology,* 125: 317–345.

86. "L'Oreal to Ask S.C. to Review Ruling on the Firing of Unattractive Worker," *Metropolitan New Enterprise,* Apr. 14, 2003, at http://www.metnews.com.

87. Tahmincioglu, E. (Jan. 26, 2007) It's Not Easy for Obese Workers, MSNBC.com, at http://www.msnbc.msn.com.

88. Dion K., Berscheid, E., & Walster, E. (1972). What is beautiful is good. *Journal of Personality and Social Psychology,* 24: 285–290.

89. Hosoda, M., Stone-Romero, E.F., & G. Coats. 2003. The effects of physical attractiveness on job-related outcomes: A meta-analysis of experimental studies. *Personnel Psychology,* 26: 431–462; Rudolph, C.W., Wells, C.L., Weller, M.D., Baltes, B. 2009. A meta-analysis of empirical studies of weight-based bias in the workplace. *Journal of Vocational Behavior,* 74: 1–10.

90. Fikkan, J., & Rothblum, E. 2005. Weight bias in employment. In K.D. Brownell, R.M. Puhl, M.B. Schwartz, & L. Rudd (Eds.), *Weight bias: Nature, consequences, and remedies* (pp. 15-28). New York: The Guilford Press.

91. Dipboye, R.L., & Colella, A. 2005. *Discrimination at work: The psychological and organizational bases.* Mahwah, NJ: Lawrence Erlbaum Associates.

92. Ibid.

93. Corbett, W.R. 2007. The ugly truth about appearance discrimination and the beauty of our employment discrimination law. *Duke Journal of Gender Law and Policy,* 14: 153–175.

94. McEnrue, M.P. 1984. Perceived competence as a moderator of the relationship between role clarity and job performance: A test of two hypotheses. *Organizational Behavior and Human Performance,* 34: 379–386.

95. Heider, F. 1958. *The psychology of interpersonal relations.* New York: John Wiley & Sons.

96. Kelley, H.H., & Michela, J. 1981. Attribution theory and research. *Annual Review of Psychology,* 31: 457–501.

97. Young, R.A. 1986. Counseling the unemployed: Attributional issues. *Journal of Counseling and Development,* 64: 374–377.

98. Harvey, J.H., & Weary, G. 1984. Current issues in attribution theory and research. *Annual Review of Psychology,* 35: 428–432.

99. Mitchell, T.R., & Green, S.G. 1983. Leadership and poor performance: An attributional analysis. In J.R. Hackman, E.E. Lawler, & L.W. Porter (Eds.), *Perspectives on behavior in organizations.* New York: McGraw-Hill.

100. Perrow, *Normal accidents: Living with high risk technologies.*

101. Ruhnka, J.C., & Feldman, H.D. 1992. The "Living Dead" phenomenon in venture capital investments. *Journal of Business Venturing,* 7: 137–155.

102. Ganzach, Y., & Pazy, A. 2001. Within-occupation sources of variance in incumbent perception of complexity. *Journal of Occupational and Organizational Psychology,* 74: 95–108.

103. Wong, C., Hui, C., & Law, K.S. 1998. A longitudinal study of the perception–job satisfaction relationship: A test of the three alternative specifications. *Journal of Occupational and Organizational Psychology,* 71: 127–146.

104. Hackman, J.R., Oldham, G., Janson, R., & Purdy, K. 1975. A new strategy of job enrichment. *California Management Review,* 17(4): 57–71.

105. Saavedra, R., & Kwun, S.K. 2000. Affective states in job characteristic theory. *Journal of Organizational Behavior,* 21 (Special Issue): 131–146.

106. Slusher, E.A., & Griffin, R.W. 1985. Comparison processes in task perceptions, evaluations, and reactions. *Journal of Business Research,* 13: 287–299.

107. Simon, D., Hitt, M.A., & Ireland, D. 2007. Managing resources in dynamic environments to create value. *Academy of Management Review,* 32:273–292.

108. Breen, B. 2004. Hidden asset. *Fast Company,* March: 93.

personality, intelligence, attitudes, and emotions

I Know She's Smart and Accomplished ... But Does She Have "Personality"?

Answer "true" or "false" to the following questions:

It's maddening when the court lets guilty criminals go free.
Slow people irritate me.
I can easily cheer up and forget my problems.
I am tidy.

I am not polite when I don't want to be.
I would like the job of a race car driver.
My teachers were unfair to me in school.
I like to meet new people.

The way you answer these questions, or similar items, could determine whether you get the job or not. These questions are examples of the types found on personality tests commonly used to hire people for jobs. One survey found that over 30 percent of employers use some form of personality test when hiring employees. Another survey found that 29 percent of adults aged 18 to 24 took a personality test in the past two years in order to be considered for a job. One of the largest testing companies, Unicru (now a part of Kronos), tested over 11 million candidates in one year for companies such as Universal Studios. Personality testing has taken the employment field by storm. Employers are no longer relying only on stellar resumes and amazing experience, they also care about whether an applicant has the right temperament to carry out the job and fit in with the organization. "Although personality-based testing has been around for years,

knowledge objectives

After reading this chapter, you should be able to:

1. Define *personality* and explain the basic nature of personality traits.
2. Describe the Big Five personality traits, with particular emphasis on the relationship with job performance, success on teams, and job satisfaction.
3. Discuss specific cognitive and motivational concepts of personality, including locus of control and achievement motivation.
4. Define *intelligence* and describe its role in the workplace.
5. Define an *attitude* and describe how attitudes are formed and how they can be changed.
6. Discuss the role of emotions in organizational behavior.

it's now in the spotlight," said Bill Byham, CEO of Development Dimensions International, a consulting firm that is a leader in the personality testing field.

So, what are the right answers? That depends on what the employer is looking for. Common things that employers look for are conscientiousness, ability to handle stress, ability to get along with others, potential leadership, problem-solving style, and service orientation. Different employers look for different personality profiles, and often it depends on the job being sought.

For example, Karen Schoch, who hires employees for Women & Infants Hospital of Rhode Island, states, "A person must be qualified to do the job, but they also require the right personality. We're a hospital that puts a premium on patient care, and we want people who can deliver the concept." Thus, she looks for people who have a blend of compassion, diplomacy, energy, and self-confidence.

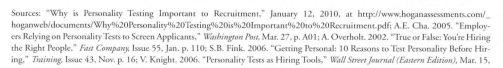

©iStockphoto

Harbor Group LLC, a Houston financial advisory firm, examines dominance, influence, steadiness, and conscientiousness to predict how its associates will handle stress. David Hanson, a founding principal at First Harbor, states "Stress can result in lower productivity, increased absenteeism, tardiness, and high employee turnover." Thus, it is important for his company to identify how people deal with stress so that they can develop ways to counteract the effects of stress.

Southwest Airlines, a company well known for its relaxed, fun culture, takes creating a relaxed, warm environment on its flights seriously. To accomplish this goal, Southwest Airlines carefully screens job applicants to ensure that only individuals with personalities and attitudes consistent with the desired culture are hired. Libby Sartain, former vice president of the People Department at Southwest, put it this way: "If we hire people who don't have the right

attitude, disposition, and behavioral characteristics to fit into our culture, we will start to change that culture." Herb Kelleher, former CEO, has said, "We look for attitudes; people with a sense of humor who don't take themselves too seriously. We'll train you on whatever it is you have to do, but the one thing Southwest cannot change in people is inherent attitudes." Thus, Southwest tests people for kindness and creativity.

These four organizations all have different cultures and work environments. Therefore, they all look for different personality traits in new employees. The extent to which the personality of associates fits with an organization's culture has been found to have a positive impact on both associates and the organization, and personality testing is one way to make sure that employees have the right disposition to mesh with the organization's culture. This emphasis on cultural fit is found in many high-involvement organizations, where identifying and selecting individuals who complement a carefully developed and maintained culture is a highly important task.

One example of a company that has used personality testing to directly impact its bottom line is Outback Steakhouse. Personality testing helped Outback to identify applicants who would fit the firm's needs. Better hiring decisions resulted in growth in revenues and higher profits over time. As a result, associate turnover was reduced by 50 percent, decreasing the company's recruitment and training costs by millions of dollars. A popular and valid personality test is the Hogan Personality Inventory (HPI). Using this test in employee selection led to 50 percent reduced turnover in a retail company, 48 percent improved productivity in an insurance company, decreased accidents resulting in lost time among hospital workers, and an increase of $308,000.00 per year in sales in a bank.

Sources: "Why is Personality Testing Important to Recruitment," January 12, 2010, at http://www.hoganassessments.com/_hoganweb/documents/Why%20Personality%20Testing%20is%20Important%20to%20Recruitment.pdf; A.E. Cha. 2005. "Employers Relying on Personality Tests to Screen Applicants," *Washington Post,* Mar. 27, p. A01; A. Overholt. 2002. "True or False: You're Hiring the Right People," *Fast Company,* Issue 55, Jan. p. 110; S.B. Fink. 2006. "Getting Personal: 10 Reasons to Test Personality Before Hiring," *Training,* Issue 43, Nov. p. 16; V. Knight. 2006. "Personality Tests as Hiring Tools," *Wall Street Journal (Eastern Edition),* Mar. 15,

Sources: *(continued from page 158)* p. B3A; B. Dattner. 2004. "Snake Oil or Science? That's the Raging Debate on Personality Testing," *Workforce Management,* Issue 83 (10), Oct., p. 90, accessed at www.workforce3.com, Mar. 2007; E. Frauenheim. 2006. "The (Would Be) King of HR Software," *Workforce Management,* Issue 85 (15), Aug. 14, pp. 34–39, accessed at www.workforce3.com, Mar. 2007; www.kronos.com, accessed Mar. 2007; K. Brooker. 2001. "The Chairman of the Board Looks Back," *Fortune* 143, no. 11: 62–76; R. Chang. 2001. "Turning into Organizational Performance," *Training and Development* 55, no. 5: 104–111; K. Ellis. 2001. "Libby Sartain," *Training* 38, no. 1: 46–50; L. Ellis. 2001. "Customer Loyalty," *Executive Excellence* 18, no. 7: 13–14; K. Freiberg & J. Freiberg. 1996. *Nuts!: Southwest Airlines' Crazy Recipe for Business and Personal Success* (Austin, TX: Bard Press); K. Freiberg & J. Freiberg. 2001. "Southwest Can Find Another Pilot," *Wall Street Journal (Eastern Edition),* Mar. 26, p. A22; H. Lancaster. 1999. "Herb Kelleher Has One Main Strategy: Treat Employees Well," *Wall Street Journal (Eastern Edition),* Aug. 31, p. B1; S.F. Gale. 2002. "Three Companies Cut Turnover with Tests," *Workforce* 81, no. 4: 66–69.

the strategic importance of Personality, Intelligence, Attitudes, and Emotions

The discussion of personality testing in *Exploring Organizational Behavior in Action* illustrates how important it is for organizations to select the right individuals. Everyone has individual differences that cannot be easily changed. As Herb Kelleher mentioned above, organizations can train people to do only so much; there are individual differences in people that are not easily influenced. In this chapter we explore three such differences: personality, intelligence, and emotions. We also explore another individual difference: attitudes that can be more easily affected by one's organizational experience. All of these human attributes influence organizational effectiveness by influencing associates' performance, work attitudes, motivation, willingness to stay in the organization, and ability to work together in a high-involvement environment.

In Chapter 1, we stated that an important part of high-involvement work systems was that organizations engage in selective hiring, illustrating the importance of hiring people with the right set of attributes. A great deal of research has been done that has shown that certain traits, such as conscientiousness[1] and intelligence,[2] are related to associates' performance. Associates' traits have also

been linked to how likely they will be to engage in counterproductive work behavior, such as being frequently absent or stealing.[3] In addition to traits directly affecting performance, the degree to which associates' traits fit the work environment and culture is also linked with how satisfied and committed associates are to their organization[4] and how likely they will be to remain in the organization.[5] Furthermore, the attributes of top leaders in the organization have a direct impact on organizational functioning by relating to the group dynamics among top decision makers[6] and the strategic decisions they make.[7] Thus, the individual traits and attitudes of everyone in the organization can have an important impact on the functioning of that organization.

Because personalities have such important effects on behavior in organizations, care must be taken in adding new people. For a manufacturing firm emphasizing stable, efficient operations because it competes on the basis of low cost, hiring newcomers who are serious, conscientious, and emotionally stable is logical. For a manufacturing firm competing on the basis of frequent process and product innovations, hiring newcomers who embrace change and are inquisitive is important. Furthermore, as

you will learn in this chapter, it is critical to hire associates who fit the characteristics of the particular jobs they will hold. Inside the same firm, personalities suitable for the tasks required in sales may be less suitable for the tasks involved in research and development. Although personality, intelligence, attitudes, and emotions are not perfect predictors of job performance and should never be used alone in selection decisions, they are important.

In this chapter, we open with a discussion of fundamentals of personality, including its origins and the degree to which it changes over time. Building on this foundation, we examine a major personality framework, the Big Five, that has emerged as the most useful for understanding workplace behaviors. Next, we discuss several cognitive and motive-based characteristics of personality not explicitly included in the major framework. Next, we examine intelligence, another individual difference that has become a controversial topic in employee selection. We then move on to an exploration of attitudes, including attitude development and change as well as several important types of workplace attitudes. Finally, we address emotions and their role in organizations.

Fundamentals of Personality

The term *personality* may be used in several ways. One common use—or, rather, misuse—of the word is in describing the popularity of our classmates or colleagues. We may think that Hank has a pleasant personality or that Susan is highly personable. In your high-school yearbook, someone was probably listed with the title of Mr. or Ms. Personality. When *personality* is used in this way, it means that person is popular or well liked. This meaning has little value, however, in understanding or predicting behavior. To know that some people are popular does not enable us to have a rich understanding of them, nor does it improve our ability to interact with them.

For our purposes, personality describes a person's most striking or dominant characteristics—jolly, shy, domineering, assertive, and so on. This meaning of personality is more useful because a set of rich characteristics tells us much about the behavior we can expect a person to exhibit and can serve as a guide in our interactions with her.

More formally, **personality** is a stable set of characteristics representing the internal properties of an individual, which are reflected in behavioral tendencies across a variety of situations.[8] These characteristics are often referred to as "traits" and have names such as dominance, assertiveness, and neuroticism. More important than the names of personality traits, however, is the meaning given to them by psychologists. The traditional meaning of personality traits rests on three basic beliefs:

1. Personality traits are individual psychological characteristics that are relatively enduring—for example, if a person is introverted or shy, he or she will likely remain so for a long period of time.

2. Personality traits are major determinants of one's behavior—for example, an introverted person will be withdrawn and exhibit nonassertive behavior.

3. Personality traits influence one's behavior across a wide variety of situations—an introverted person will be withdrawn and nonassertive at a party, in class, in sports activities, and at work.

Some researchers and managers have criticized these traditional beliefs about personality traits, believing instead that personality can undergo basic changes. They believe, for example, that shy people can become more assertive and outgoing. Furthermore, by examining our own behaviors, we may learn that sometimes we behave differently from situation to situation. Our behavior at a party, for example, may be different from our behavior at work.

Still, we often can observe consistencies in a person's behavior across situations. For example, many people at various levels of Scott Paper saw Al Dunlap act in hard-hearted ways and exhibit outbursts of temper when he served this company as CEO. Many individuals at Sunbeam, where he next filled the CEO role, observed the same behaviors. Apparently, family members also experienced similar treatment. When Dunlap was fired by the board of directors at Sunbeam, his only child said, "I laughed like hell. I'm glad he fell on his ... ."[9] His sister said, "He got exactly what he deserved."[10]

> **personality**
> A stable set of characteristics representing internal properties of an individual, which are reflected in behavioral tendencies across a variety of situations.

Determinants of Personality Development

To properly understand personality, it is important to examine how it develops. Both heredity and environment play important roles in the development of personality.

©Siri Stafford/Getty Images, Inc.

Heredity

From basic biology, we know that parents provide genes to their children. Genes in turn determine height, hair color, eye color, size of hands, and other basic physical characteristics. Similarly, genes seem to influence personality, as demonstrated in three different types of studies.

The first type of study involves examinations of identical twins. Identical twins have identical genes and should therefore have similar personalities if genes play an important role. Moreover, if genes influence personality, identical twins separated at birth should have more similar adult personalities than regular siblings or fraternal twins who have been raised apart. This is precisely the case, as has been found in a number of studies.[11] Consider identical twins Oskar and Jack, who were parented by different people. Oskar was raised in Germany by his Roman Catholic maternal grandmother, whereas Jack was raised outside Germany by his Jewish father. As adults, however, both of the brothers were domineering, prone to anger, and absentminded.[12]

The second type of study involves assessments of newborns. Because newborns have had little exposure to the world, the temperaments they exhibit—including their activity levels, adaptability, sensitivity to stimulation, and general disposition—are probably determined to a large degree by genetics. If newborn temperament in turn predicts personality later in life, a link between genes and personality is suggested. Several studies have provided evidence for this relationship. In one such study, newborns ranging in age from 8 to 12 weeks were tracked into adult life. Temperament in the early weeks of life was found to predict personality later in life.[13]

The third type of study supporting genetic effects focuses directly on genes. In several studies, researchers have identified distinct genes thought to influence personality. Gene D_4DR serves as a useful example. This gene carries the recipe for a protein known as *dopamine receptor,* which controls the amount of dopamine in the brain. Dopamine is crucial because it seems to affect initiative and adventure-seeking. Individuals with a long version of the gene, where a key sequence of DNA repeats itself six or more times, are more likely to be adventure-seeking than individuals with a short version of the gene.[14]

Although genes clearly play an important role in personality, we must be careful not to overemphasize their effects. Researchers typically believe that 50 percent of adult personality is genetically determined. Furthermore, we should not conclude that a single magical gene controls a particular aspect of personality. The best information currently available suggests that combinations of genes influence individual personality traits.[15] For example, gene D_4DR plays an important role in how much adventure a person desires, but other genes also affect this trait.

Environment

Beyond genes, the environment a person experiences as a child plays an important role in personality. In other words, what a child is exposed to and how she is treated influence the type of person she becomes. Warm, nurturing, and supportive households are more likely to produce well-adjusted, outgoing individuals.[16] Socioeconomic circumstances of the household may also play a role, with favorable circumstances being associated with value systems that promote hard work, ambition, and self-control.[17] Events and experiences outside the home can also affect personality. Schools, churches, and athletic teams are important places for lessons that shape personality.

Although research suggests that personality is reasonably stable in the adult years,[18] events and experiences later in life can affect personality. Reports have described, for example, how a heart attack survivor reaches deep inside to change himself. In addition, some psychological theories suggest that change may occur over time. One theory proposes a model of personality that includes possible transitions at various points in life, including infancy, early childhood, late childhood, the teenage years, early adulthood, middle adulthood, and late adulthood, for instance.[19] The specific changes that might occur are less important than the fact that change is possible.

The Big Five Personality Traits

For managers and associates to effectively use personality traits in predicting behavior, they must work with a concise set of traits. But thousands of traits can be used to describe a person. Which traits are most useful? Which correspond to the most meaningful behavioral tendencies in the workplace? These questions have puzzled researchers for many years. Fortunately, a consensus among personality experts has emerged to focus on five traits. These traits, collectively known as the Big Five, include extraversion, conscientiousness, agreeableness, emotional stability, and openness to experience, as shown in Exhibit 5-1.

Extraversion

The **extraversion** trait was an important area of study for many well-known psychologists in the early-to-middle portion of the twentieth century, including Carl Jung, Hans

extraversion
The degree to which an individual is outgoing and derives energy from being around other people.

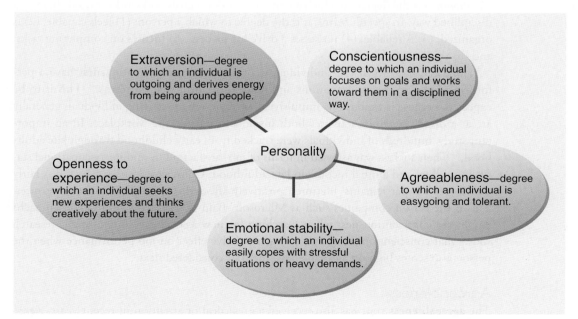

Exhibit 5-1   The Big Five Personality Traits

Eysenck, and Raymond Cattell. For Jung and many of his contemporaries, this aspect of personality was considered the most important driver of behavior. Extraversion is the degree to which a person is outgoing and derives energy from being around other people. In more specific terms, it is the degree to which a person: (1) enjoys being around other people, (2) is warm to others, (3) speaks up in group settings, (4) maintains a vigorous pace, (5) likes excitement, and (6) is cheerful.[20] Herb Kelleher of Southwest Airlines clearly fits this mold, as does Carol Bartz, current CEO of Yahoo![21]

Research has shown that people scoring high on this dimension, known as *extraverts,* tend to have a modest but measurable performance advantage over introverts in occupations requiring a high level of interaction with other people.[22] Specific occupations where extraverts have been found to perform particularly well include sales and management. In contrast, *introverts,* who do not score high on extraversion, tend to do particularly well in occupations such as accounting, engineering, and information technology, where more solitary work is frequently required. For any occupation where teams are central, or in a high-involvement organization where teams are emphasized, extraverts may also have a slight edge, as teams involve face-to-face interaction, group decision making, and navigation of interpersonal dynamics.[23] A team with a very high percentage of extraverts as members, however, may function poorly, for too many team members may be more interested in talking than in listening. Finally, research suggests that extraversion is related to job satisfaction, with extraverts exhibiting slightly more satisfaction regardless of the specific conditions of the job situation.[24]

Conscientiousness

conscientiousness
The degree to which an individual focuses on goals and works toward them in a disciplined way.

The **conscientiousness** trait has played a central role in personality research in recent years. Many current personality researchers believe this dimension of personality has the greatest effect of all personality dimensions on a host of outcomes in the workplace. *Conscientiousness* is the degree to which a person focuses on goals and works toward them in a disciplined way. In specific terms, it is the degree to which a person: (1) feels capable, (2) is organized, (3) is reliable, (4) possesses a drive for success, (5) focuses on completing tasks, and (6) thinks before acting.[25]

Research has shown that individuals scoring high on conscientiousness have a performance edge in most occupations and tend to perform well on teams.[26] This is to be expected, because irresponsible, impulsive, low-achievement-striving individuals generally are at a disadvantage in activities both inside and outside the workplace. In an important study, hundreds of individuals were tracked from early childhood through late adulthood.[27] Their success was assessed in terms of job satisfaction in midlife, occupational status in midlife, and annual income in late adulthood. Conscientiousness, which was fairly stable over the participants' lifetimes, positively affected each of these success measures. This is the reason companies such as Microsoft, Bain & Company, and Goldman Sachs emphasize conscientiousness when searching for new associates.[28] Interestingly, research shows that conscientiousness has a stronger positive effect on job performance when the person also scores high on agreeableness, the trait considered next.[29]

Agreeableness

agreeableness
The degree to which an individual is easygoing and tolerant.

The **agreeableness** trait has also received a great deal of attention in recent years. *Agreeableness* is the degree to which a person is easygoing and tolerant—the degree to which a person: (1) believes in the honesty of others, (2) is straightforward, (3) is willing to help others, (4) tends to yield under conflict, (5) exhibits humility, and (6) is sensitive to the feelings of others.[30]

Research has not shown a consistent pattern of job outcomes for individuals scoring high or low on agreeableness. After all, being agreeable and disagreeable can be valuable at different times in the same job. A manager, for example, may need to discipline an associate in the morning but behave very agreeably toward union officials in the afternoon. A salesperson may need to be tough in negotiations on one day but treat a long-standing customer with gracious deference on the next day.

Agreeable individuals do, however, seem to be consistently effective in teamwork.[31] They are positive for interpersonal dynamics, as they are sensitive to the feelings of others and often try to ensure the participation and success of all team members. Teams with many members who are agreeable have been found to perform well.[32] Having an extremely high percentage of very agreeable team members, however, may be associated with too little debate on important issues. When teams must make important decisions and solve non-routine problems, having some individuals with lower scores on agreeableness may be an advantage.

Emotional Stability

The trait of **emotional stability** relates to how a person copes with stressful situations or heavy demands. Specific features of this trait include the degree to which a person: (1) is relaxed, (2) is slow to feel anger, (3) rarely becomes discouraged, (4) rarely becomes embarrassed, (5) resists unhealthy urges associated with addictions, and (6) handles crises well.[33] Research has shown that emotionally stable individuals tend to have an edge in task performance across a large number of occupations.[34] This is reasonable, for stable individuals are less likely to exhibit characteristics that may interfere with performance, such as being anxious, hostile, and insecure. Similarly, emotionally stable individuals seem to have modest but measurable advantages as team members.[35] Several studies reveal that teams perform more effectively when composed of members scoring high on this trait.[36] Furthermore, when individuals are high on emotional stability, in combination with high extraversion and high conscientiousness, they are more likely to have team leadership potential, than those who do not have this personality profile.[37] Finally, research shows that emotional stability is positively linked to job satisfaction, independent of the specific conditions of the job situation.[38]

emotional stability
The degree to which an individual easily handles stressful situations and heavy demands.

Openness to Experience

The **openness** trait is the degree to which a person seeks new experiences and thinks creatively about the future. More specifically, openness is the degree to which a person: (1) has a vivid imagination, (2) has an appreciation for art and beauty, (3) values and respects emotions in himself and others, (4) prefers variety to routine, (5) has broad intellectual curiosity, and (6) is open to reexamining closely held values.[39] Research suggests that both individuals scoring high and individuals scoring low on openness can perform well in a variety of occupations and can function well on teams.[40] Those who score high on this dimension of personality, however, are probably more effective at particular tasks calling for vision and creativity, such as the creative aspects of advertising, the creative aspects of marketing, and many aspects of working in the arts. At W.L. Gore and Associates, maker of world-renowned Gore-Tex products (such as sealants and

openness to experience
The degree to which an individual seeks new experiences and thinks creatively about the future.

fabrics), strong openness is valued for many aspects of engineering, sales, and marketing because the company has been successful through innovation and wants to keep its culture of creativity, discovery, and initiative.[41] Individuals with lower openness scores may be more effective in jobs calling for strong adherence to rules, such as piloting airplanes and accounting.

The Big Five as a Tool for Selecting New Associates and Managers

Given the links between important competencies and specific personality traits, it is not surprising that personality assessment can play a role in hiring decisions. Although no single tool should be used as the basis for hiring new associates and managers, personality assessment can be a useful part of a portfolio of tools that includes structured interviews and skills evaluations. In some reviews of available tools, Big Five assessments have been shown to provide useful predictions of future job performance.[42] It is important, however, to develop a detailed understanding of how personality traits predict performance in a specific situation. Such understanding requires that the general information just discussed be supplemented by: (1) an in-depth analysis of the requirements of a particular job in a particular organization and (2) an in-depth determination of which traits support performance in that particular job. In some cases, only certain aspects of a trait may be important in a specific situation. For example, being slow to anger and not prone to frustration may be crucial aspects of emotional stability for particular jobs, whereas being relaxed may be much less important for these jobs. Call center operator positions call for this particular combination of characteristics. They have to respond positively to customers, even when customers are rude or hostile.[43]

The Big Five and High-Involvement Management

We now turn to competencies that are important for high-involvement management. Combinations of several Big Five traits likely provide a foundation for important competencies. Although research connecting the Big Five to these competencies has not been extensive, the evidence to date suggests important linkages.

Recall that high-involvement management focuses on developing associates so that substantial authority can be delegated to them. Available research suggests that managers' competencies in developing, delegating, and motivating are enhanced by high extraversion, high conscientiousness, and high emotional stability.[44] This research is summarized in Exhibit 5-2 and is consistent with our earlier discussion, which pointed out that conscientious, emotionally stable individuals have advantages in many situations and that extraverts have a slight advantage in situations requiring a high level of interaction with people.

As might be expected, available research also indicates that these same characteristics provide advantages to associates in high-involvement organizations. For associates, competencies in self-development, decision making, self-management, and teamwork are crucial. Conscientious, emotionally stable individuals are likely to work at these competencies, and being an extravert may present a slight advantage.[45] Agreeableness and openness do not appear to have consistent effects on the competencies discussed here.

EXHIBIT 5-2 The Big Five and High-Involvement Management

Competencies	Description	Big Five Traits*
For Managers		
Delegating to others	Patience in providing information and support when empowering others, but also the ability to confront individuals when there is a problem	E+ C+ A− ES+ O+
Developing others	Interest in sharing information, ability to coach and train, and interest in helping others plan careers	E+ (C+) A++ ES+ (O+)
Motivating others	Ability to bring out the best in other people, desire to recognize contributions of others, and in general an interest in others	E++ C+ (A+) ES+
For Associates		
Decision-making skills	Careful consideration of important inputs, little putting off of decisions, and no tendency to change mind repeatedly	E+ C++ A− ES+ O+
Self-development	Use of all available resources for improvement, interest in feedback, and lack of defensiveness	E+ C++ A+ ES+ (O−)
Self-management	Little procrastination, effective time management, and a focus on targets	E+ C+ (A−)
Teamwork	Willingness to subordinate personal interests for the team, ability to follow or lead depending on the needs of the team, and commitment to building team spirit	E+ C+ A++ ES+ O+

* Entries in the exhibit are defined as follows: E = extraversion, C = conscientiousness, A = agreeableness, ES = emotional stability (many researchers define this using a reverse scale and use the label "need for stability" or "neuroticism"), and O = openness to experience. A "+" indicates that higher scores on the trait appear to promote the listed competency. A "++" indicates that higher scores on a trait appear to have very significant effects on the listed competency. Similarly, a "−" indicates that low levels of a trait appear to promote the listed competency. Parentheses are used in cases where some aspects of a trait are associated with the listed competency but the overall trait is not. For example, only the first and fourth aspects of conscientiousness (feels capable and possesses a drive for success) have been found to be associated with the competency for developing others.

Source: Adapted from P.J. Howard and J.M. Howard. 2001. *The Owner's Manual for Personality at Work* (Austin, TX: Bard Press).

Cognitive and Motivational Properties of Personality

We turn next to several cognitive and motivational concepts that have received attention as separate and important properties related to personality. They are defined as follows (see Exhibit 5-3):

- *Cognitive properties*—properties of individuals' perceptual and thought processes that affect how they typically process information
- *Motivational properties*—stable differences in individuals that energize and maintain overt behaviors

Cognitive Concepts

Differences in how people use their intellectual capabilities may result in vastly different perceptions and judgments. Personality concepts that focus on cognitive processes help us

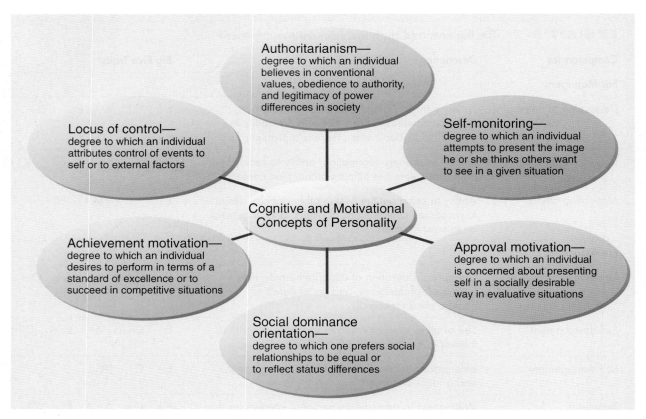

Exhibit 5-3 Cognitive and Motivational Concepts of Personality

locus of control
The degree to which an individual attributes control of events to self or external factors.

authoritarianism
The degree to which an individual believes in conventional values, obedience to authority, and legitimacy of power differences in society.

to understand these differences. Three such concepts are locus of control, authoritarianism, and self-monitoring.

The personality concept of **locus of control** refers to a person's tendency to attribute the cause or control of events either to herself or to factors in the external environment. People who tend to believe that they have control over events are said to have an "internal" locus of control. Those who consistently believe that events are controlled by outside forces in the environment have an "external" locus of control.[46]

Internals believe they can control what happens to them. This often leads them to engage in work and leisure activities requiring greater skill[47] and to conform less to group influences.[48] Internals, then, tend to think they can be successful if they simply work hard enough, and this belief may be reflected in their work habits, especially on difficult tasks. They also tend to exhibit a greater sense of well-being, a finding that holds worldwide.[49] *Externals* believe that what happens to them is more a matter of luck or fate, and they see little connection between their own behavior and success or failure. They are more conforming and may therefore be less argumentative and easier to supervise. Structured tasks and plenty of supervision suit them well. Overall, associates with an internal locus of control experience more positive work outcomes than people with an external locus of control, including higher motivation and less job stress.[50]

The original research on **authoritarianism** began as an effort to identify people who might be susceptible to anti-Semitic ideologies. Over time, the concept evolved into its present meaning—the extent to which a person believes in conventional values, obedience to authority, and the legitimacy of power and status differences in society.[51] Authoritarianism has been extensively researched. Individuals who score high on this concept tend to believe that status and the use of power in organizations are proper. They are submissive to people in power and aggressive toward those who break rules.[52] Furthermore, they may be more willing to accept unethical behavior in others when those others are in powerful or high-status positions.[53] Such people tend to adjust readily to rules and regulations and emerge as leaders in situations requiring a great deal of control by the manager.

©Janie Barrett/Fairfax photos/Redux Pictures

Related to authoritarianism, is **social dominance orientation (SDO)**.[54] SDO refers to a general attitudinal orientation concerning whether one prefers social relationships to be equal or to reflect status differences. Furthermore, people with a high SDO view their own groups as superior and dominant over other "outgroups."[55] SDO is negatively related to the Big Five personality traits agreeableness and openness to experience.[56] People high in SDO have also been found to be more likely to discriminate against job applicants from different demographic groups[57] and prefer to work in nondiverse organizations[58] as compared with people low in SDO.

Self-monitoring is an important personality concept that describes the degree to which people are guided by their true selves in decisions and actions. It determines whether people are fully consistent in behavior across different situations. Low self-monitors follow the advice given by Polonius to Laertes in Shakespeare's *Hamlet*[59]: "To thine own self be true." Low self-monitors ask, "Who am I, and how can I be me in this situation?"[60] In contrast, high self-monitors present somewhat different faces in different situations. They have been referred to as "chameleon-like," as they try to present the appropriate image to each separate audience.[61] High self-monitors ask, "Who does this situation want me to be, and how can I be that person?"[62]

High self-monitors can be quite effective in the workplace, with a tendency to outperform low self-monitors in several areas.[63] Because they are highly attentive to social cues and the thoughts of others, they are sometimes more effective at conflict resolution. Because they are attentive to social dynamics and the expectations of others, they frequently emerge as leaders. Because they are more likely to use interpersonal strategies that fit the desires of other people, they tend to perform well in jobs requiring cooperation and interaction. Management is one such job, and research indicates that high self-monitors are more effective managers. In one study, MBA graduates were tracked for five years after graduation. MBAs who were high self-monitors received more managerial promotions.[64]

Motivational Concepts

Motivational concepts of personality are reflected more in a person's basic needs than in his or her thought processes. Two important concepts in this category are achievement motivation and approval motivation.

Achievement motivation is commonly referred to as the need for achievement (or *n-Ach*). It is an important determinant of aspiration, effort, and persistence in situations where performance will be evaluated according to some standard of excellence.[65]

social dominance orientation

A general attitudinal orientation concerning whether one prefers social relationships to be equal or to reflect status differences.

self-monitoring

The degree to which an individual attempts to present the image he or she thinks others want to see in a given situation.

achievement motivation

The degree to which an individual desires to perform in terms of a standard of excellence or to succeed in competitive situations.

Thus, need for achievement is the strength of a person's desire to perform in terms of a standard of excellence or to succeed in competitive situations. Unlike most conceptualizations of personality traits, need for achievement has been related to particular situations. That is, it is activated only in situations of expected excellence or competition. The interaction of personality and the immediate environment is obvious in this theory, and it affects the strength of motivation.

Persons with a high need for achievement set their goals and tend to accept responsibility for both success and failure. They dislike goals that are either extremely difficult or easy, tending to prefer goals of moderate difficulty. They also need feedback regarding their performance. People with a high need for achievement are also less likely to procrastinate than people with a low need for achievement.[66]

This personality characteristic is often misinterpreted. For example, some may think that need for achievement is related to desire for power and control. High need achievers, however, tend to focus on task excellence rather than on power.

Approval motivation is another important motive-based personality concept. Researchers have noted the tendency for some people to present themselves in socially desirable ways when they are in evaluative situations. Such people are highly concerned about the approval of others. Approval motivation is also related to conformity and "going along to get along."[67]

Ironically, the assessment of one's own personality is an evaluative situation, and persons high in approval motivation tend to respond to personality tests in socially desirable ways. In other words, such people will try to convey positive impressions of themselves. Such tendencies lead individuals to "fake" their answers to personality questionnaires according to the perceived desirability of the responses. Many questionnaires contain "lie" scales and sets of items to detect this social approval bias. Such precautions are especially important when personality tests are used to select, promote, or identify persons for important organizational purposes.

approval motivation
The degree to which an individual is concerned about presenting himself or herself in a socially desirable way in evaluative situations.

Some Cautionary and Concluding Remarks

Personality characteristics may change to some degree, and situational forces may at times overwhelm the forces of personality. People can adjust to their situations, particularly those who are high self-monitors. An introverted person may be somewhat sociable in a sales meeting, and a person with an external locus of control may on occasion accept personal responsibility for his failure. Furthermore, some people can be trained or developed in jobs that seem to conflict with their personalities. Fit between an individual's personality and the job does, however, convey some advantages. Overall, the purpose of measuring personality is to know that some people may fit a given job situation better than others. For those who fit less well, we may want to provide extra help, training, or counseling before making the decision to steer them toward another position or type of work. We also note that personality testing in organizations should focus only on "normal" personality characteristics. According to the Americans with Disabilities Act (1990), it is illegal to screen out potential employees based on the results of personality tests designed to measure psychological disabilities (e.g., depression or extreme anxiety).

The information on personality and performance presented in this chapter has been developed largely from research in the United States and Canada. Research in Europe is reasonably consistent,[68] but other parts of the world have been studied less. Great care must be taken in applying the results of U.S.- and Canadian-based research to other regions of the world.

"I Have Ketchup in My Veins"

Patricia Harris uses the above phrase to describe her commitment and fit with the McDonald's Corporation. Ms. Harris, currently a Vice President of McDonald's Corporation, USA. and the Global Chief Diversity Officer, began her career with the company over 30 years ago. She started at McDonald's in 1976 in a secretarial position and soon began rising through the ranks, while attending college part-time and raising a family. Many of Ms. Harris's positions have been in human resource management, and she is often attributed in making McDonald's a current leader and early forerunner in promoting employee diversity, leading the company to win the coveted Equal Employment Opportunity Commission's "Freedom to Compete Award" in 2006 and the national Restaurant Association's Diversity Award in 2009, among many other honors concerning diversity.

Several attributes of Patricia Harris have led to her phenomenal career. First of all, she is high on conscientiousness. Ms. Harris's colleagues describe her as "driven," and she has often "stepped out of her comfort zone" to take on new job challenges. She is also goal-driven to develop diversity processes and programs to help build McDonald's business all over the world. While being extremely performance-focused, Ms. Harris also displays agreeableness by serving as a mentor to many other McDonald's associates

©Nathan Mandell Photography

and crediting her own mentors and team members when asked about her success. Her high need for achievement came through when, early in her career, she told her boss and mentor: "I want your job!" Ms. Harris also has a strong internal locus of control because she focuses on making her environment and the company's a better place to work. Finally, she demonstrates a great deal of intelligence in dealing with her job. In addition to a temperament that makes her very well suited for her career, she also possesses the knowledge and intelligence that have helped make McDonald's a leader in diversity. Rich Floersch, Executive Vice President in Charge of Human Relations, states: "She's very well informed, a true student of diversity. She is good at analyzing U.S. diversity principles and applying them in an international market. She's also a good listener who understands the business and culture very well."

Patricia Harris would probably be a success anywhere she worked—yet her true passion for McDonald's and its diversity initiatives seems to set her apart from most other executives. In 1985, when Ms. Harris was first asked to become an affirmative action manager, she was apprehensive about taking the job because affirmative action was not a popular issue at the time. She overcame her apprehension and started on her path to dealing with diversity issues. She states that "this job truly became my passion. It's who I am, both personally and professionally." By working on diversity issues, Ms. Harris was able to realize not only her professional goals, but also her personal goals of helping women and minorities. Ray Kroc, the founder of McDonald's, stated that "None of us is as good as all of us," focusing on the importance of inclusion and ownership by all employees. This value permeates McDonald's corporate vision and also coincides with the personal vision of Patricia Harris. Harris says that her company's mission "is to create an environment in which everyone within McDonald's global system is able to contribute fully regardless of role." Thus, not only is she extremely competent at her job, she is also passionate about her job and her organization. Patricia Harris exemplifies what happens when an individual's traits, abilities, and passion line up with the vision of the organization.

Sources: K. Whitney. Jan. 18, 2009. Diversity is everybody's business at McDonald's. *Diversity Executive*. At http://www.diversity-executive.com/article.php?article=480; McDonald's, May 14, "National Restaurant Association Honors McDonald's With Diversity Award" at http://www.aboutmcdonalds.com/mcd/csr/news/national_restaurant.5.html?DCSext.destination=http://www.aboutmcdonalds.com/mcd/csr/news/national_restaurant.5.html; A. Pomeroy. Dec. 2006. "She's Still Lovin' It," *HRMagazine*, Dec., pp. 58–61; anonymous staff writer. 2007. "An Interview with Pat Harris, Vice President Diversity Initiatives with McDonald's Corporation" at http://www.employmentguide.com/careeradvice/Leading_the_Way-in_Diversity. html, accessed Apr. 18, 2007; J. Lawn. 2006. "Shattered Glass and Personal Journeys," *FoodManagement*, July, at http://www.food-management.com/article/13670; anonymous. 2005. "Ray Kroc: Founder's Philosophies Remain at the Heart of McDonald's Success," *Nation's Restaurant News*, Apr. 11, at http://findarticles.com/p/articles/mi_m3190/is_15_39/ai_n13649039.

In conclusion, determining the personality and behavioral attributes of higher performers in an organization can help a firm to improve its performance over time, as suggested in the *Experiencing Organizational Behavior* feature. Patricia Harris, Vice President of McDonald's Corporation, USA, and Global Chief Diversity Officer, exemplifies such a high performer whose personality fits the organization's strategies and goals.

Intelligence

intelligence
General mental ability used in complex information processing.

In the preceding section, we saw how important personality is to organizational behavior and achieving a high-involvement workplace. There is another stable individual difference that can greatly affect organizational behavior, particularly job performance. This trait is *cognitive ability*, more commonly referred to as **intelligence**. *Intelligence* refers to the ability to develop and understand concepts, particularly more complex and abstract concepts.[69] Despite its importance, intelligence as an aspect of human ability has been somewhat controversial. Some psychologists and organizational behavior researchers do not believe that a meaningful general intelligence factor exists. Instead, they believe that many different types of intelligence exist and that most of us have strong intelligence in one or more areas. These areas might include the following:[70]

- *Number aptitude*—the ability to handle mathematics
- *Verbal comprehension*—the ability to understand written and spoken words
- *Perceptual speed*—the ability to process visual data quickly
- *Spatial visualization*—the ability to imagine a different physical configuration—for example, to imagine how a room would look with the furniture rearranged
- *Deductive reasoning*—the ability to draw a conclusion or make a choice that logically follows from existing assumptions and data
- *Inductive reasoning*—the ability to identify, after observing specific cases or instances, the general rules that govern a process or that explain an outcome—for example, to identify the general factors that play a role in a successful product launch after observing one product launch at a single company
- *Memory*—the ability to store and recall previous experiences

Most psychologists and organizational behavior researchers who have extensively studied intelligence believe, however, that a single unifying intelligence factor exists, a factor that blends together all of the areas from above. They also believe that general intelligence has meaningful effects on success in the workplace. Existing evidence points to the fact that general intelligence is an important determinant of workplace performance and career success.[71] This is particularly true for jobs and career paths that require complex information processing, as opposed to simple manual labor. Exhibit 5-4 illustrates the strong connection between intelligence and success for complex jobs.

Although the use of intelligence tests is intended to help organizations select the best human capital, as explained in the *Experiencing Organizational Behavior* feature on page 173, their use is controversial. It is controversial because some question the ability of these tests to accurately capture a person's true level of intelligence. Also, there can be legal problems with intelligence tests if they result in an adverse impact. However, if a test accurately reflects individual intelligence, it can help managers select higher-quality associates. The superior human capital in the organization will then lead to higher productivity and the ability to gain an advantage over competitors. A competitive advantage, in turn, usually produces higher profits for the organization.[72]

EXHIBIT 5-4 Intelligence and Success

Job	Effects of Intelligence
Military Jobs*	**Percentage of Success in Training Attributable to General Intelligence**
Nuclear weapons specialist	77%
Air crew operations specialist	70%
Weather specialist	69%
Intelligence specialist	67%
Fireman	60%
Dental assistant	55%
Security police	54%
Vehicle maintenance	49%
General maintenance	28%
Civilian Jobs**	**Degree to which General Intelligence Predicts Job Performance (0 to 1 scale)**
Sales	.61
Technical assistant	.54
Manager	.53
Skilled trades and craft workers	.46
Protective professions workers	.42
Industrial workers	.37
Vehicle operator	.28
Sales clerk	.27

* *Source:* M.J. Ree and J.A. Earles. 1990. *Differential Validity* of a Differential Aptitude Test, AFHRL-TR-89–59 (San Antonio, TX: Brooks Air Force Base).
** *Source:* J.E. Hunter and R.F. Hunter. 1984. "Validity and Utility of Alternative Predictors of Job Performance," *Psychological Bulletin* 96: 72–98.

Attitudes

It is sometimes difficult to distinguish between an individual's personality and attitudes. The behavior of Southwest associates and managers described in the opening case, for example, might be interpreted by some as based primarily on attitudes rather than personality, whereas others might believe that personality plays a larger role. Regardless, managers are concerned about the attitudes of associates because they can be major causes of work behaviors. Positive attitudes frequently lead to productive efforts, whereas negative attitudes often produce poor work habits.

An **attitude** is defined as a persistent mental state of readiness to feel and behave in a favorable or unfavorable way toward a specific person, object, or idea. Close examination of this definition reveals three important conclusions. First, attitudes are reasonably stable.

attitude
A persistent tendency to feel and behave in a favorable or unfavorable way toward a specific person, object, or idea.

Intelligence and Intelligence Testing in the National Football League

Each spring, representatives of National Football League teams join a large group of college football players in Indianapolis, Indiana. They are in town to participate in the so-called draft combine, where the players are given the opportunity to demonstrate their football skills. After showing their speed, strength, and agility, the players hope to be selected by a team early in the draft process and to command a large salary. For some, success at the combine is critical to being chosen by a team. For others, success is important because the combine plays a role in determining the amount of signing bonuses and other financial incentives.

Talented football players work to achieve the best physical condition they can in anticipation of the important evaluations. They focus on the upcoming medical examinations, weightlifting assessments, 40-yard dashes, vertical- and broad-jump tests, and tackling-dummy tests. They may be less focused on another key feature of the draft combine—the intelligence test. The practice of testing general intelligence has been a fixture of the NFL since the early 1970s. The test that is used by all teams, the Wonderlic Personnel Test, has 50 questions and a time limit of 12 minutes in its basic version.

©PCN/Corbis Images

Teams place different levels of importance on the intelligence test. The Green Bay Packers, for example, historically have not put a great deal of emphasis on it. "The Wonderlic has never been a big part of what we do here," said former Green Bay general manager and current consultant Ron Wolf. "To me, it's [just] a signal. If it's low, you better find out why it's low, and if the guy is a good football player, you better satisfy your curiosity." The Cincinnati Bengals, in contrast, have generally taken the test very seriously, in part "because it is the only test of its kind given to college players." In Atlanta, former head coach Dan Reeves showed his faith in the intelligence-testing process by choosing a linebacker who was equal in every way to another linebacker, except for higher intelligence scores. In New York, intelligence and personality testing has been taken to an extreme for the NFL. The Giants organization has used a test with nearly 400 questions. The late Giants manager, George Young, stated, "Going into a draft without some form of psychological testing on the prospects is like going into a gunfight with a knife."

Can a player be too smart? According to some, the answer is yes. "I've been around some players who are too smart to be good football players," said Ralph Cindrich, a linebacker in the NFL many years ago. Many others have the opinion that high intelligence scores are indicative of a player who will not play within the system but will want to improvise too much on the field and argue with coaches too much off the field. There isn't much evidence, however, to support this argument. Many successful quarterbacks, for example, have had high scores. Super Bowl winner Tom Brady of the New England Patriots scored well above average, as did the New York Giants' Eli Manning.

Quarterbacks score higher on the test than players in several other positions but do not score the highest. Average scores for various positions are shown below, along with scores from the business world for comparison. A score of 20 correct out of 50 is considered average and equates to approximately 100 on a standard IQ test. Any score of 15 (the lowest score shown below) or above represents reasonable intelligence.

Offensive tackles—26

Centers—25

Quarterbacks—24

Fullbacks—17

Safeties—19

Wide receivers—17

Chemists—31

Programmers—29

News reporters—26

Halfbacks—16

Salespersons—24

Bank tellers—17

Security guards—17

Warehouse workers—15

Many players become tense over the NFL intelligence test. What types of questions are causing the anxiety? A sample of the easier questions follows (to learn more, go to www.wonderlic.com):

1. The 11th month of the year is: (a) October, (b) May, (c) November, (d) February.

2. Severe is opposite of: (a) harsh, (b) stern, (c) tender, (d) rigid, (e) unyielding.

3. In the following set of words, which word is different from the others? (a) sing, (b) call, (c) chatter, (d) hear, (e) speak.

4. A dealer bought some televisions for $3,500. He sold them for $5,500, making $50 on each television. How many televisions were involved?

5. Lemon candies sell at 3 for 15 cents. How much will $1\frac{1}{2}$ dozen cost?

6. Which number in the following group of numbers represents the smallest amount? (a) 6, (b) .7, (c) 9, (d) 36, (e) .31, (f) 5.

7. Look at the following row of numbers. What number should come next? 73 66 59 52 45 38.

8. A plane travels 75 feet in $\frac{1}{4}$ second. At this speed, how many feet will it travel in 5 seconds?

9. A skirt requires $2\frac{1}{3}$ yards of material. How many skirts can be cut from 42 yards?

10. ENLARGE, AGGRANDIZE. Do these words: (a) have similar meanings, (b) have contradictory meanings, (c) mean neither the same nor the opposite?

11. Three individuals form a partnership and agree to divide the profits equally. X invests $4,500, Y invests $3,500, Z invests $2,000. If the profits are $2,400, how much less does X receive than if profits were divided in proportion to the amount invested?

Sources: D. Dillon. 2001. "Testing, Testing: Taking the Wonderlic," *Sporting News.com,* Feb. 23, at www.sportingnews.com/voices/dennis_dillon/20010223.html; K. Kragthorpe. 2003. "Is Curtis Too Smart for NFL?" Utah Online, Apr. 23, at www.sltrib.com/2003/Apr/04232003/Sports/50504.asp; J. Litke. 2003. "Smarter Is Better in the NFL, Usually: But Not Too Smart to Be Good Football Players," *National Post (Canada),* May 1, p. S2; J. Magee. 2003. "NFL Employs the Wonderlic Test to Probe the Minds of Draft Prospects," SignOnSanDiego.com, Apr. 20, at www.signonsandiego.com/sports/nfl/magee/200304209999–ls20nflcol.html; J. Merron. 2002. "Taking Your Wonderlics," ESPN Page 2, Feb. 2, at www.espn.go.com/page2/s/closer/020228.html; T. Silverstein. 2001. "What's His Wonderlic? NFL Uses Time-Honored IQ Test as Measuring Stick for Rookies," *Milwaukee Journal Sentinel,* Apr. 18, p. C1 ; A. Barra. 2006. "Do These NFL Scores Count for Anything?" *Wall Street Journal (Eastern Edition),* Apr. 25, p. D.6

Unless people have strong reasons to change their attitudes, they will persist or remain the same. People who like jazz music today will probably like it tomorrow, unless important reasons occur to change their musical preferences.

Second, attitudes are directed toward some object, person, or idea; that is, we may have an attitude toward our job, our supervisor, or an idea the college instructor presented. If the attitude concerns the job (for example, if a person dislikes monotonous work), then the attitude is specifically directed toward that job. We cannot extend that negative job attitude to an attitude toward jazz music.

Third, an attitude toward an object or person relates to an individual's behavior toward that object or person. In this sense, attitudes may influence our actions. For example, if an individual likes jazz music (an attitude), he may go to a jazz club (a behavior) or buy a jazz CD (a behavior). If an associate dislikes her work (an attitude), she may avoid coming to work (absenteeism behavior) or exert very little effort on the job (poor productivity behavior). People tend to behave in ways that are consistent with their feelings. Therefore, to change an unproductive worker into a productive one, it may be necessary to deal with that worker's attitudes.

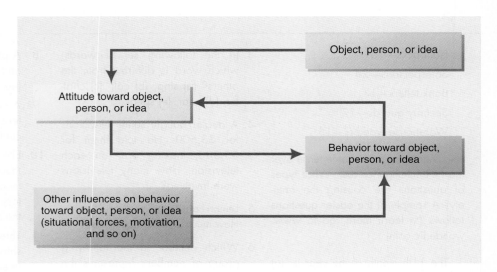

Exhibit 5-5   Influence of Attitudes on Behavior

As illustrated in Exhibit 5-5, our behavior toward an object, person, or idea is influenced by our attitudes. In turn, our attitudes are constantly developing and changing as a result of our behaviors. It is important to recognize that our behaviors are also influenced by other factors, such as motivational forces and situational factors. We therefore can understand why behaviors are not always predictable from attitudes. For example, we may have a strong positive attitude about a close friend. But we might reject an opportunity to go to a movie with that friend if we are preparing for a difficult exam to be given tomorrow. Thus, attitudes include behavioral tendencies and intentions, but our actual behaviors are also influenced by other factors.

Attitude Formation

Understanding how attitudes are formed is the first step in learning how to apply attitude concepts to organizational problems. This understanding can be developed by examining the three essential elements of an attitude: (1) cognitive, (2) affective, and (3) behavioral.[73]

- The *cognitive* element of an attitude consists of the facts we have gathered and considered about the object, person, or idea. Before we can have feelings about something, we must first be aware of it and think about its complexities.
- The *affective* element of an attitude refers to the feelings one has about the object or person. Such feelings are frequently expressed as like or dislike of the object or person and the degree to which one holds these feelings. For example, an employee may love the job, like it, dislike it, or hate it.
- Finally, most attitudes contain a *behavioral* element, which is the individual's intention to act in certain ways toward the object of the attitude. As previously explained, how we behave toward people may depend largely on whether we like or dislike them based on what we know about them.

The formation of attitudes may be quite complex. In the following discussion, we examine some ways in which attitudes are formed.

Learning

Attitudes can be formed through the learning process.[74] As explained in Chapter 4, when people interact with others or behave in particular ways toward an object, they often experience rewards or punishments. For example, if you touch a cactus plant, you may experience pain. As you experience the outcomes of such behavior, you begin to develop feelings about the objects of that behavior. Thus, if someone were to ask you how you felt about cactus plants, you might reply, "I don't like them—they can hurt." Of course, attitudes can also develop from watching others experience rewards and punishments. A person may not touch the cactus herself, but a negative attitude toward cacti could develop after she watches a friend experience pain.

Self-Perception

People may form attitudes based on simple observations of their own behaviors.[75] This is called the *self-perception effect,* and it works as follows. An individual engages in a particular behavior without thinking much about that behavior. Furthermore, no significant positive rewards are involved. Having engaged in the behavior, the person then diagnoses his actions, asking himself what the behavior suggests about his attitudes. In many instances, this person will conclude that he must have had a positive attitude toward the behavior. Why else would he have done what he did? For example, an individual may join co-workers in requesting an on-site cafeteria at work, doing so without much thought. Up to that point, the person may have had a relatively neutral attitude about a cafeteria. After having joined in the request, however, he may conclude that he has a positive attitude toward on-site cafeterias.

Influencing people through the foot-in-the-door technique is based on the self-perception effect. This technique involves asking a person for a small favor (foot-in-the-door) and later asking for a larger favor that is consistent with the initial request. After completing the small favor with little thought, the target often concludes that she has a positive view toward whatever was done, and therefore she is more likely to perform the larger favor. In one study of the foot-in-the-door technique, researchers went door-to-door asking individuals to sign a petition for safer driving.[76] The request was small and noncontroversial; thus, most people signed the petition without much thought. Weeks later, colleagues of the researchers visited these same people and asked them to put a large, unattractive sign in their yards that read "Drive Carefully." These same colleagues also approached other homeowners who had not been asked for the initial small favor. Fifty-five percent of the individuals who had signed the petition agreed to put an ugly sign in their yards, whereas only 17 percent of those who had not been asked to sign the petition agreed to the yard sign.

Need for Consistency

A major concept associated with attitude formation is consistency.[77] Two well-known theories in social psychology, *balance theory* and *congruity theory,* are important to an understanding of attitude consistency. The basic notion is that people prefer that their attitudes be consistent with one another (in balance or congruent). If we have a specific attitude toward an object or person, we tend to form other consistent attitudes toward related objects or persons.

A simple example of attitude formation based on consistency appears in Exhibit 5-6. Dan is a young accounting graduate. He is impressed with accounting theory and thinks that accountants should work with data to arrive at important conclusions for management. Obviously, he has a positive attitude toward accounting, as illustrated by the plus sign between Dan and accounting in the exhibit. Now suppose that Dan's new job requires him to work with someone who dislikes accounting (represented by the minus sign between

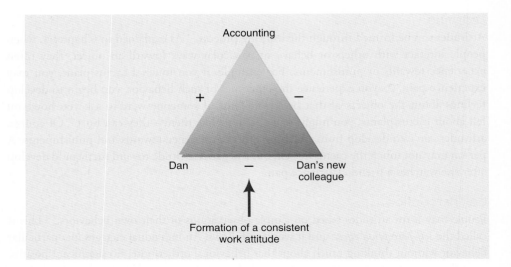

Exhibit 5-6 Formation of Consistent Attitudes

the new colleague and accounting). In this case, Dan may form a negative attitude toward the person in order to have a consistent set of attitudes. Dan likes accounting and may have a negative attitude toward those who do not.

Two Important Attitudes in the Workplace

The two most thoroughly examined attitudes in organizational behavior are job satisfaction and organizational commitment. Job satisfaction is a broad attitude related to the job. A high level of satisfaction represents a positive attitude toward the job, while a low level of satisfaction represents a negative attitude. Organizational commitment, as defined here, is a broad attitude toward the organization as a whole. It represents how strongly an individual identifies with and values being associated with the organization. Strong commitment is a positive attitude toward the organization, whereas weak commitment is a less positive attitude. As we discuss below, these two attitudes can impact behavior that is important to the functioning of an organization; thus, it is important to consider job satisfaction and organizational commitment as desirable aspects of human capital.[78]

Job Satisfaction and Outcomes

Organizations need to be concerned with the satisfaction of their associates, because job satisfaction is linked to many important behaviors that can have an impact on the bottom line of an organization's performance. Satisfaction has a highly positive effect on intentions to stay in the job and a modest effect on actually staying in the job.[79] Factors such as attractive job openings during a booming economy and reaching retirement age can cause satisfied people to leave, but in general satisfaction is associated with low turnover. With the costs of replacing a departed worker generally quite high, maintaining higher levels of satisfaction is important. High satisfaction also has a modestly positive effect on regular attendance at work.[80] Factors such as a very liberal sick-leave policy can, however, cause even highly satisfied associates and managers to miss work time. Satisfaction also has a moderately strong relationship with motivation.[81]

Job satisfaction has a reasonably straightforward relationship with intention to stay, actually staying, absenteeism, and motivation. In contrast, the specific form of the relationship between satisfaction and job performance has been the subject of a great deal of controversy. Many managers and researchers believe that high satisfaction produces strong performance. This idea seems reasonable, for a positive attitude should indeed result in strong effort and accountability. Other managers and researchers, however, believe that it is strong performance that causes workers to be satisfied with their jobs. For this second group of investigators, a positive attitude does not cause strong performance but strong performance does cause a positive attitude. Still others believe that satisfaction and performance are not related or are only weakly related. For this last group, factors other than attitudes, such as skills and incentive systems, are believed to have much stronger effects on job performance.

A recent study has helped to put these differences of opinion into perspective.[82] In this study, all previously published research on satisfaction and performance was synthesized using modern quantitative and qualitative techniques. The study concluded with an integrative model suggesting that all three of the groups mentioned above are correct to some degree. High satisfaction causes strong performance, strong performance also causes high satisfaction, and the relationship between the two is weaker in some situations. On this last point, low conscientiousness and the existence of simple work are examples of factors that may cause the relationship to be weaker. Individuals who have positive attitudes toward the job but who are lower in conscientiousness may not necessarily work hard, which weakens the effects of job satisfaction on performance. In addition, strong performance at simple work does not necessarily result in strong satisfaction, which weakens the effects of performance on satisfaction. For engineers, managers, and others with complex jobs, performance and satisfaction have a reasonably strong connection.

Organizational Commitment and Outcomes in the Workplace

Similar to satisfaction, commitment has important effects on intentions to stay in the job and modest effects on actually staying in the job and attending work regularly.[83] Commitment also is significantly related to motivation. Interestingly, length of employment plays a role in the relationship between commitment and staying in the job. A high level of organizational commitment tends to be more important in decisions to stay for associates and managers who have worked in their jobs for less time.[84] For longer-term employees, simple inertia and habit may prevent departures independent of the level of commitment to the organization. Commitment also has positive effects on job performance, but the effects are somewhat small.[85] This link to performance appears to be stronger for managers and professionals. Although the relationship between commitment and regular job performance is not extremely strong, organizational commitment does have a very strong relationship with discretionary organizational citizenship behaviors, such as helping others and taking on voluntary assignments.[86]

Causes of Job Satisfaction and Organizational Commitment

Given that job satisfaction and organizational commitment can impact on many important organizational behaviors, it is imperative that organizations understand what makes their associates satisfied and committed. Many of the same factors that lead to job satisfaction also lead to organizational commitment. These factors include:

- Role ambiguity[87]
- Supervision/leadership[88]
- Pay and benefits[89]

- Nature of the job[90]
- Organizational climate[91]
- Stress[92]
- Perceptions of fair treatment[93]

Although these factors have all been linked to satisfaction and commitment, the relationships are not always so simple. For example, in order to best understand whether someone will be satisfied with a given dimension of her work, you need to consider her comparison standard. People compare desirable facets of their work with what they expect to receive or what they think they should receive.[94] So, while one person may be very satisfied with earning $100,000 per year, another person may find this amount unsatisfactory because she was expecting to earn more.

Another complication arises when we consider that associates may be committed to their organization for different reasons. There are three general reasons why people are committed to their organizations.[95] **Affective commitment** is usually what we think of when we talk about organizational commitment because it means someone has strong positive attitudes toward the organization. **Normative commitment** means that someone is committed to the organization because he feels he should be. Someone who stays with their organization because he does not want to let his co-workers down is normatively committed. Finally, associates may experience **continuance commitment**, which means that they are committed to the organization because they do not have any better opportunities. Different factors affect different types of commitment.[96] For example, benefits may affect continuance commitment, for example, when a person is committed to an organization only because her retirement plan will not transfer to another organization. On the other hand, benefits may not influence how positive one feels about the organization, so that benefits would be unrelated to affective commitment.

One other thing to note about the factors affecting satisfaction and commitment is that the presence of high-involvement management is particularly important. Individuals usually have positive experiences working with this management approach, and thus strong satisfaction and commitment is likely to develop through the learning mechanism of attitude formation. As part of high-involvement management, individuals are selected for organizations in which their values fit, they are well trained, they are encouraged to think for themselves, and they are treated fairly (e.g., receive equitable compensation).

Finally, satisfaction and commitment are not totally dependent on situational factors; personality also can play a role. Some individuals have a propensity to be satisfied and committed, whereas others are less likely to exhibit positive attitudes, no matter the actual situation in which they work.[97] In addition to one's personality disposition, emotions can also affect job attitudes. Thus, we discuss emotions in the workplace later in this chapter.

Attitude Change

Personality characteristics are believed to be rather stable, as we have seen, but attitudes are more susceptible to change. Social forces, such as peer pressure or changes in society, act on existing attitudes, so that over time attitudes may change, often in unpredictable ways. In addition, in many organizations, managers find they need to be active in changing employee attitudes. Although it is preferable for associates to have positive attitudes toward the job, the manager, and the organization, many do not. When the object of the attitude cannot be changed (for example, when a job cannot be redesigned), managers must work

---

affective commitment
Organizational commitment due to one's strong positive attitudes toward the organization.

normative commitment
Organizational commitment due to feelings of obligation.

continuance commitment
Organizational commitment due to lack of better opportunities.

directly on attitudes. In such cases, it is necessary to develop a systematic approach to change attitudes in favorable directions. We discuss two relevant techniques next.

Persuasive Communication

Most of us experience daily attempts by others to persuade us to change our attitudes. Television, radio, and Internet advertisements are common forms of such persuasive communication. Political campaigns are another form. Occasionally, a person who is virtually unknown at the beginning of a political campaign (such as Bill Clinton) can win an election by virtue of extensive advertising and face-to-face communication.

The persuasive communication approach to attitude change consists of four elements:[98]

1. *Communicator*—the person who holds a particular attitude and wants to convince others to share that attitude
2. *Message*—the content designed to induce the change in others' attitudes
3. *Situation*—the surroundings in which the message is presented
4. *Target*—the person whose attitude the communicator wants to change

Several qualities of the communicator affect attitude change in the target. First, the communicator's overall credibility has an important effect on the target's response to the persuasion attempt. Research shows that people give more weight to persuasive messages from people they respect.[99] It is more difficult to reject messages that disagree with our attitudes when the communicator has high credibility.

Second, people are more likely to change their attitudes when they trust the intentions of the communicator. If we perceive that the communicator has something to gain from the attitude change, we are likely to distrust his or her intentions. But if we believe the communicator is more objective and less self-serving, we will trust his or her intentions and be more likely to change our attitudes. Individuals who argue against their own self-interests are effective at persuasion.[100]

Third, if people like the communicator or perceive that person to be similar to them in interests or goals, they are more likely to be persuaded.[101] This is one reason that movie stars, athletes, and other famous people are used for television ads. These people are widely liked and have characteristics that we perceive ourselves to have (correctly or incorrectly) or that we would like to have.

Finally, if the communicator is attractive, people have a stronger tendency to be persuaded. The effects of attractiveness have been discussed in studies of job seeking and political elections. The most notable example is the U.S. presidential election of 1960. By many accounts, Richard Nixon had equal, if not superior, command of the issues in the presidential debates that year, but the more handsome John Kennedy received higher ratings from the viewing public and won the election.[102]

The message involved in the communication can also influence attitude change. One of the most important dimensions of message content is fear arousal. Messages that arouse fear often produce more attitude change.[103] For example, a smoker who is told that smoking is linked to heart disease may change his attitude toward smoking. The actual amount of fear produced by the message also seems to play a role. If the smoker is told that smoking makes teeth turn yellow, rather than being told of a link to heart disease, the fear is weaker, and the resulting attitude change also is likely to be weaker.

Greater fear usually induces larger changes in attitudes, but not always. Three factors beyond amount of fear play a role:[104] (1) the probability that negative consequences will actually occur if no change in behavior is made, (2) the perceived effect of changing behavior, and (3) the perceived ability to change behavior. Returning to our smoker, even if the message regarding smoking risk arouses a great deal of fear, he still may not alter his attitude if he does not believe that he is likely to develop heart disease, if he has been smoking for so many years that he does not believe that quitting now will help the situation, or if he does not believe he can stop smoking.

So far, we have discussed how the communicator and the message affect attitude change. In general, each affects the degree to which the target believes the attitude should be changed. Frequently, however, people are motivated by factors outside the actual persuasion attempt. Such factors may be found in the situation in which persuasion is attempted. We can see a good example of this when a person is publicly reprimanded. If you have ever been present when a peer has been publicly chastised by an instructor, you may have been offended by the action. Instead of changing your attitude about the student or the student's skills, you may have changed your attitude about the instructor. Other situational factors include the reactions of those around you. Do they smile or nod their heads in approval when the communicator presents her message? Such behaviors encourage attitude change, whereas disapproving behavior may influence you to not change your attitudes.

Finally, characteristics of the target also influence the success of persuasion. For example, people differ in their personalities, their perceptions, and the way they learn. Some are more rigid and less willing to change their attitudes—even when most others believe that they are wrong. Locus of control and other characteristics also influence attitudes. People with high self-esteem are more likely to believe that their attitudes are correct, and they are less likely to change them. Therefore, it is difficult to predict precisely how different people will respond, even to the same persuasive communication. The effective manager is prepared for this uncertainty.

Cognitive Dissonance

cognitive dissonance
An uneasy feeling produced when a person behaves in a manner inconsistent with an existing attitude.

Another way in which attitudes can change involves **cognitive dissonance.** Like balance and congruity theories, discussed earlier in this chapter, dissonance theory deals with consistency.[105] In this case, the focus is usually on consistency between attitudes and behaviors—or, more accurately, inconsistency between attitudes and behaviors. For example, a manager may have a strong positive attitude toward incentive compensation, which involves paying people on the basis of their performance. This manager, however, may refuse workers' requests for such a compensation scheme. By refusing, she has created an inconsistency between an attitude and a behavior. If certain conditions are met, as explained below, this inconsistency will create an uneasy feeling (dissonance) that causes the manager to change her positive attitude.

What are the key conditions that lead to dissonance and the changing of an attitude? There are three.[106] First, the behavior must be substantially inconsistent with the attitude rather than just mildly inconsistent. Second, the inconsistent behavior must cause harm or have negative consequences for others. If no harmful or negative consequences are involved, the individual exhibiting the inconsistent behavior can more easily move on without giving much consideration to the inconsistency. Third, the inconsistent behavior must be voluntary and not forced, or at least the person must perceive it that way.

In our example, the manager's behavior satisfies the first two conditions. It was substantially inconsistent with her attitude, and it had negative consequences for the workers

MANAGERIAL ADVICE

Job Satisfaction Takes a Dive!

In 1987, a majority, 61.1 percent, of Americans responded that they were satisfied with their jobs. This was the first year that the Conference Board, a global independent membership organization that collects and disseminates information for senior executives around the world, surveyed workers about their job satisfaction. At the end of 2009, following a steady decrease over the years, that figure had plummeted to 45.3 percent. A less-scientific MSNBC poll of almost 45,000 people found that less than 34 percent of respondents were satisfied or somewhat satisfied with their jobs and 11.5 percent hated every part of their jobs.

©iStockphoto

The Conference Board survey found that while satisfaction has decreased for all age groups, it is particularly bad for younger workers. Less than 36 percent of those under 25 years old are satisfied with their jobs, as compared with a satisfaction rate of 47 percent for those 45 to 54 years old. These results also held across all income brackets. Furthermore, satisfaction decreased for all specific aspects of one's job, including: job design, organizational health, managerial quality, and extrinsic rewards.

Why are Americans so unhappy with their jobs? One could argue it is because of the economic downturn experienced during 2008 and 2009. Associates are required to do more, are afraid of losing their jobs, and are likely to receive fewer extrinsic rewards ("no raises this year!"). However, this is not the entire story. "It says something troubling about work in America. It is not about the business cycle or one grumpy generation," says Linda Barrington, managing director of human capital at the Conference Board. On of the major reasons that respondents were dissatisfied with their jobs was because the jobs were uninteresting. Ratings of interest in one's work dropped almost 19 percentage points between 1987 and 2009, with only about half of respondents currently finding their jobs interesting. Americans are finding their jobs increasingly boring and unengaging. Other reasons given for job dissatisfaction included salaries that were not keeping up with inflation, job insecurity, and health care costs.

These findings should be a wake-up call for employers. John Gibbons, program director of employee engagement research and services at the Conference Board, says "Widespread job dissatisfaction negatively affects employee behavior and retention, which can impact enterprise-level success." Lynn Franco, director of the Conference Board's Consumer Research Center, concurs, "What's really disturbing about growing job dissatisfaction is the way it can play into the competitive nature of the U.S. work force down the road and on the growth of the U.S. economy—all in a negative way." John Hollon warns, "my counsel for managers and executives is simple: If you ignore these numbers, you do so at your own peril." It is imperative that managers pay attention to these findings, given the effects that low satisfaction and commitment can have on the climate, functioning, and bottom-line success of an organization.

Sources: http://www.conference-board.org/aboutus/about.cfm; The Conference Board. Jan. 5, 2010, "U.S. Job Satisfaction at Lowest Level in Two Decades," at http://www.conference-board.org/utilities/pressDetail. cfm?press_ID=3820. MSNBC, Jan. 5, 2010. "Are you satisfied with your job?" at http://business.newsvine.com/_question/2010/01/05/3716711-are-you-satisfied-with-your-job?threadId=759420&pc=25&sp=25#short%20comment; MSNBC, Jan. 5, 2010. "Job satisfaction falls to a record low: Economists warn discontent could stifle innovation, hurt U.S. productivity," at C:\Documents and Settings\Administrator\My Documents\Americans' job satisfaction falls to record low - Careers- msnbc_com.mht; J. Hollon. Jan. 5, 2010. "A Ticking Time Bomb: Job Satisfaction Hits Record-Low Levels," *Workforce Management*, at C:\Documents and Settings\Administrator\My Documents\Workforce Blogs - The Business of Management.mht.

who wanted incentive pay. We have no way of knowing whether the third condition was met because we do not know whether someone higher in the organization ordered the manager to refuse the requests for incentive compensation or whether a union agreement prohibited such a compensation scheme. If the manager's behavior was not forced by a higher-level manager or an agreement, dissonance is more likely to occur, leading to a change of the manager's attitude toward incentive pay from positive to negative.

If an executive had wanted to change this manager's attitude toward incentive pay, he could have gently suggested that such pay not be used. If the manager acted on this suggestion, she may have experienced dissonance and changed the attitude because her behavior was at least partly voluntary. She was not required to act in a manner inconsistent with her attitude, but she did so anyway. To eliminate the uneasy feeling associated with the inconsistent behavior, she may convince herself that she does not like incentive pay as much as she previously thought.

Emotions

During a sales force team meeting, Chad became frustrated with team leader Bob's presentation. He felt that Bob was ignoring the needs of his unit. In a pique of anger, Chad yelled out that Bob was hiding something from everyone and being dishonest. Bob's reaction to Chad's outburst was to slam his fist on the table and tell him to be quiet or leave. Next door, in the same company, Susan had just learned that her team had won a coveted account. She jumped with joy and was all smiles when she ran down the hall to tell her teammates. Everyone she passed grinned and felt better when they saw Susan running past their desks.

Chad, Bob, and Susan are all displaying their emotions at work. Despite the common norms that associates should hide their emotions when they are at work,[107] people are emotional beings, and emotions play a big role in everyday organizational behavior. Indeed, organizational scholars have recently begun studying the role emotions play at work,[108] and organizations have become more concerned with the emotions of their employees. For example, Douglas Conant, CEO of Campbell Soup, says that in his company care is taken to make sure that employees focus their emotions on their jobs, so that employees "fall in love with (the) company's agenda."[109]

emotions
Complex subjective reactions that have both a physical and mental component.

Emotions are complex reactions that have both a physical and a mental component. These reactions include anger, happiness, anxiety, pride, contentment, and guilt. Emotional reactions include a subjective feeling accompanied by changes in bodily functioning such as increased heart rate or blood pressure.[110] Emotions can play a part in organizational functioning in several ways. First, associates' emotions can directly affect their behavior. For example, angry associates may engage in workplace violence[111] or happy employees may be more likely to help other people on the job.[112] Another way in which emotions come into play at work is when the nature of the job calls for associates to display emotions that they might not actually be feeling. For example, on a rocky airplane ride, flight attendants have to appear calm, cool, and collected, while reassuring passengers that everything is okay. However, these flight attendants may have to do this while hiding their own fear and panic. This dynamic is called *emotional labor*. Finally, both business scholars and organizations have become concerned with what has been termed *emotional intelligence*. We turn now to discussions of these three roles that emotions play in organizational behavior.

Direct Effects of Emotions on Behavior

Emotions can have several direct causal effects on behavior. The relationship between emotions and other important behaviors, such as job performance, is less clear. While it would seem most likely that positive emotions would always lead to high performance, this is not always the case. In some instances, negative emotions, such as anger, can serve as a motivator. Research on creativity demonstrates this point. Some researchers have found that positive emotions increase creativity,[113] while others have found that negative emotions lead to greater creativity.[114] Positive emotions should lead to greater creativity because when people feel good they are more likely to be active and inquisitive. On the other hand, negative emotions, such as fear, can serve as a signal that something is amiss, leading people to search for creative solutions to solve the problem. Indeed, a recent study found that people were most creative when they were experiencing emotional ambivalence, that is, both positive and negative emotions at the same time.[115]

The direct effects of emotions can be either beneficial or harmful to organizational effectiveness. The impact of these emotions, whether negative or positive, is even greater when one considers the phenomenon of **emotional contagion**. Emotional contagion occurs when emotions experienced by one or a few members of a work group spread to other members.[116] One study found that leaders' emotions were particularly important in influencing the emotions of followers.[117] This study indicated that charismatic leaders have a positive influence on organizational effectiveness because they are able to induce positive emotions in their followers. Thus, angry and anxious leaders are likely to develop followers who are angry and anxious, whereas leaders who are happy and passionate about their work are likely to develop followers who experience the same emotions. Exhibit 5-7 summarizes the direct effects of emotions.

emotional contagion
Phenomenon where emotions experienced by one or a few members of a work group spread to other members.

EXHIBIT 5-7   The Direct Effects of Emotion

Positive Emotions Influence:
Social activity
Altruism and helping behavior
Effective conflict resolution
Job satisfaction
Motivation
Organizational citizenship behavior

Negative Emotions Influence:
Aggression against co-workers
Aggression toward the organization
Workplace deviance
Job dissatisfaction
Decision making
Negotiation outcomes

Sources: S. Lyubomirsky, L. King, & E. Deiner. 2005. The benefits of frequent positive affect: Does happiness lead to success? *Psychological Bulletin,* 131: 803–855; T.A. Judge, B.A. Scott, & R. Ilies. 2006. Hostility, job attitudes, and workplace deviance: Test of a multilevel model. *Journal of Applied Psychology,* 91: 126–138; M.S. Hershcovis, N. Turner, J. Barling, K.A. Arnols, K.E. Dupre, M. Inness, M.M. LeBlanc, & N. Sivanathan. 2007. Predicting workplace aggression: A meta-analysis. *Journal of Applied Psychology,* 92; 228–238; A.P. Brief, H.M. Weiss. 2002. Organizational behavior: Affect in the workplace. In S.T. Fiske (Ed.), *Annual Review of Psychology,* 53: 279–307. Palo Alto, CA: Annual Reviews.

Emotional Labor

Many service and sales jobs require that individuals display certain emotions, regardless of what they are really experiencing. For example, flight attendants are expected to be warm and cordial, call center employees are expected to keep their cool when customers are hostile toward them, and sales associates are expected to be enthusiastic about the product they are selling, no matter what they actually feel. The process whereby associates must display emotions that are contrary to what they are feeling is termed **emotional labor**.[118] Organizations often indicate to employees what emotions they must express and under what circumstances. When these required emotions, or display rules, are contrary to what associates are actually feeling, they can experience stress, emotional exhaustion, and burnout.[119] Emotional labor does not always lead to overstressed employees. When associates actually come to feel the emotions they are required to display, they can experience positive outcomes such as greater job satisfaction.[120]

Even when associates may not feel the emotions they are required to express, several factors can influence whether this acting will have a negative outcome on associates' well-being. First, the manner in which supervisors enforce display rules can influence whether emotional labor is harmful to associates.[121] When supervisors are quite demanding, associates will become more exhausted. Another factor that influences the effects of emotional labor is the self-identities of associates.[122] When associates have a strong self-identity as a service worker or a caregiver then they will be less likely to experience negative effects from emotional labor. For example, a hospice care worker may feel tired and frustrated, but behave in a caring and nurturing manner with her patients. If the care worker has a strong self-identity as a caregiver, she will experience less exhaustion from her emotional labor. Finally, when associates have networks of supportive people and caring mentors, the negative effects of emotional labor will be mitigated.[123]

Emotional Intelligence

Are some people just better dealing with emotions, theirs and others, than are other people? The past decade or so has seen an explosion in what has been termed the concept of **emotional intelligence** in both the study and practice of management. The best-accepted definition of emotional intelligence (EI) is that it is the ability to

- Accurately appraise one's own and others' emotions.
- Effectively regulate one's own and others' emotions.
- Use emotion to motivate, plan, and achieve.[124]

A person displaying high emotional intelligence can accurately determine his or her own emotions and the effect those emotions will have on others, then go on to regulate the emotions to achieve his or her goals.

Emotional intelligence has been linked to career success, leadership effectiveness, managerial performance, and performance in sales jobs.[125] It also is the subject of many management development programs, popular books,[126] and articles that may at times inflate the value of emotional intelligence relative to cognitive intelligence.[127] The specific abilities generally associated with emotional intelligence include:[128]

- ***Self-awareness.*** Associates with high self-awareness understand how their feelings, beliefs, and behaviors affect themselves and others. For example, a supervisor knows that her reaction to a valuable (and otherwise high-performing)

---

emotional labor
The process whereby associates must display emotions that are contrary to what they are feeling.

emotional intelligence
The ability to accurately appraise one's own and others' emotions, effectively regulate one's own and others' emotions, and use emotion to motivate, plan, and achieve.

associate's chronic lateness and excuses is one of anger, but she realizes that if she displays this anger, it will cause the associate to withdraw even further.

- *Self-regulation.* Self-regulation is the ability to control one's emotions. The supervisor may feel like yelling at the associate or being punitive in making work assignments; however, if she is high in self-regulation, she will choose her words and actions carefully. She will behave in a manner that will more likely encourage the associate to come to work on time rather than make the associate withdraw even more.
- *Motivation or drive.* This characteristic is the same as achievement motivation, discussed previously in this chapter, and drive, discussed above under trait theories. Associates with high EI want to achieve for achievement's sake alone. They always want to do things better and seek out feedback about their progress. They are passionate about their work.
- *Empathy.* Effective empathy means thoughtfully considering others' feelings when making decisions and weighting those feelings appropriately, along with other factors. Consider again our example of the supervisor dealing with the tardy associate. Suppose she knows that the associate is frequently late because he is treated poorly by the work group. The supervisor can display empathy by acknowledging this situation and can act on it by attempting to change work arrangements rather than punishing the associate for being late. Thus, she can remove an obstacle for the associate and perhaps retain an associate who performs well and comes to work on time.
- *Social skill.* Social skill refers to the ability to build effective relationships with the goal of moving people toward a desired outcome. Socially skilled associates know how to build bonds between people. Often, leaders who appear to be

THE STRATEGIC LENS

Understanding personality, intelligence, attitudes, and emotions enables managers to more effectively manage the behavior of their associates. Selecting new associates based on personality and intelligence can have an impact on organizational performance, as demonstrated by Outback Steakhouse and the National Football League. Hiring associates who fit its culture in turn enables an organization to better implement its strategy, as illustrated by the success of Patricia Harris at McDonald's. Organizations can further increase existing associates' organizational fit, performance, and tenure by creating work environments that lead to positive attitudes and emotionally healthy environments. Furthermore, from the examples presented throughout the chapter and summarized above, we can see how knowledge of personality, intelligence, attitudes, and emotions allows executives to more effectively implement their strategies through management of behavior in their organizations.

Critical Thinking Questions

1. Specifically, how can you use knowledge of personality, attitudes, intelligence, and emotions to make better hiring decisions?

2. If top executives wanted to implement a strategy that emphasized innovation and new products, how could they use knowledge of personality, attitudes, and emotions to affect the organization's culture in ways to enhance innovation?

3. How could a manager use knowledge about personality and attitudes to form a high-performance work team?

socializing with co-workers are actually working to build relationships and exercise their influence in a positive manner.

While emotional intelligence is quite a popular concept right now, it is not without its critics.[129] One major criticism is that emotional intelligence is not intelligence at all, but rather a conglomeration of specific social skills and personality traits. Another criticism is that sometimes emotional intelligence is so broadly defined that it is meaningless. Nonetheless, the basic abilities that make up emotional intelligence are important influences on organizational behavior, whether they form one construct called *emotional intelligence* or are simply considered alone.

What This Chapter Adds to Your Knowledge Portfolio

In this chapter, we have discussed personality in some detail. We have seen how personality develops and how important it is in the workplace. We have also discussed intelligence. If an organization is to be successful, its associates and managers must understand the effects of personality and intelligence and be prepared to act on this knowledge. Moving beyond enduring traits and mental ability, we have examined attitude formation and change. Without insights into attitudes, associates and managers alike would miss important clues about how a person will act in the workplace. Finally, we have briefly examined emotions and their various roles in behavior and organizational life. More specifically, we have made the following points:

- Personality is a stable set of characteristics representing the internal properties of an individual. These characteristics, or traits, are relatively enduring, are major determinants of behavior, and influence behavior across a wide variety of situations.
- Determinants of personality include heredity and environment. Three types of studies have demonstrated the effects of heredity: (1) investigations of identical twins, (2) assessments of newborns and their behavior later in life, and (3) direct examinations of genes. Studies of environmental effects have emphasized childhood experiences as important forces in personality development.
- There are many aspects of personality. Five traits, however, have emerged as particularly important in the workplace. These traits, collectively known as the Big Five, are extraversion, conscientiousness, agreeableness, emotional stability, and openness to experience.
- Extraversion (the degree to which a person is outgoing and derives energy from being around people) tends to affect overall job performance, success in team interactions, and job satisfaction. For performance, fit with the job is important, as extraverts have at least modest advantages in occupations calling for a high level of interaction with other people, whereas introverts appear to have advantages in occupations calling for more solitary work.
- Conscientiousness (the degree to which a person focuses on goals and works toward them in a disciplined way) also affects job performance, success as a team member, and job satisfaction. Higher levels of conscientiousness tend to be positive for these outcomes.
- Agreeableness (the degree to which a person is easygoing and tolerant) does not have simple, easily specified effects on individual job performance but does appear to contribute positively to successful interactions on a team.
- Emotional stability (the degree to which a person handles stressful, high-demand situations with ease) affects job performance, success as a team member, and job satisfaction. Higher levels of emotional stability tend to be positive.
- Openness to experience (the degree to which a person seeks new experiences and thinks creatively about the future) does not have simple links to overall job performance, success at teamwork, or job satisfaction, but individuals scoring higher on this aspect

of personality do appear to have an edge in specific tasks calling for vision and creativity.

- The Big Five personality traits may play a role in high-involvement management. Certain combinations of these traits seem to provide a foundation for the competencies needed by managers and associates. Absent these trait combinations, individuals may still be effective in high-involvement systems, but they may need to work a little harder.

- A Big Five assessment can be useful in selecting new associates and managers but must be combined with other tools, such as structured interviews and evaluations of the specific skills needed for a particular job.

- Beyond the Big Five, several cognitive and motivational personality concepts are important in the workplace. Cognitive concepts correspond to perceptual and thought processes and include locus of control, authoritarianism, social dominance orientation, and self-monitoring. Motivational concepts correspond to needs in individuals and are directly involved in energizing and maintaining overt behaviors. They include achievement motivation and approval motivation.

- There are many areas of intelligence, including number aptitude, verbal comprehension, and perceptual speed. Most psychologists who have extensively studied intelligence believe these various areas combine to form a single meaningful intelligence factor. This general intelligence factor has been found to predict workplace outcomes.

- An attitude is a persistent mental state of readiness to feel and behave in favorable or unfavorable ways toward a specific person, object, or idea. Attitudes consist of a cognitive element, an affective element, and a behavioral element.

- Attitudes may be learned as a result of direct experience with an object, person, or idea. Unfavorable experiences are likely to lead to unfavorable attitudes, and favorable experiences to favorable attitudes. Attitudes may also form as the result of self-perception, where an individual behaves in a certain way and then concludes he has an attitude that matches the behavior. Finally, attitudes may form on the basis of a need for consistency. We tend to form attitudes that are consistent with our existing attitudes.

- Job satisfaction and organizational commitment are two of the most important workplace attitudes. Job satisfaction is a favorable or unfavorable view of the job, whereas organizational commitment corresponds to how strongly an individual identifies with and values being associated with the organization. Both of these attitudes affect intentions to stay in the job, actual decisions to stay, and absenteeism. They are also related to job performance, though not as strongly as some other factors. Attitudes may change through exposure to persuasive communications or cognitive dissonance. Persuasive communication consists of four important elements: the communicator, message, situation, and target. Dissonance refers to inconsistencies between attitude and behavior. Under certain

back to the knowledge objectives

1. What is meant by the term *personality*? What key beliefs do psychologists traditionally hold about personality traits?

2. What are the Big Five traits, and how do they influence behavior and performance in the workplace? Give an example of someone you know whose personality did not fit the job he or she had. This could be a person in an organization in which you worked, or it could be a person from a school club or civic organization. What was the outcome? If you had been the individual's manager, how would you have attempted to improve the situation?

3. Describe a situation in which a manager's or a friend's locus of control, authoritarianism, social dominance orientation, self-monitoring, need for achievement, or approval motivation had an impact on your life.

4. What is intelligence, and what is its effect in the workplace?

5. How are attitudes similar to and different from personality? How do attitudes form? How can managers change attitudes in the workplace? Assume that the target of the attitude cannot be changed (that is, the job, boss, technology, and so on cannot be changed). Be sure to address both persuasive communication and dissonance.

6. What is the relationship between emotions and attitudes? Describe the emotions displayed by a past or current boss and explain how those emotions affected your job.

conditions, a behavior that is inconsistent with an existing attitude causes the attitude to change. Key conditions include: (1) the behavior being substantially inconsistent with the attitude, (2) the behavior causing harm or being negative for someone, and (3) the behavior being voluntary.

- Emotions are the subjective reactions associates experience that contain both a psychological and physiological component. Emotions can influence organizational behavior directly, as the basis of emotional labor, or through associates' emotional intelligence.

Key Terms

personality, p. 157
extraversion, p. 159
conscientiousness, p. 160
agreeableness, p. 160
emotional stability, p. 161
openness to experience, p. 161
locus of control, p. 164
authoritarianism, p. 164

social dominance
    orientation, p. 165
self-monitoring, p. 165
achievement
    motivation, p. 165
approval motivation, p. 166
intelligence, p. 168
attitude, p. 169
affective commitment, p. 176

normative commitment,
    p. 176
continuance commitment,
    p. 176
cognitive dissonance, p. 178
emotions, p. 180
emotional contagion, p. 181
emotional labor, p. 182
emotional intelligence, p. 182

---

building your human capital

Big Five Personality Assessment

Different people have different personalities, and these personalities can affect outcomes in the workplace. Understanding your own personality can help you to understand how and why you behave as you do. In this installment of *Building Your Human Capital*, we present an assessment tool for the Big Five.

Instructions

In this assessment, you will read 50 phrases that describe people. Use the rating scale below to indicate how accurately each phrase describes you. Rate yourself as you generally are now, not as you wish to be in the future; and rate yourself as you honestly see yourself. Keep in mind that very few people have extreme scores on all or even most of the items (a "1" or a "5" is an extreme score); most people have midrange scores for many of the items. Read each item carefully, and then circle the number that corresponds to your choice from the rating scale.

1	2	3	4	5
Not at all like me	Somewhat unlike me	Neither like nor unlike me	Somewhat like me	Very much like me

1. Am the life of the party.	1	2	3	4	5
2. Feel little concern for others.	1	2	3	4	5
3. Am always prepared.	1	2	3	4	5

4.	Get stressed out easily.	1	2	3	4	5
5.	Have a rich vocabulary.	1	2	3	4	5
6.	Don't talk a lot.	1	2	3	4	5
7.	Am interested in people.	1	2	3	4	5
8.	Leave my belongings around.	1	2	3	4	5
9.	Am relaxed most of the time.	1	2	3	4	5
10.	Have difficulty understanding abstract ideas.	1	2	3	4	5
11.	Feel comfortable around people.	1	2	3	4	5
12.	Insult people.	1	2	3	4	5
13.	Pay attention to details.	1	2	3	4	5
14.	Worry about things.	1	2	3	4	5
15.	Have a vivid imagination.	1	2	3	4	5
16.	Keep in the background.	1	2	3	4	5
17.	Sympathize with others' feelings.	1	2	3	4	5
18.	Make a mess of things.	1	2	3	4	5
19.	Seldom feel blue.	1	2	3	4	5
20.	Am not interested in abstract ideas.	1	2	3	4	5
21.	Start conversations.	1	2	3	4	5
22.	Am not interested in other people's problems.	1	2	3	4	5
23.	Get chores done right away.	1	2	3	4	5
24.	Am easily disturbed.	1	2	3	4	5
25.	Have excellent ideas.	1	2	3	4	5
26.	Have little to say.	1	2	3	4	5
27.	Have a soft heart.	1	2	3	4	5
28.	Often forget to put things back in their proper place.	1	2	3	4	5
29.	Get easily upset.	1	2	3	4	5
30.	Do not have a good imagination.	1	2	3	4	5
31.	Talk to a lot of different people at parties.	1	2	3	4	5
32.	Am not really interested in others.	1	2	3	4	5
33.	Like order.	1	2	3	4	5
34.	Change my mood a lot.	1	2	3	4	5
35.	Am quick to understand things.	1	2	3	4	5
36.	Don't like to draw attention to myself.	1	2	3	4	5
37.	Take time out for others.	1	2	3	4	5
38.	Shirk my duties.	1	2	3	4	5
39.	Have frequent mood swings.	1	2	3	4	5
40.	Use difficult words.	1	2	3	4	5
41.	Don't mind being the center of attention.	1	2	3	4	5
42.	Feel others' emotions.	1	2	3	4	5
43.	Follow a schedule.	1	2	3	4	5
44.	Get irritated easily.	1	2	3	4	5
45.	Spend time reflecting on things.	1	2	3	4	5
46.	Am quiet around strangers.	1	2	3	4	5
47.	Make people feel at ease.	1	2	3	4	5
48.	Am exact in my work.	1	2	3	4	5
49.	Often feel blue.	1	2	3	4	5
50.	Am full of ideas.	1	2	3	4	5

Scoring Key

To determine your scores, combine your responses to the items above as follows:

Extraversion = (Item 1 + Item 11 + Item 21 + Item 31 + Item 41) + (30 − (Item 6 + Item 16 + Item 26 + Item 36 + Item 46))

Conscientiousness = (Item 3 + Item 13 + Item 23 + Item 33 + Item 43 + Item 48) + (24 − (Item 8 + Item 18 + Item 28 + Item 38))

Agreeableness = (Item 7 + Item 17 + Item 27 + Item 37 + Item 42 + Item 47) + (24 − (Item 2 + Item 12 + Item 22 + Item 32))

Emotional stability = (Item 9 + Item 19) + (48 − (Item 4 + Item 14 + Item 24 + Item 29 + Item 34 + Item 39 + Item 44 + Item 49))

Openness to experience = (Item 5 + Item 15 + Item 25 + Item 35 + Item 40 + Item 45 + Item 50) + (18 − (Item 10 + Item 20 + Item 30))

Scores for each trait can range from 10 to 50. Scores of 40 and above may be considered high, while scores of 20 and below may be considered low.

Source: International Personality Item Pool. 2001. A Scientific Collaboration for the Development of Advanced Measures of Personality Traits and Other Individual Differences (http://ipip.ori.org).

---

an organizational behavior moment
Whatever Is Necessary!

Marian could feel the rage surge from deep within her. Even though she was usually in control of her behavior, it was not easy to control her internal emotions. She could sense her rapid pulse and knew that her face was flushed. But she knew that her emotional reaction to the report would soon subside in the solitary confines of her executive office. She would be free to think about the problem and make a decision about solving it.

Marian had joined the bank eight months ago as manager in charge of the consumer loan sections. There were eight loan sections in all, and her duties were both interesting and challenging. But for some reason there had been a trend in the past six months of decreasing loan volume and increasing payment delinquency. The month-end report to which she reacted showed that the past month was the worst in both categories in several years.

Vince Stoddard, the president, had been impressed by her credentials and aggressiveness when he hired her. Marian had been in the business for 10 years and was the head loan officer for one of the bank's competitors. Her reputation for aggressive pursuit of business goals was almost legendary among local bankers. She was active in the credit association and worked long, hard hours. Vince believed that she was the ideal person for the position.

When he hired her, he had said, "Marian, you're right for the job, but I know it won't be easy for you. Dave Kattar, who heads one of the loan sections, also wanted the job. In fact, had you turned down our offer, it would have been Dave's. He is well liked around here, and I also respect him. I don't think you'll have any problems working with him, but don't push him too hard at first. Let him get used to you, and I think you'll find him to be quite an asset."

But Dave was nothing but a "pain in the neck" for Marian. She sensed his resentment from the first day she came to work. Although he never said anything negative, his aggravating way of ending most conversations with her was, "Okay, Boss Lady. Whatever you want is what we'll do."

When loan volume turned down shortly after her arrival, she called a staff meeting with all of the section heads. As she began to explain that volume was off, she thought she noticed several of the section heads look over to Dave. Because she saw Dave only out of the corner of her eye, she couldn't be certain, but she thought he winked at the other heads. That action immediately angered her—and she felt her face flush. The meeting accomplished little, but each section head promised that the next month would be better.

In fact, the next month was worse, and each subsequent month followed that pattern. Staff meetings were now more frequent, and Marian was more prone to explode angrily with threats of what would happen if they didn't improve. So far she had not followed through on any threats, but she thought that "now" might be the time.

To consolidate her position, she had talked the situation over with Vince, and he had said rather coolly, "Whatever you think is necessary." He hadn't been very friendly toward her for several weeks, and she was worried about that also.

"So," Marian thought to herself, "I wonder what will happen if I fire Dave. If I get him out of here, will the others shape up? On the other hand, Vince might not support me. But maybe he's just waiting for me to take charge. It might even get me back in good graces with him."

Discussion Questions

1. What role did personality play in the situation at the bank? Which of the Big Five personality traits most clearly

influenced Marian and Dave? Which of the cognitive and motivational aspects of personality played a role?

2. Working within the bounds of her personality, what should Marian have done when trouble first seemed to be brewing? How could she have maintained Dave's job satisfaction and commitment?

3. How should Marian proceed now that the situation has become very difficult?

---

team exercise

Experiencing Emotional Labor

Have you ever been forced to smile at someone who was annoying you? Have you ever had to be calm when you felt very afraid? If so, you have probably engaged in emotional labor. The purpose of this exercise is to examine how emotional labor can affect us in different ways and the factors that impact the toll that emotional labor can take on us.

STEPS
1. At the beginning of class, assemble into teams of six to eight people.
2. During the next 30 minutes of class, each individual will be required to follow emotional display rules for one of the following emotions:
   a. Happiness
   b. Anger
   c. Compassion and caring
   d. Fear
   Assign the display rules so that at least one person is displaying each emotion.
3. Each person is to display his or her assigned emotion during the next 30 minutes of class lecture or activity—*no matter what he or she actually feels!*
4. At the end of the 30 minutes (or when instructed by your teacher), re-form into groups and address the following questions:
   a. How difficult was it for you to display your assigned emotion? Was your assigned emotion different from how you actually felt? Did your felt emotions begin to change to coincide with your displayed emotion?
   b. To what extent did the type of emotion required (e.g., happiness versus anger) influence your reaction to this exercise?
   c. How much longer could you have continued displaying your assigned emotion? Why?
5. Appoint a spokesperson to present the group's conclusions to the entire class.

Source: Adapted from *Experiences in Management and Organizational Behavior,* 4th ed. New York: John Wiley & Sons, 1997.

Endnotes

1. Barrick, M.R., & Mount, M.K. 1991. The Big Five personality dimensions and performance: A meta-analysis. *Personnel Psychology,* 44: 1–26.
2. Hough, L.M., Oswald, F.L., & Ployhart, R.E. 2001. Determinants, detection, and amelioration of adverse impact in personnel selection procedures: Issues, evidence and lessons learned. *International Journal of Selection and Assessment,* 9: 152–194; Schmidt, F.L., & Hunter, J.E. 1998. The validity and utility of selection methods in personnel psychology: Practical and theoretical implications of 85 years of research findings. *Psychological Bulletin,* 124: 262–274.

3. Marcus, B., Lee, K., & Ashton, M.C. 2007. Personality dimensions explaining relationships between integrity tests and counterproductive behavior: Big Five, or one in addition? *Personnel Psychology*, 60: 1–35.

4. Kristof-Brown, A.L., Zimmerman, R.D., & Johnson, E.C. 2005. Consequences of individuals' fit at work: A meta-analysis of person-job, person-organization, person-group, and person-supervisor fit. *Personnel Psychology*, 58: 281–342; Arthur, W., Bell, S.T., Villado, A.J., & Doverspike, D. 2006. The use of person-organization fit in employment decision making: An assessment of its criterion related validity. *Journal of Applied Psychology*, 91: 786–801.

5. McCulloch, M.C., & Turban, D.B. 2007. Using person-organization fit to select employees for high turnover jobs. *International Journal of Selection and Assessment*, 15: 63.

6. Peterson, R.S., Smith, D.B., & Martorana, P.V. 2003. The impact of chief executive officer personality on top management team dynamics: One mechanism by which leadership affects organizational performance. *Journal of Applied Psychology*, 88: 795–808.

7. Miller, D., & Toulouse, J-M. 1986. Chief executive personality and corporate strategy and structure in small firms. *Organizational Science*, 32: 1389–1410.

8. Eysenck, H.J., Arnold, W.J., & Meili, R. 1975. *Encyclopedia of psychology (Vol. 2)*. London: Fontana/Collins; Fontana, D. 2000. *Personality in the workplace*. London: Macmillan Press; Howard, P.J., & Howard, J.M. 2001. *The owner's manual for personality at work*. Austin, TX: Bard Press.

9. Byrne, J.A. 1998. How Al Dunlap self-destructed. *Business Week*, July 6, 58–64.

10. Ibid.

11. See, for example, Bouchard, T.J., Lykken, D.T., McGue, M., Segal, N.L., & Tellegen, A. 1990. Sources of human psychological differences: The Minnesota study of twins reared apart. *Science*, 250: 223–228; Shields, J. 1962. *Monozygotic twins*. London: Oxford University Press.

12. Ibid.

13. Chess, S., & Thomas, A. 1987. *Know your child: An authoritative guide for today's parents*. New York: Basic Books.

14. Hamer, D., & Copeland, P. 1998. *Living with your genes*. New York: Doubleday; Ridely, M. 1999. *Genome: The autobiography of a species in 23 chapters*. New York: HarperCollins.

15. Ridely, M. 1999. *Genome: The autobiography of a species in 23 chapters*. New York: HarperCollins.

16. Friedman, H.S., & Schustack, M.W. 1999. *Personality: Classic theories and modern research*. Boston: Allyn and Bacon.

17. McCandless, B. 1969. *Children: Behavior and development*. London: Holt, Rinehart, & Winston.

18. Costa, P.T., & McCrae, R.B. 1993. Set like plaster: Evidence for the stability of adult personality. In T. Heatherton and J. Weimberger (Eds.), *Can personality change?* Washington, DC: American Psychology Association.

19. Erikson, E. 1987. *A way of looking at things: Selected papers from 1930 to 1980*. New York: W.W. Norton.

20. Costa, P.T., & McCrae, R.R. 1992. *NEO PI-R: Professional manual*. Odessa, FL: Psychological Assessment Resources.

21. Reuters. January 13, 2009. Yahoo names software exec Bartz as new CEO. At http://www.reuters.com/article/idUSN1340746920090113.

22. Barrick, M.R., & Mount, M.K. 1991. The Big Five personality dimensions and performance: A meta-analysis. *Personnel Psychology*, 44: 1–26; Barrick, M.R., Mount, M.K., & Judge, T.A. 2001. Personality and performance at the beginning of the new millennium: What do we know and where do we go next? *International Journal of Selection and Assessment*, 9: 9–30; Hurtz, G.M., & Donovan, J.J. 2000. Personality and job performance: The Big Five revisited. *Journal of Applied Psychology*, 85: 869–879; Mount, M.K., Barrick, M.R., & Strauss, G.L. 1998. Five-factor model of personality and performance in jobs involving interpersonal interactions. *Human Performance*, 11: 145–165.

23. de Jong, R.D., Bouhuys, S.A., & Barnhoorn, J.C. 1999. Personality, self-efficacy, and functioning in management teams: A contribution to validation. *International Journal of Selection and Assessment*, 7: 46–49.

24. Judge, T.A., Heller, D., & Mount, M.K. 2002. Five-factor model of personality and job satisfaction: A meta-analysis. *Journal of Applied Psychology*, 87: 530–541.

25. Costa, P.T., & McCrae, R.R. 1992. *NEO P-R: Professional manual*. Odessa, FL: Psychological Assessment Resources.

26. Barrick, M.R., & Mount, M.K. 1991. The Big Five personality dimensions and performance: A meta-analysis. *Personnel Psychology*, 44: 1–26; Barrick, M.R., Mount, M.K., & Judge, T.A. 2001. Personality and performance at the beginning of the new millennium: What do we know and where do we go next? *International Journal of Selection and Assessment*, 9: 9–30.

27. Judge, T.A., Higgins, C.A., Thoresen, C., & Barrick, M.R. 1999. The Big Five personality traits, general mental ability, and career success across the life span. *Personnel Psychology*, 52: 621–652.

28. Bain & Company, 2007. Springboard: People. www.bain.com/bainweb/Join_Bain/people_places.asp; Goldman Sachs Group, Inc. 2007. Our people. www2.goldmansachs.com/careers/inside_goldman_sachs/our_people/index.html; Microsoft. 2007. Meet Our People. http://members.microsoft.com/careers/mslife/meetpeople/default.aspx.

29. Witt, L.A., Burke, L.A., Barrick, M. R., & Mount, M.K. 2002. The interactive effects of conscientiousness and agreeableness on job performance. *Journal of Applied Psychology*, 87: 164–169.

30. Costa, P.T., & McCrae, R.R. 1992. *NEO P-R: Professional manual*. Odessa, FL: Psychological Assessment Resources.

31. Barrick, M.R., Mount, M.K., & Judge, T.A. 2001. Personality and performance at the beginning of the new millennium: What do we know and where do we go next? *International Journal of Selection and Assessment*, 9: 9–30.

32. Kichuk, S.L., & Weisner, W.H. 1997. The Big Five personality factors and team performance: Implications for selecting successful product design teams, *Journal of Engineering and Technology Management*, 14: 195–221; Neuman, G.A., Wagner, S.H., & Christiansen, N.D. 1999. The relationship between work-team personality composition and the job performance of teams. *Group and Organization Management*, 24: 28–45; Neuman, G.A., & Wright, J. 1999. Team effectiveness: beyond skills and cognitive ability. *Journal of Applied Psychology*, 84: 376–389.

33. Costa, P.T., & McCrae, R.R. 1992. *NEO P-R: Professional manual.* Odessa, FL: Psychological Assessment Resources.

34. Barrick, M.R., & Mount, M.K. 1991. The Big Five personality dimensions and performance: A meta-analysis. *Personnel Psychology,* 44: 1–26.

35. Barrick, M.R., Mount, M.K., & Judge, T.A. 2001. Personality and performance at the beginning of the new millennium: What do we know and where do we go next? *International Journal of Selection and Assessment,* 9: 9–30.

36. Kichuk, S.L., & Weisner, W.H. 1997. The Big Five personality factors and team performance: Implications for selecting successful product design teams. *Journal of Engineering and Technology Management,* 14: 195–221; Thomas, P., Moore, K.S., & Scott, K.S. 1996. The relationship between self-efficacy for participating in self-managed work groups and the Big Five personality dimensions. *Journal of Organizational Behavior,* 17: 349–363.

37. Hirschfeld, R.R., Jordan, M.H., Thomas, C.H., & Field, H.S. 2008. Observed leadership potential of personnel in a team setting: Big Five traits and proximal factors as predictors. *International Journal of Selection and Assessment, 16:* 385–402.

38. Judge, T.A., Heller, D., & Mount, M.K. 2002. Five-factor model of personality and job satisfaction: A meta-analysis. *Journal of Applied Psychology,* 87: 530–541.

39. Costa, P.T., & McCrae, R.R. 1992. NEO P-R: *Professional manual.* Odessa, FL: Psychological Assessment Resources.

40. Barrick, M.R., Mount, M.K., & Judge, T.A. 2001. Personality and performance at the beginning of the new millennium: What do we know and where do we go next? *International Journal of Selection and Assessment,* 9: 9–30.

41. W.L. Gore & Associates. 2007. Careers: North America. www.gore.com/careers/north_america_careers.html.

42. Hough, L.M., Oswald, F.L., & Ployhart, R.E. 2001. Determinants, detection, and amelioration of adverse impact in personnel selection procedures: Issues, evidence and lessons learned. International *Journal of Selection and Assessment,* 9: 152–194; Schmidt, F.L., & Hunter, J.E. 1998. The validity and utility of selection methods in personnel psychology: Practical and theoretical implications of 85 years of research findings. *Psychological Bulletin,* 124: 262–274; Tett, R.P., Jackson, D.N., & Rothstein, M. 1991. Personality measures as predictors of job performance. Personnel Psychology, 44: 703–742.

43. Wilk, S.L. & Moynihan, L.M. 2005. Display rule regulators: The relationship between supervisors and worker emotional exhaustion. *Journal of Applied Psychology,* 90: 917–927.

44. Howard, P.J., & Howard, J.M. 2001. *The owner's manual for personality at work.* Austin, TX: Bard Press.

45. Ibid.

46. Spector, P.E. 1982. Behavior in organizations as a function of employee's locus of control. *Psychological Bulletin,* 91: 482–497.

47. Kabanoff, B., & O'Brien, G.E. 1980. Work and leisure: A task-attributes analysis. *Journal of Applied Psychology,* 65: 596–609.

48. Spector, P.E. 1982. Behavior in organizations as a function of employee's locus of control. *Psychological Bulletin,* 91: 482–497.

49. Spector, P.E., Cooper, C.L., Sanchez, J.I., O'Driscoll, M., Sparks, K., Bernin, P., Bussing, A., Dewe, P., Hart, P., Lu, L., Miller, K.,

De Moraes, L.R., Ostrognay, G.M., Pagon, M., Pitariu, H.D., Poelmans, S.A.Y., Radhakrishnan, P., Russinova, V., Salamatov, V., Salgado, J.F., Shima, S., Siu, O., Stora, J.B., Teichmann, M., Theorell, T., Vlerick, P., Westman, M., Widerszal-Bazyl, M., Wong, P.T., & Yu, S. 2002. Locus of control and well-being at work: How generalizable are western findings? *Academy of Management Journal,* 45: 453–466.

50. Ng, T.W.H., Sorensen, K.L., & Eby, L.T. 2006. Locus of control at work: A meta-analysis. *Journal of Organizational Behavior,* 27: 1057–1087.

51. Blass, T. 1977. *Personality variables in behavior.* Hillsdale, NJ: Lawrence Erlbaum Associates.

52. Altmeyer, B. 1998. The other "authoritarian personality." In M.P. Zanna (Ed.), *Advances in experimental social psychology (Vol. 30).* San Diego: Academic Press, pp. 47–92.

53. Son Hing, L.S., Bobocel, D.R., Zanna, M.P., and McBride, M.V. 2007. Authoritarian dynamics and unethical decision making: High social dominance orientation leaders and high right-wing authoritarian followers. *Journal of Personality and Social Psychology,* 92: 67–81.

54. Sidanius, J., & Pratto, F. 1999. *Social dominance: An intergroup theory of social hierarchy and oppression.* New York: Cambridge University Press.

55. Pratto, F., Sidanius, J., Stallworth, L.M., & Malle, B.F. 1994. Social dominance orientation: A personality variable predicting social and political attitudes. *Journal of Personality and Social Psychology,* 67: 741–763.

56. Sibley, C.G., & Duckitt, J. 2008. Personality and prejudice: A meta-analysis and theoretical review. *Personality and Social Psychology Review,* 12: 248–279.

57. Umphress, E.E., Simmons, A.L., Boswell, W.R., & Triana, M.d.C. 2008. Managing discrimination in selection: The influence of directives from an authority and social dominance orientation. *Journal of Applied Psychology,* 93: 982–993; Petersen, L.E., & Dietz, J. 2000. Social discrimination in a personnel selection context: The effects of an authority's instruction to discriminate and followers' authoritarianism. *Journal of Applied Social Psychology,* 30: 206–220.

58. Umphress, E.E., Smith-Crowe, K., Brief, A.P., Dietz, J., & Watkins, M.B. 2007. When birds of a feather flock together and when they do not: Status composition, social dominance orientation and organizational attractiveness. *Journal of Applied Psychology,* 92: 396–409; McKay, P.F., & Avery, D.R. 2006. What has race got to do with it? Unraveling the role of racioethnicity in job seekers' reactions to site visits. *Personnel Psychology,* 59: 395–429.

59. Mehra, A., Kilduff, M., & Brass, D.J. 2001. The social networks of high and low self-monitors: Implications for workplace performance. *Administrative Science Quarterly,* 46: 121–146.

60. Snyder, M. 1979. Self-monitoring processes. *Advances in Experimental Social Psychology,* 12: 85–128.

61. Mehra, A., Kilduff, M., & Brass, D.J. 2001. The social networks of high and low self-monitors: Implications for workplace performance. *Administrative Science Quarterly,* 46: 121–146.

62. Snyder, M. 1979. Self-monitoring processes. *Advances in Experimental Social Psychology,* 12: 85–128.

63. Day, D.V., Schleicher, D.J., Unckless, A.L., & Hiller, N.J. 2002. Self-monitoring personality at work: A meta-analytic investigation of construct validity. *Journal of Applied Psychology*, 87: 390–401.

64. Kilduff, M., & Day, D.V. 1994. Do chameleons get ahead? The effects of self monitoring on managerial careers. *Academy of Management Journal*, 37: 1047–1060.

65. Blass, T. 1977. *Personality variables in behavior*. Hillsdale, NJ: Lawrence Erlbaum Associates.

66. Steel, P. 2007. The nature of procrastination: A meta-analytic and theoretical review of quintessential self-regulatory failure. *Psychological Bulletin*, 133: 65–94.

67. Blass, T. 1977. *Personality variables in behavior*. Hillsdale, NJ: Lawrence Erlbaum Associates.

68. See, for example, Salgado, J.F. 1997. The five factor model of personality and job performance in the European Community. *Journal of Applied Psychology*, 82: 30–43.

69. Locke, E.A. 2005. Why emotional intelligence is an invalid concept. *Journal of Organizational Behavior*, 26: 425–431.

70. Dunnette, M.D. 1976. Aptitudes, abilities, and skills. In M.D. Dunnette (Ed.), *Handbook of industrial and organizational psychology*. Chicago: Rand McNally.

71. Hunter, J.E., & Hunter, R.F. 1984. Validity and utility of alternative predictors of job performance. *Psychological Bulletin*, 96: 72–98; Hunter, J.E., & Schmidt, F.L. 1996. Intelligence and job performance: Economic and social implications. *Psychology, Public Policy, and Law*, 2: 447–472; Salgado, J.F., & Anderson, N. 2002. Cognitive and GMA testing in the European Community: Issues and evidence. *Human Performance*, 15: 75–96; Schmidt, F.L. 2002. The role of general cognitive ability and job performance: Why there cannot be a debate. *Human Performance*, 15: 187–210; Schmidt, F.L., & Hunter, J.E. 1998. The validity and utility of selection methods in personnel psychology: Practical and theoretical implications of 85 years of research findings. *Psychological Bulletin*, 124: 262–274.

72. Simon, D.G., Hitt, M.A., & Ireland, R.D. 2007. Managing firm resources in dynamic environments to create value: Looking inside the black box. *Academy of Management Review*, 32: 273–292.

73. Katz, D., & Stotland, E. 1959. Preliminary statement to a theory of attitude structure and change. In S. Kock (Ed.), *Psychology: A study of science* (3rd ed.). New York: McGraw-Hill.

74. Petty, R.E., & Cacioppo, J.T. 1981. *Attitudes and persuasion: Classic and contemporary approaches*. Dubuque, IA: Wm. C. Brown.

75. Bem, D.J. 1972. Self-perception theory. In L. Berkowitz (Ed.), *Advances in experimental social psychology (Vol. 6)*. New York: Academic Press.

76. Freedman, J.L., & Fraser, S.C. 1966. Compliance without pressure: The foot-in-the-door technique. *Journal of Personality and Social Psychology*, 4: 195–202.

77. Heider, F. 1958. *The psychology of interpersonal relations*. New York: John Wiley & Sons; Osgood, C.E., & Tannenbaum, P.H. 1955. The principle of congruity in the prediction of attitude change. *Psychological Review*, 62: 42–55.

78. Holtom, B.C., Mitchell, T.R., & Lee, T.W. 2006. Increasing human and social capital by applying embeddedness theory. *Organizational Dynamics*, 35: 316–331.

79. Mitchell, T.R., Holtom, B.C., Lee, T.W., Sablynski, C.J., & Erez, M. 2001. Why people stay: Using job embeddedness to predict voluntary turnover. *Academy of Management Journal*, 44: 1102–1121; Tett, R.P., & Meyer, J.P. 1993. Job satisfaction, organizational commitment, turnover intention, and turnover: Path analyses based on meta-analytic findings. *Personnel Psychology*, 46: 259–293.

80. Scott, K.D., & Taylor, G.S. 1985. An examination of conflicting findings on the relationship between job satisfaction and absenteeism: A meta-analysis. *Academy of Management Journal*, 28: 599–612.

81. Kinicki, A.J., McKee-Ryan, F.M., Schriesheim, C.A., & Carson, K.P. 2002. Assessing the construct validity of the Job Descriptive Index: A review and meta-analysis. *Journal of Applied Psychology*, 87: 14–32.

82. Judge, T.A., Thoresen, C.J., Bono, J.E., & Patton, G.K. 2001. The job satisfaction-job performance relationship: A qualitative and quantitative review. *Psychological Bulletin*, 127: 376–407.

83. Gellatly, I.R., Meyer, J.P., & Luchak, A.A. 2006. Combined effects of the three commitment components on focal and discretionary behaviors: A test of Meyer and Herscovitch's propositions. *Journal of Vocational Behavior*, 69: 331–345; Meyer, J.P., Stanley, D.J., Herscovitch, L., & Topolnytsky, L. 2002. Affective, continuance, and normative commitment to the organization: A meta-analysis of antecedents, correlates and consequences. *Journal of Vocational Behavior*, 61: 20–52.

84. Wright, T.A., & Bonett, D.G. 2002. The moderating effect of employee tenure on the relation between organizational commitment and job performance: A meta-analysis. *Journal of Applied Psychology*, 87: 1183–1190.

85. Riketta, M. 2002. Attitudinal organizational commitment and job performance. *Journal of Organizational Behavior*, 23: 257–266.

86. Gellatly, I.R., Meyer, J.P., & Luchak, A.A. 2006. Combined effects of the three commitment components on focal and discretionary behaviors: A test of Meyer and Herscovitch's propositions. *Journal of Vocational Behavior*, 69: 331–345.

87. Meyer, J.P., Stanley, D.J., Herscovitch, L., & Topolnytsky, L. 2002. Affective, continuance, and normative commitment to the organization: A meta-analysis of antecedents, correlates and consequences. *Journal of Vocational Behavior*, 61: 20–52; Kalbers, L.P., & Cenker, W.J. 2007. Organizational commitment and auditors in public accounting. *Managerial Auditing Journal*, 22: 354–375.

88. Vandenberghe, C., Bentein, K., & Stinglhamber, F. 2004. Affective commitment to the organization, supervisor, and work group: Antecedents and outcomes. *Journal of Vocational Behavior*, 64: 47–71.

89. Ford, M.T., Heinen, B.A., & Langkamer, K.L. 2007. Work and family satisfaction and conflict: A meta-analysis of cross-domain relations. *Journal of Applied Psychology*, 92: 57–106.

90. Meyer, J.P., Stanley, D.J., Herscovitch, L., & Topolnytsky, L. 2002. Affective, continuance, and normative commitment to the organization: A meta-analysis of antecedents, correlates and consequences. *Journal of Vocational Behavior*, 61: 20–52.

91. Schulte, M., Ostroff, C., & Kinicki, A.J. 2006. Organizational climate and psychological climate perceptions: A cross-level study of climate-satisfaction relationships. *Journal of Occupational and Organizational Psychology*, 79: 645–671.

92. Podsakoff, N.P., LePine, J.A., & LePine, M.A. 2007. Differential challenge stressor-hindrance relationships with job attitudes, turnover intentions, and withdrawal behavior: A meta-analysis. *Journal of Applied Psychology*, 92: 438–454.

93. Colquitt, J.A., Conlon, D.E., Wesson, M.J., Porter, C.O.L.H., & Ng, K.Y. 2001. Justice at the millennium: A meta-analytic review of 25 years of organizational justice research. *Journal of Applied Psychology*, 86: 425–445.

94. Locke, E. A. 1976. The nature and causes of job satisfaction. In M. D. Dunnette (Ed.), *Handbook of industrial and organizational psychology*. Chicago: Rand McNally, pp. 1297–1343.

95. Meyer, J.P., & Allen, N.J. 1997. *Commitment in the workplace:* Theory, research, and application. Thousand Oaks, CA: Sage.

96. Meyer, J.P., Stanley, D.J., Herscovitch, L., & Topolnytsky, L. 2002. Affective, continuance, and normative commitment to the organization: A meta-analysis of antecedents, correlates and consequences. *Journal of Vocational Behavior*, 61: 20–52.

97. Ilies, R., Arvey, R.D., & Bouchard, T.J. 2006. Darwinism, behavioral genetics, and organizational behavior: A review and agenda for future research. *Journal of Organizational Behavior*, 27: 121–141.

98. Deaux, K., Dane, F.C., Wrightsman, L.S., & Sigelman, C.K. 1993. *Social psychology in the 90s*. Pacific Grove, CA: Brooks/Cole.

99. Aronson, E., Turner, J., & Carlsmith, J. 1963. Communicator credibility and communication discrepancy. *Journal of Abnormal and Social Psychology*, 67: 31–36; Hovland, C., Janis, I., & Kelley, H.H. 1953. *Communication and persuasion*. New Haven, CT: Yale University Press.

100. Eagly, A.H., Chaiken, S., & Wood, W. 1981. An attributional analysis of persuasion. In J. Harvey, W.J. Ickes, & R.F. Kidd (Eds.), *New directions in attribution research (Vol. 3)*. Hillsdale, NJ: Lawrence Erlbaum Associates; Walster, E., Aronson, E., & Abrahams, D. 1966. On increasing the persuasiveness of a low prestige communicator. *Journal of Experimental Social Psychology*, 2: 325–342.

101. Berscheid, E. 1966. Opinion change and communicator–communicatee similarity and dissimilarity. *Journal of Personality and Social Psychology*, 4: 670–680.

102. McGinniss, J. 1969. *The selling of the president*, 1968. New York: Trident Press.

103. Leventhal, H. 1970. Findings and theory in the study of fear communications. In L. Berkowitz (Ed.), *Advances in experimental social psychology (Vol. 5)*. New York: Academic Press.

104. Rogers, R.W. 1983. Cognitive and physiological processes in fear appeals and attitude change: A revised theory of protection motivation. In J. Cacioppo, & R. Petty (Eds.), *Social psychophysiology*. New York: Guilford Press; Maddux, J.E., & Rogers, R.W. 1983. Protection motivation and self-efficacy: A revised theory of fear appeals and attitude change. *Journal of Experimental Social Psychology*, 19: 469–479.

105. Festinger, L.A. 1957. *A theory of cognitive dissonance*. Stanford, CA: Stanford University Press.

106. Deaux, K., Dane, F.C., Wrightsman, L.S., & Sigelman, C.K. 1993. *Social psychology in the 90s*. Pacific Grove, CA: Brooks/Cole.

107. Johnson, P.R., & Indvik, J. 1999. Organizational benefits of having emotionally intelligent managers and employees. *Journal of Workplace Learning*, 11: 84–90.

108. Fisher, C.D., & Ashkanasy, N.M. 2000. The emerging role of emotions in work life: An introduction. *Journal of Organizational Behavior*, 21: 123–129.

109. Hymowitz, C. 2006. Business is personal, so managers need to harness emotions. *Wall Street Journal (Eastern Edition)*, November 13, p. B.1.

110. Lazarus, R.S., & Lazarus, A.D. 1994. *Passion and reason: Making sense of emotions*. New York: Oxford University Press.

111. Hershcovis, M.S., Turner, N., Barling, J., Arnols, K.A., Dupre, K.E., Inness, M., LeBlanc, M.M., & Sivanathan, N. 2007. Predicting workplace aggression: A meta-analysis. *Journal of Applied Psychology*, 92: 228–238.

112. George, J.M. & Brief, A.P. 1992. Feeling good—doing good: A conceptual analysis of mood at work—organizational spontaneity. *Psychological Bulletin*, 112: 310–329.

113. Isen, A.M., Daubman, K.A., & Nowicki, G.P. 1987. Positive affect facilitates creative problem solving. *Journal of Personality and Social Psychology*, 52: 1122–1131.

114. George, J.M., & Zhou, J. 2002. Understanding when bad moods foster creativity and good ones don't: The role of context and clarity of feelings. *Journal of Applied Psychology*, 87: 687–697.

115. Ting Fong, C. 2006. The effects of emotional ambivalence on creativity. *Academy of Management Journal*, 49: 1016–1030.

116. Barsade, S. 2002. The ripple effect: Emotional contagion and its influence on group behavior. *Administrative Science Quarterly*, 47: 644–675; Hatfield, E., Cacioppo, J.T., & Rapson, R.L. 1994. *Emotional contagion*. Cambridge, England: Cambridge University Press.

117. Bono, J.E., & Ilies, R. 2006. Charisma, positive emotions and mood contagion. *The Leadership Quarterly*, 17(4): 317–334.

118. Hochschild, A.R. 1983. *The managed heart: Commercialization of human feeling*. Berkeley, CA: University of California Press; Ashforth, B.E., & Humphrey, R.H. 1993. Emotional labor in service roles: The influence of identity. *Academy of Management Review*, 18: 88–115.

119. Cropanzano, R., Weiss, H. M., & Elias, S. M. 2004. The impact of display rules and emotional labor on psychological well-being at work. In P.L. Perrewé, & D.C. Ganster (Eds.), *Research in occupational stress and well-being (Vol. 3)*. Amsterdam: Elsevier, pp. 45–89; Schaubroeck, J., & Jones, J.R. 2000. Antecedents of workplace emotional labor dimensions and moderators of their effects on physical symptoms. *Journal of Organizational Behavior*, 21: 163–183.

120. Zapf, D., & Holz, M. 2006. On the positive effect and negative effects of emotion work in organizations. *European Journal of Work and Organizational Psychology*, 15: 1–26.

121. Wilk, S.L., & Moynihan, L.M. 2005. Display rule "regulators": The relationship between supervisors and worker emotional exhaustion. *Journal of Applied Psychology*, 90: 915–927.

122. Wilk & Moynihan Display rule "regulators"; Ashforth, B.E., & Humphrey, R.H. 1993. Emotional labor in service roles: The influence of identity. *Academy of Management Review*, 18: 88–115.

123. Bozionelos, N. 2006. Mentoring and expressive network resources: Their relationship with career success and emotional exhaustion among Hellenes employees involved in emotion work. *Journal of Human Resource Management*, 17: 362–378.

124. Salovey, P., & Mayer, J. 1990. Emotional intelligence. *Imagination, Cognition, and Personality,* 9: 185–211.

125. Kerr, R., Garvin, J., Heaton, N., & Boyle, E. 2006. Emotional intelligence and leadership effectiveness. *Leadership and Organizational Development Journal,* 27: 265–279; Cote, S., & Miners, C.T.H. 2006. Emotional intelligence, cognitive intelligence, and job performance. *Administrative Science Quarterly,* 51: 1–28; Semadar, A., Robins, G., & Ferris, G.R. 2006. Comparing the validity of multiple social effectiveness constructs in the prediction of managerial job performance. *Journal of Organizational Behavior,* 27: 443–461. Rozell, E.J., Pettijohn, C.E., & Parker, R.S. 2006. *Journal of Marketing Theory and Practice,* 14: 113–125; Rooy, D.L., & Viswasvaran, C. 2004. Emotional intelligence: A meta-analytic investigation of predictive validity and nomonological net. *Journal of Vocational Behavior,* 65: 71–95.

126. Goleman, D. 1995. *Emotional intelligence.* New York: Bantam.

127. Locke, E.A. 2005. Why emotional intelligence is an invalid concept. *Journal of Organizational Behavior,* 26: 425–443.

128. Goleman, D. 2004. What makes a leader? *Harvard Business Review,* Jan. 2004: 82–91; Goleman, D. 1995, *Emotional intelligence,* New York: Bantam; Fineman, S. 2005. Appreciating emotion at work: Paradigm tensions. *International Journal of Work Organisation and Emotion,* 1: 4–19.

129. Locke, E.A. 2005. Why emotional intelligence is an invalid concept. *Journal of Organizational Behavior,* 26: 425–431; Murphy, K.R. (Ed.) 2006. *A critique of emotional intelligence: What are the problems and how can they be fixed?* Mahwah, NJ: Lawrence Erlbaum Associates; Fineman, S. 2005. Appreciating emotion at work: Paradigm tensions. *International Journal of Work Organisation and Emotion,* 1: 4–19.

work motivation

Work Motivation at W.L. Gore & Associates

On January 1, 1958, Wilbert and Genevieve Gore founded a small company to develop applications of polytetrafluoroethylene (PTFE). Wilbert, a chemist and research scientist, tended to the technical work while Genevieve handled accounting and other business matters.

Wilbert Gore initially focused on applications in the emerging computer industry, where PTFE's insulation characteristics were potentially useful in cables and circuit boards. After solving a number of technical issues, he and his company succeeded with cable and wire products. Some of these products eventually landed on the moon as part of the technology used in the Apollo space program. More recently, they have been incorporated into the U.S. space shuttle program. Moving beyond cables and wires, Gore has created a number of leading products for a number of industries. Best known among consumers for waterproof Gore-Tex fabrics, the company also places products in industries such as aerospace, automotive, chemical processing, computing, telecommunications, environmental protection, medical/health care, pharmaceutical, biotechnology, and textiles. Gore-Tex fabrics were used in the uniforms of the 2010 U.S. Olympic snowboarding team.

Having previously experienced bureaucratic roadblocks in highly structured organizations, Wilbert Gore designed a different kind of company to support the work with PTFE. Using the term *lattice structure*

knowledge objectives

After reading this chapter, you should be able to:

1. Define work motivation and explain why it is important to organizational success.
2. Discuss how managers can use Maslow's need hierarchy and ERG theory to motivate associates.
3. Describe how need for achievement, need for affiliation, and need for power relate to work motivation and performance.
4. Explain how Herzberg's two-factor theory of motivation has influenced current management practice.
5. Discuss the application of expectancy theory to motivation.
6. Understand equity theory and procedural justice, and discuss how fairness judgments influence work motivation.
7. Explain how goal-setting theory can be used to motivate associates.
8. Describe how jobs can be enriched and how job enrichment can enhance motivation.
9. Based on all major theories of work motivation, describe specific actions that can be taken to increase and sustain employee motivation.

to signify an emphasis on informal communication and fluid work networks, he set up a company that focused on equality among people as well as freedom for those people to pursue their own ideas and projects. To a significant degree, individuals were and still are expected to define their own jobs within areas that interest them. Assigned sponsors help both new and existing Gore personnel with job definition.

Formal leadership assignments are less common at Gore than in more structured companies. Instead of formal assignments, Gore looks for individuals who have attracted "followers" for their ideas and projects. Thomas Malone, a professor at Massachusetts Institute of Technology, has studied the com-

©Tyler Stableford/Stone/Getty Images

pany and summarizes the approach as follows: "The way you become a [leader] is by finding people who want to work for you. … In a certain sense, you're elected rather than appointed. It's a democratic structure inside a business organization."

Culturally, four principles govern the behavior of individuals within W.L. Gore & Associates:

- The ability to make one's own commitments and keep them
- Freedom to encourage, help, and allow other associates to grow in knowledge, skill, and scope of responsibility
- Consultation with others before undertaking actions that could impact the reputation of the company
- Fairness to each other and everyone with whom contact is made

These structural and cultural features of the company set the stage for personal fulfillment and growth. The official Gore website puts it this way: "Everyone can quickly earn the credibility to define and drive projects. Sponsors help associates chart a course in the organization that will offer personal fulfillment while maximizing their contribution to the enterprise." Current CEO Terri Kelly said this: "We work hard at maximizing individual

potential … and cultivating an environment where creativity can flourish." He later stated that "Thanks largely to the pioneering corporate culture established by our founders … Gore is a place where innovation thrives and where every individual has the ability to contribute to the success of the enterprise … our culture is our biggest competitive advantage."

Of course, Gore is not for everyone. Individuals who work at the company must tolerate a certain amount of ambiguity and must thrive in autonomous settings. Moreover, they must value personal growth in the workplace. While many or even most individuals desire personal growth, some do not. Through rigorous selection procedures, Gore tends to find the right people. The result is a highly motivated and effective workforce.

The emphasis on fairness also affects motivation and effectiveness. In many companies, pay systems promote dysfunctional internal competition and jealousy. At W.L. Gore & Associates, the pay system tends to promote a sense of equity and justice. A key aspect of the system is the sponsor. Each individual at Gore has a sponsor, either a peer or a leader, who is responsible for ensuring fair pay. The sponsor collects information on contributions and achievements from an individual's peers and leaders and then shares this information with a compensation committee. Overall, Gore's approach can be summarized as follows: "Unlike companies which base an employee's pay on the evaluations of one or two people—or supervisors' opinions alone—Gore involves many [people] in the process. Our goal: internal fairness and external competitiveness."

Recognition and success have resulted from Gore's practices. For example, W.L. Gore & Associates has been listed for 12 consecutive years on the Fortune list of the "Best 100 Companies to Work For." It has also been listed as a top company for which to work in German, Italian, and British rankings, and indeed in rankings for the entire European Union. It has received awards for many technological breakthroughs. Financially, the privately held company has enjoyed consistently strong performance.

Going forward, the company seems poised for continued success. Today Gore has approximately 9,000 associates located in 30 countries worldwide, with manufacturing facilities in the United States, Germany, Scotland, Japan, and China and sales offices around the world. Their annual revenues are $2.5 billion. As it continues to grow, the company seems intent on maintaining its current structure and culture.

Sources: D. Anfuso. 1999. "Core Values Shape W.L. Gore's Innovative Culture," *Workforce,* 78 no. 3: 48–53; A. Deutschman. 2004. "The Fabric of Creativity," *Fast Company,* no. 89: 54–59; Gore & Associates, "Compensation," 2007, at http://www.gore.com/en_xx/careers/benefits/compensation.html; Gore & Associates, "Corporate Culture," 2007, at http://www.gore.com/en_xx/aboutus/culture/index.html; Gore & Associates, "Fast Facts," 2010, at http://www.gore.com/en_xx/aboutus/fastfacts/index.html; P. Kriger. 2006. "Power of the Individual," *Workforce Management,* 85, no. 4: 1–7; F. Shipper and C.C. Manz. 1993 "W.L. Gore & Associates, Inc.," Pinnacle Management Strategy Case Base; M. Weinreb. 2003. "Power to the People," *Sales and Marketing Management,* 155, no. 4: 30–35; W.L. Gore and Associates Press Release (Jan. 22, 2009), "W.L. Gore and Associates Marks 12th Year as One of Nation's Best," at http://www.gore.com/en_xx/news/FORTUNE2009.html; Gore and Associates, "About Us." at http://www.gore.com/en_xx/aboutus/index.html.

the strategic importance of Work Motivation

Formulating strategies that can deliver competitive advantage is not easy. Senior managers working with other individuals engage in countless conversations, meetings, experiments, and analyses in order to create or modify company strategies. Implementing strategies and engaging in the day-to-day behaviors that help to create competitive advantage also are not easy tasks. Hard work is involved. Managers and associates must be willing to deliver strong efforts if a firm is to succeed.[1]

With strong efforts being so important, work motivation is a crucial topic in any discussion of organizational behavior. People must be motivated if they are to effectively engage in the behaviors and practices that bring advantage and success to a firm.

It is important to note that different strategies require different types of people and behavior, and therefore different approaches to motivation. W.L. Gore has adopted a general strategy of differentiation based on innovation and creativity. Differentiating in this way requires people who can think differently, experiment in smart ways, accept responsibility, and appreciate the learning that accompanies failed efforts. The strategy also requires people who want to be challenged and grow in the workplace. To fully motivate such people, resources for trying new ideas must be made available, including time. Opportunities to develop new skills and polish old ones are important. Recognition for successes and pats on the back for strong efforts that unexpectedly did not bear fruit also might be useful. Pay, while important, often takes a backseat.

There are many ways to motivate people. Hence, there is no simple answer to the question of what managers should do to increase and sustain their associates' motivation. A great deal is known, however, about how people are motivated. In this chapter, we describe the major theories of work motivation and the practices that are most likely to increase and sustain strong efforts. We begin by formally defining what is meant by *motivation*. Next, we describe fundamental theories of work motivation, including both content and process theories. To synthesize these theories, we close the main body of the chapter by distilling useful management practices.

What Is Motivation?

Man and machine … work in close harmony to achieve more than either could alone. Machines bring precision and capacity. They make our lives easier, perfect our processes, and in many ways, enrich our quality of life. But people possess something that machines don't—human spirit and inspiration. Our people work continuously at setting goals and tracking results for ongoing improvement as an overall business. They are an inspiration and their goals and accomplishments have won Branch-Smith Printing recognition on the highest of levels.[2]

This quotation from Branch-Smith Printing, a 2002 recipient of the Malcolm Baldrige National Quality Award, gets at the heart of motivation: it is the spirit and inspiration that leads people to apply their human capital to meet the goals of the organization. In Chapter 1, we discussed the strategic importance of human capital to the success of a firm. However, human capital alone is not enough to ensure behaviors that support organizational performance. Associates must translate their human capital into actions that result in performance important to the achievement of organizational goals. Motivation is the process through which this translation takes place.

Consider the following example. A manager has three assistants reporting to her. They have similar levels of experience and education. However, they have different levels of ability for the tasks at hand, and they perform at different levels. It is interesting that the person with the least ability has outperformed his counterparts. How can a person with less ability outperform individuals who have greater abilities? The answer may be that he is more motivated to apply his abilities than the others. The two other assistants are approximately equal to one another in their motivation to perform, judging by the fact that they work equally hard, and yet one of these assistants outperforms the other. How can this be when they are equally motivated? The answer may lie in their different ability levels. Thus, we can see that a person's level of performance is a function (f) of both ability and motivation:

$$\text{Performance} = f(\text{Ability} \times \text{Motivation})$$

Now consider another scenario. Two salespersons are equally motivated and have the same ability, yet one of them outperforms the other. How can we explain this, if performance is a function of ability and motivation? In this case, the better performer has a more lucrative sales territory than the other salesperson. Thus, environmental factors can also play a role in performance.

This brings us to our definition of work motivation. We know from the preceding discussion that ability and certain environmental factors exert influences on performance that are separate from the effects of motivation. **Motivation**, then, refers to forces coming from within a person that account for the willful direction, intensity, and persistence of the person's efforts toward achieving specific goals, where achievement is not due solely to ability or to environmental factors.[3] Several prominent theories offer explanations of motivation. Most of the theories can be separated into two groups: those concerned largely with content and those concerned largely with process. In the next two sections, we consider theories in each of these two groups.

motivation
Forces coming from within a person that account for the willful direction, intensity, and persistence of the person's efforts toward achieving specific goals, where achievement is not due solely to ability or to environmental factors.

Content Theories of Motivation

Content theories of motivation generally focus on identifying the specific factors that motivate people. These theories are, for the most part, straightforward. Four important content theories of motivation are Maslow's need hierarchy, Alderfer's ERG theory, McClelland's need theory, and Herzberg's two-factor theory.

Hierarchy of Needs Theory

One of the most popular motivation theories, frequently referred to as the **hierarchy of needs theory**, was proposed in the 1940s by Abraham Maslow.[4] According to Maslow, people are motivated by their desire to satisfy specific needs. Maslow arranged these needs in

hierarchy of needs theory
Maslow's theory that suggests people are motivated by their desire to satisfy specific needs, and that needs are arranged in a hierarchy with physiological needs at the bottom and self-actualization needs at the top. People must satisfy needs at lower levels before being motivated by needs at higher levels.

hierarchical order, with physiological needs at the bottom, followed by safety needs, social and belongingness needs, esteem needs, and, at the top, self-actualization needs. In general, lower-level needs must be substantially met before higher-level needs become important. Below, we look at each level and its theoretical implications in organizational settings.

1. *Physiological needs.* Physiological needs include basic survival needs—for water, food, air, and shelter. Most people must largely satisfy these needs before they become concerned with other, higher-order needs. Money is one organizational award that is potentially related to these needs, to the extent that it provides for food and shelter.

2. *Safety needs.* The second level of Maslow's hierarchy concerns individuals' needs to be safe and secure in their environment. These needs include the need for protection from physical or psychological harm. People at this level might consider their jobs as security factors and as a way to keep what they have acquired. These managers and associates might be expected to engage in low-risk job behaviors, such as following rules, preserving the status quo, and making career decisions based on security concerns.

3. *Social and belongingness needs.* Social needs involve interaction with and acceptance by other people. These needs include the desire for affection, affiliation, friendship, and love. Theoretically, people who reach this level have primarily satisfied physiological and safety needs and are now concerned with establishing satisfying relationships with other people. Although a great deal of satisfaction may come from family relationships, a job usually offers an additional source of relationships. Managers and associates at this level may thus seek supportive co-worker and peer-group relationships.

4. *Esteem needs.* Esteem needs relate to feelings of self-respect and self-worth, along with respect and esteem from peers. The desire for recognition, achievement, status, and power fits in this category. People at this level may be responsive to organizational recognition and awards programs and derive pleasure from having articles about them published in the company newsletter. Money and financial rewards may also help satisfy esteem needs, because they provide signals of people's "worth" to the organization.

©Ryan McVay/Getty Images, Inc.

5. *Self-actualization needs.* A person's need for self-actualization represents her desire to fulfill her potential, maximizing the use of her skills and abilities. People at the self-actualization level are less likely to respond to the types of rewards described for the first four levels. They accept their own achievements and seek new opportunities to use their unique skills and talents. They often are highly motivated by work assignments that challenge these skills, and they might even reject common rewards (salary increase, promotion) that could distract them from using their primary skills. Only a few people are assumed to reach this level.

As mentioned, these needs are arranged in hierarchical order, with physiological needs the lowest and self-actualization the highest. According to Maslow's theory, each need is prepotent over all higher-level needs until it has been satisfied. A prepotent need is one that predominates over other needs. For example, a person at the social and belongingness level will be most concerned with rewards provided by meaningful relationships and will not be so concerned with esteem-related rewards, such as public recognition or large bonuses. It follows that a satisfied need is no longer a motivator. For example, after a person's social needs are met, she will no longer be concerned with developing and maintaining relationships but will instead be motivated to seek esteem-related rewards. The need hierarchy theory is supposed to apply to all normal, healthy people in a similar way.

The need hierarchy theory has not been well supported by empirical research.[5] Research has indicated that a two-level hierarchy of lower-order and higher-order needs may exist, but it has not found much support for the five specific need categories proposed by Maslow. One reason for this finding may be the context of the studies. Most people in the United States, where the studies typically have been done, have satisfied their basic needs and are faced with a complex system of means to satisfy their higher-order ones. It may be difficult for researchers to separate the needs these people experience into the five specific categories proposed by Maslow.

In addition, the idea of prepotency has been questioned.[6] Some researchers have noted that several needs may be important at the same time. For example, a person can simultaneously have strong social, esteem, and self-actualization needs. Even Maslow's clinical studies showed that the idea of prepotency is not relevant for all individuals.[7]

A final problem with the need hierarchy theory involves a practical concern. It is difficult to determine the present need level for each associate and the exact rewards that would help satisfy that associate's specific needs. For example, a person's concern with being popular with co-workers may be related to either social and belongingness needs or esteem needs (or both). Being popular can mean that one is liked, but it can also mean that one has high status in the group. If a manager is attempting to diagnose the meaning behind a person's desire to be popular, she could make an erroneous judgment. As another example, money can be used to meet both physiological and esteem needs, but it may not have the desired effect in all cases where esteem is the key issue. In general, it is challenging for managers to apply the need hierarchy to motivate associates.

Although the need hierarchy theory has many weaknesses, it is historically important because it focused attention on people's esteem and self-actualization needs. Previously, behaviorism had been the dominant approach to understanding human motivation. As you may recall, behaviorism proposes that people's behaviors are motivated solely by extrinsic rewards. The need hierarchy, in contrast, suggests that the behavior of many people is motivated by needs reflecting a human desire to be recognized and to grow as an individual. Beyond its historical significance, the need hierarchy also continues to guide some research in fields such as humanistic psychology.[8]

ERG Theory

ERG theory Alderfer's theory that suggests people are motivated by three hierarchically ordered types of needs: existence needs (E), relatedness needs (R), and growth needs (G). A person may work on all three needs at the same time, although satisfying lower-order needs often takes place before a person is strongly motivated by higher-level needs.

ERG theory, developed by Clayton Alderfer, is similar to Maslow's need hierarchy theory in that it also proposes need categories.[9] However, it includes only three categories: existence needs (E), relatedness needs (R), and growth needs (G). The relationship of these categories to those of Maslow's need hierarchy theory is shown in Exhibit 6-1. As you can see in the exhibit, existence needs are similar to Maslow's physiological and safety needs,

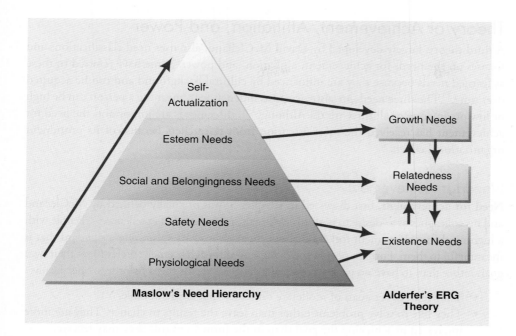

Exhibit 6-1 Maslow's Need Hierarchy and Alderfer's ERG Theory Compared

relatedness needs are similar to Maslow's social and belongingness needs, and growth needs are similar to Maslow's needs for esteem and self-actualization. Growth needs are particularly important in an organization such as W.L. Gore & Associates.

ERG theory differs from Maslow's theory in two important ways. First, the notion of prepotency is not fixed in ERG theory. A person's existence needs do not necessarily have to be satisfied before she can become concerned about her relationships with others or about using her personal capabilities. Her desire to meet the existence needs may be stronger than her desire to meet the two other types of needs, but the other needs may still be important. The need hierarchy theory proposes that the hierarchy is fixed and that physiological needs must be largely satisfied before other needs become important.

Second, even when a need is satisfied, it may remain the dominant motivator if the next need in the hierarchy cannot be satisfied. For instance, if a person has satisfied his relatedness needs but is frustrated in trying to satisfy his growth needs, his desire for relatedness needs again becomes strong (recall that a satisfied need is no longer a motivator in the need hierarchy theory). Alderfer called this the frustration-regression process.[10] Thus, it is possible that a need may never cease to be a motivator. An associate who has many friends and is very well liked may continue to seek friends and social approval if frustrated in satisfying growth needs. Understanding this is important for managers because it may provide them with the reasons for a person's behavior.

ERG theory has more research support than Maslow's hierarchy of needs. For example, some research has found evidence for the meaningfulness of the three categories of needs.[11] Support has also been found for several of Alderfer's basic propositions, such as the concept that a satisfied need may remain a motivator.[12] Indeed, relatedness and growth needs have been found to increase as they are satisfied. In other words, the more they are satisfied, the more they are desired. However, more research on ERG theory is necessary to test its usefulness under different conditions. In general, ERG theory may be viewed as a refinement of the need hierarchy theory.[13]

Theory of Achievement, Affiliation, and Power

A third theory, largely developed by David McClelland, also uses need classifications and focuses on the needs for achievement, affiliation, and power. Some have referred to these as learned needs because they are influenced by cultural background and can be acquired over time.[14] The three needs are also viewed as independent, meaning a person can be high or low on any one or all three needs. Although all three needs are important, the need for achievement has received the most attention from researchers because of its prominent organizational effects.[15]

Need for Achievement

need for achievement
The need to perform well against a standard of excellence.

Need for achievement, first discussed in Chapter 5, was originally defined by McClelland and his colleagues as a "desire to perform well against a standard of excellence."[16] People with a high need for achievement feel good about themselves when surpassing a standard that is meaningful to them. Further, people with a high need for achievement prefer to set their own goals rather than to have no goals or to accept the goals set for them by others. Specifically:

- They tend to set goals of moderate difficulty that are achievable.
- They like to solve problems rather than leave the results to chance. They are more interested in achieving the goal than in the formal rewards they may receive, although they recognize the value of their inputs and tend to earn good incomes.
- They prefer situations in which they receive regular, concrete feedback on their performance.[17]
- They are positive thinkers who find workable solutions to life's hurdles and challenges.[18]
- They assume strong personal responsibility for their work.

Some consider the achievement motive to be a component of self-actualization.[19] Consistent with this belief, people high on need for achievement tend to do well in challenging jobs but do less well in boring or routine jobs. In a study of sales and sales support personnel, individuals with high achievement needs had positive outcomes only when occupying more demanding, technically oriented roles.[20] Related to this finding, people who aspire to be entrepreneurs frequently have a high need for achievement.[21] Also, managers who have high achievement needs tend to manage differently relative to those who have lower achievement needs because of a more pronounced goal orientation.[22]

Although need for achievement is thought to be a relatively stable characteristic in adults, it is possible to train adults to increase their need for achievement. This training includes the following steps:[23]

1. Teach people how to think like persons with a high need for achievement. This includes teaching people how to imagine the achievement of desired goals and mentally rehearse the steps necessary to reach those goals.
2. Teach and encourage people to set challenging but realistic work-related goals.
3. Give people concrete feedback about themselves and their performance. Ensure that people are knowledgeable about their behavior and its outcomes.
4. Create *esprit de corps*.

In organizations such as W.L. Gore & Associates, people with high achievement needs are generally positive. Such people, however, can react negatively to the ambiguity found in these organizations. Without reasonably clear pathways to success, high achievement needs can go unmet in any given time period.

Need for Affiliation

People with a high **need for affiliation** have a strong desire to be liked and to stay on good terms with most other people. Affiliative people tend not to make good managers. They are more concerned with initiating and maintaining personal relationships than with focusing on the task at hand. In one study, managers of product development units were assessed. Those with high needs for affiliation were seen as less influential and as having less-influential units. They also had units with weaker innovation profiles.[24]

Need for affiliation is a particularly important consideration in today's world, where working from home as virtual contributors is common. About 17 percent of the U.S. workforce works from home at least two days per week. At IBM, 42 percent of the workforce works from home, on the road, or at a client location. Significant percentages of people work virtually at Sun Microsystems, Convergys, and many other companies.

Without daily contact with other associates or managers, individuals with strong affiliation needs might have difficulty developing strong relations and assessing how well they are liked. They may be particularly prone to feelings of isolation and dissatisfaction. To combat these and other issues, companies that rely heavily on virtual contributors have introduced a host of technologies and practices. To ensure satisfied and productive workers, they generally have provided key technologies that help people stay connected, such as laptops, Internet access, and a personal digital assistant. Many companies also support instant messaging and provide sophisticated collaboration software. Companies such as Sun Microsystems, Ernst & Young, and Deloitte & Touche designate office and conference space for associates who occasionally stop in. Also, some managers insist on face-to-face team meetings every now and then.[25]

Need for Power

The **need for power** can be defined as the desire to influence people and events. According to McClelland, there are two types of need for power: one that is directed toward the good of the organization (*institutional power*) and one that is directed toward the self (*personal power*).[26] People high in the need for institutional power want to influence others for altruistic reasons—they are concerned about the functioning of the organization and have a desire to serve others. They are also more controlled in their exercise of power. In contrast, those high in the need for personal power desire to influence others for their own personal gain. They are more impulsive in exercising power, show little concern for other people, and are focused on obtaining symbols of prestige and status (such as big offices).

Research has shown that a high need for institutional power is critical for high-performing managers. People with a high need for institutional power are particularly good at increasing morale, creating clear expectations, and influencing others to work for the good of the organization. Need for institutional power seems to be more important than need for achievement in creating managerial success,[27] although blending both is perhaps better than having one or the other.

As discussed in the *Managerial Advice* feature, the Hay Group has conducted a great deal of research on managers' needs. Its consultants apply this work in the firm's well-regarded global consulting practice. Importantly, Hay research shows that a strong need for achievement can create problems. Such problems, however, are less likely to occur when a

need for affiliation
The need to be liked and to stay on good terms with most other people.

need for power
The desire to influence people and events.

Managers over the Edge

The Hay Group, an internationally renowned consulting firm, studies managers' needs for achievement, affiliation, and power. Through its McClelland Center, it continues the work that David McClelland began many years ago.

In a recent report, the organization identified changes in the needs of tens of thousands of managers, most of them from the United States. In terms of average strength, need for achievement exhibited a substantial increase from the mid-1980s, with most of the increase occurring after 1995. Moreover, it became by far the strongest need. Need for affiliation exhibited little change during the key time period, but slipped from the strongest to the second strongest need. Need for power weakened and then strengthened over the time period. Overall, the average strength of this need exhibited little net change, ending the time period close to where it began. In terms of rank, it settled into a distant third place.

While increased need for achievement among managers implies many positive behaviors and outcomes, very high levels of this need can create problems for two reasons. First, a strong achievement need in a manager can set the stage for coercive tendencies, particularly when this need is paired with relatively weak needs for affiliation and institutional power. These coercive tendencies result from the manager wanting to achieve at

any cost while having limited needs to be liked and to build engaged associates. Hay research on IBM managers showed these tendencies in action. High-need-for-achievement managers with lower needs for affiliation and institutional power produced inferior work climates through less delegation, less effort in connecting associates' work to the overall strategy and mission of the organization, more command-and-control behaviors, and more instances of taking over work that should be done by others.

Second, a strong achievement need can set the stage for shortcuts and illicit actions, all in the name of achievement. Again, this is of most concern when high need for achievement is paired with relatively weak needs for affiliation and institutional power. Hay researchers cite Jeffery Skilling as a relevant example. Skilling was sentenced to prison for his role in the fall of Enron.

Scott Spreier, a senior consultant with The Hay Group; Mary Fontaine, a vice president at Hay; and Ruth Malloy, director of research at Hay's McClelland Center recently provided a set of guidelines designed to help high-achievement managers avoid problems.

- **Understand needs**. Without explicitly understanding their own personal needs in the workplace, managers cannot manage those needs. Understanding needs can

©Stockbyte/Getty Images, Inc.

be accomplished by simply thinking about valued activities and outcomes or by using available assessment tools (one popular tool will be presented in this chapter's installment of *Building Your Human Capital*).

- **Manage needs**. Having gained awareness of their needs, managers can take actions to handle them effectively. A manager with quite a strong achievement need might ask a trusted colleague to monitor his behavior for coercion. Such a manager might also seek training focused on the benefits of delegation and an empowered workforce. Finally, she might channel some of the need for achievement into nonwork pursuits (e.g., competitive golf).

Sources: Hay Group, "About Hay Group," 2007, at http://www.haygroup.com/ww/About/Index.asp?id=495; Hay Group, "A Recent Rise in Achievement Drive among Today's Executives," 2006, at http://www.haygroup.com/ww/Media/index.asp; Hay Group, "The McClelland Center Fact Sheet," 2002, at http://www.haygroup.com/wwResearch/Detail.asp?PageID=703; S.W. Spreier, M.H. Fontaine, & R.L. Malloy. 2006. "Leadership Run Amok: The Destructive Potential of Overachievers," *Harvard Business Review*, 84, no. 6: 72–82.

strong achievement need is blended and balanced with a significant need for institutional power and perhaps also with some level of need for affiliation.

Two-Factor Theory

The **two-factor theory** (sometimes called the *dual-factor theory*) is based on the work of Frederick Herzberg.[28] It has some similarities to the other need theories, but it focuses more on the rewards or outcomes of performance that satisfy individuals' needs. The two-factor theory emphasizes two sets of rewards or outcomes—those related to job satisfaction and those related to job dissatisfaction. This theory of motivation suggests that satisfaction and dissatisfaction are not opposite ends of the same continuum but are independent states. In other words, the opposite of high job satisfaction is not high job dissatisfaction; rather, it is low job satisfaction. Likewise, the opposite of high dissatisfaction is low dissatisfaction. It follows that the job factors leading to satisfaction are different from those leading to dissatisfaction, and vice versa. Furthermore, receiving excess quantities of a factor thought to decrease dissatisfaction will not produce satisfaction, nor will increasing satisfaction factors overcome dissatisfaction.

The factors related to job satisfaction have been called *satisfiers,* or **motivators**. These are factors that, when increased, will lead to greater levels of satisfaction. They include:

- Achievement
- Recognition
- Responsibility
- Opportunity for advancement or promotion
- Challenging work
- Potential for personal growth

The factors related to dissatisfaction have been called dissatisfies, or **hygienes**. When these factors are deficient, dissatisfaction will increase. However, providing greater amounts of these factors will not lead to satisfaction—only to less dissatisfaction. Hygiene factors include:

- Pay
- Technical supervision
- Working conditions
- Company policies, administration, and procedures
- Interpersonal relationships with peers, supervisors, and subordinates
- Status
- Security

Research has not generally supported Herzberg's two-factor theory.[29] One criticism is that the theory is method-bound—meaning that support can be found for the theory only when Herzberg's particular methodology is used. Researchers using different methodologies to test the theory have not found support. A second criticism is that the theory confuses job satisfaction and motivation. As discussed in Chapter 5, job satisfaction does not always lead to increased motivation. Happy associates are not always motivated associates. The causal path can also go the other way—with motivation, and consequently performance, influencing satisfaction—or there may be no relationship at all. A third criticism is that motivators and hygienes may not be uniquely different. For

two-factor theory
Herzberg's motivation theory that suggests that job satisfaction and dissatisfaction are not opposite ends of the same continuum but are independent states and that different factors affect satisfaction and dissatisfaction.

motivators
Job factors that can influence job satisfaction but not dissatisfaction.

hygienes
Job factors that can influence job dissatisfaction but not satisfaction.

example, some factors, such as pay, can affect both satisfaction and dissatisfaction. Pay can help satisfy basic food and shelter needs (hygiene), but it can also provide recognition (motivator).

Despite the criticisms of two-factor theory, managers tend to find it appealing. Indeed, Herzberg's 1965 *Harvard Business Review* article on this theory was reprinted in a more recent *Harvard Business Review* volume (January 2003), indicating that these ideas continue to be popular with managers. At a practical level, the theory is easy to understand and apply. To motivate associates, managers should provide jobs that include potential for achievement and responsibility. They should also try to maintain the hygiene factors at an appropriate level to prevent dissatisfaction. Thus, managers can motivate associates by manipulating job-content factors and can prevent associate dissatisfaction by manipulating the job context or environment.

Perhaps the most important managerial conclusion is that organizations should not expect high productivity in jobs that are weak in motivators, no matter how much they invest in hygienes. Simply providing good working conditions and pay may not result in consistently high performance. Thus, managers now give much more attention to how jobs are designed. Indeed, Herzberg's work helped launch the current focus on enriched jobs that emphasize responsibility, variety, and autonomy. This focus is consistent with high-involvement management, a key theme of our book.

Conclusions Regarding Content Theories

The four content theories we have just discussed address the factors that affect motivation. These factors include associates' needs and the various job and contextual attributes that might help them meet these needs. All four theories are popular among managers because each has an intuitive logic and is easy to understand. Although research support for the theories has not been strong overall, the theories have been useful in developing specific managerial practices that increase motivation and performance. Further, these theories can be integrated with process theories, discussed next.

Process Theories of Motivation

Whereas content theories emphasize the *factors* that motivate, process theories are concerned with the *process* by which such factors interact to produce motivation. One of the weaknesses of content theories is the assumption that motivation can be explained by only one or two factors, such as a given need or the content of a job. As we have seen, human motivation is much more complex than that. In most cases, several conditions interact to produce motivated behavior. Process theories take this complexity into account. Process theories generally focus on the cognitive processes in which people engage to influence the direction, intensity, and persistence of their behavior. Three important process theories of motivation are expectancy theory, equity theory, and goal-setting theory.

expectancy theory
Vroom's theory that suggests that motivation is a function of an individual's expectancy that a given amount of effort will lead to a particular level of performance, instrumentality judgments that indicate performance will lead to certain outcomes, and the valences of outcomes.

Expectancy Theory

The first process theory to recognize the effects of multiple, complex sources of motivation was Victor Vroom's **expectancy theory**.[30] Expectancy theory suggests that managers and associates consider three factors in deciding whether to exert effort.

First, they consider the probability that a given amount of effort will lead to a particular level of performance. For example, an associate might consider the probability that working on a report for an extra four hours will lead to a significant improvement in that report. This probability is referred to as an **expectancy**.

expectancy
The subjective probability that a given amount of effort will lead to a particular level of performance.

The second factor individuals consider is the perceived connection between a particular level of performance and important outcomes. For example, the associate cited above would consider the potential outcomes of a better report. She may believe there is a strong positive connection between a better report and (1) praise from her supervisor and (2) interesting future assignments. In other words, she may perceive that good performance makes these outcomes very likely. She may also believe that there is a weak positive connection between a better report and an increase in pay, meaning she believes that good performance makes this outcome only slightly more likely to occur. Overall, she is interested in the effects of good performance on three outcomes. Each perceived connection between performance and an outcome is referred to as an **instrumentality**.

instrumentality
Perceived connections between performance and outcomes.

The third factor is the importance of each anticipated outcome. In our example, the associate may believe that more praise from her boss, better assignments, and an increase in pay would bring her a great deal of satisfaction. As a result, these outcomes have high valence. **Valence** is defined as the value placed on an outcome.

valence
Value associated with an outcome.

In essence, expectancy theory suggests that people are rational when deciding whether to expend a given level of effort. The following equation formally states how people implement expectancy theory:

$$MF = E \times \Sigma\,(I \times V)$$

where:

MF = Motivational force.

E = Expectancy, or the subjective probability that a given level of effort will lead to a particular level of performance. It can range from 0 to +1. Further, the expectancy of interest usually corresponds to the probability that strong effort will result in good performance.[31] Thus, an expectancy of zero means that an individual thinks there is no chance that strong effort will lead to good performance. An expectancy of one means that an individual thinks it is certain that strong effort will lead to good performance. For a given person in a given situation, self-esteem, previous experience with the task, and availability of help from a manager can influence this subjective probability.[32]

I = Instrumentality, or the perceived connection between a particular level of performance and an outcome. Instrumentality can range from −1 to +1, because it is possible for a performance level to make an outcome less likely as well as make an outcome more likely. For example, an instrumentality of −.8 indicates that an individual expects that performing at a particular level would make an outcome very unlikely (e.g., praise from co-workers might be unlikely because of jealousy).

V = Valence, or the value associated with an outcome. Valence can be negative or positive, because some outcomes may be undesirable while others are desirable.

Exhibit 6-2 illustrates the expectancy theory process.

As an example, consider a car salesman who is considering the possibility of selling 15 automobiles next month. Would he attempt to sell that many cars? Assume that our salesman believes there is a .7 probability that strong effort would result in the desired performance. Also, assume that he perceives the following connections between performance

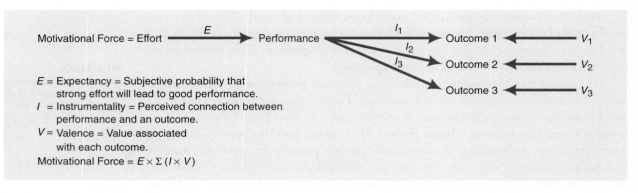

E = Expectancy = Subjective probability that
  strong effort will lead to good performance.
I = Instrumentality = Perceived connection between
  performance and an outcome.
V = Valence = Value associated
  with each outcome.
Motivational Force = $E \times \Sigma (I \times V)$

Exhibit 6-2 Expectancy Theory

and four key outcomes: +.9 for a $1,000 bonus, +.8 for strong praise from his managers, +.9 for high intrinsic satisfaction, and −.7 for meaningful praise from co-workers.[33] Finally, assume valences for these outcomes of 5, 3, 4, and 1 (on a scale from 1 to 5, where 1 means not valued at all and 5 means highly valued). Based on these beliefs and perceptions, our salesman probably would be motivated to attempt to sell the automobiles. He believes there is a good chance that his strong effort would result in success (expectancy of .7), and he perceives strong positive connections between performance and three valued outcomes (instrumentalities of .9, .8, and .9) while perceiving a strong negative connection to a nonvalued outcome (−.7) (he perceives that success probably would yield no praise, and perhaps even scorn, from co-workers, but he does not care).

Another example of expectancy theory in action is a study of over 400 police officers' productivity in terms of drug arrests.[34] This study found that officers who made the most arrests were more likely to have: (1) received specialized training in drug interdiction, and perceived that they had sufficient time in their shift to properly investigate suspected drug offenses (high expectancies); (2) perceived that drug arrests were rewarded by their agency (high instrumentality); and (3) perceived that management saw drug enforcement as a priority (high valence).

Research has generally been supportive of expectancy theory.[35] Criticisms, however, have been expressed concerning how the components of expectancy theory are measured, how they should be combined, and the impact of individual differences. For example, it has been shown that all three components of expectancy theory predict motivation better when they are considered together than when any one component is examined alone. However, the three components do not appear to have equal strength in affecting motivation. That is, the desirability of outcomes may be the most important element in the equation. Not surprisingly, valence seems to be most important.[36] Another issue results from consideration of individual differences. For example, people who have high consideration of others are less likely to engage in the rational, outcome-maximizing decision-making processes underlying expectancy theory.[37] Although subsequent research has led to revised versions of Vroom's original model, the basic components remain the same.[38]

Expectancy theory has clear implications for managers. In order to increase motivation, managers can do one or more of the following:

• Heighten expectancy by increasing associates' beliefs that strong effort will lead to higher levels of performance.

- Increase instrumentalities by clearly linking high performance to outcomes.
- Increase valence by providing outcomes that are highly valued.

We discuss specific procedures later in this chapter.

Equity Theory

The notion of fairness and justice has been of concern to human beings throughout written history and undoubtedly before that as well. Thus, it should not be surprising that people's perception of how fairly they are being treated influences their motivation to perform tasks. The study of organizational justice has been popular in recent years,[39] and its popularity is likely to continue with the increasing incidence of corporate scandals (such as those involving Enron and Arthur Andersen) and discrimination lawsuits.[40] Further, the concept of equity has taken on added importance with the demands by minority groups and women for equitable treatment on the job.[41]

The basic model for using the fairness concept to explain human motivation comes from J. Stacey Adams's **equity theory**.[42] According to this theory, motivation is based on a person's assessment of the ratio of outcomes she receives (e.g., pay, status) for inputs on the job (e.g., effort, ability) compared with the same ratio for a comparison other, frequently a co-worker. Thus, in assessing equity, the person makes the following comparison:

$$\frac{\text{My Outcomes}}{\text{My Inputs}} \text{ vs. } \frac{\text{Other's Outcomes}}{\text{Other's Inputs}}$$

After making the comparison, the person forms equity perceptions. Based on the perceptions of equity or the lack of it, people make *choices* about the action to take (e.g., how much effort to exert to perform the task). Equity exists when the person's ratio of outcomes to inputs is equal to that of the other person, and inequity exists when the ratios are not equal. Inequity may result, for example, when one person is paid more than the other for the same inputs or when one person provides less input for the same pay. Note that an individual may compare his outcome/input ratio to the average ratio of several other people, but often the comparison is to one other person.

When individuals perceive inequity, they can reduce it in several ways. Consider the following tactics (pay is the focus here, but other inputs can affect perceptions of inequity):

- *Increasing or decreasing inputs.* Underpaid associates could decrease their effort, whereas overpaid associates could increase their effort to resolve inequity. This reaction to inequity demonstrates how equity perceptions can influence motivation.
- *Changing their outcomes.* If underpaid associates convince their supervisor to increase their pay, inequity is resolved. It is less likely, but possible, that overpaid workers would seek a salary reduction. However, they may seek to reduce or give up other outcomes, such as not taking interesting assignments or taking a less desirable office.
- *Distorting perceptions of their inputs and outcomes.* If it is not possible to actually change inputs or outcomes, inequitably paid associates may distort their perceptions of the situation. One common erroneous perception by underpaid workers is that their jobs offer many psychological benefits. Overpaid workers often believe they are working much harder than they actually are.

equity theory
A theory that suggests motivation is based on a person's assessment of the ratio of outcomes she receives (e.g., pay, status) for inputs on the job (e.g., effort, ability) compared to the same ratio for a comparison other.

- *Distorting perceptions of the inputs or outcomes of the referent other.* This is similar to distorting perceptions of one's own inputs and outcomes to resolve inequity. For example, if an associate feels she is underpaid compared to her co-worker, she can reason that the co-worker really does stay late more often or has a degree from a better school and thereby the co-worker has higher inputs.
- *Changing the referent other.* If an associate perceives inequity in comparison to one co-worker, it may be easiest to find a co-worker who compares more favorably.
- *Leaving the organization.* In cases where inequity is resistant to other forms of resolution, associates may be motivated to resign from the organization and seek a more equitable situation elsewhere.

Research generally suggests that inequity is an important concept.[43] For example, some individuals have been found to respond to overpayment by increasing their effort and performance.[44] When these individuals believe they are being paid more than they deserve, they increase their inputs to bring them into balance with outcomes. In general, different individuals have been found to react differently to inequity. *Sensitives* are individuals who pay a great deal of attention to outcome/input ratios and are motivated to resolve any inequity, whether the inequity is favorable or unfavorable to them. *Benevolents* are tolerant of inequity that is unfavorable but are not comfortable with inequity that favors them. *Entitleds* do not tolerate unfavorable inequity but are comfortable with inequity that favors them.[45] In the overall population, many people exhibit behavior that seems consistent with the entitleds.

Professional athletes provide interesting case studies for the inequity concept, as indicated by frequent headlines telling us that some "star" is upset about his compensation. These highly paid athletes evidently feel that their outcome/input ratios—their salaries compared with their contributions to their teams—do not measure up to those of similar athletes in the same sport. In 2001, Alex Rodriguez, a young and talented professional baseball player, agreed to a 10-year, $252 million contract to play for the Texas Rangers. Even in the era of exceptional salaries for professional sports figures, this amount seemed almost outrageous. The contract provided Rodriguez, known as A-Rod to his fans, $25.2 million annually. However, that is not all. If by chance anyone in professional baseball negotiated a higher salary in the 10 years of his contract, A-Rod would be given that figure plus $1. In other words, his contract guaranteed that he would be the highest-paid professional baseball player for a decade.[46] Yet, partly because of this very high compensation level, he was traded to the New York Yankees, where he has had both good times and bad.[47]

Perceptions of inequity have several important effects in the workplace.[48] For example, research has found that feelings of inequity can lead to negative employee behaviors such as theft and revenge.[49] On the positive side, feelings of equity frequently lead to outcome satisfaction and job satisfaction,[50] organizational commitment,[51] and organizational citizenship behaviors.[52] *Organizational citizenship behavior* refers to an associate's willingness to engage in organizationally important behaviors that go beyond prescribed job duties, such as helping co-workers with their work or expending extra effort to bring positive publicity to the organization.[53]

Perceptions of inequity often are defined in terms of **distributive justice**, a form of justice that relates to perceptions of fairness in outcomes. Another type of justice is also important, however. **Procedural justice** is the degree to which procedures used to determine outcomes seem fair.[54] Research shows that when outcomes are unfavorable, people

distributive justice
The degree to which people think outcomes are fair.

procedural justice
The degree to which people think the procedures used to determine outcomes are fair.

are likely to be concerned with the fairness used in determining those outcomes.[55] People will be less likely to have negative reactions to unfavorable or questionable outcomes when they perceive that procedures used to arrive at the outcomes are fair. Procedures based on the following rules are more likely to be perceived as fair:[56]

- People should feel that they have a voice in the decision process. For example, good performance-appraisal systems allow associates to provide input into the evaluation process.
- Procedures should be applied consistently. For example, the same criteria should be used to decide on everyone's pay increase.
- Procedures should be free from bias.
- Procedures should be based on accurate information.
- A mechanism should be in place for correcting faulty outcome decisions. Such mechanisms sometimes involve formal grievance procedures.
- Procedures should conform to the prevailing ethical code.
- People should be treated with respect.
- People should be given reasons for the decisions. For example, survivors of a layoff are much more likely to remain motivated if the reasons for the layoff are explained.[57] Overall, equity and procedural-justice concepts can help managers understand associates' reactions to decisions about rewards. As discussed earlier, individuals at W.L. Gore & Associates have already mastered the use of equity and procedural justice.

Goal-Setting Theory

Goal-setting theory, developed by Edwin Locke, posits that goals enhance human performance because they direct attention and affect effort and persistence.[58] Given the nature of human beings, individuals are likely to be committed to the achievement of goals after they have been set and to exert effort toward goal attainment.[59] Indeed, goals serve as reference points that energize behavior.[60] The positive effects of goals on work motivation is one of the strongest findings in research on organizational behavior. Goal setting has been found to increase the motivation of associates in a multitude of jobs, such as air traffic controllers, truck drivers, faculty researchers, marine recruits, managers, social workers, nurses, research and development workers, truck maintenance workers, and weightlifters.[61] To effectively set goals for associates, managers should address several factors, including goal difficulty, goal specificity, goal commitment, participation in goal setting, and feedback:

- *Goal difficulty.* How difficult should the performance goal be? Should the goal be easy, moderately difficult, or very difficult to achieve?
- *Goal specificity.* How specific should the expected outcome be (e.g., number of parts assembled), or can goals be more loosely defined (do your best)?
- *Goal commitment.* What will make associates commit to goals?
- *Participation in setting goals.* How important is it for associates to have input in selecting the goals and levels of performance to be achieved? If important, how should they be involved?
- *Feedback.* To what extent should associates be informed of their progress as they work toward the performance goals?

goal-setting theory
A theory that suggests challenging and specific goals increase human performance because they affect attention, effort, and persistence.

Goal Difficulty

From the perspective of expectancy theory and achievement motivation theory, we might expect that associates exert the maximum effort at work when their performance goals are set at moderate levels of difficulty (i.e., somewhat difficult but achievable). Goals that are too difficult may be rejected by associates because the expectancy is low (strong effort would not lead to goal attainment). A number of researchers, however, have found that associates exert more effort when they have goals that are difficult to a significant degree. This has been found to be true of engineers and scientists, loggers, and many experimental subjects working on a variety of tasks in laboratory settings.[62] Thus, it seems that goals should be as difficult as possible, but not unreasonable. Stretch goals that are extremely difficult can be quite demotivating.

Goal Specificity

Performance goals can be explicitly stated, clear in meaning, and specific in terms of quantity or quality of performance. For example, a goal might be to "generate twenty-seven pages of edited copy with an error rate of less than one error per ten pages in each work period" or "make twelve new customer contacts each month." The nature of some tasks, however, makes it difficult to clearly determine and state the exact performance levels that should be achieved. In such cases, a performance goal can be stated only in vague terms, such as "do your best" or "increase sales during the month."

Many studies have shown that specific goals lead to better performance than do vague goals, such as "do your very best."[63] If a goal is to act as a motivator, it must establish a specific target toward which people can direct their effort. Managers are likely to find this aspect of setting goals to be challenging because many jobs involve activities that are difficult to specify. For example, it may be difficult for a manager to be specific about an engineer's goals; yet the manager must make the attempt, or the engineer's motivation could be adversely affected.

Goal Commitment

In general, associates must accept and be committed to reaching externally set goals for these goals to be motivating. A great deal of research has been conducted on the factors that influence people's commitment to externally set goals. Expectancy theory provides a useful framework for organizing these factors; people will be committed to goals that: (1) carry a reasonable expectation of being attained and (2) are viewed as desirable to attain.[64] A summary of the factors that can affect goal commitment is presented in Exhibit 6-3.

Participation in Setting Goals

A practical question for a manager, especially during performance-counseling sessions with associates, is, "Should I set performance goals for the associate on the basis of my own knowledge and judgment of her abilities, or should I allow the associate to provide input and have some degree of control over them?" Importantly, associates who participate in setting a goal rather than having it dictated to them might be more satisfied with the goal and be more committed to it, resulting in stronger performance.[65] While some researchers have failed to find a relationship between participation in goal setting and performance,[66] others have found that performance is better when associates participate in setting goals.[67] Also, as discussed earlier, individuals with high achievement needs tend to dislike assigned goals.

EXHIBIT 6-3 Factors Affecting Goal Commitment

Factors Increasing the Desirability of Attaining a Given Goal

1. The goal is set by or in conjunction with an appropriate authority figure.
2. The goal fosters a sense of self-achievement and potential for development.
3. The goal is set by or in conjunction with someone who is trustworthy.
4. The goal is set by or in conjunction with someone who is supportive and promotes self-efficacy.
5. Peers are committed to the goal.
6. The goal assigner, if there is one, provides a rationale for the goal.
7. The goal provides a challenge to prove oneself and meets ego needs.
8. The goal is public.

Factors Increasing the Perceived Ability of Attaining a Given Goal

1. There is high self-efficacy on the task.
2. There are successful role models.
3. The task is not impossibly difficult.
4. Expectancy for success is high.
5. There is competition with others.

Source: Based on E.A. Locke, & G.P. Latham. 1990. *A Theory of Goal Setting and Task Motivation* (Englewood Cliffs, NJ: Prentice Hall).

Subconscious Goals

Some management research has demonstrated that goals do not have to be consciously assigned to influence motivation and performance.[68] That is, people do not need to be consciously aware that they have been given a goal in order for the goal to influence their behavior. Studies examining this phenomenon usually use supraliminal priming to assign goals. Supraliminal priming involves consciously providing people with achievement information, but in a manner that appears to be unrelated to the task that they are about to perform.[69] For example, people may be asked to circle words in a large matrix of letters or they may be asked to unscramble words to make sentences. Those who are being assigned goals are given words or sentences having to do with motivation and achievement ("win" or "the man will succeed"), along with other neutral words or sentences. Later they are asked to perform some task. Research has found that those who are primed with achievement goals outperform those who are not primed with goals[70] and that this effect can last quite awhile.[71] It appears that subconsciously primed goals lead people to set higher self-set goals than do non-goal-oriented primes.[72] This line of research is still very new and most of it has been conducted in the laboratory, so it remains to be seen to what extent subconscious goals can be primed in actual workplace settings and to what extent these subconscious goals will affect behavior.[73] However, one preliminary study found that subconscious goals can be primed (in this case there was a picture of a woman winning a race to show achievement) and do increase motivation and performance in the workplace.[74]

Feedback

The motivational effect of providing feedback to associates about their progress toward performance goals is well established. In fact, feedback on performance, even in the absence of established goals, is likely to have a positive effect on motivation.[75] However,

Making Visible Changes

Imagine a grand ballroom filled with people in black ties and ball gowns. The crowd hushes as the award ceremony begins. A young woman in a red dress steps up on stage to receive her award: a $40,000 bonus. The woman is 25-year-old Lara Hadad, whose total pay package, including her bonus, will be almost a quarter of a million dollars. Lara is joining other colleagues who together are receiving 11 cars, a trip to Greece, and part of $8.7 million in bonuses.

Interestingly, Lara doesn't work for a large multinational firm. She is a hair stylist with Visible Changes hair salons. Visible Changes is an innovator in the hair salon industry. The company was started in 1977 in Houston, Texas. At the time, hairdressing was considered a risky business, and the McCormacks—the entrepreneurs who started the firm—had a difficult time convincing mall owners and bankers to support their project. However, the McCormacks implemented a management philosophy that has made them leaders in their field. Visible Changes has been recognized in *Inc.* magazine's list of the fastest-growing companies in the United States and won Salon Entrepreneur of the Year at the Global Salon Business Awards in Barcelona, Spain. Furthermore, in an industry plagued by high turnover and employment problems, Visible Changes associates have a low turnover rate and high satisfaction. The firm currently has 17 locations in major Texas malls with a total of over 800 associates. And each salon averages over $2 million in annual sales—well above the industry average.

How did the McCormacks build such a high-performance climate? Most of their success has been due to the way they motivate their employees:

- They provide well-defined career paths, and the performance standards required to move from one level to another are well known by stylists. For example, to move from a senior cutter to a master cutter (with an associated increase in pay and potential bonuses), a stylist must increase the total number of haircuts given from 7,000 to 14,000, be requested by 65 percent of his clients, and complete additional education. Training and encouragement help to establish positive expectancies for these performance levels.

- They provide valued rewards and benefits, showing employees that they are a part of the company "family" and that the company cares about them. For example, they have a profit-sharing plan whereby the company makes yearly contributions to associates' accounts. Associates are fully vested after 7 years, and the average person has about $100,000 in her account after 10 years. Such

©Digital Vision

a plan is highly unusual in the hair salon industry. Furthermore, in addition to bonuses, employees are rewarded with cars, public-recognition ceremonies, and travel to interesting locations. The "manager of the year" receives a one-carat diamond and the use of the company Mercedes. If she wins three times consecutively, she gets to keep the car! All these perks are based on meeting and exceeding clear performance standards. John McCormack promised his employees that should any of their children want to go to medical school, the company would pay for it. Several employees have taken him up on this offer.

- They set specific, challenging goals for each time period and reward people for achieving them. The stylists at Visible Changes make three times the industry average, with some earning six-figure incomes. The industry average is below $18,500. Beginning stylists are guaranteed $7 per hour; however, they are free to make as much as they can in commissions and bonuses.

- In order to encourage customer service performance, commissions and bonuses are based on the number of requests by customers, amount of products sold, and general performance of the stylist. When requested by name, the stylist receives an extra 10% commission. When that happens 50% of the time the bonus increases an additional 10%, and then again by another 10% when a stylist is requested by name 75% of the time. When a stylist is among the top 50 requested in the entire chain, he or she earns another super bonus.

- They provide support for their stylists to help them build their client base. For example, they provide brochures, business cards, and coupons.
- They avoid layoffs of associates.
- They engage associates in a variety of organizational decisions.

The McCormacks have been industry pioneers in the ways they motivate and provide support to their associates. Thus, their company is an industry leader. Other salons are copying their methods by introducing such things as better benefits packages and profit-sharing plans. We might say that the McCormacks have made significant Visible Changes.

Sources: D. Lauk. 2003. "Up Close: Local Company Puts Employees First," 11 News (Houston, Texas), Apr. 14, at http://www.khou.com; I. MacMillan & R.G. McGrath. 2000. *The Entrepreneurial Mindset: Strategies for Continuously Creating Opportunity in an Age of Uncertainty* (Cambridge, MA: Harvard Business School Press); Visible Changes, "Careers," 2010, at http://www.visiblechanges.com/Careers.aspx; Visible Changes, "Stylist," 2010, at http://www.visiblechanges.com/Stylist.aspx; Leadership-and-Motivation Training. Jan. 29, 2010. "Managing Change in the Workplace," at http://www.leadership-and-motivation-training.com/managing-change-in-the-workplace.html; A. Ragsdale. May 30, 2007. "Texas CEO makes big promise to employees". Houstonist.com at http://houstonist .com/2007/05/30/texas_ceo_makes.php.

feedback is especially important when performance goals exist and when they are relatively difficult to achieve. In this case, feedback permits an associate to gauge his actual progress toward the goal and make corresponding adjustments in his efforts. Such adjustments are unlikely in the absence of feedback. Thus, the presence of both goals and feedback exerts a positive influence on employee motivation.

Conclusions Regarding Process Theories

Expectancy theory, equity theory, and goal-setting theory emphasize the processes that occur in motivation. Expectancy theory focuses on people as rational decision makers: "If I exert a given amount of effort, how likely is it that my performance will result in outcomes I value?" The manager's job in this case is to develop situations in which associates have high expectancies and strong performance is rewarded. Equity theory focuses more on people's general feelings about how fairly they are being treated. This theory suggests that managers must take into account how associates are comparing themselves with others in the organization; a manager's treatment of one individual can influence the motivation of others. Finally, goal-setting theory suggests that managers can motivate associates by setting or helping to set goals.

In the *Experiencing Organizational Behavior* feature, the importance of associates' motivation is emphasized. The owners of Visible Changes, the McCormacks, ensure challenging goals for their associates and then pay them handsome bonuses for meeting those goals. They also focus on expectancies held by associates and use a variety of meaningful rewards. Finally, they support associates' growth needs through an education program, and they allow associates to participate in decisions. As a result, associates earn well above the industry average, and turnover is exceptionally low. The associates' high motivation and strong performance have made Visible Changes a top performer in its industry. Thus, Visible Changes is an industry leader both in methods of motivating associates and in company performance.

EXHIBIT 6.4 Motivation Practices Resulting from Motivation Theories

Motivation Theories	Motivation Practices				
	Find Meaningful Individual Rewards	Tie Rewards to Performance	Redesign Jobs	Provide Feedback	Clarify Expectations and Goals
Need Hierarchies Maslow ERG	X		X	X	
McClelland's Needs	X	X	X	X	X
Herzberg's Two-Factor Theory			X		
Expectancy Theory	X	X		X	X
Equity Theory	X	X		X	X
Goal-Setting Theory		X		X	X

Note: The fact that there is no X in a particular cell indicates that the theory has nothing specific to say about the practice, not that the theory says the practice is ineffective.

Motivating Associates: An Integration of Motivation Theories

Viewed as a set, the various motivation theories may suggest that motivation is highly complex and even confusing. That is not actually the case, however. Motivating associates and junior managers can be undertaken in a reasonably straightforward and meaningful way. While there are no foolproof approaches, there are sound tactics to use. Exhibit 6-4 identifies connections between the various motivation theories and five categories of motivation practices that managers can use. As shown in the exhibit, multiple theories have similar implications for managers. We discuss these implications in the remainder of the chapter.

Find Meaningful Individual Rewards

All of the content theories suggest that individuals vary in what they find motivating. Furthermore, expectancy theory implies that individuals assign different valences to outcomes. This means that by tailoring individual rewards to individual needs and desires, companies can create a competitive advantage in attracting and motivating associates. One area in which this is obvious is the provision of benefits. An unmarried 28-year-old associate with no children likely places different values on various retirement and insurance plans relative to a 50-year-old associate with three children in college, for example.

One mistake that managers often make when trying to determine what motivates individual associates involves placing too much emphasis on extrinsic rewards (e.g., pay increases, bonuses, pay level, job security, job titles) while underemphasizing intrinsic rewards (e.g., satisfaction based on exciting and challenging work, feelings of accomplishment).[76] Indeed, one survey of a random sample of U.S. adults indicated that they ranked "important work" as the most important aspect of their jobs. Pay was ranked third. When, however, these same people were asked what motivates "other people," 75 percent responded that pay was the primary motivator of others.[77] Apparently, most people feel that they are motivated by outcomes that meet higher-order growth or achievement needs, but they think others are primarily motivated by money as a way to meet physiological and security needs.

Some research has shown that if a person receives extrinsic rewards for performing an intrinsically satisfying task, he may attribute the performance to external forces, with a resulting reduction in his intrinsic interest in the job.[78] This suggests that relying too heavily on extrinsic rewards can cause people to lose any natural interest they have in performing their jobs. However, this position has been challenged by some researchers, who argue that in work situations, extrinsic rewards are necessary for motivation on any kind of task. Despite the mixed research,[79] it is clear that managers must be concerned with both extrinsic and intrinsic rewards and not overemphasize either, striving instead for an appropriate balance between the two (keeping in mind that the appropriate balance differs across different people or types of people).

Individuals may vary in what they find motivating based on their position in the organization. People in different jobs and at different levels may have different concerns. Indeed, when *Harvard Business Review* asked a dozen top leaders to state their most important thoughts on motivating people, Liu Chuanzhi, chairman of the Legend Group of Beijing, noted that a leader must establish different incentives for people at different levels in the organization.[80] He divided his organization into three groups and provided appropriate incentives for each group:

- The company's executives wanted a sense of ownership in the company, so the company gave all of its executives stock, an unusual practice in Chinese state-owned organizations. They also wanted recognition, so they were given opportunities to speak to the media.
- Midlevel managers wanted to become senior-level managers. The major incentives applied to this group involved opportunities to display and develop their knowledge, skills, and abilities, so they would be in a better position to achieve promotions within the company.
- Associates wanted outcomes that would provide a sense of stability and security. Thus, based on their performance, they received predictable bonuses. Furthermore, they were allowed to participate in decisions regarding how bonuses were allotted.

Tie Rewards to Performance

A basic characteristic of high-involvement management involves tying rewards to performance. The importance of this tactic is supported by many theories concerning human motivation and learning. One of the basic principles of operant conditioning (Chapter 4) is that rewards should be tied directly to performance to encourage the desired behavior. This basic proposition is reflected in the process theories of motivation as well. Expectancy theory proposes that motivation is a function of the perceived connections between performance and outcomes. To the extent that people have experience with performance leading to rewards, they will develop stronger instrumentalities.

Equity theory suggests that performance in the recent past (an input) should play a role in rewards (outcomes). In addition, justice research indicates that linking performance and rewards should result in greater motivation because the reward decisions will be viewed as more ethical and unbiased as people are rewarded based on their achievement and contribution. Finally, goal-setting theory suggests that providing rewards for the achievement of goals can help associates accept and become committed to those goals, although external rewards are not necessarily required for goals to affect motivation.[81]

Although tying rewards to performance may seem obvious and simple, managers often find it to be challenging. One reason for this problem is that performance is sometimes difficult to measure.[82] How does one evaluate the work of an R&D professional whose job entails developing and testing many new ideas, most of which will not result in usable products? What if an individual is highly interdependent with others? Can his individual contributions be clearly assessed? Further, some managers may supervise too many employees to closely observe and easily evaluate the contributions of all of them. If one cannot measure or evaluate performance accurately, then one cannot link performance to rewards. To partially address these issues, managers can have their direct reports undertake self-assessments and generate peer assessments. These tactics coupled with managers' knowledge of performance are often very helpful.

Another problem with tying rewards to performance is that managers may have little flexibility with rewards, particularly financial rewards. For example, a manager may be able to give an average raise of only 3 percent to her employees. If the bottom third of performers are given 2 percent increases, to adjust for the cost of living, this means the best performers can receive only 4 percent increases. Associates are not likely to see this small differential as being commensurate with performance differences. Such a small differential can produce low instrumentalities or perceptions of inequity.

Such problems with flexibility underscore the importance of nonfinancial rewards. Although managers may be restricted in how they can distribute financial rewards, they often can be more creative in assigning other types of rewards based on performance. For example, high-performing associates can be given job assignments that allow them to develop new skills, or they can be given credits toward payment of tuition at a local university. The Society for Human Resource Management surveyed its members and developed a list of over 150 creative rewards that companies offer their associates. These included the services of an ergonomics consultant, sophisticated office chairs, textbook money, funding to attend conferences in exotic locations, allowing pets at work, concierge services, free dinners, and flexible work hours.

To think more deeply about tying financial rewards to performance, consider the case of Susan. Susan supervises 10 customer call-center representatives. One of her associates, Angelo, clearly outperforms the others. Angelo's customer satisfaction ratings are much higher than those of the others, he handles the most calls, and there have been no complaints against him. Susan is highly pleased with Angelo's performance, especially because he has been on the job for only one month. Susan's worst performer is Jessica, who has the lowest customer service rating, handles an average number of calls, and has been the target of several customer complaints about rudeness. Jessica has worked in the unit for the past three years, which is a long tenure for a customer service representative. It's time to assign pay increases, and Susan's boss told her that her budget for salaries would be only 4 percent. This means that her employees can receive, on average, only a 4 percent raise. Susan is considering an 8 percent increase for Angelo and no increase for Jessica. However, when she begins to assign pay increases, she has a change of heart. She realizes that if she gives Angelo an 8 percent increase and gives no pay increase to Jessica, Angelo will receive more overall pay than Jessica, who has been on the job much longer. Susan doesn't want to alienate Jessica, because it is difficult to retain people on the job (and Jessica has a tendency to react quite negatively to bad news). In the end, Susan gives Angelo a 5 percent pay increase and Jessica a 3 percent pay increase. Three months later, Susan notices that Angelo's customer service rating has decreased and that he is handling fewer calls. Jessica's performance hasn't improved either. In fact, the number of complaints against her has increased.[83]

Susan's dilemma illustrates several common pitfalls in tying financial rewards to performance.

One problem is that Susan didn't differentiate more between Angelo's and Jessica's pay increases because of her fear that Jessica would become angry. This is a common reaction of managers when distributing financial rewards. Too often, managers are overly focused on superficial harmony, and they mistakenly distribute rewards equally or nearly equally rather than equitably based on performance. Monica Barron, a management consultant from AMR research, has stated, "You should make your best performers role models and say to others 'Here's what you can do to get one of these checks.'"[84]

A second problem was that Susan really wanted to reward performance, but instead she ended up rewarding tenure. Jessica received a larger pay increase because she had remained with the organization and in the job for a relatively long time. If Susan was asked whether mediocre, or even poor, performers should be rewarded for remaining on the job, she would probably answer "No." This might not have happened if Susan had clearly established what performance she expected from associates and how that performance would be rewarded.

A third problem was Susan's dilemma of having a budget of only 4 percent for pay increases. Her situation reflects the current state for many companies. Indeed, Robert Heneman, a compensation expert from Ohio State University, has said that managers "need a 7 percent or 8 percent [compensation increase] just to catch anybody's attention."[85] Thus, the amount of money Susan had for rewards limited her flexibility.

Beyond the simple amount of money available, how the money is used also can make a difference. A frequent issue is too much emphasis placed on merit pay increases (i.e., year-to-year pay increases). With such a focus, rewards provided for good performance in any given year are maintained in an associate's pay regardless of future performance. In addition, such an approach is often inflexible in dealing with economic downturns (because higher levels of pay are locked in for some individuals who are no longer performing among the best). Finally, the approach constrains managers from being able to provide a wide distribution of rewards. There are more creative ways to provide merit-based pay, including profit sharing and bonuses.

Redesign Jobs

Job redesign is viewed as a way to make jobs more intrinsically meaningful to people and thus more likely to satisfy higher-order needs. Job redesign generally takes one of two forms: job enlargement or job enrichment.

Job Enlargement

Job enlargement involves adding tasks with similar complexity to the current tasks. The added tasks offer more variety and often require the use of different skills. However, the additional tasks are not of greater complexity and therefore offer little opportunity for personal growth. Some refer to this practice as *horizontal job loading*.

job enlargement
The process of making a job more motivating by adding tasks that are similar in complexity relative to the current tasks.

An example of job enlargement involves giving a data entry specialist the additional task of filing correspondence. In this case, a different skill is utilized, but filing is no more complex than routine data entry. Even so, by providing variety, job enlargement may prevent boredom in simple tasks. However, the effects may be only temporary because the tasks do not offer more challenges or opportunities for personal growth. Overall, research has shown that the effects of job enlargement are mixed. Some studies have found that job enlargement produces positive results, whereas others have not.[86] Individuals with lower growth needs may benefit the most.

Job Enrichment

job enrichment
The process of making a job more motivating by increasing responsibility.

For our purposes, **job enrichment** can be differentiated from job enlargement by the complexity of tasks added to the job. Job enrichment is frequently referred to as *vertical job loading*. In enriched jobs, workers have greater responsibility for accomplishing assigned tasks; it may be said that they become "managers" of their own jobs. The concept of job enrichment was popularized by Herzberg's two-factor concept of motivation, which emphasizes responsibility, achievement, and the work itself as motivators. The concept of job enrichment also is consistent with McClelland's notion of developing a strong need for achievement and with Maslow's and Alderfer's ideas about meeting higher-order needs.

Many organizations, including AT&T, Corning, IBM, and Procter & Gamble, have implemented job enrichment programs. Usually, job enrichment involves adding tasks formerly handled at levels higher in the hierarchy. Boeing, for example, has implemented job enrichment by using work teams, empowering employees to work on their own ideas, and providing continuous learning opportunities. Because job enrichment involves giving associates greater control over their work, expanded job duties, and greater decision power, job enrichment is an integral part of high-involvement management.

Numerous studies have found positive results from job enrichment using outcome variables such as job satisfaction, commitment to the organization, and performance.[87] However, job enrichment programs are not always successful. To be effective, such programs must be carefully planned, implemented, and communicated to associates and must also take into account individual differences.[88]

Interestingly, many individuals who are currently entering the workforce may embrace enriched jobs to a greater degree than some others have. These individuals are members of Generation Y, those born between 1981 and 1993. According to Deloitte Consulting, members of Generation Y love challenges in the workplace, appreciate the opportunity to be flexible and explore new ideas, and want to make a difference.[89]

©Adrian Bradshaw/epa/Corbis

The work of two researchers, Richard Hackman and Greg Oldham, has been very influential in specifying how to enrich jobs so that the motivating potential of the jobs is increased. They identified five job characteristics important in the design of jobs—skill variety, task identity, task significance, autonomy, and feedback:[90]

- *Skill variety* refers to the degree to which associates utilize a broad array of skills in doing their jobs.
- *Task identity* is the extent to which job performance results in an identifiable piece of work. Contrast the situation in which an assembly line worker's entire job is

screwing bolts into one piece of metal versus the situation in which that associate is responsible for turning out an entire dashboard assembly.

- *Task significance* is the extent to which a job has an impact on the organization. It is important because people need to see how the work they do contributes to the functioning of the organization.
- *Autonomy* means that the associate has the independence to schedule his or her own work and influence the procedures with which it is carried out.
- *Feedback* involves obtaining accurate information about performance.

Hackman and Oldham propose that these five characteristics affect three psychological states: feeling of the work's meaningfulness, feeling of responsibility for the work done, and knowledge of results of personal performance on the job. Skill variety, task identity, and task significance affect the feeling of meaningfulness. Feeling of responsibility is affected by autonomy, and knowledge of results is affected by feedback. The following formula combines these factors to compute a motivating potential score (MPS) for a given job:[91]

$$\text{MPS} = \frac{(\text{Skill variety} + \text{Task identity} + \text{Task Significance}) \times \text{Autonomy} \times \text{Feedback}}{3}$$

Research has been generally supportive of the Hackman and Oldham model, finding that associates' perceptions of task characteristics relate to intrinsic motivation and performance.[92] However, several factors have been found to influence whether employees are motivated by enriched jobs. The most heavily researched factor is growth need strength.[93] People with high growth need strength tend to be more motivated by enriched jobs than those with low growth need strength. Perceptions of job characteristics have also been found to relate to job satisfaction and growth satisfaction.[94] Indeed, in one poll, one of the major reasons given for the decline in the job satisfaction of U.S. associates, is that they perceive their jobs to be boring and unengaging.[95] On the negative side, however, enriched jobs, which require more skill variety, responsibility, and control, can also be more stressful to certain associates.[96]

As discussed in the *Experiencing Organizational Behavior* feature, there are steps managers can take to ensure that the demands of enriched jobs are successfully handled. When managers provide a proper setting and resources, associates interested in growth and challenge usually rise to the occasion.

Provide Feedback

Feedback is critical to motivation from a variety of perspectives. Those high in need for achievement seek it, it is necessary for the development of expectancies and instrumentalities, it can influence perceptions of fairness by providing explanations for decisions, and it enhances the goal-setting process. A great deal of research has been conducted on the effects of performance feedback. A review of this research resulted in the following implications for making feedback effective:[97]

- Feedback is most effective when provided in conjunction with goals.
- Feedback should be repeated and provided at regular intervals. Robert Eckert, chairman and CEO of Mattel, states this succinctly: "People can't and won't do much for you if no one in the organization knows what's going on, what you expect of them. … And talking to them once a quarter is not enough."[98]

Connecting People in the Workplace

Enriched jobs have the potential to be highly motivating and rewarding. Such jobs, however, place significant demands on jobholders. To ensure success in dealing with these demands, individuals must rely on one another. In a recent report, Deloitte Research, an arm of Deloitte & Touche, put it this way: "Work has always been done through relationships. But as jobs become more complex, people increasingly depend on one another, whether it's to design software, lead a call center, or sell a service."

To facilitate connections among people, Deloitte recommends a number of tactics:

- *Design physical space that fosters connections.* Proximity and layout matter. Being located far away from others who have relevant knowledge and insight can be particularly harmful to those with complex jobs. A lack of face-to-face interactions, the richest type, can be harmful to those who have such jobs. Also, an absence of dedicated areas for collaborative discussions as well as areas for quiet contemplation can be detrimental.

- *Build an organizational cushion of time and space.* Overly busy associates and managers often do not have the time to consult with others. With today's leaner organizations and stretched people, connecting to other people in rich ways can be difficult. Yet, those connections can improve productivity and quality in the long run, particularly for those who have complex jobs.

- *Cultivate communities.* Without a sense of community, associates and managers may not seek out those who have relevant knowledge and insight. Communities revolve around shared interests and goals, and they foster a sense of shared identity and belonging.

- *Stimulate rich networks of high-quality relationships.* Many associates and managers have limited informal networks of colleagues. Without a rich network that stretches across departments, divisions, and hierarchical levels, individuals are blocked from key sources of information and problem solving. In some organizations, explicit mapping of informal networks is carried out and those with deficient networks are counseled on how to improve.

- *Provide collaboration tools.* A lack of interactive, real-time collaborative technologies can be a roadblock for some types of jobs. Tools such as shared whiteboards and interactive decision-support systems can be quite useful. Wikis are also becoming useful (these involve open-access information sites whose core content can be edited by anyone at any time).

©Beau Lark/Corbis

Sources: R. Athey. 2004. "It's 2008: Do You Know Where Your Talent Is?—Part 1" (New York: Deloitte & Touche USA); R. Athey. 2007. "It's 2008: Do You Know Where Your Talent Is?—Part 2" (New York: Deloitte & Touche USA); C. Mamberto. 2007. "Instant Messaging Invades the Office," *Wall Street Journal*, July 24, B.1; D. Fichter. 2005. "The Many Forms of E-Collaboration," *Online*, July-Aug., pp. 48–50.

- Feedback should contain information about how associates can improve their performance. It is not enough to tell people whether they did well or poorly; performance strategies and plans must also be part of the message.
- Feedback should come from a credible source. The person giving the feedback should have the authority to do so and should also have sufficient knowledge of the recipient's performance.

- Feedback should focus on the performance, not on the person. In other words, feedback should always refer specifically to a performance measure, as in "Your performance is poor because you missed your quota by 10 percent," not "Your performance is poor because you are not a very good salesperson."

Clarify Expectations and Goals

The importance of goal setting to associates' motivation is made explicit in goal-setting theory. However, goal setting is also important from other motivational perspectives. Goal setting can be used to strengthen the relationships important in expectancy theory. For example, because goals help people analyze and plan performance, their effort-performance expectancies may be enhanced. Also, higher goals may be associated with higher outcome valences. Furthermore, goal setting is an important part of need for achievement because people high in this characteristic tend to set moderately difficult and reachable goals for themselves.

Many organizations have adopted goal setting, for two reasons. One is the motivating potential of goals; the other is that goals often can serve to align individual motives with organizational goals. One formal management program that aims to align motives and goals is referred to as management by objectives (MBO). Throughout the organization, individuals meet with their managers to agree on expectations for the upcoming time period.

THE STRATEGIC LENS

Associates' motivation is very important in all types of organizations. In general, associates who have greater motivation perform at higher levels, and this helps to implement the organization's strategy. When the associates achieve their goals, the strategy is implemented. When the strategy is implemented effectively, the organization achieves higher performance. This result was evident in the case of W.L. Gore and later in the example of Visible Changes. The goals of associates at Visible Changes related to the strategic goal of the organization to provide high-quality service to its customers.

As part of motivation and performance, individuals must work with others to achieve success on interdependent tasks. Karl Malone, a former professional basketball player, experienced firsthand the disappointment that can occur when colleagues are unwilling to work together. He moved from the Utah Jazz to the Los Angeles Lakers in order to have a better chance to be on a championship team. He gave up a great deal of money as well as status as the sole star on a team in order to move, and he was highly motivated to perform well for the Lakers.[99] The Lakers, however, failed to play effectively as a team, and as a result they failed to win the championship. For organizations to achieve their goals and enjoy strong performance, associates and managers must be motivated not only to perform their individual tasks well but also to coordinate their activities with others in the organization to ensure that the organization's strategy is well implemented and success is ensured.

Critical Thinking Questions

1. Assume that you are managing a talented but unmotivated associate. Also assume that organizational resources needed for the job are generally sufficient. What factors would you consider first in attempting to motivate the associate? Why those factors?

2. A number of theories of motivation suggest that different rewards might be important to different people. How difficult is it to reward people differently for performing the same or similar work?

3. How will your individual motivation affect your career opportunities?

❓ back to the knowledge objectives

1. What do we mean by work motivation, and how does it relate to performance? Why is individual work motivation important to organizational success?

2. What assumptions do Maslow's need hierarchy and ERG theory make about human motivation? How can managers use these theories to motivate associates? How do need for achievement, need for affiliation, and need for power differ? How do these needs relate to work performance and motivation? How would you distinguish McClelland's notion of needs from those of other content theorists?

3. What does Herzberg's two-factor theory of motivation say about human motivation? How has it influenced current management practice?

4. What does expectancy theory suggest about people and motivation at work? When does expectancy theory best explain motivation? What implications does this theory have for managers?

5. What do equity theory and ideas from procedural justice suggest about motivation? How do fairness judgments influence work motivation, and how can managers ensure that associates perceive judgments as having been made fairly?

6. What are the basic tenets of goal-setting theory? What should a manager keep in mind when engaging in goal setting with his associates?

7. How does job enrichment affect associates' motivation to perform? To make sure job enrichment has the desired effects, what should the organization consider?

8. Considering the various theories of motivation, what can managers do to increase motivation?

What This Chapter Adds to Your Knowledge Portfolio

In this chapter, we have discussed work motivation in some detail. We have defined motivation, discussed both content and process theories of motivation, and described how these theories can be integrated and translated into managerial practice. More specifically, we have made the following points:

- Motivation refers to forces coming from within a person that account for the willful direction, intensity, and persistence of the person's efforts toward achieving specific goals, where achievement is not due solely to ability or to environmental demands.

- Content theories of motivation generally are concerned with identifying the specific factors (such as needs, hygienes, or motivators) that motivate people. They tend to be somewhat simplistic and are easily understood by managers. The basic implications of these theories suggest that managers must take individual needs into account when trying to decipher what motivates associates.

- Maslow's need hierarchy includes five levels of needs: physiological, safety, social and belongingness, esteem, and self-actualization. These needs are arranged in prepotent hierarchical order. Prepotency refers to the concept that a lower-order need, until satisfied, is dominant in motivating a person's behavior. Once a need is satisfied, the next higher need becomes the active source of motivation. Research has not been very supportive of Maslow's theory; however, this theory has served as the basis for other theories and practices that have received empirical support.

- ERG theory is similar to Maslow's hierarchy but does not consider prepotency to be relevant. The three needs in ERG theory are existence, relatedness, and growth. A person may work on all three needs at the same time, although satisfying lower-order needs often takes place before a person is strongly motivated by higher-level needs.

- Achievement, affiliation, and power needs are the focus of McClelland's theory. Practitioners have given the most attention to the need for achievement. People with a high need for achievement like to establish their own goals and prefer moderately difficult ones. They seek feedback on their achievements and tend to be positive thinkers. However, the need that most distinguishes effective managers from nonmanagers is the need for institutionalized power.

- Herzberg's two-factor theory identifies two types of organizational rewards: those related to satisfaction (motivators) and those related to dissatisfaction (hygienes). It also raises the issue of intrinsic and extrinsic rewards. One important application of this theory, job enrichment, is widely practiced today.

- Whereas content theories emphasize the factors that motivate, process theories are concerned with the process by which such factors interact to produce motivation. They generally are more complex than content theories and offer substantial insights and understanding. Their application frequently results in highly motivated behaviors.

- Expectancy theory suggests that motivation is affected by several factors acting together. This theory emphasizes associates' perceptions of the relationship between effort and performance (expectancy), the linkage between performance and rewards (instrumentalities), and anticipated satisfaction with rewards (valence). Managers can influence employee motivation by affecting one of these areas but can have greater impact by affecting more than one.

- Equity theory considers the human reaction to fairness. According to this theory, a person compares her outcome/input ratio with that of another person, often a co-worker, to determine whether the relationship is equitable. An inequitable situation causes an individual to alter inputs or outcomes, distort his or her perception of inputs or outcomes, change the source of comparison, or leave the organization. Associates' perceptions of procedural justice can also influence how they react to perceived inequities.

- Goal-setting theory is concerned with several issues that arise in the process of setting performance goals for employees, including goal difficulty, goal specificity, goal commitment, associates' participation, and feedback. In general, goals should be difficult but realistic and specific. Participation and feedback are also useful for increasing the effectiveness of goals in influencing motivation.

- Motivation theories support the use of several managerial practices to increase associates' motivation: (1) find meaningful individual rewards; (2) tie rewards to performance; (3) redesign jobs through enlargement or enrichment; (4) provide feedback; and (5) clarify expectations and goals.

Key Terms

building your human capital
Assessing Your Needs

©John-Francis Bourke/Corbis

Look at the picture to the right for 60 seconds. *Turn the picture over or close your book* and take 15 to 20 minutes to write a story about what you see happening in the picture. Your story should be at least one to two pages in length and it should address the following issues:

1. Who are the people in the picture? What is their relationship?
2. What is currently taking place in the picture? What are the people doing?
3. What took place in the hour preceding the taking of the picture?
4. What will take place in the hour following the taking of the picture?

This exercise is based on a tool, the Thematic Apperception Test, used by McClelland and associates to assess people's needs for achievement, affiliation, and power. The Hay Group and other leading consulting and development firms continue to use this type of tool. To determine where you fall on the three needs, do the following:

1. Give yourself one point for need for achievement every time one of the following themes appears in your story:
   • Your story involves a work or competitive situation.
   • Feedback is being given or received.
   • Goals or standards are being discussed.
   • Someone is taking responsibility for his or her work.
   • Someone is expressing pride over his or her own accomplishments or those of another person.

2. Give yourself one point for need for affiliation every time one of the following themes appears in your story:
   • The relationship between the characters is personal.
   • Help is being given or received.
   • Encouragement, comfort, empathy, or affection is being given or received.
   • Someone is expressing a desire to be close to the other person.
   • The characters are engaged in or talking about social activities

3. Give yourself one point for need for power every time one of the following themes appears in your story:
   • The relationship between the characters is hierarchical. Someone has higher status than the others.
   • Someone is trying to get someone else to do something.
   • Someone is attempting to get others to work together.
   • Someone is concerned about reaching organizational goals.
   • Someone is evoking rules, policies, or regulations.

Add up your points for each of the needs, and answer the following questions.

1. What is your dominant need? That is, in which category did you have the most points? What does this suggest about you?
2. Does this assessment seem valid to you? Why or why not?
3. If you are not as high on need for achievement as you thought you would be, what can you do to increase it?

Sources: D.C. McClelland et al. 1958. "A Scoring Manual for the Achievement Motive," in J.W. Atkinson (Ed.), *Motives in Fantasy, Action and Society* (New York: Van Nostrand); C.D. Morgan & H.A. Murray. 1935. "A Method for Investigating Fantasies: The Thematic Apperception Test," *Archives of Neurology and Psychiatry*, 34: 289–306.

an organizational behavior moment

The Motivation of a Rhodes Scholar

Frances Mead, compensation director for Puma Corporation, was pleased because she had just hired an individual whom she considered to be highly qualified to fill the position of benefits administrator. Dan Coggin was an extremely bright fellow. He had graduated summa cum laude with a B.S. degree in finance from the University of Chicago. He had then traveled to England for a year of study as a Rhodes Scholar. After returning from England, he had worked for a large bank in the investments area for a year. He had then accepted the position of benefits administrator in the corporate personnel department at Puma, headquartered in Salt Lake City, Utah.

Dan felt good about his new job. He would be well paid and have a position of some status. Most importantly, the job was located in Utah. Dan had always enjoyed the outdoors, and he liked to backpack, camp, and do some mountain climbing. Salt Lake City was the perfect location for him.

He arrived on the job happy and ready to tackle his new responsibilities. Dan's financial background aided him greatly in his new job, where he was responsible for the development and administration of the pension plan, life and health insurance packages, employee stock purchase plan, and other employee benefit programs. Within a month, Dan had learned all of the program provisions and had things working smoothly. Frances was satisfied with her selection for benefits administrator. In fact, she expected Dan to move up in the department ranks rapidly. Dan was enjoying himself, particularly his opportunities to get into the mountains. His only concern was that he did not seem to have enough time to enjoy his outdoor activities. After six months, he had his job mastered. He was quite talented, and the job did not present a strong challenge to him.

Frances recognized Dan's talents and wanted him to evaluate Puma's complete benefits package for the purpose of making needed changes. Frances believed that Puma's benefits package was outdated and needed to be revised. With Dan's abilities, Frances thought new programs could be designed without the help of costly outside consultants.

She held several discussions with Dan, encouraging him to evaluate the total benefits package. However, at the end of a year on the job, Dan had accomplished little in the way of evaluation. He seemed to be constantly thinking of and discussing his outdoor activities. Frances became concerned about his seeming lack of commitment to the job.

In the ensuing months, Dan's performance began to slack off. He had had the current programs running smoothly shortly after his arrival, but complaints from employees regarding errors and time delays in insurance claims and stock purchases began to increase. Also, he was making no progress in the evaluation of the benefit package and thus no progress in the design of new benefit programs. In addition, he began to call in sick occasionally. Interestingly, he seemed to be sick on Friday or Monday, allowing for a three-day weekend.

It was obvious that Dan had the ability to perform the job and even more challenging tasks. However, Frances was becoming concerned and thought that she would have to take some action.

Discussion Questions

1. Using ERG theory, explain the reasons for the situation described in the case.
2. Using expectancy theory, explain the reasons for the situation.
3. Using the integration framework found in the last major section of the chapter, describe what actions Frances should and should not take.

Workplace Needs and Gender

Do women and men have similar needs in the workplace? Do they exhibit similar levels of need for achievement, need for affiliation, and need for power? In this exercise, you will have the opportunity to address these questions.

STEPS
1. As an individual, think about women's and men's achievement, affiliation, and power needs. On average, do women and men exhibit similar levels of these needs? Spend five minutes on this step.

2. Assemble into groups of four or five. Each group should consist of both women and men (two or three of each). Spend 15 minutes completing the next steps.
3. Decide as a group whether:
   a. Women and men exhibit similar levels of the need for achievement.
   b. Women and men exhibit similar levels of the need for affiliation.
   c. Women and men exhibit similar levels of the need for institutional power.
   d. Women and men exhibit similar levels of the need for personal power.
4. Identify the reasons for your group's beliefs.
5. Appoint a spokesperson to present the group's ideas to the class.

Endnotes

1. Hitt, M.A., Ireland, R.D., & Hoskisson, R.E. 2007. *Strategic management: Competitiveness and globalization* (7th ed.). Cincinnati, OH: South-Western.
2. Branch-Smith Printing. 2007. Accomplishments & Quality Awards. At http://www.branchsmith.com/bsaawards.html.
3. Kanfer, R. 1995. Motivation. In N. Nicholson (Ed.), *Encyclopedic dictionary of organizational behavior*. Cambridge, MA: Blackwell Publishing, pp. 330–336.
4. Maslow, A.H. 1943. A theory of human motivation. *Psychological Review,* 50: 370–396; Maslow, A.H. 1954. *Motivation and personality.* New York: Harper.
5. Wahba, M.A., & Bridwell, L.G. 1976. Maslow reconsidered: A review of the research on the need hierarchy theory. *Organizational Behavior and Human Performance,* 15: 212–225; Kanfer, R. 1990. Motivation theory and industrial and organizational psychology. In M.D. Dunnette & L. Hough (Eds.), *Handbook of industrial and organizational psychology (Vol. 1).* Palo Alto, CA: Consulting Psychologists Press, pp. 75–170.
6. Ibid.
7. Ibid.
8. See, for example, Laas, I. 2006. Self-actualization and society: A new application for an old theory. *Journal of Humanistic Psychology,* 46: 77–91; Zalenski, R.J., & Raspa, R. 2006. Maslow's hierarchy of needs: A framework for achieving human potential in hospice. *Journal of Palliative Medicine,* 9: 1120–1127.
9. Alderfer, C.P. 1972. *Existence, relatedness and growth human needs in organizational settings.* New York: The Free Press.
10. Ibid.
11. See, for example, Wanous, J.P., & Zwany, A. 1977. A cross sectional test of need hierarchy theory. *Organizational Behavior and Human Performance,* 16: 78–97.
12. See, for example, Alderfer, C.P., Kaplan, R.E., & Smith, K.K. 1974. The effect of variations in relatedness need satisfaction on relatedness desires. *Administrative Science Quarterly,* 19: 507–532.
13. Arnolds, C.A., & Boshoff, C. 2002. Compensation, esteem valence and job performance: An empirical assessment of Alderfer's ERG theory. *International Journal of Human Resource Management,* 13: 697–719.
14. McClelland, D.C. 1966. That urge to achieve. *Think,* 32: 19–23.
15. McClelland, D.C. 1961. *The achieving society.* Princeton, NJ: Van-Nostrand.
16. McClelland, D.C., Atkinson, J.W., Clark, R.A., & Lowell, E.L. 1953. *The achievement motive.* New York: Appleton-Century-Crofts.
17. McClelland, That urge to achieve.
18. Korn, E.R., & Pratt, G.J. 1986. Reaching for success in new ways. *Management World,* 15 (7): 6–10.
19. Hershey, P., & Blanchard, K.H. 1972. *Management and organizational behavior.* New York, NY: Prentice-Hall.
20. Eisenberger, R., Jones, J.R., Stinglhamber, F., Shanock, L., & Randall, A.T. 2005. Flow experiences at work: For high achievers alone? *Journal of Organizational Behavior,* 26: 755–775.
21. See Shaver, K.G. 1995. The entrepreneurial personality myth. *Business and Economic Review,* 41 (3): 20–23.
22. Hall, J. 1976. To achieve or not: The manager's choice. *California Management Review,* 18: 5–18.
23. McClelland, D.C. 1965. Toward a theory of motivation acquisition. *American Psychologist,* 20: 321–333; Steers, R.M. 1981. *An introduction to organizational behavior.* Glenview, IL: Scott, Foresman, & Co.
24. Frischer, J. 1993. Empowering management in new product development units. *Journal of Product Innovation Management,* 10: 393–401.
25. Material related to virtual workers was drawn from: King, R. 2007. Working from home: It's in the details. *BusinessWeek,* special report at http://www.businessweek.com/technology/content/feb2007/tc20070212_457307.htm.
26. McClelland, D.C. 1975. *Power: The inner experiences.* New York: Irvington; McClelland, D.C., & Burnham, D.H. 1976. Power is the great motivator. *Harvard Business Review,* 54 (2): 100–110 (reprinted in 1995 and in 2003).
27. McClelland & Burnham, Power is the great motivator.
28. Herzberg, F., Mausner, B., & Synderman, B. 1959. *The motivation to work.* New York: John Wiley & Sons; Herzberg, F. 1966. *Work and the nature of man.* Cleveland, OH: World Publishing.
29. House, R., & Wigdor, L. 1967. Herzberg's dual-factor theory of job satisfaction and motivation: A review of the empirical evidence and a criticism. *Personnel Psychology,* 20: 369–380; Dunnette, M.D., Campbell, J., & Hakel, M. 1967. Factors contributing to job dissatisfaction in six occupational groups. *Organizational Behavior and Human Performance,* 2: 143–174.
30. Vroom, V.H. 1964. *Work and motivation.* New York: John Wiley & Sons.

31. See, for example, Ferris, K.R. 1977. A test of the expectancy theory of motivation in an accounting environment. *The Accounting Review,* 52: 605–615; Reinharth, L., & Wahba, M.A. 1975. Expectancy theory as a predictor of work motivation, effort expenditure, and job performance. *Academy of Management Journal,* 18: 520–537.

32. See Pinder, C.C. 1984. *Work motivation.* Glenview, IL: Scott & Foresman.

33. In Vroom's original theory, extrinsic rewards were the focus. In some later work, intrinsic rewards were also a point of emphasis.

34. Johnson, R.R. 2009. Explaining patrol officer drug arrest activity through expectancy theory. *Policing: An International Journal of Police Strategies & Management,* 32: 6–20.

35. Durocher, S., Fortin, A., & Cote, L. 2007. Users' participation in the accounting standard-setting process: A theory-building study. *Accounting, Organizations, and Society,* 32: 29–59; House, R.J., Shapiro, H.J., & Wahba, M.A. 1974. Expectancy theory as a predictor of work behavior and attitudes: A reevaluation of empirical evidence. *Decision Sciences,* 5: 481–506; Kanfer, R. 1990. Motivation theory and industrial and organizational psychology. In Dunnette & Hough (Eds.), *Handbook of industrial and organizational psychology (Vol. 1);* Landy, F.J., & Trumbo, D.A. 1980. *Psychology of work behavior* (2nd ed.). Homewood, IL: Dorsey Press, pp. 343–351; Wahba, M.A., & House, R.J., 1972. Expectancy theory in work and motivation: Some logical and methodological issues. *Human Relations,* 27: 121–147; Watson, S. 2006. "A multi-theoretical model of knowledge transfer in organizations: Determinants of knowledge contribution and knowledge reuse." *Journal of Management Studies,* 43: 141–173.

36. Landy & Trumbo, *Psychology of work behavior.*

37. Korsgaard, M.A., Meglino, B.M., & Lester, S.W. 1997. Beyond helping: Do other-oriented values have broader implications in organizations? *Journal of Applied Psychology,* 82: 160–177.

38. For one revised model, see: Porter, L.W., & Lawler, E.E. 1968. *Managerial attitudes and performance.* Homewood, IL: Irwin-Dorsey.

39. See, for example, Camerman, J. 2007. The benefits of justice for temporary workers. *Group & Organization Management,* 32: 176–207; Cropanzano, R., Rupp, D.E., Mohler, C.J., & Schmincke, M. 2001. Three roads to organizational justice. In G. Ferris (Ed.), *Research in personnel and human resources management.* Oxford, UK: Elsevier Science, pp. 1–113; Greenberg, J., Ashton-James, C.E., & Ashkanasy, N.M. 2007. Social comparison processes in organizations. *Organizational Behavior and Human Decision Processes,* 102: 22–41; Wong, Y.-T., Ngo, H.-Y., & Wong, C.-S. 2006. Perceived organizational justice, trust, and OCB: A study of Chinese workers in joint ventures and state-owned enterprises. *Journal of World Business,* 41: 344–355.

40. Pasturis, P. 2002. The corporate scandal sheet. At http://www. Forbes.com.

41. See Cox, T. 2001. *Creating the multicultural organization: A strategy for capturing the power of diversity.* San Francisco: Jossey-Bass.

42. Adams, J.S. 1965. Inequity in social exchange. In L. Berkowitz (Ed.), *Advances in experimental social psychology (Vol. 2).* New York: Academic Press, pp. 267–299.

43. Colquitt, J.A., Conlon, D.E., Wesson, M.J., Porter, C.O.L.H., & Ng, K.Y. 2001. Justice at the millennium: A meta-analytic review of 25 years of organizational justice research. *Journal of Applied Psychology,* 86: 425–445; Greenberg, Ashton-James, & Ashkanasy, Social comparison processes in organizations.

44. Greenberg, J., & Leventhal, G. 1976. Equity and the use of over-reward to motivate performance. *Journal of Personality and Social Psychology,* 34: 179–190.

45. See, for example, Bing, M.N., & Burroughs, S.M. 2001. The predictive and interactive effects of equity sensitivity in teamwork-oriented organizations. *Journal of Organizational Behavior,* 22: 271–290; Huseman, R.C., Hatfield, J.D., & Miles, E.W. 1987. A new perspective on equity theory: The equity sensitivity construct. *Academy of Management Review,* 12: 222–234.

46. For details of this story, see: Boswell, T. 2000. A Texas-sized mistake involving no lone star. *The Washington Post,* December 12, p. D.01; Simmons, M. 2003. A-Rod hits the jackpot, super Mario returns. At www.askmen.com.

47. White, P. 2007. How A-Rod learned to relax and enjoy N.Y.: In a turnabout he's on a roll but Yankees aren't. *USA Today,* May 4, p. 1A.

48. Colquitt, Conlon, Wesson, Porter, & Ng, Justice at the millennium.

49. Greenberg, J. 1993. Stealing in the name of justice: Informational and interpersonal moderators of theft reactions to underpayment inequity. *Organizational Behavior and Human Decisions Processes,* 54: 81–103; Umphress, E.E., Ren, L.R., Bingham, J.B., & Gogus, C.I. 2009. The influence of distributive justice on lying and stealing from a supervisor. *Journal of Business Ethics,* 86: 507–518; Hershcovis, M.S. et al. 2007. Predicting workplace aggression: A meta-analysis. *Journal of Applied Psychology,* 92: 228–238; Jones, D.A. 2009. Getting even with one's supervisor and one's organization: Relationships among types of injustice, desires for revenge, and counterproductive work behaviors. *Journal of Organizational Behavior,* 30, 525–542.

50. Loi, R., Yan, J., & Diefendorff, J.M. 2009. Four-factor justice and daily job satisfaction: A multilevel investigation. *Journal of Applied Psychology,* 94, 770–781; Colquitt, Conlon, Wesson, Porter, & Ng, Justice at the millennium.

51. Colquitt, Conlon, Wesson, Porter, & Ng, Justice at the millennium.

52. Colquitt, Conlon, Wesson, Porter, & Ng, Justice at the millennium.

53. Borman, W. C., & Motowidlo, S. J. 1993. Expanding the criterion domain to include elements of contextual performance. In N. Schmitt & W. C. Borman (Eds.), *Personnel selection in organizations.* San Francisco: Jossey-Bass, pp. 71–98. Organ, D. W. 1988. *Organizational citizenship behavior: The good soldier syndrome.* Lexington, MA: Lexington Books.; Organ, D.W. 1997. Organizational citizenship behavior: It's construct clean-up time. *Human Performance,* 10: 85–97.

54. Distributive and procedural justice are the two most studied types of justice. A third type, however, has been distilled and has received some attention. This third type, interactional justice, relates to quality of interpersonal treatment, typically from the supervisor. In our chapter, we focus on the main two anchors of justice phenomena. For additional discussion, see, for example, Olkkonen, M.-E., & Lipponen, J. 2006. Relationships between organizational justice, identification with the organization and

work unit, and group related outcomes. *Organizational Behavior and Human Decision Processes,* 100: 202–215; Roch, S.G., & Shanock, L.R. 2006. Organizational justice in an exchange framework: Clarifying organizational justice distinctions. *Journal of Management,* 32: 299–322.

55. Brockner, J., & Wiesenfeld, B.M. 1996. An integrative framework for explaining reactions to decisions: Interactive effects of outcomes and procedures. *Psychological Bulletin,* 120: 189–208; Thibaut, J., & Walker, L. 1975. *Procedural justice: A psychological analysis.* Hillsdale, NJ: Lawrence Erlbaum.

56. Bies, R.J., & Moag, J.F. 1986. Interactional justice: Communication criteria of fairness. In R.J. Lewicki, B.H. Sheppard, & M.H. Bazerman (Eds.), *Research on negotiations in organizations (Vol. 1).* Greenwich, CT: JAI Press, pp. 43–55; Leventhal, G.S. 1980. What should be done with equity theory: New approaches to the study of fairness in social relationships. In K. Gergen, M. Greenberg, & R. Willis (Eds.), *Social exchange: Advances in theory and research.* New York: Plenum, pp. 27–55; Thibaut & Walker, *Procedural justice.*

57. Brockner, J., DeWitt, R.L., Grover, S., & Reed, T. 1990. When it is especially important to explain why: Factors affecting the relationship between managers' explanations of a layoff and survivors' reactions to the layoff. *Journal of Experimental Social Psychology,* 26: 389–407.

58. Locke, E.A., & Latham, G.P. 1990. *A theory of goal setting and task performance.* Englewood Cliffs, NJ: Prentice Hall.

59. Locke, E.A. 1968. Toward a theory of task motivation and incentives. *Organizational Behavior and Human Performance,* 3: 157–189.

60. Heath, C., Larrick, R.P., & Wu, G. 1999. Goals as reference points. *Cognitive Psychology,* 38: 79–109.

61. Locke & Latham, *A theory of goal setting and task performance.*

62. Locke, E.A., & Latham, G.P. 1979. Goal setting: A motivational technique that works. *Organizational Dynamics,* 8 (2): 68–80.

63. See, for example: Motowidlo, S.J., Loehr, U., & Dunnette, M.D. 1978. A laboratory study of the effects of goal specificity on the relationship between probability of success and performance. *Journal of Applied Psychology,* 63: 172–179.

64. Locke & Latham, *A theory of goal setting and task performance.*

65. Locke, Toward a theory of task motivation and incentives; Renn, R.W. 1998. Participation's effects on task performance: Mediating roles of goal acceptance and procedural justice. *Journal of Business Research,* 41: 115–125.

66. Latham, G.P., & Marshall, H.A. 1982. The effects of self-set, participatively set and assigned goals on the performance of government employees. *Personnel Psychology,* 35: 399–404; Latham, G.P., Steele, T.P., & Saari, L.M. 1982. The effects of participation and goal difficulty on performance. *Personnel Psychology,* 35: 677–686.

67. Renn, Participation's effect on task performance.

68. Latham, G.P., Stajkovic, A.D., & Locke, E.A. 2010. The relevance and viability of subconscious goals in the workplace. *Journal of Management,* 36: 234–255.

69. Chartrand, T. L, & Bargh, J. A. 2002. Nonconscious motivations: Their activation, operation, and consequences. In D. Tesser, A. Stapel, & J. V. Wood (Eds.), *Self and motivation: Emerging psychological perspectives.* Washington, DC: American Psychological Association, pp. 13–41.

70. Stajkovic, A. D., Locke, E. A., Bandura, A., & Greenwald, J. 2009a. *Effects of subconscious self efficacy on performance.* Paper presented at the Academy of Management, Philadelphia; Stajkovic, A.D., Locke, E.A., Bandura, A., & Greenwald, J. 2009b. The effects of subconscious self-efficacy on performance and mediation of conscious self-efficacy and conscious self-set goals. In A.D. Stajkovic (Chair), *Subconscious goals, self efficacy, need for achievement: The latest priming research.* Symposium at the annual meeting of the Society of Industrial-Organizational Psychology, New Orleans; Stajkovic, A. D., Locke, E. A., & Blair, E. S. 2006. A first examination of the relationships between primed subconscious goals, assigned conscious goals, and task performance. *Journal of Applied Psychology,* 91: 1172–1180.

71. Shantz, A., & Latham, G. P. 2009. An exploratory field experiment on the effect of subconscious and conscious goals on employee performance. *Organizational Behavior and Human Decision Making Processes,* 109: 9–17.

72. Stajkovic, Locke, Bandura, & Greenwald, The effects of subconscious self-efficacy on performance and mediation of conscious self-efficacy and conscious self-set goals.

73. Latham, Stajkovic, & Locke, The relevance and viability of subconscious goals in the workplace.

74. Shantz, A., & Latham, G.P. 2009. An exploratory field experiment on the effect of subconscious and conscious goals on employee performance.

75. Becker, L.J. 1978. Joint effect of feedback and goal setting on performance: A field study of residential energy conservation. *Journal of Applied Psychology,* 63: 428–433.

76. Morse, G. 2003. Why we misread motives. *Harvard Business Review,* 81 (1): 18.

77. Ibid.

78. Deci, E.L. 1972. Effects of noncontingent rewards and controls on intrinsic motivation. *Organizational Behavior and Human Performance,* 8: 217–229.

79. See, for example: Pate, L.E. 1978. Cognitive versus reinforcement views of intrinsic motivation. *Academy of Management Review,* 3: 505–514.

80. Chuanzhi, L. Set different incentive levels. *Harvard Business Review,* 81 (1): 47.

81. Locke & Latham, *A theory of goal setting and task performance.*

82. Kerr, S. 1975. On the folly of rewarding A, while hoping for B. *Academy of Management Journal,* 18: 769–783.

83. This story is based on the following materials: Bates, S. 2003. Top pay for best performers. *HR Magazine,* 48 (1): 31–38; Leventhal, G.S. 1976. The distribution of rewards and resources in groups and organizations. In L. Berkowitz & E. Walster (Eds.), *Advances in Experimental Social Psychology (Vol. 9).* New York: Academic Press, pp. 91–131; Mizra, P., & Fox, A. 2003. Reward the best, prod the rest. *HR Magazine,* 48 (1): 34–35.

84. Bates, Top pay for best performers

85. Ibid.

86. Aldag, R.J., & Brief, A.P. 1979. *Task design and employee motivation.* Glenview, IL: Scott, Foresman, pp. 42–43.

87. See, for example, Ford, R. 1969. *Motivation through the work itself.* New York: American Management Association; Fried, Y., & Ferris, G.R. 1987. The validity of the job characteristics model:

A review and meta-analysis. *Personnel Psychology,* 40: 287–322; Walton, R.E. 1972. How to counter alienation in the plant. *Harvard Business Review,* 50 (6): 70–81; Whittington, J.L., Goodwin, V.L., & Murray, B. 2004. Transformational leadership, goal difficulty, and job design: Independent and interactive effects on employee outcomes. *The Leadership Quarterly,* 15: 593–606.

88. Hulin, C.L. 1971. Individual differences and job enrichment: The case against general treatments. In J. Maher (Ed.), *New perspectives in job enrichment.* Berkeley, CA: Van Nostrand Reinhold; Aldag & Brief, *Task design and employee motivation.*

89. Deloitte Consulting. 2005. *Who are the millennials (aka Generation Y)?* New York: Deloitte & Touche USA.

90. Hackman, J.R., & Oldham, G.R. 1974. *The job diagnostic survey: An instrument for the diagnosis of jobs and the evaluation of job design projects,* Technical Report No. 4. New Haven, CT: Yale University, Department of Administrative Sciences.

91. Hackman, J.R., & Oldham, G.R. 1976. Motivation through the design of work: Test of a theory. *Organizational Behavior and Human Decision Performance,* 16: 250–279.

92. See, for example, Abbott, J.B., Boyd, N.G., & Miles, G. 2006. Does type of team matter? An investigation of the relationships between job characteristics and outcomes within a team-based environment. *The Journal of Social Psychology,* 146: 485–507; Fried & Ferris, The validity of the job characteristics model.

93. Kanfer, Motivation; Fried & Ferris, The validity of the job characteristics model.

94. Fried & Ferris, The validity of the job characteristics model.

95. The Conference Board, January 5, 2010, "U.S. Job Satisfaction at Lowest Level in Two Decades" at http://www.conference-board. org/utilities/pressDetail.cfm?press_ID=3820; Hollon, J. January 5, 2010. "A Ticking Time Bomb: Job Satisfaction Hits Record-Low Levels," Workforce Management at http://www.workforce. com/wpmu/bizmgmt/category/recession/.

96. Schaubroeck, J., Ganster, D.C., & Kemmerer, B.E. 1994. Job complexity, "type A" behavior, and cardiovascular disorder: A prospective study. *Academy of Management Journal,* 37: 426–439; Dwyer, D.H., & Fox, M.L. 2000. The moderating role of hostility in the relationship between enriched jobs and health. *Academy of Management Journal,* 43: 1086–1096.

97. Kluger, A.N., & DeNisi, A.S. 1996. The effects of feedback interventions on performance: A historical review, a meta-analysis, and a preliminary feedback intervention theory. *Psychological Bulletin,* 119: 254–284.

98. Eckert, R.A. 2003. Be a broken record. *Harvard Business Review,* 81 (1): 44.

99. Miller, P. 2003. Signed, delivered: Malone cannot hide his excitement about playing for a title in L.A. *Salt Lake Tribune,* July 18, at http://www.sltrib.com.

stress and well-being

Striking for Stress at Verizon

The pay is good, and sales bonuses can be generous. So why did Verizon call-center service representatives go on strike for 18 days several years ago? The answer in part is excessive stress.

Verizon, a *Fortune* 100 telecommunications company with revenues of more than $107 billion, depends on call-center representatives to provide positive customer service. These representatives provide the service link between the company and its customers. They answer many calls each day, covering a wide range of service issues. In addition, they sell products to the customers who call (such as caller ID services and DSL high-speed Internet access). The representatives are monitored electronically and in person on such factors as courtesy, length of calls, and sales of products. They are also closely monitored for tardiness, break times, and attendance. Failure to meet strict performance standards can lead to severe penalties, such as probation, suspension, or "separation from the payroll." Finally, service representatives are required to work overtime.

Call-center representatives are well paid and can earn commissions on sales. Over the years, they have voiced few complaints about the pay associated with the job. They have, however, voiced complaints about other issues. Associates said the following a few years ago:

> You are constantly monitored on everything that you do. Every call is timed …, If you go to the bathroom too long they say something about it.
>
> It is very stressful because we don't have enough people. … People aren't treated as people anymore. The company only sees us as numbers and dollar signs. …
>
> You're worried that before you let the customer go, you have to offer [sell] him something, no matter how upset he is, because the person sitting next to you or in that observation room is going to mark you off.

knowledge objectives

After reading this chapter, you should be able to:

1. Define *stress* and distinguish among different types of stress.
2. Understand how the human body reacts to stress and be able to identify the signs of suffering from too much stress.
3. Describe two important models of workplace stress and discuss the most common work-related stressors.
4. Recognize how different people experience stress.
5. Explain the individual and organizational consequences of stress.
6. Discuss methods that associates, managers, and organizations can use to manage stress and promote well-being.

In addition to the above issues, one associate complained of being forced to sell a product to a person who was calling to have phone service shut off for a dead relative.

Several associates complained that managers monitored employees for personal reasons rather than to evaluate performance.

The Communication Workers of America (CWA), representing the call-center associates, and Verizon settled the strike that partially resulted from these workplace conditions. The settlement attempted to alleviate some of the more stressful conditions. Some of the changes included:

©AP/Wide World Photos

- Advance notification of monitoring and limits on the number of calls that can be monitored based on associates' performance.
- Monitoring only during regular working hours—not during overtime hours.
- Face-to-face feedback on monitoring within 24 hours of observation.
- Permission to be away from phones for 30 minutes per day to do paperwork.
- The formation of a CWA–Verizon committee to examine stressful conditions.
- Funding for work and family support programs.
- At some locations, recording of performance at the team level rather than the individual level.

- Split shifts, job sharing, and limited flextime at various locations.
- Limits on overtime at some locations—for example, 24-hour advance notice of overtime, 7.5 hours per week limit on mandatory overtime, and 15-minute breaks for every three hours of overtime worked.

Although the new contract addressed many of the call-center associates' complaints, some still argue that not enough has been done. To that end, some call-center associates and other employees have threatened to strike again over the last few years.

Overall, though, Verizon seems to have addressed these issues. Verizon has received awards and recognition recently from *Working Mother, LATINAStyle, CEO, Training*, and several other periodicals. Yet contention still remains. Verizon call-center employees still express frustration with the stress experienced on their jobs. For example, Abbey Bailey-Parrish recently stated that her call center job in Roanoke Virginia was a source of "constant pressure" due to an atmosphere of fear about being fired and the push to get callers to buy new products that they could not afford. She said "If you check your values at the door, this is a great job for you because the pay is great."

Sources: Anonymous, "Union Rejects Contract Offer—Verizon Communication Workers Speak on Issues in Strike," Aug. 2000, at http://www.wsws.org/articles/2000/aug2000/cwa-a15.shtml; Communication Workers of America, "Protections against Abusive Monitoring, Adherence, and Sales Quotas in CWA Contracts," 2003, at http://www.cwa-union.org/workers/customers/protections.asp; Communication Workers of America, "Contract Improvements for CWA Customer Service Professionals: 1999–Spring 2001," 2003, at http://www.cwa-union.org/workers/customers/improv_99-01.asp; K. Maher. 2001. "Stressed Out: Can Worker Stress Get Worse?" *Wall Street Journal*, Jan. 16: B1; L. Caliri. 2003. "'The Call Center Is a Gold-Plated Sweatshop': A Retired Employee of Roanoke Center Says Verizon Strike Likely as Workers Complain about Work Stress," *roanoke.com*, August, at www.roanoke.com/roatimes/news/story152897.html; Verizon Communications, "Executive Center: Awards and Honors," 2007, at http://www22.verizon.com/about/executivecenter/besttoflists/besttoflists_index.html; Verizon Communications, "Verizon Careers," 2007, at http://www22.verizon.com/jobs/. A. Sharma. 2008. "Verizon-Union Deal Averts Strike Three-Year Pact Will Create Jobs; Ratification Awaits," *Wall Street Journal*, Aug. 11, at http://online.wsj.com/article/SB121840111215927955.html. Verizon News Release. Verizon named to working mother magazine's List of 100 Best Companies." Sept. 23, 2009, at http://newscenter.verizon.com/press-releases/verizon/2009/verizon-named-to-working.html. D. Adams. "Views differ on call-center experience" July 19, 2009, Roanoke.com at http://www.roanoke.com/news/roanoke/wb/212332.Verizon Website. "Investor Relations" February 9, 2010 at http://investor.verizon.com/profile/overview.aspx

the strategic importance of Workplace Stress

By most standards, call-center service representatives have stressful jobs. Of course, individuals in other jobs also can experience stress, and such stress can lead to poor performance, workplace violence, sabotage, substance abuse, and other types of maladaptive behaviors; depression; and increased health-care costs.[1] It has been estimated that 75 percent of all medical problems are directly attributable to stress.[2] Time away from work is also an issue. According to the U.S. Bureau of Labor Statistics, individuals with substantial occupational stress missed 23 days of work per person (the median number), with 44 percent of absences lasting more than 31 days—much longer than absences resulting from injuries and illnesses.[3]

As suggested by the Verizon call-center case, many jobs and organizational policies can cause stress. Rapid technological changes, long work hours, repetitive computer work, work–family issues, and a growing service economy can also lead to stress. Given the many sources of stress, it is not surprising that a National Institute for Occupational Safety and Health (NIOSH) report on stress at work indicates that 26 to 40 percent of Americans find their work to be very or extremely stressful.[4] A survey by Northwestern National Life found that 25 percent of people believe their jobs to be the most stressful aspect of their lives.[5] A 2009 Gallup survey indicated that 31 percent of respondents were somewhat or completely dissatisfied with the stress produced in their jobs.[6] Finally, a Marlin Company survey of attitudes in the American workplace found that 43 percent of respondents believed managers at their companies did not help associates deal with stress.[7]

Although not all stress is bad (some of it can have positive outcomes, as explained later in this chapter), much of it is dysfunctional and, as we have seen, costly to organizations in terms of lost human capital and lower productivity. As a result, managers at all levels are increasingly aware of the effects of their decisions and actions on the stress of others. Indeed, it is imperative that managers effectively deal with the stress of those around them if they are to develop/maintain a high-involvement, high-performance workforce.

Given the prevalence of stress in the workplace and the high direct and indirect costs of stress at work, it should be a priority item on the agenda of top executives. In fact, many top executives also experience significant stress. The CEO makes decisions that affect many people. The strategy adopted by the organization affects the jobs performed by managers and associates. Poor decisions concerning strategy may mean that some people lose their jobs because of decreased demand for the organization's products or services, for example.

Top executives also make decisions to acquire or merge with other firms, and they must decide how many people will be laid off as a result of an acquisition or merger. Sometimes, too, they make decisions to lay off employees simply to cut costs. Layoffs create stress for the associates and managers who lose their jobs and for the survivors as well. Survivors experience stress because of job insecurity. In addition, research shows that they often feel guilty because their friends and co-workers were chosen to lose their jobs and they were not.[8] For stress to be as low as possible, those chosen to be laid off as well as survivors must view the actions of the senior leaders to be fair and humane. Research has shown that communicating effectively about the layoffs, implementing layoffs by careful selection of the units (those less valuable to the organization), and helping those laid off (e.g., providing severance pay, providing services to help them find new jobs) produces better outcomes.[9] For example, these actions result in investors seeing managers as more effective and more likely to produce higher performance, and thus stock price is positively affected.[10]

In the first section of this chapter, we define stress and related concepts. In the two sections that follow, we (1) present two important models of workplace stress that explain why and when people experience stress, and (2) discuss common workplace stressors. Next, we discuss individual characteristics that can cause people to experience more stress or help them cope with stressors. We then describe individual and organizational outcomes resulting from stress reactions. Finally, we present methods that associates, managers, and organizations can use to combat the effects of stress.

Workplace Stress Defined

Unfortunately, we all know what it feels like to be stressed. For some people, stress manifests itself as an upset stomach. For others, heart palpitations and sweaty palms signal stress. The list of stress reactions is almost endless and differs from individual to individual. Even though we know what stress feels like, we may not know just how to define it. In fact, stress is a difficult concept to define, and researchers have argued over its definition and measurement for many years.[11]

For our purposes, **stress** can be defined as a feeling of tension that occurs when a person perceives that a given situation is about to exceed her ability to cope and consequently could endanger her well-being.[12] In such situations, people first ask themselves: "Am I in trouble or danger?" and then ask, "Can I successfully cope with this situation?" If people respond with "yes" to the first question and "no" to the second, they are likely to experience stress. Extending this definition, we can define **job stress** as the feeling that one's capabilities, resources, or needs do not match the demands or requirements of the job.[13]

Consider a call-center representative who has a child in day care who must be picked up at 5:30 P.M. The representative has sole responsibility for picking up his child because his wife is out of town. At 4:58 P.M., as the representative is beginning to close down his station, his supervisor walks over and tells him that he must stay and work for another two hours. If the representative refuses to stay, he can be put on probation or even be fired, but he cannot think of anyone to call to pick up his child for him. Clearly, the demands of this situation are taxing his ability to cope, and therefore stress results. It is easy to see why being notified about overtime at least 24 hours in advance was such an important issue for Verizon's call-center representatives.

There are several important issues regarding the definition of stress. First, the level of stress experienced depends on *individual* reactions to a situation. Therefore, an event experienced by one person as stressful may not be as stressful to another person. For example, some people find stopping at a traffic light while driving to be stressful, whereas others do not. A second issue is that the source of stress, or *stressor,* can be either real or imagined. People do not actually need to be in danger to experience stress—they have only to *perceive* danger.

Stress can be defined as acute or chronic.[14] **Acute stress** is a short-term reaction to an immediate threat. For example, an associate might experience acute stress when being reprimanded by a supervisor or when not able to meet a deadline. **Chronic stress** results from ongoing situations. For example, it can result from living in fear of future layoffs or from having continuing problems with a supervisor. The constant monitoring in the call centers also is an example of a stressor likely to result in chronic stress.

Reactions involving chronic stress are potentially more severe than those involving acute stress because of the way the body responds. Stress makes demands that create an imbalance in the body's energy supply that is difficult to restore. The body reacts with a special physiological response commonly referred to as the **stress response**. A stress response is an unconscious mobilization of the body's energy resources that occurs when the

stress
A feeling of tension that occurs when a person perceives that a situation is about to exceed her ability to cope and consequently could endanger her well-being.

job stress
The feeling that one's capabilities, resources, or needs do not match the demands or requirements of the job.

acute stress
A short-term stress reaction to an immediate threat.

chronic stress
A long-term stress reaction resulting from ongoing situations.

stress response
An unconscious mobilization of energy resources that occurs when the body encounters a stressor.

©Somos/Veer/Getty Images, Inc.

> **EXHIBIT 7-1** Some Stress-Related Conditions
>
> **Conditions That Can Result from Acute Stress**
>
> Alertness and excitement
> Increase in energy
> Feelings of uneasiness and worry
> Feelings of sadness
> Loss of appetite
> Short-term suppression of the immune system
> Increased metabolism and burning of body fat
>
> **Conditions That Can Result from Chronic Stress**
>
> Anxiety and panic attacks
> Depression
> Long-term disturbances in eating (anorexia or overeating)
> Irritability
> Lowered resistance to infection and disease
> Diabetes
> High blood pressure
> Loss of sex drive
>
> Source: Adapted from: Mayo Clinic, "Managing Work Place Stress: Plan Your Approach." 2003, at http://www.mayoclinic.com/invoke.cfm?id=HQ01442.

body encounters a stressor.[15] The body gears up to deal with impending danger by releasing hormones and increasing the heartbeat, pulse rate, blood pressure, breathing rate, and output of blood sugar from the liver.[16] If stress is short-lived, or acute, then stress responses tend to be short term. If, on the other hand, stress lasts over a period of time, with little relief, stress responses begin to wear down the body and result in more serious problems. Exhibit 7-1 displays some of the conditions that can be caused by acute and by chronic stress.

Not all demands that associates and managers encounter on the job lead to negative stress responses. Sometimes people become energized when faced with difficulties. Hans Seyle, one of the most influential stress researchers, distinguished between eustress and dystress.[17] **Eustress** is positive stress that results from facing challenges and difficulties with the expectation of achievement. Eustress is energizing and motivating.[18] Stressors do not necessarily have to be perceived in a negative manner, since they are often the result of a positive experience or result in positive outcomes.[19] For example, a promotion may result in more stressful responsibility but is viewed in a very favorable light, or completing a stressful assignment may lead to a feeling of achievement. Indeed, some research suggests that a certain level of stress is necessary for maximum performance.[20] Too little stress can produce boredom and even apathy, whereas reasonable levels of stress increase alertness and concentration. However, as stress increases, it reaches a point at which the effects become negative. If a high level of stress continues for prolonged periods, **dystress**, or bad stress, results. Note that we use the general term *stress* to refer to dystress throughout the book. This type of stress overload can lead to the physiological and psychological problems discussed here.

eustress
Positive stress that results from facing challenges and difficulties with the expectation of achievement.

dystress
Negative stress; often referred to simply as stress.

How can you tell when stress is reaching a negative level? Dr. Edward Creagan, an oncologist at the Mayo Clinic, identifies five basic signs in everyday life that indicate you are under too much stress:[21]

1. You feel irritable.

2. You have sleeping difficulties. Either you are sleepy all the time, or you have problems falling asleep and/or staying asleep.

3. You do not get any joy out of life.

4. Your appetite is disturbed. Either you lose your appetite, or you cannot stop eating.

5. You have relationship problems and difficulties getting along with people who are close to you.

Two Models of Workplace Stress

We have seen that workplace stress, or job stress, can occur when individuals perceive the demands of the workplace to outweigh their resources for coping with those demands. We turn now to two popular and important models of workplace stress—the **demand–control** model[22] and the **effort–reward imbalance model**.[23]

Demand–Control Model

The demand–control model is focused on two factors that can create situations of job strain and ultimately the experience of stress. Job strain is a function of the following two factors:

1. The workplace demands faced by an associate or manager

2. The control that an individual has in meeting those demands

Workplace demands are aspects of the work environment that job holders must handle. Examples of workplace demands abound in the call-center example at the beginning of this chapter and include long hours, pressure to handle calls quickly, and being subjected to monitoring. *Control* refers to the extent to which individuals are able to (or perceive themselves as able to) affect the state of job demands and to the amount of control they have in making decisions about their work. In the call-center example, one issue of the greatest concern to associates was their lack of control over how many hours they worked.

The demand–control model suggests that job strain is highest when job demands are high and control is low. In this condition, individuals face stressors but have little control over their situation. Call-center associates who must try to sell a product to every caller—with no authority to decide whether a particular caller needs or can afford the product—operate in a state of high strain and consequently experience stress. Compare this with a situation in which a call-center associate has a sales quota but also has the power to decide what products to try to sell and to whom to sell them. In this situation, the associate could exercise a great deal of creativity in determining how to classify customers so that their needs are met and still meet her sales goals. This situation exemplifies the "Active" condition in which both demands and control are high. The result is similar to the notion of eustress discussed earlier. Individuals are most likely to be energized, motivated, and creative in this condition.[24] Less research has been done on the other two conditions, labeled

demand–control model
A model that suggests that experienced stress is a function of both job demands and job control. Stress is highest when demands are high but individuals have little control over the situation.

effort–reward imbalance model
A model that suggests that experienced stress is a function of both required effort and rewards obtained. Stress is highest when required effort is high but rewards are low.

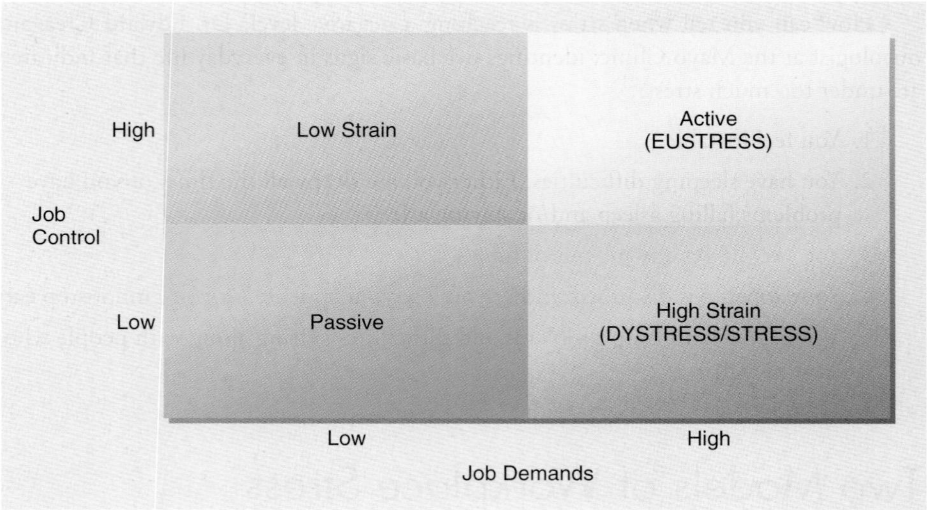

Exhibit 7-2 The Demand–Control Model of Workplace Stress

Source: R. Karasek. 1989. Control in Workplace and its Health-Related Aspects. In S.L. Sauter, J.J. Hurrell, Jr., & C.L. Cooper (Eds.), *Job Control and Worker Health*. New York: John Wiley & Sons, pp. 129–159.

"Low Strain" and "Passive," which are characterized by low demands. In any event, people facing these conditions are unlikely to experience stress. The demand–control model is depicted in Exhibit 7-2.

Research on the demand–control model has yielded somewhat mixed results. Some research has found that people in the high-strain condition are more likely to experience stress-related health problems, such as coronary heart disease and high blood pressure.[25] Other research has found less support for the model.[26] On balance, most researchers agree that both demands and control are important factors in explaining stress. However, how they work together, what constitutes job control, and the role of other variables (such as social support) must be considered in refining the demand–control model of workplace stress.[27] Furthermore, control may have only a buffering effect if it serves to reduce a person's perception of job demands.[28]

Effort–Reward Imbalance Model

The effort–reward imbalance model is focused on two factors, as depicted in Exhibit 7-3:

1. The effort required by an associate or manager
2. The rewards an individual receives as a result of the effort

Exhibit 7-3 The Effort–Reward Imbalance Model of Stress

Source: Adapted from: J. Siegrist. 1999. Occupational Health and Public Health in Germany, In P.M. Le Blanc, M.C.W. Peeters, A. Bussing, & W.B. Schaufeli (Eds.), *Organizational Psychology and Healthcare: European Contributions*. Munchen: Rainer Hampp Verlag.

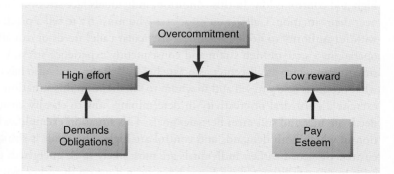

Effort required relates to the performance demands and obligations of the job. It is very similar to the demand dimension in the demand–control model, but it is somewhat more narrowly focused on the job itself rather than on broader aspects of the overall work environment. Rewards include extrinsic (e.g., pay) and intrinsic (e.g., esteem) outcomes of the work.

The effort–reward imbalance model highlights the fact that a combination of strong required efforts and low rewards violates the principle of reciprocity. Ongoing violation of this principle results in strong negative emotions and harmful changes in the autonomic nervous system. Although an individual facing such a situation could simply exit, many stay because of: (1) limited opportunities in the labor market, (2) hope for changes in the situation, and (3) excessive work-related overcommitment.[29] Overcommitment, the factor that most researchers have focused on, is driven by achievement motivation and approval motivation.

Research has yielded generally supportive results for the effort–reward imbalance model. For example, in a study of hospital workers, effort–reward imbalance predicted musculoskeletal injury.[30] In a synthesis of 45 studies, effort–reward imbalance predicted a variety of negative outcomes.[31] The relevance of overcommitment has been questioned (it may not play an important role), but other aspects of the model appear to be valid.

Organizational and Work-Related Stressors

A great deal of research has focused on identifying the specific aspects of the work environment likely to cause associates and managers to experience stress—that is, the factors that act as **stressors**. Organizational and work-related causes of stress include role conflict, role ambiguity, work overload, occupation, resource inadequacy, working conditions, management style, monitoring, job insecurity, and incivility.[32] We examine these factors next.

stressors
Environmental conditions that cause individuals to experience stress.

Role Conflict

All of us have many roles (student, fraternity/sorority member, athlete, spouse, associate). Many times, these roles are reasonably compatible. Sometimes, however, they are not compatible and create conflicting demands and requirements. This situation, known as **role conflict**, has been demonstrated to be a significant work stressor and is often associated with dissatisfaction, tardiness, absenteeism, and turnover.[33] It has been labeled a hindrance stressor in recent stress research.[34]

A specific example of role conflict and its connection to stress is provided by the case of flight attendants after the September 11 terrorist attacks.[35] Prior to the attacks, the flight attendants' role focused on providing service to passengers—"service with a smile." However, since September 11, flight attendants, under federal rulings, have been required to perform extraordinary security procedures and to scrutinize passengers. It is difficult to provide friendly service (customer service role) while taking extreme security precautions (security role). Pat Friend, president of the Association of Flight Attendants, noted that before the attacks, flight attendants could ignore or "grin and bear" unruly passenger behavior. Now, however, they are required to treat the mildest infraction as a "level-one" threat. This approach has produced an increase in passenger complaints,

role conflict
A situation in which different roles lead to conflicting expectations.

stress-management programs for flight attendants, and a study of job stress sponsored by a major flight attendants' union.

Apart from conflict among work roles, it is not uncommon for a person's work and nonwork roles to conflict. For example, a person's job demands may conflict with a role as a spouse and mother or father. Such conflict was seen in the Verizon case, and it can be quite serious. One study, for example, connected work–family conflict to mental issues. Individuals with high levels of such conflict exhibited mood problems, anxiety, and substance use. This was true for women and men, with single mothers and married fathers having the highest levels of work–family tension.[36] Overall, men and women seem to exhibit similar levels of work–family issues.[37]

The discussion in the *Managerial Advice* feature highlights a number of useful ideas for managing work–life conflict. Ensuring an appropriate balance between work and personal lives is crucial to the well-being and productivity of associates and managers. Because high-involvement organizations expect a great deal from associates, these organizations must pay particular attention to work–life balance among those individuals.

Role Ambiguity

role ambiguity
A situation in which goals, expectations, and/or basic job requirements are unclear.

Role ambiguity refers to the situation in which jobholders are unclear about the goals, expectations, or requirements of their jobs. Under ambiguous job demands, people are unsure of what is expected of them and how they will be evaluated. A number of management jobs have high role ambiguity; thus, ambiguity is another contributor to the high stress often experienced in managerial jobs.

Ambiguity on the job creates tension and anxiety.[38] Reactions to this stress are likely to be emotional. Moreover, role ambiguity has been shown to have strong negative effects on job motivation and performance, even stronger than role conflict in many instances. Further, it often has stronger effects on tardiness, absenteeism, and turnover than does role conflict.[39] Finally, role ambiguity seems to be most problematic when the job demands are perceived as quite challenging.[40]

Work Overload

Another common cause of stress in organizations is work overload. Overload can be quantitative (too much work) or qualitative (work is too complex). Research suggests that qualitative overload creates more stress than quantitative overload. For example, qualitative work overload has been found to create greater depression, less enjoyment of work, and greater hostility.[41] In a study of nurses, those with an overload of complex cases were sick more frequently.[42] Therefore, managers should be very sensitive to overloading associates with work that is too complex for them.

Evidence suggests that workload has been increasing over the past few decades.[43] In one study of high earners, 62 percent reported working more than 50 hours per week, 35 percent reported working more than 60 hours per week, and 10 percent reported working more than 80 hours per week.[44] The majority of these respondents also reported qualitative overload such as unpredictability, a fast pace with tight deadlines, and 24/7 client demands. U.S. workers are not the only ones experiencing overload, it appears to be a global phenomenon. The problem of work overload and its ensuing

Restoring and Maintaining Work–Life Balance

Work–life conflict is a serious source of stress in many parts of the world. Work demands have increased for many people because of longer working hours, heightened speed and complexity of the work world, and advances in communication technology that tie together workplaces and workers 24 hours per day. At the same time, personal lives have become more complex, particularly for those with families. Families have become complicated by increases in dual-career couples, increases in the number of long-distance relationships, greater needs for taking care of parents and other older family members, and more time-consuming non–school activities for children. Work–family conflict leads to role conflict, interpersonal conflict, dissatisfaction, exhaustion, time pressures, and guilt, all of which can lead to increased stress.

To help individuals cope in today's world, organizations such as the Mayo Clinic, the National Mental Health Association, and WebMD have developed useful ideas. Their advice is particularly important for managers, professionals, and other white-collar workers who have high-demand jobs. Here is our adaptation of their advice:

- *Focus on what is truly important.* Track and record all activities for one week, those that are work-related and those that are not. Prioritize the items on the list. At work, delegate tasks that are less important or personally less enjoyable. At home, outsource less enjoyable tasks. If mowing the lawn is not an enjoyable task, outsource it if possible. At both work and home, delete nonessential tasks. Less important, non-enjoyed, and nonessential tasks clutter the days of a surprising number of people.
- *Take advantage of work-related options.* If commuting is time-consuming and stressful, consider telecommuting some days, or request longer working hours on some days to avoid going to the office on other days. If onsite day-care is offered, consider using it to simplify drop-off and pickup routines. If financial services are offered onsite or nearby through a credit union, consider using those services to avoid traveling to a financial institution for face-to-face transactions.
- *Protect nonwork time.* Do not allow work-related matters to creep into nonwork time. Rejuvenation is crucial. Attempt to complete less desirable personal tasks (e.g., laundry, changing the bed linen) on work days so that days off can be spent on more enjoyable activities.

©Photodisc/Getty Images, Inc.

- *Manage your personal time.* Rather than going out multiple times to handle different errands, use multipurpose outings. Cook multiple meals for the week during a single evening. Complete multiple chores simultaneously whenever possible and comfortable (such as washing clothes and preparing dinner).
- *Set aside specific time each week for recreation.* Stay away from cell phones and work-related computing while enjoying activities with family and friends.

If stress becomes unmanageable, employee-assistance programs might be helpful. Given the complexity of today's world, some companies now offer programs designed specifically to help managers and associates strengthen relationships with spouses and significant others. For a suite of helpful tools, techniques, and resources, see the Mayo Clinic Stress Center at http://www.mayoclinic.com/health/stress/SR99999.

Sources: Mayo Clinic. 2006, "Work-life balance: Ways to Restore Harmony and Reduce Stress," at http://www.mayo-clinic.com/health/work-life-balance/WL00056; National Mental Health Association, 2007, "Finding Your Balance: At Work and at Home," at http://www.nmha.org/go/finding-your-balance-at-work-and-home; R. Silverman. 2007. "Working on Your Marriage—At Work," *Wall Street Journal*, May 31, p. D.1; E. White. 2006. "How to Balance Home-Life Issues with Work Duties," *Wall Street Journal*, Aug. 22, p. B.8; WebMD. 2006, "5 Tips for Better Work-Life Balance," at http://www.webmd.com/balance/guide/5-strategies-for-life-balance?page=1; Livingston, B.A., & Judge, T. 2008. Emotional responses to work-family conflict: An examination of gender role orientation among working men and women. *Journal of Applied Psychology*, 93: 207–216; Cooper, C, Lu, L., Kao, S., Chang, T. & Wu, H. 2008. Work-family demands, work flexibility, work/family conflict and their consequences for work. *International Journal of Stress Management*, 15: 1–21; Eby, L.T., Maher, C.P., & Butts, M.M. 2010. The intersection of work and family life: The role of affect. *Annual Review of Psychology*, 61: 599–622.

stress-related health consequences has become so prevalent in Japan that they have special terms to describe the phenomenon: "karoshi," which means "work to death" and "karo-jisatsu," which means "suicide by overwork."[45] Causes for the growth in overload are far ranging, from economic downturns leading to more work for fewer employees, more competitive work environments, and the increasing ease with which employees are available because of technology. "BlackBerry Thumb" has become an actual medical condition.

Occupation

In accordance with the models of stress discussed above, occupations characterized by high demands and strong required efforts can generate stress. Statistics from the U.S. Department of Labor indicate that white-collar occupations are associated with a higher proportion of stress cases than the blue-collar and service occupations combined.[46] Technical, sales, and administrative support personnel contribute most of these cases, but managerial and professional occupations also contribute a substantial number of them. Although the white-collar occupations may allow greater control and offer substantial rewards, demands and requirements for people holding these jobs are typically much greater than in other occupations. On the other hand, the effects of control and rewards are demonstrated in research findings that suggest senior managers (upper-level executives, such as CEOs) experience less stress than middle managers. Even though demands on the senior managers may be greater, these managers are also likely to have more control,[47] and they frequently have generous reward packages.

Resource Inadequacy

People may also experience job stress when they lack needed resources.[48] Having inadequate resources makes it difficult to accomplish tasks effectively and efficiently and can therefore increase job demands or lessen control. There may be too few people, too little support, or inadequate material to accomplish a task, placing pressure on the person who has responsibility for the task. Severe resource shortages caused by situations such as loss of sales may lead to other stressful events, such as layoffs. As mentioned earlier, layoff decisions are stressful for the managers who make them, for those who lose their jobs, and even for those who stay. Those who remain on the job experienced stress before the layoff decision (because of uncertainty about who would be laid off), experienced the loss of friends and co-workers who were laid off, and then must endure added pressures to accomplish tasks with fewer workers.

Working Conditions

The job environment can have major effects on job attitudes and reactions. The job environment includes both physical surroundings (lighting, temperature, noise, office arrangements, and so on) and psychological aspects (such as peer relationships, warmth, and perceived rewards). If the working conditions are unpleasant, they can be stressful. For example, working with inadequate lighting, loud noise, or uncomfortable temperatures or working in isolation from others creates pressure and stress.[49]

Management Style

Management style significantly affects the psychological climate of the workplace, and certain styles of dealing with subordinates create more stress than others. For example, one study found that high scores on Machiavellianism (managing through fear) were negatively related to job satisfaction and positively related to job tension.[50] Certain types of jobs and associate personalities may interact with managerial style to produce stress. For example, directive managerial styles may produce less stress on routine jobs and with associates who prefer a more structured environment. However, for people in professional jobs and for those who prefer more personal involvement and self-determination in their jobs, a less directive managerial style produces less stress.

Monitoring

Relatively recent developments in technology have led to an explosion of stricter monitoring of associates' behavior—both work-related and non-work-related. Organizations are able to read associates' e-mail, detect websites they visit, listen to phone conversations, and keep track of any work they do electronically. As illustrated in our opening feature, Verizon's call-center associates frequently mentioned phone monitoring as a source of stress. Monitoring can cause associates to experience increased demands and loss of control at the same time, making monitoring extremely stressful.[51] Demands are increased because associates feel that they must always be "on" and that any mistake will be noticed. Control is lessened because associates who are being monitored may feel that they have little discretion in how they do their jobs. Call-center associates, for example, complained about having to follow strict scripts when they felt that it was inappropriate and would even hinder performance.

Job Insecurity

In the early part of the twenty-first century, the U.S. unemployment rate increased somewhat, and more organizations became involved in mergers and acquisitions, downsizing, and moving work offshore. The economic downturn beginning in 2008 has led to record numbers of jobs lost and unemployment rates over 9 percent. As a result, U.S. associates today are more likely to experience insecurity about keeping their jobs. Job insecurity can be an enormous stressor.[52]

Incivility in the Workplace

Have you ever been annoyed by someone taking a cell phone call while you were in a meeting, or by someone sending rude jokes over the Internet, or by someone purposefully failing to include you in a conference call? If so, then you have experienced **incivility** at work. *Incivility* is defined as slightly deviant behavior with ambiguous intent to harm another person.[53] Slightly deviant behavior means that the behavior is not overtly aggressive, physical, or violent. Ambiguous intent means that the perpetrator behaves in a way so that he or she can deny the intent to harm someone else. Incivility at work has been found to be related to job stress, mental health, and physical health of employees,[54] as well as other outcomes that impact an organization's bottom line.[55] Incivility in the workplace is discussed in more detail in the *Experiencing Organizational Behavior* feature.

incivility
Slightly deviant behavior with ambiguous intent to harm another person.

Incivility on the Job: The Cost of Being Nasty

On September 9, 2009, President Barack Obama was giving a speech to a joint session of congress about health care issues. In the middle of the President's speech, Republican Representative Joe Wilson from South Carolina very loudly and angrily said "You lie!" President Obama paused and said "That's not true." and then continued on.

Wilson's behavior went against all the norms and mores for decorum and respect in this type of event, where proper behavior is somewhat ritualized. After receiving pressure from his colleagues, Wilson came back an hour later with the following apology: "This evening I let my emotions get the best of me. While I disagree with the President's statement, my comments were inappropriate and regrettable. I extend sincere apologies to the President for this lack of civility." Several days later, when Wilson refused to apologize to his colleagues in Congress about his outburst, House Democrats, and some Republicans, reprimanded him. *New York Times* columnist, Maureen Dowd, wrote of the incident "It was a rare triumph for civility in a country that seems to have lost all sense of it."

Have we become an uncivil society, and does this behavior generalize to the workplace (outside of congressional meetings with the President)? A 10-year-long study by Christine Pearson and Christine Porath suggests that we have. In their survey of thousands of employees, 96 percent reported experiencing incivility at work, and nearly half reported that were treated rudely once or more a week. Ninety-nine percent reported that they had witnessed incivility being inflicted on other people. Another study by Lilia Cortina and her colleagues found that 71 percent of employees reported being the targets of incivility in the past five years. Examples of incivility include:

- passing blame for our own mistakes
- taking credit for other's efforts
- checking e-mail or texting during meetings
- talking down to others
- belittling others
- withholding information
- paying little attention to others' opinions
- making demeaning remarks about someone
- avoiding someone

Clearly, workplace incivility is a common occurrence, and according to Porath and Pearson's study, an expensive one for organizations. They found that associates who were

©Radius Images/Alamy

victims of uncivil treatment reacted by generally withdrawing from work. About half of the respondents said they decreased effort, time at work, or the quality of their work, so not surprisingly, 66 percent reported that their performance declined. Almost 80 percent said they became less committed to their organizations and 12 percent said they quit their jobs as a direct result of being the victim of incivility. Lilia Cortina and Vicki Magley's studies of thousands of other people in several professions found further costs of incivility in that it was a major stressor and was related to negative mental and physical health outcomes.

Sources: C. Pearson & C. Porath. 2009. *The cost of bad behavior: How incivility is costing your business and what you can do about it.* New York: Penguin Group; C.L. Porath, & C.M. Pearson. 2010. The cost of bad behavior. *Organizational Dynamics, 39:* 64–71; M. Dowd. Sept. 15, 2009. "Rapping Joe's Knuckles." *The New York Times,* at http://www.nytimes.com/2009/09/16/opinion/16dowd.html; A. Graves. Sept. 16, 2009. "Joe Wilson." *The New York Times,* at http://topics.nytimes.com/top/reference/timestopics/people/w/addison_graves_wilson/index.html; L. M. Cortina, V. J. Magley, J. H. Williams, & R. D. Langhout. 2001. Incivility at the workplace: Incidence and impact. *Journal of Occupational Health Psychology, 6* (1): 64–80; S. Lim, L. M Cortina, & V. J Magley. 2008. Personal and workgroup incivility: Impact on work and health outcomes. *Journal of Applied Psychology, 93:* 95–107; L. M. Cortina, & V. J. Magley. 2009. Patterns and profiles of response to incivility in the workplace. *Journal of Occupational Health Psychology, 14:* 272–288.

Individual Influences on Experiencing Stress

Earlier, in defining *stress,* we noted that individuals vary in how they respond to external stressors. For example, some individuals may be energized by quite demanding workloads, whereas others respond with negative stress reactions. A great deal of research has examined characteristics that are likely to influence how an individual reacts to stress. These characteristics include Type A versus Type B personality, self-esteem, hardiness, and gender.

Type A versus Type B Personality

Many researchers have studied people with Type A and Type B personalities and how they respond to stress. People with **Type A personalities** are competitive, aggressive, and impatient. Type A's may push themselves to achieve higher and higher goals until they become frustrated, irritated, anxious, and hostile. Type A behavior is exemplified by the driver who blasts the car horn when the car in front of him is a second too slow in moving through an intersection after the light has turned green. In the words of the two physicians who focused attention on this phenomenon:

> The Type A pattern is an action–emotion complex that can be observed in any person who is aggressively involved in a chronic, incessant struggle to achieve more and more in less and less time, and if required to do so, against the opposing efforts of other things or other persons. It is not psychosis or a complex of worries or fears or phobias or obsessions, but a socially acceptable—indeed often praised—form of conflict.[56]

People with Type B personalities are quite different. They tend to be less competitive, less aggressive, and more patient.

People with Type A personalities are more susceptible to stress-induced illness.[57] Type A individuals may experience more stress for two reasons. First, given their competitive and aggressive tendencies, they may actually create more stressors in their environments. For example, Type A people have been known to increase work overload on their own, whereas Type B people are more reasonable.[58] Second, Type A people are more likely to appraise any given event as a stressor than are Type B people.[59]

Type A personality
A personality type characterized by competitiveness, aggressiveness, and impatience.

Self-Esteem

Research has found that people with high self-esteem suffer fewer negative effects from stress than people with low self-esteem.[60] People with high self-esteem, in general, experience greater well-being and may be more resistant to the effects of stressors. Furthermore, people with high self-esteem are more likely to engage in active coping behaviors when they experience stressful demands relative to those with low self-esteem. For example, when faced with a heavy workload, people with high self-esteem may break tasks down into manageable units and prioritize their work so that they can begin to tackle excessive work demands. In contrast, someone with low self-esteem may withdraw from the work or procrastinate, making the work overload even worse. Consequently, people with high self-esteem are more likely to gain control over stressful situations and decrease the amount of stress they experience.

Hardiness

Individuals who are high in **hardiness** tend to have a strong internal commitment to their activities, have an internal locus of control, and seek challenge in everyday life. Research

hardiness
A personality dimension corresponding to a strong internal commitment to activities, an internal locus of control, and challenge seeking.

has shown that people who are high in hardiness experience less severe negative stress reactions than those who are low in hardiness.[61] For example, one study showed that managers in a public utility who had scored high on hardiness had fewer illnesses following exposure to significant stress.[62]

Perhaps the most important aspect of hardiness is locus of control. Recall from Chapter 5 that people with an internal locus of control are likely to view themselves as responsible for the outcomes they experience. Those with an external locus of control are more likely to view themselves as victims of fate or luck. It is not surprising that people with an internal locus of control are more likely to develop active coping strategies and to perceive that they have control when experiencing stressful work demands. However, research has shown that the relationship between stress and locus of control may be more complex because people who have an extreme internal locus of control are likely to blame themselves for negative events and thus experience more responsibility, a stressor.[63]

Gender

Although the evidence is not entirely conclusive, women and men do not seem to differ in how stressful they perceive a given stressor to be.[64] They do, however, seem to cope differently. More specifically, women seek more emotional social support (comfort and a shoulder to lean on), seek more instrumental social support (specific support to solve a problem), engage in more positive self-talk, and exhibit rumination (thinking over the situation).[65] Social support tends to be an effective coping strategy.[66]

Beyond the above issues, women might be exposed to more stressors in the workplace. In some cases, women are paid less than men are for similar work. They are more likely than men to experience discrimination and stereotyping and to work in service industries that are stressful (such as nursing). Research suggests that women experience a greater variety of stressors in the workplace than men.[67] Some studies directly comparing the stress experienced by men and women at work also suggest that women experience more stress overall.[68] The U.S. Bureau of Labor Statistics reported that for every case of stress leading to work absence for men, there were 1.6 cases for women.[69]

Individual and Organizational Consequences of Stress

It should be clear by now that stress can be detrimental to developing a high-involvement, high-performance work organization. High-involvement organizations require that associates be engaged and motivated to perform at high levels and that their individual capabilities be used in the most productive and efficient manner. However, the consequences of work stress can sabotage managerial attempts to develop such an environment. The following discussion focuses on the individual and organizational consequences of stress.

Individual Consequences

Individual consequences of stress can be classified as psychological, behavioral, or physiological.

Psychological Consequences

Psychological responses to stress include anxiety, depression, low self-esteem, sleeplessness, frustration, family problems, and burnout.[70] Some of these psychological reactions are more severe than others. Their importance and overall effect on individual behavior and physical condition depend on their degree or level. Extreme frustration or anxiety can lead to other, more severe behavioral and physiological problems.

One important psychological problem is **burnout**. Associates and managers experiencing burnout show little or no enthusiasm for their jobs and generally experience constant fatigue. These individuals often complain bitterly about their work, blame others for mistakes, are absent from work more and more often, are uncooperative with co-workers, and become increasingly isolated.[71] Burnout often occurs in jobs that require individuals to work closely and intensely with others under emotionally charged conditions (nursing is an example). Burnout is a major concern in American industry and governmental organizations.

burnout
A condition of physical or emotional exhaustion generally brought about by stress; associates and managers experiencing burnout show various symptoms, such as constant fatigue, or lack of enthusiasm for work, and increasing isolation from others.

Behavioral Consequences

Behavioral consequences of stress include excessive smoking, substance abuse (alcohol, drugs), accident proneness, appetite disorders, and even violence.[72] Probably the most severe behavioral consequences are substance abuse and violence.

Substance abuse, unfortunately, has become much more common in the United States in recent years. The Department of Health and Human Services has reported that alcohol, tobacco, and other drug-related problems cost U.S. businesses over $100 billion every year.[73] Studies have shown that alcoholics and other drug users in the workforce exhibit the following characteristics:[74]

- They are much less productive than other associates.
- They use three times as many sick days as other associates.
- They are more likely to expose themselves and co-workers to serious safety hazards because of poor judgment and coordination. Up to 40 percent of industrial fatalities are linked to alcohol and drug consumption.
- They are five times more likely to file worker's compensation claims. In general, they are subject to higher rates of absenteeism, accidents, and sickness.
- They report missing work frequently because of hangovers.
  Each year, 500 million workdays are lost because of alcoholism.

©John Sleeman/Photodisc/Getty Images, Inc.

Although there are many reasons for alcoholism and drug abuse, many people use alcohol and drugs as a means of handling stress. Alcohol and some drugs are depressants that can substantially reduce emotional reactions. Studies have shown that in small doses, alcohol has little effect. However, with moderate-to-heavy consumption, alcohol can substantially reduce tension, anxiety, fear, and other emotional reactions to disturbing situations.[75] Drugs can have the same effects. Alcohol and drugs, then, give people a means of blocking stress reactions when they cannot control the situation. Of course, emotions are suppressed only as long as the individual continues to consume large quantities of alcohol or drugs. Because the disturbing situation still exists, emotional reactions return when the effects of drugs or alcohol wear off, leading to continued usage of these substances.

Another serious behavioral consequence of stress is workplace violence. The Occupational Safety and Health Administration (OSHA) reports that approximately two million workers are victims of workplace violence every year. Homicide is the third leading cause of workplace fatalities. Workplace violence can be either physical or mental, as in the case of excessive taunting or harassment. Many cases of tragic outbursts at work are related to stressful working conditions. The case of Mark O. Barton offers an example.

On July 31, 1999, Barton shot and killed 9 people and injured 13 more at two Atlanta day-trading organizations. In the previous days, he had killed his wife and two children by hammering them to death. After being spotted by the police at a gas station a few hours after the shootings, Barton shot and killed himself. What caused Barton to commit these unspeakable acts of violence? While the causes of such behavior are highly complex, one contributing factor was the extreme stress involved in day trading.[76]

Day trading involves the buying and selling of stocks on a very-short-term basis. Traders often use their own money, and they can experience heavy gains and losses daily. In the month before the killings, Mark Barton had lost $105,000. Day traders have no security and no regular paycheck. Some have said that day traders must have a casino mentality.[77] Christopher Farrell, author of *Day Trading Online,* states: "A day trader makes a living at the game; you live or die by your profit and loss. You never get away from it. It's on your mind twenty-four hours a day. You don't have a steady paycheck."[78] Although day trading is not as popular as it once was, it continues to be a widespread phenomenon.[79]

Stress probably was not the only factor that led to Barton's deadly outburst; he most likely suffered from personality disorders. However, the stress of trading may have been one factor that set him off. And while Barton's behavior may have been extreme, workplace violence is so prevalent that we have nicknames for it, such as "going postal," "desk rage," and "air rage" to describe it.

Physiological Consequences

Physiological reactions to stress include high blood pressure, muscle tension, headaches, ulcers, skin diseases, impaired immune systems, musculoskeletal disorders (such as back problems), and even more serious ailments, such as heart disease and cancer.[80] Stress has also been linked to obesity, a rising health epidemic worldwide.[81] Stress can be directly related to physiological problems, or it can make existing conditions worse. As we mentioned earlier, it has been estimated that 75 percent of all medical problems are directly attributable to stress.[82] The physical ailments noted above may lower productivity while on the job and increase absences from work (thereby reducing overall productivity even more).

Rick Speckmann exemplifies the debilitating physiological effects that can result from stress.[83] Speckmann was a hard-driving entrepreneur, burned out from the stress of running his executive search company in Minneapolis. One day, at age 40, Speckmann experienced an intense tightness in his chest after exercising. He was promptly sent to the hospital in an ambulance, where he received a battery of tests. The final diagnosis: acute overstress. Luckily, Speckmann paid attention to this lesson and changed his lifestyle to a less stressful one. It is important to note that physiological stress begins with normal biological mechanisms. Recall from our earlier discussion that the stress response prepares the body to deal with impending danger by releasing hormones and increasing the heartbeat, pulse rate, blood pressure, breathing rate, and output of blood sugar from the liver. These physiological changes helped primitive human beings respond to danger.[84] Such a physiological response to stress is often referred to as the *fight-or-flight response*. However, the stress response is best adapted for dealing with acute stress. As noted earlier, it is chronic stress, and the physiological responses to it, that can lead to physical ailments. The human body has not yet adapted well to an environment of continuous stress. Therefore, individual responses to stress can be severe and costly.

Organizational Consequences

Stress has consequences for organizations as well as for individuals. These consequences follow from the effects on individuals that include lower motivation, dissatisfaction, lower job performance, increased absenteeism, increased turnover, and lower quality of relationships at work. Research has shown strong connections between stress, job dissatisfaction, turnover, and health-care costs.[85] Stress-related illnesses cost companies millions of dollars in insurance and worker's compensation claims. Employees who report high levels of stress have health-care expenditures that are 50 percent higher than those reporting lower levels of stress.[86] Exhibit 7-4 gives some perspective to these costs.

Furthermore, individual consequences of stress may interact to cause organizational problems. For example, behavioral problems, such as violence, and psychological consequences, such as anxiety, can lower the quality of the relationships between co-workers, resulting in distrust, animosity, and a breakdown in communications. When individuals frequently miss work because of stress-related illness, their colleagues may become resentful at having to take over their work while they are absent.[87] We have already discussed the increased safety risks for everyone that result from one person's alcohol or drug use. Thus, the organizational consequences of stress can be dangerous as well as costly. Fortunately, many organizations and professionals, including companies, government agencies (NIOSH, OSHA), medical doctors, and psychologists, have recognized the importance of addressing stress in the workplace, and a variety of techniques have been developed to combat stress-induced problems. We now turn to a discussion of actions that can be taken to alleviate the debilitating effects of stress on individuals and organizations.

EXHIBIT 7-4   *Managerial Costs of Job Stress*

The cost of job stress to American industry can be estimated at $200 billion per year due to:

Absenteeism
Diminished productivity
Compensation claims
Health insurance
Direct medical expenses

To put this figure into perspective, consider the following:

Total U.S. corporate profits were $897.6 billion in 2006 (after taxes, with inventory valuation and capital accounted for).

The entire U.S. gross domestic product (the market value of the nation's goods and services) was approximately $13,246 billion in 2006.

Sources: 2007, at http://www.bca.gov/national/txt/dpga.txt; Bureau of Economic Analysis, 2007, at http://www.bea.gov/national/xls/gdplev.xls; J. Cahill, P.A. Landsbergis & P.L. Schnall. 1995. "Reducing Occupational Stress," at http://workhealth.org/prevention/prred.html.

Managing Workplace Stress

Individual associates and managers can implement a number of tactics to more effectively deal with stress. Similarly, organizations can be helpful in alleviating stress. They also can be mindful of stressful working conditions that cause stress in the first place.

Individual Stress Management

Based on the models of stress discussed earlier in this chapter, associates and managers can avoid workplace stress by finding jobs that provide a personally acceptable balance between demands and control, and between effort required and rewards. They can also propose that a dysfunctional job be redesigned. Further, they can avoid or reduce some stress by following the tactics for work–life balance presented in the earlier *Managerial Advice* feature. Beyond these tactics, individuals can adopt several positive tactics for coping with existing stress. The goal is to develop healthy ways of coping. Because individuals experience multiple sources of stress, using multiple tactics for coping is beneficial.

One of the most important tactics is regular exercise. Three areas are important: endurance, strength, and flexibility.[88] Endurance activities maintain or increase aerobic capacity. Key activities include regular walking, treadmill walking, jogging, running, cycling, and swimming. Extreme amounts of endurance exercise are not required. Moderate amounts improve fitness and reduce mortality.[89] Moderate exercise has been defined as 30 minutes of sustained activity three to four times per week, at a heart rate that is above the normal rate but below the maximum rate. An individual's target heart rate can be calculated by subtracting his age from 220, and then taking 65 to 80 percent of that number.[90]

Strength activities maintain or improve muscle mass and can prevent loss of bone mass as well. Key activities include weight training and aqua-aerobics. Twenty minutes of these types of exercises three times per week can provide important benefits.[91] Flexibility activities maintain or improve range of motion and energy. Stretching is the key activity. Stretching various muscle groups three times per week provides important and sustainable benefits.[92]

A second tactic for coping with stress is proper diet. Diet affects energy, alertness, and overall well-being. According to research conducted at the Cooper Institute, four key areas should be considered.[93] First, it is important to monitor fat intake. Adults over 30 should obtain no more than 20 to 25 percent of calories from fat per day. Younger adults also should be careful with fat consumption. Fifty to 70 percent of calories should come from complex carbohydrates (drawn from fruits, vegetables, and whole grain foods, not from candy and cakes). Ten to 15 percent of calories should come from protein (drawn from fish, poultry, and meats). Second, it is important to consume a reasonable amount of fiber, both insoluble and soluble. Third, consumption of calcium is important. Fourth, consumption of foods rich in antioxidants can be helpful. Antioxidants seem to be helpful in preventing damage caused by normal bodily operations involving oxygen.

In today's world, implementing a proper diet can be difficult. Time for grocery shopping and cooking is often limited. Many companies (not to mention school cafeterias) make the situation worse by providing or facilitating the consumption of junk food. In a poll conducted by Harris Interactive for the Marlin Company (a workplace communications company), 63 percent of respondents reported that vending machines on the job mostly contain junk food, such as potato chips, candy bars, and cookies. In a second poll, 74 percent of respondents reported that it is common for special occasions to be celebrated with candy, cookies, or cake. Even on routine workdays, accessible candy bowls are in many cubicles and offices.

A third tactic for coping with stress involves the development and use of social-support networks.[94] Social support is very important. Research has shown that such support is positively related to cardiovascular functioning and negatively related to perceived stress, anxiety, and depression.[95] Having friends and family to talk with about problems can be quite useful (emotional social support). Having friends and family who can offer specific suggestions, provide resources, and break down barriers can also be quite useful (instrumental social support).

A fourth tactic involves the use of relaxation techniques. For some, meditation, yoga, and visualization of serene settings work very well. For others, a simple walk in the park is more useful.

Other tactics include developing and using planning skills, being realistic about what can be accomplished, and avoiding unnecessary competition.

Organizational Stress Management

Organizations can help to reduce stress or help managers and associates deal more effectively with stress. To reduce stress, the following actions can be taken. These actions are consistent with high-involvement management:

- Increase individuals' autonomy and control. According to the demand–control model, increased control should help to keep experienced stress to manageable levels.
- Ensure that individuals are compensated properly. According to the effort–rewards imbalance model, proper compensation should help to keep experienced stress to manageable levels.
- Maintain job demands/requirements at healthy levels.
- Ensure that associates have adequate skills to keep up-to-date with technical changes in the workplace.
- Increase associate involvement in important decision making.
- Improve physical working conditions. For example, use ergonomically sound equipment and tools.
- Provide for job security and career development. Provide educational opportunities so that associates can continue to improve their skill sets. Use job redesign and job rotation to expand associates' skill sets.
- Provide healthy work schedules. Avoid constant shifting of schedules. Allow for flextime or other alternative work schedules.
- Improve communication to help avoid uncertainty and ambiguity.

In addition to actions taken to reduce stress, organizations can help associates and managers cope with stress and its effects. Specifically, they can encourage some managers to be "toxin handlers" and they can implement wellness programs. These are discussed next.

Toxin handlers, a term coined by renowned educator and consultant Peter Frost, are people who take it upon themselves to handle the pain and stressors that are part of everyday life in organizations.[96] Frost argues that toxin handlers are necessary for organizations to be successful, even though their contributions are often overlooked. Without the efforts of these organizational heroes, both individual and organizational well-being and productivity would suffer.

Managers can become more efficient, compassionate toxin handlers. Frost lists the following behaviors as necessary for handling the pain, strain, and stress of others:

- Read your own and others' emotional cues and understand the impact that emotional cues have on others. For example, be aware that when you show signs of anger, the most common response will be defensiveness or hostility. This can begin a cycle of negative emotions and nonproductive behavior that could have been avoided. The ability to avoid negative behaviors is one of the major components of emotional intelligence.
- Keep people connected. Devise ways in which people at work can react to each other as human beings. This can be accomplished by encouraging intimacy and fun.
- Empathize with those who are in pain. Actively listen with compassion.
- Act to alleviate the suffering of others. Providing a shoulder to cry on might be appropriate. Arranging for discreet financial aid to an associate in need might be useful.
- Mobilize people to deal with their pain and get their lives back on track. Actively acknowledge problems, encourage helping behavior, and celebrate achievements.
- Create an environment where compassionate behavior toward others is encouraged and rewarded.

Wellness programs are very popular and important tools that organizations use to manage stress and its effects.[97] These programs include health screenings, health advice, risk-management programs, smoking cessation, weight control, and exercise. The main goal is to develop/maintain a healthy and productive workforce. In some organizations, health coaches are used to proactively monitor participating associates and managers. These coaches, often nurses, offer advice based on health-screening information as well as ongoing medical events and drug prescriptions.[98]

The wellness program at Johnson & Johnson (J&J) is one of the oldest and most recognized. Originally called "Live for Life," the program has helped thousands of people lead healthier lives. In terms of company benefits, assessments have shown positive returns to the bottom line through enhanced productivity and lower health-care costs. In 2002, one estimate suggested that savings just from reduced medical expenditures have been approximately $224 per person per year, which translates into a total of $22.4 million per year based on J&J's employment base of 100,000.[99]   In 2008, J&J estimates that it avoided $15.9 million in health care costs for its U.S. employees alone. J&J has exceeded its program goals given that:

- 96 percent of employees are tobacco-free.
- 94 percent of employees have blood pressures of 140/90 or better.
- 93 percent of employees have total cholesterol levels below 240.
- 68 percent of employees are physically active, defined as 30 minutes of activity three or more times each week.[100]

Evidence suggests that wellness programs provide benefits to both individuals and organizations. As such, organizations want as many people as possible to participate. Participation, though, is voluntary. As discussed in the next *Experiencing Organizational Behavior* feature, incentives have been used to raise participation levels. These incentives, however, have a dark side, and legal issues have arisen.

Incentives for Participating in Wellness Programs

Evidence supporting the bottom-line impact of wellness programs has begun to accumulate. Overall, research suggests a return of three dollars for every one dollar spent, with some recent estimates suggesting a return of six dollars per dollar spent on a wellness program. In one recent evaluation of programs at organizations such as LL Bean, Duke University, and General Motors, returns on investment were very positive.

With substantial benefits available, incentives designed to increase participation are now offered by many companies. Indeed, according to a 2008 Harris Interactive poll, 91 percent of employers "believed they could reduce their health care costs by influencing employees to adopt healthier lifestyles." Because participation by associates and managers is voluntary, these incentives are very important. At Baptist Health Florida, individuals who complete the wellness program's health assessment receive an additional $10,000 in life insurance survivor benefits. At IBM, individuals who complete a health risk assessment at the start of the year are given up to two $150 payments. At Scotts Miracle-Gro, associates receive a $10 monthly fitness center membership fee, which is reimbursable after 120 uses of the center, free health coaching,

free medical services for employees and covered dependents, and free prescriptions for generic drugs.

At some companies, however, incentives have become heavy-handed, and this is a source of growing concern. Employees at Weyco who failed to have mandated medical tests and evaluations in 2006 paid an additional $65 per month for insurance premiums. After 2006, additional increases have come into play for those who continue to resist the program. Employees at Scotts Miracle-Gro Company who failed to have "requested" evaluations saw $40 per month added to their insurance premiums. Moreover, all employees were subjected to investigation by an outside health-management company. This company used data-mining techniques and available databases to uncover any health problems or risks. Those who had issues/risks were assigned a health coach and an action plan was developed. Individuals who failed to comply with the action plan saw $67 per month added to their insurance premiums.

Although it makes sense to have people with higher risks pay more for insurance, there are some problems to consider. First, health assessments are becoming less and less voluntary and seek very personal information (e.g., information on depression, the quality

of a relationship with a spouse/partner, parents' causes of death). Is it appropriate to provide, directly or indirectly, this information to an employer? Second, the use of financial incentives tied to health plan costs and the pushing of action plans based on health status may bring legal issues. Certainly, charging people in certain categories (i.e., smokers) more for health insurance can be a complex undertaking. In the United States, the Health Insurance Portability and Accountability Act (HIPAA), the Americans with Disabilities Act (ADA), and Bona Fide Wellness Program Exceptions (BFWP) must be considered, along with applicable state laws.

Overall, the use of heavy-handed incentives (and indeed punishments) is becoming more common as companies strive for a smarter, fitter workforce. Only time will tell how accepted these practices become.

©Ryan McVay/Stone/Getty Images, Inc.

Sources: L. Chapman. 2006. "Wellness Programs Hitting Their Stride," *Benefits & Compensation Digest*, 43, no. 2: 15–17; M. Conlin. 2007. "Get Healthy or Else: One Company's All-out Attack on Medical Costs," *BusinessWeek*, Feb. 26, pp. 58–69; R. Dotinga. 2006. "Can Boss Insist on Healthy Habits?" *Christian Science Monitor*, Jan. 11, p. 15; D. Koffman, R. Goetzel, V. Anwuri, K. Shore, D. Orenstein, & T. Lapier. 2005. "Heart Healthy and Stroke Free," *American Journal of Preventive Medicine*, 29: 113–121; L. McGinley. 2006. "Health Costs: The Big Push for Wellness," *Wall Street Journal*, July 16, p. 2A; M. McQueen. 2006. "The Road to Wellness Is Starting at the Office: Employers' Efforts to Push Preventative Care Begin to Show Both Health and Cost Benefits," *Wall Street Journal*, Dec. 5, p. D1; T.M. Simon, F. Bruno, N. Grossman, & C. Stamm. 2006. "Designing Compliant Wellness Programs: HIPAA, ADA, and State Insurance Laws," *Benefits Law Journal*, 19, no. 4: 46–59; T. Walker. 2007. "Businesses Justify Worker Incentives," *Managed Healthcare Executive*, 17, no. 5: 18; L. Hand. Winter, 2009. Employer health incentives: Employee wellness programs prod workers to adopt healthy lifestyles. *Harvard Public Health Review*. At http://www.hsph.harvard.edu/ news/hphr/winter-2009/winter09healthincentives.html.

THE STRATEGIC LENS

Stress is an important component of organizational life. Although some stress has positive effects on people's behavior, much stress is dysfunctional. Stress affects everyone in the organization—top executives, middle and lower-level managers, and associates at all levels. All of these individuals represent human capital to an organization. We know that human capital is important because it represents much of the knowledge and skill in an organization and affects task performance. Effective task performance and problem solving are necessary for an organization to gain and hold a competitive advantage, which in turn results in positive outcomes for the organization and its external stakeholders. However, dysfunctional stress prevents associates and managers from fully utilizing their knowledge and applying it in their jobs. When this occurs, their productivity suffers, and organizational performance is harmed. If many associates and managers are overstressed, the organization may suffer millions of dollars in extra costs and lower profits. In short, top executives who want the strategies they develop to be successfully implemented must manage the stress in their organizations. Overall, managers' ability to prevent stress and help associates cope with the stress they experience will have a major impact on the performance of individuals and the organization as a whole.

Critical Thinking Questions

1. How can good stress be distinguished from bad stress? How much stress is too much stress?

2. How can managing stress in an organization contribute to improved strategy implementation and organizational performance?

3. How much stress do you currently experience? How can reducing your stress increase your performance in school and enhance your life in general?

What This Chapter Adds to Your Knowledge Portfolio

In this chapter, we have discussed workplace stress, focusing on its causes and consequences and what can be done to help manage it. A high-involvement, high-performance workplace requires that associates perform at their best; however, stress can prevent them from doing so. If an organization is to compete successfully, it is important both to manage the stress experienced by associates and to eliminate some of the sources of stress. In summary, we have made the following points.

- Stress is a feeling of tension experienced by an individual who feels that the demands of a situation are about to exceed her ability to cope. It can also be acute (short-term) or chronic (long-term). Not all stress has negative effects; eustress is positive stress that results from facing challenges with an expectation of achievement.
- The demand–control model of stress suggests that experienced stress is a function of both job demands and job control. Stress is highest when demands are high but control is low. The effort–reward imbalance model suggests that stress comes about when effort required is high but rewards are low.
- Organizational and work-related stressors include role conflict, role ambiguity, work overload, occupation, resource inadequacy, working conditions, management style, monitoring, job insecurity, and incivility.
- Individual differences can influence how people experience stress, react to stress, and cope with stress. These individual differences include Type A versus

Type B personalities, self-esteem, hardiness, and gender.

- The consequences of stress are serious for both individuals and organizations. For the individual, stress can lead to psychological consequences, such as burnout; behavioral consequences, such as substance abuse and violence; and physiological consequences, such as high blood pressure, impaired immune systems, and heart disease. Many medical problems are attributed to stress.
- Organizational consequences of stress include lower job performance across a number of people, higher absenteeism and turnover rates, lower quality of work relationships, increased safety risks, and increased health-care and insurance costs.
- Associates and managers can do many things to help manage their own stress. Coping tactics include exercise, healthy diets, social support, and relaxation techniques.
- Organizations can reduce the stress experienced by associates and managers by reducing stressors. They also can encourage toxin handlers and implement wellness programs.

back to the knowledge objectives

1. What do we mean by *stress*? What are the distinguishing features of acute and chronic stress, and eustress and dystress? Does all stress result in negative consequences?
2. How does the human body react to stress? What are the outcomes of this reaction? How can you tell if you or someone you know may be suffering from too much stress?
3. What are the general causes of workplace stress according to the demand–control model? What are the general causes of stress according to the effort–reward imbalance model? What implications do these models have for creating a high-involvement workplace? What are the most common workplace stressors?
4. What types of people are likely to experience the most stress at work? If you are experiencing too much stress, what can you do to help manage it?
5. What specific effects does workplace stress have on individuals and organizations?
6. What can organizations do to prevent and manage workplace stress? What specific changes can they make?

Key Terms

stress, p. 235
job stress, p. 235
acute stress, p. 235
chronic stress, p. 235
stress response, p. 235
eustress, p. 236

dystress, p. 236
demand–control model, p. 237
effort–reward imbalance model, p. 237
stressors, p. 239

role conflict, p. 239
role ambiguity, p. 240
incivility, p. 243
Type A personality, p. 245
hardiness, p. 245
burnout, p. 247

building your human capital
How Well Do You Handle Stress?

One of the most famous stress studies was published in 1960 and illustrated that it was possible to predict the likelihood that a person would succumb to stress-related illnesses within two years. The study resulted in the following list of life events with assigned points that can be used to predict a person's chances of becoming ill. The list is slightly modified to reflect modern life. Even though this research is almost 40 years old, the questionnaire still predicts stress-related illness.

To find out how likely you are to experience health problems due to stress, mark each life event that you have experienced in the last 12 months.

RANK	LIFE EVENT	POINT VALUE
1	Death of a spouse or life partner	100
2	Divorce or breakup with life partner	73
3	Marital separation or separation from life partner	65
4	Jail term	63
5	Death of close family member	63
6	Personal injury or illness	53
7	Marriage	50
8	Fired from job or laid off	47
9	Relationship reconciliation	45
10	Retirement	45
11	Change in health of family member	44
12	Pregnancy	40
13	Sex difficulties	39
14	Gain of new family member	39
15	Major business readjustment	39
16	Change in financial state	38
17	Death of close friend	37
18	Change in one's line of work	36
19	Change in number of arguments with spouse or partner	35
20	Taking on large mortgage or debt	31
21	Foreclosure of mortgage or loan	30
22	Change in work responsibilities	29
23	Child leaving home	29
24	Trouble with in-laws	29
25	Outstanding personal achievement	28
26	Spouse or partner's work begins or stops	26
27	Beginning or ending schooling	26
28	Change in living conditions	25
29	Revision of personal habits (e.g., diet, quit smoking)	24
30	Trouble with boss	23
31	Change in work hours or conditions	20
32	Change in residence	20
33	Change in schools	20
34	Change in recreation	19
35	Change in church activities	19
36	Change in social activities	18
37	Taking on a small mortgage or debt	17
38	Change in sleep habits	16
39	Change in number of family get-togethers	15
40	Change in eating habits	15
41	Vacation	13
42	Christmas (or other major holiday)	12
43	Minor violations of the law	11

Scoring

Total the point values of the life events that you marked. Use the total to assess your risk of health problems, as follows:

Up to 150 points   You are unlikely to experience health problems due to stress.

151–300 points   You have a 50 percent chance of experiencing health problems due to stress.

301 or more points   You have an 80 percent chance of experiencing health problems due to stress.

Source: Adapted from T. Holmes & R. Rahe. 1967. "Holmes-Rahe Social Readjustment Rating Scale," *Journal of Psychosomatic Research*, 11: 213–218.

an organizational behavior moment

Friend or Associate?

Walt strode angrily to the kitchen to see Tony. Tony had begun showing up late for work and had missed several shifts altogether. In fact, Walt had had to cover his shift last night. The problem was that Walt really liked Tony despite the drinking problem. "I even named my kid after him," Walt thought to himself.

He had first met Tony when they both worked at the old Frontier Hotel. Tony was the chef, and Walt was head-waiter. Perhaps because they were both in their late thirties and headed nowhere, they really hit it off. Even in those days, Tony had a taste for the booze. Tony's marriage was breaking up, and he seemed to be lost. Walt often traveled the bars looking for Tony when he had missed a few days of work. He would get Tony sobered up and help him straighten it out with the boss. Tony would be okay for two or three months, and then it would happen all over again. Throughout all this time, Walt remained a faithful friend, believing that some day Tony would straighten himself out.

It was during one of Tony's good periods that the idea of starting a restaurant came up. Tony encouraged Walt to start a place of his own. Walt thought the idea was crazy, but Tony insisted on having Walt meet another friend, Bill, who might be interested in backing the idea. After several meetings and a lot of planning, they opened a small place, converting an old two-story home into a quaint Italian restaurant.

Walt and Bill were full partners, and Tony was to be the chef. They had both tried to convince Tony to join them in partnership, but he had refused. It had something to do with losing his freedom, but Walt was never sure what Tony had meant by that.

The restaurant had been an almost-instant success. Within a year, they had to move to a larger location. Walt couldn't believe how much money he was making. He took care of his associates, sharing his revenues generously with them and frequently acknowledging their efforts. Tony was earning nearly twice what he had made at the Frontier and seemed to be happy.

Then, about a week ago, Tony didn't come in to work. He hadn't called in sick; he just didn't show up. Walt was a little worried about him, but he covered the shift and went over to Tony's the next morning. Tony answered the door still half asleep, and Walt demanded an explanation.

Groggily, Tony explained, "I met the nicest woman you ever saw. Things were going so well, I just couldn't leave her. You understand, don't you?"

Walt laughed. It was all right with him if his friend had met someone and was happy. After all, Tony was a friend first and an associate second. "Sure, Tony. Just meet her a little earlier next time, okay? Can't do without a chef every day, you know."

Tony came to work late the next couple of nights, showed up the third night on time, but missed the last two. Although Walt was a patient man, he found it irritating to have to work Tony's shifts. After all, he was the boss. And then it happened. While complaining about Tony's "love life" to one of the other cooks, Walt nearly dropped a pizza platter when the cook said, "What love life, Walt? Tony's drinking again. I saw him last night over at Freddie's place on my way home. He was so drunk he didn't even recognize me."

Walt was worried. It had been almost two years since Tony had "gone on the wagon." He was concerned and irritable when a waitress, Irene, came up to the front and said, "Walt, Tony's in the back—drunk. He says he wants his money. He looks awful."

Discussion Questions

1. Could Tony's problem with alcohol be stress-related? Explain why or why not.
2. What should Walt do in this circumstance to help Tony cope?
3. Is Tony savable? Do the benefits outweigh the costs of trying to save him?

team exercise

Dealing with Stress

1. If you have not done so already, complete the assessment presented in *Building Your Human Capital.* In addition to the periodic stressors identified in that assessment, identify and list any ongoing stressors (demanding classes, a teacher who is not treating you appropriately, etc.).
2. Write down what you currently do to cope with stress. Be specific in commenting on each element found in the section entitled "Individual Stress Management" (e.g., endurance exercise, instrumental social support, meditation).

3. Give your results from Steps 1 and 2 to two classmates, as identified by your instructor (if you have privacy concerns, consult with your instructor).
4. Receive results from the same two classmates, and evaluate the effectiveness of their coping strategies in light of their stressors.
5. Team up with the other two people and discuss your evaluations.

Steps 1–4 should take about 30 minutes to complete, and step 5 should take about 20–30 minutes.

Endnotes

1. Manning, M.R., Jackson, C.N., & Fusilier, M.R. 1996. Occupational stress, social support, and the costs of health care. *Academy of Management Journal,* 39: 738–751; Webster, J.R., Beehr, T.A., & Christianson, N.D. 2009. Toward a better understanding of the effects of hindrance and challenge stressors on work behavior. *Journal of Vocational Behavior,* 76: 68–77. Netterstrøm, B., Conrad, N., Bech, P., Fink, P., Olsen, O., Rugulies, R., & Stansfeld, S. 2008. The relation between work-related psychosocial factors and the development of depression. *Epidemiologic Reviews, 30*:118–132.

2. Hughes, G.H., Person, M.A., & Reinhart, G.R. 1984. Stress: Sources, effects, and management. *Family and Community Health,* 7: 47–58.

3. U.S. Bureau of Labor Statistics. 2006. Occupational stress and time away from work. At http://www.bls.gov/opub/ted/1999/oct/wk3/art03.htm (originally published in 1999).

4. Sauter, S, Murphy, L., Colligan, M., Swanson, N., Hurrell, J., Scharf, F., Sinclair, R., Grubb, P., Goldenhar, L., Alterman, T., Johnston, J., Hamilton, A., & Tisdale, J. 1999. *Stress … At Work.* Publication No. 99–101. Washington, D.C.: National Institute for Occupational Safety and Health.

5. Ibid.

6. The Gallup Poll. 2009. Work and Work Place. At http://www.gallup.com/poll/1720/Work-Work-Place.aspx.

7. The Marlin Company. 2003. Workplace behavior: Gossip, stress, rudeness. At http://www.themarlincompany.com/Media Room/PollResults.aspx.

8. Brockner, J., Grover, S., Reed, T.F., & DeWitt, R.L. 1992. Layoffs, job insecurity and survivors' work effort: Evidence of an inverted-U relationship. *Academy of Management Journal,* 35: 413–425.

9. See, for example, Hopkins, S.M., & Weathington, B.L. 2006. The relationship between justice perceptions, trust, and employee attitudes in a downsized organization. *The Journal of Psychology,* 140: 477–498; Mishra, K.E., Spreitzer, G.M., & Mishra, A.K. 1998. Preserving employee morale during downsizing. *Sloan Management Review,* 39(2): 83–95.

10. Nixon, R.D., Hitt, M.A., Lee, H., & Jeong, E. 2004. Market reactions to announcements of corporate downsizing actions and implementation strategies. *Strategic Management Journal,* 25: 1121–1129.

11. Dewe, P. 1991. Primary appraisal, secondary appraisal and coping: Their role in stressful work encounters. *Journal of Occupational and Organizational Psychology,* 64: 331–351.

12. See, for example, Lazarus, R.S., & Folkman, S. 1984. *Stress, appraisal and coping.* New York: Springer; Medline Plus Medical Encyclopedia. 2007. Stress and Anxiety. At http://www.nlm.nih.gov/medlineplus/ency/article/003211.htm.

13. Sauter et al., *Stress … At Work.*

14. Mayo Clinic. 2003. Managing work place stress: Plan your approach. At http://www.mayoclinic.com/invoke.cfm?id=HQ01442; Mayo Clinic. 2006. Understand your sources of stress. At http://www.mayoclinic.com/health/stress-management/SR00031.

15. Quick, J.C., & Quick, J.D. 1984. *Organizational stress and preventive management.* New York: McGraw-Hill.

16. Mayo Clinic, Managing work place stress.

17. Seyle, H. 1982. History and present status of the stress concept. In L. Goldberger and S. Breiznitz (Eds.), *Handbook of stress.* New York: Free Press, pp. 7–17.

18. Simmons, B.L., & Nelson, D.L. 2007. Eustress at work: Extending the holistic stress model. In D.L. Nelson & C.L. Cooper (eds.), *Positive organizational behavior.* London: Sage, pp. 40–54.

19. Beehr, T.A. & Grebner, S.I. 2009. When stress is less (harmful). In A.-S.G. Antiniou, C.L. Cooper, G.P. Chrousos, C.D. Speilberger, & M.W. Eysenck (Eds.) Handbook of managerial behavior and occupational health. Northhampton, MA: Edward Elgar Publishing, Inc., pp. 20–34.

20. McGrath, J.E. 1976. Stress and behavior in organizations. In M.D. Dunnette (Ed.), *Handbook of industrial and organizational psychology.* Chicago: Rand McNally, pp. 1351–1395.

21. From Mayo Clinic, Managing work place stress.

22. Karasek, R. 1979. Job demands, job decision latitude, and mental strain: Implications for job redesign. *Administrative Science Quarterly,* 24: 285–306; Karasek, R. 1989. Control in the workplace and its health related aspects. In S.L. Sauter, J.J. Hurrell, & C.L. Cooper (Eds.), *Job control and worker health.* New York: John Wiley & Sons, pp. 129–159; Karasek, R., Theorell, T., 1990. Healthy Work: Stress, Productivity, and the Reconstruction of Working Life. Oxford, United Kingdom: Basic Books.

23. Siegrist, J. 1996. Adverse health effects of high-effort/low-reward conditions. *Journal of Occupational Health Psychology,* 1: 27–41; Siegrist, J. 1999. Occupational health and public health in Germany. In P.M. Le Blanc, M.C.W. Peeters, A. Büssing, & W.B. Schaufeli (Eds.), *Organizational psychology and healthcare: European contributions.* München: Rainer Hampp Verlag, pp. 35–44; Siegrist, J., Siegrist, K., & Weber, I. 1986. Sociological concepts in

the etiology of chronic disease: The case of ischemic heart disease. *Social Science & Medicine*, 22: 247–253.

24. Ibid.

25. See, for example, Karasek, Control in the workplace and health related aspects; Stansfeld, S., & Candy, B. 2006. Psychosocial work environment and mental-health: A meta-analytic review. *Scandinavian Journal of Work Environment & Health*, 32: 443–462.

26. Daniels, K., & Guppy, A. 1994. Occupational stress, social support, job control, and psychological well-being. *Human Relations*, 47: 1523–1544; Ganster, D.C., & Schaubroeck, J. 1991. Work stress and employee health. *Journal of Management*, 17: 235–271; Perrewe, P.L., & Ganster, D.C. 1989. The impact of job demands and behavioral control on experienced job stress. *Journal of Organizational Behavior*, 10: 213–229.

27. Daniels & Guppy, Occupational stress, social support, job control, and psychological well-being.

28. Flynn, N, James, J.E. 2009. Relative effects of demand and control on task-related cardiovascular reactivity, task perceptions, performance accuracy, and mood. *International Journal of Psychophysiology*, 72, 217–227.

29. Siegrist, Adverse health effects of high-effort/low-reward conditions; van Vegchel, N., de Jonge, J., Bosma, H., & Schaufeli, W. 2005. Reviewing the effort-reward imbalance model: Drawing up the balance of 45 empirical studies. *Social Science & Medicine*, 60: 1117–1131.

30. Gillen, M., Yen, I.H., Trupin, L., Swig, L., Rugulies, R., Mullen, K., Font, A., Burian, D., Ryan, G., Janowitz, I., Quinlan, P.A., Frank, J., & Blanc, P. 2007. The association of status and psychosocial and physical workplace factors with musculoskeletal injury in hospital workers. *American Journal of Industrial Medicine*, 50: 245–260.

31. van Vegchel, de Jonge, Bosma, & Schaufeli, Reviewing the effort-reward imbalance model.

32. Kahn, R.L., & Byosiere, P. 1992. Stress in organizations. In M.D. Dunnette & L.M. Hough (Eds.), *Handbook of industrial and organizational psychology (Vol. 3)*. Palo Alto, CA: Consulting Psychologists Press, pp. 571–650.

33. Jackson, S.E., & Schuler, R. 1985. A meta-analysis and occupational critique of research on role ambiguity and role conflict in work settings. *Organizational Behavior and Human Decision Processes*, 36: 16–78; Jamal, M. 1984. Job stress and job performance controversy: An empirical assessment. *Organizational Behavior and Human Performance*, 33: 1–21; Kalliath, T., & Morris, R. 2002. Job satisfaction among nurses: A predictor of burnout levels. *Journal of Nursing Administration*, 32: 648–654; O'Driscoll, M.P., & Beehr, T.A. 1994. Supervisor behaviors, role stressors and uncertainty as predictors of personal outcomes for subordinates. *Journal of Organizational Behavior*, 15: 141–155; Piko, B.F. 2006. Burnout, role conflict, job satisfaction and psychosocial health among Hungarian health care staff. *International Journal of Nursing Studies*, 43: 311–318.

34. Podsakoff, N.P., LePine, J.A., & LePine, M.A. 2007. Differential challenge stressor-hindrance stressor relationships with job attitudes, turnover intentions, turnover, and withdrawal behavior: A meta-analysis. *Journal of Applied Psychology*, 92: 438–454.

35. Barnes, B. 2003. The new face of air rage. *Wall Street Journal (Eastern Edition)*, Jan. 10: W1.

36. Wang, J.L., Afifi, T.O., Cox, B., & Sareen, J. 2007. Work-family conflict and mental disorders in the United States: Cross-sectional findings from the National Comorbidity Survey. *American Journal of Industrial Medicine*, 50: 143–149.

37. Byron, K. 2005. A meta-analytic review of work-family conflict and its antecedents. *Journal of Vocational Behavior*, 67: 169–198.

38. Glazer, S., & Beehr, T.A. 2005. Consistency of implications of three role stressors across four countries. *Journal of Organizational Behavior*, 26: 467–487; Jackson & Schuler, A meta-analysis and occupational critique of research on role ambiguity and role conflict in work settings.

39. Jamal, Job stress and job performance controversy.

40. Lang, J., Thomas, J.L., Bliese, P.D., & Adler, A.B. 2007. Job demands and job performance: The mediating effect of psychological and physical strain and the moderating effect of role clarity. *Journal of Occupational Health Psychology*, 12: 116–124.

41. Shaw, J.B., & Weekley, J.A. 1985. The effects of objective workload variations of psychological strain and post-work-load performance. *Journal of Management*, 11: 87–98; Ganter & Schaubroeck, Work stress and employee health.

42. Rauhala, A., Kivimäki, M., Fagerström, L., Elovainio, M., Virtanen, M., Vahtera, J., Rainio, A., Ojaniemi, K., & Kinnunen, J. 2007. What degree of work overload is likely to cause increased sickness absenteeism among nurses? Evidence from the RAFAELA patient classification system. *Journal of Advanced Nursing*, 57: 286–295.

43. Hewlett, S.A. & Luce, C.B. December 2006. Extreme jobs: The dangerous allure of the 70-hour workweek. *Harvard Business Review*, 43: 49–59.

44. Ibid.

45. Kanai, A. 2009. "Karoshi (Work to Death)" in Japan. *Journal of Business Ethics*, 84:209–216.

46. U.S. Bureau of Labor Statistics. 1999. Issues in labor statistics: Summary 99-10. At http://www.bls.gov/opub/ils/pdf/opbils35.pdf.

47. Ivancevich, J.M., Matteson, M.T., & Preston, C. 1982. Occupational stress, Type A behavior, and physical well-being. *Academy of Management Journal*, 25: 373–391.

48. Jamal, Job stress and job performance controversy.

49. Kahn & Byosiere, Stress in organizations.

50. Holton, C.J., 1983. Machiavellianism and managerial work attitudes and perceptions. *Psychological Reports*, 52: 432–434.

51. Aiello, J.R., & Kolb, K.J. 1995. Electronic performance monitoring and social context: Impact on productivity and stress. *Journal of Applied Psychology*, 80: 339–353.

52. Reisel, W., & Banai, M. 2002. Job insecurity revisited: Reformulating with affect. *Journal of Behavioral and Applied Management*, 4: 87–96.

53. Andersson, L. M., & Pearson, C. M. 1999. Tit for tat? The spiraling effect of incivility in the workplace. *Academy of Management Review*, 24: 452–471.

54. Lim, S., Cortina, L.M., & Magley, V.J. 2008. Personal and work-group incivility: Impact on work and health outcomes. *Journal of Applied Psychology*, 93: 95–107.

55. C. Pearson & C. Porath. 2009. *The cost of bad behavior: How incivility is costing your business and what you can do about it*. New York: Penguin Group.

56. Friedman, M., & Rosenman, R.H. 1974. *Type A behavior and your heart.* New York: Knopf, p. 47.

57. Kahn & Byosiere, Stress in organizations; Ganster & Schaubroeck, Work stress and employee health; Sanz, J., Garcia-Vera, M.P., Magan, I., Espinosa, R., & Fortun, M. 2007. Differences in personality between sustained hypertension, isolated clinic hypertension and normotension. *European Journal of Personality,* 21: 209–224.

58. Froggatt, K.L., & Cotton, J.L. 1987. The impact of Type A behavior pattern on role overload-induced stress and performance attributions. *Journal of Management,* 13: 87–90.

59. Ganster & Schaubroeck, Work stress and employee health.

60. Ibid.

61. Jimenez, B.M., Natera, N.I.M., Munoz, A.R., & Benadero, M.E.M. 2006. Hardy personality as moderator variable of burnout syndrome in firefighters. *Psicothema,* 18: 413–418; Kobasa, S.C.O., & Puccetti, M.C. 1983. Personality and social resources in stress resistance. *Journal of Personality and Social Psychology,* 45: 839–850; McCalister, K.T., Dolbier, C.L., Webster, J.A., Mallon, M.W., & Steinhardt, M.A. 2006. Hardiness and support at work as predictors of work stress and job satisfaction. *American Journal of Health Promotion,* 20: 183–191.

62. Kobasa, S.C., Maddi, S.R., & Kahn, S. 1982. Hardiness and health: A prospective study. *Journal of Personality and Social Psychology,* 42: 168–177.

63. Ganster & Schaubroeck, Work stress and employee health.

64. See, for example, Martocchio, J.J., & O'Leary, A.M. 1989. Sex differences in occupational stress: A meta-analytic review. *Journal of Applied Psychology,* 74: 495–501; Tamres, L.K., Janicki, D., & Helgeson, V.S. 2002. Sex differences in coping behavior: A meta-analytic review and an examination of relative coping. *Personality and Social Psychology Review,* 6: 2–30; Vagg, P.R., Speilberger, C.D., & Wasala, C.F. 2002. Effects of organizational level and gender on stress in the workplace. *International Journal of Stress Management,* 9: 243–261.

65. Tamres, Janicki, & Helgeson, Sex differences in coping behavior; Torkelson, E., & Muhonen, T. 2004. The role of gender and job level in coping with occupational stress. *Work and Stress,* 18: 267–274.

66. Daniels & Guppy, Occupational stress, social support, job control, and psychological well-being.

67. McDonald, K.M., & Korabik, K. 1991. Sources of stress and ways of coping among male and female managers. In R.L. Perrewe (Ed.), *Handbook on job stress.* New York: Select Press, pp. 185–199; Lim, V.K.G., & Thompson, S.H.T. 1996. Gender differences in occupational stress and coping strategies among IT personnel. *Women in Management Review,* 11: 20–29.

68. Nelson, D.L., & Quick, J.C. 1985. Professional women: Are distress and disease inevitable? *Academy of Management Review,* 10: 206–213.

69. Webster, Y., & Bergman, B. 1999. Occupational stress: Counts and rates. *Compensation and Working Conditions,* Fall: 38–41.

70. Nelson & Quick, Professional women.

71. For a more extensive list, see: Mayo Clinic. 2006. Job burnout: Know the signs and symptoms. At http://www.mayoclinic.com/health/burnout/WL00062.

72. Quick, J.C., & Quick, J.D. 1985. *Organizational stress and preventive management.* New York: McGraw-Hill.

73. U.S. Department of Health and Human Services. 1995. Alcohol, tobacco and other drugs in the workforce. At http://www.health.org/govpubs/m1006; U.S. Department of Health and Human Services. 2010. Division of Workplace Programs: Drugs in the workplace. At http://workplace.samhsa.gov/DrugTesting/Files_Drug_Testing/FactSheet/factsheet041906.aspx

74. Ibid

75. Bandura, A. 1969. *Principles of behavior modification.* New York: Holt, Rinehart & Winston; Cook, R., Walizer, D., & Mace, D. 1976. Illicit drug use in the Army: A social-organizational analysis. *Journal of Applied Psychology,* 61: 262–272.

76. Colarusso, D. 1999. Over the edge: Amateur traders stressed beyond capacity to cope. *ABC News.com,* at http://abcnews.go.com/sections/business?TheStreet/daytraders_990729.html; Immelman, A. 1999. The possible motives of Atlanta day-trading mass murderer Mark O. Barton. *Unit for the Study of Personality in Politics,* at http://www.csbsju.edu/uspp/Research/Barton.html.

77. Harmon, A. 1999. "Casino mentality" linked to day trading stresses. *New York Times,* Aug. 1, p. 1.16.

78. Colarusso, Over the edge: Amateur traders stressed beyond capacity to cope.

79. For additional information on day trading, go to http://www.daytraders.com.

80. Quick & Quick, *Organizational stress and preventive management;* Sauter et al., *Stress … At Work.*

81. Chrousos, G.P., & Gold, P.W. 1992. The concepts of stress and stress system disorders: Overview of physical and behavioral homeostasis. *Journal of the American Medical Association,* 267: 1244–1252. Peeke, P. 2000. *Fight fat after forty.* New York: Penguin.

82. Hughes, G.H., Pearson, M.A., & Reinhart, G.R. 1984. Stress: Sources, effects, and management. *Family and Community Health,* 6: 47–58.

83. Margoshes, P. 2001. Take the edge off. *Fortune Small Business,* June 23, at http://www.fortune.com/smallbusiness/articles/0,15114,358931,00.html.

84. Quick & Quick, *Organizational stress and preventive management.*

85. Kemery, E.R., Bedeian, A.G., Mossholder, K.W., & Touliatos, J. 1985. Outcomes of role stress: A multisample constructive replication. *Academy of Management Journal,* 28: 363–375; Manning & Jackson, Occupational stress, social support, and the costs of health care; Parasuraman, S., & Alluto, J.A. 1984. Sources and outcomes of stress in organizational settings: Toward the development of a structural model. *Academy of Management Journal,* 27: 330–350.

86. Sauter et al., *Stress … At work.*

87. Colella, A. 2001. Coworker distributive fairness judgments of the workplace accommodation of employees with disabilities. *Academy of Management Review,* 26: 100–116.

88. Neck, C.P., & Cooper, K.H. 2000. The fit executive: Exercise and diet guidelines for enhancing performance. *Academy of Management Executive,* 14 (2): 72–83.

89. Blair, S.N., Kohl, H.W., Paffenbarger, R.S., Clark, D.G., Cooper, K.H., & Gibbons, L.W. 1989. Physical fitness and all-cause mortality: A prospective study of healthy men and women. *Journal of the American Medical Association,* 262: 2395–2401.

90. Neck & Cooper, The fit executive: Exercise and diet guidelines for enhancing performance.

91. For additional details, see Cooper, K.H. 1995. *It's better to believe.* Nashville: Thomas Nelson, Inc.

92. For additional details, see Neck & Cooper, The fit executive. For important safety tips, see Blake, R. 1998. Don't take muscle flexibility for granted. *Executive Health's Good Health Report,* 34 (12): 7–8. In general, individuals with any health concerns should consult a physician prior to beginning a new exercise program.

93. For details, see: Cooper, K.H. 1996. *Advanced nutritional therapies.* Nashville: Thomas Nelson, Inc.; Neck & Cooper, The fit executive.

94. R. Cieslak. 2009. Social support in the work stress context. In A.-S.G. Antiniou, C.L. Cooper, G.P. Chrousos, C.D. Speilberger, & M.W. Eysenck (Eds.) *Handbook of managerial behavior and occupational health.* Northhampton, MA: Edward Elgar Publishing, Inc., pp. 427-436.

95. Clay, R.A. 2001. Research to the heart of the matter. *Monitor on Psychology,* 32: 42–45; Schirmer, L.L., & Lopez, F.G. 2001. Probing the social support and work strain relationship among adult workers: Contributions of adult attachment orientations. *Journal of Vocational Behavior,* 59: 17–33.

96. Frost, P.J. 2003. *Toxic emotions at work.* Boston: Harvard Business School Press.

97. For general information, see: Wellness Councils of America, 2007, WELCOA Overview. At http://www.welcoa.org/presskit/index.php. Note that we are using the term "wellness" broadly to include a number of health and general well-being initiatives.

98. See, for example: Schoeff, M. 2006. UPS employees get advice from health coaches. *Workforce Management,* 85 (16): 14.

99. Ozminkowski, R.J., Ling, D., Goetzel, R.Z., Bruno, J.A., Rutter, K.R, Isaac, F., & Wang, S. 2002. Long-term impact of Johnson & Johnson's Health and Wellness Program on health care utilization and expenditures. *Journal of Occupational and Environmental Medicine,* 44: 21–29.; Edwards, J.R., & Greenwood, P. Johnson & Johnson: The Live for Life Program (a). Darden Case No. UVA-OB-0412. At http://www.jnj.com/connect/caring/employee-health/?flash=true; Johnson & Johnson webpage. 2010. Protecting our people. At http://ssrn.com/abstract=1421087. Note that some controversy exists over the exact benefits received by J&J, but most analysts agree that the impact has been substantially positive.

100. Johnson & Johnson. 2010. Protecting our people. At http://ssrn.com/abstract=1421087. Note that some controversy exists over the exact benefits received by J&J, but most analysts agree that the impact has been substantially positive.

PART 3

groups, teams, and social processes

In Part II, we examined individual-level processes that affect organizational behavior. In Part III, we explore group, team, and social processes, which can directly or indirectly affect behavior in organizations. Knowledge of each of these types of processes helps managers achieve and maintain a competitive advantage. Therefore, each has important strategic implications for the organization.

Chapter 8, the first chapter in Part III, discusses various concepts related to leadership and explains what makes a leader effective. In the chapter, we pay special attention to the effects of leadership on motivation and productivity. Chapter 9 explores communication in organizations. Communication is critical for achieving objectives because it provides the information on which people in organizations act. In addition, leaders communicate in order to motivate individuals and teams and to obtain the behavior desired.

Chapter 10 describes individual and group decision making. Decision making is a critical dimension of leadership and has substantial effects on organizational behavior. In Chapter 11, we turn to an examination of group dynamics and teams. Because organizations make frequent use of teams (groups of associates integrated to accomplish specified goals), understanding and managing teams can be essential to organizational success. Finally, in Chapter 12, we explore power, conflict, politics, and negotiations within organizations. Both the exercise of power and occurrences of conflict can have either functional or dysfunctional consequences. Chapter 12 provides an understanding of how managers can achieve functional outcomes.

leadership

exploring behavior in action

exploring behavior in action

Maria Yee and the Green Furniture Revolution

A number of issues confront the global furniture industry. Perhaps the most important of these is the loss of hardwood forests in many parts of the world. This loss threatens the supply of raw materials for furniture makers, and it also affects the air-cleansing capacity of the earth's tree stock and the potential for rainfall downwind of lost timberland. In addition, toxic lacquers and adhesives are commonplace in furniture manufacturing. Ethylene oxide is one example. Problematic fabric-embedded chemicals are ubiquitous as well, including perfluorooctanoic acid for stain and water resistance as well as decabromodiphenyl ether for flame retardation.

To combat these problems, a number of forward-thinking entrepreneurs have worked on green (i.e., sustainable) technologies for high-quality furniture materials and manufacturing. Their work, however, has been an uphill struggle. Hardwoods from sustainable sources are not always easy to find. Alternatives to traditional hardwoods, such as bamboo, can be difficult to transform into attractive, durable tables, chairs, and dressers. Alternatives to traditional adhesives can be challenging to develop. Safe and easy-to-produce compounds offering important flame-retardant qualities are not readily available. Perhaps most difficult, the costs of green technologies are typically greater than traditional methods, and consumers are not necessarily ready to pay higher prices. In a survey conducted by the market-research firm NPD Group, 64 percent of respondents supported green products but only 38 percent were willing to pay for them.

Against this difficult backdrop, Maria Yee has attempted to successfully implement green technologies in the furniture industry. Born in mainland China, Ms. Yee immigrated to the United States, where she founded

? knowledge objectives

After reading this chapter, you should be able to:

1. Define *leadership* and distinguish between formal and informal leaders.
2. Demonstrate mastery of the trait concept of leadership.
3. Compare and contrast major behavioral theories of leadership.
4. Explain contingency theories of leadership, emphasizing how they relate leadership effectiveness to situational factors.
5. Describe transformational leaders.
6. Integrate concepts and ideas from behavioral, contingency, and transformational leadership.
7. Discuss several additional topics of current relevance, including leader–member exchange, servant leadership, gender effects on leadership, and global differences in leadership.

her company, Maria Yee Inc., in 1988. With manufacturing located in China, the company initially relied on wood reclaimed from destroyed Chinese buildings. Later, it used hardwoods grown by reasonably managed Chinese growing companies. From there, the company moved toward hardwoods sourced only from growers using principles of true sustainable production, including preservation of biological diversity, limited harvesting, and respect for forest workers and local communities. Along with the pursuit of sustainably produced hardwoods, the company began in 2002 to experiment with bamboo boards. By 2009, approximately 50 percent of its products were based on innovative materials called BambooTimbre and

©iStockphoto

RidgeBamboo. Because bamboo is a grass rather than a tree, a stand of bamboo can be harvested and replanted in five-year cycles, which makes it a rapidly renewable resource under prevailing standards. Beyond its approach to wood and boards, Maria Yee Inc. also has taken seriously the challenge of developing or encouraging others to develop nontoxic or less toxic lacquers, adhesives, sealers, water guards, stain guards, and flame retardants. Finally, the company has used a number of recycled raw materials for fuel and other inputs in the manufacturing process.

In 2009, Maria Yee Inc. had grown from a one-person hobby to a 30-million-dollar business with two manufacturing sites and hundreds of employees. A number of successful patent applications had been filed for a variety of materials and processes. Key customers included Crate & Barrel, Room & Board, and Magnolia Home Theatre. How has this success been achieved, given the tremendous competition in the furniture industry and the difficulties associated with green strategies in that industry?

The key to Ms. Yee's success seems to lie at least partially in her passion for a sustainable world and her ability to inspire others to share in her pursuit of such a world

through the activities of the company. Her vision demands a company that follows a moral path of protecting the environment while delighting end users with safe and elegantly designed furniture, and to produce that furniture in a way that ensures that associates in the manufacturing plants are healthy and happy. Commenting on the vision, Ms. Yee said this, "Being green is not just for marketing. ... Because I'm a human, I want to take a very small step to protect the environment. We actually did so much more on green than we told people. We did it because of our beliefs."

Beyond the compelling vision and the ability to enlist others in pursuit of that vision, Ms. Yee is known for her coaching and development of others. She has, for example, helped to develop local Chinese management talent for her manufacturing facilities. She has also insisted on well-trained associates, and has paid them wages above average for the area while offering a full range of benefits.

Ms. Yee, however, is not just a people-oriented person. She can also be a tough taskmaster when necessary. During a recent visit to one of the manufacturing sites, an observer noted that she was "both encouraging and tough, insisting they sweat the details and strive for perfection." After discovering a table that had not been sanded properly, she asked, "Which one of you is going to be responsible for this?"

Overall, Ms. Yee is a smart, confident, high-energy person with insight into both people and technical issues. One observer had this to say, "I have not met a lot of people like Maria. ... She clearly is someone who is very focused, very hard-working, gives incredible attention to detail, very customer-focused, respectful of the environment, and a strong leader. Clearly a very strong leader with impeccable standards." Another put it this way: "We love her intense level of working. ... She's always available to us directly. ... That's something that makes the relationship special." Indeed, Ms. Yee is a special person on a mission.

Sources: S. Fornoff. 2007. "What's in Furniture? It's Enough to Make You Sick," *San Francisco Chronicle,* Oct. 24, p. G.1; Maria Yee Inc., "Maria's Story," 2010, at http://www.mariayee.com/about/maria/index.php; Maria Yee Inc., "Who We Are," 2010, at http://www.mariayee.com/about/index.php; M. Shao. 2009. "A Fine Green Niche," *Stanford Social Innovation Review,* Fall, pp. 68–71; M. Shao & G. Carroll. 2009. *Maria Yee Inc.: Making 'Green' Furniture in China* (Stanford, CA: Stanford Graduate School of Business).

the strategic importance of Leadership

Maria Yee has displayed remarkable leadership for a number of years. As a visionary who can inspire others, she has provided important direction and energy. Although not operating at the same level or with the same scope, she is similar in many ways to Mohandas Gandhi and Margaret Thatcher in the political domain and Bill Hewlett and Dave Packard in the business world. Beyond vision, Ms. Yee also demonstrates a crucial balance between people and technical issues. As discussed in this chapter, strong leadership involves attention to both.

Ms. Yee's leadership has had a profound impact on her company. Research has not always revealed such a strong link between the leadership of senior executives and organizational performance,[1] but the overall body of evidence does provide a number of supportive studies. One study focused on the leadership of chief executives and showed positive effects for performance among *Fortune* 500 firms. These effects were especially strong for firms operating in uncertain environments.[2] In another study, chief executives of major league baseball clubs were examined in the United States. Again, leadership had positive effects, in this case on team winning percentage and fan attendance.[3] In both of these studies, the leaders who exhibited a transformation, which includes vision creation, had the strongest positive effect on performance. We discuss transformational leadership in this chapter.

Consistent with these studies, a survey of chief executive officers (CEOs) conducted by the Center for Creative Leadership showed that almost 80 percent of respondents believe leadership development throughout the organization is the most important factor or one of the top five factors in achieving a competitive advantage in the market.[4] The survey respondents also reported that leadership quality is linked to a firm's financial performance. CEOs of firms with superior performance were more likely to indicate that their companies support the development of leadership skills through human resource systems, that there is a shared understanding of the nature of effective leadership, and that their leadership development practices are tailored to meet individual needs.

Actions taken by senior managers correspond to the original definition of *strategic leadership*.[5] Certainly, the CEO and those working directly with him are very important given the substantial influence they have in designing the organization's strategy and overseeing its implementation. Effective implementation, however, involves all leaders in the organization. Thus, the concept of strategic leadership has been extended in recent years to include leaders from all levels.

In this context, strategic leadership covers a spectrum of behaviors for those below the rank of senior management. For example, this type of leadership might entail developing a vision for the unit or group being led, a vision that is consistent with the overall strategy of the firm.[6] Furthermore, recent work has focused on the importance of strategic leaders' managing the resources under their direction, to include financial capital but especially human capital and valuable interpersonal relationships (social capital). Particular emphasis has been placed on the importance of providing effective leadership that enhances associates' productivity (i.e., managing human capital well) and building and maintaining important relationships both within the organization (with associates and other leaders) and externally (e.g., with alliance partners). Those who manage this human and social capital well are effective leaders.[7] Based on this work, we assert that leadership is necessary in building and maintaining a high-involvement, high-performance workforce.

In this chapter, we examine the concept of leadership. We begin by describing its fundamental nature. Next, we address three types of theories that have historically been used to explain leadership effectiveness: trait theories, behavioral theories, and contingency approaches. We then focus on more recent developments in leadership theory: the transformational and charismatic approaches. We close with a discussion of several additional topics of current relevance and importance.

The Nature of Leadership

We usually attribute the success or failure of an organization to its leaders. When a company or an athletic team is successful, for example, it is the president or coach who receives much of the credit. These individuals are also subject to criticism if the company does not meet its goals or the team has a losing season.

leadership
The process of providing general direction and influencing individuals or groups to achieve goals.

Leadership has been defined in many ways, but most definitions emphasize the concept of influence. Here, we define **leadership** as the process of providing general direction and influencing individuals or groups to achieve goals.[8] A leader can be formally designated by the organization (formal leader) or can provide leadership without such formal designation (informal leader).

Leaders can do many things to provide direction and to influence people. These activities include providing information, resolving conflicts, motivating followers, anticipating problems, developing mutual respect among group members, and coordinating group activities and efforts.[9] Warren Bennis, who has studied leadership for a number of years, suggests that effective leaders are concerned with "doing the right things" rather than "doing things right."[10] The right things, according to Bennis, include the following:

- Creating and communicating a vision of what the organization should be
- Communicating with and gaining the support of multiple constituencies
- Persisting in the desired direction even under bad conditions
- Creating the appropriate culture and obtaining the desired results

From this definition of leadership, company presidents and many managers can be identified as leaders. Coaches, basketball captains, and football quarterbacks are leaders. Army drill sergeants are leaders. The person who organizes a social gathering is also a leader. In other words, many people serve as either formal or informal leaders, and almost anyone can act as a leader. However, some positions provide more opportunities to display leadership behavior than others. And not all people in positions that call for leader behavior (e.g., managerial positions) act as leaders. For example, a manager who merely follows rules and fails to provide direction to and support for his associates is not acting as a leader.

Trait Theory of Leadership

At one time, it was thought that some people were born with certain traits that made them effective leaders, whereas others were born without leadership traits.[11] The list of traits generated by this early research was substantial (in the thousands) and included physical characteristics (such as height and appearance), personality characteristics (such as self-esteem and dominance), and abilities (such as intelligence and verbal fluency). Additional traits that were thought to characterize leaders are presented in Exhibit 8-1.

Early trait research has been criticized for several reasons. For example, the methodology used to identify the traits was poor. Investigators simply generated lists of traits by loosely comparing people who were labeled as leaders with those who were not—without actually measuring traits or systematically testing for meaningful differences. A second criticism is that the list of traits associated with leadership grew so large it became meaningless. A third criticism is that the results of this research were inconsistent—different leaders possessed different traits. Finally, no leadership trait was found to relate consistently to unit or organizational performance, and different situations seemed to require different

> ## EXHIBIT 8-1   Traits Associated with Leadership
>
> | | | | |
> |---|---|---|---|
> | Energy | Achievement drive | Initiative | Sense of humor |
> | Appearance | Adaptability | Insightfulness | Tolerance for stress |
> | Intelligence | Aggressiveness | Integrity | Interpersonal skill |
> | Judgment | Enthusiasm | Persistence | Prestige |
> | Verbal fluency | Extraversion | Self-confidence | Tact |
>
> Source: Based on A.C. Jago. 1982. "Leadership: Perspectives in Theory and Research," *Management Science*, 28: 315–336.

traits.[12] Although famous leaders (e.g., Abraham Lincoln, Gandhi, Martin Luther King, Jr.) had "special" traits, a close examination reveals differences among them. Numerous studies conducted to determine the traits that relate to effective leadership found that not all leaders possess the same traits.

Nevertheless, the notion of leadership traits has been revived in recent years.[13] Research has demonstrated that leaders usually are different from other people. It is now believed, however, that many of the traits (or characteristics) that are possessed by leaders can be learned or developed (i.e., leaders are not born but are made). Moreover, possessing leadership traits is not enough to make a person a successful leader; he must also take specific actions necessary for strong leadership.[14] The measurement and understanding of personal characteristics have improved since the early twentieth century, and modern researchers have proposed that important leadership traits can be categorized as follows:[15]

- *Drive.* Drive refers to the amount of ambition, persistence, tenacity, and initiative that people possess. Leaders must have the energy and will to continue to act during turbulent and stressful times. Drive and ambition are also important to a leader's ability to create a vision and engage in behavior to achieve the vision.
- *Leadership motivation.* Leadership motivation refers to a person's desire to lead, influence others, assume responsibility, and gain power. We must distinguish here between two types of motives. Leaders can have a *socialized power motive,* whereby they use power to achieve goals that are in the organization's best interests or in the best interests of followers. In contrast, a leader with a *personalized power motive* desires power solely for the sake of having power over others.
- *Integrity.* Leaders with honesty are truthful and maintain consistency between what they say and what they do. Followers and others in the organization are not likely to trust a leader who does not have these characteristics.
- *Self-confidence.* Leaders must be confident in their actions and show that confidence to others. People who are high in self-confidence are also able to learn from their mistakes, react positively to stress, and remain even-tempered and display appropriate emotions.
- *Cognitive ability.* Leaders who possess a high degree of intelligence are better able to process complex information, solve problems, and deal with changing environments.
- *Knowledge of the domain.* Knowledge of the domain in which they are engaged allows leaders to make better decisions, anticipate future problems, and understand the implications of their actions.

Reforming a Rotten Apple and an Evil City

©Brian Harkin/Getty Images, Inc.

*W*illiam Bratton was appointed police commissioner of New York City in 1994 at perhaps one of the worst times in the history of the huge New York City Police Department (NYPD). New York City had experienced three decades of increasing crime rates, and some critics claimed that there was nothing the police department could do about it. Bratton, who had previously worked his way up through the Boston Police Department, faced a challenge that had been unresolved by his predecessors, and he had to handle the problem without an increase in resources.

Mr. Bratton became the head of the Los Angeles Police Department in 2002 at one of the worse times in its history. Los Angeles had just become the murder capital of the United States. The city was operating under federal supervision because of a number of corruption scandals and civil rights violations. Relations between the police and citizens were strained. As in New York, many questioned whether Bratton could handle the situation.

To say that William Bratton exhibited successful leadership would be an understatement. Within two years, his leadership of the NYPD made New York City one of the safest large cities in the world. Felony crimes fell 39 percent, theft decreased 35 percent, and murders dropped 50 percent. Public confidence in the police department, reported in Gallup polls, soared from 37 percent to 73 percent. Not only was the NYPD effective in fighting crime, but police

officers were also happier with their jobs, reporting record levels of job satisfaction. In Los Angeles, violent crimes declined by nearly 50 percent during Bratton's leadership from 2002 to 2009. The federal supervision ended. Approval ratings from the public soared to 83%.

Does William Bratton exhibit the leadership traits suggested by modern research? Yes, he does:

Drive. Bratton has been called a "cannonball," which provides an idea of his drive and ambition. Bratton shows passion for his vision that police should be held accountable for reducing crime and that success should be measured by how much crime, disorder, and fear are reduced.

Leadership motivation. From his early years in the Boston Police Department, Bratton expressed the desire to lead it some day. When he was leaving the New York City police commissioner's job, he entertained the idea of running for mayor. Today, he is considering various leadership posts. He has been mentioned as a possible candidate for the U.S. senate, governor of New York, and director of the FBI.

Integrity. Bratton's actions have always supported his words. Even in the face of opposition from political contingencies and civil liberties groups, he has remained committed to police accountability and zero-tolerance policies. Bratton has not tailored his messages

to his audiences. For example, he has said, "One of the things people like about me is that when I'm talking to a black audience I'm not talking any different than when I'm talking to a white audience." Furthermore, he has been tough on corruption, firing officers who are dishonest.

Self-confidence. Bratton has always displayed self-confidence, particularly in the face of adversity. His self-confidence has sometimes been interpreted as arrogance; however, over his career he has learned the difference between the two.

Cognitive ability. One of the most telling indications of Bratton's strong cognitive ability is the strategic manner in which he has approached managing the country's largest police departments.

Knowledge of the domain. Bratton worked his way through the ranks of the Boston Police Department, gaining knowledge about how policing works from the bottom up. As the NYPD police commissioner, he would ride the subway to work so that he had a better understanding of what was going on in the street. In Los Angeles, he would regularly visit barbershops, parks, and other gathering places to better understand the community.

Openness to new experiences. Bratton has been open to new ideas and change. He has frequently adopted the new ideas of others during his career. In Los Angeles, he changed his approach to minority relations, as the situation was quite different relative to what he had experienced in New York.

Extraversion. One of the key attributes that Bratton has brought to the policing is his hands-on approach and vigorous pace. From informal chats with community leaders to Sunday dinners with his inner circle in New York, he has embraced people and the energy they create for him.

Beyond the traits listed above, Bratton undertook a number of specific actions that led to success and

to his being named "Police Executive of the 20th Century" (and having his photo on the cover of Time). His success has been attributed to four major actions:

1. He endorsed decentralization, giving strong authority and autonomy to precinct/division commanders. Instead of having to deal with bureaucratic policies that prevented them from combating crime, commanders were able to deal more aggressively and decisively with it and do so with more understanding, involvement, and commitment from the communities in which they served.

2. He engaged in systematic strategic planning to analyze crime patterns and use of resources. The end result was more efficient use of resources. More police officers were assigned to higher-crime areas, and more focus was placed on common and serious crimes.

3. He adopted the *Compstat process.* This process uses computerized crime statistics, electronic maps,

and management meetings where precinct/division heads are held accountable (and rewarded or reprimanded) for the crime activity in their precincts.

4. He instigated a controversial policy known as zero-tolerance crime fighting. Police officers were required to arrest people for seemingly petty crimes such as graffiti writing, panhandling, and minor vandalism. The philosophy behind this policy is that if a neighborhood is plagued by petty crime, it appears to be out of control—reducing the felt presence of the police and making criminals feel freer to commit more serious crimes.

Although there are critics of Bratton's zero-tolerance style of policing and questions about some of his other tactics, the fact remains that crime was substantially reduced in both New York and Los Angeles, and police relations with their communities were strengthened. Few doubt that Bratton is an effective leader.

Sources: W.J. Bratton, & P. Knobler. 1998. *The Turnaround: How America's Top Cop Reversed the Crime Epidemic* New York: Random House; G. Kahn. 2009. "Bratton Joins Private Sector after 7 Years as L.A.'s Top Cop," *Wall Street Journal*, Aug. 6, p. A.2; W.C. Kim, & R. Mauborgne. 2003. "Tipping Point Leadership," *Harvard Business Review*, 81, no. 4: 60–69; J. Newfield & M. Jacobson. 2000. "An Interview with William Bratton," at http://www.tikkun.org/magazine/index.cfm/action/tikkun/issues/tik0007/article/000727.html; J. Zengerie. 2009. "Repeat Defender: After Taming Crime in Los Angeles Bill Bratton Has Won Over Skeptics Who Doubted His Success in New York," *New York*, Nov. 30, pp. 12–16.

- *Openness to new experiences.* Being open to new ideas and approaches is associated with flexibility, which can be very important in today's dynamic world.
- *Extraversion.* Leaders who enjoy being around people, prefer to maintain a vigorous pace, and seek excitement are more likely to be proactive in engaging both problems and opportunities.

William Bratton, former chief of police for New York City and now retired head of the Los Angeles Police Department, exhibits these traits. As discussed in the *Experiencing Organizational Behavior* feature, he has leveraged them to create positive outcomes in the areas of enhanced public safety and reduced crime. He also has exhibited the characteristics of strategic leaders that were explained earlier. For example, he engaged in strategic planning in both New York and Los Angeles and effectively implemented the resulting strategies. To implement these strategies, he decentralized authority to leverage the talents of various leaders and used effective communication processes to enhance co-ordination. He used his knowledge of policing to have a strong positive effect on police-department performance.

Most studies of leaders have concluded that the traits focused on here are important. As noted, however, although specific traits may be necessary for a person to be an effective leader, ultimately she must take action to be successful.

Before ending this discussion of trait theory, it is important to mention charisma. Think of famous (or infamous) leaders such as John F. Kennedy, Adolf Hitler, Winston Churchill, Eleanor Roosevelt, Martin Luther King, Jr., Ronald Reagan, and Barbara Jordan. Many people believe that all of these individuals possessed charisma. *Charisma* is usually defined by the effect it has on followers. Charismatic leaders inspire their followers to change their needs and values, follow visionary quests, and sacrifice their own personal interests for the good of the cause. Traditionally, charisma was thought of as a personality trait. However, conceptualizing charisma as a simple personality trait has been subject to criticism. In addition, charisma has been difficult to define precisely, and different leaders have displayed charisma in different ways.

The notion of charisma has become popular again in modern theories. Charismatic leadership, though possibly based in personality to some degree, can be learned over time (at least partially) and is ultimately reflected in a leader's behavior. Thus, it is best described by the leader's behavior and her relationship to followers.[16] We discuss charisma in more detail later in this chapter in the section on transformational leadership.

Behavioral Theories of Leadership

In response to the heavy reliance in the earlier part of the twentieth century on trait theory and the notion that leaders are born and not developed, large research projects were conducted at the University of Michigan and the Ohio State University to examine what leaders actually did to be effective. This research concentrated largely on leadership style. Although both managerial thought and scholarly investigation have progressed beyond these two lines of research, this work provided the foundation for more contemporary theories of leadership, such as the transformational leadership approach discussed later in the chapter.

University of Michigan Studies

job-centered leadership style
A behavioral leadership style that emphasizes employee tasks and the methods used to accomplish them.

employee-centered leadership style
A behavioral leadership style that emphasizes employees' personal needs and the development of interpersonal relationships.

The leadership studies at the Institute for Social Research of the University of Michigan were conducted by such scholars as Rensis Likert, Daniel Katz, and Robert Kahn. The studies involved both private and public organizations, including businesses from numerous industry groups. These studies examined two distinct styles of leader behavior: **the job-centered** and **employee-centered styles**.[17]

The job-centered leader emphasizes employee tasks and the methods used to accomplish them. A job-centered leader supervises individuals closely (provides instructions, checks frequently on performance) and sometimes behaves in a punitive manner toward them. Alternatively, an employee-centered leader emphasizes employees' personal needs and the development of interpersonal relationships. An employee-centered leader frequently delegates decision-making authority and responsibility to others and provides a supportive environment, encouraging interpersonal communication.

To measure these styles, leaders completed a questionnaire consisting of a number of items. Based on their responses, they were classified as either job-centered or employee-centered. The effectiveness of these leaders was then examined by measuring factors such as the productivity, job satisfaction, absenteeism, and turnover rates of those being led.

The results of these studies were inconsistent. In some cases, units whose leaders used a job-centered style were more productive, whereas in other cases units with employee-centered leaders were more productive. The job-centered style, however, resulted in less-productive units more often than did the employee-centered style. In addition, even when productivity was high, employees with job-centered leaders had lower levels of job satisfaction than those who worked with employee-centered leaders. Therefore, many of the researchers involved in the studies concluded that the employee-centered style was more effective.

The situations in which job-centered leaders were effective could not be explained well. In addition to style, then, other factors seemed to affect a leader's effectiveness. In addition, the leadership style examined in these studies was unidimensional. A leader was classified as either job-centered or employee-centered but could not possess characteristics of both styles. This oversimplification no doubt affected the results of the research.

If we consider the case of Police Commissioner William Bratton, discussed in the earlier *Experiencing Organizational Behavior* feature, it is clear why the unidimensional view of leadership behavior is problematic. Although Bratton displayed a job-centered style by carefully monitoring police officers' performance and providing rewards or punishment based on that performance, he also demonstrated an employee-centered style by decentralizing authority and opening communication channels within the department. Similarly, Maria Yee from the opening case displayed both the job-centered and employee-centered styles.

Ohio State University Studies

At around the same time that the University of Michigan studies were being conducted, leadership studies were underway at Ohio State University led by such scholars as Ralph Stogdill and Edwin Fleishman. These studies emphasized a two-dimensional view of leaders' behavior. The two independent dimensions of leadership behavior were initiating structure and consideration.

Initiating structure indicates behavior that establishes well-defined patterns of organization and communication, defines procedures, and delineates the leader's relationships with those being led. Leaders who initiate structure emphasize goals and deadlines and ensure that employees are assigned tasks and know what performance is expected from them.

Consideration refers to behavior that expresses friendship, develops mutual trust and respect, and builds strong interpersonal relationships with those being led. Leaders who exhibit consideration offer support to their employees, use employees' ideas, and frequently allow them to participate in decisions.[18]

These two concepts are similar to the ones used in the Michigan studies—initiating structure is similar to job-centered leadership, while consideration is similar to employee-centered leadership. The important difference is that leaders can exhibit characteristics of both. Thus, an individual could be classified in any of the four cells shown in Exhibit 8-2,

initiating structure
A behavioral leadership style demonstrated by leaders who establish well-defined patterns of organization and communication, define procedures, and delineate their relationships with those being led.

consideration
A behavioral leadership style demonstrated by leaders who express friendship, develop mutual trust and respect, and have strong interpersonal relationships with those being led.

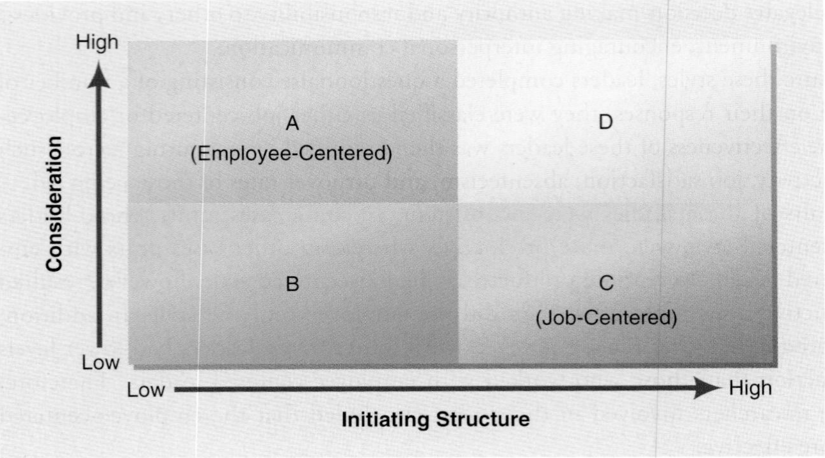

Exhibit 8-2 Comparison of Initiating Structure and Consideration with Job-Centered and Employee-Centered Concepts

whereas the Michigan approach artificially forced a person to be classified in either Cell A or Cell C.

Various studies have examined the linkage between these two dimensions of leader behavior and effectiveness. Results of early research suggested that leaders high in both initiating structure and consideration were more effective than other leaders. However, further studies showed that the relationship between leaders' behavior and their effectiveness, as measured by factors such as employee productivity, satisfaction, and turnover, was more complicated. In addition, each of the leader-behavior dimensions might affect various outcomes in different ways (structuring might have stronger effects on productivity, whereas consideration seems to have stronger effects on satisfaction, for example). A 2004 review of studies on initiating structure and consideration showed that the basic ideas of the Ohio State studies still applied.[19] Newer theories of leadership, however, present a more complex and complete view.

Contingency Theories of Leadership

Studies of trait and behavioral leadership concepts hinted at the importance of situational factors in leader effectiveness. Those studies led other researchers to conclude that effective leadership practices are "contingent" on the situation. Contingency leadership concepts were then developed. The two best known are the aptly named *contingency theory of leadership effectiveness* and the *path–goal theory of leadership*.

Fiedler's Contingency Theory of Leadership Effectiveness

contingency theory of leadership effectiveness
A theory of leadership that suggests that the effectiveness of a leader depends on the interaction of his style of behavior with certain characteristics of the situation.

The **contingency theory of leadership effectiveness** was developed by Fred Fiedler.[20] According to this theory, the effectiveness of a leader depends on the interaction of the leader's behavioral style with certain characteristics of the situation.

Leader Style

Different leaders may, of course, exhibit different styles of behavior. Fiedler explains that leaders' behavior is based on their motivational needs. The most important needs of leaders, according to Fiedler, are interpersonal-relationship needs and task-achievement needs. As you can see, these are similar to the concepts used in the Michigan and Ohio State studies.

The relative importance of these needs to a leader determines the leader's style. In determining which need is strongest, the esteem for the least-preferred co-worker (LPC) must be assessed.[21] If leaders describe their least-preferred co-worker mainly in negative terms (uncooperative, unfriendly), they obtain a low LPC score, which indicates a task-oriented leader whose task-achievement needs have first priority. Leaders who describe their least-preferred co-worker in positive terms (cooperative, friendly) receive a high LPC score. A high score indicates that the leader has a relationship-oriented style where interpersonal relationship needs have first priority.

Perhaps you have had a supervisor who focused mainly on the work to be done and did not engage in much personal interaction with those being led. This supervisor would probably have a low LPC score and be considered task-oriented. Contrast this person with another leader you have known who really cared about others and put a great deal of effort into maintaining positive relationships with everyone. This leader would have a high LPC score and be considered relationship-oriented. Which of these styles is most effective? That depends on situational characteristics.

Situational Characteristics

In some situations, leaders have more control over the work environment. In the context of Fiedler's contingency theory, this means that leaders can influence events in a straightforward way and work systematically toward desired outcomes. Important situational characteristics that determine a leader's level of control include leader–member relations, task structure, and position power.

- **Leader–member relations** correspond to the degree to which a leader is respected, is accepted as a leader, and has friendly interpersonal relations. When a leader has the respect and admiration of those who are led, he tends to have more control over the situation. He can more easily influence events and outcomes. This is the most important of the three situational variables.
- **Task structure** is the degree to which tasks can be broken down into easily understood steps or parts. When a leader deals with structured tasks, she has more control over the situation. She can more easily influence events and drive for goal achievement.
- **Position power** is the degree to which a leader can reward, punish, promote, or demote individuals in the unit or organization. When a leader can reward and punish, he has greater control and influence over the situation.[22]

leader–member relations
The degree to which a leader is respected, is accepted as a leader, and has friendly interpersonal relations.

task structure
The degree to which tasks can be broken down into easily understood steps or parts.

position power
The degree to which a leader can reward, punish, promote, or demote individuals in the unit or organization.

Situational Favorableness

The amount of control a leader has determines the favorableness of the situation. In the most favorable situations, leader–member relations are good, the tasks are highly structured, and the leader has strong position power. In the least favorable situations, leader–member relations are poor, tasks are unstructured, and leader position power is weak. Situations may, of course, vary between these two extremes.

Consider leading a project team for this course. Suppose that you have the respect of the team members, you are engaged in a set of tasks that can be easily managed, and you

Effective Leader	Task-Oriented (Low LPC)			Relationship-Oriented (High LPC)			Task-Oriented (Low LPC)	
Situational Favorableness	Favorable			Intermediate Favorableness			Unfavorable	
Leader–Member Relations	Good	Good	Good	Good	Poor	Poor	Poor	Poor
Task Structure	Structured	Structured	Un-structured	Un-structured	Structured	Structured	Un-structured	Un-structured
Leader Position Power	Strong	Weak	Strong	Weak	Strong	Weak	Strong	Weak
Situation	I	II	III	IV	V	VI	VII	VIII

Exhibit 8-3 Fiedler's Contingency Model of Leadership Effectiveness

are able to assign participation grades. This represents a favorable situation in which you, as leader, could easily influence events and outcomes. Now suppose instead that you do not get along with the members of the team, you are engaged in a set of tasks that are difficult to manage, and you have no power to reward or punish team members. This would be a very unfavorable situation, in which you would have much less influence over events and probably would have more difficulty working toward goal achievement.

Leadership Effectiveness

The leader's effectiveness is determined by the interaction of the leader's style of behavior and the favorableness of the situational characteristics. The leader's effectiveness is judged by the performance of the group being led. The linkages involving the leader's effectiveness, her style of behavior, and situational favorableness are shown in Exhibit 8-3.

Fiedler's research on the contingency model has shown that task-oriented leaders are more effective in highly favorable (I, II, III) and highly unfavorable (VII, VIII) situations, whereas relationship-oriented leaders are more effective in situations of intermediate favorableness (IV, V, VI). More specifically, the correlations between LPC scores and group performance in favorable and unfavorable situations is negative (performance was higher when LPC was lower). The correlation between LPC and group performance in situations of intermediate favorableness is positive (performance was higher when LPC was higher).[23]

Fiedler has also found that leaders may act differently in different situations. Relationship-oriented (high-LPC) leaders often display task-oriented behaviors under highly favorable conditions and display relationship-oriented behaviors in situations that are unfavorable or intermediate in favorableness. Conversely, task-oriented (low-LPC) leaders often display task-oriented behaviors in situations that are unfavorable or intermediate in favorableness but display relationship-oriented behaviors in favorable situations.[24] These findings help to explain why various leadership styles are effective in different situations, as discussed below.

Favorable situations do not require leaders to provide strong oversight or frequent task-focused inputs. Tasks can be accomplished with less direction from the leader. The task-oriented (low-LPC) leader's interpersonal needs are activated in favorable situations; however, the relationship-oriented (high-LPC) leader's needs for task achievement are activated in favorable situations. The low-LPC leader is thus more effective in favorable situations because they require leaders to provide encouragement, support, and interpersonal trust (relationship-oriented behavior).

Unfavorable situations require stronger oversight and more task-focused inputs. In such situations, the high-LPC leader's natural needs for interpersonal relations are activated, which creates difficulties. On the other hand, the low-LPC leader's natural needs for task achievement are activated. This matches the requirements of the situation.

Situations of intermediate favorableness provide neither of these extremes. Where the task is unstructured, a naturally relationship-oriented leader may be necessary to get the group to use its creativity to solve problems. Where leader-member relations are poor, a naturally relationship-oriented leader may be better able to overcome the negative relations with the group and build trust.

According to the contingency model, then, a leader cannot be effective in all situations by exhibiting only one leadership style. Fiedler believes that individuals should be matched with situations in which their leadership styles are likely to be most effective. Lacking the ability to reassign leaders, the characteristics of the situation should be changed to provide an effective match between the leader's style and the favorableness of the situation.

Fiedler conducted extensive research on the contingency model, and most of his research provided support for it.[25] Furthermore, the general observation that previously successful leaders do not always perform well after moving to a new job provides some support for a central idea in Fiedler's theory—leaders have a certain style and cannot easily adjust to a new context. In a study of senior managers who had departed from GE, lack of fit with a new job situation was cited as a cause of difficulties.[26] Still, the overall pool of research has provided only mixed support for Fiedler's ideas.[27] One issue is the simplicity of the model. It incorporates only two narrow behavioral styles (task and relationship). Moreover, it does not explain outcomes for the middle-LPC leader. Interestingly, some research suggests that the middle-LPC leader may be more effective than either the high- or low-LPC leader. Because the middle-LPC leader is more flexible and is not constrained by one orientation, she may better adapt to multiple situations.[28] Another concern has been the validity of the LPC measure. Critics believe that other measures of leader behavior are more reliable and valid.[29] A final concern has been the model's failure to explicitly address followers' satisfaction with leaders. Some research, however, has found the model to predict follower satisfaction.[30]

These criticisms do not reduce the importance of Fiedler's model. It represents one of the first comprehensive attempts to explain a complex subject. In addition, a significant amount of research supports the model, and researchers continue to investigate and attempt to extend it.

The Path–Goal Leadership Theory

The **path–goal leadership theory** was originally developed by Martin Evans[31] and Robert House.[32] The theory, which is based on expectancy concepts from the study of motivation, emphasizes a leader's effects on subordinates' goals and the paths used to achieve those goals. It provides a bridge to the modern study of leadership.

path–goal leadership theory
A theory of leadership based on expectancy concepts from the study of motivation, which suggests that leader effectiveness depends on the degree to which a leader enhances the performance expectancies and valences of her subordinates.

Recall from Chapter 6 that *expectancies* relate to the perceived probability of goal attainment and *valences* correspond to the value or attractiveness of goal attainment. Leadership can affect employees' expectancies and valences in several ways:

- Facilitating employees' efforts to achieve task goals (effort → performance expectancy). Effective leaders help employees (through encouragement, training, and technical direction, for example) believe that their efforts on a task will lead to goal attainment. As part of this, leaders address any barriers perceived by a given employee.
- Tying extrinsic rewards (pay raise, recognition, promotion) to accomplishment of task goals (performance → reward instrumentality).
- Linking individuals to tasks for which goal attainment is personally valuable (valence). In other words, leaders can assign individuals to tasks that they will find rewarding.

These tactics used by leaders increase effectiveness; employees achieve higher performance because of their increased motivation on the job. Specific behaviors through which these tactics are implemented must be tailored, however, to the situation. More so than Fielder's theory, the path–goal theory highlights the ability of managers to tailor their behaviors.[33]

Leader Behavior and Situational Factors

The path–goal leadership theory focuses on several types of leader behavior and situational factors. The main types of leader behavior are as follows:[34]

directive leadership
Leadership behavior characterized by implementing guidelines, providing information on what is expected, setting definite performance standards, and ensuring that individuals follow rules.

supportive leadership
Leadership behavior characterized by friendliness and concern for individuals' well-being, welfare, and needs.

achievement-oriented leadership
Leadership behavior characterized by setting challenging goals and seeking to improve performance.

participative leadership
Leadership behavior characterized by sharing information, consulting with those who are led, and emphasizing group decision making.

- **Directive leadership** behavior is characterized by implementing guidelines, providing information on what is expected, setting definite performance standards, and ensuring that individuals follow the rules.
- **Supportive leadership** behavior is characterized by being friendly and showing concern for well-being, welfare, and needs.
- **Achievement-oriented leadership** behavior is characterized by setting challenging goals and seeking to improve performance.
- **Participative leadership** behavior is characterized by sharing information, consulting with those who are led, and emphasizing group decision making.

Directive leadership and achievement-oriented leadership are related to the earlier concepts of job-centered style (Michigan studies), initiating structure (Ohio State studies), and task orientation (Fiedler's contingency theory of leadership effectiveness). Supportive leadership and participative leadership are related to the concepts of employee-centered style (Michigan studies), consideration (Ohio State studies), and interpersonal orientation (Fiedler's contingency theory of leadership effectiveness).

There are two sets of situational factors: subordinates' characteristics (such as needs, locus of control, experience, and ability) and characteristics of the work environment (such as task structure, interpersonal relations in the group, role conflict, and role clarity). The effectiveness of various leader behaviors depends on these situational factors.

Interaction of Leader Behavior and Situational Factors

Path–goal theory specifies a number of interactions between leader behavior and situational factors, with these interactions influencing outcomes. Researchers, however, have provided only mixed support for the theory,[35] with some studies supporting it and others failing to support it.[36] Relationships that appear to be valid are listed below:

- Associates with an internal locus of control (who believe outcomes are a function of their own behavior) are likely to be more satisfied with a participative leader. Individuals with an external locus of control (who believe outcomes are a function of chance or luck) are more likely to be effective with directive leaders.
- Associates who have a high need for affiliation are likely to be more satisfied with a supportive leader. Supportive leaders fulfill their needs for close personal relationships.
- Associates with a high need for security probably will be more satisfied with a directive leader who reduces uncertainty by providing clear rules and procedures.
- Supportive and participative leaders are more likely to increase satisfaction on highly structured tasks. Because the tasks are routine, little direction is necessary. Directive leaders are more likely to increase satisfaction on unstructured tasks, where individuals (particularly those with less experience and ability) often need help in clarifying an ambiguous task situation.
- Directive leadership is often more effective on unstructured tasks because it can increase an employee's expectation that effort will lead to task-goal accomplishment (particularly when employees have less experience and/or ability). Supportive leadership is often more effective on structured tasks because it can increase a person's expectation that accomplishing goals will lead to extrinsic rewards.[37]
- Associates with a high need for growth who are working on a complex task probably perform better with a participative or achievement-oriented leader. Because they are intrinsically motivated, they appreciate information and difficult goals that help in achievement. Individuals with a low growth need strength working on a complex task perform better with directive leaders.[38]

A summary of these interactions involving leader behavior and situational factors is presented in Exhibit 8-4. Although any number of situational factors could play roles in leader effectiveness,[39] those discussed here have been shown to be important.

Situational Factors		
Subordinate Characteristics	Characteristics of the Work Environment	Effective Leader Behaviors
Internal Locus of Control		Participative
External Locus of Control		Directive
High Need for Affiliation		Supportive
High Need for Security		Directive
	Structured Task	Supportive
	Unstructured Task	Directive
High Growth Need Strength	Complex Task	Participative Achievement Oriented
Low Growth Need Strength	Complex Task	Directive
High Growth Need Strength	Simple Task	Supportive
Low Growth Need Strength	Simple Task	Supportive

Exhibit 8-4 Interaction of Leader Behavior and Situational Factors

Phil Jackson and Leadership Success

Phil Jackson's success as a coach in the National Basketball Association (NBA) is legendary. He has won eleven championships, six with the Chicago Bulls and five with the Los Angeles Lakers. He has more playoff victories than anyone else in the history of the league and has the best winning percentage in playoff games among coaches with significant playoff experience. He also sports the best winning percentage in regular season games.

Some have suggested that Jackson's success is due only to having great players, such as Michael Jordan, Shaquille O'Neal, and Kobe Bryant. But the facts do not support this. In both Chicago and Los Angeles, the great players did not win championships until Jackson arrived.

So what makes him special? One answer to this question is his philosophy of leadership. His philosophy, which has been influenced by Zen Buddhism, embraces humility, respect for others, and a belief in the interconnected nature of humankind. Jackson said this:

In terms of leadership, this means treating everyone with the same care and respect you give yourself—and trying to understand their reality without judgment. When we can do that, we begin to see that we all share human struggles, desires, and dreams.

In essence, Jackson applies a philosophy that suggests less directive leadership, which fits the situation he faces in the NBA. His players typically have strong ability, a great deal of experience, and strong growth needs in terms of wanting to achieve on the basketball court. In addition, the relevant tasks are relatively structured. Under these conditions, directive leadership behaviors would be less desirable, and Jackson is known to be one of the least-directive coaches during basketball games.

In Los Angeles, Jackson helped his star player, Kobe Bryant, rebuild respect with his fellow players after a tumultuous period. Although tensions continue to arise from time to time, Jackson helped to make the situation better. He did so by advising Bryant to exhibit fewer directive behaviors in his own leadership. In Bryant's words:

Sometimes it's best if you just step back and kind of guide

©AP/Wide World Photos

them a little bit and allow them to learn on their own. Very subtle. That's ... one of the things he taught me. ...

Within his overall approach, Jackson tailors his leadership to circumstances. If players are less experienced or have growth needs that are dormant, he is more directive. His goal is to be "invisible," but he would not advise such invisibility in all situations.

Sources: Basketball-Reference.com, "Phil Jackson," 2009, at http://www.basketball-reference.com/coaches/jacksph01c.html; M. Bresnahan. 2007. "Leader Counsel," Los Angeles Times, Feb. 20, p. D.1; D. Dupree. 2002. "Phil Jackson: Zen and Now," USA Today.com, June 6, at http://www.usatoday.com/sports/nba/02playoffs/2002-06-05-cover-jackson.htm; P. Jackson, & H. Delehanty. 1995. "Sacred Hoops" New York: Hyperion; NBA Encyclopedia, "All-Time Regular Season Victories-Coaches," 2009, at http://www.nba.com/history/records/victories_coaches.html; J.P. Pfeffer, & R.I. Sutton. 2006. "Hard Facts, Dangerous Half-truths, & Total Nonsense" Boston: Harvard Business School Press.

Conclusions Regarding Contingency Theories

Contingency leadership concepts are more difficult to apply than the trait or behavioral concepts because they are more complex. But when appropriately used, they are more practical and should therefore lead to higher levels of effectiveness. In essence, they require that leaders correctly diagnose a situation and identify the behaviors that are most appropriate (those that best fit the characteristics of the situation). Also, contingency theories imply that a leader might need to change her approach over time. Among those being led, abilities and experience levels change, as do other features of the situation, suggesting that leaders must change their approaches.[40] Finally, path–goal theory implies that leaders might need to treat individuals differently within the same unit or organization.[41] If individuals in a unit are different, then leaders can benefit from approaching them in different ways, at least to some degree.

In order to be successful, leaders must act in ways that fit the situation in which they find themselves. Phil Jackson, one of basketball's great coaches, leads in a way that fits his situation. His story is presented in the *Managerial Advice* feature.

Although important and useful, contingency theories of leadership have received less attention in recent years. The dynamic business environment and rapid technological advancements of the past two decades have combined to create the need for a new approach to leadership.[42] We next turn to one of the most significant contemporary paradigms for leadership.

Transformational Leadership

The need for organizations to change and adapt rapidly while creating a high-performance workforce has become increasingly apparent in recent years. To stay competitive, business leaders must be able to inspire organizational members to go beyond their ordinary task requirements and exert extraordinary levels of effort and adaptability. As a result, new approaches to leadership have emerged.

Transactional leadership[43] provides a useful starting point in this discussion. This type of leadership focuses primarily on leaders' extrinsic exchange relationships with followers—that is, the degree to which leaders provide what followers want in response to good performance. Followers comply with leaders' wishes to gain desired rewards. Transactional leaders have the following four specific characteristics:[44]

> **transactional leadership**
> A leadership approach that is based on the exchange relationship between followers and leaders. Transactional leadership is characterized by contingent reward behavior and active management-by-exception behavior.

1. They understand what followers want from their work, and they attempt to deliver these rewards if deserved.

2. They clarify the links between performance and rewards.

3. They exchange rewards and promises of rewards for specified performance.

4. They respond to interests of followers only if performance is satisfactory.

Transactional leaders are characterized by contingent reward behavior and active management-by-exception behavior.[45] *Contingent reward behavior* involves clarifying performance expectations and rewarding followers when those expectations are met. *Active management-by-exception* behavior is demonstrated when a leader clarifies minimal performance standards and punishes those who do not perform up to the standards. Transactional leaders consistently monitor the performance of their followers.

In contrast to this extrinsic exchange-based approach, **transformational leadership** involves motivating followers to do more than expected, to continuously develop and

> **transformational leadership**
> A leadership approach that involves motivating followers to do more than expected, to continuously develop and grow, to increase self-confidence, and to place the interests of the unit or organization before their own. Transformational leadership involves charisma, intellectual stimulation, and individual consideration.

grow, to increase their level of self-confidence, and to place the interests of the unit or organization before their own.[46] Transformational leaders do the following three things:

1. They increase followers' awareness of the importance of pursuing a vision or mission and the strategy required.
2. They encourage followers to place the interests of the unit, organization, or larger collective before their own personal interests.
3. They raise followers' aspirations so that they continuously try to develop and improve themselves while striving for higher levels of accomplishment.

Transformational leadership results from both personal characteristics and specific actions. Three characteristics have been identified with transformational leaders: charisma, intellectual stimulation, and individual consideration.[47] **Charisma** refers specifically to the leader's ability to inspire emotion and passion in his followers and to cause them to identify with the leader.[48] A charismatic leader displays confidence, goes beyond self-interest, communicates and lives up to organizational values, draws attention to the purpose of the organization or mission, and speaks optimistically and enthusiastically. The second characteristic, *intellectual stimulation,* is the leader's ability to increase the followers' focus on problems and to develop new ways of addressing them. Leaders who provide intellectual stimulation reexamine assumptions, seek out different views, and try to be innovative. Finally, individual consideration involves supporting and developing followers so that they become self-confident and desire to improve their performance. Leaders showing *individual consideration* provide individualized attention to followers, focus on followers' strengths, and act as teachers and coaches.

A great deal of research has focused on how transformational leaders behave—that is, what they do to become transformational leaders. The list of common behaviors includes the following:[49]

- Transformational leaders articulate a clear and appealing vision, which is beneficial to the followers.
- They communicate the vision through personal action, emotional appeals, and symbolic forms of communication (such as metaphors and dramatic staged events).
- They delegate significant authority and responsibility.
- They eliminate unnecessary bureaucratic constraints.
- They provide coaching, training, and other developmental experiences to followers.
- They encourage open sharing of ideas and concerns.
- They encourage participative decision making.
- They promote cooperation and teamwork.
- They modify organization structure (such as resource allocation systems) and policies (such as selection and promotion criteria) to promote key values and objectives.

The proactive and energetic nature of transformational leadership hints at an opposite approach, called *laissez-faire* or *passive-avoidant* leadership.[50] Leaders displaying a laissez-faire style are not proactive, react only to failures or chronic problems, avoid making decisions, and are often absent or uninvolved in followers' activities. Such leaders typically do not have positive outcomes.[51] Leaders who strongly display transformational leadership do not display laissez-faire behaviors.

---

charisma

A leader's ability to inspire emotion and passion in his followers and to cause them to identify with the leader.

Commander D. Michael Abrashoff exemplified transformational leadership during his days on the USS *Benfold*.[52] First, Abrashoff's charisma was evident in several different ways. He demonstrated confidence with his informal but passionate manner. Consistent with this, he said the following: "I divide the world into believers and infidels. What the infidels don't understand … is that innovative practices combined with true empowerment produce phenomenal results." He focused on the vision of extreme readiness in order to protect the United States, and he communicated that vision clearly to all crew members, often meeting with them individually. He tried to link each crew member's tasks to the vision. He also went beyond self-interest, saying, "Anyone on my ship will tell you that I'm a low maintenance CO. It's not about me; it's about my crew."

©Reuters/Corbis

Abrashoff demonstrated his ability to create intellectual stimulation by continuously reexamining the way things were done on the ship and changing procedures when a better way was found. He stated, "There is always a better way to do things." During his first few months on the *Benfold,* he thoroughly analyzed all operations. He questioned everyone involved in each operation to find out whether they had suggestions for how to do things better. They almost always did.

Finally, Abrashoff displayed individual consideration by meeting individually with all new recruits on the ship and asking three questions: "Why did he/she join the Navy? What's his/her family situation like? What are his/her goals while in the Navy—and beyond?" He said that getting to know the sailors as individuals and linking that knowledge to the vision for the ship was critical. He always treated the sailors with respect and dignity. For example, he had the ship's cooks train at culinary schools so that the food would be the best of any ship in the Navy. Furthermore, he created learning opportunities for the crew. He wanted the crew to take the time to thoroughly learn their jobs and develop the skills necessary for job success and promotion.

The *Benfold* achieved notable performance, both in terms of reduced maintenance and repair budgets and in terms of combat-readiness indicators such as gunnery scores. At one point, the ship was considered the best in the U.S. Navy's Pacific Fleet, and it was awarded the prestigious Spokane Trophy. Furthermore, the commitment and satisfaction of the crew was quite high. One hundred percent of the crew signed up for a second tour of duty (the average for the Navy at the time was 54 percent).

Systematic research on transformational leadership is still being conducted. However, several conclusions have become apparent. First, leaders can be trained to exhibit transformational leadership behaviors.[53] Second, leaders can display both transformational and transactional leadership styles.[54] William Bratton provides a clear example of this. While exhibiting many charismatic qualities and decentralizing authority (transformational leadership), he also closely monitored officers' performance and rewarded or punished that performance accordingly (transactional leadership). Likewise, Maria Yee provides a clear example. While inspiring a shared vision and empowering individuals to make decisions (transformational leadership), she has also rewarded key performers and generally held people accountable (transactional leadership).

Third, both transformational and transactional leadership can be positive.[55] Transactional leadership has been associated with follower satisfaction, commitment, performance, and in some cases organizational citizenship (contingent reward behavior appears to be more positive than active management by exception).[56] Transformational leadership has also been linked to follower satisfaction and commitment, unit performance, organizational performance, and individual performance.[57] There are some differences. For example, the effects of transformational leadership seem to be stronger at the unit level than at the individual level (collective unit outcomes versus the outcomes of individuals). Furthermore, transformational leaders are viewed as better leaders by their followers and are more likely to enhance the self-concepts of followers.[58] This can pay important dividends in terms of confidence and sustained efforts. Finally, transformational leaders seem to be more effective in bringing about significant change in a unit or organization,[59] which explains why this form of leadership receives so much attention in today's fast-paced world. By focusing on shared visions of the future and collective interests, transformational leaders promote change.[60]

A unique study used historical data to assess U.S. presidents' charismatic leadership (part of transformational leadership). The study found that presidential charisma was positively related to presidential performance (measured by the impact of the president's decisions and various ratings by historians).[61] Another particularly interesting study found that the market value (stock price) of companies led by charismatic leaders was higher than the market value of other companies. This study also found that external stakeholders were more likely to make larger investments in a firm led by a charismatic leader than in firms whose leaders did not display charismatic qualities.[62] In another study, transformational leaders positively affected the outcomes of a strategic acquisition.[63] Because diversification and growth strategies often involve acquisitions of other firms, this is an important finding. As mentioned, however, it appears that both types of leadership can be effective; the organizational context may determine which one should be emphasized.[64] Transactional leadership perhaps should be a greater part of the leadership mix in stable situations, where significant change is not required. Transformational leadership perhaps should be a greater part of the mix in more dynamic situations, where associates must perform outside of explicit expectations, in terms of either providing extraordinary effort or being innovative. Overall, though, an integration of transformational and transactional leadership approaches seems to provide the most effective leadership strategy.[65] The basic relationships are shown in Exhibit 8-5.

Very recently, transformational leadership theory has been put to use in the pursuit of more ethical behavior in organizations. We describe this work in the *Experiencing Organizational Behavior* feature.

The scandals described in the *Experiencing Organizational Behavior* feature dramatically illustrate the effects of leaders on the performance of an organization. Unfortunately, they show the negative effects of leadership. The leaders at Enron, for example, destroyed all value in a multibillion-dollar corporation, and many people lost their jobs and all retirement savings because of the unethical leadership.

Additional Topics of Current Relevance

In closing our discussion of leadership, we cover several additional topics relevant to leading in today's workplaces. We discuss leader–member exchange, servant leadership, gender effects on leadership, and global differences in leadership.

Ethical Leadership? Authentic Leadership!

The twenty-first century seems to have brought an all-time low in ethical behavior by corporate leaders. A record number of top executives have been caught in outrageous scandals, leading to a large drop in public confidence in business leadership. Here are some examples:

- In one of the most widely reported scandals, numerous Enron executives—including former CEO Kenneth Lay; former COO, president, and CEO Jeffrey Skilling; and former CFO Andrew Fastow—were indicted on various charges, including conspiracy, fraud, and money laundering. Fastow alone was indicted on 788 charges and was sentenced to a 10-year prison term in return for pleading guilty to conspiracy and agreeing to help prosecutors with the rest of the cases. Enron declared bankruptcy in December 2001—the scandal involved, among other things, outrageous attempts to cover up the company's poor performance. Arthur Andersen LLP, the accounting firm that served as Enron's auditor, was convicted in June 2002 of obstruction of justice for destroying Enron documents. The Enron fiasco had a terrible financial impact on thousands of employees, who had most of their retirement in Enron stock, as well as on shareholders and on the company's creditors, who have received little of what they are owed.

- Samuel D. Waksal, founder of ImClone Systems, pleaded guilty in October 2002 to charges of securities fraud, perjury, and obstruction of justice. He played a major role in the flurry of stock sales that occurred after he learned that the Food and Drug Administration was not going to approve one of ImClone's new cancer drugs.

- The Waksal case led to the even-more-publicized trial of Martha Stewart, the popular lifestyle guru, who stood trial on charges related to her sale of ImClone stock. As part of the trial, many personally embarrassing details about Stewart's behavior were revealed (e.g., her tendency to treat employees badly). She was convicted and sent to prison.

- Bernard Madoff was jailed in 2009 for running a giant Ponzi scheme that cost investors billions of dollars. Paying earlier investors with the money of later investors rather than generating actual investment returns has been a popular crime over the years, but the scale of Madoff's fraud was epic. Charities that had entrusted funds to Madoff were among the hardest hit. Several had to close their doors. Retirees were also hard hit.

- In an alleged Ponzi scheme, financier R. Allen Stanford of the Stanford Financial Group was indicted in 2009. Laura Pendergest-Holt, the firm's chief investment officer, was also indicted not only for possible involvement in the Ponzi scheme but also for obstruction of justice. Billions of investor dollars have been lost.

©Stan Honda/AFP/Getty Images, Inc.

The large number of scandals (and there were many more than reported here) has led to a public outcry demanding that the management community, including business schools, place more emphasis on the ethical behavior of leaders. In response to this demand, new conceptualizations of leadership have been advanced. One such conceptualization is authentic leadership, proposed by Fred Luthans and Bruce Avolio.

Building on the research regarding transformational leadership, which partially addresses the quality of moral behavior, Luthans and Avolio posit the need to focus attention on developing leaders who are not only transformational but also authentic. An authentic leader is someone who is genuine, trustworthy, and truthful. Authentic leaders "own" their thoughts, emotions, and beliefs and act according to their true selves. These leaders have the following qualities:

- They are guided by values that focus on doing what's right for their constituencies.

- They try to act in accordance with their values.
- They remain transparent. That is, they are aware of their own shortcomings and discuss these shortcomings with others. Others are free to question them.
- They "walk the talk." That is, they model confidence, hope, optimism, and resiliency.

- They place equal weight on getting the task accomplished and developing associates.
- They continuously develop themselves.
- They have developed the values and personal strength they need to deal with ambiguous ethical issues.

The concept of authentic leadership is important in today's complex business environment. Future

leadership development and training should encompass authentic qualities so that leaders will be less likely to succumb to greed and dishonesty. Perhaps with this new stage in leadership development, images of executives from major companies being led away in handcuffs and innocent people being emotionally and financially devastated by corporate corruption will be a less common sight!

Sources: Associated Press, "Timeline of Events in Enron Scandal," press release, Feb. 19, 2004; A. Efrati, T. Lauricella, & D. Searcey. 2008. "Top Broker Accused of $50 Billion Fraud," *Wall Street Journal*, Dec. 12, p. A.1; B. George, P. Sims, A. McLean, & D. Mayer. 2007. "Discovering Your Authentic Leadership," *Harvard Business Review*, 85, pp. 129–138; F. Luthans & B.J. Avolio. 2003 "Authentic Leadership," in K.S. Cameron, J.E. Dutton, & R.E. Quinn (Eds.), *Positive Organizational Scholarship* San Francisco: Berrett-Koehler; E. Perez, & S. Stecklow. 2009. "Stanford is Indicted in Fraud, Surrenders," *Wall Street Journal*, June 19, p. C.1; "The Perp Walk," *BusinessWeek Online*, Jan. 13, 2003, at http://www.businessweek.com/print/magazine/content/03_02/bb3815660.htm.

Leader–Member Exchange

leader–member exchange
A model of leadership focused on leaders developing more positive relationships with some individuals and having more positive exchanges with these individuals.

The **leader–member exchange** (LMX) model builds on a simple idea: leaders develop different relationships with different followers.[66] A leader develops positive relationships with some followers but develops less positive relationships with others. An individual's ability to contribute at a high level is one factor that determines the relationship with the leader. An individual's similarity to the leader, in terms of personality and interests, is another factor.[67]

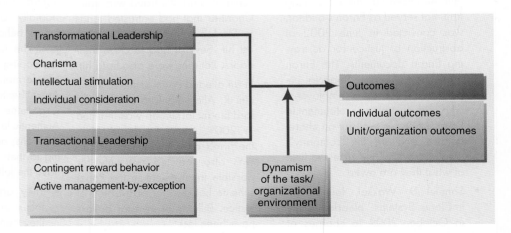

Exhibit 8-5 The Effects of Transformational and Transactional Leadership

Individuals who have positive relationships with the leader are members of an in-group. They experience leader–member exchange characterized by mutual trust, mutual support, and the provision of substantial resources. Individuals who have less positive relationships with the leader are members of an out-group. They experience out-group leader–member exchange characterized by more formality, less respect, lack of mutual support, and fewer opportunities for growth. Research on the LMX model indicates that members of an out-group tend to have lower levels of satisfaction, commitment, and performance.[68]

The existence of an out-group is inconsistent with high-involvement management. The high-involvement approach requires selection and retention of qualified individuals, proper training and coaching for each of them, and meaningful work for each of them. This is not simply a moral imperative. As explained in Chapter 1, organizational performance is at stake. Leaders should provide opportunities for all employees, or at least for as many as possible.

Servant Leadership

Similar to authentic leadership, **servant leadership** overlaps with the transformational tradition.[69] It includes elements such as valuing individuals, developing people, building community, conceptualizing, exhibiting foresight, and displaying wisdom.[70] Its distinctive focus, however, lies with an emphasis on serving others, both inside and outside the organization. Servant leaders want to serve others. They want to serve those who follow them. Their self-concepts are those of servants rather than leaders. And they often do not seek out leadership roles. Rather, such roles are thrust upon them.

servant leadership
An approach to leadership focused on serving others.

Max De Pree, former CEO of Herman Miller, often told a story that illustrates the key idea. In his words:

> I arrived at the local tennis club just after high school students had vacated the locker room. Like chickens, they had not bothered to pick up after themselves. Without thinking too much about it, I gathered up all their towels and put them in a hamper. A friend of mine quietly watched me do this and then asked me a question that I've pondered many times over the years. "Do you pick up towels because you're the president of the company? Or are you the president because you pick up towels?"[71]

The premise of the first question is more consistent with servant leadership. It suggests a mentality of "I am the leader, therefore I serve," rather than "I am the leader, therefore I lead."[72]

Systematic research into the effects of servant leadership is very limited. Even so, the research that is available suggests positive effects on associates' job satisfaction and commitment to the organization.[73] James Blanchard, former CEO of Synovus Financial Corporation, put it this way:

> The heart of the servant-leader brings order, brings meaning to employees. When employees feel order and meaning and that they are part of a team that stands for something good, that there is a higher calling than just working to get a paycheck, that they are improving mankind, there is an energy level that explodes and great things happen.[74]

Gender Effects on Leadership

Do women lead differently relative to men? Given the increase in the number of women in the U.S. workforce since the 1970s and the concern over the glass ceiling facing women who wish to advance in U.S. corporations,[75] it is not surprising that a great deal of attention has been focused on this question. For over three decades, researchers have investigated the issue of gender and leadership, and this research has been characterized by a great deal of debate.[76] There are reasons to believe that women often lead differently (for better or worse) than men, and there are also reasons to expect no differences in how men and women lead, particularly in U.S. work organizations.

One argument suggesting that women and men behave differently as leaders is referred to as the **structural–cultural model** of leader behavior.[77] This model suggests that because women often experience lack of power, lack of respect, and certain stereotypical expectations that result from cultural norms and stereotypes, they must behave differently from men to be effective leaders.[78] For example, followers are likely to expect different behaviors from women than from men. Thus, a female leader who acts aggressively might be viewed as mean-spirited or overly emotional, whereas a man behaving in the same way might be thought of as strong, confident, or passionate. Women may also be pressured to conform to certain gender-role stereotypes, such as being more interpersonally oriented and nurturing.[79] In essence, they are required to find a way to lead while making associates comfortable by exhibiting behavior consistent with gender-role stereotypes. Women who do this will not necessarily be less effective leaders because, as we discussed above, the effectiveness of specific leader behaviors depends on situational factors. Therefore, when the situation calls for a leader who emphasizes concern and caring for followers, women exhibiting nurturing behavior and strong interpersonal skills are likely to be effective and perhaps will be better at leading than men.[80]

In contrast, the **socialization model** suggests that there should be no differences in the way male and female leaders behave.[81] According to this argument, when all newcomers enter an organization, they are socialized into the organization's norms and accepted ways of behaving. Regardless of gender, all who advance to leadership positions have experienced the same organizational socialization and therefore are likely to display similar leader behaviors.[82] Therefore, women and men who have advanced into leadership positions will behave in the same way in a given organization. Across all organizations, both women and men will display a variety of behaviors.

Research evidence exists for both points of view. On the one hand, some studies have found that women display more interpersonal and social behaviors in small groups assembled as part of formal experiments, whereas men display more task-oriented behaviors.[83] Other studies have found women to be more democratic and participative than men in both experimental situations and in real organizations.[84] On the other hand, some research examining female leaders in organizational work settings has found no differences in the way male and female leaders behave.[85] Interestingly, in one study of almost 700 middle-level and executive managers, female managers and executives engaged more frequently in both stereotypical female behaviors (interpersonal behaviors) and stereotypical male behaviors (task-oriented behaviors).[86] In this case, the organization highly valued both types of behaviors—and it appeared that female leaders had to demonstrate those behaviors to a greater degree than did men. In conclusion, answering the question of whether women and men lead differently is not simple.[87] Overall, a number of studies support the idea that some stereotypical differences exist among managers, but the evidence is not quite as clear as we would like it to be. Moreover, studies that are supportive of this idea tend to reveal differences that are quite small in magnitude (i.e., women and men might differ but only to a small degree).

structural–cultural model

A model holding that because women often experience lack of power, lack of respect, and certain stereotypical expectations, they develop leadership styles different from those of the men.

socialization model

A model proposing that all leaders in a particular organization will display similar leadership styles, because all have been selected and socialized by the same organization.

The arguments concerning the differences or lack thereof between male and female leaders could be extended to differences between racial/ethnic minority leaders and white majority leaders. However, less research has been done on this issue than on gender differences. Results tend to show weak differences or no differences.[88] However, to address this issue more fully we need to better understand glass-ceiling issues that also affect racial/ethnic minority group members.

©AP/Wide World Photos

Global Differences in Leadership

As discussed in greater detail in Chapters 2 and 3, the U.S. workforce has become more diverse. In particular, globalization has produced situations in which U.S. managers lead associates socialized in different cultures, international managers lead U.S. associates, and work groups are made up of people from different cultures who must work together. Most of the theories and findings discussed so far in this chapter have focused primarily on the North American workforce, which values participation in decision making, narrow power distance (power should be equally shared), a high-performance orientation (people should be rewarded for good performance), significant individualism, and reasonably strong orientation toward the future (planning, investing, delaying gratification).[89] We can easily understand why leaders who are charismatic, engender participation, and provide relevant rewards for high performance are effective with this workforce.

But what happens in a culture that values collectivism (i.e., the group is viewed as more important than individuals) or has a high power distance (where people believe that power should be hierarchically distributed)? Such views are common in Arabic cultures such as Egypt and Morocco.[90] Would effective leadership take a different form? Or are there universal truths about what makes a good leader? As Michael Marks, CEO of Flextronics, a multinational manufacturing company, points out, "I have learned that in every place we operate, in every country, the people want to do a good job [and] there is no place where people can't do a world class job. ... This isn't to say we approach every region with cookie-cutter uniformity."[91]

The U.S. National Science Foundation funded a worldwide project, headed by Robert House, to examine whether leadership differs across different cultures and whether the effectiveness of different types of leadership varies by culture. This study is referred to as the *GLOBE* project (Global Leadership and Organizational Behavior Effectiveness).[92] It was first introduced in Chapter 3. Findings from the GLOBE project, based on surveys of thousands of people, cluster countries into groups with shared histories and values. Below is a description of the ideal leader for four cultural clusters:

1. *Anglo cluster*[93] (Australia, Canada, England, Ireland, New Zealand, South Africa [white sample], and United States): The ideal leader demonstrates charismatic influence and inspiration while encouraging participation. Ideal leaders are viewed as being diplomatic, delegating authority, and allowing everyone to have their say.

2. *Arabic Cluster*[94] (Egypt, Morocco, Kuwait, and Qatar, with Turkey also being included with these Arabic countries): Ideal leaders need to balance a paradoxical set of expectations. On one hand, they are expected to be charismatic and powerful, but on the other, they are expected not to differentiate themselves from others and to have modest styles. Leaders are also expected to have a great deal of power and to direct most decisions and actions.

3. *Germanic cluster*[95] (Austria, Germany, the Netherlands, and Switzerland): The ideal leader is one who is charismatic and participative, and who conceptualizes her relationships in a team-like fashion.

THE STRATEGIC LENS

Leadership is a critically important concept in organizational behavior and equally important for the performance of organizations. As demonstrated in this chapter, leaders have direct and strong effects on the performance of the individuals and teams they lead. At all levels in the organization, leaders often have major goals for performance, and they provide the context and take actions that affect and support efforts to achieve those goals. Leaders at the top of organizations, with input from lower-level leaders and associates, establish the strategies designed to achieve the organization's overall goals. Furthermore, the actual achievement of those goals is based strongly on the quality of the leadership they and other leaders throughout the organization provide in the implementation of strategies. In such implementations, leaders may need to be directive while simultaneously exhibiting compassion for their associates.

For strategies to be effective, they need to be formulated and implemented within a context of appropriate organizational values and with a working knowledge of the global environment. In addition, organizational strategies can be more effectively implemented when the value of diversity is understood and used to advantage. Research has shown that entering international markets with current products helps the firm achieve economies of scale (reduces the cost for each product sold), but selling goods in international markets has additional benefits that are even greater. For example, organizations operating in international markets often gain access to new knowledge. People from different cultures develop different ways of thinking and operating. As a result, leaders can obtain new ideas from employees, customers, and suppliers in international markets and incorporate them into their domestic operations and other foreign operations as well.[99]

International operations provide an excellent opportunity to gain benefits from diversity, as discussed in Chapters 2 and 3. For example, some firms develop teams composed of people from multiple ethnic and cultural backgrounds. With effective leadership, these heterogeneous teams often produce more creative ideas and solutions to problems. Also, they can better understand diverse customers and satisfy their needs.[100] Although the global context is complex, effective leadership adjusts to it and uses the multicultural environments to benefit the organization. Thus, leaders who espouse and exhibit ethical values, understand and use a diverse workforce to benefit the organization, and adapt to and extract knowledge from different environments in international markets contribute to an organization's capability to achieve and sustain a competitive advantage. These leadership characteristics contribute to the formulation of better strategies and to more effective implementation of those strategies.[101]

Critical Thinking Questions

1. How should leaders approach individuals, units, and organizations suffering from poor performance?

2. Why is ethical leadership often of utmost importance to various stakeholders?

3. Should women and men lead in different ways?

4. *Southern Asia cluster*[96] (India, Indonesia, Iran, Malaysia, Philippines, and Thailand): The ideal leader is humane, participative, and charismatic. Leaders are expected to be benevolent while maintaining a strong position of authority.

The findings from the GLOBE project suggest that charismatic leadership is viewed as effective and desirable across all cultures. Other dimensions of leadership, such as participation, humaneness, and team orientation, vary in importance across cultures. As numerous CEOs of multinational firms have indicated,[97] today's managers need to develop the cultural sensitivity required to understand differences in leadership requirements across national boundaries and cultures in order to develop highly productive multinational workforces.[98]

What This Chapter Adds to Your Knowledge Portfolio

In this chapter, we have discussed ideas about what makes a leader effective. We have covered trait theories, behavioral theories, contingency theories, and transformational leadership theory. All of these theories are related and build on one another. In specific terms, the following points were made:

- Leadership is the process of providing general direction and influencing individuals or groups to achieve goals.
- Trait theories of leadership propose that a person must possess certain characteristics to become a leader. Older trait theories held that leaders were born, not made. More modern trait theories state that certain characteristics are necessary but not sufficient for a person to be an effective leader and that many leadership characteristics can be developed or learned. Eight core traits of leaders are drive, leadership motivation, integrity, self-confidence, cognitive ability, knowledge of the relevant domain, openness to new experiences, and extraversion. Charisma may also be important.
- The Michigan studies focused on two distinct behavioral leadership styles—job-centered and employee-centered. The job-centered leader emphasizes tasks and the methods used to accomplish them. The employee-centered leader emphasizes employees and their needs and the development of interpersonal relationships. Research on which style is more effective has been inconclusive.
- The Ohio State studies focused on two dimensions of leader behavior: initiating structure and consideration. Leaders exhibiting initiating structure establish well-defined patterns of structure and communication, defining both the work activities and the relationship between leaders and subordinates. A leader showing consideration expresses friendship and develops mutual trust and strong interpersonal relationships with subordinates. Leaders may possess any combination of these two dimensions. Early research indicated that leaders exhibiting high levels of both initiating structure and consideration were most effective. However, later research showed that leadership effectiveness is more complex than this simple idea suggests.
- Fiedler's contingency model of leadership suggests that effectiveness depends on the match between a leader's style and the degree of favorableness of the situation. The important situational characteristics in this model are leader–member relations, task structure, and the leader's position power. Situational favorableness is determined by the amount of control a leader has. Fiedler's research indicates

❓ back to the knowledge objectives

1. What is leadership, and why is it important for organizations?
2. Are leaders born or made? Explain your answer. What are the core traits possessed by effective leaders?
3. Considering the findings from the Michigan and Ohio State studies, what do you think is the most effective leadership style? Give reasons to support your choice.
4. What key situational variables are related to leadership effectiveness in Fiedler's model of leadership effectiveness and in the path–goal model of leadership? In what ways do contingency models fall short in specifying a complete picture of effective leadership?
5. How do transformational and transactional leaders differ? What kind of results can be expected from each type of leader?
6. How do the leader–member exchange and servant–leadership models differ?
7. Explain why male and female leaders might engage in different leadership behaviors. What does the evidence show with respect to differences in leadership?
8. Describe the characteristics of an effective leader in each of the following clusters of countries: Anglo, Arabic, Germanic, and Southern Asia.

that task-oriented leaders are more effective in highly favorable or highly unfavorable situations, whereas relationship-oriented leaders are more effective in situations of intermediate favorableness. Fiedler's model has been criticized, but it is one of the first contingency concepts proposed and is supported by some research.

- The path–goal leadership model proposed by Robert House is based on the expectancy concept of motivation. Leaders positively influence individuals by enhancing their beliefs about the attainability of goals, giving consistent rewards for task-goal achievement, and assigning tasks that have valuable rewards for people being managed. Research has provided support for many of the specific predictions of the theory.

- Transformational leadership has been the subject of recent attention. Transactional leaders, who provide a useful contrast to transformational leaders, provide clear expectations and reward or punish followers based on their performance. Followers comply with leaders' wishes to gain desired rewards. Transformational leaders motivate followers to do more than expected, to continuously develop and grow, to build up their own confidence, and to put the interests of the team or organization before their own. They display charisma, intellectual stimulation, and individual consideration of followers. Research shows that both types of leadership can be positive and even necessary, with the appropriate degree of emphasis on each varying with the context (stable versus dynamic situations).

- Leader–member exchange is focused on the nature of the relationship between a leader and an individual in his unit/organization. When a positive relationship exists, the individual is a member of an in-group and experiences positive interactions. When a less positive relationship exists, the individual is a member of an out-group and experiences less positive interactions. Research shows that out-group members have lower satisfaction, commitment, and performance.

- Servant leadership means serving others. Research has been scant, but a number of individuals report success with the approach.

- Whereas the structural–cultural model suggests that there are significant differences in the leadership styles used by men and women, the socialization model holds that men and women experience the same organizational socialization and therefore exhibit the same leadership behaviors in U.S. work organizations. Research is mixed.

- The globalization of business has helped us understand that leaders must exhibit different styles to be effective in different regions of the world. For example, in the

Anglo region, the ideal leader demonstrates charismatic influence and inspiration while encouraging participation, whereas in the Arabic region leaders are expected to have a great deal of power and to direct most decisions and actions.

Key Terms

leadership, p. 268
job-centered leadership style, p. 272
employee-centered leadership style, p. 272
initiating structure, p. 273
consideration, p. 273
contingency theory of leadership effectiveness, p. 274
leader–member relations, p. 275
task structure, p. 275
position power, p. 275
path–goal leadership theory, p. 277
directive leadership, p. 278
supportive leadership, p. 278
achievement-oriented leadership, p. 278
participative leadership, p. 278
transactional leadership, p. 281
transformational leadership, p. 281
charisma, p. 282
leader–member exchange, p. 286
servant leadership, p. 287
structural–cultural model, p. 288
socialization model, p. 288

building your human capital

Are You a Transformational Leader?

Individuals lead in different ways. Understanding your own leadership behavior is very useful in assessing its appropriateness. In this chapter's *Building Your Human Capital,* we provide an assessment tool for transformational, transactional, and laissez-faire leadership.

Instructions

If you currently hold or have recently held a leadership position, ask several individuals who have experienced your leadership to respond to the questions that appear below. Your leadership position could involve managing a formal work unit in a company, leading a temporary team in an organization, being captain of an intramural basketball team, being pledge chairwoman for a sorority, and so on. If you do not have recent leadership experience, then complete a self-assessment, being very honest with yourself about the behaviors that you probably would exhibit in a future leadership role. Alternatively, you could complete the assessment with another leader in mind (i.e., rate someone who has been a leader for a unit or organization in which you have been a member).

For each item, tell your respondents to rate the frequency with which you engage in the behavior described. Also tell them that few people have extreme scores (low or high) on all or even most items (a "1" or a "4" is an extreme score). Have each respondent circle the appropriate number beside the item, using the following scale (note that "L" stands for Leader):

1	2	3	4
Never	Infrequently	Frequently	Always

1. L goes beyond self-interest.	1	2	3	4
2. L has my respect.	1	2	3	4
3. L displays power and confidence.	1	2	3	4

4. L talks of values.	1	2	3	4
5. L models integrity.	1	2	3	4
6. L considers the integrity dimension of situations.	1	2	3	4
7. L emphasizes the collective mission.	1	2	3	4
8. L talks optimistically.	1	2	3	4
9. L expresses confidence.	1	2	3	4
10. L talks enthusiastically.	1	2	3	4
11. L arouses awareness about important issues.	1	2	3	4
12. L reexamines assumptions.	1	2	3	4
13. L seeks different views.	1	2	3	4
14. L suggests new ways.	1	2	3	4
15. L suggests different angles.	1	2	3	4
16. L individualizes attention.	1	2	3	4
17. L focuses on your strengths.	1	2	3	4
18. L teaches and coaches.	1	2	3	4
19. L differentiates among us.	1	2	3	4
20. L clarifies rewards.	1	2	3	4
21. L assists based on effort.	1	2	3	4
22. L rewards your achievements.	1	2	3	4
23. L recognizes your achievements.	1	2	3	4
24. L focuses on your mistakes.	1	2	3	4
25. L puts out fires.	1	2	3	4
26. L tracks your mistakes.	1	2	3	4
27. L concentrates on failures.	1	2	3	4
28. L reacts to problems but only when very serious.	1	2	3	4
29. L reacts to only the biggest failures.	1	2	3	4
30. L displays a philosophy of "If it's not broke, don't fix it."	1	2	3	4
31. L reacts to problems, if chronic.	1	2	3	4
32. L avoids involvement.	1	2	3	4
33. L is absent when he or she is needed.	1	2	3	4
34. L avoids deciding.	1	2	3	4
35. L delays responding.	1	2	3	4

Scoring

Items 1–11: These items measure **charisma**. To calculate your score, sum the points given to you by each respondent and then divide by the number of respondents (i.e., calculate the average total score given by the respondents). If your score is above 29, then you display significant charisma. If the score is greater than 41, then you score very high on charisma.

Items 12–15: These items measure **intellectual stimulation**. If the total score for these items (averaged across respondents) is greater than 10, then you display significant intellectual stimulation. If the score is greater than 14, you score very high on intellectual stimulation.

Items 16–19: These items measure **individualized consideration**. If you scored higher than 11 (averaged across respondents), you display individual consideration to a significant degree. If the score is greater than 15, then you score very high on individual consideration.

Items 20–23: These items measure **contingent reward behavior**. If you scored higher than 10 (averaged across respondents), you display contingent reward behavior to a significant degree. If the score is greater than 14, then you score very high on contingent reward behavior.

Items 24–27: These items measure **management-by-exception behavior**. If you scored higher than 7 (averaged across respondents), you demonstrate management-by-exception behavior to a significant degree. If the score is greater than 11, then you score very high on management-by-exception behaviors.

Items 28–35: These items measure tendencies toward **laissez-faire** leadership. If you scored more than 8 (averaged across respondents), you display passive behavior to some degree. If the score is greater than 16, then you score very high on passive leadership.

Transformational leaders are characterized by charisma, intellectual stimulation, and individualized consideration. If you scored high on these three scales, then you are a good example of a transformational leader.

Transactional leaders provide contingent rewards and exhibit management-by-exception behaviors. If you scored high on these two scales, then you engage in transactional leadership. It is possible for a leader to be high on both transformational and transactional leadership.

Laissez-faire managers score high on avoidant/passive behaviors. If you scored high on the last set of items, then you are most likely a passive leader.

Source: Based on B.J. Avolio, B.M. Bass, and D.I. Jung. 1999. "Re-examining the Component of the Transformational and Transactional Leadership Using the Multifactor Leadership Questionnaire," *Journal of Occupational and Organizational Psychology*, 72: 441–462.

an organizational behavior moment
The Two Presidents

Frances Workman had been president of Willard University for less than two years, but during that time she had become very popular throughout the state. Frances was an excellent speaker and used every opportunity to speak to citizen groups statewide. She also worked hard to build good relationships with the major politicians and business leaders in the state. This was not easy, but she managed to maintain favorable relationships with most.

She also had worked on the internal structure of the organization, streamlining the administrative component. She started a new alumni club to help finance academic needs, such as new library facilities and higher salaries for faculty and staff. In addition, she lobbied the state legislature and the state university coordinating board for a larger share of the state's higher education budget dollars. Her favorable image in the state and her lobbying efforts resulted in large increases in state funding for Willard. Interestingly, Frances was so busy with external matters that she had little time to bother with the daily operations of the university. However, she did make the major operational decisions. She delegated the responsibility for daily operations to her three major vice presidents.

Before Frances's arrival, Willard University had several presidents, none of whom had been popular with the state's citizens or particularly effective in managing the university's internal affairs. The lack of leadership resulted in low faculty morale, which affected student enrollment. Willard had a poor public image. Frances worked hard to build a positive image, and she seemed to be succeeding.

Another state university, Eastern State, had Alvin Thomas as president. Al had been president about three years. He was not as popular externally as Frances. He was not a particularly effective speaker and did not spend much time dealing with the external affairs of the university. Al delegated much of that responsibility to a vice president. He did work with external groups but in a quieter and less conspicuous way than Frances did.

Al spent much of his time working on the internal operation of the university. When he arrived, he was not pleased to find that Eastern was under censure by the American Association of University Professors (AAUP) and that the university had a large number of students without adequate faculty. In addition, Eastern was not involved in externally funded research. Al was committed to developing a quality university. Although he did not change the fundamental administrative structure of Eastern, he did extend considerable responsibilities to each of his vice presidents. He had high performance expectations for those on his staff, set ambitious goals, and reviewed every significant decision made in the university, relying heavily on his vice presidents and deans to implement them effectively. He developed a thorough planning system, the first of its kind at Eastern. He maintained good relations with the board of regents, but faculty viewed him as somewhat "stilted" and indifferent.

Frances projected a positive image to people in the state and along with that had built a positive image of Willard. The results of her efforts included an increase in enrollment of more than a thousand students in the past year. This occurred when enrollments were declining for most other colleges and universities in the state. Willard received the largest budget increase ever from the state university coordinating board and the state legislature. Finally, the outside funds from her special alumni club totaled almost $2 million in its first year. Faculty morale was higher, but faculty members viewed Frances warily because of her external focus.

In contrast, Eastern received an average budget increase similar to those it had received in the past. Although Eastern still had more students than Willard, its student enrollment declined slightly (by almost 300 students). However, the university was removed from AAUP censure. Externally funded research had increased by approximately $2 million during the previous year. Faculty morale was declining, and most faculty members did not believe they had an important voice in the administration of the university.

Discussion Questions

1. Based on the information provided, describe Frances's and Al's leadership styles.
2. What are the important factors that the leaders of Willard and Eastern must consider in order to be effective?
3. Compare and contrast Frances's and Al's effectiveness as leaders of their respective universities. What did each do well? What could each have done to be more effective?

---

team exercise

Coping with People Problems

The purpose of this exercise is to develop a better understanding of leadership through participation in a role-play in which a leader must cope with an employee problem.

Procedure

1. Assemble into three-person teams.
2. Within each team, one person should be selected as Don Martinez, the manager; one person selected as John Williams, the subordinate; and one person as the observer.
3. Each person should read his or her role and prepare to role-play the situation (allow 10 minutes for reading and preparing for roles). Each person, except the observer, should read only the role assigned. The observer should read all role materials.
4. After preparation, each team will engage in the role-play for approximately 20 minutes.
5. Following the role-play, each observer will answer the relevant questions and prepare to discuss how the leader (Don Martinez) handled the subordinate's (John Williams') problem.
6. Reassemble as a class. Each observer will describe the leadership situation in his or her team.
7. The instructor will present additional points for consideration.

Role for Don Martinez

You are manager of material control for Xenex Corp. You have had the job for five years and have almost 15 years of managerial experience. You enjoy working at Xenex, although advancement opportunities have become somewhat limited in the firm and budget constraints have been nontrivial in recent months. Four supervisors report to you, and John Williams is one of them. John is supervisor of inventory control. He has 22 people under his direction and has held the position for nine years. He is a good supervisor, and his unit performance has never been a problem.

However, in recent weeks you've noticed that John seems to be in a bad mood. He doesn't smile and has snapped back at you a couple of times when you've made comments to him. Also, one of his lead persons in the warehouse quit last week and claimed John had been "riding" him for no apparent reason. You think there must be some problem (maybe at home) for John to act this way. It is uncharacteristic.

John made an appointment to see you today and you hope that you can discuss this problem with him. You certainly want to deal with the problem because John has been one of your best supervisors.

Role for John Williams

You have been supervisor for inventory control for Xenex Corp. for almost nine years. You've had this job since about six months after graduating from college. When you took the job, Xenex was much smaller, but the job was a real challenge for a young, inexperienced person. The job has grown in complexity and number of people supervised (now 22).

Don Martinez, your boss, is manager of material control. He has held the job for about five years. When he was selected for the position, you were a little disappointed that you were not promoted to it, because you had done a good job. However, you were young and needed more experience, as the director of manufacturing told you.

Overall, Don has been a fairly good manager, but he seems to have neglected you during the past couple of years. You have received good pay increases, but your job is boring now. It doesn't present any new challenges. You just turned 31 and have decided that it's time to move up or go elsewhere. In past performance-appraisal sessions, you tried to talk about personal development and your desire for a promotion, but Don seemed unresponsive.

You've decided that you must be aggressive. You have done a good job and don't want to stay in your present job forever. You believe that you have been overlooked and ignored and don't intend to allow that to continue.

The purpose of your meeting today is to inform Don that you want a promotion. If the company is unable or unwilling to meet your needs, you are prepared to leave. You intend to be aggressive.

Role for Observer

You are to observe the role-play with Don Martinez and John Williams without participating. Please respond to the following based on this role-play:

1. Briefly describe how the situation evolved between Don and John.

2. What leadership style did Don use in trying to deal with John?

3. How was the problem resolved?

4. How could Don have handled the situation more effectively?

Endnotes

1. Pfeffer, J., & Sutton, R.I. 2006. *Hard facts, dangerous half-truths, & total nonsense: Profiting from evidence based management.* Boston: Harvard Business School Press, pp. 187–214.

2. Waldman, D.A., Ramirez, G.C., House, R.J., & Puranam, P. 2001. Does leadership matter? CEO leadership attributes and probability under conditions of perceived environmental uncertainty. *Academy of Management Journal,* 44: 134–143.

3. Resick, C.J., Whitman, D.S., Weingarden, S.A., & Hiller, N.J. 2009. The bright-side and the dark-side of CEO personality: Examining core self-evaluations, narcissism, transformational leadership, and strategic influence. *Journal of Applied Psychology,* 94: 1365–1381.

4. Haapniemi, P. 2003. Leading indicators: The development of executive leadership. At http//www.ccl.org.

5. Finkelstein, S., & Hambrick, D. 1996. *Strategic leadership.* St Paul, MN: West Publishing Co.

6. For additional insights related to vision creation as an aspect of strategic leadership, see Ireland, R.D., & Hitt, M.A. 1999. Achieving and maintaining strategic competitiveness in the 21st century: The role of strategic leadership. *Academy of Management Executive,* 13(1): 43–57.

7. Hitt, M.A., & Ireland, R.D. 2002. The essence of strategic leadership: Managing human and social capital. *Journal of Leadership and Organizational Studies,* 9(1): 3–14.

8. Wesley, K.N., & Yukl, G.A. 1975. *Organizational behavior and industrial psychology.* New York: Oxford University Press, pp. 109–110.

9. Kouzes, J.M., & Posner, B.Z. 2002. *The leadership challenge.* San Francisco: Jossey-Bass.

10. Bennis, W. 1982. The artform of leadership. *Training and Development Journal,* 36(4): 44–46.

11. Kirkpatrick, S.A., & Locke, E.A. 1991. Leadership: Do traits matter? *Academy of Management Executive,* 5: 48–60.

12. Stogdill, R.M. 1974. *Handbook of leadership: A survey of theory and research.* New York: Free Press.

13. Judge, T.A., Piccolo, R.F., & Kosalka, T. 2009. The bright and dark sides of leader traits: A review and theoretical extension of the leader trait paradigm. *Leadership Quarterly,* 20: 855–875; Zaccaro, S.J. 2007. Trait-based perspectives of leadership. *American Psychologist,* 62: 6–16.

14. Kirkpatrick & Locke, Leadership: Do traits matter?

15. Our list of important traits is based heavily on the work of Kirkpatrick & Locke, Leadership: Do traits matter? It also reflects the following: Judge, T.A., Hono, J.E., Ilies, R., & Gerhardt, M.W. 2002. Personality and leadership: A qualitative and quantitative review. *Journal of Applied Psychology,* 87: 765–780; Judge, Piccolo, & Kosalka, The bright and dark sides of leader traits: A review and theoretical extension of the leader trait paradigm; Peterson, S.J., Walumbwa, F.O., Byron, K., & Myrowitz, J. 2009. CEO Positive psychological traits, transformational leadership, and firm performance in high-technology start-up and established firms. *Journal of Management,* 35: 348–368.

16. Bass, B.M., & Avolio, B.J. 1990. The implications of transactional and transformational leadership for individual, team, and organizational development. In W.A. Pasmore, & R.W. Woodman (Eds.), *Research in organizational change and development,* Vol. 4. Greenwich, CT: JAI Press, pp. 231–272; House, R.J., Spangler, W.D., & Woycke, J. 1991. Personality and charisma in the U.S. presidency: A psychological theory of leader effectiveness. *Administrative Science Quarterly,* 36: 364–396.

17. Likert, R. 1961. *New patterns of management.* New York: McGraw-Hill.

18. Stogdill, *Handbook of leadership.*

19. Judge, T.A., Piccolo, R.F., & Illies, R. 2004. The forgotten ones? The validity of consideration and initiating structure in leadership research. *Journal of Applied Psychology,* 89: 36–51.

20. Fiedler, F.E. 1967. *A theory of leadership effectiveness.* New York, NY: McGraw-Hill.

21. Ibid.

22. For additional information on situational factors, see Fiedler, F.E. 1993. The leadership situation and the black box in contingency theories. In M.M. Chemers, & R.Y. Ayman (Eds.), *Leadership theory and research: Perspectives and directions.* New York, NY: Academic Press, pp. 2–28.

23. Fiedler, F.E. 1971. Validation and extension of the contingency model of leadership effectiveness: A review of empirical findings. *Psychological Bulletin,* 76: 128–148.

24. Fiedler, F.E. 1972. Personality, motivational systems, and behavior of high and low LPC persons. *Human Relations,* 25: 391–412.

25. Chemers, M.M., & Skrzypek, C.J. 1972. Experimental test of the contingency model of leadership effectiveness. *Journal of Personality and Social Psychology,* 24: 173–177; Fiedler, F.E., & Chemers, M.M. 1972. *Leadership and effective management.* Glenview, IL: Scott, Foresman.

26. Groysberg, B., McLean, N., & Nohria, N. 2006. Are leaders portable? *Harvard Business Review,* 84 (5): 92–100.

27. For meta-analyses of LPC research, see Peters, L.H., Hartke, D.D., & Pohlmann, J.T. 1985. Fiedler's contingency theory of leadership: An application of the meta-analysis procedures of Schmidt and Hunter. *Psychological Bulletin,* 97: 274–285; Schriesheim, C.A., Tepper, B.J., & Tetrault, L.A. 1994. Least-preferred co-worker score, situational control, and leadership effectiveness: A meta-analysis of contingency model performance predictions. *Journal of Applied Psychology,* 79: 561–573.

28. Kennedy, J.K. 1982. Middle LPC leaders and the contingency model of leadership effectiveness. *Organizational Behavior and Human Performance,* 30: 1–14.

29. Green, S.C., & Nebeker, D.M. 1977. The effects of situational factors and leadership style on leader behavior. *Organizational Behavior and Human Performance,* 20: 368–377; Hare, A.P., Hare, S.E., & Blumberg, H.H. 1998. Wishful thinking: Who has the least preferred co-worker? *Small Group Research,* 29: 419–435; Shiflett, S. 1981. Is there a problem with the LPC score in leader match? *Personnel Psychology,* 34: 765–769; Singh, B. 1983. Leadership style and reward allocation: Does Least Preferred Co-Worker scale measure task and relation orientation? *Organizational Behavior and Human Performance,* 32: 178–197.

30. Rice, R.W. 1981. Leader LPC and follower satisfaction: A review. *Organizational Behavior and Human Performance,* 28: 1–25.

31. Evans, M.C. 1970. The effects of supervisory behavior on the path-goal relationship. *Organizational Behavior and Human Performance,* 7: 277–298.

32. House, R.J. 1971. A path-goal theory of leadership effectiveness. *Administrative Science Quarterly,* 16: 321–338.

33. Liden, R.C., & Antonakis, J. 2009. Considering context in psychological leadership research. *Human Relations,* 62: 1587–1605.

34. For work that followed the original specification of the theory, see: Fulk, J., & Wendler, E.R. 1982. Dimensionality of leader-subordinate interactions: A path-goal investigation. *Organizational Behavior and Human Performance,* 30: 241–264; House, R.J., & Mitchell, T.R. 1974. Path-goal theory of leadership. *Journal of Contemporary Business,* 3: 81–99; Podsakoff, P.M., Todor, W.D., Grover, R.A., & Huber, V.L. 1984. Situational moderators of leader reward and punishment behaviors: Fact or fiction? *Organizational Behavior and Human Performance,* 34: 21–63.

35. For a quantitative synthesis of research, see: Wofford, J.C., & Liska, L.Z. 1993. Path-goal theories of leadership: A meta-analysis. *Journal of Management,* 19: 857–876. For a supportive study in Taiwan, see: Silverthorne, C. 2001. A test of path-goal leadership theory in Taiwan. *Leadership and Organizational Development Journal,* 22: 151–158.

36. For additional insight on the mixed results, see: House, R.J. 1996. Path-goal theory of leadership effectiveness: Lessons, legacy, and a reformulated theory. *Leadership Quarterly,* 7: 305–309.

37. For additional insight, see: House, R.J., & Dessler, G.A. 1974. Path-goal theory of leadership: Some post hoc and a priori tests. In J.G. Hunt & L.L. Larsen (Eds.), *Contingency approaches to leadership.* Carbondale: Southern Illinois University Press, pp. 29–59.

38. For additional insight, see: Griffin, R.W. 1979. Task design determinants of effective leader behavior. *Academy of Management Review,* 4: 215–224; and Johnsen, A.L., Luthans, F., & Hennessey, H.W. 1984. The role of locus of control in leader influence behavior. *Personnel Psychology,* 37: 61–75.

39. Podsakoff, P.M., MacKenzie, S.B., Ahearne, M., & Bommer, W.H. 1995. Searching for a needle in a haystack: Trying to identify illusive moderators of leadership behaviors. *Journal of Management,* 21: 422–470.

40. For details of one framework emphasizing this point, see: Hersey, P., & Blanchard, K.H. 1988. *Management of organizational behavior: Utilizing human resources* (5th ed.). Englewood Cliffs, NJ: Prentice Hall.

41. See, for example: Schriesheim, C.A., Castro, S.L., Zhou, X., & DeChurch, L.A. 2006. An investigation of path-goal and transformational leadership theory at the individual level of analysis. *Leadership Quarterly,* 17: 21–38.

42. For related commentary from the key figure in path-goal theory, see: House, R.J. 1999. Weber and the neocharismatic paradigm. *Leadership Quarterly,* 10: 563–574.

43. Bass & Avolio, The implications of transactional and transformational leadership for individual, team, and organizational development; Whittington, J.L., Coker, R.H., Goodwin, V.L., Ickes, W. 2009. Transactional leadership revisited: Self-other agreement and its consequences. *Journal of Applied Social Psychology,* 39: 1860–1886.

44. Bass, B.M. 1985. *Leadership and performance beyond expectations.* New York: Free Press.

45. Bass & Avolio, The implications of transactional and transformational leadership for individual, team, and organizational development.

46. Bass, *Leadership and performance beyond expectations;* Bass & Avolio, The implications of transactional and transformational leadership for individual, team, and organizational development.

47. Others have specified four or more characteristics, but our three are grounded in the original work and have proven useful. For additional details, see: Judge, T.A., & Piccolo, R.F. 2004. Transformational and transactional leadership: A meta-analytic test of their relative validity. *Journal of Applied Psychology,* 89: 755–768; Rafferty, A.E., & Griffin, M.A. 2004. Dimensions of transformational leadership: Conceptual and empirical extensions. *Leadership Quarterly,* 15: 329–354.

48. Charisma has been studied as a standalone concept by a number of researchers and has spawned its own research tradition. It is, however, an integral part of the broader concept of transformational leadership. For details of the origins of charismatic leadership research, see House, R.J. 1977. A 1976 theory of charismatic leadership. In J.G. Hunt, & L.L. Larsen (Eds.), *Leadership: The cutting edge.* Carbondale, IL: South Illinois University Press, pp. 189–207. For example research studies, see: Howell, J.M., & Hall-Merenda, K.E. 1989. A laboratory study of charismatic leadership. *Organizational Behavior and Human Decision Process,* 43: 243–269; Shamir, B., Zakay, E., Breinin, E., & Popper, M. 1998. Correlates of charismatic leader behavior in military units: Subordinates' attitudes, unit characteristics, and superiors' appraisals of leader performance. *Academy of Management Journal,* 41: 387–409.

49. Yukl, G., & Van Fleet, D.D. 1992. Theory and research on leadership in organizations. In M.D. Dunnette & L.M. Hough (Eds.), *Handbook of industrial and organizational psychology* (2nd Ed.), Vol. 3. Palo Alto, CA: Consulting Psychologists Press, pp. 147–197.

50. Avolio, B.J., Bass, B.M., & Jung, D.I. 1999. Re-examining the components of transformational and transactional leadership using the Multifactor Leadership Questionnaire. *Journal of Occupational and Organizational Psychology,* 72: 441–462.

51. Hinkin, T.R., & Schriesheim, C.A. 2008. An examination of "nonleadership": From laissez-faire leadership to leader reward omission and punishment omission." *Journal of Applied Psychology,* 93: 1234–1248; Judge & Piccolo, Transformational and transactional research; Skogstad, A., Einarsen, S., Torsheim, T., Assland, M.S., & Hetland, H. 2007. The destructiveness of laissez-faire leadership behavior. *Journal of Occupational Health Psychology,* 12: 80–92.

52. LaBarre, P. 1999. The agenda–Grass roots leadership. *Fast Company,* 23 (April): 114–120.

53. Bass & Avolio, The implications of transactional and transformational leadership for individual, team, and organizational development.

54. Bass, B.M., Avolio, B.J., Jung, D.I., & Berson, Y. 2003. Predicting unit performance by assessing transformational and transactional leadership. *Journal of Applied Psychology,* 88: 207–218.

55. Bass, Avolio, Jung, & Berson, Predicting unit performance by assessing transformational and transactional leadership; DeGroot, T., Kiker, D.S., & Cross, T.C. 2000. A meta-analysis to review organizational outcomes related to charismatic leadership. *Canadian Journal of Administrative Sciences,* 17: 356–371; Judge & Piccolo, Transformational and transactional research; Lowe, K.B., Kroeck, K.G., & Sivasubramaniam, N. 1996. Effectiveness correlates of transformational and transactional leadership: A meta-analytic review. *Leadership Quarterly,* 7: 385–425.

56. Lowe, Kroeck, & Sivasubramaniam, Effectiveness correlates of transformational and transactional leadership; Podsakoff, P.M., Bommer, W.H., Podsakoff, N.P., & MacKenzie, S.B. 2006. Relationships between leader reward and punishment behaviour and subordinate attitudes, perceptions, and behaviors: A meta-analytic review of existing and new research. *Organizational Behavior and Human Decision Processes,* 99: 113–142.

57. Bass & Avolio, The implications of transactional and transformational leadership for individual, team, and organizational development; Lowe, Kroeck, & Sivasubramaniam, Effectiveness correlates of transformational and transactional leadership; Peterson, Walumbwa, Byron, & Myrowitz. CEO positive psychological traits, transformational leadership, and firm performance in high-technology start-up and established firms; Rowold, J., & Laukamp, L. 2009. Charismatic leadership and objective performance indicators. *Applied Psychology—An International Review,* 58: 602–621; Shamir, B., House, R.J., & Arthur, M.B. 1993. The motivational effects of charismatic leadership: A self-concept based theory. *Organizational Science,* 4: 577–594.

58. Ruggieri, S. 2009. Leadership in virtual teams: A comparison of transformational and transactional leaders. *Social Behavior and Personality,* 37: 1017–1021; Shamir, House, & Arthur, The motivational effects of charismatic leadership.

59. See, for example: Nemanich, L.A., & Keller, R.T. 2007. Transformational leadership in an acquisition: A field study of employees. *Leadership Quarterly,* 18: 49–68.

60. Bass & Avolio, The implications of transactional and transformational leadership for individual, team, and organizational development.

61. House, R.J., Spangler, W.D., & Woycke, J. 1991. Personality and charisma in the U.S. presidency: A psychological theory of leader effectiveness. *Administrative Science Quarterly,* 36: 364–396.

62. Flynn, F.J., & Staw, B.M. 2004. Lend me your wallets: The effect of charismatic leadership on external support for an organization. *Strategic Management Journal,* 25: 309–330.

63. Nemanich & Keller, Transformational leadership in an acquisition.

64. Ibid.

65. Bass, Avolio, Jung, & Berson, Predicting unit performance by assessing transformational and transactional leadership.

66. Graen, G.B. 1976. Role-making processes within complex organizations. In M.D. Dunnette (Ed.), *Handbook of industrial and organizational psychology.* Chicago: Rand McNally, pp. 1201–1245; Graen, G., Novak, M., & Sommerkamp, P. 1982. The effects of leader-member exchange and job design on productivity and satisfaction: Testing a dual attachment model. *Organizational Behavior and Human Performance,* 30: 109–131.

67. For research related to factors that influence leader-member relationships, see Sparrowe, R.T., & Liden, R.C. 1997. Process and structure in leader-member exchange. *Academy of Management Review,* 22: 522–552.

68. Chen, Z., Lam, W., & Zhong, J.A. 2007. Leader-member exchange and member performance: A new look at individual-level negative feedback-seeking behavior and team-level empowerment climate. *Journal of Applied Psychology,* 92: 202–212; DeConinck, J.B. 2009. The effect of leader-member exchange on turnover among retail buyers. *Journal of Business Research,* 62: 1081–1086; Gerstner, C.R., & Day, D.V. 1997. Meta-analytic review of leader-member exchange theory: Correlates and construct issues. *Journal of Applied Psychology,* 82: 827–844; Ilies, R., Nahrgang, J.D., & Morgeson, F.P. 2007. Leader-member exchange and citizenship behaviors: A meta-analysis. *Journal of Applied Psychology,* 269–277.

69. Barbuto, J.E., & Wheeler, D.W. 2006, Scale development and construct clarification of servant leadership. *Group & Organization Management,* 31: 300–326.

70. Ibid.; Smith, B.N., Montagno, R.V., & Kuzmenko, T.N. 2004. Transformational and servant leadership: Content and contextual comparisons. *Journal of Leadership & Organizational Studies,* 10 (4): 8091; Spears, L. 1995. Servant leadership and the Greenleaf legacy. In L.C. Spears (Ed.), *Reflections on leadership.* New York: John Wiley & Sons.

71. Max De Pree, quoted in: Sendjaya, S., & Sarros, J.C. 2002. Servant leadership: Its origin, development, and application in organizations. *Journal of Leadership & Organizational Studies,* 9 (2): 57–64.

72. Ibid.

73. Avolio, B.J., Walumbwa, F.O., & Weber, T.J. 2009. Leadership: Current theories, research, and future directions. *Annual Review of Psychology,* 60: 421–449.

74. James Blanchard, quoted in: Sendjaya & Sarros, Servant leadership.

75. Cleveland, J.N., Stockdale, M., & Murphy, K.R. 2000. *Men and women in organizations: Sex and gender issues at work.* Mahwah, NJ: Lawrence Erlbaum.

76. Ibid.

77. Dobbins, G.H., & Platz, S.J. 1986. Sex differences in leadership: How real are they? *Academy of Management Review,* 11: 118–127; Powell, G.N. 1990. One more time: Do female and male managers differ? *Academy of Management Executive,* 4: 68–75.

78. Kanter, R.M. 1977. *Men and women of the corporation.* New York: Basic Books.

79. Heilman, M.E. 1995. Sex stereotypes and their effects in the workplace: What we know and what we don't know. *Journal of Social Behavior and Personality,* 10: 3–26; Eagly, A.H., & Karau, S.J. 2002. Role congruity theory of prejudice toward female leaders. *Psychological Review,* 109: 573–598.

80. Bass, B.M., & Avolio, B.J. 1997. Shatter the glass ceiling: Women may make better managers. In K. Grint (Ed.), *Leadership: Classical, contemporary, and critical approaches.* Oxford, United Kingdom: Oxford University Press, pp. 199–210.

81. Bartol, K.M., Martin, D.C., & Kromkowski, J.A. 2003. Leadership and the glass ceiling: Gender and ethnic group influences on leader behaviors at middle and executive managerial levels. *Journal of Leadership and Organizational Studies,* 9: 8–16.

82. Eagly, A.H., & Johnson, B.T. 1990. Gender and leadership style: A meta-analysis. *Psychological Bulletin,* 108: 233–256; Ragins, B.R., & Sundstrom, E. 1989. Gender and power in organizations: A longitudinal perspective. *Psychological Bulletin,* 105: 51–88.

83. Wheelan, S.A., & Verdi, A.F. 1992. Differences in male and female patterns of communication in groups: A methodological artifact? *Sex Roles,* 27: 1–15.

84. Eagly & Johnson, Gender and leadership style.

85. Dobbins & Platz, Sex differences in leadership; Powell, One more time. Also, see van Engen, M.L., & Willemsem, T.M. 2004. Sex and leadership styles: A meta-analysis of research published in the 1990s. *Psychological Reports,* 94: 3–18.

86. Bartol, Martin, & Kromkowski, Leadership and the glass ceiling.

87. For an additional point of view see: Eagly, A.H. 2007. Female leadership advantage and disadvantage: Resolving the contradictions. *Psychology of Women Quarterly,* 31: 1–12.

88. Bartol, Martin, & Kromkowski, Leadership and the glass ceiling.

89. Hofstede, G. 1980. *Culture's consequences: International differences in work related values.* London: Sage; Ashkanasy, N.M., Trevor-Roberts, E., & Earnshaw, L. 2002. The Anglo cluster: Legacy of the British Empire. *Journal of World Business,* 37: 28–39.

90. Kabasakal, H., & Bodur, M. 2002. Arabic cluster: A bridge between East and West. *Journal of World Business,* 37: 40–54.

91. Marks, M. In search of global leaders. *Harvard Business Review,* 81 (8): 43–44.

92. House, R.J., Hanges, P.J., Javidan, M., Dorfman, P.W., Gupta, V., & GLOBE Associates. 2004. *Cultures, leadership, and organizations: GLOBE—a 62 nation study (Vol. 1).* Thousand Oaks, CA: Sage Publishing; House, R.J., Javidan, M., Dorfman, P.W., & de Luque, M.S. 2006. A failure of scholarship: Response to George Graen's critique of GLOBE. *Academy of Management Perspectives,* 20 (4): 102–114; Javidan, M., House, R.J., Dorfman, P.W., Hanges, P.J., & de Luque, M.S. 2006. Conceptualizing and measuring cultures and their consequences: A comparative review of Globe's and Hofstede's approaches. *Journal of International Business Studies,* 37: 897–914.

93. Ashkanasy, Trevor-Roberts, & Earnshaw, The Anglo cluster.

94. Kabasakal & Bodur, Arabic cluster.

95. Szabo, E., Brodbeck, Den Hartog, D.N., Reber, G., Weibler, J., & Wunderer, R. 2002. The Germanic Europe cluster: Where employees have a voice. *Journal of World Business,* 37: 55–68.

96. Gupta, V., Surie, G., Javidan, M., & Chhokar, J. 2002. Southern Asia Cluster: Where the old meets the new? *Journal of World Business,* 37: 16–27.

97. Marks, In search of global leaders.

98. For additional information related to the GLOBE project, go to http://www.thunderbird.edu/wwwfiles/ms/globe. Also see: Chhokar, J.S., Brodbeck, F.C., & House, R.J. 2007. *Culture and leadership across the world.* Mahwah, NJ: Lawrence Erlbaum Associates.

99. Hitt, M.A., Hoskisson, R.E., & Kim, H. 1997. International diversification: Effects on innovation and firm performance in product diversified firms. *Academy of Management Journal,* 40: 767–798.

100. Hitt, M.A., Keats, B.W., & DeMarie, S. 1998. Navigating in the new competitive landscape: Building strategic flexibility and competitive advantage in the 21st century. *Academy of Management Executive,* 12 (4): 22–42.

101. Hitt, M.A., Ireland, R.D., & Hoskisson, R.E. 2007. *Strategic management: Competitiveness and globalization* (7th ed.). Cincinnati, OH: South-Western.

communication

exploring behavior in action
IBM and Virtual Social Worlds

For a recent IBM conference, participants arrived at a wonderful facility featuring a plush reception area, well-equipped meeting rooms, a support library, informal mingling spaces, picnic grounds, and relaxing gardens. Greeters offered directions to meeting rooms as well as other assistance. Kiosks also offered important information on conference activities. Once underway, the conference itself included three keynote speakers and 37 breakout sessions.

The individuals attending the conference were not physically present. Instead, they participated remotely in a virtual social world. Unlike social media such as YouTube (a simple content community), Facebook (a social networking site), or Wikipedia (an asynchronous knowledge-building endeavor), virtual worlds offer real-time interactions where people exist in a three-dimensional setting as self-generated representations of themselves (i.e., avatars). Participants can communicate using voice rather than text, utilize virtual equipment of all kinds, walk around in cleverly constructed settings, and sit down with others in venues such as cafés. Providers of virtual social worlds such as Second Life have created sophisticated systems (http://secondlife.com).

Although most often thought of as places that individuals go to socialize or live secret alternative lives, virtual social worlds can be used for collaborative meetings, training, and a number of other organizational purposes. In fact, virtual worlds are becoming viable alternatives to face-to-face meetings and training sessions even in cases where complex and important information must be exchanged. The ability for back-and-forth conversations and the ability to read body language is very helpful in this regard. Participants can offer ideas, ask questions, and even show a limited range of emotions within the virtual world.

Was IBM's conference successful? Yes it was! IBM estimates that it saved several hundred thousand U.S. dollars in comparison to what the conference would have

knowledge objectives

After reading this chapter, you should be able to:

1. Explain why communication is strategically important to organizations.
2. Describe the fundamental communication process.
3. Discuss important aspects of communication that affect the organization or its units, including networks and the direction of communication flow.
4. Define interpersonal communication and discuss the roles of formal versus informal communication, communication media, communication technology, and nonverbal communication.
5. Describe organizational and individual barriers to effective communication.
6. Understand how organizations and individuals can overcome communication barriers.

cost had it been done on a face-to-face basis. Moreover, the presentations were well received, with many sessions running long as participants continued to chat. Also, participants met on their own at the end of each day for conversations over virtual cocktails. This meant that people were informally networking, which is one reason to have a conference. Overall, the learning, information development, and social outcomes were much greater than they would have been with less rich substitutes for face-to-face interactions such as web chats, teleconferences, and videoconferences.

Based on its success, IBM is now actively using virtual social worlds for a number of purposes, including:

©Carol & Mike Werner/Visuals Unlimited, Inc./Getty Images, Inc.

- Events (e.g., Human Capital Management University)
- White-board Brainstorming (e.g., metaverse-brainshare application integration)
- Mentoring (e.g., mentoring from the corporate learning group)
- New employee orientation (e.g., Fresh Blue Program in China)
- Simulations and rehearsals (e.g., energy-efficient data center)
- Software development (e.g., Bluegrass-Rational Jazz Team)

In a different type of virtual social world, participants engage in games known as massively multiplayer online role playing games (MMORPG). World of Warcraft and Star Wars Galaxies are examples. World of Warcraft describes itself this way: "Players assume the roles of Warcraft heroes as they explore, adventure, and quest across a vast world. … Whether adventuring together or fighting against each other in epic battles, players will form friendships, forge alliances, and compete with enemies for power and glory."

IBM has partnered with Seriosity, a software company that develops organizational tools, to study leadership in MMORPGs. Opportunities to lead abound in these online games, where it is crucial to craft a vision for the future, create ways to attain that future through raids and other techniques, motivate others to join and sustain the fight, and make sense of events and outcomes in a complex and fluid setting. Individuals who are successful and move up the game-world hierarchies may have leadership skills that can generalize to the real world, particularly to situations that are dynamic and uncertain.

Although this work is in its early stages, the research carried out by IBM suggests that successful gamers can be effective corporate leaders. One participant said this,

I've grown more accustomed now to directing various aspects of running the [on-line battle coalition] and providing a vision and leadership to members, Follow-up and assertiveness now feel more natural to me, even in real life. It has been an amazing opportunity to push myself beyond my boundaries.

Another participant had this to say,

Finally, I … rallied the troops to revive one another and try again, mostly because I didn't know what else to do. It was me, this girl, talking to a room of 39 guys. And to my shock and surprise, everyone complied. … That was a defining moment for me.

Surveys also provide useful evidence. A survey of IBM managers and associates active in online games revealed that 50 percent of respondents believed game-playing had improved their real-world leadership. Forty percent indicated that they had applied specific techniques from the gaming world to improve leadership outcomes at IBM.

IBM clearly has benefited from the interactions that occur in virtual social worlds. What does the future hold? With developments occurring so rapidly, it is difficult to say.

Sources: L. Cherbakov, R. Brunner, R. Smart, & C. Lu. 2009. "Virtual Spaces: Enabling Immersive Collaborative Enterprise, Part 1," at http://www.ibm.com/developerworks/webservices/library/ws-vitualspaces; IBM Global Innovation Outlook, "Virtual Worlds, Real Leaders: Online Games Put the Future of Business Leadership on Display," 2007, at http://www.ibm.com/ibm/ideasfromibm/us/giogaming/073007/index.shtml; A.M. Kaplan, & M. Haenlein. 2009. "The Fairyland of Second Life: Virtual Social Worlds and How to Use Them," *Business Horizons*, 52, no. 6, pp. 563–572; Linden Lab, "Case Study: How Meeting in Second Life Transformed IBM's Technology Elite into Virtual World Believers," 2009, at http://secondlifegrid.net/casestudies/IBM; S. Morrison. 2009. "A Second Chance for Second Life: Northrop, IBM Use Virtual World as Setting for Training, Employee Meetings," *Wall Street Journal*, Aug. 19, p. B.5; World of Warcraft, "Intro to WOW," 2010, at http://www.worldofwarcraft.com/info/beginners/index.html.

the strategic importance of Communication

Good communication is vital to better organizational performance. Effective communication is important because few things are accomplished in organizations without it.[1] Managers must communicate with their subordinates in order for jobs to be performed effectively. Top management must communicate organizational goals to the associates who are expected to achieve them. Many jobs require coordination with others in the organization, and coordination requires communication. In fact, communication is such an important part of a manager's job that managers spend between 50 and 90 percent of their time at work communicating.[2] Top managers must digest information, shape ideas, coordinate tasks, listen to others, and give instructions. Decisions and policies are of little value unless they are fully understood by those who must implement them.[3] Good communication is also the basis for effective leadership, the motivation of subordinates, and the exercise of power and influence. It is also necessary for establishing effective relations with important external entities, such as suppliers, consumers, and government agencies.

Communication systems in organizations affect numerous outcomes that are central to an organization's functioning and competitive advantage, These include productivity,[4] quality services and products,[5] reduced costs, creativity, job satisfaction, absenteeism, and turnover.[6] In other words, organizational communication is interrelated with organizational effectiveness.[7] Indeed, surveys asking managers to give the reasons for project failures cite communication problems as an important, if not the most important, explanation.[8]

Given the importance of organizational communication, it is troubling that a number of managers find communication a challenging task. One study found that many managers underestimate the complexity and importance of superior–subordinate communications.[9] In addition, although research confirms that communication is an integral part of corporate strategy,[10] an important survey showed that only 22 percent of line associates and 41 percent of their supervisors understand the organization's strategy and that 54 percent of organizations do a poor job of communicating their strategy.[11] Thus, it appears that organizations and managers at middle and high levels have much to learn about effective communication. Also, it is not surprising that a recent survey of corporate trainers found that 44 percent of their organizations planned to greatly increase their budgets for communication training for managers and senior leaders.[12]

Communication can take many forms, such as face-to-face discussions, phone calls, e-mails, letters, memos, notes posted on electronic bulletin boards, and presentations to people who are physically in the same room. As seen in the case of IBM, communication can also occur inside virtual social worlds. These worlds offer a number of advantages that can address some of the problems plaguing communication. For example, the use of virtual social worlds might help managers and associates express themselves more freely when facing contentious issues. The use of this new creative medium could unlock previously frozen interactions, and it could facilitate the inputs of shy or conflict-avoidant people. For discussing or conveying the organization's strategy, the use of virtual social worlds might help senior managers to more effectively and less expensively reach various groups of geographically dispersed managers and associates. The fundamental purposes of communication are to provide information and instructions, to influence others, and to integrate activities.[13] Virtual social worlds have a great deal to offer in accomplishing these tasks.

In this chapter, we examine a variety of issues related to communication in organizations. In the first section, we discuss the fundamental communication process. Next, we describe aspects of communication that affect the organization or major units within it. We then discuss interpersonal communication—that is, communication between and among individual associates. Finally, after describing various barriers to effective communication, we present ways in which these barriers can be overcome to build a successful communication process.

The Communication Process

Communication involves the sharing of information between two or more people to achieve a common understanding about an object or situation. Successful communication occurs when the person receiving the message understands it in the way that the sender intended. Thus, communication does not end with the message sent. We also need to consider the message that is received. Think of a time when you meant to compliment someone, but the person understood your remark as an insult. This was not successful communication—the message received was not the same as the one sent.

Communication can be viewed as a process, as shown in Exhibit 9-1. The starting point in the communication process is the sender—the person who wishes to communicate a message. To convey information, the sender must first encode it. **Encoding** involves translating information into a message or a signal.[14] The encoded message is then sent through a **communication medium**, or **communication channel**, to the intended receiver. Communication media are numerous and include writing, texting, face-to-face verbal exchanges, verbal exchanges without face-to-face contact (e.g., phone conversations), and e-mail.

Once the message has been received, the receiver must decode it. In **decoding**, the receiver perceives the message and interprets its meaning.[15] To ensure that the meaning the receiver attaches to the message is the same as the one intended by the sender, feedback is necessary. **Feedback** is the process through which the receiver encodes the message received and sends it or a response to it back to the original sender. Communication that includes feedback is referred to as *two-way* communication. If feedback is not present (resulting in *one-way* communication), the receiver may walk away with an entirely different interpretation from that intended by the sender.

communication
The sharing of information between two or more people to achieve a common understanding about an object or situation.

encoding
The process whereby a sender translates the information he or she wishes to send in a message.

communication medium or communication channel
The manner in which a message is conveyed.

decoding
The process whereby a receiver perceives a sent message and interprets its meaning.

feedback
The process whereby a receiver encodes the message received and sends it or a response to it back to the original sender.

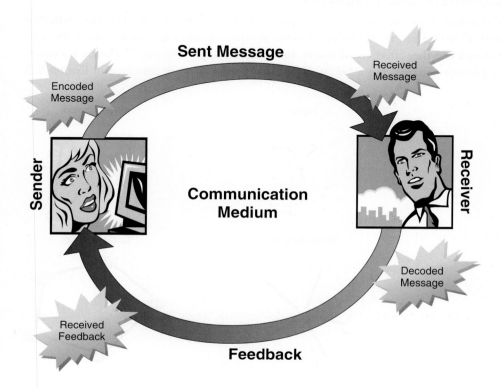

Exhibit 9-1 Sent Message

All parts of the communication process are important. A communication breakdown can occur in any part of the process. For example, information must be encoded into a message that can be understood as the sender intended. In addition, some forms of media may not be as effective as others in communicating the meaning of a particular message. Some communication media are richer than others—that is, they provide more information.[16] Consider e-mail as an example. People often use symbols such as ":)" to indicate intent (in this case, humor) because the medium is not very rich. If the message had been spoken, the humorous intent could have been indicated by the sender's tone of voice or facial expression. We describe more barriers to effective communication, as well as more details about media richness, later in the chapter.

Organizational Communication

Communication occurs at several different levels. On one level is the communication that occurs between and among individuals. This is referred to as *interpersonal communication,* and we discuss it in the next section. Here, we focus on *organizational communication*—that is, the patterns and types of communication that occur at the organizational and unit levels. The purpose of organizational communication is to facilitate the achievement of the organization's goals. As we have already seen, communication is a necessary part of almost any action taken in an organization, ranging from transmitting the organization's strategy from top executives to integrating operations among different functional areas or units. Organizational communication involves the use of communication networks, policies, and structures.[17]

Communication Networks

Communication networks represent patterns of communication (who communicates with whom). Thus, they correspond to the structure of communication flows in the organization and they affect coordination, innovation, and performance.[18] There are a variety of possible patterns, and a few of the more common ones are presented in Exhibit 9-2.

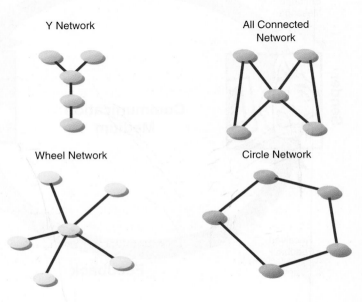

Y Network

All Connected Network

Wheel Network

Circle Network

Exhibit 9-2 Communication Networks

Each line shown in the exhibit represents two-way communication and, as such, counts as two network connections for the purposes of this chapter.

Networks can be characterized in terms of their density.[19] In **sparse networks**, there are few connections among members. In **dense networks**, there are many connections. The wheel, Y, and circle networks depicted in Exhibit 9-2 are sparse. In the wheel, for example, most members communicate regularly with only one other person, resulting in a density score of only .33 (10 connections among 6 people divided by 30 possible connections). In contrast, the well-connected network is dense, with a density score of .80 (16 connections among 5 people divided by 20 possible connections.

Networks can also be characterized in terms of their centralization.[20] In **centralized networks**, all communications pass through a central point or points, so that one or a few members of the network control most of the information exchanges. The wheel and the Y networks depicted in Exhibit 9-2 are examples of centralized networks. In the wheel, one member of the network communicates with every other member while the other members do not communicate with one another. In the Y network, one network member communicates with three other members while most of the others communicate with only one other member. Traditional organizational hierarchies, where subordinates communicate mostly or only with their bosses, who in turn communicate with their bosses, represent centralized networks. Companies in which units do not communicate with one other but only with a central headquarters, which then simultaneously coordinates all the units, are also centralized.

In **decentralized networks**, no single member of the network dominates information exchanges. The circle and the well-connected networks are examples. In the circle, each member of the network talks with two others. In the well-connected network pictured here, one member of the network communicates with each of the other four, but those other four members also communicate with almost everyone else. Centralization is somewhat higher in the well-connected network relative to the circle, but it is not excessively high.

To some degree, the effectiveness of networks depends on situational factors such as type of work and goals of the unit or organization.[21] For example, sparse highly centralized networks such as the wheel and the Y can be effective in accomplishing simple tasks. These structures promote efficiency, speed, and accuracy by channeling communication through a central person. On the other hand, dense networks with some degree of centralization in the leader role might be more effective for complex tasks. The well-connected network fits here. Communication among most or many parties facilitates trust and rich exchanges of information, which are helpful in solving complex problems. Also, having a leader with some degree of centrality is helpful to ensure that proper direction is given to the unit/organization and to ensure that a clear resolution point exists for disagreements. Overall, independent of the situational context, reasonably dense networks with some degree of leader centrality tend to be the most effective.[22] This is consistent with high-involvement management, where associates exist in a somewhat egalitarian system and have bounded authority to coordinate and solve problems among themselves.

In addition to effects on unit or organizational performance, network structure affects individual outcomes. As discussed above, in sparse networks many individuals do not directly communicate with one another. This creates an opportunity for brokerage, where one or more members of a network act as a conduit or go-between for information exchanges between members without direct ties. For example, if member B does not communicate with member C but member A communicates with both of them, then

sparse networks
A communication network in which most or all network members communicate with only a few other members.

dense networks
A communication network in which most or all network members communicate with many other members.

centralized networks
A communication network in which one or a few network members dominate communications.

decentralized networks
A communication network in which no single network member dominates communications.

member A is said to be a broker of the B–C relationship. Individuals who broker a number of relationships tend to have more positive outcomes in terms of power, job performance, and financial compensation, even after controlling for factors such as hierarchical level and education.[23] Importantly, brokers in networks are not necessarily in formal leadership positions.

The networks depicted in Exhibit 9-2 involve five or six individuals; however, networks are often considerably larger. For example, the manufacturing department in a mid-sized company might have hundreds of people in it. Social scientists have been developing theories that can be used to explain and predict outcomes in these large organizational networks. In recent years, scientists and mathematicians also have been developing sophisticated network models and analytical techniques to study diverse phenomena such as stock market crashes, the relationships among CEOs, the spread of disease, and the spread of computer viruses.[24]

For example, in the late 1990s, Toyota had a brief brush with disaster that has been attributed to its heavy reliance on affiliated companies. Interestingly, the situation was resolved quickly through the network structure that connected the affiliates.[25]

To accomplish its goals, Toyota depends on a large number of affiliated companies. Those companies provide Toyota with the parts it needs to manufacture vehicles. They are independent, and each one focuses on making a unique part (such as electrical components or seat covers). At the same time, the companies are integrated because all of them must endorse Toyota's strict production system guidelines and protocols.

One of the companies in the Toyota network is Aisin Seiki, which produces a number of products including P-valves—brake devices that help prevent cars from skidding. The production of P-valves requires high precision, and the P-valves are a necessary component of every vehicle. If production of P-valves stops, Toyota cannot complete the manufacture of any vehicles. Aisin Seiki was the sole provider of P-valves for Toyota, and all the valves were made in one plant. In 1997, this plant burned down, and it was predicted that production would stop for at least a month—which would have severely harmed Toyota. However, because of the close coordination and effective communication among the various parts of the network, other plants were able to pick up the production of the precision P-valves with only about three days' preparation! Within a week, Toyota was once more manufacturing cars. Toyota's amazingly quick recovery can be attributed to the integration of all the members of its network.

Direction of Organizational Communication

Communication within organizations can occur in any of three directions: downward, upward, or horizontally.

Downward Communication

Downward communication, which refers to communication from senior managers to junior managers and from junior managers to associates, is necessary to provide job instructions, information on organization policies, and performance feedback. Downward communication can also be used to inform those at lower levels about the organization's goals and about changes faced by the organization. Downward communication, however, is

downward communication
Communication that flows from superior to subordinate.

©Michael Hitoshi/Digital Vision/ Getty Images, Inc.

frequently deficient in this regard. Lower-level managers and associates often complain about the lack of information on goals and changes being made in the organization, as mentioned in the earlier discussion of potential uses of communication through virtual social worlds.

An example of the importance of downward communication can be seen in the acquisition of a large consumer-goods manufacturing company. The company was acquired by a large conglomerate, but no downward communication had taken place informing associates of the effects they would experience. A rumor began to circulate among the acquired company's highly professional finance department staff suggesting that the department was to be reduced to a record-keeping function. All major financial responsibilities were supposed to be transferred to the financial staff at the conglomerate's headquarters. Because of this rumor, many of the finance department's professional staff members sought and obtained jobs with other organizations. When top management realized the problem, it immediately announced that the rumor was false and assured associates that the financial responsibilities would remain in their organization. Even so, the acquired company had lost almost 50 percent of its financial staff before this downward communication occurred. With a large number of acquisitions and mergers occurring in the current time period, particularly in the financial area with such combinations as Wachovia and Wells Fargo, downward communication regarding merger details must be proactively managed.[26]

Upward Communication

Upward communication, which flows from associates to junior managers and from junior managers to senior managers, is necessary to provide feedback on downward communication and to provide ideas and information. It can, however, be difficult to achieve in an effective way. Thus, it is one of the less frequently used forms of communication in organizations. Common channels for upward communication include departmental meetings, "open-door" policies, suggestion boxes, attitude surveys, participation in decisions, grievance procedures, and exit interviews. Upward communication may be necessary for hierarchical superiors to monitor the effectiveness of decisions, gather information on problems and opportunities, ensure that jobs are being done properly, and maintain morale among those lower in the organization. However, it will not occur in organizations where superiors give the impression that they do not want to hear negative feedback or where subordinates do not trust superiors and fear reprisals. Upward communication can also be costly to organizations because policies and procedures must be developed to carry it out and also because it requires managers' time.[27]

Upward communication seems to be particularly difficult in larger organizations, probably because relationships in large organizations are more complex and formalized.[28] Certainly, larger size may inhibit the quantity of interactions between superiors and subordinates; however, the quality of the interaction is the most critical element.[29] Meg Whitman, the CEO of eBay until recently, fostered upward communication through her practice of enabling those at lower levels in the organization to be totally honest with her. So successful was this approach that a newly minted MBA associate at eBay once felt free to proclaim that almost anyone could manage the company—implying that Whitman's job as CEO was easy. Because Whitman enabled associates to communicate upward, this brash young MBA is still an associate with the company.[30] Another organization, Connecticut Bank, encouraged upward communication through employee attitude surveys. When survey results revealed that associates were dissatisfied with written communications in the

upward communication
Communication that flows from subordinate to superior.

Communication at J. Crew: Mickey Drexler

Zena Olijnyk became extremely frustrated when responding to a promotional e-mail from J. Crew advertising the "retro-dot" mini skirt. She immediately tried to order the skirt online, but her size was not available. In a pique, she fired off an e-mail to J. Crew's customer service department complaining about sending promotional e-mail ads for items that were sold out. She received a response immediately from a customer service representative who told her that the demand was much larger than expected and then apologized. She was still annoyed, so she asked that her complaint be forwarded to someone higher up—maybe even the CEO. The next day, Zena received the following e-mail from someone named Millard Drexler:

> Thx much for taking time to send email-have copied our team-it has been somewhat difficult for us to forecast demand on our fashion merchandise as have not expected the reaction we have been getting-your points about how we handle are right on-have been trying to communicate more effectively than doing right now, and obviously not doing a great job. If one of [our] team members not already searching your size, please let know if still interested.

Millard "Mickey" Drexler is the chairman and CEO of J. Crew. He took over the company after being forced out of the GAP in 2002, where he had been for 19 years. Drexler left the GAP because of a 29-month decline in profits. However, Drexler is the person credited with putting the GAP on the map, turning the company into a $14.5 billion business, and revolutionizing the way the world dresses (some say he invented "casual chic"). He has done the same for J. Crew, taking the company from a failing business that lost $40 million in 2002 to one of the most profitable retail clothing companies in 2010. Even Michelle Obama has endorsed the company by wearing and discussing a J. Crew outfit on NBC's *Tonight Show*. Drexler turned J. Crew around by bringing in his own team, raising prices while raising quality, applying his uncanny talent for spotting clothing trends, cutting operating costs, and engaging in a communication style that is somewhat unique among CEOs.

Not only does Drexler e-mail and call unhappy customers, he habitually drops by J. Crew stores around the country to get a feel for what's selling, what's not, and what is happening in individual stores and to get input from sales associates in those stores. He walks into stores and quizzes customers about what they think and what they want. He also keeps in close contact with individual store managers. Once a week Drexler holds a conference call with store managers across the country. He asks them specific questions about what's going on in their stores, such as how customers reacted to a window display featuring suits (they liked it; sales rose dramatically). While Drexler is in his office at J. Crew

©Ben Baker/Redux Pictures

headquarters, he spends most of his time running around, sticking his head into cubicles to personally talk with all associates. A recent survey found that most associates complain about a lack of face-to-face contact with the "higher-ups" and about not being asked their opinion. It seems unlikely that J. Crew team members would ever feel this way.

Drexler's communication style is also unique. He's loud, boisterous, infectiously passionate about the business, and incredibly honest when he voices his frequent opinions. A colleague from his GAP days described him as letting it all hang out—he does victory dances when pleased and yells when frustrated. In response to a pair of shorts shown to him by the design team, Drexler responded, "This is a monster! No one is doing these!" Another colleague stated "Mickey's fun, but he was making so much noise we had to close the doors. He yells and screams. ..."

In the end, it is not surprising that Mickey Drexler has taken what was known as a failing, staid, preppy clothing company and turned it into an exciting, profitable, and much-talked-about success story. Through his direct and passionate communication with all stakeholders in the business, he seems to have channeled his energy and excitement.

Sources: B. Ebenkamp. 2009. "Marketer of the Year: Mickey Drexler," *Mediaweek*, 19, no. 32: pp. 26–27; M. Gordon. 2004. "Mickey Drexler's Redemption," *New York*, Nov. 29, pp. 40–41; L. Lee. 2006. "J. Crew's Smart-Looking IPO," *BusinessWeek*, June 28, at http://www.businessweek.com/print/investor/content/jun2006/pi20060628_109690. htm; A. Maitland. 2006. "Employees Want to Hear It Straight from The Boss's Mouth," *Financial Times*, Dec. 1, p. 12; Z. Olijnyk. 2007. "Now That's Service," *Canadian Business Online*, Feb. 20, at http://candianbusiness.com/shared/print.jsp?content= 20070220_130900_5412; T. Rozhon. 2004. "A Leaner J. Crew Is Showing Signs of a Turnaround," *New York Times*, June 24, at http://query.nytimes.com/gst/fullpage.html?res=9D02EFD6123F937A35755C0A96 29C8; S.M. Sears. 2009. "The Queen of J. Crew," *Barron's*, 89, no. 14: M9.

organization, the bank focused on reducing the quantity and improving the quality of written information transfers. Communication quality improved, and so did employee satisfaction and productivity. Finally, as illustrated in the *Experiencing Organizational Behavior* feature, J. Crew CEO Mickey Drexler makes it quite easy for his subordinates to communicate directly with him by frequently dropping by J. Crew stores.

Horizontal Communication

Horizontal communication, which takes place between and among people at the same level, is also important but is frequently overlooked in the design of organizations. Coordination among organizational units is facilitated by horizontal communication. For example, the manufacturing and marketing departments must coordinate and integrate their activities so that goods will be available for sales orders. This frequently is achieved through face-to-face conversations, phone conversations, and e-mail. Formal integrating positions may also be used to facilitate horizontal communications between units. These positions are often referred to as "boundary-spanning positions" because the position holders cross the boundaries that separate different units.[31] For example, some human resource departments have representatives or liaison members in each functional unit of the organization to coordinate and communicate staffing, compensation, and performance-management activities.[32]

Some time ago, organizations began to use communication from all three directions in the area of performance appraisal. Almost all *Fortune* 500 companies use 360-degree multi-rater feedback to evaluate senior managers.[33] Such feedback includes performance appraisals from peers (horizontal communication), subordinates (upward communication), and superiors (downward communication).[34] Evaluations from customers/clients, and suppliers are also sought in some cases.

There are, however, some problems with 360-degree feedback. One problem with subordinates evaluating superiors is that retaliation for negative performance evaluations can occur. Another problem is that peers may be politically motivated to either overrate or underrate their co-workers. Thus, it is usually recommended that upward and horizontal appraisals be used only for training and development purposes and that the superiors' evaluation be given more weight when appraisals are used to make personnel decisions

horizontal communication
Communication that takes place between and among people at the same level.

(such as those involving promotions and pay raises).[35] However, if superiors do take their own 360-degree feedback seriously, and change their behavior as a result of feedback from subordinates and peers, the loyalty of subordinates will also increase.[36]

Interpersonal Communication

interpersonal communication
Direct verbal or nonverbal interaction between two or more active participants.

We now move from the organizational level to the interpersonal level of communication. **Interpersonal communication** involves a direct verbal or nonverbal interaction between two or more active participants.[37] Interpersonal communication can take many forms, both formal and informal, and be channeled through numerous media and technologies. Furthermore, people can communicate without even intending to do so, through nonverbal communication. In this section, we discuss each of these issues: formal versus informal communication, communication media, technology, and nonverbal communication.

Formal versus Informal Communication

formal communication
Communication that follows the formal structure of the organization (e.g., superior to subordinate) and entails organizationally sanctioned information.

informal communication
Communication that involves spontaneous interaction between two or more people outside the formal organization structure.

Interpersonal communication can be formal or informal. **Formal communication** follows the formal structure of the organization (e.g., superior to subordinate) and entails organizationally sanctioned information. A major drawback of formal communication is that it can be slow. In contrast, **informal communication** involves spontaneous interaction between two or more people outside the formal organization structure. For example, communication between peers on their coffee break may be considered informal communication.

The informal system frequently emerges as an important source of communication for organization members.[38] Managers must recognize it and be sensitive to communication that travels through informal channels (such as the grapevine). In addition, managers may find that the informal system enables them to reach more members than the formal one. Another benefit of informal communication is that it can help build solidarity and friendship among associates.[39]

Effective communication is crucial in implementing the organization's strategy. However, there is a downside to informal interpersonal communication—rumors and gossip. **Rumors** entail unsubstantiated information of universal interest. People often create and communicate rumors to deal with uncertainty.[40] This is why rumors are so prevalent during times of organizational upheaval, particularly during mergers and acquisitions. For example, in 2000, the Coca-Cola Company undertook a major restructuring to overcome its lagging financial performance.[41] During this period, persistent (and untrue) rumors flourished—such as "Coke is leaving Atlanta," "They're removing the flagpoles so that the American flag doesn't fly over the company," and "The CEO is leaving." These rumors resulted in dissatisfaction, loss of morale, and turnover, and senior management had to spend a great deal of time overcoming and eliminating them.

rumors
Unsubstantiated information of universal interest.

gossip
Information that is presumed to be factual and is communicated in private or intimate settings.

Gossip is information that is presumed to be factual and is communicated in private or intimate settings.[42] Often, gossip is not specifically work-related and focuses on things such as others' personal lives. Furthermore, gossip usually reflects information that is third-hand, fourth-hand, and even farther removed from the person passing it along. Gossip can cause problems for organizations because it reduces associates' focus on work, ruins reputations, creates stress, and can lead to legal problems. People are thought to engage in gossip in order to gain power or friendships or to enhance their own egos. For example, groups of low-status office workers may try to keep their supervisor in check by continuously gossiping about him and thus threatening his reputation. Interestingly, good performers might also use gossip as an indirect weapon against poor performance. Even this use of gossip does not help unit performance and in fact can harm it.[43]

To avoid rumors in the workplace, managers are advised to provide honest, open, and clear information in times of uncertainty. Rumors should be addressed by those in a position to know the truth. To combat gossip, managers can include questions in 360-degree evaluations to identify individuals who habitually traffic in irrelevant, unsubstantiated information. Offenders can then be asked to end their dysfunctional behavior. Some organizations have dealt with rumors by placing restrictions on idle chatter.

Communication Media

Interpersonal communication, as already mentioned, can be based on many different media, and different media vary in degree of richness. Recall that *richness* describes the amount of information a medium can convey. Richness depends on: (1) the availability of feedback, (2) the use of multiple cues, (3) the use of effective language, and (4) the extent to which the communication has a personal focus.[44] Face-to-face verbal communication is the richest medium.[45] Think about all that happens during a face-to-face interaction. Suppose that you (the sender) are talking to a friend. If your friend does not understand the message or interprets it inaccurately, she can let you know either verbally or nonverbally (e.g., with a puzzled expression). In the interaction, you use multiple cues, including tone of voice, semantics (the words that are used), facial expressions, and body language. You use natural language and thus communicate more precise meaning. Finally, because you and your friend are face-to-face, it is easy to create a personal focus in the message.

Research has ordered common communication media in terms of richness.[46] In order of richest to least rich, they are:

1. Face-to-face communication
2. Telephone communication
3. Electronic messaging (such as e-mail and instant messaging)
4. Personal written text (such as letters, notes, and memos)
5. Formal written text (such as reports, documents, bulletins, and notices)
6. Formal numerical text (such as statistical reports, graphs, and computer printouts)

Virtual social worlds have not been included in the research discussed above because communication through this medium is too new. The experiences of IBM discussed in the opening case suggest, however, that this medium scores well in terms of richness. Immediate feedback is possible, multiple cues are available, including some emotional reactions, effective language can be used, and the communication can be personalized.[47]

For a particular communication task, choosing from among available media involves a trade-off between the richness of a medium and the cost (especially in time) of using it. For example, it is much easier and quicker to send someone a brief e-mail rather than to find his phone number, call him, and have a phone conversation, yet the phone conversation would likely yield richer information exchange. Research on media richness has not produced consistent results, but much of it suggests that effective managers will use richer media as the message becomes more equivocal.[48] Equivocal messages are those that can be interpreted in multiple ways. "We're having a meeting in the boardroom at 2 P.M. on Thursday" is an unequivocal message. "Your performance is not what I expected" is an equivocal message. Research has also shown that managers will use richer media when the message is important and when they feel the need to present a positive self-image.[49]

Another factor that influences the choice of media corresponds to organizational norms that indicate which types of communication media are desirable.[50] Some organizations have strong norms that employees communicate in a face-to-face manner, resulting in many meetings and chatting in the office. Other organizations have strong norms for using electronic communications and the Internet. One study found that associates' use of e-mail and instant messaging was highly dependent on their organization's norms for the use of these approaches.[51]

Communication Technology

Modern technology allows organizations and their members to communicate quickly, across any distance, and to collaborate more effectively than ever before.[52] Indeed, in order for organizations to remain competitive, they need to constantly keep up–to-date on modern communication technologies.[53] For example, after the great blackout of 2003 struck the eastern United States and Canada, IBM employees were able to fall back on instant messaging to continue working, while many other organizations, which did not use wireless technology, were crippled.

Communication technology will continue to rapidly advance. The world wide web, private intranets, virtual private networks (VPNs), web-based conferencing technologies, cell phones, and multifeatured mobile communication devices (e.g., iPhones) did not exist or were not commonly used 15 years ago.[54] Today, these technologies and the new forms of communication they support are all around us. For example, billions of e-mail messages are sent via the Internet each day from company accounts. Instant messaging is now used by the vast majority of companies worldwide. Even blogging has become more popular within the business world:

- As of December 2009, approximately 16 percent of *Fortune* 500 companies had created blogs (informal electronic communication sites that reach a wide audience) and made them available to the public. Many more had blogs that were available only internally for use by the company's managers and associates.[55] Examples of publicly available blogs are:
  - Coca Cola Conversations (Coca Cola)
  - Fast Lane Blog (General Motors)
  - Nuts about Southwest (Southwest Airlines)
- Hundreds if not thousands of CEOs and top executives worldwide now have personal blogs to communicate with associates, clients/customers, and the general public.[56] Individuals with blogs available to the public include:
  - John Mackey, CEO, Whole Foods Market
  - Tom Glocer, CEO, Reuters
  - Marc Cuban, Chairman, HDNet, and Owner, Dallas Mavericks Basketball Club

Organizations have been creating blogs to provide information related to advertising and corporate decisions and to seek information related to consumer thinking in the

EXHIBIT 9-3 Communicating with Customers

22-February-2007
Dear JetBlue Customers,

We are sorry and embarrassed. But most of all, we are deeply sorry.

Last week was the worst operational week in JetBlue's seven year history. Following the severe winter ice storm in the Northeast, we subjected our customers to unacceptable delays, flight cancellations, lost baggage, and other major inconveniences. The storm disrupted the movement of aircraft, and, more importantly, disrupted the movement of JetBlue's pilots and in-flight crewmembers who were depending on those planes to get them to the airports where they were scheduled to serve you. With the busy President's Day weekend upon us, rebooking opportunities were scarce and hold times at 1-800-JETBLUE were unacceptably long or not even available, further hindering our recovery efforts.

Words cannot express how truly sorry we are for the anxiety, frustration and inconvenience that we caused. This is especially saddening because JetBlue was founded on the promise of bringing humanity back to air travel and making the experience of flying happier and easier for everyone who chooses to fly with us. We know we failed to deliver on this promise last week.

We are committed to you, our valued customers, and are taking immediate corrective steps to regain your confidence in us. We have begun putting a comprehensive plan in place to provide better and more timely information to you, more tools and resources for our crewmembers and improved procedures for handling operational difficulties in the future. We are confident, as a result of these actions, that JetBlue will emerge as a more reliable and even more customer responsive airline than ever before.

Most importantly, we have published the **JetBlue Airways Customer Bill of Rights**—our official commitment to you of how we will handle operational interruptions going forward—including details of compensation. I have a video message to share with you about this industry leading action.

You deserved better—a lot better—from us last week. Nothing is more important than regaining your trust and all of us here hope you will give us the opportunity to welcome you onboard again soon and provide you the positive JetBlue Experience you have come to expect from us.

Sincerely,

David

Source: http://www.jetblue.com/aboutourcompany/flightlog/archive_February2007/.html.

general marketplace.[57] For example, Stonyfield Farm, the largest organic yogurt company in the world, uses blogs to interact with its customers on health-related topics relevant to the yogurt business.[58] When JetBlue Airways canceled half of its flights and kept passengers waiting in planes on the runway for up to 11 hours, they had a great deal of apologizing to do—especially for a company known for its customer service.[59] One way in which the company regained its service reputation was through Chairman David Neeleman's blog message to the passengers and the general public. This message is presented in Exhibit 9-3.

Although the adoption of communication technologies and the new forms of communication they support can be beneficial, new communication technologies can also create issues for organizations and individuals. One common problem is *information overload,* which is discussed later in this chapter. Another problem is that the new technology makes it easier to leak private or secret information to an unintended audience, often with unintended consequences. For example, Mark Jen, a programmer at Google, blogged about the company's unfavorable health plan.[60] This blog caused Jen to be fired and served as a warning to other bloggers at Google. Finally, as illustrated in the *Managerial Advice* feature, personal privacy concerns that did not exist 10 years ago are now very apparent.

Surfing for Applicants

Eva Montibello, a marketing manager with a Boston-based firm, was sorting through job applications, when a member of her staff came up and told her to check out a particular applicant's MySpace page. Eva did, and was quite shocked to find many compromising photos of the applicant, including one involving Jell-O wrestling. When this applicant was asked about the photos in her interview, she laughed it off and was quite silly about them. In the end, the unprofessional photos and unprofessional response to the photos were a factor in why this applicant was not hired by Eva's firm.

In recent years, the way in which companies recruit associates has gone through a revolution because of the availability of technology that allows employers to connect with and get information about potential job applicants. It used to be that when an individual applied for a job, the hiring organization had access only to information provided by past employers, schools, and/or the applicant. Now, for many people, there exists an abundance of information in cyberspace, and organizations are using this information to evaluate job candidates. Employers have access to information about candidates that they would never dream of asking about in an interview, such as social activities, religious activities, friends, and what people really think about their old bosses.

In a 2006 survey by executive search firm ExecuNet, 77 percent of recruiters said they use search engines to check out job candidates. In a 2009 Career-Builder.com survey of 2,600 hiring managers, 45 percent reported using search engines to gather information on applicants, with many specifically checking social networking sites such as Facebook and MySpace. According to the CareerBuilder survey, recruiters found these searches quite informative. Thirty-five percent indicated that candidates had been rejected based on information found in social networking sites. Among those recruiters screening out candidates, the following issues were cited:

©AP/Wide World Photos

- Candidate posted provocative/inappropriate photos or information (53 percent).
- Candidate posted content about drinking or drug use (44 percent).
- Candidate bad-mouthed one or more previous employers, co-workers, or clients (35 percent).
- Candidate demonstrated poor communication skills (29 percent).
- Candidate made discriminatory remarks (26 percent).
- Candidate posted information on qualifications that conflicted with information provided directly to the company (24 percent).
- Candidate shared confidential information from one or more previous employers (20 percent).

To avoid problems and to present a positive image, job seekers must be proactive. Rosemary Haefner (Vice President of Human Resources at CareerBuilder), Dave Willmer (Executive Director of a talent management company), and a number of other experts in recruiting and job searches have offered helpful advice. Collectively, they suggest the following:

- Conduct a comprehensive search of your name using major search engines (for common names, the search can be narrowed by adding employer names and/or relevant cities).
- For any web-based content that can be directly controlled, delete entries that could cast a negative light on your candidacy (see list of items presented above).
- For content that cannot be directly controlled (e.g., information someone else has posted about you), contact the relevant parties and request that the information be deleted or modified. If some negative content cannot be deleted, be prepared to discuss it in an interview.
- Reconsider your friends. Searches of social networking sites will turn up information not only on you but also on your friends and their comments to you.

- Consider creating your own professional group on sites such as Facebook or BrightFuse.com. Such a group would cast a positive light on your candidacy and might lead to important contacts.
- Present yourself in a positive way by: (1) communicating effectively when blogging and posting to social networking sites; (2) providing evidence of creativity and initiative in your web-based content; and (3) mentioning awards, accolades, and positive references in your web-based content.

Overall, the message is quite clear: people must be aware of the electronic image that they project. Not only do recruiters screen people out based on negative information found in cyberspace, they also look for positive information there.

Sources: D. Aucoin. 2007. "MySpace vs. Workplace," *Boston Globe*, May 29, at http://www.boston.com/news/globe/living/articles/2007/05/29/myspace_vs_workplace; M. Brandel. 2007. "How to 'Get Found' On the Web," *Computerworld*, March 26, vol. 41, no. 13, p. 30; W.M. Bulkeley. 2006. "Technology (A Special Report)—The Inside View: Employee Blogs Can Put a Human Face on Companies, But That's Not Always a Good Thing," *Wall Street Journal (Eastern Edition)*, New York: April 3, p. R.7;.R. Haefner. 2009. "More Employers Screening Candidates via Social Networking Sites," at http://www.careerbuilder.com/Article/CB-1337-Getting-Hired-More-Employers-Screening-Candidates-via-Social-Networking-Sites/; D. Willmer. 2009. "Managing Your Digital Footprint," *T + D*, 63 no. 6: pp. 84–85.

Nonverbal Communication

We can easily understand the concept of verbal communication, which involves written or spoken language; however, **nonverbal communication** is frequently as important or even more important. Forms of nonverbal communication include facial expressions, tone of voice, personal appearance (such as dress), contact or touch, and various mannerisms. In general, nonverbal communications fall into three categories: body language, paralanguage, and gestures. *Body language* (sometimes referred to as "kinesics") includes facial expressions; the use of hands, arms, and legs; and posture. *Paralanguage* refers to how something is said, such as how tone of voice, pitch of voice, and silence are used. *Gestures* are signs used to convey specific meanings (such as making a circle with your fingers to indicate "okay" or shrugging your shoulders to indicate "I don't know").

nonverbal communication
Communication that takes place without using spoken or written language, such as communication through facial expressions and body language.

All of us have had a great deal of experience with nonverbal communication. In fact, between 60 and 90 percent of all interpersonal communication is nonverbal.[61] You have probably heard the adage "actions speak louder than words" or heard someone say they received "good vibes" from someone else. These phrases refer to nonverbal communication. One of the reasons that we place so much weight on nonverbal behavior is that it is "leaky behavior." Leaky behaviors are those that we cannot control. Therefore, people may be more likely to express their true feelings through nonverbal means rather than through verbal means, which are easy to control.

Nonverbal communication is important because, along with the sender's verbal expressions, it provides information about the person's attitudes and emotional or mental state. For example, a person's tone of voice, facial expression, and body movements can give us information about the person's feelings (timidity, enthusiasm, anger), which may either support or conflict with the words used. Nonverbal communication can also provide a useful form of feedback. Facial expressions can show whether the receiver understands the sender's message and how he or she feels about it. For this reason, face-to-face communication is frequently more effective than written communication, as we have already seen. In general, therefore, a manager should try to provide job directions and discuss performance through face-to-face communication with associates.

Because nonverbal behavior is more difficult to control than verbal behavior, it can reveal whether a person is lying. This issue has been given a great deal of attention, especially in light of its practical implications. For example, U.S. Customs officials were able to increase their hit rate in spotting drug carriers from 4.2 percent to 22.5 percent after they had been trained to read body language.[62] In the area of business negotiations, it is particularly important that people be able to read body language to identify when others are being deceptive. It is also important for negotiators to be aware of their own nonverbal cues.[63] For example, experienced negotiators often are able to determine whether the other party is lying through nonverbal cues such as the following:

- Subtle shifts in the pitch or tone of a person's voice[64]
- Long pauses before answering a question[65]
- Certain mannerisms, such as shifting limbs, licking one's lips repeatedly, scratching, or grooming[66]
- Fleeting smiles[67]

Another issue involves cultural differences in nonverbal communication. Given the increase in diversity within U.S. organizations and the globalization of the business world, it has become very important for people to understand these differences. Members of different cultures vary a great deal in how they present themselves and in their norms for nonverbal communication. Some of these differences are discussed later in the chapter. However, one aspect of nonverbal communication appears to be the same for all human beings. People of all cultures seem to discern and label facial expressions showing certain basic emotions in the same way.[68] These basic emotions include fear, disgust, surprise, happiness, and anger. Therefore, people in a variety of countries such as the United States, Spain, Argentina, New Guinea, and Japan are all likely to recognize a smile as a sign of happiness and a scowl as a sign of disgust.

Barriers to Effective Communication

At the beginning of this chapter, we emphasized how important timely, accurate, and informative communication is to an organization's overall performance and to the individuals who work within the firm. We also pointed out that organizations experience many communication problems. Here, we address the barriers to effective communication. These barriers can be categorized into organizational and individual sources.[69]

Organizational Barriers

Organizational barriers to effective communication include information overload, information distortion, jargon, time pressures, cross-cultural barriers, and breakdowns in the communication network.

Information Overload

In our present-day organizations, managers and associates are frequently burdened with more information than they can process. This overload occurs for several reasons. First, organizations face higher levels of uncertainty because of escalating change and turbulence in the external environment, so they obtain more information to reduce the uncertainty. Second, the increasing complexity of tasks and organizational structures creates a need for more information. Again, organizations employ more specialists to provide the needed information, placing greater information-processing burdens on organizational members. Third, ongoing developments in technology increase the amount of information available to associates and managers.

As mentioned, when associates or managers are overloaded with information, they cannot process all of it. Instead, they may try to escape the situation, or they may prioritize information so that some is attended to and the rest is ignored. Consider what happens when you are at a party and there are several conversations going on around you, music is playing, and someone is watching the game on TV. It is impossible to focus on everything. In order to focus on a specific conversation, you need to tune out everything else. Selecting only a portion of the available information for use, however, can result in inaccurate or incomplete communication in the organizational context.[70]

In recent years, the development and widespread use of cell phones, e-mail, and instant messaging has further increased the information overload problem—anyone can contact anyone anywhere. People in most organizations send and receive e-mail messages at work on a regular basis. Therefore, even associates at lower levels can quickly and easily send messages to higher-level managers, although this is frowned upon in many organizations. Similarly, top executives can communicate messages almost instantaneously to all associates regardless of their location. Obviously, this technology contributes to information overload, particularly for managers at higher levels. With these advances in technology, we are facing two overload problems that were not so common only a few years ago: forwarding frenzies and spamming.

Forwarding frenzies occur because electronic communication makes it very easy to pass on information to everyone. One common behavior is to forward messages to anyone who might have even the remotest interest. Thus, we receive many messages that we need to process but in which we do not have any real interest.

As you are no doubt aware, spam is unsolicited electronic junk mail. Despite anti-spam legislation in many states and increasingly sophisticated filtering systems that guard against offensive spam, the amount of spam with which people must cope at work is increasing at an alarming rate. Indeed, *InformationWeek* reported that almost 80 percent of all e-mail sent in a recent month was spam mail.[71] A study conducted by researchers at the University of Maryland estimated that spam mail cost U.S. businesses almost $22 billion due to time lost by associates reading and deleting junk mail.[72]

One way in which organizations are trying to deal with the overload caused by electronic messaging and e-mail is by adopting newer, web-based interactive technologies for internal communications. These include blogs, wiki sites, and social networking sites. With this technology, messages are all posted in one place, avoiding redundancy.

Information Distortion

It is common for information to be distorted, either intentionally or unintentionally. Unintentional distortion can occur because of honest mistakes or time pressure. On the other hand, intentional distortion often occurs because of competition between work units in an organization. Departments frequently have to compete for scarce resources in their operating budgets. Research has suggested that some units may believe that they can compete more effectively by distorting or suppressing information, thus placing their competitors at a disadvantage by keeping accurate information from them.[73] This is not a healthy situation, but it can occur if managers are not careful.

Suppression or distortion of information can (and does) also occur when a subordinate has more information than his manager. One study found that some subordinates suppress or misrepresent information about budgets when they have private information unknown to the manager.[74] For example, associates may suppress information about the amount of travel expenses, leaving the supervisor to discover the problem at audit time.

Specialty Area Jargon

One problem in large, complex organizations concerns the proliferation of specialists. Specialists are highly knowledgeable within their own fields but often have limited understanding of other fields. In addition, they often have their own "language," or jargon. It may be difficult for two specialists in different fields to communicate effectively with one another because they use different terminology. For example, a financial specialist may use terms such as *EBITA*, *accelerated depreciation*, and *P and L statement*. An information-systems specialist may use terms such as *firmware, hexadecimal, bytes,* and *PLII*. Each must understand the other's terminology if the two are to communicate.

Time Pressures

In most organizations, work needs to be done under deadlines, which create time pressures and constrain an individual's ability to communicate. When people are under time pressure, they sometimes do not carefully develop a message before sending it.[75] In addition, the pressure of a deadline often does not allow time to receive feedback, so the sender may not know whether the receiver accurately perceived the message.

Cross-Cultural Barriers

As discussed in Chapter 3, the business world is becoming more global, increasing the amount of regular cross-cultural communication. Effective cross-cultural communication is necessary for the financial success of international ventures.[76] Communication problems cause many expatriate managers to fail in their international assignments, leading to the removal of the manager or the failure of the international venture. These failures cost multinational corporations billions of dollars.[77] Many U.S. firms compete in foreign markets, and increasing numbers of foreign firms have moved into the U.S. market in recent years. Also, millions of U.S. workers are foreign-born. Thus, North American workers must deal with cross-cultural communication issues even in domestic locations. Exhibit 9-4 lists common differences in communication patterns in the United States and other cultures.

Cross-cultural barriers involve lack of language fluency or a broader lack of cultural fluency.[78] Even though English is frequently used for business around the world,[79] the potential for language barriers continues to exist in cross-cultural communications. Independently of whether English is used, one or more parties to a conversation might not speak the chosen language as well as others. Also, research has shown that many messages coming into a foreign unit of a firm arrive in the local language.[80] If knowledge of that language is weak, then trouble can ensue. Those who learn the local language often earn more respect within the culture.

Because many products are sold internationally, language is a very important consideration in product names and slogans. Major companies have experienced poor results by trying to use North American English names for products sold in foreign countries, especially when they have ignored how the name translated into other languages. For example, Enco (the former name of Exxon petroleum company) means "stalled car" in Japanese. Direct translation of advertising slogans presents similar problems. The slogan "Come alive with Pepsi," for instance, translated into "Come out of the grave" in German.

EXHIBIT 9-4   Examples of Cultural Differences between the United States and Other Cultures

Communication	In the United States	Elsewhere
Eye contact	Direct	In many Asian countries, extended eye contact is unacceptable.
Time orientation	Punctual—"Time is money"	Asian and Latin American cultures have longer time horizons; resolving issues is more important than being on time.
Answering questions	Direct and factual	Many Asian cultures view being direct as rude and aggressive.
Self-presentation	Self-promotion rewarded	Many other cultures (e.g., Asian, Russian) find this rude.
Posture	Open body posture preferred (e.g., arms relaxed)	In Japan, a closed body posture is preferred (e.g., crossed arms and legs).
Indicating "no"	Shaking one's head from side to side	In Bulgaria, the "no" signal means "I'm listening," rather than "I disagree."

Language fluency is one dimension of what is known as **cultural fluency**—the ability to identify, understand, and apply cultural differences that influence communication.[81] Language fluency is necessary for cultural fluency but is not enough by itself. Take, for example, the situation faced by Sue, an expatriate manager. When she was in Singapore, she asked a hotel clerk, who spoke English fluently, for the location of the health spa. She had seen several signs indicating that the hotel had opened a new spa, but none of the signs gave the location. The clerk responded that the hotel had no spa, although Sue kept arguing, "But I saw the signs!" After asking others and finally finding the spa, Sue concluded that the first clerk either had lied to her or was totally incompetent. Had she understood that many Asian cultures uphold the value of "face," or unwillingness to experience the embarrassment of saying "I don't know," she might have interpreted the situation differently.

cultural fluency
The ability to identify, understand, and apply cultural differences that influence communication.

Network Breakdowns

Breakdowns in the communication network frequently occur in large organizations because so much information flows through those networks. Many things can interfere with the flow—mail can be misplaced, messages may not be received by those targeted, and people can forget to relay pieces of information. Larger organizations have more problems because messages must flow through more people, increasing the probability that a message will be transmitted inaccurately at some point.

Breakdowns can also involve technology. The aftermath of Hurricane Katrina provides a vivid example. The *Experiencing Organizational Behavior* feature illustrates the strategic importance of managing communications technology and the information exchanges they support. When companies lose servers due to power outages or when malware infects intranets or when BlackBerrys will not function because of systemwide failure, the results might not be death and mayhem on the scale of Hurricane Katrina, but the chaos and financial losses can be substantial.

Communication Casualties

©AP/Wide World Photos

On August 29, 2005, Hurricane Katrina ripped through the Gulf Coast, devastating hundreds of thousands of homes, leveling entire towns, and resulting in over 1,800 deaths. After the storm, several levees surrounding Lake Pontchartrain failed, causing 80 percent of the city of New Orleans to be covered in water. For blocks and blocks, all that was visible from aerial views were rooftops, often with desperate people on top trying to flag down rescue helicopters. Cars and refrigerators floated down main streets. In many areas, the only way to get around was by boat. Swimming in the toxic, sludgy floodwater was extremely dangerous, even though it was the only way many people were able to save their lives. Some weren't so lucky, as dead bodies were often found floating down the streets of once-active and charming neighborhoods.

As if the disaster weren't enough, the attempt by authorities to respond to the disaster was shockingly inept, with a few exceptions, such as the efforts of the U.S. Coast Guard. Thousands of people waited on rooftops or overpasses for days to be rescued from the flood, without adequate food or water in insufferable heat. Looting was rampant in the city, with reports that even some New Orleans police officers were taking part in the activities. About 30,000 people were trapped in the Superdome without basic necessities, under a leaking roof, and in filthy conditions. It took five days to rescue these people. Another 15,000 to 20,000 people were stranded at the Ernest N. Morial Convention Center, right outside the famed French Quarter, suffering from the same heat, filth, and lack of food and water as those in the Superdome. People who needed medicine for diseases such as diabetes, hypertension, and asthma became critically ill because of the lack of medical care. Rumors of rape and murder terrified the crowds. Approximately 15 percent of the police force deserted. The rest of the nation looked on in horror while watching TV reports of scenes that one would never imagine taking place in a major U.S. city.

Since that late-summer week in 2005, a great deal of examination of what went wrong has taken place. Why weren't agencies, such as the Federal Emergency Management Association (FEMA), the Red Cross, or the New Orleans Police Department able to come to the aid of New Orleanians sooner and more effectively? Blame can be, and has been, placed on many. One factor, however, that everyone agrees thwarted rescue attempts and fostered the chaos following Katrina was a major failure of communications.

In order to deal effectively with such a crisis, rescue agencies and first responders, such as FEMA, the New Orleans Police Department, the Red Cross, the Louisiana National Guard, and local rescue organizations, must be able to work together, which means they must be able to communicate among themselves. There is a need for strong communication related to the extent and form of damage, what type of problems are emerging, where the damage has occurred, and what type of aid is needed and where. Also, in order to prevent panic, people affected by the crisis must be provided with communications about what has happened, safety procedures, potential dangers, and instructions for further action. In the case of Katrina, the communication system needed to accomplish these tasks was broken:

- Millions of telephone lines were knocked down.
- Thirty-eight 911 call centers went down.
- Local wireless networks had considerable damage, making most cell phones in the area useless.
- Thirty-seven of 41 radio stations in New Orleans were unable to broadcast.
- The NOPD's communications system was inoperable for three days.

Six out of eight police headquarters were flooded, making it impossible to establish command centers. There was a severe shortage of satellite phones that allowed for communication.

- Hundreds of first responders were able to communicate through only two radio channels, jamming the system and causing great delays in the communication of vital information.
- Verizon Wireless did have generators for its cell towers; however, a number of these were stolen and a fuel truck bringing fuel to the generators was stopped at gunpoint and its fuel taken.
- FEMA did not provide New Orleans with a mobile multimedia communications unit (used in emergencies) until four days after the storm.

In the case of Katrina, the breakdown of communication technology proved to be disastrous. What could have prevented this situation? Clearly, technology could have been more up-to-date and in better condition. More redundancies in communication systems also would have been helpful. Beyond these technology issues, better planning before the storm hit would have been beneficial.

Were lessons learned? Perhaps. The City of New Orleans and the entire Gulf Coast seemed better prepared for Gustav, which struck as a Category 2 hurricane just southwest of New Orleans in 2008. Houston and most of the surrounding areas of Texas seemed to be reasonably well prepared for Ike, which also struck as a Category 2 hurricane in 2008.

Sources: Select Bipartisan Committee to Investigate the Preparation for and Response to Hurricane Katrina, "A Failure of Initiative," U.S. Government Printing Office, Feb. 15, 2006, at http://www.gpoaccess.gov/congress/index.html; D. Brinkley. 2006. *The Great Deluge* New York: Harper Collins; W. Haygood, & A.S. Tyson. 2005. "It Was as If All of Us Were Already Pronounced Dead," *Washington Post*, Sept. 15, p. A01; M. Hunter. 2006. "Deaths of Evacuees Push Death Toll to 1,577," *Times Picayune*, May 19, at http://www.nola.com; C. Landry. 2008. "After the Storms," *Oil & Gas Journal*, 106 no. 48: A7–A9; M. Williams. 2008. "Thousands Flee from New Orleans: Hurricane Gustav Described as 'The Storm of the Century,'" *The Glasgow Herald*, Sept. 1, p. A2.

Individual Barriers

We have examined several organizational factors that can make effective communication difficult. Individual factors, however, are the most commonly cited barriers to effective communication. These factors include differing perceptual bases, semantic differences, status differences, consideration of self-interest, issues related to personal space, and poor listening skills.

Differing Perceptions

One of the most common communication problems occurs when the sender has one perception of a message and the receiver has another. Differing perceptions are caused by differing frames of reference. Our expectations or frames of reference can influence how we recall and interpret information.[82]

This communication problem is vividly displayed in an exchange that occurred between a coach and a quarterback in a hotly contested U.S. football game. There were 16 seconds left in the game. The team was behind by one point and had the ball on its opponent's 20-yard line with no timeouts remaining. A field goal would win the game. The safest thing to do would be to call a running play and then kick a field goal. The coach decided, however, that it was necessary to risk a pass play because no timeouts were left. (If the pass was dropped, the clock would stop. If it was caught in the end zone, the game would be won.)

The coach told the quarterback to call the play that they had discussed in practice for just such a situation. But they had discussed two plays (one a pass into the end zone and the other a running play). The quarterback assumed the coach wanted to take the safest course and called the running play. He handed off to the fullback, who carried the ball into the middle of the line. A big pileup ensued, and the clock continued to run. Before the quarterback could get off another play, time had run out, and the team lost the game. The coach and the quarterback had two different perceptions of the meaning of one message.

Semantic Differences

Semantics refers to the meaning people attach to symbols, such as words and gestures. Because the same words may have different meanings to different people, semantic differences can create communication problems. For example, the word *profit* has a positive connotation to most professionals in business, but for others it has a negative connotation as they interpret it to mean "rip-off" or "exploitation." Such differences are evident in the problems U.S. oil, pharmaceutical, and insurance companies have had in explaining their profits to the general public in the face of political attacks from Washington.

One reason for semantic differences inside organizations relates to the proliferation of specialists, as we mentioned earlier. Specialists tend to develop their own jargon; such terminology may have little meaning or a different set of meanings to a person outside the specialist's field. A second reason for semantic differences relates to variance in cultural background. This issue was also discussed earlier.

Status Differences

Status differences can result from both organizational and individual factors. Organizations create status differences through titles, offices, and support resources, but individuals attribute meaning to these differences. Status differences can lead to problems of source credibility and can create problems that block upward communication.[83] Sometimes, for example, subordinates are reluctant to express an opinion that is different from their managers', and managers—because of either time pressures or arrogance—may strengthen status barriers by not being open to feedback or other forms of upward communication. To be effective communicators, managers must overcome status differences with those who report to them.

Consideration of Self-Interest

Often, information provided by a person is used to assess her performance. For example, it is not uncommon for firms to request information from managers about their units' performance. Data such as forecasts of future activity, performance standards, and recommendations on capital budgets are often used in determining the managers' compensation. Research shows that where data accuracy cannot be independently verified, managers sometimes provide information that is in their own self-interest.[84] Although they might not intentionally distort the information that is sent, they might provide incomplete data, selecting only information that is in their own best interests.

Personal Space

All of us have a *personal space* surrounding our bodies. When someone enters that space, we feel uncomfortable. The size of the personal space differs somewhat among individuals; it also differs by gender and across cultures.[85] Women seem to have smaller personal spaces than men. Similarly, the typical personal space in some cultures (such as some European and South American cultures) is smaller than that in other cultures (such as the United States). Personal space affects, for example, how close together people stand when conversing. Suppose someone from a culture where the norm is to stand close together is talking with someone from a culture where the norm is to stand farther apart. The first person will tend to move forward as the second backs away, with each trying to adjust the space according to a different cultural norm. Each may consider the other discourteous, and it will be difficult for either to pay attention to what the other is saying. In this case, the difference in personal space can be a barrier to communication.

Poor Listening Skills

A frequent problem in communication rests not with the sender but with the receiver. The receiver must listen in order to hear and understand the sender's message, just as the sender must listen to feedback from the receiver. Managers spend more than 50 percent of their time in verbal communication, and some researchers estimate that they spend as much as 85 percent of this time talking. This does not leave much time for listening and receiving feedback. Perhaps more importantly, it has been estimated that managers listen with only about 25 percent efficiency.[86] Therefore, they hear and understand only 25 percent of what is communicated to them verbally. This can lead the speaker to become annoyed and discouraged, thus creating a bad impression of the listener.[87] Poor listening is not conducive to high-involvement management, because it breaks down the communication process and limits information sharing. Later we discuss ways in which listening can be improved.

Overcoming Communication Barriers

Several actions can be taken to address the problems identified in this chapter. We discuss those actions next.

Conduct Communication Audits

Analyzing the organization's communication needs and practices through periodic communication audits[88] is an important step in establishing effective communication. A **communication audit** examines an organization's internal and external communication to assess communication practices and capabilities and to determine needs. Communication audits can be conducted in-house (for example, by the Human Resource Management department) or by external consulting firms. Communication audits often are used to ascertain the quality of communication and to pinpoint any deficiencies in the organization. Audits can be conducted for the entire organization or for a single unit within the organization.

Communication audits usually examine the organization's communication philosophy and objectives, existing communication programs, communication media, quantity and quality of personal communications, and employee attitudes toward existing communications. The following is a recommended method for conducting a communication audit:

- Hold a planning meeting with all major parties to determine a specific approach and gain commitment to it.

communication audit
An analysis of an organization's internal and external communication to assess communication practices and capabilities and to determine needs.

- Conduct interviews with top management.
- Collect, inventory, and analyze communication material.
- Conduct associate interviews.
- Prepare and administer a questionnaire to measure attitudes toward communication.
- Communicate survey results.[89]

Improve Communication Climates

communication climate
Associates' perceptions regarding the quality of communication within the organization.

An organization's **communication climate** corresponds to associates' perceptions of the quality of communication within the organization.[90] The communication climate is important because it influences the extent to which associates identify with their organization.[91] Organizations can overcome communication barriers by establishing a communication climate where mutual trust exists between senders and receivers, communication credibility is present, and feedback is encouraged. Managers also should encourage a free flow of downward, upward, and horizontal communication.[92] People must be comfortable in communicating their ideas openly and in asking questions when they do not understand or they want to know more. Information should be available and understandable. People in organizational units should be allowed to develop their own communication systems independently for an effective communication climate.[93]

Encourage Individual Actions

Managers and associates can also act as individuals to help overcome communication barriers. Experts recommend the following ways to improve interpersonal communication.

Know Your Audience

People often engage in what communication expert Virgil Scudder refers to as "me to me to me" communication.[94] With this phrase, Scudder is describing communicating with others as if you were communicating with yourself. Such communication assumes that others share your frame of reference and, in the absence of feedback, that people interpret the message as you intend it. Take, for example, an information technology expert trying to explain to his technologically unsophisticated colleagues how to use new computer software. He may use jargon that they do not understand, not fully explain the steps, and mistake their dumbfounded silence for understanding. In the end, the IT professional believes he has done his job and taught others how to use the new program. However, because of poor communication, his colleagues learned little and are frustrated. To communicate effectively, people must know their audience, including the audience's experience, frames of references, and motivations.

Select an Appropriate Communication Medium

Earlier, we discussed how various communication media differ in richness. When messages are complex and/or important, use of rich media, such as face-to-face communication, should be considered.[95] Also, when dealing with complex/important information, it can be beneficial to use several media—for example, by following a face-to-face communication with an e-mail message summarizing the discussion.

Regulate Information Flow and Timing

Regulating the flow of information can help to alleviate communication problems. Regulating flow involves discarding information of marginal importance and conveying only significant information. That is, do not pass on irrelevant information, or else important messages may be buried by information overload or noise.

The proper timing of messages is also important. Sometimes people are more likely to be receptive to a message and to perceive it accurately than at other times. Thus, if you have an important message to send, you should not send it when recipients are about to leave work, are fully engaged in some other task, or are receiving other communication.

Encourage Feedback Related to Understanding

Communication should be a two-way process. To ensure that the received message is interpreted as intended, feedback from the recipient is necessary. Some guidelines that individuals can use to obtain feedback are as follows:

- Ask recipients to repeat what they have heard.
- Promote and cultivate feedback, but don't try to force it.
- Reward those who provide feedback and use the feedback received. For example, thank people for providing feedback.
- Respond to feedback, indicating whether it is correct.[96] In other words, obtain feedback, use it, and then feed it back to recipients.

Listen Actively

As mentioned earlier, poor listening skills are a common barrier to effective communication. Listening is not a passive, naturally occurring activity. People must actively and consciously listen to others in order to be effective communicators. Exhibit 9-5 outlines the steps in being an active listener.

EXHIBIT 9-5   Steps to Effective Listening

1. *Stop talking.* Often, we talk more than we should without giving the other person a chance to respond. If we are thinking about what we will say when we talk, we cannot focus attention on the person to whom we wish to listen. Do not interrupt.

2. *Pay attention.* Do not allow yourself to be distracted by thinking about something else. Often, we need to make an active effort to pay attention when others are speaking.

3. *Listen empathetically.* Try to take the speaker's perspective. Mirror the speaker's body language and give him or her nonjudgmental encouragement to speak.

4. *Hear before evaluating.* Do not draw premature conclusions or look for points of disagreement. Listen to what the person has to say before jumping to conclusions or judgment.

5. *Listen to the whole message.* Look for consistency between the verbal and the nonverbal messages. Try to assess the person's feelings or intentions, as well as just facts.

6. *Send feedback.* In order to make sure that you have heard correctly, paraphrase what was heard and repeat it to the person you were listening to.

Organizations cannot accomplish their goals without using effective communication practices. Managers and leaders must communicate with associates to ensure that they understand the tasks to be done. In doing so, they need to use a two-way communication process to make certain that communication is understood as intended. Without effective communication, human capital in the organization will be underutilized and will not be leveraged successfully. Organizations that do not use their human capital well usually implement their strategies ineffectively, and so their performance suffers. In this circumstance, a firm might unnecessarily change its strategy because senior managers do not realize that strategy implementation—not the actual strategy—was the problem. Of course, with continued poor performance, CEOs are likely to lose their jobs.[97]

Information serves as a base for developing organizational strategies. Usually, the organization gathers significant amounts of information on its markets, customers, and competitors to use in the development of the best strategy. Interestingly, some organizations use blogging to gather intelligence on their competitors. In addition, before selecting a strategy, managers frequently obtain information on the organization's strengths and weaknesses. To get all of this information requires substantial communication with internal and external parties. If managers do not communicate well, they are unlikely to obtain the information needed to develop the correct strategy. Therefore, top executives must ensure that they communicate effectively and that all managers (and hopefully associates) do so as well. Good communication is the base on which most of what happens in the organization depends.

Critical Thinking Questions

1. For which tasks in a manager's job is effective communication critical? Explain.
2. Which contributes more to an organization's performance—oral communication or written communication? Justify your answer.
3. What are the strengths and weaknesses in your personal communication abilities? How can you best take advantage of your strengths and overcome your weaknesses to have a successful career?
4. What impact is rapidly developing communication technology likely to have on communication in organizations?

What This Chapter Adds to Your Knowledge Portfolio

In this chapter, we have discussed the communication process and have examined both organizational and interpersonal communication issues. We have also described organizational and individual barriers to communication, along with ways of overcoming these barriers. To summarize, we have covered the following points:

- The communication process is a two-way process in which a sender encodes a message, the message travels through a communication medium to the receiver, and the receiver decodes the message and returns feedback to the sender. Effective communication occurs when the received message has the same meaning as the sent message.
- Two important aspects of organizational communication are communication networks and the direction of communication flow. Networks can be sparse or dense and centralized or decentralized. Communication can occur in a downward, upward, or horizontal direction; in the case of 360-degree feedback, it occurs in all three directions.

- Important aspects of interpersonal communication include its formal or informal nature, media choices, communication technology, and nonverbal dynamics.
- Common barriers to effective communication that occur at the organizational level are information overload, information distortion, jargon, time pressures, cross-cultural barriers, and breakdowns in the communication network.
- Common individual barriers to effective communication include differing perceptions, semantic differences, status differences, self-interest, issues related to personal space, and poor listening skills.
- Organizations can improve communication effectiveness by conducting communication audits and creating positive communication climates.
- Individuals can improve their interpersonal communication by knowing their audience, selecting appropriate communication media, regulating information flow and timing, encouraging feedback, and engaging in active listening.

? back to the knowledge objectives

1. Why is communication strategically important to organizations?
2. How would you describe an effective communication process?
3. What are the advantages and disadvantages of the various types of communication networks?
4. How are upward, downward, and horizontal communication accomplished?
5. Define *interpersonal communication*. How do formal and informal communication processes differ?
6. What is media richness, and how do different communication media vary in richness?
7. How can technology affect the communication process?
8. How does nonverbal communication contribute to the communication process?
9. What are six organizational barriers to effective communication?
10. What are six individual barriers to effective communication?
11. What are communication audits, and how are they conducted?
12. What specific actions can individuals take to overcome communication barriers?

Key Terms

communication, p. 305
encoding, p. 305
communication medium or communication channel, p. 305
decoding, p. 305
feedback, p. 305
sparse networks, p. 307
dense networks, p. 307
centralized networks, p. 307

decentralized networks. p. 307
downward communication, p. 308
upward communication, p. 309
horizontal communication, p. 311
interpersonal communication, p. 312

formal communication, p. 312
informal communication, p. 312
rumors, p. 312
gossip, p. 312
nonverbal communication, p. 317
cultural fluency, p. 321
communication audit, p. 325
communication climate, p. 326

---

building your human capital

Presentation Dos and Don'ts

Making presentations can be one of the most challenging communication exercises faced by anyone, especially those who are not accustomed to presenting. Below is a quiz to help you determine how you fare in giving public presentations. The first 16 questions are presentation "dos" while the second 16 questions are presentation "don'ts."

Answer the questions based on your own recollections of presentations you have given. Perhaps an even better assessment of your presentation effectiveness would involve having a friend in the audience fill out this questionnaire for you when you are giving a presentation. In answering the questions, use the following scale:

1	2	3	4	5
Rarely	Seldom	Sometimes	Frequently	Almost Always

Presentation "Dos"

When you are making a presentation to a group of people, how often do you:
1. Think about the audience's collective point of view?
2. Acknowledge that the audience may be different from you?
3. Do research on who constitutes your audience?
4. Tailor your message to suit the audience?
5. Provide a clear outline of what you are going to discuss?
6. Provide illustrative visual information?
7. Summarize your main points?
8. Make between three and six major points?
9. Gauge the audience's reaction as you proceed?
10. Ask the audience for feedback?
11. Stop and provide clarification when the audience seems confused?
12. Solicit questions?
13. Use body language to get your points across?
14. Maintain eye contact with the audience?
15. Modulate your tone of voice to keep people interested?
16. Show enthusiasm for your topic?

Presentation "dos" scoring:
Add together your scores on the items for each section below. If you scored less than 16 in a particular section, you need to work on that aspect of your presentation style.

Questions 1–4: Knowing your audience. Total score on questions 1–4: _____

Questions 5–8: Structure. Total score on questions 5–8: _____

Questions 9–12: Feedback. Total score on questions 9–12: _____

Questions 13–16: Animation. Total score on questions 13–16: _____

Presentation "Don'ts"

When you are making a presentation to a group of people, how often do you:
1. Present information at the most difficult level possible, because it will make you appear knowledgeable?
2. Assume everyone in the audience agrees with you?
3. Make the presentation as simple as possible so even the least-educated person will understand?
4. Believe that if a presentation works with one crowd, it will work with another?
5. Present very detailed visual information to make sure the audience picks up on all the details?
6. Avoid a summary because it should be obvious what you have already said?
7. Get distracted by random questions?
8. Attempt to be extremely thorough in getting all of your points across, even if it means you don't have time to explain all of them?
9. Look out over the heads of the people in the audience?

10. Refuse questions in order to get your message across?
11. Ignore signs of confusion or lack of interest in the audience because it will just get you off your point?
12. Focus all your attention on a friendly face in the audience?
13. Read from your notes?
14. Make nervous gestures (fidget with your hair, tap your foot, rattle your change, or the like)?
15. Speak in monotone because it is more authoritative?
16. Speak as quickly as possible?

Presentation "don'ts" scoring:

Add together your scores on the items for each section below. If you scored more than 8 in a particular section, you need to work on that aspect of your presentation style.

Questions 1–4: Knowing your audience. Total score on questions 1–4: _____

Questions 5–8: Structure. Total score on questions 5–8: _____

Questions 9–12: Feedback. Total score on questions 9–12: _____

Questions 13–16: Animation. Total score on questions 13–16: _____

Explanation of Section Topics

Knowing your audience: In order to reach audience members and engage their interest, you must understand their point of view, their motivation for hearing your presentation, their attitudes about what you are saying, and their level of knowledge about your topic.

Structure: To get your message across, it is usually best to keep it organized and fairly simple—stick to a few major, important points. If some members of the audience want more details, offer to speak to them later, provide handouts, or give them a source of further information. If your visual presentation is too complicated, the audience will be reading your slides rather than listening to you.

Feedback: Remember that feedback is an essential part of the communication process. You need to be aware of how your audience is responding so that you can further tailor your presentation to ensure that audience members understand or are engaged with what you are telling them. Do not ignore their reactions.

Animation: Everyone has experienced both "good speakers" and "boring speakers." Don't be one of the latter. Be lively, animated, and show enthusiasm for your subject. If you don't, your audience won't either.

---

an organizational behavior moment
Going North

"Roll 'em!"

"Take number 64. Lights. Camera. Action!"

"Jane, I've missed you so much these past few weeks."

"I know, my darling. I've missed you, too."

"We must make up for lost time."

"Cut, cut, cut! Tom, you're playing this scene like a frozen polar bear. This is a tender love scene!" Helen screamed in her loudest, shrillest voice. "You're supposed to play it with feeling and tenderness. You want to make people think you love Jane."

"Helen, I could play the part better if you'd just get off my back. I knew more about romance when I was a teenager than you do now. Who are you to tell me how to play a love scene?" Tom shot back.

Helen called out, "That's all for today, everybody. We can let our mechanical lover calm down and maybe get in a better mood for this scene tomorrow."

With that Tom stomped off the set, and everyone began to disperse.

Helen Reardon is the producer and director of the film *Going North*, based on a novel that had stayed on the bestseller list for 16 months. Helen is considered to be one of the best directors in Hollywood. She already has two Academy Awards to her credit and many hit motion pictures.

Tom Nesson is a promising young actor. His most recent film, *The Western Express*, was well received at the box office and thrust him into the limelight. In fact, one of the reasons he was chosen to play the leading male part in *Going North* was his current popularity. He is considered by industry insiders as a potential superstar.

All went well on the set for the first few weeks. But then problems began to arise. First came arguments between the set-design and wardrobe staff. There were feelings that the sets and the costumes didn't match. Some thought that the colors even clashed at times. The question was, "Whose fault is it?" Of course, each group blamed the other.

Later, the makeup staff walked off the job, claiming that they were being asked to work unreasonable hours. Helen did have a penchant for shooting movies at odd hours, particularly if the scene called for it. The makeup staff claimed that they had an informal agreement with studio management about the hours they would work and that this agreement had been violated. Although studio executives convinced them to return to work, the "peace" was an uneasy one. Now there was this blowup between Helen and Tom. Everyone hoped that the problems between the two were temporary.

The next day, everybody was back on the set on time except Tom. He came in about 10 minutes late. He explained that the makeup people were slow in getting his makeup on. No one questioned this, and they began where they had left off the previous day.

"Take number one. Lights. Camera. Action! ... Take number 9. ... Take number 19. ... Take number 31. ... " Finally, Helen yelled "Cut! Tom, we've got to find a way to get this right. We can't go on like this forever. What do you suggest?"

"I suggest you shoot it like it is. The scene was good. I've done it well several times, but you seem to keep finding small things wrong."

"Tom, do you really know what love is? Your acting doesn't show it."

With that Tom exploded. "Yes, I know what love is, but you obviously don't." He then left the set, shouting, "I'm not coming back on the set until you're gone!"

Helen left the set immediately, going straight to the studio executive offices. She barged into the president's office and stated, "Either you get rid of Tom Nesson on this movie, or I go!"

The studio executives were in a quandary. They did not want to lose either Helen or Tom. Neither had a history of being difficult to work with. They were not sure what was causing the problem. This movie seemed to be causing all kinds of problems, with the wildcat strike by makeup staff and the disagreements between wardrobe and set design. They obviously needed to examine all of the circumstances involved in the making of this film.

Discussion Questions

1. What do you suppose is really causing the problem between Helen and Tom? Explain.
2. Discuss the problems between the set design and wardrobe staff and those with the makeup department.
3. Could any of the problems in this case have been prevented? If so, how? How can the problems now be solved?

---

team exercise

Communication Barriers

This exercise demonstrates the importance of communication in organizations and shows how barriers affect communications.

Procedure

1. With the aid of the instructor, the class will be divided into teams of three to five persons.
2. The teams will perform the following tasks:
   - Identify all of the major ways in which your institution communicates with students (catalog, registration, advising, etc.). Be as specific as possible. Write each of these down.
   - Determine instances in which communication problems arise between the institution and students (for example, where students need more or better information). Write these down.
   - Identify specific barriers that make effective communication between students and the institution difficult. Write these down.
   - Development recommendations to overcome the barriers and solve the communication problems previously noted.

The instructor will allow 30 minutes for the teams to complete their analyses.

3. The teams will present their lists of means of communication, communication problems, and recommendations, in that order. First, each team will present one item from the means-of-communication list, then the next team will present one, and so on, until all communication means have been presented. This same procedure will be followed for communication problems and recommendations, respectively. The instructor will compile a list of all the teams' responses.

4. The instructor will guide a discussion of this exercise, noting the similarity of communication problems in all types of organizations.

The presentation and discussion should require about 30 minutes.

Endnotes

1. Monge, P.R., Farace, R.V., Eisenberg, E.M., Miller, K.I., & White, L.L. 1984. The process of studying process in organizational communication. *Journal of Communication,* 34: 234–243.
2. Whitely, W. 1984. An exploratory study of managers' reactions to properties of verbal communication. *Personnel Psychology,* 37: 41–59.
3. Shapiro, I.S. 1984. Managerial communication: The view from inside. *California Management Review,* 27: 157–172.
4. Clampitt, P.G., & Downs, C.W. 1993. Employee perceptions of the relationship between communication and productivity: A field study. *Journal of Business Communication*s, 30: 5–28.
5. Pinto, M.B., & Pinto, J.K. 1991. Determinants of cross-functional cooperation in the project implementation process. *Project Management Journal,* 22: 13–20.
6. Ammeter, A.P., & Dukerich, J.M. 2002. Leadership, team building, and team member characteristics in high performance project teams. *Engineering Management Journal,* 14: 3–10; Henderson, L.S. 2004. Encoding and decoding communication competencies in project management—an exploratory study. *International Journal of Project Management,* 22: 469–476.
7. Snyder, R.A., & Morris, J.H. 1984. Organizational communication and performance. *Journal of Applied Psychology,* 69: 461–465.
8. Thomas, D. 2005. Poor communication makes UK workers less productive. April 6, 2005, at www.PersonnelToday.com; Computing Technology Industry Association Press Release. March 6, 2007. "Poor communications is the most frequent cause of project failure, CompTIA web poll reveals." At http://www.comptia.org/pressroom/get_pr.aspx?prid=1227.
9. Whitely, W. 1984. An exploratory study of managers' reactions to properties of verbal communication. *Personnel Psychology,* 37: 41–59.
10. Hinske, G. 1985. The uneven record of the corporate communicators. *International Management,* 40: 2.
11. Collison, J., & Frangos, C. 2002. Aligning HR with organization strategy survey. Society for Human Resource Management Research Report. Alexandria, VA: Society for Human Resource Management.
12. Dewhurst, S. 2007. Key findings from the pulse survey. *Strategic Communication Management,* 11 (1): 6–7.
13. Humphreys, M.A. 1983. Uncertainty and communication strategy formation. *Journal of Business Research,* 11: 187–199.
14. Clevenger, T., Jr., & Matthews, J. 1971. *The speech communication process.* Glenview, IL: Scott Foresman.
15. Ibid.
16. Daft, R.L., & Lengel, R.H. 1986. Organizational information requirements: Media richness and structural design. *Management Science,* 32: 554–571.
17. Greenbaum, H.H. 1974. The audit of organizational communication. *Academy of Management Journal,* 17: 739–754.
18. Cross, R., Ehrlich, K., Dawson, R., & Helferich, J. 2008. Managing collaboration: Improving team effectiveness through a network perspective., *California Management Review,* 50 (4): 74-98; Shaw, M.E. 1964. Communication networks. In L. Berkowitz (Ed.), Advances in experimental social psychology. New York: Academic Press, pp. 111–147.
19. Gargiulo, M., Ertug, G., & Galunic, C. 2009. The two faces of control: Network closure and individual performance among knowledge workers. *Administrative Science Quarterly,* 54: 299-333; Wong, S.-S. 2008. Task knowledge overlap and knowledge variety: The role of advice network structures and impact on group effectiveness. *Journal of Organizational Behavior,* 29: 591–614.
20. Friedrich, T.L., Vessey, W.B., Schuelke, M.J., Ruark, G.A., & Mumford, M.D. 2009. A framework for understanding collective leadership: The selective utilization of leader and team expertise within networks. *The Leadership Quarterly,* 20: 933–958; Wong, Task knowledge overlap and knowledge variety.
21. Leavitt, H.J. 1951. Some effects of certain communication patterns on group performance. *Journal of Abnormal and Social Psychology,* 46: 38–50.
22. Balkundi, P. & Harrison, D.A. 2006. Ties, leaders, and time in teams: Strong inference about network structure's effects on team viability and performance. *Academy of Management Journal,* 49: 49–68; Friedrich, Vessey, Schuelke, Ruark, & Mumford, A framework for understanding collective leadership. Also see: Balkundi, P., Barsness, Z., & Michael, J.H. 2009. Unlocking the Influence of leadership network structures on team conflict and viability. *Small Group Research,* 40: 301–322.
23. Burt, R.S. 2007. Secondhand brokerage: Evidence on the importance of local structure for managers, bankers, and analysts. *Academy of Management Journal,* 50: 119–148; Burt, R.S. 2006.

Brokerage and closure. New York: Oxford University Press; Pfeffer, J. 2008. A note on social networks and network structure. Stanford, CA: Stanford Graduate School of Business.

24. Watts, D. 2003. *Six degrees: The science of a connected age.* New York: W.W. Norton.

25. Ibid.

26. Sidel, R. 2009. Next crisis for U.S. Banks? Integration: Merger waves poses test to system. *Wall Street Journal,* Jan. 9: C.1; Whittaker, K.D. 2009. Wachovia fades to black. *Atlanta Tribune: The Magazine,* 22 (10): 46–47.

27. Bolton, P., & Dewatripont, M. 1994. The firm as a communication network. *Quarterly Journal of Economics,* 109: 809–839.

28. Freibel, G., & Raith, M. 2004. Abuse of authority and hierarchical communications. *Rand Journal of Economics,* 35: 224–244.

29. Jablin, F.M. 1982. Formal structural characteristics of organizations and superior–subordinate communication. *Human Communication Research,* 8: 338–347.

30. Sellers, P. 2004. Most powerful women in business. *Fortune,* October 4, at http://www.fortune.com.

31. Katz, D., & Kahn, R.L. 1978. *The social psychology of organizations* (2nd ed.). New York: John Wiley & Sons.

32. Collison & Frangos, Aligning HR with organization strategy survey.

33. Ghorpade, J. 2000. Managing five paradoxes of 360-degree feedback. *Academy of Management Executive,* 14: 140–150.

34. Lussier, R.N., & Achua, C.F. 2004. *Leadership: Theory, application, skill development* (2nd ed.). Eagan, MN: Thomson Southwestern.

35. Bettenhausen, K.L., & Fedor, D.B. 1997. Peer and upward appraisals: A comparison of their benefits and problems. *Group and Organization Management,* 22: 236–263; Freibel & Raith, Abuse of authority and hierarchical communications.

36. Atwater, L.E., & Brett, J.F. 2006. 360-degree feedback: Does it relate to changes in employee attitudes? *Group and Organization Management,* 31: 578–600.

37. Huseman, R.C., Lahiff, J.M., & Hatfield, J.D. 1976. *Interpersonal communication in organizations.* Boston, MA: Holbrook Press, p. 5.

38. Kurland, N.B., & Pelled, L.H. 2000. Passing the word: Toward a model of gossip and power in the workplace. *Academy of Management Review,* 25: 428–439.

39. Michelson, G., & Mouly, V.S. 2004. Do loose lips sink ships? The meaning, antecedents, and consequences of rumor and gossip in organizations. *Corporate Communications: An International Journal,* 9: 189–201.

40. Ibid.

41. McKay, B. 2000. At Coke layoffs inspire all manner of peculiar rumors, *Wall Street Journal (Eastern Edition),* October 17: p. A1.

42. Kurland, N.B., & Pelled, L.H. 2000. Passing the word.

43. Loughry, M.L., & Tosi, H.L. 2008. Performance implications of peer monitoring. *Organization Science,* 19: 876–890.

44. Sheer, V.C., & Chen, L. 2004. Improving media richness theory: A study of interaction goals, message valence, and task complexity in manager–subordinate communication. *Management Communication Quarterly,* 18: 76–93.

45. Daft, R.L., & Lengel, R.H. 1986. Organizational information requirements: Media richness and structural design. *Management Science,* 32: 554–571.

46. Trevino, L.K., Lengel, R.H., Bodensteiner, W., Gerloff, E., & Muir, N. 1990. The richness imperative and cognitive style: The role of individual differences in media choice behavior. *Management Communication Quarterly,* 4: 176–197.

47. Davis, A., Khazanchi, D., Murphy, J., Zigurs, I., & Owens, D. 2009. Avatars, people, and virtual worlds: Foundations for research in metaverses. *Journal of the Association for Information Systems,* 10: 90–117.

48. Daft, R.L., & Lengel, R.H. 1986. Organizational information requirements: Media richness and structural design. *Management Science,* 32: 554–571.

49. Sheer, V.C., & Chen, L. 2004. Improving media richness theory: A study of interaction goals, message valence, and task complexity in manager–subordinate communication. *Management Communication Quarterly,* 18: 76–93.

50. Fulk, J. 1993. Social construction of communication technology. *Academy of Management Journal,* 36: 921–950.

51. Turner, J.W., Grube, J.A., Tinsley, C.H., Lee, C., & O'Pell, C. 2006. Exploring the dominant media: How does media use reflect organizational norms and affect performance? *Journal of Business Communication,* 43: 220–250.

52. Fontaine, M.A., Parise, S., & Miller, D. 2004. Collaborative environments: An effective tool for transforming business processes. *Ivey Business Journal Online,* May–June: 1–7.

53. Desanctis, G., & Fulk, J. (Eds.). 1999. *Shaping organizational form: Communication, connection, and community.* Thousand Oaks, CA: Sage Publications.

54. Fontaine, M.A., Parise, S., & Miller, D. 2004. Collaborative environments: An effective tool for transforming business processes. *Ivey Business Journal Online,* May–June: 1–7.

55. Fortune 500 Business Blogging Wiki. At http://www.socialtext.net/bizblogs/index.cgi.

56. For more information, see CEO Blogwatch, at http://www.ceoblogwatch.com.

57. Baker, S., & Green, H. 2005. Blogs will change your business. *BusinessWeek online.* May 2. At www.businessweek.com/print/magazine/content/05_18/b3931001_mz001.htm.

58. Gard, L. 2005. Online extra: Stonyfield Farm's blog culture. May 2. At www.businessweek.com/print/magazine/content/05_18/b3931005_mz001.htm.

59. CBS/AP. 2007. JetBlue Attempts to calm passenger furor. CBS News. February 15. At http://www.cbsnews.com.stories/2007/02/15/national/printable2480665.shtml.

60. Baker, S., & Green, H. 2005. Blogs will change your business. *BusinessWeek online.* May 2. At www.businessweek.com/print/magazine/content/05_18/b3931001_mz001.htm.

61. Mehrabian, A. 1968. Communication without words. *Psychology Today,* 2: 53–55.

62. Davis, A., Pereira, J., & Buckley, W.M. 2002. Silent signals: Security concerns bring new focus on body language. *Wall Street Journal,* Aug. 15, p. A.1.

63. Schweitzer, M.E., Brodt, S.E., & Croson, R.T.A. 2002. Seeing and believing: Visual access and strategic use of deception. *International Journal of Conflict Management,* 13: 258–275.

64. Streeter, L.A., Krauss, R.M.N., & Geller, V. 1977. Pitch changes during attempted deception. *Journal of Personality and Social Psychology,* 35: 345–350.

65. Kraut, R.E. 1978. Verbal and nonverbal cues in the perception of lying. *Journal of Personality and Social Psychology,* 36: 380–391.

66. Ibid.

67. Davis, Pereira, & Buckley, Silent signals.

68. Ekman, P., & Oster, H. 1979. Facial expressions of emotion. *Annual Review of Psychology,* 30: 527–554.

69. Brown, D.S. 1975. Barriers to successful communication: Part 1. *Management Review,* 64: 24–29; Brown, D.S. 1976. Barriers to successful communication: Part 2. *Management Review,* 65: 15–21.

70. Marcus, H., & Zajonc, R.B. 1985. The cognitive perspective in social psychology. In G. Lindzey & E. Aronson (Eds.), *The handbook of social psychology* (3rd ed). New York: Random House, pp. 137–230.

71. Gaudin, S. 2007. Report: Spam levels rise for fifth month in a row. *InformationWeek,* March 1. At http://www.informationweek.com/story/showArticle.jhtml?articleID=197700567.

72. Claburn, T. 2005. Spam costs billions. *InformationWeek.* February 3. At http://www.informationweek.com/story/showArticle.jhtml?articleID=59300834.

73. Morgan, C.P., & Hitt, M.A. 1977. Validity and factor structure of House and Rizzo's effectiveness scales. *Academy of Management Journal,* 20: 165–169.

74. Bairman, S., & Evans, J.H., III. 1983. Pre-decision information and participative management control systems. *Journal of Accounting Research,* 21: 371–395.

75. Graham, J.R. 2002. Who do we thank (and curse) for e-mail? *Agency Sales,* November, 32: 23–26.

76. Harvey, M.G., & Griffith, D.A. 2002. Developing effective intercultural relationships: The importance of communication strategies. *Thunderbird International Business Review,* 44: 455–476.

77. Fisher, G.B., & Hartel, C.E.J. 2003. Cross-cultural effectiveness of Western expatriate–Thai client interactions: Lessons learned from IHRM research and theory. *Cross Cultural Management,* 10: 4–29.

78. Beamer, L. 1992. Learning intercultural communication competence. *Journal of Business Communication,* 29: 285–303.

79. Kranhold, K. 2004. Lost in translation?: Managers at multinationals may miss the job's nuances if they speak only English. *Wall Street Journal (Eastern Edition),* May 18, p. B.1.

80. Kilpatrick, R.H. 1984. International business communication practices. *Journal of Business Communication,* 21: 33–44.

81. Scott, J.C. 1999. Developing cultural fluency: The goal of international business communication instruction in the 21st century. *Journal of Education for Business,* 74: 140–144.

82. Marcus, H., & Zajonc, R. 1985. The cognitive perspective in social psychology. In G. Lindzey & E. Aronson (Eds.), *The handbook of social psychology* (3rd ed.), Vol. 1. New York: Random House, pp. 127–230.

83. Athanassiades, J.C. 1973. The distortion of upward communication in hierarchical organization. *Academy of Management Journal,* 16: 207–226.

84. Dye, R.A. 1983. Communication and post-decision information. *Journal of Accounting Research,* 21: 514–533.

85. Cohen, L.R. 1982. Minimizing communication breakdowns between male and female managers. *Personnel Administrator,* 27: 57–58.

86. Inman, T.H., & Hook, B.V. 1981. Barriers to organizational communication. *Management World,* 10: 34–35.

87. McKechnie, D.S., Grant, J., & Bagaria, V. 2007. Observation of listening behaviors in retail service encounters. *Managing Service Quality,* 17 (2): 116–113.

88. Kopec, J.A. 1982. The communication audit. *Public Relations Journal,* 38: 24–27; Quinn, D., & Hargie, O. 2004. Internal communication audits: A case study. *Corporate Communications: An International Journal,* 9: 146–158.

89. Ibid.

90. Goldhaber, G.M. 1993. *Organizational communication.* Dubuque, IA: Brown and Benchmark.

91. Bartels, J., Pruyn, A., De Jong, M., & Joustra, I. 2007. Multiple organizational identification levels and the impact of perceived external prestige and communication climate. *Journal of Organizational Behavior,* 28: 173–190.

92. Monge, Farace, Eisenberg, Miller, & White, The process of studying process in organizational communication.

93. Poole, M.S. 1978. An information-task approach to organizational communication. *Academy of Management Review,* 3: 493–504.

94. Scudder, V. 2004. The importance of communication in a global world. *Vital Speeches of the Day,* 70: 559–562.

95. Trevino, Lengel, Bodensteiner, Gerloff, & Muir, The richness imperative and cognitive style.

96. Gelb, B.D., & Gelb, G.M. 1974. Strategies to overcome phony feedback. *MSU Business Topics,* 22: 5–7.

97. Colvin, G. 2005. CEO knockdown. *Fortune,* April 4: 19–20.

decision making by individuals and groups

exploring behavior in action

Dawn Ostroff's Decision Making at the CW Television Network

As president of the new CW Television Network, Dawn Ostroff faced many challenges in the spring of 2006. Chief among these was programming the lineup of shows for the network's first season. One issue making this a difficult task was the newness of the operation. Recently created through a combination of the WB network and UPN, the combined entity had no viewer base. What mix of existing shows versus exciting new shows would draw former WB and UPN viewers? What mix of shows would motivate former WB and UPN viewers to find and watch the new network? In some markets, WB viewers would need to find the old UPN station. In other markets, UPN viewers would need to find the old WB station. In still other markets, both WB and UPN viewers would need to find a completely new station carrying CW.

A second issue was the reduction in primetime hours available. The combination of WB and UPN had resulted in a shift from 23 centrally scheduled primetime hours to 13 centrally scheduled hours. Which existing shows should be cut? With a lineup of shows such as *America's Next Top Model* (UPN), *WWE Smackdown* (UPN), *Veronica Mars* (UPN), *Gilmore Girls* (WB), *Reba* (WB), *Smallville* (WB), and *One Tree Hill* (WB), this issue was noteworthy.

Ostroff attacked the programming task with her usual zeal. As an individual, she considered a number of factors, such as the importance of retaining current WB and UPN viewers, the passion that WB and UPN viewers displayed in lobbying for particular shows, the overall popularity of existing shows as assessed by Nielsen ratings,

❓ knowledge objectives

After reading this chapter, you should be able to:

1. Describe the fundamentals of decision making, including the basic steps and the need to balance ideal and satisfactory decisions.
2. Discuss four important decision-making styles, emphasizing the effectiveness of each one.
3. Explain the role of risk-taking propensity and reference points.
4. Define cognitive bias and explain the effects of common types of cognitive bias on decision making.
5. Explain the role of moods and emotions in decision making.
6. Discuss common pitfalls of group decision making.
7. Describe key group decision-making techniques.
8. Explain the factors managers should consider in determining the level of associate involvement in managerial decisions.

and the current and future preferences of the new network's demographic target group (18-to-34-year-olds). As a leader, she considered the views of others as well. Two dozen individuals were involved in the decision making, with a group of six providing strong inputs for the final lineup of shows. Given the nonroutine and complex nature of the situation, incorporating information and opinions from other people was crucial.

Although Ostroff had a great deal of information at her disposal, she did not become mired in evaluating detailed information. Instead, she tended to keep the big picture in mind and used her judgment in evaluating alternatives. In her words,

©CW Network, Timothy White/The Kobal Collection, Ltd.

> Ultimately the people who are successful in this business have a tacit ability to make right decisions based on a wide variety of inputs; they are able to integrate those inputs into what seems to be a gut decision. Deciding on programming is not formulaic.

In the end, Ostroff and her group decided to use mostly existing shows, emphasizing the more popular ones. Although some of these shows had begun to fade and none were top performers in the overall Nielsen ratings, they believed their strategy to be the best one for developing an audience quickly. Exciting new shows would have to wait.

The new CW network performed as well as could be expected in its first season of operation. Although the network had no established track record, no direct ownership of stations in large markets, and limited resources, it attracted a small but meaningful audience. Some were disappointed with the performance, believing that the network had used too many fading shows and had not established a consistent identity, but most saw a foundation for the future. CW executives and affiliate stations remained optimistic.

To aggressively pursue success over the long run, Ostroff has maintained her focus on the big picture and has continued to draw from her group of advisors, particularly John Maatta, the chief operating officer of the network. Taking into account factors such as Nielsen ratings, web-based use of their shows, affiliate interests, and repositioning of the CW brand toward young women, they have made a number of changes to the lineup since the early days. Some of the shows from the first season have been dropped, particularly those such as *WWE Smackdown* that did not fit the new focus on young women. A few shows have been retained, such as *Smallville* and *One Tree Hill*. New shows have been added, including *Gossip Girl, Vampire Diaries,* and remakes of *90210* and *Melrose Place.* For the 2008–2009 season, these changes produced some success, with the CW network having the largest percentage increase in DVR use among broadcast networks, an 18 percent increase in ratings within its target demographic of 18-to-34-year-old women, more than 200 million Internet streams from CW.com, and strong download traffic from Apple's iTunes for shows such as *Gossip Girls* and *Vampire Diaries* (within iTunes, these two shows are among the most popular purchases on a per-episode basis). For the 2009–2010 season, CW scheduled as much prime-time scripted programming as NBC. This is an indicator of maturity and growth at the network.

Has success been ensured for the long run? This is a difficult question. The situation remains challenging at the small network, but as of mid-2010 Ostroff has made and continues to make decisions that have the potential to pay off. Given her history of accomplishments and awards, she may have created a viable network for many years to come.

Sources: J. Benson. 2007. "Is This the CW's New Reality?" *Broadcasting & Cable,* March 26, p. 12; A. Elberse and S.M. Young. 2008. The CW: *Launching a Television Network* (Boston: Harvard Business School Press); M. Fernandez. 2007. "Youth Must Be Served: The Revitalized CW Seeks to Regain the 18 to 34 Crowd," *Los Angeles Times,* July 11, p. E.1; M. Guthrie. 2009. "The CW: New Year, New Focus," *Broadcasting & Cable,* May 25, p. 16; C. Littleton. 2006. "Dialogue with Dawn Ostroff and John Maatta," *Hollywood Reporter,* Feb. 28, pp. 1–2; M. Miller. 2007. "CW Forms a Plan of Action: 'Online Nation' and 'Gossip Girls,' with Web Components, Are Meant to Woo the 18–34 Group," *Los Angeles Times,* July 21, p. E.17; S. Schechner, & Y.I. Kane. 2009. "Apple TV Proposal Gets Some Nibbles, " *Wall Street Journal,* Dec. 22, p. B.1; M. Schneider. 2007. "Young CW Makes Brand Stand," *Variety,* Jan. 8, p. 22.

the strategic importance of Decision Making

Individuals in charge of businesses make very important decisions. When we think about these decisions, we tend to think of decisions that are strategic in nature, such as adding or deleting products and services. However, these individuals also make other important decisions that have strategic implications. For example, deciding to outsource a function can have implications for effectively implementing a strategy. As another example, deciding to hire a particular person as a senior manager can affect strategy implementation.

The decisions made by individuals at the top of an organization are important because they often have the greatest effects on the organization's performance. However, the decisions of other managers also affect performance; frequently, even decisions by lower-level managers have significant effects on the success of the organization.[1] In particular, managers throughout the organization make decisions about the actions needed to implement strategic decisions. The quality and speed of those decisions affect the success of strategy-implementation efforts.

The example of Dawn Ostroff at the CW Network provides important insights into decision making, and not only for those at the top. Ostroff made many important decisions related to programming, advertising formats, organizational structure, personnel, logos, and trademarks. Other managers in the firm made decisions that supported her efforts. Managers in charge of web-based offerings made some of the decisions related to the availability and timing of online links to episodes of television shows. Managers courting and working with advertisers made decisions related to commercials. Beyond the many managerial decisions, associates made choices in areas ranging from broadcast standards to development resources of new shows. And in many instances, joint decisions were made by groups of people.

Faced with numerous challenges in her job, Ostroff gathered information, discussed issues with managers and associates, and made choices based on the big picture and even intuition. This approach can be effective. As you will learn in this chapter, however, not all decision makers follow this approach. Indeed, personal styles vary, and different situations call for different approaches. Furthermore, cognitive biases affect decision makers, causing them to collect less information or poor information in some cases. The cognitive models used by managers to make decisions are affected by the amount and type of their education and experience. For example, a manager with an engineering degree and several years of experience in an engineering unit and a manager with a degree in marketing and several years of experience in a marketing unit are likely to approach the same problem in very different ways.[2]

In this chapter, we open with a discussion of the fundamentals of decision making, including the basic steps and the need for balance between ideal and satisfactory decisions. Following this, we cover individual decision making, focusing on individual decision styles, risk taking, cognitive biases, and moods and emotions. Next, we examine the important area of group decision making. Key topics include techniques for improving group decisions and tools for evaluating how well groups have done. Finally, we address a crucial question: To what extent should a manager involve associates in a particular decision? While high-involvement management, an important concept presented in this book, requires managers to delegate many decisions to associates and to involve them in many others, under some circumstances a manager should make a decision alone or with limited input from associates. A framework is offered to guide managers in addressing this issue.

Fundamentals of Decision Making

decisions
Choices of actions from among multiple feasible alternatives.

Decisions are choices. We make decisions every day. We decide when we want to get up in the morning, what clothes we will wear, what we will eat for breakfast, and what our schedule of activities will be. We also make more important decisions. We decide what college or university to attend, what our major will be, what job to accept, what career path to follow, and how to manage our finances. Each time we make a purchase, a decision is involved. Clearly, decision-making activities are important to each of us.

They are also important to organizations. Making decisions is one of the primary activities for senior managers. Senior managers make decisions related to things such as entering new businesses, divesting existing business, and coordinating the units of the firm. Other managers in the firm make decisions regarding how a unit should be organized, who should lead various work groups, and how job performance should be evaluated. In a high-involvement organization, associates also make many important decisions. They may decide on scheduling of work, job-rotation schedules, vacation time, approaches to various tasks, and ways to discipline an individual for problem behavior. Overall, decision-making skills are critical to organizational effectiveness.

Basic Steps in Decision Making

As a process, decision making involves multiple steps, as shown in Exhibit 10-1. First, effective decision making begins with a determination of the problem to be solved. Problems are typically gaps between where we are today and where we would like to be tomorrow. We need a new associate in the work group but do not have one. We have excess cash in the firm but do not know where to invest it. We are experiencing quality problems and must correct them.

Two individuals examining the same situation may see the problem differently. Consider the following example. A manufacturing unit has a broken machine. One person might define the problem in terms of the need to repair the machine or perhaps buy a new

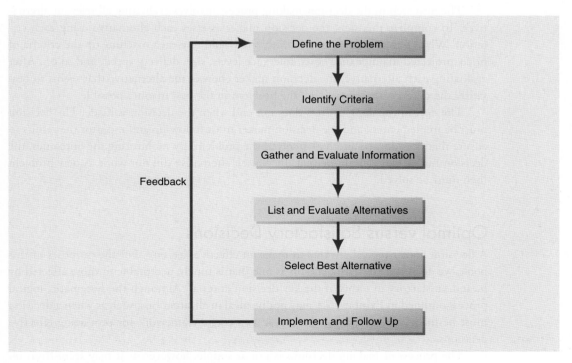

Exhibit 10-1   The Decision-Making Process

one. When developing possible solutions later in the process, she would focus either on a set of possible companies to do the repair work or a set of possible new machines. Another person might define the problem very broadly in terms of a need to return the manufacturing unit to an operational status. By broadening the problem, this person would gain access to a larger range of alternative solutions. Alternatives might include buying a new machine, repairing the existing machine, outsourcing the work, using a different type of machine already on hand to do the work, redesigning the workflow so that the machine is no longer needed, and so on. Overly narrow problem definitions are a chief concern in decision making, as they restrict options.[3]

The next step in decision making, identification of decision criteria, requires the decision maker to determine exactly what is important in solving the problem. In the case of purchasing a new machine to replace a broken one, she might consider price, maintenance costs, tolerance levels that can be achieved, size, delivery speed, and so on. Decision criteria determine what information the decision maker needs to collect in order to evaluate alternatives, and they help her explain the choice that she ultimately makes.[4] Failure to thoroughly identify important criteria results in faulty decision making.

After the decision criteria have been identified, the decision maker must gather and process information to better understand the decision context and to discover specific alternatives that might solve the problem. In discovering or identifying possible alternatives, she should be careful not to constrain or evaluate the alternatives to any significant degree, because in so doing she may prematurely eliminate more creative or novel approaches. In this context, two truisms should be understood.[5] First, a decision maker cannot choose an alternative that has not been considered. Second, a decision maker cannot choose an alternative that is better than the best alternative on the list. Therefore, careful attention to developing the list of alternatives is important.

The next step in the decision-making process involves evaluating all relevant alternatives. To complete this step, the decision maker assesses each alternative using each criterion. When purchasing a new machine, she would rate each machine on the criteria of price, projected maintenance costs, tolerance levels, size, delivery speed, and so on. After evaluating each alternative, the decision maker chooses the alternative that seems to best satisfy the criteria , thereby solving the problem in the best manner possible.

The decision-making process does not end when the decision is made. The decision must be implemented, and the decision maker must follow up and monitor the results to ensure that the adopted alternative solved the problem. By monitoring the outcomes, the decision maker may determine that the chosen alternative did not work. A new problem then must be solved.

Optimal versus Satisfactory Decisions

A decision maker typically wants to make an effective decision. For the purposes of this book, we define an effective decision as one that is timely, acceptable to those affected by it, and satisfactory in terms of the key decision criteria.[6] Although the systematic, logical process outlined in Exhibit 10-1 may not be ideal in all situations, such as when a decision must be made very quickly, it does serve as a useful framework for producing effective decisions.

The process of making decisions is not as simple, however, as it may seem from reviewing standard decision-making steps like those shown in the exhibit. Each step is more complex than it appears on the surface. Furthermore, individuals and groups cannot always make decisions that maximize their objectives, because to make such decisions we must have complete knowledge about all possible alternatives and their potential results. Complete knowledge would allow us to choose the best possible alternative, but it is unlikely that we actually would have complete knowledge for any real-world decisions. Thus, we tend to make **satisficing decisions**, or what many psychologists and economists refer to as boundedly rational decisions.[7]

There are two important reasons that people often make satisfactory decisions rather than optimal, maximizing ones. First, as already suggested, we do not have the capability to collect and process all of the information relevant for a particular decision. In theory, the number of alternatives that could be considered for most decisions is very large, as are the number of people who could be consulted and the number of analyses that could be completed. However, most of us, and certainly managers, lack the time and other resources required to complete these activities for most decisions. Consider the simple situation of hiring an individual to head a new public relations unit. Literally millions of people could possibly fill that role. Would the company consider millions of people so that the absolute best person could be found? No! Most likely, a convenient group of perhaps two dozen people would be considered.

Second, we often display a tendency to choose the first satisfactory alternative discovered. Because we are busy and typically want to conserve the resources used in making any one decision, we often stop searching when we find the first workable alternative. Research has indicated, however, that some individuals are more likely than others to choose the first satisfactory option.[8] Some continue to search for additional alternatives after encountering the first satisfactory one, thereby increasing their odds of finding a better solution. This is an important individual difference that is of interest to managers and those interested in organizational behavior.

satisficing decisions
Satisfactory rather than optimal decisions.

Individual Decision Making

Decision making is a cognitive activity that relies on both perception and judgment. If two people use different approaches to the processes of perception and judgment, they are likely to make quite different decisions, even if the facts and objectives are identical. Although many individual characteristics can affect an individual's decision process, the four psychological predispositions isolated by noted psychologist Carl Jung are of special importance for decision making in organizations. We consider these next and then turn to other factors that influence an individual's decision making, including degree of acceptable risk and cognitive biases.

Decision-Making Styles

According to Jung's theory, an individual's predispositions can affect the decision process at two critical stages: (1) the perceiving of information and (2) the judging of alternatives. Decisions, then, reflect the person's preference for one of two perceptual styles and one of two judgment styles. How these styles relate to the decision process is illustrated in Exhibit 10-2. Although some have questioned the usefulness of Jung's ideas, research has offered reasonable support for those ideas,[9] and assessment tools based on his work are very popular in the corporate world.

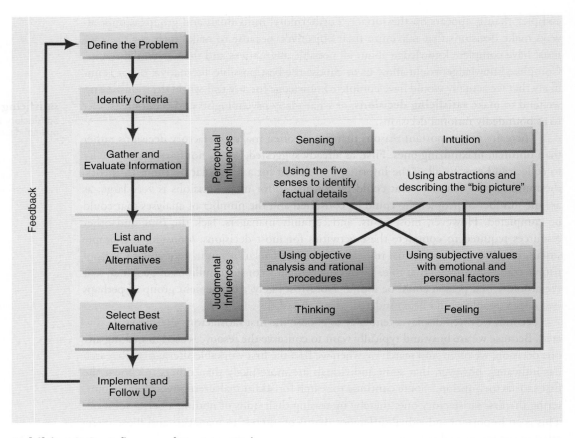

Exhibit 10-2 Influence of Decision Styles

Gathering Information

Individuals may differ in how they gather information to use in making decisions. As described in Chapter 4, gathering information involves perceptual processes. Some individuals prefer information that is concretely grounded and readily accessible through the five basic senses, whereas others prefer abstractions and figurative examples as sources.

An associate or manager who relies on facts gathered directly by the five senses is said to use a **sensing** style.[10] Such a person believes in experience and typically wants to focus on rules and regulations, step-by-step explanations, and fact checking. Decision makers who use a sensing style are concerned primarily with developing a factual database that will support any resulting decision.

People who prefer this style of gathering information see themselves as practical and realistic. They work steadily in the early stages of the decision process and enjoy the information-gathering stage. Such persons observe the actual situation very carefully: specific details, concrete examples, real experiences, practicalities, and literal statements. They are down-to-earth people who believe that creativity involves much effort. Steve Ballmer, CEO of Microsoft, seems to fit this profile. He is attracted to facts and hard data and sees things as "black or white, on or off."[11]

Decision makers who use the **intuition** style dislike details and the time required to sort and interpret them.[12] These people become impatient with routine details and often

sensing
A decision style focused on gathering concrete information directly through the senses, with an emphasis on practical and realistic ideas.

intuition
A decision style focused on developing abstractions and figurative examples for use in decision making, with an emphasis on imagination and possibilities.

perceive information in large chunks—for example, as holistic, integrated abstractions. A decision made using this style is often based on imagination. Intuitive people believe that creativity comes from inspiration rather than concentrated effort.

Although this second style may appear to be illogical and risky, many consultants and senior managers believe that it can be an effective approach. Managers with good intuition may be better able to cope with rapid change and crisis situations. They frequently have a vision for the future and can react quickly to urgent needs. Former U.S. president Bill Clinton has been classified as having the intuition style,[13] as has former British prime minister Margaret Thatcher.[14] Dawn Ostroff of the CW network also seems to fit the profile.

Overall, both the sensing and intuition styles of perception can be effective, but their effectiveness may vary depending on the context. The sensing style may be most appropriate for jobs where routine decisions are typical.[15] In one relevant study, researchers examined how loan officers handled a number of lending decisions.[16] Individuals with a sensing style used more information and made better choices. The intuition style may be most appropriate for jobs where novel decisions and a need for creativity are common. Research on innovation illustrates this point. In one important study, individuals responsible for new business ideas in a *Fortune* 500 company were divided into two groups of equal size, with one group representing the sensing style and the other representing the intuition style.[17] In the sensing group, individuals displayed less creativity and identified ideas that resulted in only $15.2 million of profit during the period of the study. Individuals in the intuition group displayed more creativity and delivered $197.5 million in profit.

Specific situations in which the intuition style may prove valuable include the following:

- When a high level of ambiguity exists
- When few or no precedents exist
- When facts are limited
- When facts don't clearly indicate which way to go
- When time is limited and there is pressure to make the right decision
- When several plausible alternative solutions exist with good arguments for each

Evaluating Alternatives

Jung proposed that once information has been gathered, decision makers again diverge in their approaches, tending to adopt either a thinking style or a feeling style to make judgments. As seen in Exhibit 10-2, there is no fixed relationship between a person's information-gathering style and his judgment style. A person using a sensing style of gathering information may use either a thinking or a feeling style in evaluating and judging the alternatives. Similarly, an intuitive information gatherer may use either of the judgment styles.

Managers and associates who use an impersonal, rational approach to arrive at their judgments are said to prefer a **thinking** style.[18] Decision makers who use the thinking style to derive conclusions from their perceptions are objective, analytical, logical, and firm.

People who use this style are concerned with principles, laws, and objective criteria. They find it easy to critique the work and behavior of others but are often uncomfortable dealing with people's feelings. Thinkers prefer objective analysis and fair decisions based on standards and policies. They are able to discipline and reprimand people, even fire them, if necessary. They are firm and may seem detached and impersonal to subordinates. Their apparently detached nature is likely due to the organized and structured approach

thinking
A decision style focused on objective evaluation and systematic analysis.

they prefer. They would seldom leap to a conclusion without fully evaluating a substantial number of alternatives. They are often conservative in their decisions.

feeling
A decision style focused on subjective evaluation and the emotional reactions of others.

At the other extreme, people who prefer to rely on their emotions and personal, subjective judgments are said to use a **feeling** style.[19] People concerned with feelings emphasize the maintenance of harmony in the workplace. Their judgments are influenced by their own or others' personal likes and dislikes. Such persons are subjective, sympathetic, and appreciative in their decisions. They also dislike decision problems that would require them to say unpleasant things to people. Managers who use a feeling approach frequently give more weight to maintaining a friendly climate in the work group than to effective task achievement. These managers often interpret problems as having been caused by interpersonal factors rather than by other issues.

Both the thinking and feeling styles are important in organizations. The thinking style is consistent with careful decision making, and a number of studies have shown this style to be effective. In one study, for example, real estate agents were asked to provide information on decision style as well as performance in selling properties.[20] Those who used the thinking style tailored their approach to selling based on circumstances and reported stronger performance. The feeling style, however, also can have positive effects. Concern for the feelings and morale of those around us is important.

To take advantage of the positive outcomes of each style and to balance the factors considered in a decision, a decision maker who emphasizes the feeling style should consult with one or more others who emphasize the thinking style. Similarly, decision makers who emphasize the thinking style should consult with those who use the feeling style. Because most managers at all levels in an organization tend to emphasize the thinking style,[21] they are likely to benefit from seeking out a feeling type. In addition, when a manager creates a team to address a problem and make a decision, she is likely to benefit from including both styles on the team.

Using Decision Styles

Although it may seem that decision-making styles are fixed, there is some flexibility in the styles used by managers and associates. As stated by Jung and later researchers, a decision style is simply a preference.[22] Many experienced decision makers are able to adjust their styles as need dictates, at least to some degree. Microsoft's Steve Ballmer, for example, clearly emphasizes the thinking style but at times seems capable of adopting the feeling style. As a thinker, he tends to be objective, logical, and analytical, and perhaps a bit impersonal as well, but he can also take into account the feelings of others. He has been known to scream, yell, and even be sarcastic and then feel badly about the behavior and attempt to make amends.[23] Dawn Ostroff appears to emphasize the thinking style, but not as strongly as Ballmer. She, therefore, probably moves more easily between thinking and feeling.

The accounting and marketing examples discussed in the *Managerial Advice* feature represent a larger problem involving many functional areas. Associates and managers in many areas can have personal styles that work well most of the time but interfere with effectiveness on occasion. Although not all individuals working in a given functional area think in the same way, they often share some general tendencies. The mind-stretching techniques briefly discussed in the advice segment can be quite helpful in addressing the problem of limited styles by extending ways of thinking about situations and broadening the decision styles used. Using the Six Thinking Hats technique, for example, enabled MDS SCIEX to save $1 million on a single project. Similarly, Hermann International's

Nurturing Alternative Decision Styles

©Digital Vision

Many accounting students and practicing accountants combine the sensing and thinking styles. In fact, many accountants are attracted to the accounting field because it allows them to emphasize rules, procedures, facts, and analysis. The structure in professional accounting activities appeals to them. They must, for example, follow generally accepted accounting principles in creating and analyzing financial data for their companies or clients. In contrast, many marketing students and practicing marketers combine the intuition and feeling styles. Marketers are often drawn to the marketing field because it allows them to engage in creative problem solving and requires an understanding of the feelings of others.

Although accountants and marketers may need to emphasize the decision styles that fit the type of work they generally do, they must be careful not to overemphasize those styles. Accountants, for example, can be too narrowly focused on standard data and analysis, thereby failing to take a strategic view of financial information in the firm. In one case, a controller was asked by the CEO to provide a summary of the firm's financial position. She proceeded to tell him about debits and credits that had been recorded on certain dates. The firm's chief financial officer, who was also present at the meeting, described the CEO's reaction this way:

As she continued, you could literally see the CEO's eyes cross.

He turned in frustration and said, "No, what I mean is, where are we ... ? What do we need to work on?"

In reflecting on this experience, the chief financial officer concluded that: (1) many accountants are biased toward a belief that having more data is better and (2) many accountants hide behind "a mass of data." He recommended that accountants focus on the strategic objectives of the firm and provide written or oral communications that interpret analyses in light of those objectives.

Some marketers also have "blind spots." For those marketers who work in the more strategic, creative areas of marketing, detailed study of a statistical market analysis is often not appealing, but such work may provide key insights. Even in areas of marketing that are more quantitative, such as marketing research, individuals may not be evaluating the data carefully enough. In the words of a successful consultant:

[M]any, both within and outside the profession, don't think marketing research has fulfilled its mandate. ... Researchers have become too long on observation, description and problem identification, and too short on rigorous hypothesis testing, analysis-based conclusions and accurate predictions.

In reflecting on the state of marketing research, this consultant suggested additional training in rigorous methods, among other tactics.

To maximize effectiveness, accountants and marketers must be comfortable with alternative decision styles. They must use their "whole brains," in the words of a *Harvard Business Review* article. To support such efforts, several companies offer training programs and materials. The de Bono Group, for example, offers training called Six Thinking Hats. The purpose is to promote the use of different ways of thinking (go to http://debonogroup.com). Numerous companies have used de Bono resources, including 3-M, AT&T, Federal Express, Intel, Microsoft, PPG, The New York Times, and Procter & Gamble. Herrmann International offers a brain dominance assessment and creative ideas for working with decision styles (go to http://www.hbdi.com). Many companies have also utilized Herrmann resources, including American Express, Citibank, Coca-Cola, DuPont, General Electric, IBM, MTV, Starbucks, and Weyerhaeuser. Overall, 70 percent of *Fortune* 500 companies have used Herrmann resources.

Sources: K.A. Brown, & N.L. Hyer. 2002. "Whole-Brain Thinking for Project Management," *Business Horizons, 45*, no. 3: 47–57; de Bono Group, "What We Do," 2010, at http://debonogroup.com/what_we_do.php; B. Hamilton. 2003. "How to Be a Top Strategic Advisor," *Strategic Finance, 84*, no. 12: 41–43; Herrmann International, "Why Herrmann International," 2010, at http://www.hbdi.com/WhyUs/index.cfm; D. Leonard & S. Straus. 1997. "Putting Your Company's Whole Brain to Work," *Harvard Business Review, 75*, no. 4: 112–121; W.D. Neal. 2002. "Shortcomings Plague the Industry," *Marketing News, 36*, no. 19: 37–39; P.D. Tieger, & B. Barron-Tieger. 2001. *Do What You Are: Discover the Perfect Career for You Through the Secrets of Personality Type*, 3rd ed. New York: Little, Brown; P. Wheeler. 2001. "The Myers-Briggs Type Indicator and Applications to Accounting Education and Research," *Issues in Accounting Education*, 16: 125–150.

brain dominance technique has been credited with helping DuPont-Mexico gain new clients, worth millions of dollars in total additional revenue. Overall, the use of these techniques can enhance organizational performance.

Degree of Acceptable Risk

Risk exists when the outcome of a chosen course of action is not certain.[24] Most decisions in business carry some degree of risk. For example, a manager may be considering two candidates for a new position. One of them has a great deal of experience with the type of work to be performed and has been very steady, though not outstanding, in her prior jobs, whereas the other has limited experience but seems to have great potential. If the manager chooses the first candidate, the likelihood of poor work performance is relatively low but not zero. If he chooses the second candidate, the likelihood of poor work performance is higher, but there is also a chance of excellent performance, performance that would be out of reach for the first candidate. Who should be chosen?

risk-taking propensity
Willingness to take chances.

In choosing between less and more risky options, an individual's **risk-taking propensity**, or willingness to take chances, often plays a role.[25] Two persons with different propensities to take risks may make vastly different decisions when confronted with identical decision situations and information. One who is willing to face the possibility of loss, for example, may select a riskier alternative, whereas another person will choose a more conservative alternative. U.S. businessman Donald Trump is known for taking risks. Over the years, he has made and lost and made again significant amounts of money in buying and selling real estate.[26]

In making decisions, individuals with lower risk-taking propensities may collect and evaluate more information. They may even collect more information than they need to make the decision. In one study, managers made hiring decisions in a practice exercise.[27] Managers with low risk-taking propensity used more information and made decisions more slowly. Although information is important, managers and associates with low risk-taking propensities must avoid becoming paralyzed by trying to obtain and consider too much detailed information. Conversely, those with high risk-taking propensities must avoid making decisions with too little information.

reference point
A possible level of performance used to evaluate one's current standing.

Beyond general risk-taking propensity, reference points play an important role in many decisions.[28] A **reference point** can be a goal, a minimum acceptable level of performance, or perhaps the average performance level of others, and it is used to judge one's current standing. If a particular individual's current position in an ongoing activity is below his reference point, he is more likely to take a risk in an attempt to move above the reference point. If his current position is above the reference point, he is less likely to take risks. For example, a manager of a division in a consumer products firm who is below the goal she has set for profitability may undertake a risky project in order to meet her goal. A manager who is above a reference point she has adopted is less likely to take on such a project. In an extreme case, a student in a finance course who is performing below the level he considers minimally acceptable may decide to take drugs to help him stay awake all night studying for the next exam, or he may even decide to cheat. A student who is above his reference point is less likely to engage in these types of risky behavior. A poker player who has just lost a big hand, and is therefore below his performance goals, may adopt a riskier approach to the game, while a player who has just won a big hand is less likely to exhibit such a shift, even though he is better positioned to take on more risk.[29]

Each individual chooses, consciously or unconsciously, his own reference point in a given situation. Two different students are likely to have different minimally acceptable performance levels for a class, and these different levels can serve as their respective reference points. In a recent study, senior managers from small firms subjectively rated disappointment with their firms' business performance.[30] In some cases, managers were disappointed with a level of performance that other leaders endorsed as very positive. Clearly, reference points differed. Moreover, managers expressing dissatisfaction based on their individual reference points were more likely to undertake particularly risky projects.

Cognitive Biases

Individuals often make mistakes in decision making. Although carelessness, sloppiness, fatigue, and task overload can be contributing factors, some mistakes are caused by simple **cognitive biases**. Such biases represent mental shortcuts.[31] Although these shortcuts can be harmless and save time, they often cause problems. Being aware of their existence is an important step in avoiding them.

> **cognitive biases**
> Mental shortcuts involving simplified ways of thinking.

The **confirmation bias** is particularly important, because it often has strong effects on the type of information gathered. This bias leads decision makers to seek information that confirms beliefs and ideas formed early in the decision process.[32] Rather than also search for information that might disconfirm early beliefs, as a thorough decision process requires, individuals subconsciously seek only information that supports their early thinking. Failing to look for disconfirming information is particularly likely if a decision maker is revisiting a decision that has already been made and partially or fully implemented.

> **confirmation bias**
> A cognitive bias in which information confirming early beliefs and ideas is sought while potentially disconfirming information is not sought.

The following story illustrates the problem. An equities broker is concerned about a company in which many of his clients have invested. Because of some recent R&D failures, the company's long-term growth prospects are not as strong as originally expected. The broker's initial position, however, is to recommend that his clients retain the stock; he believes in the company's management and does not want to recommend divesting based only on one sign of possible trouble. Before making a decision, he calls two other brokers who are acquaintances and who also remain supporters of the company. He wants to understand why they continue to be positive about the firm. In the end, he decides to stay the course without seeking the opinions of other brokers who have recommended divesting the company's stock. In other words, he makes his decision having contacted only those who were likely to agree with his initial thinking. Research suggests that this is a common occurrence.[33]

In addition to business domains, research also reveals the presence of confirmation bias in medicine, where doctors may have some tendency to seek only confirming data after forming initial diagnostic impressions.[34] Similarly, research reveals the confirmation bias in the legal system, where police investigators and prosecutors may have some tendency to seek only confirming data after forming initial opinions.[35] Clearly, the potential for problems caused by confirmation tendencies is quite significant.

The **ease-of-recall bias** is also important because it affects the amount and type of information that is gathered and evaluated. In the context of this bias, a decision maker gathers information from his own memory and relies on information that he can easily recall.[36] Unfortunately, easily recalled information may be misleading or incomplete. Vivid and recent information tends to be easily recalled but may not be indicative of the overall situation. In performance appraisals, for example, a supervisor may recall a vivid incident

> **ease-of-recall bias**
> A cognitive bias in which information that is easy to recall from memory is relied upon too much in making a decision.

such as an angry disagreement between two associates while forgetting many common instances of good performance. When selecting a new supplier for a key raw material, a manager may find one or two informal stories of poor performance easier to remember than the comprehensive numbers in an evaluative report on the various alternative suppliers. As the brutal despot Joseph Stalin once said, "A single death is a tragedy, a million deaths is a statistic."[37]

anchoring bias
A cognitive bias in which the first piece of information that is encountered about a situation is emphasized too much in making a decision.

Another bias is the **anchoring bias**. Here, decision makers place too much emphasis on the first piece of information they encounter about a situation.[38] This initial information then has undue influence on ideas, evaluations, and conclusions. Even when decision makers acquire a wide range of additional information (thereby avoiding the confirmation bias), initial information can still have too much influence.

In one study of this phenomenon, auditors from the largest accounting firms in the United States were asked about management fraud.[39] Some of the auditors were asked if executive-level fraud occurred in more than 10 out of every 1,000 client organizations. Then they were asked to estimate the actual incidence rate. Others in the study were asked if executive-level fraud occurred in more than 200 out of every 1,000 client organizations. Auditors in this latter group also were asked to estimate the actual incidence rate. Interestingly, auditors in the first group estimated the actual fraud rate to be 16.52 per 1,000 client organizations whereas auditors in the second group estimated the fraud rate to be 43.11. Despite answering the same question about actual fraud, trained auditors in the most prestigious accounting firms appear to have anchored on arbitrary and irrelevant numbers (10 in the first group and 200 in the second).

sunk-cost bias
A cognitive bias in which past investments of time, effort, and/or money are heavily weighted in deciding on continued investment.

Finally, the **sunk-cost bias** causes decision makers to emphasize past investments of time and money when deciding whether to continue with a chosen course of action.[40] Decision makers are reluctant to walk away from past investments, preferring to build on them and make them successful. Decision makers should, however, treat a past investment as a *sunk cost*—a cost that is unrecoverable and irrelevant—and focus on the future costs and benefits of continued investment. For example, when the CEO of a small business returns to a loan officer at the local bank saying that he needs another $250,000 to succeed, the loan officer should not consider the first $250,000 that was loaned. She should consider the likelihood that a new $250,000 will truly help the small firm succeed. What is the probability of success going forward? What has occurred in the past is not directly relevant to the new decision.

The power of the sunk-cost bias is illustrated by its role in the deaths of a number of Mt. Everest climbers. Rob Hall's ill-fated 1996 expedition provides one of the best known examples.[41] Hall was co-founder of Adventure Consultants, a company specializing in guiding individuals to the highest peaks in the world. By the mid-1990s, he had guided 39 clients to the summit of Everest. To avoid problems, Hall used a prespecified turnaround time for the final leg of the journey. If the summit could not be reached by a particular time in the afternoon, the party returned to the intermediate camp used during the previous night. Although the technology of climbing—clothing, supplemental oxygen, tents, and so on—has improved dramatically since the early days of Everest climbs, it still is crucial to avoid being anywhere near the uninhabitable summit as darkness approaches.

Even with the prespecified turnaround time, Rob Hall lost his life and the lives of several in his party in May 1996. In part, these deaths happened because Hall ignored his turnaround rule. In this fateful ascent, he and his party encountered delays and slow progress on the final leg. Despite the delays and the slipping schedule, Hall pressed on and failed to send back clients who were obviously struggling. These clients had invested a great deal in the effort to climb Mount Everest and did not want to be sent down after coming so far. Several members of the party did, however, decide to turn around without being forced down by Hall, prompting the following observation:

> In order to succeed you must be exceedingly driven, but if you're too driven you're likely to die. Above 26,000 feet, moreover, the line between appropriate zeal and reckless summit fever becomes grievously thin. Thus, the slopes of Everest are littered with corpses. Taske, Huthchison, Kasischke, and Fischbeck [party members who turned back] had each spent as much as $70,000 and endured weeks of agony to be granted this one shot at the summit … and yet, faced with a tough decision, they were among the few who made the right choice that day.[42]

Moods and Emotions

Moods and emotions are two aspects of affective phenomena in organizations.[43] **Moods** are affective states that correspond to general feelings disconnected from any particular event or stimulus in the workplace. Moods typically are described in generic terms, such as positive or negative, good or bad. **Emotions** correspond to more specific feelings that are often tied to particular events, people, or other stimuli. Also, emotions typically are described in terms of discrete forms, such as fear and anger. Research in the field of organizational behavior has increasingly emphasized moods and emotions in the workplace.

Mood appears to have important effects on decision making, but those effects are complex and not fully understood at this point.[44] On the one hand, individuals in positive moods seem to neglect the details of decision situations. This can lead to poor outcomes when such details are crucial. On the other hand, individuals in positive moods seem to exhibit more breadth in ideas considered, which can create more exploration, less conservatism, more creativity, and perhaps more risk taking. These decision attributes are positive in situations calling for fresh ideas or bold steps. In one study of the mood phenomenon, foreign exchange traders with positive moods were found to exhibit more confidence and risk taking, but their overall performance was lower than those in bad moods presumably because details mattered in the trading context.[45] In another study, auditors with positive moods were found to be less conservative than auditors in bad moods.[46]

Emotion also appears to have important effects on decision making. In recent years, one of the most studied emotions has been regret. Regret is an aversive emotion involving self-blame that comes from unwanted outcomes.[47] One possible reaction to this aversive emotion involves avoiding in the future a choice that has led to a poor outcome (i.e., not repeating a choice associated with failure when faced with a similar decision situation in the future). Although this reaction often is appropriate, it can be dysfunctional. For example, bad luck can create an unwanted outcome even though a good choice has been made. In that situation, a viable choice might be ruled out of future consideration when it should not be.[48] In contrast to the above circumstances, decision makers sometimes avoid full feedback so as to limit their knowledge of bad outcomes, which makes avoiding a truly poor choice difficult in the future.[49]

Another reaction to regret involves self-management. This reaction can protect the ego of the decision maker. When engaged in self management, decision makers may:[50]

1. Attempt to reverse the decision
2. Run from the decision by denying responsibility for it

moods
Affective states corresponding to general positive or negative feelings disconnected from any particular event or stimulus.

emotions
Affective states corresponding to specific feelings, such as anger, that tend to be associated with particular events, people, or other stimuli.

Anger and Fear in Recent U.S. Elections

©Joe Raedle/Getty Images, Inc.

Barack Obama earned an impressive victory in the U.S. presidential election of 2008. In part, his success was based on personal qualities such as charisma and strong oratorical skills. His success also was driven by a strong team of strategic advisors, including David Axelrod and David Plouffe. These advisors helped to develop important strategies, such as the very strong emphasis on being consistent with the political message even when setbacks and unexpected problems occurred. Energized grassroots organizations also played a role in the election outcome, as did unprecedented use of web-based media and a focus on young people.

Despite all of those positives, the victory was improbable in many ways. Obama had little leadership experience. He also had somewhat limited political experience, having served for only a few years in the U.S. Senate and roughly eight years in the Illinois state legislature. Obama also

had a number of friends and political connections that made many mainstream Americans more than a little uneasy. Reverend Jeremiah Wright is the most famous example. Wright had a long history of controversial remarks on a wide range of issues.

Scott Brown also recently earned an impressive political victory. In Brown's case, the election focused on one of Massachusetts's two seats in the U.S. Senate. Although perhaps not as gifted a campaigner as Obama, Brown worked hard to generate a win in the January 2010 special election to replace the deceased Edward Kennedy. Brown traveled widely in the state and talked with potential voters in a down-to-earth style that won high praise. He successfully applied lessons from a number of effective previous campaigns for local and state offices. He also drew on his lengthy and dedicated service in the National Guard, where he had achieved the rank of lieutenant colonel.

Scott Brown's victory was even more improbable than Obama's. He ran as a Republican in a heavily Democratic state. Moreover, he sought the Senate seat formerly held by the popular Democrat Kennedy, which meant many voters for sentimental reasons thought a Democratic candidate should have the seat. Also, his legislative record was somewhat undistinguished, and his opponent had Obama campaigning for her, albeit late in the game.

3. Argue that other alternative choices would not have led to a better outcome
4. Attempt to suppress self-knowledge of the unwanted outcome
5. Engage in after-the-fact justifications of the decision by using, for example, a self-affirmation such as "I did the best that I could".

A second often-studied emotion is anger. This emotion is widely believed to have important, potentially problematic effects on decision making. First, anger may cause decision makers to be less effective gatherers and evaluators of information.[51] Second, anger may lead to lower perceived risk unwanted decision consequences, particularly in comparison to the effects that other negative emotions have on perceived risk (e.g., fear).[52] A study of public attitudes and beliefs concerning terrorism illustrates the connection to risk.[53] Individuals who were angry about terrorism estimated the probability of future attacks as relatively small.

Obama and Brown overcame strong odds to earn their victories. Personal styles and abilities as well as strong campaign teams certainly played important roles, but the reinforcement of existing anger or the creation of new anger among voters also played a role, and a very strong one. For Obama, a key element of his overall strategy entailed positioning his opponent as an extension of then president George Bush, which leveraged the anger many American's felt toward Bush over the Iraq war, perceived corporate favoritism, and enormous government spending. Beyond simply linking the opponent to Bush to leverage existing anger, the Obama team also actively sought to create more anger related to the state of the country.

In the case of Brown, a key element of his overall strategy entailed leveraging existing anger over tactics being used in the U.S. Congress and also leveraging existing anger and creating more of it over economic conditions. He positioned himself as a Washington outsider while criticizing those working in the nation's capital. His success prompted one reporter to say this, "People are so angry out here in the real world, they can't see straight."

The strategic use of anger by Obama and Brown was no doubt critical to their success. Both candidates had a substantial number of potentially damaging attributes, as well as potentially formidable opponents. Anger among voters, though, can result in relatively low perceived

risks for bold actions that address the anger, which means such voters may be willing to take a chance on a newcomer with substantial negatives. Obama and Brown could have reduced their focus on anger, while putting greater emphasis on people's fears over where the country was heading, but that approach may not have worked as well. Further, these candidates could have deemphasized anger to some degree while focusing even more on inspiring visions for the future (both candidates did put a great deal of energy into visions for the future). While inspiring visions are very powerful, this approach also may not have worked as well in their political situations.

Sources: M. Creamer. 2008. "Barack Obama and Audacity of Marketing," *Advertising Age*, Nov. 10, pp. 1–2; R. W. Forsyth. 2010. "The New Dismal," *Barron's*, Jan. 25, pp. 7–8; E. Hornick. 2010. "Independents' Anger in Massachusetts: A sign of Things to Come?," *CNN.com*, Jan. 21, at http://www.cnn.com/2010/POLITICS/01/21/mass.independent.vote/index.html; R. Lizza. 2008. "Battle Plans: How Obama Won," *The New Yorker*, Nov. 17, pp. 46–55; D. Weigel. 2010. "Conservative Grassroots Strategy Propels Brown to the Senate," *Washington Independent*, Jan. 20, at http://washingtonindependent.com/74251/conservative-grassroots-strategy-propels-brown-to-senate.

Nonetheless, they preferred relatively bold, risky preventive measures and had relatively little concern for the consequences. Those who were fearful of terrorism estimated the probability of attacks as relatively large. Even so, they preferred less direct, less risky preventive measures as they were concerned about the consequences of bolder actions. These dynamics are explored further in the *Experiencing Organizational Behavior* feature.

Group Decision Making

We often view decision making as an individual activity, with thoughtful individuals making good or bad organizational decisions. For example, it is easy to credit the success of Intel in the 1990s microchip industry to the effective decision making of

©Karen Moskowitz/Getty Images, Inc.

Andy Grove, the CEO for many years. But it is common for a number of people to participate in important organizational decisions, working together as a group to solve organizational problems. This is particularly true in high-involvement organizations, where associates participate in many decisions with lower-level and middle-level managers and where lower-level and middle-level managers participate in decisions with senior-level managers. In high-involvement organizations, teams of associates also make some decisions without managerial input. In this way, human capital throughout the organization is utilized effectively.

Group decision making is similar in some ways to the individual decision making we described earlier. Because the purpose of group decision making is to arrive at a preferred solution to a problem, the group must use the same basic decision-making process—define the problem, identify criteria, gather and evaluate information, list and evaluate alternatives, and choose the best alternative and implement it.

On the other hand, groups are made up of multiple individuals, resulting in dynamics and interpersonal processes that make group decision making different from decision making by an individual.[54] For instance, some members of the decision group will arrive with their own expectations, problem definitions, and predetermined solutions. These characteristics are likely to cause some interpersonal problems among group members. Also, some members will have given more thought to the decision situation than others, members' expectations about what is to be accomplished may differ, and so on. Thus, a group leader may be more concerned with turning a collection of individuals into a collaborative decision-making team than with the development of individual decision-making skills. In this section, we consider these and other issues in group decision making.

Group Decision-Making Pitfalls

Although group decision making can produce positive outcomes, the social nature of group decisions sometimes leads to undesired results. In fact, group processes that occur during decision making often prevent full discussion of facts and alternatives. Group norms, member roles, dysfunctional communication patterns, and too much cohesiveness may deter the group, thereby producing ineffective decisions. Researchers have identified several critical pitfalls in decision-making groups. These include groupthink, common information bias, diversity-based infighting, and the risky shift (see upper half of Exhibit 10-3).

Groupthink

groupthink
A situation in which group members maintain or seek consensus at the expense of identifying and debating honest disagreements.

When group members maintain or seek consensus at the expense of identifying and earnestly debating honest disagreements, **groupthink** is said to occur.[55] Focusing too much attention on consensus, especially early in a decision process, can result in a faulty decision. Many important ideas and alternative courses of action may not be seriously considered.

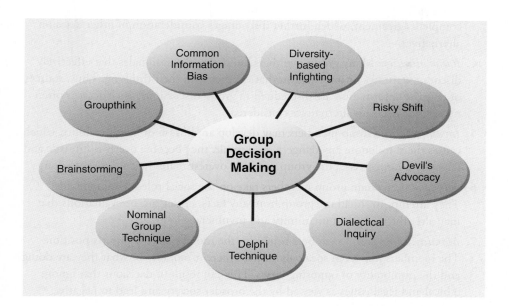

This type of group phenomenon can occur under a number of different conditions, including the following:

- Group members like one another and therefore do not want to criticize each other's ideas.[56]
- Group members have high regard for the group's collective wisdom and therefore yield to early ideas or the ideas of a leader.[57]
- Group members derive satisfaction from membership in a group that has a positive self-image and therefore try to prevent the group from having any serious divisions.[58]

In essence, then, a variety of factors can cause group members to avoid surfacing divergent opinions and ideas within the group.

Groupthink may be most likely when a group that has a positive image is under threat, such as when a management team faces a tough competitor or when a presidential administration faces possible military engagement.[59] At Enron, the failed energy company, managers valued being part of the leadership of a company perceived as progressive, innovative, and sophisticated. Being employed by Enron, and especially being a part of the favored group in the company, was powerfully reinforcing. This seems to have contributed to managers' tendency to agree with increasingly risky investments and accounting tricks.[60]

At least eight specific symptoms are associated with groupthink:

1. *Self-censorship.* Group members who recognize flaws or errors in the group position tend to remain quiet during group discussions and avoid issues that might upset the group.

2. *Pressure.* Group members apply pressure to any member who expresses opinions that threaten group consensus and harmony.

3. *Unanimity.* Censorship and pressure lead to the illusion of unanimous support for the final group decision. Members who have been quiet are assumed to be in

complete agreement, which further discourages consideration of other decision alternatives.

4. *Rationalization.* Many group members build complex rationales that effectively discount warnings or information that conflict with their thinking. Thus, sources of negative information are discredited in group discussions. Such actions often narrow the decision alternatives considered.

5. *Invulnerability.* Group members may develop an illusion of invulnerability, which causes them to ignore any dangers. As a result, they become overly optimistic and take unwarranted risks; the group seriously overestimates its collective wisdom.

6. *Mindguards.* Certain group members take on the social role of "mindguard." They attempt to shield the group from any facts, criticisms, or evaluations that may alter the illusion of unanimity and invulnerability.

7. *Morality.* Most group members believe in the morality of the group's position. The members may even speak about the inherent morality of what they are doing and the immorality of opposing views. This can result in decisions that ignore ethical and legal issues as viewed by the broader society and lead to negative consequences for others.

8. *Stereotypes.* Group members may develop negative stereotypes of other people and groups. These stereotypes can protect their own position and block the possibility of reasonable negotiations with outsiders.

As the most discussed group decision-making phenomenon, groupthink has been linked to a number of actual decisions.[61] Many of these have been U.S. government or military decisions, in part because a great deal of groupthink research has been conducted in the United States and access to important materials for assessing U.S. decision making is reasonably good. Examples include the decision of Admiral Kimmel and his advisors to focus on training instead of defense of Pearl Harbor prior to its being attacked in 1941, the decision of President John F. Kennedy and his cabinet to authorize an invasion of Cuba at the Bay of Pigs in 1960, and the decision of President Lyndon Johnson and his inner circle to escalate the war in Vietnam in the mid-1960s.[62] At NASA, examples in which groupthink may have played a role include the decision to launch the *Challenger* Shuttle in 1986[63] and the handling of the Hubble telescope.[64] For business firms, examples abound, with many of them involving boards of directors.[65] Groupthink has also been found in self-managing work teams.[66] This has implications for high-involvement organizations.

Groupthink does not guarantee a poor decision but simply increases the likelihood of such a result. When good judgment and discussion are suppressed, the group can still be lucky. However, because the purpose of group decision making is to increase the likelihood of a good decision, managers must take steps to reduce groupthink. Such steps are discussed later in this chapter.

common information bias
A bias in which group members overemphasize information held by a majority or the entire group while failing to be mindful of information held by one group member or a few members.

Common Information Bias

Some information a group might consider in making a decision may be held by one or a few group members. Other pieces of information are held by most or all group members. The **common information bias** leads groups to unconsciously neglect information held by one group member or a few members while focusing on more commonly held information in the group, thereby neglecting potentially important issues and ideas.[67]

The common information bias defeats one of the presumed advantages of group decision making—the availability of unique information, ideas, and perspectives brought to the process by individual group members.

The following study illustrates this phenomenon.[68] First, managers were asked to evaluate PeopleSoft as an alternative to the firm's existing accounting and enterprise management software. Next, these managers assembled to discuss whether adopting PeopleSoft would be positive for the firm. Concerns and ideas held by one or a few members received less attention than concerns and ideas held by most or all group members, resulting in a very limited group discussion.

Diversity-based Infighting

When groupthink is an issue, one or more members of the group typically act to suppress diverse ideas, and many members censor themselves. With the common information bias, individuals subconsciously focus on common information and ideas. Thus, in many groups, diverse ideas are not discussed. In other groups, however, diverse ideas are emphasized. Although this is generally positive for group decision making, it can become extreme.

Instead of creating rich discussions and insight, diverse ideas can create ill will and fractured groups.[69] Such **diversity-based infighting** is likely to occur when individuals feel very strongly about their ideas and no mechanisms to channel disagreement in productive ways have been instituted. As discussed in the next section, mechanisms that can help channel diversity include formal brainstorming procedures and the formal use of devil's advocacy.

diversity-based infighting
A situation in which group members engage in unproductive, negative conflict over differing views.

Risky Shift

As discussed earlier, most decisions involve some degree of risk. Because decision-making groups are composed of individuals, it would seem that risk taken by a group should be the same as the average risk that would have been taken by the individual group members acting alone. But the social forces involved in group decisions make this assumption incorrect.

Research on the risk taken by groups in making decisions began in the 1960s, when investigators compared individual and group decisions on the same problems.[70] Possible solutions to the problems ranged from relatively safe alternatives with moderate payoffs to relatively risky options with higher potential payoffs. Contrary to expectations, groups consistently made riskier decisions than individuals. This finding has since been called the **risky shift** phenomenon.

Subsequent analysis of these findings and additional research have determined that decisions made by groups are not always riskier. In fact, they are sometimes more cautious. However, group decisions seem to shift toward increased risk more often than toward increased cautiousness.[71] Several explanations for such shifts have been offered, but the most common and most powerful explanation involves diffusion of responsibility. Because individual group members believe that no single person can be blamed if the decision turns out poorly, they can shift the blame entirely to others (the group). This diffusion of individual responsibility may lead members to accept higher levels of risk in making a group decision.[72]

risky shift
A process by which group members collectively make a more risky choice than most or all of the individuals would have made working alone.

Group Decision-Making Techniques

As the preceding discussion makes clear, groups may flounder when given a problem to solve. It is important, therefore, to understand the techniques that can be used to encourage full and effective input and discussion before the group reaches a decision. Several

©Andreas Pollok/Getty Images, Inc.

brainstorming
A process in which a large number of ideas are generated while evaluation of the ideas is suspended.

techniques have been developed, including brainstorming, the nominal group technique, the Delphi technique, dialectical inquiry, and devil's advocacy (see Exhibit 10-3).

Brainstorming

For major decisions, it is usually important to generate a wide variety of new ideas during the data-gathering and alternative-generation phases of decision making. Increasing the number of ideas during these phases helps ensure that important facts or considerations are not overlooked. Unfortunately, if the group evaluates or critiques each new idea as it is introduced in a group meeting, individual members may withhold other creative ideas because they fear critical comments. In contrast, if ideas are not evaluated immediately, members may offer a number of inputs, even if they are uncertain of the value of their ideas. This is the essence of **brainstorming**.[73]

Brainstorming within groups has the following basic features:

- Imagination is encouraged. No idea is too unique or different, and the more ideas offered the better.
- Using or building on the ideas of others is encouraged.
- There is no criticism of any idea, no matter how bad it may seem at the time.
- Evaluation is postponed until the group can no longer think of any new ideas.

Many companies—such as IDEO, a Silicon Valley product design firm—use this basic approach.[74] Research supports the approach, as it suggests that groups using brainstorming often generate more ideas than groups that do not use brainstorming.[75] However, research also suggests that groups following this approach do not do as well as individuals brainstorming alone.[76] In one study, for example, a brainstorming group developed 28 ideas, and 8.9 percent of them were later judged as good ideas by independent experts.[77] The same number of people engaging in solitary brainstorming developed a total of 74.5 ideas, with 12.7 percent judged as good ideas.

Why is group brainstorming often less effective than individual brainstorming? One problem may be that group members believe criticism will not be entirely eliminated but will simply remain unspoken.[78] In other words, if a member contributes a unique idea, she may believe that others are silently ridiculing it. Another problem may be that some group members are simply distracted by the significant amount of discussion in a group brainstorming session.[79]

Two techniques may be helpful in overcoming the problems of standard group brainstorming. First, *brain-writing* can be used. In a common version of brain-writing, group members stop at various points in a group meeting and write down all of their ideas.[80] Then the written ideas are placed on a flipchart or whiteboard by an individual assigned the task of pooling the written remarks. By moving from an oral to a written approach, and by introducing anonymity, this method makes many individuals feel less inhibited. Furthermore, less talking takes place in the room, so distractions are reduced. Second, *electronic brainstorming (EBS)* can be used. In a common version of EBS, group members sit around a table with computer stations in front of them.[81] Each individual attempts to develop as many ideas as possible and enter them into a database. As an idea is entered, it is projected onto a large screen that everyone can see. Because there is anonymity, individuals feel less inhibited, and because there is less talking in the room, they are not distracted. Individuals can, however, build on the ideas of others as they appear on the screen.

Nominal Group Technique

Another technique used to overcome some of the inhibiting forces in group decision making is called the **nominal group technique**. This technique shares some features of brainwriting and electronic brainstorming. In its basic form, it calls for a decision meeting that follows four procedural rules:[82]

1. At the outset, individuals seated around a table write down their ideas silently and without discussion.

2. Each member presents one idea to the group. After the initial round has been completed, each member presents a second idea. The process is repeated until all ideas have been presented. No group discussion is permitted during this period.

3. After the ideas have been recorded on a blackboard or a large flipchart or in a computer database for projection, the members discuss them. The major purpose here is to clarify and evaluate.

4. The meeting concludes with a silent and independent vote or ranking of the alternative choices. The group decision is determined by summing or pooling these independent votes.

The nominal group technique eliminates a great deal of interaction among group members. Discussion and interaction occur only once during the entire process. Even the final choice of an alternative occurs in silence and depends on an impersonal summing process. Proponents of this technique believe that inhibitions are overcome at crucial stages, whereas group discussion occurs at the time it is needed for evaluation. Research has suggested that the technique yields better results than a standard group brainstorming session.[83]

Delphi Technique

Brainstorming and the nominal group technique generally require group members to be in close physical proximity (seated around a table, for example). However, groups using the **Delphi technique** do not meet face-to-face. Instead, members are solicited for their judgments at their various homes or places of business.[84] In the most common approach, group members respond to a questionnaire about the issue of interest. Their responses are summarized and the results are fed back to the group. After receiving the feedback, individuals are given a second opportunity to respond and may or may not change their judgments.

Some Delphi approaches use only two sets of responses, whereas others repeat the question–summary–feedback process several times before a decision or conclusion is reached. The final decision is derived by averaging or otherwise combining the members' responses to the last questionnaire; often, the members' responses become more similar over time. Although some research has been supportive of this technique,[85] it is a highly structured approach that can inhibit some types of input, especially if some individuals feel constrained by the particular set of questions posed. Even so, the Delphi technique is an option to consider, especially when members of the group are geographically dispersed.

nominal group technique
A process for group decision making in which discussion is structured and the final solution is decided by silent vote.

Delphi technique
A highly structured decision-making process in which participants are surveyed regarding their opinions or best judgments.

Dialectical Inquiry and Devil's Advocacy

The techniques for group decision making explained above are more concerned with increasing the number of ideas generated than with directly improving the quality of the final solution. Although having a greater number of ideas enhances the possibility that a superior alternative will be identified, other techniques can help the group find the best choice.

Two key approaches are dialectical inquiry and devil's advocacy. These approaches counter the tendency of groups to avoid conflict when evaluating alternative courses of action and to prematurely smooth over differences within the group when they occur.[86] In its basic form, **dialectical inquiry** calls for two different subgroups to develop very different assumptions and recommendations in order to encourage full discussion of ideas. The two subgroups debate their respective positions. **Devil's advocacy** calls for an individual or subgroup to argue against a recommended action put forth by other members of the group. Thus, both dialectical inquiry and devil's advocacy use "constructive" conflict. Proponents assert that both are learning-oriented approaches because the active debates can help the group to discover new alternatives and to develop a more complete understanding of the issues involved in the decision problems.[87] In spite of these similarities, however, there are important differences between the two approaches.

The dialectical inquiry technique requires group members to develop two distinct points of view. More specifically, one subgroup develops a recommendation based on a set of assumptions, and a second subgroup develops a significantly different recommendation based on different assumptions. Debate of the two opposing sets of recommendations and assumptions maximizes constructive conflict, and the resulting evaluation of the two points of view helps ensure a thorough review and also helps to promote the development of new recommendations as differences are bridged. Devil's advocacy, however, requires the group to generate only one set of assumptions and a single recommendation, which are then critiqued by the devil's advocate (or advocates) (this devil's advocacy process can be repeated over time with additional recommendations).

Research on these techniques suggests that both are effective in developing high-quality solutions to problems.[88] At the same time, however, they can result in somewhat lower levels of group satisfaction than approaches such as brainstorming.[89] This outcome is probably due to the intragroup conflict that can arise when these methods are used. Still, both approaches are apt to be effective in controlling undesirable group phenomena that suppress the full exploration of issues. Because both approaches aim to create constructive conflict through assigned roles, they are not likely to cause major dissatisfaction among group members.

dialectical inquiry
A group decision-making technique that relies on debate between two subgroups that have developed different recommendations based on different assumptions.

devil's advocacy
A group decision-making technique that relies on a critique of a recommended action and its underlying assumptions.

Who Should Decide? Individual versus Group Decision Making

In this closing section, we first provide guidance on how a manager should approach a decision that he must make. Should he make the decision alone, should he invite limited participation by associates, or should he use a group decision-making approach with associates? Following the discussion of associate involvement in managerial decisions, we summarize the general advantages and disadvantages of having an individual versus a group make a decision.

Associate Involvement in Managerial Decisions

Although associates in high-involvement firms make many important decisions, other decisions remain for managers to address, perhaps with the assistance of associates. For these latter decisions, managers must determine the correct level of associate involvement in the decision-making process. Two researchers, Victor Vroom and Philip Yetton, point out that the correct level of involvement depends on the nature of the decision problem itself.[90] If the manager can diagnose the nature of the problem, he can determine the degree to which a group of associates should participate.

The Vroom–Yetton method requires the manager first to diagnose the problem situation and then to determine the extent to which associates will be involved in the decision-making process. The optimal extent of involvement depends on the probable effect participation will have on: (1) the quality of the decision, (2) the acceptance or commitment subordinates exhibit when implementing the decision, and (3) the amount of time needed to make the decision.[91]

As you can see in Exhibit 10-4, there are several levels of involvement, ranging from the manager's making the decision alone to a fully participative group approach. Vroom and Yetton suggest that managers can determine the best strategy for associate participation by asking seven diagnostic questions. This procedure yields a decision tree that indicates the most effective level of participation, as shown in Exhibit 10-5. It is not always necessary, however, to ask all seven questions to determine the level of involvement because some branches of the decision tree end after a few questions are asked.

Research has supported the Vroom–Yetton method. The method predicts the technical quality, subordinate acceptance, and overall effectiveness of final solutions.[92]

EXHIBIT 10-4 Managerial Approaches to Associate Involvement in Decision Making

Approach

Low ↑	AI—Manager solves the problem or makes the decision alone, using the information to which she has current access.
	AII—Manager requests information but may not explain the problem to associates. The associates' role in the process is to provide specific information; associates do not generate or evaluate alternatives.
Level of Associate Involvement in Decision	CI—Manager explains the problem to the relevant associates one by one, requesting their input without discussing the problem as a group. After discussing it with each of the relevant associates, the manager makes the decision alone. It is unclear whether the decision reflects the associates' input.
	CII—Manager explains the problem to associates as a group. The manager obtains group members' ideas and suggestions. Afterward, the manager makes the decision alone. The associates' input may or may not be reflected in the manager's decision.
↓ High	GII—Manager explains the problem to the associates in a group setting. They work together to generate and evaluate alternatives and agree on a solution. The manager acts as a facilitator, guiding the discussion, focusing on the problem, and ensuring that the important issues are examined. The manager does not force the group to accept her solution and will accept and implement a solution supported by the group.

Source: Adapted from V.H. Vroom, & A.G. Jago. 1978. "On the validity of the Vroom–Yetton Model," *Journal of Applied Psychology,* 69: 151–162; V.H. Vroom, & P.W. Yetton. 1973. *Leadership and Decision Making.* Pittsburgh, PA: University of Pittsburgh Press.

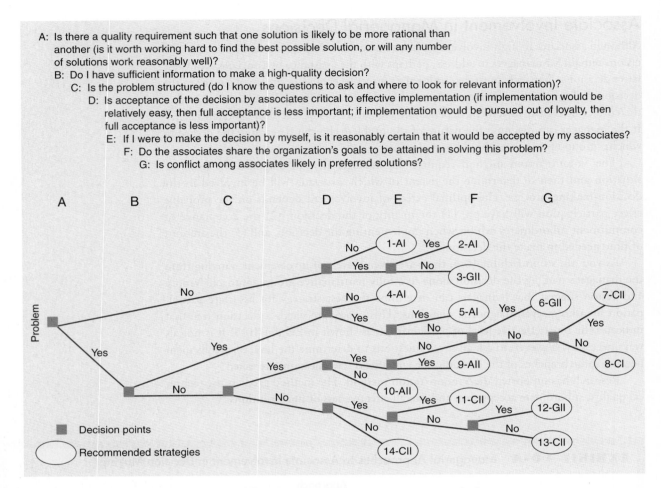

A: Is there a quality requirement such that one solution is likely to be more rational than another (is it worth working hard to find the best possible solution, or will any number of solutions work reasonably well)?

B: Do I have sufficient information to make a high-quality decision?

C: Is the problem structured (do I know the questions to ask and where to look for relevant information)?

D: Is acceptance of the decision by associates critical to effective implementation (if implementation would be relatively easy, then full acceptance is less important; if implementation would be pursued out of loyalty, then full acceptance is less important)?

E: If I were to make the decision by myself, is it reasonably certain that it would be accepted by my associates?

F: Do the associates share the organization's goals to be attained in solving this problem?

G: Is conflict among associates likely in preferred solutions?

Exhibit 10-5 Decision Tree Method for Diagnosing the Appropriate Level of Subordinate Involvement in Decisions

Source: V.H. Vroom & P.W. Yetton, 1973. *Leadership and Decision Making.* Pittsburgh, PA: University of Pittsburgh Press.

As shown in the *Experiencing Organizational Behavior* feature, the success of many U.S. Civil War generals was at least partially determined by a proper level of subordinate involvement in decisions. Like a top general during the Civil War, a CEO must decide on the proper level of involvement for the other senior managers. When, for example, the CEO needs to address a complex strategic decision (such as whether to enter a new market), she probably should fully involve other managers in the decision, given the need for a variety of inputs. The input from other top-level managers can be especially valuable when the team members are heterogeneous in their backgrounds and knowledge.[93] As you can see, the Vroom–Yetton model is useful not only for lower-level managers deciding on the appropriate level of involvement for associates but also for generals deciding on the level of involvement for subordinate officers and for senior managers deciding on the level of involvement for those who report directly to them.

One final point is important. When a group decision approach is to be used (Type GII), the manager must determine how much agreement should exist within the group.

Must all the members agree on the decision, or will the manager accept the decision even though some members disagree? Typically, managers seek either a majority or a unanimous decision from the decision-making group.[94] Seeking agreement from a majority has several advantages over seeking unanimous agreement, including increased speed and reduced risk of impasse.[95] Trying to obtain unanimity, however, generally creates more discussion and often causes group members to explore the assumptions that underlie the positions and preferences held within the group.[96] Managers must balance these factors when deciding which approach to use for group decision making.

Value of Individual versus Group Decision Making

Under the proper conditions, group decision making should increase the number of ideas generated and improve the evaluation of alternatives. Such outcomes are desirable because they generally produce better decisions. However, our earlier discussion of group decision

EXPERIENCING ORGANIZATIONAL BEHAVIOR

The Vroom–Yetton Model and Military Decisions during the U.S. Civil War

The U.S. Civil War remains one of the bloodiest conflicts in human history. Both the North and the South sustained heavy losses in this fight over the abolition of slavery, economic issues, and states' rights. Eventually, the North won the conflict, preserving the national union that had been established only decades earlier.

In deciding how and when to conduct battles, Northern and Southern generals needed information on the opposing side's troop locations, troop strength, and logistical weaknesses. They also needed information on the condition of their own forces, the nature of terrain where a battle might be fought, and so on. After considering the available information and after collecting as much new information as desired, the generals made decisions related to battle strategy.

As in business-related decision making, these generals could have involved others in making decisions or could have made decisions alone. General McClellan of the North, for example, orchestrated the Battle of Antietam without much input from others, using information he had available (in terms of Exhibit 10-4, the AI approach). General Robert E. Lee of the South followed this same approach at the Battle of Antietam (AI approach) but used a different approach at the Battle of Chancellorsville. At Chancellorsville, he collected substantial information from his subordinate commanders before making the decision on his own (AII approach).

Interestingly, the Vroom–Yetton framework seems to predict the success of generals in Civil War battles. For example, at the Battle of Shiloh,

©Mark Wilson/Getty Images

General Grant of the North faced a situation in which: (1) the quality of the decision was important, (2) the decision maker (Grant himself) did not have enough information to make a quality decision, (3) the problem was not well structured, and (4) acceptance by subordinate officers was not crucial for implementation (Situation 14 in Exhibit 10-5). Grant sought information but not ideas from his officers and made the battle-strategy decision alone (AII approach). Group discussion and idea generation would have been beneficial, however, because the problem was unstructured. Grant did not meet his objectives at Shiloh.

At the Battle of Gettysburg, General Meade of the North faced a situation in which: (1) the quality of the decision was important, (2) the decision maker (Meade himself) had the crucial information, and (3) acceptance by subordinate officers was not crucial for implementation (Situation 4 in Exhibit 10-5). Meade alone made the key decision related to strategy, without collecting substantial new information from others (AI approach, perhaps close to an AII approach). As predicted by the Vroom–Yetton model, he met his objectives.

In the following table, a number of battles are profiled. As shown, the model correctly predicts outcomes in 10 of 12 cases.

Battle/ Commanders	Problem Type	Recommended Decision Approach	Style Used	Outcome (Relative to Original Objective)
Battle of Shiloh				
General Grant	14	CII	**All**	Not Achieved
General Johnston	12	GII	**All**	Not Achieved
Battle of Antietam				
General McClellan	5	AI	**AI**	Achieved
General Lee	9	AII	**AI**	Not Achieved
Battle of Chancellorsville				
General Hooker	14	CII	**AI**	Not Achieved
General Lee	5	AI	**All**	Achieved
Battle of Gettysburg				
General Meade	4	AI	**AI**	Achieved
General Lee	11	CII	**AI**	Not Achieved
Battle of Chickamauga				
General Rosecrans	11	CII	**All**	Not Achieved
General Bragg	11	CII	**AI**	Not Achieved
Battle of Nashville				
General Thomas	11	CII	**All**	Achieved
General Hood	13	CII	**AI**	Not Achieved

Sources: Adapted from W.J. Duncan, K.G. LaFrance, & P.M. Ginter. 2003. "Leadership and Decision Making: A Retrospective Application and Assessment," *Journal of Leadership and Organizational Studies*, 9: 1–20 (principal source); B.J. Murphy. 2004. "Grant versus Lee," *Civil War Times Illustrated*, 43, no. 1: 42–52; United States War Department, *The War of the Rebellion: A Compilation of the Official Records of the Union and Confederate Armies*, multiple series and volumes within series (Washington, DC: Government Printing Office, 1880–1891).

making suggested that these results are not guaranteed. Furthermore, the generation of ideas and their evaluation are not the only outcomes from group decision making. Commitment and satisfaction of participants must also be considered.

Important considerations for judging the overall value of group decision making as opposed to individual decision making include the time needed to reach the decision, the costs of making it, the nature of the problem, the satisfaction and commitment of employees affected by the decision, and opportunities for personal growth (see Exhibit 10-6).

Time

Not surprisingly, groups typically take more time to reach decisions than do individuals. There are several reasons for this difference:

- Many social needs are met by the group (exchanging greetings, talking about the weekend, and so forth). The time required to meet these needs increases the time needed to reach a decision.
- More ideas and opinions are held by the group, and discussing these increases the time required. The use of techniques such as brainstorming and dialectical inquiry also adds to the time required.

ADVANTAGES	DISADVANTAGES
Groups can accumulate more knowledge and facts and thus generate more and better alternatives.	Groups take more time to reach decisions than do individuals.
Groups often display superior judgement when evaluating alternatives, especially for complex problems.	Group social interactions may lead to premature compromise and failure to consider all alternatives fully.
Group involvement in decisions leads to a higher level of acceptance of the decisions and greater satisfaction.	Groups are sometimes dominated by one or two "decision leaders," which may reduce acceptance, satisfaction, and quality.
Group decision making can result in growth for members of the group.	Managers may rely too much on group decisions, leading to loss of their own decision and implementation skills.

Exhibit 10-6 Advantages and Disadvantages of Group Decision Making

- Arrangements for the group meeting place, format, and assembly must be made, taking more time.

Managers must consider the importance of time in their decisions, as well as the potential quality of the decisions. Some decisions must be made immediately. In other situations, time may be available for decision making. When time is an important consideration, the manager may elect to do one of the following:

- Make the decision alone.
- Use the group for advice only.
- Use an already-existing group to minimize the arrangement time.
- Use a majority-decision rule rather than requiring unanimity.
- Use the nominal group technique to reduce lengthy discussion time.

Cost

It is also inevitable that group decision making costs more than individual decision making. Time costs money, especially when expensive managers and associates are involved. The additional time must be multiplied by the number of members in the group and their respective financial compensation levels to arrive at the total cost. The additional cost of group decision making can be substantial. Therefore, managers must determine whether the decision is important enough to warrant the extra cost.

Nature of the Problem

Members of a group typically have more information and ideas than does a single individual.[97] If the information and ideas are discussed and integrated, group decisions will often be better informed than individual decisions. Many groups, however, have difficulty managing their collective knowledge. Groupthink and common information bias can prevent information from coming to the surface. Diversity-based infighting and the risky shift can prevent sound integration of information. However, the decision-making techniques discussed in this chapter, such as devil's advocacy, can help the group to overcome these negative social forces and create high-quality decisions.

The nature of the problem being examined should be considered in choosing the approach to use. Complex problems that require many different types of input tend to be solved more effectively by groups than by individuals. Deciding whether to develop a new product, for example, may require specialized knowledge of production facilities, engineering and design capabilities, market forces, government legislation, labor markets, and financial considerations. Thus, a group should be better at making this decision. In one study focused on new-product decision making, groups were in fact more effective than individuals.[98]

Satisfaction and Commitment

Even though quality is not consistently improved by group decision making, individual satisfaction and commitment to the final solution are often enhanced.[99] These outcomes may result from several factors. First, group members may change their attitudes toward the various alternatives as a result of the group's discussions. In addition, "team spirit" may develop as group members discover similarities among themselves.

Finally, it simply may be that people who share in an important activity such as decision making feel more "ownership" of the decision than when they are excluded from it. Commitment as a result of sharing in decision making has been consistently demonstrated by research, as seen in the classic work of Kurt Lewin. During World War II in the United States, there was a scarcity of good cuts of meat but an abundance of organ meats (liver, kidneys, and so forth). Lewin thought that households could be persuaded to buy organ meats if they participated in the decision to do so. He arranged to meet with two groups to test his belief.[100] One group was given an informative lecture on the value of using organ meats. The other group was given the same information, but members then were asked to discuss it among themselves and arrive at a group decision on whether to use such meat. It was found that the group decision resulted in a much higher rate of consumption (32 percent versus 3 percent). The implementation of the decision was more effective because the group had arrived at the decision. Members of the group were satisfied and committed to it because it was their decision, not someone else's.

Personal Growth

The opportunity for personal growth provided by participation in group decision making is a benefit that is often overlooked. Advancement in a career depends on the ability to learn new skills. One of the most important skills to be learned is how to make decisions, and participation in group decision making may be an ideal opportunity for individuals to acquire this skill.

What This Chapter Adds to Your Knowledge Portfolio

In this chapter, we have discussed individual and group decision making. We have covered the major steps in decision making, taking note of decision makers' tendencies to make satisficing rather than optimal decisions. In discussing individuals, we have emphasized decision styles, approaches to risk, cognitive biases, and moods and emotions. To be successful, an organization's associates and managers must understand these elements

THE STRATEGIC LENS

Decision making is the essence of management. The primary task of managers is to make decisions. Top-level managers decide what products and services to provide and what markets to enter. Middle managers decide where to locate facilities and how many products to manufacture. Lower-level managers decide what tasks should be assigned to particular associates and when certain associates should be laid off. Therefore, the quality of managers' decisions at all levels has a major effect on the success of an organization. If managers decide to enter the wrong markets or to hire less than the best applicants, the organization's performance is likely to suffer. If, however, they decide on excellent products for the market and hire outstanding associates and motivate them to achieve, the organization is likely to flourish. Thus, understanding how to make effective decisions is necessary to be a successful manager; and organizations must have managers who are effective decision makers if they are to achieve their goals.[101] All strategic decisions—down to decisions regarding what holidays to allow for associates—affect the organization's performance.

Critical Thinking Questions

1. You are a manager of a unit with 25 associates. You have just been informed that you must lay off 20 percent of the associates in your unit. What process will you follow to make the decision and to implement it?

2. If you made a decision that your manager told you was important for the organization and later you learned that you made an error in that decision, what actions would you take? Assume that others will not notice the error for some time.

3. You make decisions on a daily basis. Do you find it difficult to make decisions, especially those of importance? What can you do to improve your decision-making abilities?

---

of individual decision making. In discussing groups, we have focused on a set of problems that can affect group decision making and have described techniques for avoiding or overcoming these problems. Finally, we have discussed a model for assessing the extent to which associates should be involved in managerial decisions. In summary, we have made the following points:

- Decisions are choices. Decision making is a process involving several steps: defining the problem, identifying criteria for a solution, gathering information, evaluating alternatives, selecting the best alternative, and implementing the decision.

- Satisfactory rather than optimal decisions are common. Satisficing occurs because: (1) individuals cannot gather and process all information that might be relevant for a particular decision and (2) individuals have a tendency to stop searching after the first acceptable solution has been found.

- Decision styles represent preferred ways of gathering information and evaluating alternatives. For gathering information, associates and managers can have either a sensing style or an intuition style. With the sensing style, individuals focus on concrete information that is directly available through the five senses. They also tend to focus on rules and facts and are usually practical and realistic. They often are effective in jobs requiring routine decision making. With the intuition style, individuals dislike details and tend to focus on abstractions and figurative examples. They are often effective in jobs that require nonroutine decisions and creativity. For evaluating alternatives, associates and managers can have either a thinking or

back to the knowledge objectives

1. What are the basic steps in decision making? How should a decision maker approach the problem-definition step? Why do decision makers usually fail to achieve optimal decisions?

2. What are the four Jungian decision styles, and how do they influence decisions and effectiveness in the workplace? Give an example of a person you know who had a decision style that did not seem to fit his or her role in an organization. This could be a person in an organization in which you have worked, or it could be a person from a school club or civic organization. What were the outcomes for this person in terms of satisfaction and performance? If you had been the individual's manager, how would you have managed the situation?

3. Describe a personal situation involving a reference point. Were you above or below your reference point? What was the effect on your behavior?

4. Which cognitive bias worries you the most, and why?

5. Compare the four primary pitfalls of group decision making. If you had to choose one, which would you prefer to deal with as a manager, and why?

6. What are the major group decision-making techniques? If you were dealing with diversity-based infighting, which of these techniques would you try first, and why?

7. What factors should a manager consider when deciding on the level of associate involvement in a decision? What shortcomings do you see in the Vroom–Yetton model?

a feeling style. With the thinking style, individuals focus on objective criteria and systematic analysis. With the feeling style, individuals use subjective approaches and are concerned with the emotional reactions of others. Although the thinking style is consistent with careful decision making, organizations need both thinkers and feelers to achieve a balance.

• Risk-taking propensity and reference points affect an individual's overall approach to risk. Risk-taking propensity relates to a person's willingness to take chances, whereas a reference point refers to a possible level of performance that a person uses to evaluate current standing. When a person has a strong propensity for risk and is below his reference point, risk taking is likely.

• Cognitive biases represent mental shortcuts that often cause problems. Four important biases are: confirmation bias (information confirming early beliefs and ideas is sought, but potentially disconfirming information is not sought), ease-of-recall bias (information that is easy to recall from memory is relied on too much), anchoring bias (the first piece of information encountered about a situation is emphasized too much), and the sunk-cost bias (past investments are weighted much too heavily).

• Moods and emotions are both part of the affective make-up of an individual. Moods correspond to general positive or negative feelings, while emotions correspond to more specific, discrete feelings such as anger and fear. Both moods and emotions can affect decision making.

• Several pitfalls are associated with group decision making. First, groupthink occurs when group members are too focused on consensus, particularly early in a decision process. This problem may occur because: (1) group members like one another and do not want to criticize each other's ideas, (2) group members have high regard for the group's collective wisdom and therefore yield to early ideas or the ideas of a leader, and (3) group members derive satisfaction from membership in a group that possesses a positive self-image and therefore they try to prevent the group from having any serious divisions. Second, the common information bias leads group members to unconsciously focus on information that is held by many members of the group while ignoring information held by only one or a few group members. Third, diversity-based infighting relates to disagreements being channeled in unproductive ways. Finally, the risky shift occurs when a group makes a more risky choice than individuals would have made (on average) when working separately.

- Several techniques exist to address the problems that may arise in group decision making. Brainstorming is a heavily used technique, but in its traditional form it fails in comparisons with individual brainstorming. Brain-writing and electronic brainstorming are useful alternatives. Nominal group technique, Delphi technique, dialectical inquiry, and devil's advocacy also can be very useful.
- Associates make many decisions in high-involvement firms. Managers address many other decisions but may involve associates in those decisions. The Vroom–Yetton model offers advice for assessing the proper level of involvement. To diagnose the situation, seven key questions are asked, and then a suggested approach is found through a decision tree.
- Groups have both advantages and disadvantages in decision making. One advantage is better quality, or at least a significant chance of better quality, particularly when complex decisions are being made. This advantage is based on the fact that groups bring more knowledge and facts to the decision and engage in a richer assessment of alternatives. Other advantages include better acceptance of decisions, greater satisfaction in the organization, and personal growth for group members. Time is one of several disadvantages associated with using a group to make a decision.

Key Terms

decisions, p. 338
satisficing decisions, p. 341
sensing, p. 342
intuition, p. 342
thinking, p. 343
feeling, p. 344
risk-taking propensity, p. 346
reference point, p. 346
cognitive biases, p. 347

confirmation bias, p. 347
ease-of-recall bias, p. 347
anchoring bias, p. 348
sunk-cost bias, p. 348
moods, p. 349
emotions, p. 349
groupthink, p. 352
common information
   bias, p. 354

diversity-based infighting,
   p. 355
risky shift, p. 355
brainstorming, p. 356
nominal group technique,
   p. 357
Delphi technique, p. 357
dialectical inquiry, p. 358
devil's advocacy, p. 358

building your human capital
Decision Style Assessment

Different people use different decision styles. Understanding how you approach the gathering of information and the evaluation of alternatives can help make you a better decision maker. Such an understanding clarifies your strengths and weaknesses, which better positions you to deal effectively with them. Below, we present an assessment tool for decision styles.

Instructions

In this assessment, you will read 24 phrases that describe people. Please use the rating scale below to indicate how accurately each phrase describes *you*. Rate yourself as you generally are now, not as you wish to be in the future. Rate yourself as you honestly see yourself. Please read each item carefully, and then circle the number that corresponds to your choice from the rating scale.

1	2	3	4	5
Not at all like me	Somewhat unlike me	Neither like nor unlike me	Somewhat like me	Very much like me

1. Do things in a logical order	1	2	3	4	5
2. Do things that others find strange.	1	2	3	4	5
3. Come straight to the point.	1	2	3	4	5
4. Like to get lost in thought.	1	2	3	4	5
5. Sympathize with the homeless.	1	2	3	4	5
6. Do things by the book.	1	2	3	4	5
7. Believe in a logical answer for everything.	1	2	3	4	5
8. Enjoy wild flights of fantasy.	1	2	3	4	5
9. Am not as strict as I could be.	1	2	3	4	5
10. Seldom daydream.	1	2	3	4	5
11. Get a head start on others.	1	2	3	4	5
12. Love to daydream.	1	2	3	4	5
13. Let people pull my leg.	1	2	3	4	5
14. Seldom get lost in thought.	1	2	3	4	5
15. Dislike imperfect work.	1	2	3	4	5
16. Swim against the current.	1	2	3	4	5
17. Do things in a halfway manner.	1	2	3	4	5
18. Take deviant positions.	1	2	3	4	5
19. Let my attention wander off.	1	2	3	4	5
20. Do unexpected things.	1	2	3	4	5
21. Believe in an eye for an eye.	1	2	3	4	5
22. Have no sympathy for criminals.	1	2	3	4	5
23. Reason logically.	1	2	3	4	5
24. Believe that criminals should receive help rather than punishment.	1	2	3	4	5

Scoring Key for Decision Style Assessment

To create scores, combine your responses to the items as follows:

Sensing vs. intuition = (Item 2 + Item 4 + Item 8 + Item 12 + Item 16 + Item 18 + Item 20) + (18 − (Item 6 + Item 10 + Item 14))

Thinking vs. feeling = (Item 1 + Item 3 + Item 7 + Item 11 + Item 15 + Item 21 + Item 22 + Item 23) + (36 − (Item 5 + Item 9 + Item 13 + Item 17 + Item 19 + Item 24))

Scores for sensing versus intuition can range from 10 to 50. Scores below 30 suggest a sensing style, while scores of 30 and above suggest an intuition style. More extreme scores (very low or very high) indicate a stronger preference for one style over another. Scores from 26 to 34 suggest weaker preferences for a particular style.

Scores for thinking versus feeling can range from 14 to 70. Scores of 42 and above suggest a thinking style, while scores below 42 suggest a feeling style. More extreme scores (very low or very high) indicate a stronger preference for one style over another. Scores from 37 to 47 suggest weaker preferences for a particular style.

Source: International Personality Item Pool (2001). A Scientific Collaboration for the Development of Advanced Measures of Personality Traits and Other Individual Differences (http://ipip.ori.org).

an organizational behavior moment
Decision Making at a Nuclear Power Facility

Part A. Harry, the Reluctant Maintenance Man

Harry opened his lunch bucket and was disappointed to find two tuna fish sandwiches again. "Damn," he muttered to himself, "four days in a row." He would have to get on his daughter, Susan, again. She graciously prepared his lunch most days but did not always provide the variety he liked. Of course, Susan would explain that she had other things to do besides providing him with a full lunch menu.

Across the cafeteria, Dan Thompson was eating with one of the design engineers, Marty Harris. Dan didn't like to talk shop while eating, but today had decided to continue a previous discussion over lunch. Dan was the supervisor of technical maintenance and had noticed that several of his people were reluctant to follow maintenance procedures. He had been told that the specifications were too complex to understand, that the procedures were often unnecessary, and that the plant engineers did not really appreciate maintenance problems. On the one hand, Dan realized that most of their complaints were just excuses for "doing things their own way." On the other hand, he didn't really know which procedures were important and which were not. That's why he had asked Marty to meet with him.

"Look, Dan," Marty was saying, "I know these procedures are complex. But damn it, nuclear power plants are complex—and potentially risky. Every specification, every procedure has a reason for being there. If your maintenance people ignore one procedure, they might get by with it and nothing happens. But one of them just might do it at the wrong time, and something could go haywire. You might explain that we have safety and cost to consider. If we lost expensive equipment, how'd they like to pay for it? Not much, I bet. If they lose a finger or get exposed to too much radiation, they wouldn't like that either. Now, just tell your people that the specifications and procedures, if followed, are the guarantee that things won't go wrong. They can count on it. If they take shortcuts, I won't guarantee a thing."

Dan nodded. This really wasn't what his maintenance staff wanted. They had hoped for a little flexibility, but he was going to have to tell them to follow the procedures. They wouldn't like it, but they would have to do it.

Later that afternoon, Dan met with his unit and relayed the instructions. He reminded them of the rules and disciplinary actions for not following procedures. At the end of the meeting, he couldn't decide whether it had done any good.

On Thursday, Harry noticed that he had been assigned the routinely scheduled maintenance on the three auxiliary feedwater (AFW) pumps. These pumps were normally used only for startup and shutdown and as emergency backup. When the main feedwater system malfunctioned, these pumps would activate to keep the system from "drying out." The procedure also specified that the pumps should be serviced and tested one at a time and that, at most, one pump should be out of service at a time.

"That's horse manure," Harry thought. "Takes three hours to service the pumps that way. I can do it in two if I shut 'em down together. Two's better than three. Those stupid design people have probably never tried to service one of these things."

Harry didn't bother to open the manual for pump servicing. He had serviced these pumps several times in the past and felt no need to do it from the book any longer. He reached over and shut off three discharge valves, set out his equipment, and got to work. Two hours later he was done. He packed up his tools and hurried to get home.

Part B. System Breakdown

Marv Bradbury was working the graveyard shift. Most technicians didn't like this shift, but Marv didn't mind it at all. In fact, he thrived on it. Over the past few months, he had discovered that he enjoyed the solitude. He also liked to sleep in the mornings. Many of his co-workers thought he was nuts, but he didn't mind. He especially liked the extra responsibility that the graveyard shift put on the technician position.

Marv's job in the nuclear generating plant was particularly important. His primary job was to monitor a series of dials and readouts in the control room. Most of the time, the job was a little monotonous because the system was so automatic. However, if the readings indicated some variance in the system, Marv's responsibilities were great. He would have to interpret the readings, diagnose the problem, and—if the automatic correcting system failed—initiate corrective actions. For two reasons, Marv never worried about the enormous responsibilities of his job. First, the system was fault-free and self-correcting. It was a good system with no weaknesses. Second, Marv was exceptionally qualified and had a great deal of understanding about the system. He always knew what he had to do in the event of a problem and was capable of doing it. Several years of training had not been wasted on him.

It was about 4 A.M. when he noticed the feedwater dial reading begin to move rapidly. Temperature in the system was increasing quickly. The readings alerted Marv that the main system was malfunctioning, and he knew just what to do. He glanced over to the AFW indicator lights to be sure they were activated. The lights switched on, and he knew everything was in order. Obviously, he would have to find the malfunction in the main system, but for the time being everything was okay. The temperature in the cooling system should drop back down to normal as the AFW pumps took over.

Suddenly, the indicator light for the pressurizer relief valve showed that it had opened. In rapid succession the high reactor tripped, and the hot leg temperature in the primary loop increased to about 607 degrees Fahrenheit.

Marv knew the system was in severe trouble and got on the phone to get help. Before he could get back, the high-pressure injection pump had started, and he could feel an unusual and threatening vibration that shouldn't be there. Indicators showed that the steam generators were drying out, but that didn't make sense—the auxiliaries were running. He knew that if they dried out, the temperature was really going to go up and that the core was going to be damaged. "Why the hell isn't that secondary loop running?" he yelled to himself.

It took eight minutes to get someone down to the auxiliary pump room and discover that the three valves were still closed. They opened the valves, but it was too late. Now no one seemed to know what to do.

Discussion Questions

1. Analyze the critical problem in Part A of the case. Did Dan handle it in the best way? What decision styles did he use?
2. In what important ways is Harry's behavior different from Marv's?
3. How might group decision making be applied at the end of Part B?
4. What alternatives do you see for reducing the possibility of a similar problem in the future?

---

team exercise

Group Decision Making in Practice

In this chapter, we discussed several techniques for group decision making. The purpose of this exercise is to demonstrate two of the techniques and to show how they facilitate group decision activities. The exercise should take about 40 minutes to complete.

Procedure

1. The instructor will assign you to either a group that will use brain-writing and dialectical inquiry (BD group) or a group that will engage in general discussion (GD group).
2. All groups will list as many ideas as possible concerning the general problem, "How can the college of business enhance its reputation among the business leaders in the regional business community?" This should take no more than 20 minutes. Each BD group will follow the rules of brain-writing to generate the list of ideas. Each GD group will discuss the issue in a group setting.
3. All groups will develop a final recommendation. Each BD group will follow the dialectical inquiry method. Each GD group will again engage in general discussion.
4. The instructor will lead a discussion about your experiences.

Endnotes

1. Hitt, M.A., Ireland, R.D., & Hoskisson, R.E. 2009. *Strategic management: Competitiveness and globalization* (8th ed.). Cincinnati, OH: South-Western.
2. Hitt, M.A., & Tyler, B.B. 1991. Strategic decision models: Integrating different perspectives. *Strategic Management Journal,* 12: 327–351.
3. Bazerman, M.H., & Moore, D.A. 2009. *Judgment in managerial decision making* (7th ed.). New York: John Wiley & Sons.
4. Hammond, J.S., Keeney, R.L., & Raiffa, H. 1999. *Smart choices: A practical guide to making better decisions.* Boston: Harvard Business School Press.
5. Ibid.
6. Based on Huber, G.P. 1980. *Managerial decision making.* Glenview, IL: Scott, Foresman.
7. Simon, H. 1957. *Administrative behavior.* New York: Macmillan.
8. Cecil, E.A., & Lundgren, E.F. 1975. An analysis of individual decision making behavior using a laboratory setting. *Academy of Management Journal,* 18: 600–604; Schwartz, B., Ward, A., Monterosso, J., Lyubomirsky, S., White, K., & Lehman, D.R. 2002. Maximizing versus satisficing: Happiness is a matter of choice. *Journal of Personality and Social Psychology,* 83: 1178–1197.

9. Most research based on Jung's ideas has used the Myers–Briggs Type Indicator (MBTI). For a review of relevant research in organizational behavior, see Gardner, W.L., & Martinko, M.J. 1996. Using the Myers-Briggs Type Indicator to study managers: A literature review and research agenda. *Journal of Management,* 22: 45–83. For a recent study based on the MBTI, see Davies, J., & Thomas H., 2009. What do business school deans do? Insights from a UK study. *Management Decision,* 47: 1396–1419; For supportive research on the internal consistency and test–retest reliability associated with the MBTI, see Capraro, R.M., & Capraro, M.M. 2002. Myers-Briggs Type Indicator score reliability across studies: A meta-analytic reliability generalization study. *Educational and Psychological Measurement,* 62: 590–602; and see Myers, I.B., & McCaulley, M.H. 1989. *Manual: A guide to the development and use of the Myers-Briggs Type Indicator.* Palo Alto, CA: Consulting Psychologists Press. For research on the construct validity associated with the MBTI, see Carlyn, M. 1977. An assessment of the Myers-Briggs Type Indicator. *Journal of Personality Assessment,* 41: 461–473; and see Thompson, B., & Borrello, G.M. 1986. Construct validity of the Myers-Briggs Type Indicator. *Educational and Psychological Measurement,* 60: 745–752. For research on temporal stability, see Salter, D.W., Evans, N.J., & Forney, D.S. 2006. A longitudinal study of learning style preferences on the Myers-Briggs type indicator and learning style inventory. *Journal of College Student Development,* 47: 173–184; For criticism of the MBTI, see, for example, Pittenger, D.J. 1993. The utility of the Myers-Briggs Type Indicator. *Review of Educational Research,* 63: 467–488.

10. Gardner & Martinko, Using the Myers-Briggs Type Indicator to study managers; Jaffe, J. 1985. Of different minds. *Association Management,* 37 (October): 120–124.

11. Leibovich, M. 2000. Alter egos: Two sides of high-tech brain trust make up a powerful partnership. *The Washington Post,* December 31, p. A.01.

12. Gardner & Martinko, Using the Myers-Briggs Type Indicator to study managers; Jaffe, Of different minds.

13. Lyons, M. 1997. Presidential character revisited. *Political Psychology,* 18: 791–811.

14. Kiersey.com. 2007. The rationals. At http://keirsey.com/personality/nt.html.

15. Gardner & Martinko, Using the Myers-Briggs Type Indicator to study managers.

16. Rodgers, W. 1991. How do loan officers make their decisions about credit risks? A study of parallel distributed processing. *Journal of Economic Psychology,* 12: 243–365.

17. Stevens, G.A., & Burley, J. 2003. Piloting the rocket of radical innovation. *Research Technology Management,* 46: 16–25.

18. Gardner & Martinko, Using the Myers-Briggs Type Indicator to study managers; Jaffe, Of different minds.

19. Ibid.

20. McIntyre, R.P. 2000. Cognitive style as an antecedent to adaptiveness, customer orientation, and self-perceived selling performance. *Journal of Business and Psychology,* 15: 179–196.

21. Gardner & Martinko, Using the Myers-Briggs Type Indicator to study managers; Jaffe, Of different minds.

22. Jaffe, Of different minds.

23. See the following: Leibovich, Alter egos; Lohr, S. 2007. Preaching from the Ballmer pulpit. *The New York Times,* January 28, p. 3.1; Schlender, B. 2004. Ballmer unbound. *Fortune,* 149 (2): 117–124; Schlender, B. 2007. The wrath of Ballzilla. *Fortune,* 155 (8): 70.

24. Bazerman & Moore, *Judgment in managerial decision making;* Hammond, Keeney, & Raiffa, *Smart choices.*

25. Dahlback, O. 1990. Personality and risk taking. *Personality and Individual Differences,* 11: 1235–1242; Dahlback, O. 2003. A conflict theory of group risk taking. *Small Group Research,* 34: 251–289; March, J.G. 1994. *A primer on decision making.* New York: The Free Press.

26. Lashinsky, A. 2004. For Trump, fame is easier than fortune. *Fortune,* 149 (4): 38; Shawn, T. 1996. Donald Trump: An ex-loser is back in the money. *Fortune,* 134 (2): 86–88.

27. Taylor, R.N., & Dunnette, M.D. 1974. Influence of dogmatism, risk-taking propensity, and intelligence on decision-making strategies for a sample of industrial managers. *Journal of Applied Psychology,* 59: 420–423.

28. Jegers, M. 1991. Prospect theory and the risk-return relation. *Academy of Management Journal,* 34: 215–225; Kahneman, D., & Tversky, A. 1979. Prospect theory: An analysis of decision under risk. *Econometrica,* 47: 263–291; Larrick, R.P., Heath, C., Wu, G. 2009. Goal induced risk taking in negotiation and decision making. *Social Cognition,* 27: 342–364; Tversky, A., & Kahneman, D. 1986. Rational choice and the framing of decisions. *Journal of Business,* 59: 251–278; Wakker, P.P. 2003. The data of Levy and Levy (2002) "Prospect theory: Much ado about nothing?" actually support prospect theory. *Management Science,* 49: 979–981.

29. Smith, G., Levere, M., & Kurtzman, R. 2009. Poker player behavior after big wins and big loses. *Management Science,* 55: 1547–1555.

30. Simon, M., Houghton, S.M., & Savelli, S. 2003. Out of the frying pan...? Why small business managers introduce high-risk products. *Journal of Business Venturing,* 18: 419–440.

31. Tversky, A., & Kahneman, D. 1974. Judgment under uncertainty: Heuristics and biases. *Science,* 185: 1124–1131.

32. Bazerman & Moore, *Judgment in managerial decision making;* Hammond, Keeney, & Raiffa, *Smart choices;* Hogarth, R. 1980. *Judgment and choice.* New York: John Wiley & Sons.

33. Einhorn, H.J., & Hogarth, R.M. 1978. Confidence in judgment: Persistence in the illusion of validity. *Psychological Review,* 85: 395–416; Jones, M., & Sugden, R. 2001. Positive confirmation bias in the acquisition of information. *Theory and Decision,* 50: 59–99; Wason, P.C. 1960. On the failure to eliminate hypotheses in a conceptual task. *Quarterly Journal of Experimental Psychology,* 12: 129–140.

34. Pines, J.M. 2006. Profiles in patient safety: Confirmation bias in emergency medicine. *Academic Emergency Medicine,* 13: 90–94; Tschan, F, Semmer, N.K., Gurtner, A., Bizzari, L., Spychiger, M., Breuer, M., & Marsch, S.U. 2009. Explicit reasoning, confirmation bias, and illusory transactive memory. *Small Group Research,* 40: 271–300; Schawb, A.P. 2008. Putting cognitive psychology to work: Improving decision making in the medical encounter. *Social Science and Medicine,* 67: 1861–1869.

35. Ask, K., & Granhag, P.A. 2007. Motivational bias in criminal investigators' judgments of witness reliability. *Journal of Applied*

Social Psychology, 37: 561–591; Ask, K., Rebelius, A., Granhag, P.A. 2008. The 'elasticity' of criminal evidence: A moderator of investigator bias. *Applied Cognitive Psychology,* 22: 1245–1259; O'Brien, B. 2009. Prime suspect: An examination of factors that aggravate and counteract confirmation bias in criminal investigations. *Psychology, Public Policy, and Law,* 15: 315–334.

36. Bazerman & Moore, *Judgment in managerial decision making.*

37. Time.com. 2004. Person of the year: Notorious leaders— Joseph Stalin. http://www.time.com/time/personoftheyear/archive/ photohistory/stalin.html.

38. Bazerman & Moore, *Judgment in managerial decision making.*

39. Joyce, E.J., & Biddle, G.C. 1981. Anchoring and adjustment in probabilistic inference in auditing. *Journal of Accounting Research,* 19: 120–145.

40. Hammond, Keeney, & Raiffa, *Smart choices;* Roberto, M.A. 2002. Lessons from Everest: The interaction of cognitive bias, psychological safety, and system complexity. *California Management Review,* 45 (1): 136–158.

41. Coffey, M. 2006. The ones left behind. *Outside,* 31 (9): 80–82; Roberto, M.A. 2002. Lessons from Everest: The interaction of cognitive bias, psychological safety, and system complexity. *California Management Review,* 45 (1): 136–158; Roberto, M.A., & Carioggia, G.M. 2003. *Mount Everest—1996.* Boston: Harvard Business School Publishing; Turner, P.S. 2003. Going up: Life in the death zone. *Odyssey,* 12 (8): 19.

42. Krakauer, J. 1997. *Into thin air: A personal account of the Mount Everest disaster.* New York: Villard Books.

43. Andrade, E.B., Ariely, D. 2009. The enduring impact of transient emotions on decision making. *Organizational Behavior and Human Decision Process,* 109: 1–8; Brief, A.P., & Weiss, H.M. 2002. Organizational behavior: Affect in the workplace. *Annual Review of Psychology,* 53: 279–307.

44. Bramesfeld, K.D., & Casper, K. 2008. Happily putting the pieces together: A test of two explanations for the effects of mood on group-level information processing. *British Journal of Social Psychology,* 47: 285–309; Cianci, A.M., & Bierstaker, J.L. 2009. The impact of positive and negative mood on the hypothesis generation and ethical judgments of auditors. *Auditing—A Journal of Practice & Theory,* 28 (2): 119–144; Englich, B., & Sodor, K. 2009. Moody experts—How mood and expertise influence judgmental anchoring. *Judgment and Decision Making,* 4: 41-50; Forgas, J.P. 2006. Affect in social thinking and behavior. New York: Psychology Press; Martin, L.L., & Clore, G.L. 2001. Theories of mood and cognition: A user's guidebook. Mahwah, NJ: Erlbaum.

45. Au K., Chan F., Wang D., & Vertinsky I. 2003. Mood in foreign exchange trading: Cognitive processes and performance. *Organizational Behavior and Human Decision Processes,* 91:322–338.

46. Chung, J.O.Y., Cohen, J.R., & Monroe, G.S. 2008. The effects of moods on auditors inventory valuation decisions. *Auditing—A Journal of Practice and Theory,* 27 (2): 137–159.

47. Zeelenberg, M. & Pieters, R. 2007. A theory of regret regulation 1.0. *Journal of Consumer Psychology,* 17: 3–18.

48. Ratner, R.K., & Herbst, K.C. 2005. When good decisions have bad outcomes: The impact of affect on switching behavior. *Organizational Behavior and Human Decision Processes,* 96: 23–37.

49. Reb, J., & Connolly, T. 2009. Myopic regret avoidance: Feedback avoidance and learning in repeated decision making. *Organizational Behavior and Human Decision Processes,* 109: 182–189;

50. Zeelenberg, & Pieters, A theory of regret regulation 1.0.

51. Lerner, J.S., & Tiedens, L.Z. 2006. Portrait of the angry decision maker: How appraisal tendencies shape anger's influence on cognition. *Journal of Behavioral Decision Making,* 19: 115–137.

52. Lerner, & Tiedens, Portrait of the angry decision maker: How appraisal tendencies shape anger's influence on cognition; Weber, E.U., & Johnson, E. J. 2009. Mindful judgment and decision making. *Annual Review of Psychology,* 60: 53–85.

53. Lerner, J.S., Gonzalez, R.M., Small, D.A, & Fischoff, B. 2003. Affects of fear and anger on perceived risks of terrorism: A natural field experiment. *Psychological Science,* 14: 144–150.

54. For an excellent example of social interactions in decision making, see Anderson, P.A. 1983. Decision making by objection and the Cuban missile crisis. *Administrative Science Quarterly,* 28: 201–222.

55. For the original formulation of groupthink, see the following: Janis, I.L. 1972. *Victims of groupthink: A psychological study of foreign-policy decisions and fiascos.* Boston: Houghton Mifflin; Janis, I.L. 1982. *Groupthink: Psychological studies of policy decisions and fiascos* (revised version of *Victims of groupthink).* Boston: Houghton Mifflin. For later variants of the groupthink model, see the following examples: Hart, P.T. 1990. *Groupthink in government: A study of small groups and policy failure.* Amsterdam: Swets & Zeitlinger; Turner, P.E., & Pratkanis, A.R. 1998. A social identity maintenance model of groupthink. *Organizational Behavior and Human Decision Processes,* 73: 210–235; Whyte, G. 1998. Recasting Janis's groupthink model: The key role of collective efficacy in decision fiascos. *Organizational Behavior and Human Decision Processes,* 73: 163–184. For an interesting critique of some past groupthink research, see Henningsen, D.D., Henningsen, M.L.M., Eden, J., & Cruz, M.G. 2006. Examining the symptoms of groupthink and retrospective sensemaking. *Small Group Research,* 37: 36–64. Also see: Haslam, S.A., Ryan, M.K., Postmes, T., Spears, R., Jetten, J., & Webley, P. Sticking to our guns: Social identity as a basis for the maintenance of commitment to faltering organizational projects. *Journal of Organizational Behavior,* 27: 607–628.

56. See, for example: Callaway, M.R., & Esser, J.K. 1984. Groupthink: Effects of cohesiveness and problem-solving procedures on group decision making. *Social Behavior and Personality,* 12: 157–164; Courtright, J.A. 1978. A laboratory investigation of groupthink. *Communication Monographs,* 45: 229–246; Janis, *Victims of groupthink.*

57. Whyte, Recasting Janis's groupthink model.

58. See, for example, Turner & Pratkanis, A social identity maintenance model of groupthink; Turner, M.E., & Pratkanis, A.R. 1997. Mitigating groupthink by stimulating constructive conflict. In C. De Dreu, & E. Van de Vliert (Eds.), *Using Conflict in Organizations.* London: Sage.

59. Turner & Pratkanis, A social identity maintenance model of groupthink; Turner & Pratkanis, Mitigating groupthink by stimulating constructive conflict.

60. Stephens, J., & Behr, P. 2002. Enron's culture fed its demise: Groupthink promoted foolhardy risks. *The Washington Post,* January 27, p. A.01.

61. For summaries of published case research, see: Esser, J.K. 1998. Alive and well after 25 years: A review of groupthink research. *Organizational Behavior and Human Decision Processes,* 73: 116–141; Park, W. 2000. A comprehensive empirical investigation of the relationships among variables of the groupthink model. *Journal of Organizational Behavior,* 21: 873–887.

62. Janis, *Victims of groupthink;* Tetlock, P.E., Peterson, R.S., McGuire, C., Chang, S., & Field, P. 1992. Assessing political group dynamics: A test of the groupthink model. *Journal of Personality and Social Psychology,* 63: 403–425.

63. Moorehead, G., Ference, R., & Neck, C.P. 1991. Group decision fiascos continue: Space Shuttle *Challenger* and revised groupthink framework. *Human Relations,* 44: 539–550.

64. Chisson, E.J. 1994. *The Hubble wars.* New York: Harper-Perennial.

65. Horton, T.R. 2002. Groupthink in the boardroom. *Directors and Boards,* 26(2): 9; Hymowitz, C. 2003. Corporate governance: What's your solution? *Wall Street Journal,* February 24: R8.

66. Manz, C.C., & Sims, H.P. 1982. The potential for "groupthink" in autonomous work groups. *Human Relations,* 35: 773–784.

67. Kim, P.H. 1997. When what you know can hurt you: A study of experiential effects on group discussion and performance. *Organizational Behavior and Human Decision Processes,* 69: 165–177; Stasser, G., & Titus, W. 1985. Pooling of unshared information in group decision making: Biased information sampling during discussion. *Journal of Personality and Social Psychology,* 48: 1467–1478.

68. Hunton, J.E. 2001. Mitigating the common information sampling bias inherent in small-group discussion. *Behavioral Research in Accounting,* 13: 171–194.

69. De Dreu, C.K.W., & Weingart, L.R. 2003. Task versus relationship conflict, team performance, and team member satisfaction: A meta-analysis. *Journal of Applied Psychology,* 88: 741–749; Miller, C.C., Burke, L.M., & Glick, W.H. 1998. Cognitive diversity among upper-echelon executives: Implications for strategic decision processes. *Strategic Management Journal,* 19: 39–58.

70. Stoner, J. 1968. Risky and cautious shifts in group decisions: The influence of widely held values. *Journal of Experimental Social Psychology,* 4: 442–459.

71. See, for example: Dahlback, A conflict theory of group risk taking.

72. Dahlback, A conflict theory of group risk taking; Mynatt, C., & Sherman, S.J. 1975. Responsibility attribution in groups and individuals: A direct test of the diffusion of responsibility hypothesis. *Journal of Personality and Social Psychology,* 32: 1111–1118; Wallach, M.A., Kogan, N., & Bem, D.J. 1964. Diffusion of responsibility and level of risk taking in groups. *Journal of Abnormal and Social Psychology,* 68: 263–274.

73. Osborn, A.F. 1957. *Applied imagination* (revised edition). New York: Scribner.

74. Thompson, L. 2003. Improving the creativity of organizational work groups. *Academy of Management Executive,* 17 (1): 96–109.

75. Bouchard, T. 1971. Whatever happened to brainstorming? *Journal of Creative Behavior,* 5: 182–189.

76. Mullen, B., Johnson, C., & Salas, E. 1991. Productivity loss in brainstorming groups: A meta-analytic integration. *Basic and Applied Social Psychology,* 12: 3–23; Stroebe, W., & Nijstad, B.A. 2004. Why brainstorming in groups impairs creativity: A cognitive theory of productivity losses in brainstorming groups. *Psychologische Rundschau,* 55: 2–10; Taylor, D.W., Berry, P.C., & Block, C.H. 1958. Does group participation when using brainstorming facilitate or inhibit creative thinking? *Administrative Science Quarterly,* 3: 23–47.

77. Diehl, M., & Stroebe, W. 1987. Productivity loss in brainstorming groups: Toward a solution of a riddle. *Journal of Personality and Social Psychology,* 53: 497–509.

78. Camacho, L.M., & Paulus, P.B. 1995. The role of social anxiousness in group brainstorming. *Journal of Personality and Social Psychology,* 68: 1071–1080; Thompson, Improving the creativity of organizational workgroups.

79. Thompson, Improving the creativity of organizational workgroups.

80. Ibid. Also see: Heslin, P.A. 2009. Better than brainstorming? Potential contextual boundary conditions to brainwriting for idea generation in organizations. *Journal of Occupational and Organizational Psychology,* 82: 129–145.

81. Ibid. Also see: DeRosa, D.M., Smith, C.L., & Hantula, D.A. 2007. The medium matters: Mining the long-promised merit of group interaction in creative idea generation tasks in a meta-analysis of the electronic group brainstorming literature. *Computers in Human Behavior,* 23: 1549–1581; Lynch, A.L., Murthy, U.S., & Engle, T.J. 2009. Fraud brainstorming using computer-mediated communication: The effects of brainstorming technique and facilitation. *The Accounting Review,* 84: 1209–1232.

82. Van de Ven, A., & Delbecq, A. 1974. The effectiveness of nominal, Delphi, and interacting group decision processes. *Academy of Management Journal,* 17: 605–621.

83. For supporting evidence, see: Gustafson, D.H., Shukla, R., Delbecq, A., & Walster, W. 1973. A comparative study in subjective likelihood estimates made by individuals, interacting groups, Delphi groups, and nominal groups. *Organizational Behavior and Human Performance,* 9: 280–291. Also see: Asmus, C.L., & James, K. 2005. Nominal group technique, social loafing, and group creative project quality. *Creativity Research Journal,* 17: 349–354.

84. Van de Ven & Delbecq, The effectiveness of nominal, Delphi, and interacting group decision processes.

85. See, for example, Landeta, J. 2006. Current validity of the Delphi method in social sciences. *Technology Forecasting & Social Change,* 73: 467–482; Van de Ven & Delbecq, The effectiveness of nominal, Delphi, and interacting group decision processes.

86. For early research on these two techniques, see the following: Mason, R. 1969. A dialectical approach to strategic planning. *Management Science,* 15: B403–B411; Mason, R.O., & Mitroff, I.I. 1981. *Challenging strategic planning assumptions,* New York: Wiley; Schweiger, D.M., Sandberg, W.R., & Ragan, J.W. 1986. Group approaches for improving strategic decision making: A comparative analysis of dialectical inquiry, devil's advocacy, and consensus. *Academy of Management Journal,* 29: 51–71.

87. Cosier, R.A. 1983. Methods for improving the strategic decision: Dialectic versus the devil's advocate. *Strategic Management Journal,* 4: 79–84; Mitroff, I.I. 1982. Dialectic squared: A fundamental difference in perception of the meanings of some key concepts in social science. *Decision Sciences,* 13: 222–224.

88. Schwenk, C. 1989. A meta-analysis on the comparative effectiveness of devil's advocacy and dialectical inquiry. *Strategic*

Management Journal, 10: 303–306; Valacich, J.S., & Schwenk, C. 1995. Structuring conflict in individual, face-to-face, and computer-mediated group decision making: Carping versus objective devil's advocacy. *Decision Sciences,* 26: 369–393.

89. Schweiger, Sandberg, & Ragan, Group approaches for improving strategic decision making.

90. Vroom, V.H., & Yetton, P.W. 1973. *Leadership and decision making.* Pittsburgh, PA: University of Pittsburgh Press.

91. Ibid.

92. Field, R.H.G. 1982. A test of the Vroom-Yetton normative model of leadership. *Journal of Applied Psychology,* 67: 523–532; Field, R.H.G., & House, R.J. 1990. A test of the Vroom-Yetton model using manager and subordinate reports. *Journal of Applied Psychology,* 75: 362–366; Tjosvold, D., Wedley, W.C., & Field, R.H.G. 1986. Constructive controversy, the Vroom–Yetton model, and managerial decision-making. *Journal of Occupational Behaviour,* 7: 125–138; Vroom, V.H., & Jago, A.G. 1978. On the validity of the Vroom-Yetton Model. *Journal of Applied Psychology,* 69: 151–162; Vroom, V.H., & Jago, A.G. 2007. The role of the situation in leadership. *American Psychologist,* 62: 17-24.

93. Hitt, Ireland, & Hoskisson, *Strategic management.*

94. For discussions of consensus vs. majority rule, see: Hare, A.P. 1976. *Handbook of small group research* (2nd ed.). New York: Free Press; Miller, C.E. 1989. The social psychological effects of group decision rules. In P.B. Paulus (Ed.), *Psychology of Group Influence.* Hillsdale, NJ: Erlbaum; Mohammed, S., & Ringseis, E. 2001. Cognitive diversity and consensus in group decision making: The role of inputs, processes, and outcomes. *Organizational Behavior and Human Decision Processes,* 85: 310–335.

95. Mohammed & Ringseis, Cognitive diversity and consensus in group decision making.

96. Ibid.

97. Maier, N.R.F. 1967. Assets and liabilities in group problem solving: The need for an integrative function. *Psychological Review,* 74: 239–249.

98. Schmidt, J.B., Montoya-Weiss, M.M., & Massey, A.P. 2001. New product development decision-making effectiveness: Comparing individuals, face-to-face teams, and virtual teams. *Decision Sciences,* 32: 575–600.

99. Maier, Assets and liabilities in group problem solving.

100. Weiner, B. 1977. *Discovering psychology.* Chicago: Science Research Associates.

101. For an interesting history of the study of decision making, see: Buchanan, L., & O'Connell, A. 2006. A brief history of decision making. *Harvard Business Review,* 84 (1): 32-41.

groups and teams

exploring behavior in action
Teamwork at Starbucks

Although a few setbacks have occurred in recent years, Starbucks remains one of the most successful business stories in history. The company's growth and financial success have been nothing short of phenomenal. As of early 2010, Starbucks has more than 16,000 retail outlets in more than 45 countries. For the 2009 fiscal year, sales were $9.7 billion. In the most recent quarter for which data are available, the company's profits soared as the global recession eased. In addition to its retail coffee shops and kiosks, with which you are probably familiar, the company has entered several successful joint ventures and partnerships. For example, a partnership with PepsiCo produces the

bottled coffee drink Frappuccino, and a joint venture with Unilever produces Starbucks coffee-flavored ice cream, which is sold in grocery stores. A partnership with Capitol Records resulted in a series of Starbucks jazz CDs. Furthermore, Starbucks has partnered with other companies, including United Airlines and Barnes & Noble Bookstores—all of which exclusively serve or sell Starbucks coffee. The list of industry awards is also impressive, including national and international awards for best management, humanitarian efforts, brand quality, and workplace experiences.

Much has been written about the sources of success at Starbucks. Several factors have been singled out for attention—effective branding, superior product quality, product innovation, superior customer service, innovative human resource practices, effective real estate strategies, and exceptional corporate social responsibility, for example. However, to anyone who has ever visited a Starbucks, another factor for its success is apparent—the teamwork of Starbucks "baristas" (the associates who take orders and who make and serve coffee and food).

knowledge objectives
After reading this chapter, you should be able to:

1. Describe the nature of groups and teams and distinguish among different types of teams.
2. Explain the criteria used to evaluate team effectiveness.
3. Discuss how various aspects of team composition influence team effectiveness.
4. Understand how structural components of teams can influence performance.
5. Explain how various team processes influence team performance.
6. Describe how teams develop over time.
7. Know what organizations can do to encourage and support effective teamwork.
8. Understand the roles of a team leader.

Watching the baristas at work in a busy Starbucks can be like watching a well-choreographed ballet. Baristas are making elaborate coffee drinks, serving up dessert, taking orders at record speed, answering customer questions, helping each other out when needed, and seemingly enjoying their work. Starbucks is legendary for its customer service, and teamwork is an important part of how this service is delivered. The extent to which baristas work together as a team, then, is an important aspect of Starbucks' success. And baristas are not only part of their shop's team—they are also part of the corporate Starbucks team.

Starbucks fosters a teamwork-based culture in many ways. It begins by hiring baristas who have the desires and skills to be successful team players. For potential job applicants, Starbucks puts it this way:

©Kevin P. Casey/©AP/Wide World Photos

> What's it like to work at Starbucks? We call each other "partners." We understand, respect, appreciate and include different people. We hear each partner's voice. And we learn from each other.

Training is an important element in this culture as well. Within their first month, all baristas receive many hours of training (most other coffee shops barely train their counter staff). New baristas are trained in the exact methods for making Starbucks drinks, care and maintenance of machinery, and customer service practices. In addition, they receive training in how to interact with each other. One of the guiding principles in Starbucks' mission statement involves providing a great work environment where people treat each other with respect and dignity. Historically, all baristas have been trained in the "Star Skills": (1) maintain and enhance (others') self-esteem; (2) listen and acknowledge; and (3) ask questions.

Another factor leading to increased teamwork and commitment to the company is Starbucks' generous benefits package. Baristas receive higher pay, better health benefits, and more vacation time than the industry norm. Even part-time employees receive benefits. Furthermore, Starbucks has a stock option plan (the Bean Stock plan) in which baristas can participate if they wish to.

Yet another way in which Starbucks fosters teamwork is by providing numerous communication channels so that every barista can communicate directly with headquarters. These communication channels include e-mail, suggestion cards, and regular forums with executives.

These are some of the most telling signs of Starbucks' desire to create a teamwork culture.

Sources: M. Gunther. 2006. "How UPS, Starbucks, Disney Do Good," *Fortune,* Feb. 25, at http://money.cnn.com/2006/02/23/news/companies/mostadmired_fortune_responsible/index.htm; D. Kesmodel. 2009. "Earnings: Starbucks Says Demand Perking Up: Coffee Retailer Reports Surge in Earnings as Cost Cuts Pay Off, Raises Outlook for 2010," *Wall Street Journal,* Nov. 6, p. B.5; Starbucks, "Our Starbucks Mission," 2010, at http://www.starbucks.com/mission/default.asp; Starbucks, "Starbucks Posts Strong Fourth Quarter and Fiscal 2009 Results," 2009, at http://investor.starbucks.com; Starbucks, "The Partner Experience," 2010, at http://www.starbucks.com/aboutus/jobcenter_partner_experience.asp; A.A. Thompson, J.E. Gamble, & A.J. Strickland. 2006. *Strategy: Winning in the Marketplace* (Chicago: McGraw-Hill); G. Weber. 2005. "Preserving Starbucks Counter Culture," *Workforce Management,* Feb., pp. 28–34

the strategic importance of Groups and Teams

U.S. organizations, following popular practice in other countries such as Japan, have adopted teamwork as a common way of doing work. The focus on teams in U.S. organizations developed during the 1980s. By 1993, 91 percent of *Fortune* 1000 companies used work teams, and 68 percent used self-managed work teams.[1] The presence of teamwork in business has only become greater since then. Indeed, after complaints from recruiters and advice from executives concerning the lack of interpersonal skills and teamwork skills of new graduates, many elite MBA programs have added teamwork training to the MBA curricula.[2]

Effective work teams have a synergistic effect on performance. **Synergy** means that the total output of a team is greater than the output that would result from adding together the outputs of the individual members working alone. Working in a team can produce synergy for several reasons. Team members are given more responsibility and autonomy; thus, they are empowered to do their jobs. Greater empowerment can produce higher motivation and identification with the organization.[3] Work teams also allow employees to develop new skills that can increase their motivation and satisfaction.[4] In addition, work teams can provide a means for employees to be integrated with higher levels in the organization, thereby aligning individual goals with the organization's strategy.[5] Finally, work teams can promote creativity, flexibility, and quick responses to customer needs.[6] These outcomes can be seen in the teams of baristas that work in Starbucks' stores.

Organizations have reported a great deal of success with work teams. Studies have documented tenfold reductions in error rates and quality problems, product-to-market cycles cut in half, and 90 percent reductions in response times to problems.[7] Extremely effective teams, often known as *high-performance work teams*, are able to achieve extraordinary results. A team of this kind seems to act as a whole rather than as a collection of individuals.[8]

In many companies, the organization's strategy is developed by a team of senior managers. Research has shown that heterogeneous teams that work together effectively develop strategies that lead to higher organizational performance.[9] Heterogeneity of backgrounds and experiences among team members has been shown to produce more and diverse ideas, helping to resolve complex problems more effectively. The quality of strategic decisions made by the management team affects the organization's ability to innovate and to create strategic change. Teams of top executives are used to make strategic decisions because of the complexity and importance of such decisions.[10] The senior management team at Starbucks, for example, made the strategic decisions to develop new products (such as Cinnamon Dolce Latte) and to enter new international markets (such as Russia and India). To make such important decisions, the team must work together effectively.

For the reasons noted above, the development and management of teams is highly critical to organizational performance. However, simply having people work together as a team does not guarantee positive outcomes. Teams must be effectively composed, structured, developed, managed, and supported in order to become high-performance work teams. In this chapter, we begin by exploring the nature of teams and their effectiveness. We then examine the factors that affect team performance. Next, we describe how teams develop and change overtime. Finally, we explain how to develop an effective team and how to manage teams.

The Nature of Groups and Teams

For over 100 years, social science research has focused on studying collections of people interacting together. It is often said that human beings are social animals and that we seek out interactions with others. Organizations provide many opportunities for such interactions. Business transactions such as planning and coordinating require that individuals interact. Also, because associates are assigned to work units on the basis of their work skills and backgrounds, they are likely to find others with whom they share common interests.

synergy
An effect wherein the total output of a team is greater than the combined outputs of individual members working alone.

Furthermore, organizations frequently structure work so that jobs are done by associates working together. Two terms are used to define these clusters of associates: *groups* and *teams*.

Groups and Teams Defined

There are many definitions for both *group and team,* with most researchers using the terms interchangeably.[11] For our purposes, the term **group** can be defined in very general terms as "two or more interdependent individuals who influence one another through social interaction."[12] In this chapter, however, our focus is more specific: we are mainly interested in teams—groups of individuals working toward specific goals or outcomes.[13] The common elements in the definition of a **team** are as follows:[14]

group
Two or more interdependent individuals who influence one another through social interaction.

team
Two or more people with work roles that require them to be interdependent, who operate within a larger social system (the organization), performing tasks relevant to the organization's mission, with consequences that affect others inside and outside the organization, and who have membership that is identifiable to those on the team and those not on the team.

1. Two or more people,
2. with work roles that require them to be interdependent,
3. who operate within a larger social system (the organization),
4. performing tasks relevant to the organization's mission,
5. with consequences that affect others inside and outside the organization,
6. and who have membership that is identifiable to those who are in the team and to those who are not in the team.

This definition helps us understand what a team is and is not. For example, mere assemblies of people are not teams. A crowd watching a parade is not a team because the people have little, if any, interaction, nor are they recognized as a team. A collection of people who interact with and influence each other, such as a sorority or a book club, can be thought of as a general group. When the goals of a group become more specific, such as winning a game, we refer to the group as a team (baseball team, project team, senior management team, and so forth). The baristas at Starbucks work as a team because they work interdependently toward the goal of serving customers, are recognized by others as a team, and most likely perceive themselves as a team.

Several types of groups and teams exist within organizations that differ in important ways. These differences may affect how the group or team is formed, what values and attitudes are developed, and what behaviors result. In the discussion that follows, we describe various types of groups and teams.

Formal and Informal Groups

formal groups
Groups to which members are formally assigned.

Both formal and informal groups exist within organizations. People become members of **formal groups** because they are assigned to them. Thus, in our terminology, teams are formal groups. To complete their tasks, members of these teams must interact. They often share similar task activities, have complementary skills, and work toward the same assigned goals. They recognize that they are part of the team, and the team exists as long as the task goals remain.[15] Examples of such teams are a faculty department, a highway crew, a small unit of production workers in an aircraft plant, and an assigned project team for class.

informal groups
Groups formed spontaneously by people who share interests, values, or identities.

Many groups that are not formally created by management arise spontaneously as individuals find others in the organization with whom they wish to interact. These **informal groups** form because their members share interests, values, or identities. Membership in an informal group depends on voluntary commitment. Members are not assigned, and they may or may not share common tasks or task goals. They do, however, share other social values and attitudes, and their group goals are often related to individual social needs. For example, groups of employees may gather to go to Happy Hour on Friday afternoons or to play in a fantasy football league. The informal group may exist regardless of any formal purpose, and it endures as long as social satisfaction is achieved. Because of their various characteristics, informal groups are not considered teams.

Identity Groups

In Chapter 2, we discussed the importance of social identity. Associates often form groups based on their social identities, such as gender identity, racial identity, or religious identity. These groups are referred to as **identity groups**.[16] Individuals belong to many identity groups that are not based on membership in the work organization (e.g., Hispanic, female, Catholic). Thus, any member of a team is also a member of several identity groups. Effective team performance can be more difficult to achieve when team members belong to different identity groups or when their identification with these groups conflicts with the goals and objectives of the team.[17] For example, suppose most of the members of a team are white North Americans who prefer a decision-making process in which all arguments are open and group members are encouraged to debate and question each other publicly. Some of the team members, however, identify with the Japanese culture, in which publicly contradicting someone is viewed as impolite. These team members will likely find the team's decision-making process to be uncomfortable and disrespectful, and they may not participate. Thus, team functioning will be impaired.

identity groups
Groups based on the social identities of members.

Virtual Teams

First discussed in Chapter 3, a **virtual team** is made up of associates who work together as a team but are separated by time, distance, or organizational structure.[18] Exhibit 11-1 displays common tools through which virtual teams operate. The benefits of virtual

virtual teams
Teams in which members work together but are separated by time, distance, or organizational structure.

EXHIBIT 11-1   Tools Commonly Used by Virtual Teams

Audio conferencing (traditional or Internet-based)
Videoconferencing (room to room from two or three locations or via dispersed micro-electronic equipment)
Online chat rooms
E-mail and online bulletin boards
Keypad voting systems
Project-management software
Instant messaging
Messaging boards
Web conferencing
Blogs and wiki sites

Sources: D. Mittleman, & R.O. Briggs. 1999. "Communicating Technologies for Traditional and Virtual Teams." In E. Sundstrom, & Associates (Eds.), *Supporting Work Team Effectiveness*, pp. 246–270; W. Combs, & S. Peacocke. 2007. "Leading Virtual Teams," *T&D*, 61, no. 2, pp. 27–28; B. Williamson. 2009. "Managing at a Distance," *BusinessWeek*, July 27, p. 64.

teams are obvious—they allow people who are physically separated to work together. Virtual teams, however, have been shown to be less effective than face-to-face teams in many instances.[19]

There are several reasons for this outcome. First, because fewer opportunities exist for informal discussions, trust can be slower to develop among virtual team members. Second, virtual team members rely on communication channels that are less rich than face-to-face interactions. (Chapter 9 discussed communication richness.) Consequently, misunderstandings are more likely to occur among team members. Third, it is more difficult for virtual teams to develop behavioral norms. Finally, it is easier for some members to be free riders (those who do not contribute effectively to the team's work), thereby causing frustration among other team members. Thus, it is very important that virtual teams be managed well, because they have a tendency to fall apart if care is not taken to maintain the team.

Research has shown that the effectiveness of virtual teams increases as a function of the number of face-to-face meetings members actually have.[20] Also, virtual teams in which members have a great deal of empowerment (authority to make their own decisions and act without supervision) are more effective than virtual teams with little empowerment. The impact of empowerment becomes even more important when virtual teams have little face-to-face interaction.[21] Finally, virtual teams are more effective when led by transformational leaders.[22] In fact, transformational leadership (involving vision, attention to collective interests, and lofty aspirations) seems to be more important for the success of virtual teams than for the success of face-to-face teams.[23] This type of leadership facilitates the development of trust, positive team norms, and commitment to the team and team task, each of which is particularly difficult in virtual situations.

When implemented properly, virtual teams can increase productivity and save companies millions of dollars.[24] For example, IBM has shortened its project completion times and reduced person-hours with virtual teams. Marriott Corporation has saved millions of dollars by reducing the number of person-hours required for certain tasks. By using same-time, different-place technology, Hewlett-Packard has connected research and development teams in California, Colorado, Japan, Germany, and France so that all teams can participate in the same presentation.

Functional Teams

Teams can be distinguished by the type of work they do and the purpose they serve. Types of functional teams include the following:[25]

- *Production teams*—groups of associates who produce tangible products (e.g., automotive assemblers or a team of restaurant chefs)
- *Service teams*—groups of associates who engage in repeated transactions with customers (e.g., sales teams or Starbucks baristas)
- *Management teams*—groups of managers who coordinate the activities of their respective units (e.g., senior management teams)
- *Project teams*—groups of associates (often from different functional areas or organizational units) who temporarily serve as teams to complete a specific project (e.g., new-product development teams)
- *Advisory teams*—groups of associates formed to advise the organization on certain issues (e.g., disability groups who advise on the technical aspects of various products)

Self-Managing Teams

Self-managing teams have a great deal of autonomy and control over the work they do.[26] Usually self-managing teams are responsible for completing a whole piece of work, an entire project, or a significant portion of a product or service delivery process. For example, rather than working only on one part of an automobile, a self-managing auto-assembly team might build the whole automobile or a significant portion of it. Although a self-managing team typically has formal supervision from above, the supervisor's role is to facilitate team performance and member involvement rather than to direct the team. The members of the team make important decisions that in other types of teams are made by the supervisor, such as assigning members to specific tasks, setting team performance goals, and even deciding the team's pay structure. Team members are also held more accountable for team performance.

Self-managed work teams can lead to many benefits, including more satisfaction for workers, lower turnover and absenteeism, increased productivity, and higher-quality work.[27] These benefits result because members of self-managed work teams are more engaged in their work and more committed to the team. However, the effectiveness of self-managed teams can be thwarted by several factors, including leaders who are too autocratic.[28]

A well-known example of a self-managed work team is the Orpheus Chamber Orchestra, the orchestra without a conductor. Orpheus musicians collaborate to take on leadership roles usually reserved for the conductor. The orchestra is incredibly flexible, with members moving into and out of roles as the need arises. As a result of this collaboration and flexibility, orchestra members always give their best performance, rather than acting passively as they might when working under the direction of a conductor. The Orpheus Chamber Orchestra is more successful (sells more tickets, takes in more money, and receives more positive reviews) and has lower turnover and greater member loyalty than many other orchestras.[29]

In this chapter's first *Experiencing Organizational Behavior* feature, teams at McKinsey & Company are highlighted. Unlike the barista teams at Starbucks, the consulting teams at McKinsey are temporary project teams. While both the barista and consulting teams operate predominantly in a face-to-face mode, there is a substantial amount of virtual work for McKinsey teams as they access supporting resources from offices dispersed globally (and some virtual work is also carried out between/among team members). Further, both sets of teams experience empowerment, although in McKinsey's case the teams are more clearly in the self-managing category. For McKinsey, there is also a great deal of complexity. This is often the case with project teams inside and outside consulting. Project teams typically have diverse members who must bridge differences against the backdrop of a temporary existence. A well-developed, time-tested and globally deployed approach to project work helps McKinsey address the inherent difficulties.

Team Effectiveness

How do we know when a team is effective? When a team reaches its performance goals, does this alone mean it was effective? Consider a class project in which a team turns in one report and everyone on the team receives the same grade. If the project earns an A, can we say the team was effective? What if only one person on the team did all the work and

Teams at McKinsey & Company

McKinsey & Company is one of the most revered consulting firms in the world. Through 90 offices in more than 50 countries, it offers a broad array of services in areas such as competitive strategy, organizational behavior and change, risk management, and corporate finance. Its mission is simple:

To help leaders make distinctive, lasting, and substantial improvements in performance, and constantly build a great firm that attracts, develops, excites, and retains exceptional people.

Similar to other major firms in the consulting industry, McKinsey & Company relies on project teams to accomplish its objectives. These teams are small, usually comprising fewer than 10 members. They are also temporary. Once a project has been completed, the team disbands and its members join new teams working with different clients. Each team generally has a mix of tenures represented, including a partner, an associate partner, an engagement manager, several associates, and one or more business analysts. Members of the team are drawn from more than 7,000 individuals positioned globally.

In addition to these core elements, McKinsey emphasizes dissent within its teams. If anyone on a team believes that inappropriate choices are being made, that individual has a responsibility to speak up. The firm says this to candidates for positions:

All McKinsey consultants are obligated to dissent if they believe something is incorrect or not in the best interests of the client. Everyone's opinion counts. While you might be hesitant to disagree with the team's most senior member or the client, you're expected to share your point of view.

©JEON HEON-KYUN/ epa/Corbis

In a typical work week, team members fly on Monday morning or Sunday evening to the client's site. During the week, individuals complete technical tasks working alone; create presentation materials alone or with others; join face-to-face team meetings; and participate in face-to-face meetings with representatives of the client. They use teleconferences, video conferences, and e-mail exchanges to access supporting resources at various McKinsey offices. Late nights are common. Lunches and dinners often involve substantive tasks or socializing with the client. On Friday afternoon or evening, team members fly home.

Clearly, the life of a consultant is complex and dynamic. Consultants must work effectively with teammates who are diverse in many ways, including their areas of expertise, national origins, levels in the firm, religions, races, and genders. They must travel constantly and work long hours. They must move to a newly forming team every two to six months. And they must live up to very high performance expectations. To ensure that consultants and their teams perform well and avoid undue stress, McKinsey & Company emphasizes the fundamentals that we would expect: sophisticated selection systems for new hires, proper training, sound information technology, and effective leadership. Perhaps more important than these tactics, McKinsey emphasizes consistent consulting methodologies at each of the more than 90 offices worldwide. This is difficult but crucial, as it allows each consultant who joins a new project team to know what to expect from others and to provide what others expect from him (recall that team members for a project are drawn from various locations around the world). The familiarity and predictability created by this approach adds structure to an otherwise complex and dynamic situation.

Also, McKinsey has addressed a history of stress and voluntary turnover by reducing travel to some degree and by generally being more attentive to work–life balance. These efforts have paid off, but stress and turnover remain issues in the consulting industry.

To further experience the complex McKinsey team environment, take the company's leadership test at http://www.mckinsey.com/locations/swiss/career/team_leader/index.asp.

Sources: H. Coster. 2007. "Baby Please Don't Go," *Forbes*, Oct. 15, p. 86; McKinsey & Company, "About Us: What We Believe," 2010, at http://www.mckinsey.com/aboutus/whatwebelieve/index.asp; McKinsey & Company, "McKinsey Careers: Teams," 2010, at http://www.mckinsey.com/careers/what_will_it_be_like_if_i_join/the_day_to_day/teams.aspx; McKinsey & Company, "McKinsey Careers: The Day-to-Day," 2010, at http://www.mckinsey.com/careers/what_will_it_be_like_if_i_join/the_day_to_day.aspx; A. Taylor. 1998. "Consultants Have a Big People Problem," *Fortune*, April 13, pp. 162–166.

everyone else loafed? The person who did all the work is likely to be angry and dissatisfied, while the others have learned nothing and walk away with the idea that it pays to loaf, especially when they have a conscientious teammate. In this case, it would have been better to have individuals work separately, even though the final product was successful. Because outcome by itself is not enough, team effectiveness is measured on several dimensions: knowledge criteria, affective criteria, and outcome criteria. A final consideration in team effectiveness is whether a team is even needed to perform the work, or whether the work is best performed by individuals.

Knowledge Criteria

Knowledge criteria reflect the degree to which the team continually increases its performance capabilities.[30] Teams are more effective when team members share their knowledge with one another and develop a collective understanding of the team's task, tools and equipment, and processes, as well as members' characteristics.[31] This shared knowledge is referred to as the team's *mental model*.[32] Shared mental models allow team members to have common expectations and agreed-upon courses of action, improve information processing and decision making, and facilitate problem solving.[33] Another knowledge-based criterion for team effectiveness is team learning—the ability of the team as a whole to learn new skills and abilities over time.[34] Clearly, in the class project example discussed above, this criterion was not met.

Affective Criteria

Affective criteria address the question of whether team members have a fulfilling and satisfying team experience.[35] One important affective criterion is the team's affective tone, or the general emotional state of the team.[36] It is important that the team, as a whole, have a positive, happy outlook on their work. Unfortunately, it is easy for even one member to contaminate the mood of a team.[37] The team's affect influences the way they communicate and their cohesion, as discussed later.

Outcome Criteria

Outcome criteria refer to the quantity and quality of the team's output[38] or the extent to which the team's output is acceptable to clients.[39] The outcome should reflect synergy, as described earlier in the chapter. Another important outcome criterion is team viability—that is, the ability of the team to remain functioning as long as needed.[40] Research has shown that teams have a tendency to "burn out" over time. One study, for example, found that the performance of research-and-development teams peaks at around years 2 to 3 and shows significant declines after year 5.[41] This decline in performance can be due to teams becoming overly cohesive (which can lead to groupthink, as discussed in Chapter 10) or to breakdowns in communication between team members. Often teams are created to deal with changing environments and uncertainty. Consider, for example, a military special operations team that must operate secretly in a foreign and hostile environment. In this case, a team's ability to adapt to the environment becomes an extremely important outcome.[42]

Is the Team Needed?

As stated earlier, teamwork has become very popular in business, as well as other types of organizations. However, is teamwork always the best way to accomplish a job? According to

Jon Katzenbach, a popular team consultant to companies such as Citicorp, General Electric, and ExxonMobil, some situations do not call for teamwork and are better handled by individuals working alone.[43] He argues that because teams are popular, managers often "jump on the team bandwagon" without giving a thought to whether a team is needed in the first place. He offers the following diagnostic checklist to determine whether a team should be created:

- Does the project really require collective work? If the work can be done by individuals working alone without any need for integration, teamwork is not necessary and merely adds to the burden by creating additional coordination tasks.
- Do team members need to focus on collective work a significant portion of the time? Can they instead focus on different aspects of the project most of the time? If the latter, then it might be more efficient to assign specific duties to individuals, rather than make the team responsible for all duties.
- Do people on the team hold one another accountable? Mutual accountability signals greater commitment to the team.

If there is a situation where these criteria are not met, then perhaps it is better to not use a team to accomplish the job.

Factors Affecting Team Effectiveness

As discussed in the opening section on the strategic importance of teams, when used properly, teams can yield great performance benefits to organizations. Teams can create synergy for several reasons, including greater goal commitment, a greater variety of skills and abilities applied to task achievement, and a greater sharing of knowledge. However, teamwork can also lead to poorer performance than individuals working alone, as suggested earlier. In addition to performing their regular work-related tasks and achieving organizational goals, team members must also deal with any interpersonal problems that arise, overcome the propensity to be lazy that some individuals might exhibit, coordinate tasks between/among individuals, and implement effective communication within the team. This extra "teamwork" can be quite substantial and can produce a significant **process loss**,[44] which is the difference between actual and potential team performance. If teams are not able to achieve synergy, less positive outcomes will result.

To ensure that the benefits of teamwork outweigh the process loss that occurs from it, teams must be structured and managed properly. Literally thousands of studies in almost every type of organizational context have examined factors that influence team effectiveness. We focus on three factors: team composition, team structure, and team processes.

process loss
The difference between actual and potential team performance that is caused by diverting time and energy into maintaining the team as opposed to working on substantive tasks.

Team Composition

Team composition is important because it addresses who members of the team are and what human resources (skills, abilities, and knowledge) they bring to the team. When managers assign associates to teams, they often make three questionable assumptions, which can lead to mistakes:[45]

1. They assume that people who are demographically similar and share beliefs will work better together, and so they attempt to compose teams that are somewhat homogeneous in these areas.

2. They assume that everyone knows how or is suited to work in a team.

3. They assume that a larger team size is always better.

In this section, we address these issues.

Diversity

In Chapter 2, we explored in depth the impact of demographic diversity on group performance. Some studies have found negative effects for demographic diversity,[46] others have found positive effects,[47] and still others have found no effect.[48] Another type of diversity that can impact team performance corresponds to differences in important beliefs among team members. Much of the research on belief diversity has taken place in the context of senior management teams, exploring how differences in beliefs regarding the attractiveness of various strategies/goals impact management-team performance and consequently firm performance. Consistent with research on demographic diversity, the impact of belief diversity on performance has been mixed.[49] Overall, the effects of demographic and belief diversity on team performance seem to depend on several factors:[50]

- *Type of task.* Diversity seems to have more positive effects when the team's tasks require complex problem solving such as that demanded by the pursuit of innovation and creativity.[51] Experiences with diverse teams at McKinsey are consistent with this idea.
- *Outcome.* Diversity may have a positive effect on performance but a negative effect on members' reactions to the team and subsequent behaviors, such as turnover.[52]
- *Time.* Diversity can have negative effects in the short run but positive effects in the long run.[53]
- *Type of diversity.* If team members are diverse on factors that lead them to have different performance goals or levels of commitment to the team the relationship between diversity and performance can be negative.[54]
- *Fault lines.* If team members exhibit diversity along two or more dimensions and those dimensions converge, then diversity can be negative.[55] For example, team members on a product development team might fall into the following two camps: (1) older male engineers and (2) younger female marketers. In this case, age, gender, and functional background converge such that two quite different subgroups exist.

Personality

The relationship between members' personalities and team performance can be quite strong, but the exact relationship depends on the type of task that the team is trying to accomplish. Researchers have several ways of determining the personality of the team; however, all methods are based on aggregating individuals' scores. The personality traits that have important effects on team performance include agreeableness (the ability to get along with others and cooperate) and emotional stability (the tendency to experience positive rather than negative emotions).[56] Also, the greater the degree of conscientiousness among team members, the higher the team's performance tends to be.[57] This is particularly true when the team's task involves planning and performance rather than creativity. It appears that agreeable team members contribute to team performance by fulfilling team maintenance roles, whereas conscientious team members perform critical task roles.[58] Finally, team-level extraversion and openness to experience can be positively related to

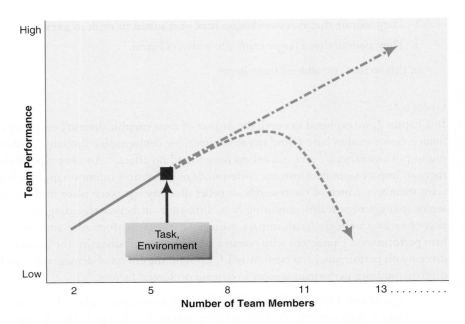

Exhibit 11-2 The
Relationship between
Team Size and Team
Performance

performance in situations requiring nonroutine decision making and creative tasks.[59] (All
of these personality traits are discussed in Chapter 5.)

Team Orientation

team orientation
The extent to which an
individual works well with
others, wants to contribute
to team performance, and
enjoys being on a team.

Some individuals are better at working on teams than others because they like working
on teams and have the requisite skills. **Team orientation** refers to the extent to which an
individual works well with others, wants to contribute to team performance, and enjoys
being on a team.[60] When a team comprises many members who have a positive team
orientation, that team will adapt and perform better than a team whose members do not
have such an orientation.[61] Notice that both Starbucks and McKinsey & Company hire
associates based on their teamwork orientation, among other things.

Size

There is no one ideal number of team members for all situations. Many studies have examined the relationship of team size and team performance, and two lines of thought have
emerged. These two ideas are depicted in Exhibit 11-2.

The first suggests that the relationship between team size and team performance is
shaped like an inverted U.[62] As teams become larger, the diversity of skills, talents, ideas, and
individual associate inputs into the task is greater, leading to improved performance. However, as the number of team members continues to increase, the need for cooperation and
coordination also increases. At some point, the effort that goes into managing the team will
outweigh the benefits of having more members, and team performance will begin to decline.

Other researchers, however, have found that performance increases linearly with team
size without ever showing a downturn.[63] This linear relationship most likely results when a
team avoids the problems associated with too many members, such as social loafing (to be
discussed later in the chapter), poor coordination, and worsening communication. Thus,
the relationship between team size and performance probably depends on team skill at
process management, and it also no doubt depends on factors such as the scope of the task

or the complexity of the environment.[64] When task scope and environmental complexity are high, more team members are needed for task accomplishment and strong performance.

Team Structure

Team structure refers to the ongoing means of coordinating formal team efforts. The contribution of structure to team achievement is evident. For example, consider a bank with a loan department and a collection department (each department can be considered a team). One department is assigned tasks related to making loans, such as credit analysis, interest computation, loan closing, and filing. These are somewhat dissimilar tasks but they form a sequential chain related to the lending process—loans cannot be closed until credit analysis has been performed and interest computed. Thus, grouping the tasks in one department under one leader makes sense. The other department is assigned phone collections, field collections, and repossessing tasks. These tasks are less sequential but they are very similar to one another. Task similarity is another basis for grouping tasks under one leader.

Beyond grouping together tasks and the individuals assigned to them, it is necessary to use additional structural methods to coordinate the efforts of individuals. Otherwise, tasks may not be performed in the best manner possible, and employees may duplicate their efforts or work against each other. Important aspects of team structure include roles, norms and task structure.

Team Member Roles

Team **roles** are expectations shared by team members about who will perform what types of tasks and under what conditions.[65] Roles can be formally assigned, or they can be informally adopted by team members. Some members primarily serve in leadership roles, and others take the roles of followers. The leadership role does not need to be formally assigned or to be a function of formal authority. Leaders can emerge informally in groups.

Apart from leadership roles, all teams need to have members fulfilling both task roles and socioemotional, or expressive, roles.[66] **Task roles** involve behaviors aimed at achieving the team's performance goals and tasks. **Socioemotional roles** require behaviors that support the social aspects of the team. A team member may also emphasize **destructive individual roles**, which involve behaviors that place that individual's needs and goals above those of the team.[67] As we would expect, these roles impede team performance rather than facilitate it. Exhibit 11-3 depicts examples of specific task, socioemotional, and individual roles.

As a team becomes more stable and structured, the roles of individual members often become resistant to change.[68] Group social pressures tend to keep members "in their place," and the team resists outside forces that would change members' roles, even if these roles were not the ones assigned by the formal organization.

Norms

Norms are informal rules or standards that regulate the team's behavior. Norms tend to emerge naturally in a team and are part of the team's mental model, although occasionally they are systematically recorded. Norms serve the purpose of regulating team members' behavior and providing direction. When individual team members violate team norms, some type of punishment or sanction is usually applied. For example, Hudson Houck, the offensive line coach for the 1996 Dallas Cowboys, stated that anyone on the team who didn't work hard all the time (a team norm) was shunned.[69]

roles
Expectations shared by group members about who is to perform what types of tasks and under what conditions.

task roles
Roles that require behaviors aimed at achieving the team's performance goals and tasks.

socioemotional roles
Roles that require behaviors that support the social aspects of the organization.

destructive individual roles
Roles involving self-centered behaviors that put individual needs and goals ahead of the team.

norms
Informal rules or standards that regulate the team's behavior.

EXHIBIT 11-3 Team Member Roles

Role	Function
Task Roles	
Initiator/Contributor	Suggests new ideas, solutions, or ways to approach the problem
Information Seeker	Focuses on getting facts
Information Giver	Provides data for decision making
Elaborator	Gives additional information, such as rephrasing, examples
Opinion Giver	Provides opinions, values, and feelings
Coordinator	Shows the relevance of various specific ideas to the overall problem to be solved
Orienter	Refocuses discussion when the team gets off topic
Evaluator/Critic	Appraises the quality of the team's work
Energizer	Motivates the team when energy falters
Procedural Technician	Takes care of operational details, such as technology
Recorder	Takes notes and keeps records
Socioemotional Roles	
Encourager	Provides others with praise, agreement, warmth
Harmonizer	Settles conflicts among other members
Compromiser	Changes his or her position to maintain team harmony
Gatekeeper	Controls communication process so that everyone gets a chance to participate
Standard Setter	Discusses the quality of the team process
Observer	Comments on the positive or negative aspects of the team process and calls for changes
Follower	Accepts others' ideas and acts as a listener
Destructive Individual Roles	
Aggressor	Attacks others
Blocker	Unnecessarily opposes the team
Dominator	Manipulatively asserts authority
Evader	Focuses on expressing own feelings and thoughts that are unrelated to the team goals
Help Seeker	Unnecessarily expresses insecurities
Recognition Seeker	Calls unnecessary attention to himself or herself

Sources: K.D. Benne and P. Sheets. 1948. "Functional Roles of Group Members," *Journal of Social Issues*, 4: 41–49. D.R. Forsyth. 1999. *Group Dynamics* (Belmont, CA: Wadsworth Publishing Company).
Copyright 2006 John Wiley & Sons, Inc. All rights reserved.

Team norms can become very powerful and resistant to change. Witness a situation such as a regular team meeting, or even a college class, where everyone sits in the same seat at every meeting. Any change in seating can cause unease on the part of group or team members. In these situations, seating norms develop to curb the social unease that could result from choosing a different seat at every meeting. No one has to wonder why someone is or is not sitting next to her. Nor does anyone have to worry about how others will interpret his motives for a seating choice.

Although norms allow teams to function smoothly, they can sometimes be harmful to team members. Research on the causes of eating disorders in young women illustrates this fact.[70] Certain groups, such as cheerleading squads, sororities, and dance troupes, have particularly high rates of bulimia among their members. Examination of these groups has indicated that they often develop group norms of binging and purging. Instead of considering this behavior to be abnormal and unhealthy, team members come to view it as a normal way of controlling weight. Because norms are not always positive, it is important that teams develop norms that foster team productivity and performance and promote the welfare of individual members.

Task Structure

Task structure has been shown to be an important determinant of how teams function and perform.[71] Several typologies have been proposed for categorizing tasks. One of the most popular typologies emphasizes the following: (1) whether tasks can be separated into subcomponents, (2) whether tasks have quantity or quality goals, and (3) how individual inputs are combined to achieve the team's product.[72]

First, then, we consider whether a task can be broken down into parts. Tasks such as playing baseball, preparing a class project, and cooking a meal in a restaurant are **divisible tasks** because they can be separated into subcomponents. Thus, different individual associates can perform different parts of the task. **Unitary tasks** cannot be divided and must be performed by a single individual. Examples of unitary tasks are reading a book, completing an account sheet, and talking to a customer on the phone. If a particular goal or mission requires the completion of unitary tasks, it may not be advantageous for a team to complete the mission.

Second, we consider the goals of the task. Tasks with a quantity goal are called maximization tasks. Examples of **maximization tasks** include producing the most cars possible, running the fastest, and selling the most insurance policies. Tasks with a quality goal are referred to as optimization tasks. **Optimization tasks** often require innovation and creativity. Examples of optimization tasks include developing a new product and developing a new marketing strategy. As mentioned earlier, diverse teams tend to perform better on optimization tasks.

Finally, we consider how individual inputs are combined to achieve the team's product. The manner in which this is done places a limit on how well the team can perform. We can classify how inputs are combined by determining whether a task is additive or compensatory and whether it is disjunctive or conjunctive.

Additive tasks are those in which individual inputs are simply added together—for example, pulling a rope or inputting data. When members' inputs are additively combined, team performance will often be *better than the best individual's performance* because of social facilitation processes (discussed later in the chapter).[73] *Compensatory tasks* are those in which members' individual performances are averaged together to arrive at the team's overall performance. For example, members of a human resource management team may individually estimate future labor demands in the organization, and the total projection may then be based on the average of the managers' estimates. The potential team performance on this type of task is likely to be *better than the performance of most of the individual members*.

Disjunctive tasks are those in which teams must work together to develop a single, agreed-upon product or solution. A jury decision is an example of a disjunctive task. Usually, disjunctive tasks result in team performance that is *better than that of most of the individual members but not as good as the best member's performance*.[74] *Conjunctive tasks* are those in which all members must perform their individual tasks to arrive at the team's overall performance. Examples of conjunctive tasks are assembly lines and trucks moving in a convoy. Teams working on conjunctive tasks *cannot perform any better than their worst*

divisible tasks
Tasks that can be separated into subcomponents.

unitary tasks
Tasks that cannot be divided and must be performed by an individual.

maximization tasks
Tasks with a quantity goal.

optimization tasks
Tasks with a quality goal.

individual performers. For example, an assembly line cannot produce goods at a rate faster than the rate at which its slowest member performs.

Team Processes

Team processes are the behaviors and activities that influence the effectiveness of teams. Team processes have strong effects on outcomes. Team processes include cohesion, conflict, social facilitation, social loafing, and communication.

Cohesion

interpersonal cohesion
Team members' liking or attraction to other team members.

task cohesion
Team members' attraction and commitment to the tasks and goals of the team.

Team cohesion refers to members' attraction to the team.[75] **Interpersonal cohesion** is the team members' liking or attraction to other team members. **Task cohesion** is team members' attraction and commitment to the tasks and goals of the team.[76] Team cohesion is an important criterion because research indicates that cohesion affects team performance outcomes and viability.[77] Furthermore, members of cohesive teams are more likely to be satisfied with their teams than are members of noncohesive teams.[78]

Cohesive teams are likely to have strong performance when there is task cohesion.[79] When there is only interpersonal cohesion, performance is likely to be low. In fact, if team members really like each other and enjoy spending time together but are not committed to their organizational tasks and goals, they will perform worse than if they were not interpersonally cohesive. A classic study of factory workers illustrates these effects.[80] Interpersonally cohesive teams committed to organizationally sanctioned performance goals performed the best, whereas interpersonally cohesive teams without commitment to such goals performed the worst—even worse than non–interpersonally cohesive teams lacking commitment to the performance goals. Finally, it is worth noting that cohesion also has stronger effects on performance when there is a great deal of interdependence among team members.[81]

In the *Experiencing Organizational Behavior* feature, we discuss a form of behavior that is consistent with both task and interpersonal cohesion—*backing-up behavior.* As in many jobs, performers in the Cirque du Soleil must be ready to take over for their team members at a moment's notice and do more than their fair share.

The support that team members provide to each other can be quite important in the performance of the team and the unit in which it operates. The *Experiencing Organizational Behavior* feature describes the necessity of backing-up behavior by Cirque du Soleil performers. However, this behavior is necessary in almost all teams. Think of the need for backup among police officers. Backing-up behavior may be one of the strongest indicators of team effectiveness, because not only is everyone on the team doing his or her share, but each member is willing to take on others' work when assistance is needed or to fill in any gaps. Teams that engage in backing-up behavior are displaying the spirit of high-involvement management by going beyond what is merely necessary to get the job done.

Conflict

When the behaviors or beliefs of a team member are unacceptable to other team members, conflict occurs. Several types of intragroup (within-team) conflict exist; they include personal conflict (sometimes referred to as "relationship conflict"), substantive conflict (sometimes referred to as "task conflict"), and procedural conflict (sometimes referred to as "process conflict").

Backup at Cirque Du Soleil

Chances are that you have seen a performance by Cirque du Soleil (approximately 15 million people saw their performances in 2009). What started out as a band of street performers in 1984 in Quebec, Canada, has grown into a business with over 5,000 employees (1,200 are performing artists), a number of touring companies that perform all over the world, and resident shows in Las Vegas, Orlando, New York, Tokyo, and Macau. Cirque du Soleil has come to redefine what we mean by the term *circus*. There are no animals, the shows are aimed at adult audiences, and performances provide visuals not seen before, such as the shows conducted under water ("O") and the amazing costumes. The company builds its brand on creativity and teamwork.

Cirque du Soleil hires people from all over the world, searching for people with various talents, ranging from being an acrobat and scuba-certified, to doing gymnastics on rollerblades. It does not just look for run-of-the mill acrobats, jugglers, and trapeze artists. Everyone must meet certain artistic qualifications and be predisposed to teamwork. Indeed, because about 20 percent of the artists turn over (due to injury or retirement) every year, Cirque has resorted to creating its own training camps, such as a camp for contortionists in Mongolia, to make sure it has a constant supply of talent.

Once artists are cast, they go through an eight-week boot camp where they learn how to operate as a team. One important aspect of this teamwork is the ability to be flexible, creative, and work off of other performers. Their coach, Boris Verkhovsky, states that this is not always easy, because many are trained athletes who are accustomed to performing on their own using strict protocols rather than engaging in artistic performances. An important part of a Cirque performer's job is to be able to back up other performers. As with many jobs, such as police officers or retail sales clerks, it is important that these performers be able to monitor the performance of all of their team members and be able to step in when there is trouble, a team member is overtaxed, or the artistic role requires it. Thus, providing backup to other performers is an essential component of all Cirque du Soleil artists' jobs. Consider the job of an aerialist who relies on her team members for safety support should she make a mistake during her routine.

©ALFREDO ALDA/epa/Corbis

Research has addressed the issue of who is likely to provide backup, who is likely to receive it, and under what conditions backing-up behaviors are likely to occur. When team members are highly conscientious and emotionally stable, they are more likely to provide backup to team members in need. Team members must also be knowledgeable about others' job responsibilities, as well as their own, in order to provide backup. When the team member who needs help is highly conscientious and extraverted, he or she will more likely receive backup from other team members. Finally, when team members perceive that the person who needs backing up has a larger workload or fewer resources to accomplish his or her work, they are more likely to provide the support needed.

Sources: Cirque du Soleil, "Cirque Du Soleil at a Glance," 2009, at http://www.cirquedusoleil.com/cirquedusoleil/pdf/pressroom/en/cds_en_bref_en.pdf; R.M. McIntyre, & E. Salas. 1995. "Measuring and Managing for Team Performance: Emerging Principles from Complex Environments," in R.A. Guzzo et al. (Eds.), *Team Effectiveness and Decision Making in Organizations* (San Francisco: Jossey-Bass, pp. 9–45); C.O.L.H. Porter et al. 2003. "Backing Up Behaviors in Teams: The Role of Personality and Legitimacy of Need," *Journal of Applied Psychology*, 88: 391–403; L. Tischler. 2005. "Join the Circus," *Fast Company*, July 5, at http://www.fastcompany.com/magazine/96/cirque-du-soleil.

Personal conflicts result when team members simply do not like each other. As we might expect, people assigned to a team are more likely to experience this sort of conflict than are people who choose to belong to the same informal group. Personal conflict may be based on personality clashes, differences in values, and differences in likes and dislikes. No disagreement over a specific issue is necessary for personal conflict to occur. One study of business executives found that 40 percent of their conflicts resulted from personal dislike rather than disagreement over a specific issue.[82]

Substantive conflicts occur when a team member disagrees with another's task-related ideas or analysis of the team's problem or plans. For example, a design team whose task is developing a better product may disagree about whether they should focus on making the product more attractive or making it easier to use. Substantive conflicts can often lead to greater creativity and innovation, if they do not become personal conflicts.[83]

Finally, *procedural conflicts* occur when team members disagree about policies and procedures. That is, they disagree on how to work together. For example, a member of a virtual team may believe that the correct way to work as a team is to check in by e-mail with other members at least twice a day. Furthermore, he may believe that team members should respond immediately to such e-mails. Other team members, however, may believe that checking in so frequently is a waste of time and may want to contact others only when necessary. Group norms develop as a way to avoid procedural conflicts. Teams may also develop specific policies or rules to avoid conflicts of this kind. Robert's Rules of Order are one such device because they specifically define how group meetings should be conducted.

Depending on the specific type, conflict can have negative or positive consequences for team effectiveness.[84] Personal conflict tends to be negative because it interferes with cooperation and a healthy task focus. On the other hand, substantive conflict can be positive, particularly for tasks involving creativity and innovation. This type of conflict generates multiple ideas and sets the stage for the best ones to be emphasized. Openly confronting and discussing the different task ideas is important, however. Ignoring differences of opinion is less helpful. Overall, substantive conflict can be beneficial when teams cooperatively problem solve, develop positive norms, and create a consistent team mental model.[85] Procedural conflict has not been studied often enough for firm conclusions to be drawn, but it certainly would have negative effects if not addressed to some degree.

Social Facilitation

In the late 1890s, Norman Triplett, a bicyclist and early social scientist, noticed that cyclists performed better racing against others than when they were timed cycling alone.[86] This effect—that is, when the presence of others improves individual performance—has been termed the **social facilitation effect**. Social facilitation suggests that teamwork can lead to increased performance because others are present.

Several reasons for the social facilitation effect have been suggested. One is that the presence of human beings creates general arousal in other human beings.[87] This general arousal then leads to better performance. Another explanation is that the presence of others arouses evaluation apprehension, so that people perform better because they think they are being evaluated.[88] Whatever the reason, social facilitation seems to occur only when people are performing well-learned, simple, or familiar tasks.[89] The presence of others can actually decrease performance on tasks that are complex or unfamiliar. For example, someone who is not accustomed to giving speeches is likely to perform more poorly when speaking in front of others relative to practicing alone.

social facilitation effect
Improvement in individual performance when others are present.

Social Loafing

Research suggests that the simple act of grouping individuals together does not necessarily increase their total output; in fact, people working together on a common task may actually perform at a lower level than they would if they were working alone. This phenomenon is called **social loafing**[90] or shirking,[91] and it can obviously result in serious losses. There are three primary explanations for the social loafing effect. First, if individual outputs are not identifiable, associates may shirk because they can get away with poor performance. Second, if associates, when working in teams, expect their teammates to loaf then they may reduce their own efforts to establish an equitable division of labor.[92] In this case, individual team members do not have a team identity and place their own good (working less) over the good of the team. Finally, when many individuals are working on a task, some individuals may feel dispensable and believe that their own contributions will not matter.[93] This is likely to happen when individuals think that they have low ability and cannot perform as well as other team members.[94]

Research on shirking supports these explanations. In one study, individuals were asked to pull alone as hard as possible on a rope attached to a strain gauge. They averaged 138.6 pounds of pressure while tugging on the rope. When the same individuals pulled on the rope in groups of three, however, they exerted only 352 pounds of pressure, an average of 117.3 pounds each. In groups of eight, the individual average dropped even lower, to an astonishing 68.2 pounds of pressure. This supports the first explanation of social loafing—that the less identifiable the individual's output is, the more the individual loafs.[95] Also, if the people with the least physical strength decrease their pressure the most, then there would also be support for the dispensability explanation.

In a second study, participants expected to work on a group task. Some of the subjects were told by a co-worker (a confederate of the researchers) that the co-worker expected to work as hard on the group task as she had on an individual task. Other participants were told that the co-worker expected to work less hard on the group task than on the individual task. In a third condition, nothing was said about the co-worker's intention. In the group task, the participants who had been told to expect lower performance from their co-worker reduced their efforts. However, the participants who had been told to expect no slacking of effort from the co-worker maintained their effort during the group task.[96] This supports the second explanation of social loafing—that individuals reduce their efforts to establish an equitable division of labor when they expect their co-workers to slack off in their efforts.

Students often experience social loafing. It occurs frequently when students are assigned to team projects in one of their courses. Inevitably, when student teams work on a class project, one or two members coast along, not "pulling their own weight." These "loafers" frequently miss the project team's meetings, fail to perform their assigned tasks, and so on. They rely on the fact that the more motivated members will complete the project without their help. The loafers still expect to share the credit and obtain the same grade, because the professor may not be concerned about determining who worked and who did not. One study examining social loafing in student groups found that the most common reasons for loafing were perceptions of unfairness (i.e., others were loafing) and perceived dispensability because one was not as talented as others.[97]

Social loafing is always a possibility in work teams, especially in teams that have limited task cohesion. For example, in a study of almost 500 work team members, 25 percent expressed concern that members of their teams engaged in social loafing. This can be extremely costly to organizations, because creating and supporting work teams requires

social loafing
A phenomenon wherein people put forth less effort when they work in teams than when they work alone.

investments in such things as new technology to aid teamwork, coordination efforts, more complicated pay systems, and restructuring of work. Thus, when teams perform worse than individuals, not only are performance and productivity lower, but costs are also higher.

Social loafing can occur in any team at any level in an organization. And because social loafing clearly results in lower productivity, it is a serious problem. At the least, when social loafing occurs, the organization's human capital is underutilized. Fortunately, managers can use several methods to address this problem.[98] First they can make individual contributions visible. This can be accomplished by using smaller rather than larger teams, using an evaluation system where everyone's contributions are noted, and/or appointing someone to monitor and oversee everyone's contributions. The second thing that can be done is to foster team cohesiveness by providing team-level rewards, training members in teamwork, and selecting "team players" to be on the team.

Communication

Team members must communicate to effectively coordinate their productive efforts. Task instructions must be delivered, results must be reported, and problem-solving discussions must take place. Because communication is crucial, teams create many formal communication processes, which may include formal reports (such as profit-and-loss statements), work schedules, interoffice memoranda, and formal meetings.

But informal communication also is necessary. Associates need and want to discuss personal and job-related problems with each other. Informal communication is a natural consequence of group processes. The effectiveness and frequency of communication are affected by many of the same factors that lead to group formation and group structure. For example, frequency of communication is partially the result of the opportunity to *interact*. People who share the same office, whose jobs are interconnected, and who have the same working hours are likely to communicate more frequently. Thus, the opportunity to interact leads to both group formation and frequent communication. This is why virtual teams are more likely to be effective when they have more face-to-face interaction.[99]

In addition to affecting task performance, communication frequency and effectiveness are related to team member satisfaction, particularly in cohesive teams. Increased communication enhances team members' satisfaction with their membership on the team. Also, communication becomes more rewarding as team membership increases in importance and satisfaction to associates.[100] Thus, communication is both a cause and a consequence of satisfaction with the team.

Team Development

The nature of interactions among team members changes over time. Teams behave differently when they meet for the first time relative to when they have been together long enough to be accustomed to working together. At the beginning of a team's life cycle, members may spend more time getting to know each other than they do on the task. As time progresses, however, the team often becomes more focused on performance. According to Bruce Tuckman's group development model, teams typically go through four stages over their life cycle: forming, storming, norming, and performing.[101]

During the *forming* stage, associates come to teams without established relationships but with some expectations about what they want in and from the team. The new team members focus on learning about each other, defining what they want to accomplish, and determining how they are going to accomplish it. Sometimes personality conflicts or disagreements arise about what needs to be done or how the team should go about doing it. At this point, the team has entered the *storming* stage, marked by conflict among team members. If the team is to be successful, team members need to resolve or manage personal conflicts and work through substantive and procedural conflicts in order to reach sufficient agreement on desired performance outcomes and processes. In working through substantive and procedural conflicts, the team will come to some understanding concerning desired outcomes, rules, procedures, and norms for team behavior. This is the *norming* stage, in which team members cooperate with each other and become more cohesive. Once the team has established norms and is working as a cohesive whole, it enters the *performing* stage. In this stage, team members are more committed to the team, focus on task performance, and are generally more satisfied with the team experience.[102]

Most teams experience some sort of end. Individual members may leave, or the team may be formally disbanded when its mission has been accomplished. Thus, teams ultimately go through a fifth stage, *adjourning,* when individuals begin to leave the team and terminate their regular contact with other team members. Adjourning can result from voluntary actions on the part of team members, as when a team member takes a job with another organization or retires. It can also result from actions over which team members have little control, such as reassignment by the parent organization or the end of a project. When individual members of a cohesive team leave, the remaining members often experience feelings of loss, and the team becomes less cohesive and less structured, until it no longer exists, unless new members replace the members who have left. In this instance, the team is similar to a new team, and the process of team development is likely to begin again.

Teams may not go through all of the stages described above in all situations. For example, the members of a newly formed team belong to the same organization and may already know each other. They are also likely to be familiar with performance expectations and may even share similar work-related values. Thus, the forming and storming stages are not needed. Furthermore, the nature of the team's work can influence the formation of the team. Most research on Tuckman's stage theory has focused on simple teams that worked on a single project and whose members were relative strangers.[103] Thus, the theory may not apply to teams that work on complex projects or that have members who have had a long history together.

The **punctuated equilibrium model (PEM)** of team development provides an alternative view of development over time.[104] This model suggests that teams do not go through linear stages but that team formation depends on the deadlines for the task at hand. The PEM is essentially a two-stage model representing two periods of equilibrium "punctuated" by a shift in focus. In the first stage, team members get to know one another and engage in norming activities. The focus at this stage is the development of socioemotional roles. When the deadline for the team's work approaches, the team undergoes a dramatic change in functioning. This is the point at which the "punctuation" occurs. After this point is reached, the team refocuses its activities on performing the task. Thus, the focus shifts to task roles. This model contrasts with Tuckman's stage model because it suggests that team life-cycle stages are determined by temporal aspects of the task, not by social dynamics within the team. Exhibit 11-4 compares the two models. Overall, research suggests that the PEM model best describes the development of teams working on a very specific, clearly time-bounded task.[105]

punctuated equilibrium model (PEM)
A model of team development that suggests that teams do not go through linear stages but that team formation depends on the task at hand and the deadlines for that task.

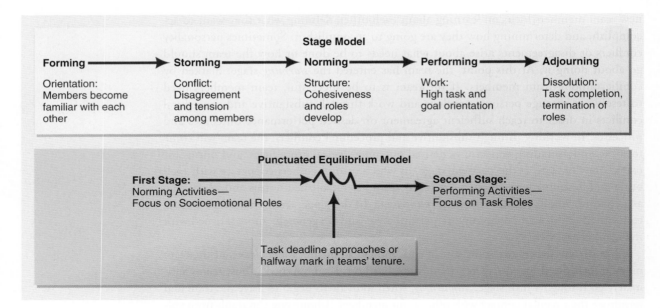

Exhibit 11-4 Models of Team Development

Sources: B.W. Tuckman. 1965. "Developmental Sequences in Small Groups," *Psychological Bulletin,* 6: 384–399; B.W. Tuckman, & M.A.C. Jensen. 1977. "Stages of Small Group Development," *Group and Organizational Studies,* 2: 419–427; C.J.G. Gersick. 1988. "Time and Transition in Work Teams: Toward a New Model of Group Development," *Academy of Management Journal,* 31: 9–41; C.J.G. Gersick. 1989. "Marking Time: Predictable Transitions in Task Groups," *Academy of Management Journal,* 32: 274–309; D.R. Forsyth. 1999. *Group Dynamics* (Belmont, CA: Wadsworth Publishing Company).

Managing for Effective Teams

To experience the potential gains of teamwork, organizations must provide support for teams to work effectively. An organization cannot simply declare that it will increase the level of teamwork without planning, training, selecting, and rewarding people for teamwork. Following are several "best practices" for managing effective teams.

Top Management Support

Effective teamwork requires support from the top of the organization.[106] All organizations that are known for their teamwork, such as Xerox, Harley-Davidson, FedEx, and Boeing, have senior management teams that actively promote teamwork. Several management practices can help senior management to support team effectiveness:[107]

- Have an explicit vision and strategic plan that serves as the basis for determining desirable team outcomes.
- Use results-oriented measurement of team outcomes and expect all leaders in the organization to do the same.
- Actively include associates and managers at all levels in the decision-making process related to the use of teams.
- Make an explicit decision about using teams and tie the decision to business objectives.
- Actively manage and review support systems for teams.

Senior management at Starbucks, described in the chapter-opening case, clearly follows these recommended practices. For example, two of the company's stated missions are to make profits and to be environmentally sensitive. These missions are incorporated into the baristas' performance assessments. The company also provides mechanisms that enable baristas to regularly communicate and share their ideas with senior management.

Support Systems

Support systems are aspects of organizational life that allow a team to function well. Support systems include technology, information systems, selection of team members, training, rewards, and leadership.

Technology

It is important that teams have access to the technology they need to do their work. This includes the technology necessary to carry out tasks (such as tools and computer software) and also technology to help team members coordinate their work. Many technologies are designed to help teams communicate and interact more fully and efficiently. Examples can be found at McKinsey & Company. Each team member has access to personal computing technology as well as mobile communication devices. Each member has access to the Internet for web-conferencing and other tasks. Also important for success, team members should have input into the adoption or development of communication technologies.[108]

Information Systems

Teams must have the necessary information to act, but they frequently need more information than they possess. An example is provided by the now-defunct People Express Airlines, which used customer service teams to conduct much of the airline's business.[109] The customer service teams needed important information, such as future bookings, to do their work; however, executives were reluctant to allow them access to this information because they were afraid that it might leak out to their competitors.

Teams can also suffer from receiving too much information.[110] Often, information technology can provide people with a flood of information; but as discussed in Chapter 9, too much information creates overload. In such situations, associates may not know to what information they should attend. They may become overwhelmed and attend to only a portion of the information, or perhaps attend to none of it, or they may even shut the system down entirely. A related problem is information unavailable in the form most useful to the team. To address this problem, it is important that teams have "user-friendly" information systems.

Selection of Team Members

Traditionally, it is recommended that organizations select team members with the knowledge, skills, and abilities to perform their individual jobs and with values that fit well with the organizational culture.[111] However, team members also have other roles to fulfill. For example, they may perform teamwork roles, such as energizing the team or soliciting and elaborating on the ideas of others. Furthermore, because teamwork often involves a variety of activities, a broader set of skills may be necessary for team-based jobs. Thus, teamwork selection needs to consider more factors than selection for a traditional job. Following are some suggestions for selecting team members:[112]

- Tailor the staffing process to the type of team. For example, paper-and-pencil personality tests may be appropriate for service teams but not for senior management teams.
- Conduct a teamwork analysis to identify the knowledge, skills, and abilities needed to perform both individual task work and teamwork.
- Consider political issues. It may be important to have members representing different constituencies on a team. For example, a university's internal review board that evaluates whether faculty research is ethical in its treatment of human subjects includes a community member who does not have ties to the university community and does not do research.
- Carefully consider who is to do the assessment of potential team members' knowledge, skills, and abilities and who will decide whom to select. It is often useful to have members of the team itself involved in the selection process.

Rewards

If people are to work together effectively as a team, they must be rewarded as a team. Team members have little motivation to engage with and support each other if they are rewarded only for their individual performance. Thus, it is important that the reward system for teams have multiple components, some of which reflect team performance. One such reward system is a profit-sharing plan in which associates receive bonuses based on the profits generated by their team. Furthermore, if the teamwork requires cross-functional work and knowledge, team members may receive skill-based or knowledge-based pay. Such pay is determined by what skills and knowledge associates acquire rather than by how they perform on specific tasks. Finally, team-based pay should be provided for only those aspects of performance under the team's control.[113]

Leadership

A team's leadership is crucial to the effectiveness of the team.[114] Team leaders can naturally emerge, or they can be assigned based on special skills or authority. Successful team leaders must fulfill three roles.[115]

The first role, team liaison, requires the leader to network with information sources both inside and outside the team, creating a bridge between the two. Outside sources include suppliers, clients, customers, other teams, and higher levels of management. In the liaison role, a team leader also acts as a representative of the team and watches out for the team's interests. In essence, the team leader connects the team to the outside world.

Another leader role involves direction setting. The leader must ensure the development of a direction for team action. This means that the leader must develop or help to develop short-term action strategies based on the long-term organizational strategies developed by the senior management team. Overall, the leader must help to translate those long-term strategies into directions, goals, and action plans for team members.

Finally, the team leader must serve as the team's operational coordinator. This role represents the management of the team's work and processes. The major responsibilities of this role are to recognize each member's contributions and decide how to best integrate the various team members' contributions; to monitor team performance and functioning

The Pros and Cons of Experiential Teambuilding

©Michael Pole/Corbis

Experiential teambuilding is used by many organizations around the world. The general idea is to move a team outside of its day-to-day routines and place it in a situation where fun and challenging activities are offered. The goal is to create stronger camaraderie and commitment among team members. Strengthening skills in the areas of problem solving and goal setting are also a part of the plan in many cases. Example activities include:

- Murder mysteries—Participants attempt to solve a murder staged by actors.
- Improv sessions—Participants engage in comedic improvisation exercises.
- Ropes courses—Participants help one another to navigate a series of challenges involving ropes that range from ground level to 10 to 12 feet above the ground.
- Scavenger hunts—Participants compete in subteams to decipher clues that lead to valuable items.
- Family feuds—Participants engage in a version of the storied game show.
- Boats—Participants form subteams to build and race boats made from barrels, boards, and ropes.

These types of activities are very popular in the business world. Despite their popularity, critics have questioned their effectiveness. Judith Mair, a German entrepreneur in the communication and advertising field,

famously complained that corporate fun and games blurred the distinction between business and personal lives, eroded the German work ethic, and imperiled the German economy. Other critics have not been quite this harsh, but have questioned the ability of experiential teambuilding to create real behavioral change in the workplace. The key concern is that teambuilding activities often are not tied to specific workplace problems.

Merrick Rosenberg, Chief Learning Officer at Team Builders Plus, understands the issues but believes they are not insurmountable. In his view, the first step is to score teams in terms of the degree to which they have deep problems with conflict, lack of trust, and lack of cooperation. For teams with few problems, simple participation in a teambuilding activity can provide a valued break from routine and a boost to morale. For teams with many problems, the basic experience is not enough. Instead, preactivity personality tests and surveys to determine specific problems must be emphasized so that teambuilding can be tailored to specific needs. Based on these assessments, particular activities can be chosen, particular individuals can be selected for certain subteams or leadership roles, and particular points can be made when instructors debrief the activities. Also, follow-up contacts, either virtually or through face-to-face meetings, become quite important for reinforcing lessons from the teambuilding experience.

Studies suggest that well-executed experiential teambuilding does in fact provide reasonable benefits. A recent participant put it this way:

We had a wonderful time! Facing a set of challenges that were very different than what we do 50–60 hours a week, we all learned different and surprising things about each other. ... I think we will be a closer, better team for it.

David Goldstein, founder of a very successful company called Teambonding, certainly agrees with this assessment. He points out that well-designed team-based play delivers results because it: (1) is involving, (2) is low risk, (3) explores team dynamics, (4) promotes self-awareness, (5) builds trust, (6) shows the value of the team, (7) promotes pleasure, and (8) provides specific problem-solving and communication lessons. Based on scientific analysis and real-world applications, the power of experiential teambuilding for creating better attitudes and performance seems to be reasonably strong.

Sources: D. Goldstein. 2009. "The Power of Play," at http://www.teambonding.com/blog; H.L. Gillis, & E. Speelman. 2008. "Are Challenge (Ropes) Courses an Effective Tool? A Meta-Analysis," *The Journal of Experiential Education*, 31: pp. 111–135; J. Harkin. 2003. "Executives Go Out To Play," *New Statesmen*, Feb. 10, p. 18; C. Klein, D. DiazGranados, E. Salas, H. Le, C.S. Burke, R. Lyons, & G.F. Goodwin. 2009. "Does Team Building Work?" *Small Group Research*, 40: pp. 181–222; M. Rosenberg. 2007. "Beyond the Basics of Experiential Learning," *T&D* 61, no. 12: pp. 26–28; Teambonding, "Programs," 2010, at http://www.teambonding.com/programs.

and make necessary changes if feedback indicates problems; and to ensure that the team is operating in a psychological climate that will enable it to function effectively.

Training

The thousands of team training programs and methods that exist speak to the criticality of adequate team training. Recall from an earlier section that one of the assumptions often held by managers is that people know how and are suited to work on teams. This is questionable in many cases. Team-building training generally focuses on four different types of skills:[116] (1) interpersonal skills, especially communication, supportiveness, and trust; (2) problem-solving skills, which allow team members to identify problems, generate solutions, and evaluate solutions; (3) goal-setting skills, and (4) role-clarification skills, which allow members to articulate role requirements and responsibilities.

A great deal of research has been done on the effectiveness of team training in improving team performance. This research shows that training has positive but somewhat weak effects on performance outcomes while having stronger positive effects on team members' evaluations of their team.[117] We should note that most of this research has been conducted on intact teams whose members had considerable experience working together. As a result, these teams had existing structures, roles, and norms, which probably made them more difficult to change. Training is likely to have a greater impact on the performance of newly formed teams.

In the *Managerial Advice* feature, a specific and important type of team training is profiled.

THE STRATEGIC LENS

In recent times much of the organization's work has been accomplished by teams. Some teams correspond to formal units of the firm (e.g., a department), some teams exist within formal units, and some teams cut across formal units. The work begins with the senior management team, which develops the organization's vision and the strategies intended to help realize the vision. These strategies are implemented by teams throughout the organization. For example, when the organization's goal is innovation, cross-functional teams are often assigned to develop new products. Members of these teams commonly represent research and development, marketing, and manufacturing units. Sometimes additional team members are drawn from customers and also external suppliers, who will provide materials for the new products.

Because of the pervasive use and importance of teams, an organization's performance ultimately depends on its teams' effectiveness. The effectiveness of the baristas in Starbucks stores, for example, has been largely responsible for the success of the overall organization. The design of teams, the selection of team members, and team leadership and management are all critical for organizational success. As a result, strategic leaders should invest significant effort in developing and managing teams.

Critical Thinking Questions

1. Think of some teams of which you have been a member. How successful were they? To what do you attribute your teams' success or lack thereof?

2. Why do organizations use teams to accomplish the work that needs to be done? What value do teams provide?

3. Someday you will be a leader of a team. What processes will you use to select team members? What specific actions will you take to manage the team to ensure high team productivity?

What This Chapter Adds to Your Knowledge Portfolio

This chapter discussed the importance of teams and teamwork in organizations. We began by discussing the nature of groups and teams and their different forms. Then, we addressed the criteria that should be used to determine whether a team is effective and the factors that influence team effectiveness. Next, we examined how teams develop over time. Finally, we described ways in which organizations and leaders can promote team effectiveness. To summarize, we focused on the following points:

- A group can be defined in very general terms as "two or more interdependent individuals who influence one another through social interaction." A team is a group that consists of two or more people who work interdependently within an organization, with tasks that are relevant and consequential for the organization's mission, and who are identified as a team by people within and outside the team.

- Groups and teams can be classified in a number of ways. Both formal and informal groups arise in organizations. People in organizations often belong to identity groups based on their social identities, such as gender identity, racial identity, or religious identity. Types of teams include virtual teams, functional teams, and self-managing teams. The type and purpose of the team can affect how the team develops and functions.

- Team effectiveness is measured in terms of the team's learning and cognition, team members' feelings about the team, and team outputs and viability.

- The composition of the team influences the team's effectiveness. The diversity of members, their personality, and the size of the team all influence team effectiveness.

- The structure of a team, including the roles held by members, the norms, and the task structure, can all influence a team's effectiveness.

- The processes used and experienced by the team also influence team performance. Team processes include team cohesion, conflict among team members, social facilitation, social loafing, and communication.

- Teams change and develop over time. The stage model of development proposes that teams experience four developmental stages: forming, storming, norming, and performing. A fifth stage, in which the team disbands, is adjourning. The punctuated equilibrium model of team development holds that teams undergo a shift from interpersonally focused to task-focused when the deadline for the team project moves closer.

back to the knowledge objectives

1. What makes a collection of people a team? How does a team differ from a group? What are some different types of teams?
2. To determine whether a team is effective, what should be measured?
3. What composition factors should a manager consider in designing an effective team? Would these factors differ depending on the type of team being formed?
4. What are the important aspects of team structure? How does each affect team performance?
5. What types of team processes can have a positive influence on team performance? What processes can have negative effects?
6. How do the stage model and the punctuated equilibrium model of team development differ?
7. What can organizations do to encourage and support effective teamwork?
8. What are some important team leader roles? Describe an example from your own experience of a team leader who filled one or more of these roles.

- Organizations can promote effective teamwork through senior management support, technical and informational support, selecting appropriate people for teamwork, training people in teamwork skills, and rewarding team performance.
- Effective team leaders are also important for teamwork. They act as liaisons, ensure proper direction, and operationally coordinate team activities.

Key Terms

synergy, p. 377
group, p. 378
team, p. 378
formal groups, p. 378
informal groups, p. 378
identity groups, p. 379
virtual teams, p. 379
process loss, p. 384
team orientation, p. 386

roles, p. 387
task roles, p. 387
socioemotional roles, p. 387
destructive individual roles, p. 387
norms, p. 387
divisible tasks, p. 389
unitary tasks, p. 389

maximization tasks, p. 389
optimization tasks, p. 389
interpersonal cohesion, p. 390
task cohesion, p. 390
social facilitation effect, p. 392
social loafing, p. 393
punctuated equilibrium model (PEM), p. 395

---

building your human capital

Do You Have a Team?

The benefits of teamwork are clearly outlined in this chapter. Not only can teams increase organization-related performance and contribute to the competitive advantage of the organization, they can also increase individual well-being. This has led the business world to adopt teamwork whenever possible. However, sometimes what we call a team does not really function as a team. Think of a team that you belong to, whether it is a sports team, a class project team, or a work team. Answer the following questions below to determine whether your team is really operating as a team:

1. To what extent is your team working interdependently?
   - Do team members work well together?
   - Are there problems in coordinating the team's activities?
   - Do people work together, or do they mostly do their work independently of one another?
   - What happens when a team member does not perform up to standards?
2. Is your team structured as a team?
   - Is the team organized?
   - Is it clear who is supposed to be doing what?
   - Are there conflicts over who is in charge?
3. Is your team interpersonally cohesive?
   - Is your team close or tight-knit?
   - Do team members like each other?
   - Do team members frequently quit the team?
4. Does your team have an identity?
   - Does your team have a name (either formal or informal)?
   - Are team members proud to tell others that they are a part of this team?
   - Do the team members have a sense of shared identity with each other?
   - Do team members put the team goals above their own personal goals?
   - Do team members work hard to reach the team's goals?
   - Does the team have a specific mission that everyone is clear about?

Source: Information adapted from and based on D.R. Forsyth. 1999. *Group Dynamics* (Belmont, CA: Wadsworth).

an organizational behavior moment
The New Quota

"One club." Jack closed his hand and, almost imperceptibly, leaned forward a little. To most people, such a movement would have gone unnoticed. But all three of the others knew that Jack's opening bid was a little weak.

"Pass."

"Three no trump." Bill was gleeful. He had 16 points, and this would be the first hand he had played this lunch hour. He watched as Jack spread his hand and noted that the play would be uneventful.

"Bid three, making four," Dennis said as he penciled down the score. "Got time for another?"

"Not really. Gotta get back to the grind," Steve grimaced as he spoke. "Listen, what do you guys think about the new quota?"

"It's ridiculous!" Bill was anxious to find out how his co-workers felt, and he also wanted to express his own opinion. "When I came here five years ago, we were supposed to wire three assemblies an hour. Now we're supposed to do eight. They aren't paying me that much more. I think it stinks."

"I do, too." Dennis was usually pretty low key. But as he spoke, his eye began to twitch, revealing his anxiety. "I'm not sure that I could meet it even if I tried, and I'm sure as hell not going to try. They can have my stinking job if they want. Only reason I stick around here, anyway, is because you guys are such lousy bridge players."

They all laughed. Then Jack, seeing that Steve was waiting, said, "Eight's possible, but I think some of us are going to be laid off if we all do it. I was talking to this guy over in engineering the other day, and he explained how to make a jig that lets you just lay those wires in real easy. I tried it and it really works. It saved me about six minutes on the first assembly. Of course, I went back and told him it didn't work. I just don't want to do eight—won't help any of us if we do."

Steve looked curiously at Jack. "So that's what you were up to! I saw you really pushing a couple of days ago and

thought you'd lost your screws. Anyway, I'm glad you guys feel the same as me. It makes me feel a lot better. Don't figure the boss will do much to us if he thinks an old pro like Jack can't do eight."

It was several days later when Dave, the shop supervisor, was called to the manager's office. Dave knew that it was going to be about the quota, and he didn't know exactly what he was going to say. Mr. Martin was on the phone but motioned for him to sit down.

When he hung up, he faced Dave and said, "That was Pacific Electronics. They want to know if we can meet the shipping schedule or not. What do I tell them when I call back?"

"I don't know, honestly. The guys have picked their speed up some, but I don't think we're going to do better than six-and-a-half, maybe seven."

"That won't cut it, Dave. This new business is important. If we can't handle it, we'll have to cut back some workers. We have too many budget problems without it. Are you sure they're really trying?"

"Yes!" Dave responded. "Jack even tried a new jig that engineering thought up, but it didn't seem to help. Maybe if we added some more incentive bonus it would help. I don't know."

"We can't do that. Costs are already too high. We're being hurt on scrap rate, too. You just go back there and really push them. I'm going to tell Pacific that we can meet the schedule. Now you get that crew of yours to do it!"

Discussion Questions

1. What factors seem to be influencing team performance here?
2. Identify the team norms and goals. Are they compatible with organizational objectives?
3. How does the team function to meet individual needs? If you were Dave, what team concepts would you apply? Why?

team exercise
Virtual versus Real Teams

As discussed in this chapter, the use of virtual teams is common in the business world. Although virtual teams can save an organization time and money, they can also have their disadvantages. The purpose of this exercise is to explore the different dynamics that occur between face-to-face teams and virtual teams.

Procedure

DAY 1

1. The instructor will randomly divide the class into teams of five to seven people. The instructor will designate half of the teams as face-to-face teams and the other half as virtual teams.
2. Each team is responsible for developing a new school logo and branding slogan. They will have approximately one week to do this.

INTERIM PERIOD (APPROXIMATELY ONE WEEK)

1. Each team is responsible for completing its task outside class. Face-to-face teams can meet any time they desire and can also use electronic means of communication. Virtual teams may not meet face-to-face but can use any form of electronic communication to complete their task. Virtual teams also should not discuss the task in class. In addition, it is not necessary for all team meetings to include everyone on the team but several members should be present and all members should participate in some of the meetings.
2. The task is to develop a new school logo and branding slogan. Each team must also develop a three- to five-minute presentation of its product to present in class on Day 2 of the exercise.
3. Before class, each team should prepare answers to the following questions:
   a. How many meetings between team members took place? To what extent were these meetings productive?
   b. What were the most frustrating aspects of working on this project?
   c. To what extent did everyone contribute to the project?
   d. What type of communication problems arose in your team?
   e. To what extent was your team congenial? Were there misunderstandings? How well do team members now understand each other?
   f. How difficult was it to coordinate your work?

DAY 2 (APPROXIMATELY ONE WEEK AFTER DAY 1)

1. Each team presents its logo and slogan to the class.
2. The class votes on which team has the best logo and slogan.
3. The instructor leads the class in a discussion of their answers to the above questions and the different dynamics between face-to-face and virtual teams.

Endnotes

1. Lawler, E.E., III, Mohrman, S.A., & Ledford, G.E. 1995. *Creating high performance organizations: Practices and results in Fortune 1000 companies*. San Francisco: Jossey-Bass.
2. Fisher, A. 2007. The trouble with MBAs. *Fortune*, April 23, at http://cnnmoney.printhis.clikckability.com/pt/cpt?action=cpt&title+The trouble+with+MBAs.
3. Kirkman, B.L., Rosen, B., Tesluk, P.E., & Gibson, C.B. 2004. The impact of team empowerment on virtual team performance: The moderating role of face-to-face interaction. *Academy of Management Journal*, 47: 175–192.
4. Hackman, J.R., & Oldham, G.R. 1980. *Work redesign*. Reading, MA: Addison-Wesley.
5. Cohen, S.G., Ledford, G.E., & Spreitzer, G.M. 1996. A predictive model of self-managed work team effectiveness. *Human Relations*, 49: 643–679.
6. Sundstrom, E. 1999. The challenges of supporting work team effectiveness. In E. Sundstrom, & Associates (Eds.), *Supporting work team effectiveness: Best management practices for fostering high performance*. San Francisco: Jossey-Bass, pp. 3–23.
7. Ibid.
8. Labich, K. 1996. Elite teams get the job done. *Fortune*, February 19: 90–99.
9. Finkelstein, S., & Hambrick, D.C. 1996. *Strategic leadership: Top executives and their effects on organizations*. St. Paul, MN: West Publishing Company.
10. Ireland, R.D. Hoskisson, R.E., & Hitt, M.A. 2005. *Understanding business strategy*. Mason, OH: South-Western Thomson Publishing.
11. Koslowski, S.W.J., & Bell, B.S. 2004. Work groups and teams in organizations. In W.C. Borman, D.R. Ilgen, & R.J. Klimoski, (Eds.), *Handbook of psychology, Vol. 12: Industrial and organizational psychology*. Hoboken, NJ: Wiley, pp. 333–374; West, M.A. 1996. Preface: Introducing work group psychology. In M.A. West (Ed.), *Handbook of work group psychology*. Chichester, United Kingdom: John Wiley & Sons, pp. xxvi–xxxiii; Guzzo,

R.A. 1995. Introduction: At the intersection of team effectiveness and decision making. In R.A. Guzzo, E. Salas, & Associates (Eds.), *Team effectiveness and decision making in organizations*. San Francisco: Jossey-Bass, pp. 1–8.

12. Forsyth, D.R. 1999. *Group dynamics*. Belmont, CA: Wadsworth, p. 5.

13. Guzzo, Introduction.

14. Ibid.

15. Mitchell, T. 1978. *People in organizations: Understanding their behavior*. New York: McGraw-Hill, p. 176.

16. Alderfer, C.P. 1987. An intergroup perspective on group dynamics. In J. Lorsch (Ed.), *Handbook of organizational behavior*. Upper Saddle River, NJ: Prentice Hall, pp. 190–210.

17. Chao, G.T. 2000. Levels issues in cultural psychology research. In K.J. Klein & S.W.J. Koslowski (Eds.), *Multilevel theory, research, and methods in organizations*. San Francisco: Jossey-Bass, pp. 308–346.

18. See, for example, Furumo, K. 2009. The impact of conflict and conflict management style on deadbeats and deserters in virtual teams. *Journal of Computer Information Systems*, 49 (4): 66–73; Mittleman, D., & Briggs, R.O. 1999. Communicating technologies for traditional and virtual teams. In E. Sundstrom & Associates (Eds.), *Supporting work team effectiveness*. San Francisco: Jossey-Bass, pp. 246–270.

19. Furst, S.A., Reeves, M., Rosen, B., & Blackburn, R.S. 2004. Managing the life cycle of virtual teams. *Academy of Management Executive*, 18: 6–20.

20. Kirkman, Rosen, Tesluk, & Gibson, The impact of team empowerment on virtual team performance. Also, see Hill, N.S., Bartol, K.M., Tesluk, P.E., & Langa, G.A. 2009. Organizational context and face-to-face interaction: Influences on the development of trust and collaborative behaviors in computer-mediated groups. *Organizational Behavior and Human Decision Processes*, 108: 187–201.

21. Kirkman, Rosen, Tesluk, & Gibson, The impact of team empowerment on virtual team performance.

22. Joshi, A., Lazarova, M.B., & Liao, H. 2009. Getting everyone on board: The role of inspirational leadership in geographically dispersed teams. *Organization Science*, 20: 240–252; Ruggieri, S. 2009. Leadership in virtual teams: A comparison of transformational and transactional leaders. *Social Behavior and Personality*, 37: 1017–1021.

23. Purvanova, R.K., & Bono, J.E. 2009. Transformational leadership in context: Face-to-face and virtual teams. *The Leadership Quarterly*, 20: 343–357.

24. Mittleman, & Briggs, Communicating technologies for traditional and virtual teams.

25. Sundstrom, E., McIntyre, M., Halfhill, T., & Richards, H. 2000. Work groups: From the Hawthorne studies to work teams of the 1990s and beyond. *Group Dynamics: Theory, Research, and Practice*, 4: 44–67.

26. Hackman, J.R. 1986. The psychology of self-management in organizations. In M.S. Pollack, & R.O. Perlogg (Eds.), *Psychology and work: Productivity change and employment*. Washington, DC: American Psychological Association, pp. 85–136; Manz, C.C. 1992. Self-leading work teams: Moving beyond self-management myths. *Human Relations*, 45: 1119–1140.

27. Cohen, S.G., & Ledford, G.E., Jr., 1994. The effectiveness of self-managing teams: A quasi-experiment. *Human Relations*, 47: 13–43; Manz, C.C., & Sims, H.P., Jr. 1987. Leading workers to lead themselves: The external leadership of self-managing work teams. *Administrative Science Quarterly*, 32: 106–128.

28. Druskat, V.U., & Wheeler, J.V. 2003. Managing from the boundary: The effectiveness leadership of self-managing work teams. *Academy of Management Journal*, 46: 435-457; Stewart, G.L., & Manz, C.C. 1995. Leadership for self-managing work teams: A typology and integrative model. *Human Relations*, 48: 347–370.

29. Orpheus Chamber Orchestra. 2010. History. http://www.orpheusnyc.com/history.html; Pfeffer, J. 2007. *What were they thinking?: Unconventional wisdom about management*. Boston: Harvard Business School Press; Seifert, H. 2001. The conductor-less orchestra. *Leader to leader*, No. 21, http://www.pfdf.org/leaderbooks/121/summer2002/seifter.html.

30. Hackman, J.R. 2002. *Leading teams: Setting the stage for great performances*. Boston; Harvard Business School Press.

31. Canon-Bowers, J.A., Salas, E., & Converse, S.A. 1993. Shared mental models in expert team decision making. In N.J. Castellan (Ed.), *Individual and group decision making*. Hillsdale, NJ: Erlbaum, pp. 221–246.

32. Klimoski, R.J., & Mohammed, S. 1994. Team mental model: Construct or metaphor? *Journal of Management*, 20: 403–437.

33. Edwards, B.D., Day, E.A., Arthur, W., Jr., & Bell S.T. 2006. Relationships among team ability composition, team mental models, and team performance. *Journal of Applied Psychology*, 91: 727–736.

34. Koslowski & Bell, Work groups and teams in organizations.

35. Hackman, *Leading teams*.

36. George, J.M. 1990. Personality, affect, and behavior in groups. *Journal of Applied Psychology*, 75: 107–116.

37. Barsade, S.G., Ward, A., Turner, J., & Sonnenfeld, J. 2000. To your heart's content: A model of affective diversity in top management teams. *Administrative Science Quarterly*, 45: 802–836.

38. Shea, G.P., & Guzzo, R.A. 1987. Groups as human resources. In K.M. Rowland, & G.R. Ferris (Eds.), *Research in personnel and human resource management (Vol. 5)*. Greenwich, CT: JAI Press, pp. 323–356.

39. Hackman, *Leading teams*.

40. Hackman, J.R. 1987. The design of work teams. In J. Lorsch (Ed.), *Handbook of organizational behavior*. New York: Prentice Hall, pp. 315–342.

41. Katz, R., & Allen, T.J. 1988. Investigating the not invented here (NIH) syndrome: A look at performance, tenure, and communication patterns of 50 R&D project groups. In M.L. Tushman, & W.L. Moore (Eds.), *Readings in the management of innovation*. New York: Ballinger, pp. 293–309.

42. Burke, C.S., Stagl, K.C., Salas, E., Pierce, L., & Kendall, D. 2006. Understanding team adaptation: A conceptual analysis and model. *Journal of Applied Psychology*, 91: 1189–1207.

43. Katzenbach, J., 1997. *Teams at the top*. Boston, MA: Harvard Business Press.

44. Steiner, I.D. 1972. *Group processes and productivity*. New York: Academic Press.

45. Hackman, *Leading teams*.

46. Kochan, T., et al. 2003. The effects of diversity on business performance: Report of the diversity research network. *Human Resource Management,* 42: 3–21.

47. Ely, R.J., & Thomas, D.A. 2001. Cultural diversity at work: The effects of diversity perspectives on work group processes and outcomes. *Administrative Science Quarterly,* 46: 229–274; Bantel, K.A., & Jackson, S.E. 1989. Top management and innovations in banking: Does the composition of the top team make a difference? *Strategic Management Journal,* 10: 107–124; Jackson, S.E., Brett, J.F., Sessa, V.I., Cooper, D.M., Julin, J.A., & Peyroonnin, K. 1991. Some differences make a difference: Individual dissimilarity and group heterogeneity as correlates of recruitment, promotions, and turnover. *Journal of Applied Psychology,* 76: 675–689; Pelled, L.H., Eisenhardt, K.M., & Xin, K.R. 1999. Exploring the black box: An analysis of work group diversity, conflict, and performance. *Administrative Science Quarterly,* 44: 1–28.

48. Campion, M.A., Medsker, G.J., & Higgs, A.C. 1993. Relations between work group characteristics and effectiveness: Implications for designing effective work groups. *Personnel Psychology,* 46: 823–850.

49. Barkema, H.G., & Shvyrkov, O. 2007. Does top management team diversity promote or hamper foreign expansion? *Strategic Management Journal,* 28: 663–680; Miller, C.C., Burke, L.M., & Glick, W.H. 1998. Cognitive diversity among upper-echelon executives: Implications for strategic decision processes. *Strategic Management Journal,* 19: 39–58; Perretti, F., & Giacomo, N. 2007. Mixing genres and matching people: A study in innovation and team composition in Hollywood. *Journal of Organizational Behavior,* 28: 563–586; Simons, T., Pelled, L.H., & Smith, K.A. 1999. Making use of difference: Diversity, debate, and decision comprehensiveness in top management teams. *Academy of Management Journal,* 42: 662–673; Ward, A.J., Lankau, M.J., Amason, A.C., Sonnenfeld, J.A., & Agle, B.R. 2007. Improving the performance of top management teams. *MIT Sloan Management Review,* Spring: 84–90.

50. Argote, L., & McGrath, J.E. 1993. Group processes in organizations: Continuity and change. In C.L. Cooper, & I.T. Robertson (Eds.), *International review of industrial and organizational psychology (Vol. 8).* New York: John Wiley & Sons, pp. 333–389.

51. Jackson, S.E., May, K.E., & Whitney, K. 1995. Understanding the dynamics of diversity in decision making teams. In R.A. Guzzo, E. Salas, & Associates (Eds.), *Team effectiveness and decision making in organizations.* San Francisco: Jossey-Bass, pp. 204–261.

52. Koslowski & Bell, Work groups and teams in organizations.

53. Watson, W.E., Kumar, K., & Michaelson, L.K. 1993. Cultural diversity's impact on interaction process and performance: Comparing homogeneous and diverse task groups. *Academy of Management Journal,* 36: 590–602.

54. Barkema, H.G., & Shvyrkov, O. 2007. Does top management team diversity promote or hamper foreign expansion?

55. Bezrukova, K., Jehn, K.A., Zanutto, E.L., & Thatcher, S.M.B. 2009. Do workgroup faultlines help or hurt? A moderated model of faultlines, team identification, and group performance; Lau, D.C., & Murnighan, J.K. 1998. Demographic diversity and faultlines: The compositional dynamics of organizational groups. *Academy of Management Review,* 23: 325–340.

56. Mount, M.K., Barrick, M.R., & Stewart, G.L. 1998. Five-Factor model of personality and performance in jobs involving interpersonal interactions. *Human Performance,* 11: 145–165.

57. Barrick, M.R., Stewart, G.L., Neubert, M.J., & Mount, M.K. 1998. Relating member ability and personality to work-team processes and team effectiveness. *Journal of Applied Psychology,* 83: 377–391; Bell, S.T. 2007. Deep-level composition variables as predictors of team performance: A meta-analysis. *Journal of Applied Psychology,* 92: 595.

58. Stewart, G.L. 2003. Toward an understanding of the multilevel role of personality in teams. In M.R. Barrick, & A.M. Ryan (Eds.), *Personality and work: Reconsidering the role of personality in organizations.* San Francisco: Jossey-Bass, pp. 183–204.

59. Neuman, G.A., & Wright, J. 1999. Team effectiveness: Beyond skills and cognitive ability. *Journal of Applied Psychology,* 84: 376–389.

60. Burke, Stagl, Salas, Pierce, & Kendall, Understanding team adaptation.

61. Ibid.

62. Nieva, V.F., Fleishman, E.A., & Reick, A. 1985. *Team dimensions: Their identity, their measurement, and their relationships. (Research Note #12).* Washington, DC: U.S. Army Research Institute for the Behavioral and Social Sciences.

63. Campion, M.A., Medsker, G.J., & Higgs, A.C. 1993. Relations between work group characteristics and effectiveness: Implications for designing effective work groups. *Personnel Psychology,* 46: 823–850.

64. Koslowski & Bell, Work groups and teams in organizations.

65. Porter, L., Lawler, E., III, and Hackman, J. 1975. *Behavior in organizations.* New York: McGraw-Hill, p. 373.

66. Forsyth, D.R. 1999. *Group dynamics.* Belmont, CA: Wadsworth, p. 5.

67. Benne, K.D., & Sheets, P. 1948. Functional roles of group members. *Journal of Social Issues,* 4: 41–49.

68. Hackman, *Leading teams.*

69. Labich, K. 1996. Elite teams get the job done. *Fortune,* February 19: 90–99.

70. Crandall, C.S. 1988. Social contagion of binge eating. *Journal of Personality and Social Psychology,* 55: 588–598.

71. Hackman, The design of work teams.

72. Steiner, *Group processes and productivity.*

73. Forsyth, D.R. 1999. *Group dynamics. Belmont,* CA: Wadsworth.

74. Ibid.

75. Evans, C.R., & Jarvis, P.A. 1980. Group cohesion: A review and re-evaluation. *Small Group Behavior,* 11: 359–370.

76. Ibid.

77. Barrick, Stewart, Neubert, & Mount, Relating member ability and personality to work-team processes and team effectiveness; Hambrick, D.C. 1995. Fragmentation and other problems CEOs have with their top management teams. *California Management Review,* 37: 110–127; Mullen, B., & Copper, C. 1994. The relationship between group cohesiveness and performance: An integration. *Psychological Bulletin,* 115: 210–227.

78. Hackman, J.R. 1992. Group influences on individuals in organizations. In M.D. Dunnette & L.M. Hough (Eds.), *Handbook of industrial and organizational psychology (Vol. 3).* Palo Alto, CA: Consulting Psychologists Press, pp. 199–267.

79. Mullen, & Copper, The relationship between group cohesiveness and performance.

80. Seashore, S.E. 1954. *Group cohesiveness in the industrial work group.* Ann Arbor: University of Michigan, Institute for Social Research.

81. Gully, S.M., Devine, D.J., & Whitney, D.J. 1995. A meta-analysis of cohesion and performance: Effects of levels of analysis and task interdependence. *Small Group Research,* 26: 497–520.

82. Morrill, C. 1995. *The executive way.* Chicago: University of Chicago Press.

83. Forsyth, *Group dynamics..*

84. Amason, A.C., & Schweiger, D.M. 1994. Resolving the paradox of conflict, strategic decision making and organizational performance. *International Journal of Conflict Management,* 5: 239–253; Jehn, K.A. 1995. A multimethod examination of the benefits and detriments of intragroup conflict. *Administrative Science Quarterly,* 40: 256–282; Jehn, K.A., Greer, L., Levine, S., & Szulanski, G. 2008. The effects of conflict types, dimensions, and emergent states on group dynamics. *Group Decision and Negotiation,* 17: 465–495; Tekleab, A.G., Quigley, N.R., Tesluk, P.E. 2009. A longitudinal study of team conflict, conflict management, cohesion, and team effectiveness. *Group & Organizational Management,* 34: 170–205.

85. Forsyth, *Group dynamics.*

86. Ibid.

87. Zajonc, R.B. 1980. Compresence. In P.B. Paulus (Ed.), *Psychology of group influence.* Hillsdale, NJ: Erlbaum, pp. 35–60.

88. Cottrell, N.B. 1972. Social facilitation. In C.G. McClintock (Ed.), *Experimental social psychology.* New York: Holt, Rinehart, & Winston, pp. 185–236.

89. Bond, M.H., & Titus, L.J. 1983. Social facilitation: A meta-analysis of 241 studies. *Psychological Bulletin,* 94: 265–292.

90. Latane, B., Williams, K., & Harkins, S. 1979. Many hands make light the work: The causes and consequences of social loafing. *Journal of Personality and Social Psychology,* 47: 822–832.

91. Alcian, A.A., & Demsetz, H. 1972. Production information costs, and economic organization. *American Economic Review,* 62: 777–795.

92. Price, K.H., Harrison, D.A., & Gavin, J.A. 2006. Withholding inputs in team contexts: Member composition, interaction processes, evaluation structure, and social loafing. *Journal of Applied Psychology,* 91: 1375–1384; Jackson, J.M., & Harkins, S.G. 1985. Equity in effort: An explanation of the social loafing effect. *Journal of Personality and Social Psychology,* 49: 1199–1206.

93. Karau, S.J., & Williams, K.D. 1993. Social loafing: A meta-analytic review and theoretical integration. *Journal of Personality and Social Psychology,* 65: 681–706.

94. Kerr, N., & Bruun, S. 1983. Dispensability of effort and group motivational losses: Free rider effects. *Journal of Personality and Social Psychology,* 44: 78–94.

95. Latane, Williams, & Harkins, Many hands make light the work.

96. Jackson, J.M., & Harkins, S.G. 1985. Equity in effort: An explanation of the social loafing effect. *Journal of Personality and Social Psychology,* 49: 1199–1206.

97. Price, Harrison,, & Gavin, Withholding inputs in team contexts.

98. Vermeulen, P. and Benders, J. 2003. A reverse side of the team medal. *Team Performance Management: An International Journal,* 9: 107–114.

99. Kirkman, Rosen, Tesluk, & Gibson, The impact of team empowerment on virtual team performance.

100. Reitz, J. 1977. *Behavior in organizations.* Homewood, IL: Richard D. Irwin, p. 301.

101. Tuckman, B.W. 1965. Developmental sequences in small groups. *Psychological Bulletin,* 63: 384–399; Tuckman, B.W., & Jensen, M.A.C. 1977. Stages of small group development. *Group and Organizational Studies,* 2: 419–427.

102. Koslowski, & Bell, Work groups and teams in organizations.

103. Ibid.

104. Gersick, C.J.G. 1988. Time and transition in work teams: Toward a new model of group development. *Academy of Management Journal,* 31: 9–41; Gersick, C.J.G. 1989. Marking time: Predictable transitions in task groups. *Academy of Management Journal,* 32: 274–309.

105. Chang, A., Bordia P., & Duck, J. 2003. Punctuated equilibrium and linear progression: Toward a new understanding of group development. *Academy of Management Journal,* 46: 106–117.

106. Hitt, M.A., Nixon, R.D., Hoskisson, R.E., & Kochhar, R. 1999. Corporate entrepreneurship and cross-functional fertilization: Activation, process and disintegration of a new product design team. *Entrepreneurship, Theory & Practice,* 23: 145–167.

107. Sundstrom, E. 1999. Supporting work team effectiveness: Best practices. In E. Sundstrom, & Associates (Eds.), *Supporting work team effectiveness: Best management practices for fostering high performance.* San Francisco: Jossey-Bass, pp. 301–342.

108. Sundstrom, Supporting work team effectiveness.

109. Hackman, Group influences on individuals in organizations.

110. Ibid.

111. Heneman, H.G. III, & Judge, T.A. 2003. *Staffing organizations.* Middleton, WI: Mendota House.

112. Klimoski, R.J., & Zukin, L.B. 1999. Selection and staffing for team effectiveness. In E. Sundstrom, & Associates (Eds.), *Supporting work team effectiveness: Best management practices for fostering high performance.* San Francisco: Jossey-Bass, pp. 63–91.

113. Sundstrom, Supporting work team effectiveness.

114. McIntyre, R.M., & Salas, E. 1995. Measuring and managing for team performance: Emerging principles from complex environments. In R.A. Guzzo, E. Salas, & Associates (Eds.), *Team effectiveness and decision making in organizations.* San Francisco: Jossey-Bass, pp. 9–45.

115. Chen, G., Kirkman, B.L., Kanfer, R., Allen, D., & Rosen, B. 2007. A multilevel study of leadership, empowerment, and performance in teams. *Journal of Applied Psychology,* 92: 331–346; Zaccaro, S.J., & Marks, M.A. 1999. The roles of leaders in high-performance teams. In E. Sundstrom, & Associates (Eds.), *Supporting work team effectiveness: Best management practices for fostering high performance.* San Francisco: Jossey-Bass, pp. 95–125.

116. Salas, E., Rozell, D., Driskell, J.D., & Mullen, B. 1999. The effect of team building on performance: An integration. *Small Group Research,* 30: 309–329.

117. Ibid; Klein, C., DiazGranados, D., Salas, E., Le, H., Burke, C.S., Lyons, R., & Goodwin, G.F. 2009. Does Team Building Work? *Small Group Research,* 40. 181–222

conflict, negotiation, power, and politics

Green Conflict

In November 2007, Thomas Falk, the CEO of Kimberly-Clark Corporation, arrived at the University of Wisconsin where he would deliver an address on corporate governance as part of the annual Director's Summit (a meeting designed for the continuing education of board members from various companies). As he began to work through his PowerPoint presentation, the audience noticed some peculiar slides, slides that pointedly protested Kimberly-Clark's use of old-growth forests for its tissue paper products (Kleenex, Cottonelle, Scott, and other brands). After terminating the presentation and adjourning early for lunch, the directors and others in attendance found interesting menus at their tables. Those menus included entries such as "Songbird Stir-fry" and "Caribou Clearcut Cake." The appetizer was "Social Conflict Scramble." Clearly, Greenpeace activists had been active that day!

After speaking at the Consumer Electronics show in Las Vegas in 2003, Michael Dell was confronted by a group of angry environmental activists from the Silicon Valley Toxics Coalition. They were dressed as prisoners and shackled to PCs. The protest was against Dell's then-practice of using prison labor and unsafe practices to recycle old computers while competitors such as Hewlett-Packard were using much safer and more effective means. In 2005, Greenpeace activists dumped hundreds of used PCs outside of Wipro headquarters in Bangalore, India, to protest the computer assembler's lack of a "take-back" recycling practice. Greenpeace mounted a different type of campaign to motivate Apple to become more environmentally

knowledge objectives

After reading this chapter, you should be able to:

1. Explain how conflict can be either functional or dysfunctional and distinguish among various types of conflict.
2. Discuss common causes of conflict.
3. Describe conflict escalation and the various outcomes of conflict.
4. Explain how people respond to conflict and under what circumstances each type of response is best.
5. Understand how organizations can manage conflict.
6. Describe the basic negotiation process as well as effective strategies and tactics for negotiating.
7. Explain why organizations must have power to function, and discuss how people gain power in organizations.
8. Define organizational politics and the tactics used to carry out political behavior.

responsive by creating the "Green My Apple" website in 2006. In 2007, the Center for Health, Environment, and Justice staged a huge protest against Target stores for using PVC vinyl. The protest included newspaper ads against Target, a petition to the CEO, letters to store managers, and picketing at individual stores. In 2009, the World Wildlife Federation presented a petition with 50,000 signatures to ExxonMobil protesting activities that endanger the Western gray whale.

These are just six out of thousands of examples where conflict between environmental groups and business corporations has surfaced. Traditionally, the goals of the environmental groups have included reducing carbon emissions, protecting wildlife and natural habitats, avoiding the use of poisonous substances, recycling, and the development and use of sustainable products and energy sources. Corporate goals have usually centered on providing value to shareholders—meaning companies typically benefit from using the least expensive products, processes, energy sources, and labor practices to produce their goods and services. Typically, environmentally sound business practices have not been the most cost (or profit) effective. Thus, it is no surprise that there is a long history of conflict between environmental groups and business firms.

However, things are beginning to change, with environmentalist organizations working together with business corporations to obtain mutual benefit. In fact, in order for many organizations to survive now, they must work with environmental groups. For example, when William K. Reilly was contemplating a private equity takeover of TXU corporation, a Texas utilities firm, a major drawback was that TXU did not have support from environmentalist organizations. In order for the deal to go through, TXU had to win support from those organizations. TXU had been doing battle with Environmental Defense, a major environmentalist organization, over the opening of 11

©DIETER NAGL/AFP/Getty Images, Inc.

coal-fired power plants. As part of the deal negotiation, Environmental Defense was brought in. After harrowing negotiations, the new owners of TXU agreed to Environmental Defense's terms and dropped 8 of the original 11 proposed plants. When asked why environmentalists' support was so important for the TXU deal, Reilly responded, "We all swim in the same culture—and the culture is going green."

TXU is not the only company forming partnerships with environmentalist organizations. Shortly after the 2003 protest against their recycling policies, Dell joined together with Silicon Valley Toxics Coalition to develop a state-of-the-art recycling plan. DuPont, which is known as a green leader in its industry, employs Paul Gilding, the former head of Greenpeace, to work on its environmental policies and practices. In a much-publicized campaign, Walmart is working with Conservation International and the consulting firm BlueSkye to become a leader in environmentally sound retail practices. Walmart's former CEO, Lee Scott, stated that what started out as a defensive strategy in response to public protests over Walmart's environmental practices has turned out to be exactly the opposite.

Kimberly-Clark also has been working with environmental groups. In 2009, it agreed to alter its procurement policy by: (1) avoiding the use of fiber from the world's most sensitive forests, (2) giving preference to FSC (Forest Stewardship Council) certified fiber over other virgin wood, and (3) using postconsumer recycled fiber (e.g., from office paper) in some products rather than virgin fiber or preconsumer recycled fiber (e.g., wood chips from furniture manufacturing). For Kimberly-Clark, these changes will reduce the protests and pressure from activists while not substantially affecting the bottom line. For activists, the agreement is not perfect but the changes do mean more protection for ancient forests and their wildlife. For example, the National Resource Defense Council estimates that 425,000 trees would be saved annually if each U.S. household replaced once per year a 500-sheet roll of non-recycled bathroom tissue with a roll made from 100 percent recycled material. In 2009, an iPhone app was introduced to help consumers determine which tissue and bath tissue products are the most positive for the environment.

Sources: Anonymous. 2008. "Gotcha: CEO's Presentation Foiled," *Greenpeace Update*, Spring, p. 7; Associated Press. 2003. "Environmentalists at Vegas Trade Show Protest Dell's Recycling," press release, Jan. 9; J. Carey & M. Arndt. 2007. "Hugging the Tree-Huggers: Why So Many Companies Are Suddenly Linking Up with Eco Groups—Hint: Smart Business," *Business Week*, Mar. 12, pp. 66–67; Center for Health, Environment, and Justice. 2007. "Target Faces Mounting Pressure to Phase Out Toxic Products & Packaging on Day of Annual Shareholder Meeting," news release, May 24, at http://www.besafenet.com/pvs/ newsreleases/target_may_24_doa_ release. htm; Greenpeace, "About Kimberly-Clark's Campaign, Aug. 5, 2009, at http://www.greenpeace.org/canada/en/recent/kimberly-clark-and-greenpeace/about-kimberly-clark-s-campain; Greenpeace. 2007. "Green My Apple Bears Fruit," June 1, at http://www.greenpeace. org/ use/news/green-my-apple-bears-fruit; M. Gunther. 2006. "The Green Machine," *Fortune*, July 31, pp. 42–45; J. Ribeiro. 2005. "Greenpeace Protests Recycling Policies," *PCWorld*, Sept. 6, at http://www.pcworld.com/printable/article/ id.122419/printable.html; B. Walsh. 2009. "A Delicate Undertaking," *Time*, June 22, p. 97; World Wildlife Fund. 2009. "Exxon Ignores Pleas from 50,000 People to Stop Threatening Rare Whales," Aug. 9, at http://worldwildlife.org/who/media/press/2009/WWFPresitem13143b.html.

the strategic importance of Conflict, Negotiation, Power, and Politics

The *Exploring Behavior in Action* feature illustrates a fundamental conflict between environmental organizations and businesses that was once believed to be a zero-sum game, where one side had to win and the other had to lose. It was thought that businesses could either act responsibly toward the environment and thus decrease profits (environmentalists win) or they could operate to increase profits at the expense of the environment (business wins). However, today many environmental organizations and businesses are handling this conflict in a different manner so that effective compromises or even win–win outcomes are achieved. Environmentalists have learned to work with businesses to develop more environmentally friendly practices rather than to protest and embarrass them. At the same time, many businesses have come to view being environmentally responsible as a profitable business strategy.[1]

For those businesses that have been able to solve this conflict, the payoff has been immense. First, many practices that are environmentally sound have also served to save businesses money. For example, DuPont has saved over $2 billion from reductions in energy use since 1990.[2] Another way in which companies benefit is by improving sustainability of the environment. This is a long-term perspective whereby companies operate so as not to deplete their resources thereby ensuring that they can operate in the future. For example, Walmart, one of the largest purveyors of seafood, has developed a program of sustainable fishing practices to maintain commercial stocks of fish, which can become depleted.[3] Finally, companies' reputations are bolstered by acting in an environmentally responsible manner.[4] There are many very public "report cards" (e.g., the Dow Jones Sustainability Index and the FTSE4Good Index) that evaluate how well companies perform in terms of environmental responsibility as well as other types of social responsibility.[5] Company reputation has been linked to profits,[6] associates' morale,[7] and the ability to recruit top talent.[8] In this case, effectively dealing with and resolving conflict has been shown to have a very important strategic impact on firm performance.

In this chapter, we examine the nature of conflict, the process of negotiation, the exercise of power, and the political behavior that is common in organizations. We begin by defining conflict and differentiating among different types of conflict. We then turn to the causes of conflict, its outcomes, and various responses to it. After discussing conflict-resolution techniques in organizations, we conclude with a discussion of power and politics.

The Nature of Conflict

Conflict is a "process in which one party perceives that its interests are being opposed or negatively affected by another party."[9] In this chapter, we focus on conflict between individuals and between organizational units, with some attention given to interorganizational conflict as well. As we noted in the opening discussion, some conflicts are dysfunctional and some are not. In this section, we look more closely at the difference between functional and dysfunctional conflict and then describe three major types of conflict.

conflict
A process in which one party perceives that its interests are being opposed or negatively affected by another party.

Dysfunctional and Functional Conflict

Dysfunctional conflict is conflict that interferes with performance. Conflict can be dysfunctional for several reasons. First, conflict with important constituencies can create doubt about the organization's future performance in the minds of shareholders, causing stock prices to drop.[10] For example, this happened when Greenpeace protested Shell Oil's sinking of the oil rig, Brent Spar, in the North Sea.[11] Second, conflict can cause people to exercise their own individual power and engage in political behavior directed toward achieving their own goals at the expense of attaining organizational goals. Third, conflict can have negative effects on interpersonal relationships, as shown in Exhibit 12-1. Finally, it takes time, resources, and emotional energy to deal with conflict, both on an interpersonal and an organizational level. Thus, resources that could be invested in achieving the organization's mission are used in the effort to address the conflict. One survey showed that managers spend approximately 25 percent of their time dealing with conflict. In some fields (such as hospital administration and management of municipal organizations), managers can spend as much as 50 percent of their time managing conflict. Managers have rated conflict management as equal to or higher in importance than planning, communicating, motivating, and decision making.[12]

dysfunctional conflict
Conflict that is detrimental to organizational goals and objectives.

As mentioned, however, conflict need not be dysfunctional. Conflict that has beneficial results for both the organization and the individual is considered **functional conflict**.[13] An organization without functional conflict frequently lacks the energy and ideas to create effective innovation. Indeed, to encourage functional conflict in groups, some managers have implemented a formal dialectical-inquiry or devil's advocacy approach (described in

functional conflict
Conflict that is beneficial to organizational goals and objectives.

EXHIBIT 12-1   Effects of Conflict

Effects on Individuals	Effects on Behavior	Effects on Interpersonal Relationships
• Anger	• Reduced motivation and productivity	• Distrust
• Hostility	• Avoidance of other party	• Misunderstandings
• Frustration	• Emotional venting	• Inability to see other's perspective
• Stress	• Threats	• Questioning of other's intentions
• Guilt	• Aggression (psychological or physical)	• More negative attitudes toward others
• Low job satisfaction	• Quitting	• Changes in the amount of power
• Embarrassment	• Absenteeism	• Changes in the quality of communication
	• Biased perceptions	• Changes in the amount of communication
	• Stereotyped thinking	
	• Increased commitment to one's perspective	
	• Demonizing others	

Chapter 10). For example, the person serving as devil's advocate has the responsibility of questioning decisions to ensure that as many alternatives as possible are considered.[14]

By stimulating energy and debate, conflict can have a number of functional consequences for organizations, including the following:

- Facilitation of change
- Improved problem solving or decision making
- Enhanced morale and cohesion within a group (based on conflict with other groups)
- More spontaneity in communication
- Stimulation of creativity and, therefore, productivity[15]

Types of Conflict

Three types of conflict occur in the workplace: personal conflict, substantive conflict, and procedural conflict.[16] As shown in Exhibit 12-2, unresolved personal conflict and procedural conflict tend to be dysfunctional, but ongoing or periodic substantive conflict can prove constructive.

personal conflict
Conflict that arises out of personal differences between people, such as differing values, personal goals, and personalities.

As mentioned in Chapter 11, **personal conflict** refers to conflict that arises out of personal and relationship differences between people—differing values, personal goals, personalities, and the like. Individuals involved in personal conflict often report disliking one another, making fun of one another, being angry with or jealous of one another, having problems with each other's personalities, or perceiving each other as enemies.[17] Personal conflict is likely to result in poor performance.[18] This form of conflict creates distrust, misunderstanding, and suspicion and reduces goodwill.[19] As a result, associates have trouble focusing their attention fully on their job responsibilities and find it difficult to work together toward organizationally relevant goals.

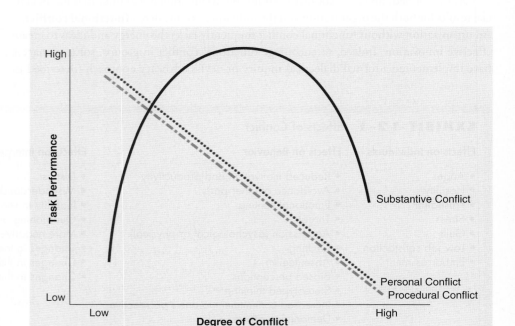

Exhibit 12-2 The Effects of Different Types of Conflict on Task Performance

The second type of conflict, **substantive conflict**, occurs over work content, tasks, and task goals.[20] In essence, differing opinions exist for task-related issues. One example of substantive conflict relates to an event described as the "Great Petunia War."[21] Two types of military retailers sell goods to military personnel: commissaries and post exchanges. In 1997, these retailers entered into a turf war over who had the right to sell garden plants and flowers. The battle soon escalated to include cooking oil, fruits and vegetables, and other types of food. These retailers were in conflict over their work goals. The conflict became so heated that two generals had to get involved because the conflict was threatening a proposal to reduce costs by integrating the operations of both retailers in the same facility

©Libby Welch/Alamy

on some bases. Substantive conflicts do not have to result in poor performance, if managed correctly.[22] Moderate levels of substantive conflict can actually increase performance. Even somewhat higher levels might lead to creative, positive outcomes if collaborative problem solving is emphasized. We discuss these issues later in this chapter.

The third type of conflict, **procedural conflict**, concerns how work should be completed.[23] Procedural conflict occurs, for example, when students working together on a project disagree about who will work on which parts of the project or whether they should meet face to face or communicate by e-mail. Unresolved procedural conflict has been found to negatively affect performance. If individuals cannot decide who should be responsible for completing a task or how it should be done, there is little chance that they will accomplish their goals or even complete the project.[24]

substantive conflict
Conflict that involves work content, tasks, and task goals.

procedural conflict
Conflict that arises over how work should be completed.

Causes of Conflict

Conflict within organizations can be caused by many factors, which are frequently interrelated. To manage conflict effectively, managers should understand the causes of conflict and be able to diagnose them. Some of the more common causes are structural factors, communication factors, cognitive factors, individual characteristics, and the history of relations between the parties.

Structural Factors

Among the structural factors that can lead to conflict are increased specialization, interdependency among parties, centralization versus decentralization, and physical layout.

Increased Specialization

As organizations become larger and more diverse, they require more specialization for effective operation. For example, smaller organizations may have general human resource managers who perform most or all of the Human Resource Management functions, but larger organizations frequently have specialists for employment, labor relations, training, compensation, and affirmative action. This situation represents specialization within one function. Organizations also add new functional areas as they serve a more diverse public. Dividing up the work in this manner is referred to as *differentiation*. Effective organizations become more differentiated as they grow larger or as their external environment becomes more complex.[25]

Increasing specialization has many positive benefits, but it also creates a greater potential for conflict. Specialists frequently view issues from different perspectives. They also often differ with regard to time perspectives and goals. For example, within a human resource unit the training specialists may have different perspectives relative to the compensation specialists. Also, a research and development department often operates within a long-term time frame because developing a product and preparing it for manufacture often require several years. However, a production department operates within a much shorter time frame, perhaps a few weeks (the time required to produce the products for a given order). Conflict can result when the research and development department is late in developing and testing product prototypes, thereby creating scheduling delays for the production department.

Interdependency

In most organizations, work must be coordinated between/among units and between/among individuals inside those units. The more interdependent units or individuals are, the more the potential for conflict exists. A good example of interdependence can be found within state governments. Many state employees work under what is referred to as a *merit system*. This system is designed to alleviate political patronage; employment is based on a person's merit. A Human Resource Management agency based on the merit system is used to screen applicants for state employment and to maintain lists of those who are eligible for certain jobs within state government. When a state agency has a job opening, it must request a list of eligible applicants from the merit system. The state agency, then, depends on the merit system, and the merit system exists to serve state agencies. If the merit system is slow in responding to a request, conflict can occur.

Interdependency can result from limited resources or from required coordination in the timing and sequencing of activities. All organizations have limited resources and attempt to find the most efficient way to divide the resources and accomplish tasks. For example, an organization orders new computers for many of its associates. However, before the associates can use the computers, the company computer technician must hook them up. If there is only one technician and each job takes an hour, competition will arise among associates for the technician's time. One study found that competition for limited resources often leads to dysfunctional conflict. In this case, such competition caused units to distort and suppress information needed by other units.[26]

Centralization Versus Decentralization

Both centralization and decentralization of authority can cause conflict, but each causes a different form of conflict. At the level of the overall organization, centralized authority means that one individual makes decisions for all units or that one higher unit makes decisions for all other units. Centralization can lessen conflict between units because all units are more likely to share the same goals and perspectives in a centralized system. However, conflict between individuals and their supervisors within units or between individual units and the decision-making unit can arise because individuals and units have less control over their own work situations.

For example, many organizations have centralized recruiting; that is, the human resource department recruits associates for jobs in all departments. Centralized recruiting has many advantages for the organization. It ensures that Equal Employment Opportunity Commission rules are followed, and it can save the organization money by avoiding duplication of effort.[27] However, many units may resent the human resource department's control over whom they hire (after all, the people in the unit have to work with the new hires). The hiring goals of the human resource department may be different from those of the individual units. Thus, conflict can arise between individual units and the human resource department.

Decentralized authority means that each unit manager can make important decisions. Although decentralized authority can reduce conflict between superiors and subordinates within a unit, because subordinates have more control over their work situations, it also creates the potential for more conflict between units because decisions made by one unit may conflict with decisions made by another. Furthermore, these decisions may reflect biased perceptions associated with the separate units.

Physical Layout

The physical layout of work environments can produce conflict through several mechanisms. In Chapter 11, we discussed how virtual work teams, whose members are physically separated from one another, are more likely to suffer from poor communication that can lead to conflict. Conflict can also arise when associates must work too closely together.[28] Associates commonly work in small, crowded cubicles that do not allow for privacy or personal space—a phenomenon sometimes termed the "Dilbertization effect" (after the comic-strip character).[29] Associates in such environments experience a stressful type of interdependency. Because everyone is continuously in view and can be easily overheard when talking, even in private conversations, conflict can arise. Conflict is especially likely if associates are unaware of the effect their behavior is having on others around them. For example, someone with a loud phone voice can be particularly irritating to co-workers. Furthermore, such environments do not allow associates to handle sensitive matters in private, a situation that can further increase conflict.[30] In the *Experiencing Organizational Behavior* feature, Herman Miller's approach to physical layout for teamwork is discussed. Their ideas offer substantial benefits.

Communication

As discussed in Chapter 9, a common cause of conflict is poor communication, which can lead to misunderstandings and allow barriers to be erected.[31] Probably the easiest way to prevent conflict is to ensure good communication. One of the authors observed conflict caused by poor communication a few years ago in a consulting case. The situation involved two company vice presidents who did not communicate well with one another. They would *talk* to each other, but neither of them would *listen* to the other. As a result, misunderstandings occurred and were never resolved. There were frequent heated arguments in meetings. This hostility extended to their respective departments, and problems of coordination became evident. The conflict became so bad that the chief executive officer asked one of the vice presidents to resign.

Both too little and too much communication can lead to conflict.[32] On the one hand, when there is too little communication, associates do not know enough about each other's intentions, goals, or plans. Coordination becomes difficult, and misunderstandings are more likely to occur, which can result in conflict. On the other hand, too much

Herman Miller, Designing for Teamwork

Herman Miller, Inc. was voted onto *Fortune* magazine's list of most admired companies in 2009, for the 21st time in the past 23 years. The company, which designs furniture, primarily for the workplace, and provides consulting and research services for office design, consistently wins awards for being a great place to work. Herman Miller, founded in 1923 by D.J. DePree, is one of the largest office furniture companies in the world and had sales of $1.63 billion in its most recent fiscal year. Thus, the company itself serves as its own best advertisement for the products and services it sells. Overall, its purpose is quite simple: "To Design and Build a Better World."

Part of its foundation for providing great work environments involves fostering teamwork through the physical design of the company's offices. The company has made the following suggestions for arranging an area that is conducive to teamwork:

First it is important to delineate boundaries, so that everyone has their own private space over which they feel ownership. At the same time, associates should always be able to see each other, which makes for easier collaboration. Next, a collaborative workspace should be created in a quiet secluded space. Holding team meetings in more public, central spaces, allows "outsiders" to intrude on the team's meeting. It is also important that team members be provided with furniture they can arrange themselves. This allows

©Michael L. Abramson/
Time & Life Pictures/Getty Images, Inc.

the team to reconfigure itself to suit the task. For example, when one person on the team is presenting information to the others, that would require a different furniture arrangement than if everyone were working collectively on the same document. Finally, it is important for team members to create ways to signal each other that they are unavailable and should not be disturbed.

Herman Miller follows these suggestions in the design of its own workspaces, particularly those in which creative teams are working. However, the design team is quick to point out that simply arranging the physical layout of the office space is not enough to support teamwork, although it greatly facilitates it. Rather, the company must also have a culture, management system, and reward system that fosters positive personal and task relationships. Herman Miller incorporates these types of elements in several ways. For example, the company has an employee-participation and profit-sharing plan. To complement this plan, all employees are taught during orientation about how to link their team's performance to the profits of the company.

Looking to the future, the company believes that balancing more effectively the needs for interaction and solitude will depend on advances in cognitive science. New developments connecting cognitive processing and the design of the work environment are likely to better identify factors that contribute to distraction. These developments are also likely to yield more sophisticated aids and tactics for cognitive processing in the work place. Clearly, Herman Miller is thinking ahead.

Sources: Herman Miller. 2010. "About Us: Overview," at http://www.hermanmiller.com/About-Us/Overview; Herman Miller. 2010. "About Us: For Our Investors," http://www.hermanmiller.com/About-Us/For-Our-Investors; Herman Miller. 2008. "Making Room for Collaboration," at http://www.hermanmiller.com/MarketFacingTech/hmc/research_summaries/pdfs/wp_Collaboration.pdf; Herman Miller. 2007. "Making Teamwork Work," at http://www.hermanmiller.com; J.C. Sarros, B.K. Cooper, & J.C. Santora. 2007, May–June. "The Character of Leadership," *Ivey Business Journal*, at http://www.iveybusinessjournal.com/article.asp?intArticle_ID=689.

communication can also result in information overload and misunderstandings that cause conflict. Other factors leading to poor communication are discussed in Chapter 9.

Cognitive Factors

Certain beliefs and attitudes can lead to conflict. Two such cognitive factors involve differing expectations and one party's perceptions of the other party.

Differing Expectations

People sometimes differ in their expectations about jobs, careers, and managerial actions. A common example of such differences involves professional associates (such as research scientists, accountants, or attorneys) and managers. Professional associates often perceive themselves as being loyal to their professions and define their careers as extending beyond a particular organization. In so doing, they focus on those activities valued by the profession, which the management of the organization does not necessarily value. This can lead to lower organizational loyalty and potentially to conflict between these associates and management. If the differences in expectations are great and conflict ensues, the associates may even leave the organization.[33] Thus, managers must be aware of this potential problem and work to reduce differences in expectations.

Perceptions of the Other Party

The perceptions that one party holds about another can set the stage for conflict. One person may perceive that another has extremely high goals and that these goals will interfere with his own goal attainment.[34] For example, if Smith perceives that a co-worker, Johnson, desires to be promoted at any cost, Smith might fear that Johnson will try to steal his work or sabotage his performance to "beat the competition." In general, perceptions that result in conflict include the perception that the other party's intentions are harmful, violate justice norms, are dishonest, or are counter to one's own intentions.[35]

Individual Characteristics

Individual characteristics that may lead to conflict include personality factors, differences in the value placed on conflict, and differences in goals.

Personality

The Type A personality trait has been linked to increased conflict. Recall from Chapter 7 that people with Type A personalities are competitive, aggressive, and impatient.[36] One study found that managers with Type A personalities reported more conflict with subordinates.[37] Because people with Type A personalities are more competitive, they are more likely to perceive others as having competing goals, even when this is not the case.

Another type of personality characteristic likely to influence how people experience and react to conflict is *dispositional trust*. People who are low in trust are less likely to cooperate with others[38] and less likely to try to find mutually beneficial solutions when conflict arises.[39] When people are high in trust, they are more likely to concede to another party during conflicts, especially when it appears that the other party is upset or disappointed.[40] High-trust individuals are more likely than others to become vulnerable because they have positive expectations about the motives of others.[41]

Differences in personality across people can also facilitate conflict. People high in conscientiousness plan ahead, are organized, and desire feedback. While working on a project, a person high in conscientiousness wants to plan the project out, start early, set clear goals, and consistently seek feedback. Someone who is low in conscientiousness may see these actions as unnecessary, creating the potential for procedural conflict. Note that it is not the degree of conscientiousness per se that leads to conflict here; it is the difference in this trait between two people who must work together.

Differences Across People in the Perceived Value of Conflict

People vary in the degree to which they value conflict. Some people think conflict is necessary and helpful, whereas others avoid it at all costs. There are important cultural differences as well in the way people view conflict.[42] People in Western cultures tend to view conflict as an inevitable and sometimes beneficial aspect of life. Those in some Asian cultures (such as Chinese) believe that conflict is bad and should be avoided.[43] These value differences make it more difficult to resolve conflicts when the parties are from different cultures. Value differences are most likely to get in the way of conflict resolution when the parties have a high need for closure.[44] That is, when people desire for there to be closure to a situation, they will resort to their strongest cultural norms to guide their decision making. So an American with a high need for closure might seek out solutions that put her at the best advantage for prevailing, whereas a Chinese associate with a high need for closure would focus on avoiding the conflict and maintaining harmony.

Goals

By definition, when individuals have competing or contrary goals, they often engage in conflict. In addition, certain aspects of individual goals make conflict more likely.[45] Associates with lofty goals, rigid goals, or competitive goals are more likely to experience conflict, especially when they are strongly committed to the goals.

Differences in goals can result from structural characteristics of the organization, such as increased specialization and interdependency. Recall our earlier example of the merit system for state-government employees. The merit system has the goal of ensuring that only qualified candidates are on the eligible-for-hire list and that all applicants are given a fair chance. A state agency wants qualified applicants for a job opening, but it also needs the position filled quickly so that the required work is done. It takes time to be fair to all and to be cautious about who is on the eligible list, which can delay getting the list to the state agency. Meanwhile, the agency may have a vacant job and a work backlog during the delay. In this case, differences in goals generate conflict. As the difference between the goals of two units becomes greater, the likelihood that conflict will occur increases. Organizations with structures that align individual and subgroup goals with those of the organization experience less conflict.[46]

History

Previous relationships between two parties can influence the likelihood of conflict in the future. Past performance and previous interactions are two such relationship factors.

Past Performance

When individuals or groups receive negative feedback because of poor past performance, they often perceive it as a threat.[47] When a threat is perceived, individuals frequently attempt to deal with it by becoming more rigid, exerting more control over deviant group members and ideas, and restricting the flow of communication.[48] When people become more rigid and communicate less, personal, substantive, and procedural issues can become heated. Thus, when past performance is poor, the chances for conflict are greater.[49]

Previous Interactions

Individuals who have experienced conflict in the past are more likely to experience it in the future.[50] Previous conflict can influence the probability of future conflict in several ways. First, the parties often engage in the same conflict-inducing behaviors. Second, the parties likely distrust one another. Third, they may expect conflict, and this expectation may become a self-fulfilling prophecy. Think of the old story of the warring Hatfield and McCoy families. These two families had been fighting so long that younger members of each family did not know what had caused the initial conflict. All they had learned was to engage in conflict with the other family.

Later in the chapter we discuss the negotiation process, which is an illustration of how associates and managers attempt to resolve conflict. Negotiation situations are influenced by the negotiators' previous interactions. Research has shown that negotiators' history of negotiation in terms of the quality of deals they arranged influences how they negotiate in other situations—even if they are negotiating with a different person.[51] Negotiators who have a history of not being able to reach a satisfactory conclusion during previous negotiations are much more likely to reach unfavorable solutions in future negotiations than those who have had a successful negotiation history.

Conflict Escalation and Outcomes

As we have just seen, conflict has many causes, and they are often interrelated. For example, structural factors such as specialization are related to differences in goals and perceptions. The physical environment can cause conflict because it can interfere with communication. However a conflict begins, though, there are only a certain number of ways in which it can end.

Fortunately, most cases of conflict are resolved, although not necessarily in a manner satisfactory to both parties or to the organization (as in the earlier example, where two vice presidents were in conflict and one was fired by the CEO). In this section, we discuss conflict escalation and then focus on conflict outcomes.

Conflict Escalation

Conflict escalation is the process whereby a conflict intensifies over time. Escalation is characterized by several features. Tactics become increasingly severe on both sides, and the number of issues grows. In addition, the parties become more and more deeply involved in the conflict. Eventually, as their goals shift from caring about their own welfare and outcomes to trying to harm the other party, they lose sight of their own self-interests.[52]

Many reasons have been proposed for conflict escalation. Some experts feel that escalation is inevitable unless direct measures are taken to resolve the conflict.[53] Others believe

conflict escalation
The process whereby a conflict grows increasingly worse over time.

that conflicts do not have to escalate. Rather, there are certain general conditions that make escalation more likely. These include the following:

- Cultural differences exist between the parties.[54]
- The parties have a history of antagonism.[55]
- The parties have insecure self-images.[56]
- Status differences between the parties are uncertain.[57]
- The parties have informal workplace ties to one another.[58]
- The parties do not identify with one another.[59]
- One or both parties have the goal of escalating the conflict in order to beat the other party.[60]

Conflict escalation might involve overt expressions of workplace aggression. This aspect of escalation may be one-sided, where one party becomes more hostile than the other(s). These issues are taken up in the next *Experiencing Organizational Behavior* feature.

Conflict Outcomes

There are five ways in which conflict can end in terms of how the outcome satisfies each party's concerns, interests, or wishes: lose–lose, win–lose, lose–win, compromise, and win–win.

Lose–Lose

In this conflict outcome, neither party gets what was initially desired. In aggression situations, lose–lose outcomes are often seen. The aggressor often fails to obtain an initially desired goal such as a promotion or continued employment, and he also frequently fails to obtain true satisfaction through the aggressive behavior. The aggrieved sometimes fails to achieve desired peace in the workplace, and can suffer many negative consequences beyond that.

Win–Lose or Lose–Win

In either of these outcome scenarios, one party's concerns are satisfied, whereas the other party's concerns are not. This type of outcome is obviously not advantageous for the losing party, and it often is not particularly advantageous for the organization. Such outcomes can be difficult to avoid, however. When conflicts involve "zero-sum," or distributive, issues, one party can gain only at the expense of the other. This can cause each party to attempt to fully satisfy its concerns at the expense of the other party. For example, consider a situation in which two opposing parties are competing for a limited number of resources. The more of the resources one party obtains, the less of the resources the other party obtains. When United Airlines fought its unions following the 9/11 attacks on New York, distributive issues were at the heart of the conflict.[61] Each dollar obtained by the unions for salaries and pension benefits represented a dollar out of the pocket of the airline.

Compromise

Compromise occurs when both parties give in to some degree on an issue or set of issues. Had management at United Airlines been willing to agree to somewhat less drastic pay cuts, then the unions in exchange could have moderated their demands in other strongly contested areas, such as pensions. Indeed, compromise was actually achieved several times

Workplace Aggression

On January 12, 2010, a disgruntled ex-employee of an Atlanta-area Penske truck rental facility visited his former employer. He arrived at the start-time of his former shift wearing camouflage clothing. According to police reports, the ex-employee then entered the work site and began shooting. Two individuals were killed and several others were critically injured, including the former supervisor of the alleged assailant.

On January 7, 2010, an employee of ABB's St. Louis–area transformer plant arrived at work with more than his lunch pail. He also had an assault rifle, two shotguns, and two handguns. He proceeded to kill three co-workers, seriously wound five others, and kill himself. The individual had been a party to a lawsuit related to the retirement plan.

In an office situation, a disagreement erupted. Soon, one party had the other pinned against a wall with punch after punch being delivered to the individual's face. Blood was everywhere. In another situation, an unhappy subordinate led his supervisor to a vault under false pretenses. He then locked the supervisor in the vault and turned the lights off. In another instance, a disagreement arose between two supervisors over who would deliver layoff notices. One supervisor threw a large, filled envelope at the other.

The events discussed above represent workplace aggression. This type of aggression involves behavior by one or more individuals that is designed to physically or psychologically harm a worker or multiple workers in a workplace setting. Including murders involving co-workers (or former co-workers) as well as murders committed by customers, clients, and the general public, several hundred to over one thousand workplace murders occur in any given year in the United States. Other physical forms of aggression such as fights or shoving affect millions each year. Milder acts of aggression, such as psychological bullying, affect even more. In one survey, the U.S. Bureau of Labor Statistics reported that about 50 percent of establishments with more than 1,000 employees had experienced some form of noteworthy workplace aggression in the previous 12-month period, with roughly 34 percent of the establishments having experienced co-worker–on–co-worker aggression.

The stereotypical portrait of workplace aggressors involves young white males who have poor self-esteem and/or aggressive personalities, perhaps coupled with substance abuse issues. This stereotype seems to be both right and wrong. Males with self-esteem issues and/or aggressive personalities (or anger as a general trait) do seem to be somewhat more likely to commit acts of workplace aggression. Abusers of alcohol also are more likely to commit such acts. On the other hand, individuals who are young and/or white do not appear to carry a higher likelihood of aggression in the workplace. Beyond demographic and personality factors, lack of justice in the organization and constraints on task performance are predictive of aggression.

In addition to the human suffering, the financial costs of workplace aggression are staggering (billions of dollars each year). To reduce these costs, many tactics have been suggested. The president of PCM Consultants, Chuck Mannila, suggests the following actions, with a particular emphasis on reducing or avoiding the most severe forms of aggression:

- Adopt a zero-tolerance policy
- Implement a formal workplace prevention program
- Train managers and associates to address the issues
- Take every threat seriously
- Immediately investigate all threats
- Implement tighter security
- Provide access to employee assistance programs

Sources: J. Barling, K.E. Dupre, & E.K. Kelloway. 2009. "Predicting Workplace Aggression and Violence," *Annual Review of Psychology*, 60:671–692; Bureau of Labor Statistics. 2005. "Survey of Workplace Prevention, 2005," at http://www.bls.gov/iif/oshwc/osnr0026.pdf; A. Gomstyn. 2009. "Workplace Horror Stories: Yale and Beyond," *ABC News.com*, Sept. 21, at http://abcnews.go.com/Business/workplace-horror-stories-yale/story?id=8615343; C. Mannila. 2008. "How to Avoid Becoming a Workplace Violence Statistic," *T + D*, 62(7): 60–66; K. Nolan, V. Dagher. 2010. "Workplace Shooting in St. Louis Leaves Four Dead, *Wall Street Journal*, Jan. 8, p. A.5; K. Rowson. 2010. "Police Sources: Penske Gunman Was Fired," *11Alive.com*, Jan. 13, at http://www.11alive.com/rss/rss_story.aspx?storyid=139675; D. Yusko. 2010. "Official Drops Claim Over Tossed Envelope," Timesunion.com, Jan. 16, at http://www.timesunion.com/ASPStories/Story.asp?StoryID=889607.

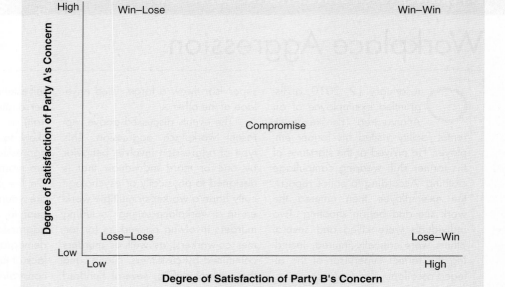

Exhibit 12-3 Possible Conflict Outcomes

Source: Adapted from K.W. Thomas. 1992. "Conflict and Negotiation Processes." In M.D. Dunnette, & L.M. Hough (Eds.), *Handbook of Industrial and Organizational Psychology, Vol. 3* Palo Alto, CA: Consulting Psychologists Press, pp. 651–717.

during the travails at United. For example, a compromise resulted in employees' accepting more substantial pay cuts than they wanted while management agreed to more employee stock ownership than it wanted. Compromise can be a desirable solution to conflict.

Win–Win

A win–win situation occurs when both parties get what they want. Consider a situation in which a union bargains for increased pay, but management does not have the resources to increase pay. A win–win situation would occur if the union decided to accept specific productivity incentives. Increases in productivity would be accompanied by cash bonuses, thus increasing union members' pay to the levels they desired in the first place. Management would win because productivity (and consequently profit) would be expected to increase, in turn covering the higher pay. Exhibit 12-3 depicts the five conflict outcomes.

Responses to Conflict

People respond to conflict in different ways. One person may try to win at all costs, whereas another person may try to ensure that both her own concerns and those of the other party are met. There are five potential responses to conflict, as well as situations in which each response is appropriate.[62] Each response is described in terms of assertiveness and cooperativeness.[63] Here, *assertiveness* refers to the extent to which a party tries to satisfy his, her, or its own concerns. *Cooperativeness* refers to the extent to which a party attempts to satisfy the other party's concerns.

1. *Competing.* A party with a competing response attempts to win at the expense of the other party. Other names for this response include *forcing* and *dominating*. This style is useful when quick, decisive action is required, when an unpopular course of action must be taken, or when the other party will take advantage

of noncompetitive behavior. For example, some countries have more lenient copyright laws than the United States, leading to a proliferation of imitative (knockoff) goods (such as fake Gucci purses, Adidas sneakers, and Rolex watches). The Calvin Klein Company used a competing conflict response in dealing with counterfeiters by establishing a worldwide network to investigate and take legal action against any organization counterfeiting its goods.[64]

2. *Accommodating.* An accommodating response is the opposite of a competitive style. A person using an accommodating response will forgo his own concerns so that the concerns of the other party can be met. For example, when someone has to work on a holiday, an associate may agree to work on the holiday so that a co-worker can have the holiday off, in order to avoid conflict. An accommodating style may be used by a party who believes that he cannot win. It may also be useful when the issue is less important to one party than to the other. An individual or unit can adopt an accommodating style in return for a favor at a future time.

3. *Avoiding.* A party who exhibits an avoiding response neglects both her own concerns and those of the other party. An avoiding style may be necessary to allow emotions to cool down or as a means of delaying decisions until effective solutions can be found. IBM has avoided conflict by refusing to do business in countries that allow bribery of public officials.[65]

4. *Compromising.* Compromising responses are those in which a party tries to partially meet both his own concerns and those of the other party. A compromising response is best used when the parties are of relatively equal power, when temporary settlements to complex problems are required, when there is time pressure, and as a backup when collaboration (described next) is unsuccessful.

5. *Collaborating.* Collaborating responses are attempts to fully meet the concerns of both parties. To use a collaborating response, the parties must work together to identify solutions in which both parties can win.[66] This type of response is most likely to result in the win–win outcome described earlier. A collaborating response is best used when both parties' concerns are too important to ignore and when the objective is to learn and to gain commitment.

Negotiation

The resolution of conflict usually requires negotiations between the conflicting parties. **Negotiation** is a process through which two or more parties with different preferences and interests attempt to agree on a solution through back-and-forth communication. Furthermore, the parties are committed to achieving a peaceful means of dispute resolution.[67]

In the resolution of conflict, the parties often engage in bargaining that requires them to engage in several reactions to conflict such as compromise, collaboration, accommodation, or competition. Although each party usually approaches negotiations with the intent to gain the most benefits for its side, for negotiations to be successful, all parties must bargain in good faith. Managers should build their skills in negotiation because they will be called on to negotiate in many situations. The political skills explained later can be useful to managers in negotiations if they use them for the benefit of the organization to achieve a negotiated agreement whereby both or all parties gain benefit and agree to abide

negotiation
A process through which parties with different preferences and interests attempt to agree on a solution.

by the decision. Depending on the circumstances, a manager can serve as a mediator or an arbitrator in negotiations. A mediator acts as a neutral third party who facilitates a positive solution to the negotiations, whereas an arbitrator acts as a third party with the authority to require an agreement. In reality, managers often serve in both roles simultaneously, and require tact and strong interpersonal skills to achieve negotiated agreement in a conflict situation. The skills and means of negotiation depend on the negotiator's bargaining strategy.

Negotiation Strategies

distributive bargaining
A strategy that: (1) involves a competing, win–lose approach and (2) tends to be used when one party's goals are in direct conflict with the goals of another party.

integrative bargaining
A strategy that: (1) involves a collaborative, win–win approach and (2) tends to be used when the nature of the problem permits a solution that is attractive to both parties.

Negotiators typically emphasize one of two strategies.[68] The **distributive bargaining** strategy involves a competing, win–lose approach. It tends to be used when one party's goals are in direct conflict with the goals of another party. For example, if a buyer and a supplier are negotiating over the price of a product, the higher the agreed-upon price, the bigger the win for the supplier and the bigger the loss for the buyer. On the other hand, the **integrative bargaining** strategy involves a collaborative, win–win approach. This strategy tends to be used when the nature of the problem permits a solution that is attractive to both parties. Sometimes what appears to be a distributive situation at the beginning can be turned into an integrative strategy by broadening the issues under consideration. For example, if the above buyer were to also offer the supplier bigger orders and offer to buy additional products in return for a lower price on the product under negotiation, then an integrative solution could be reached. The buyer would get a lower price; the supplier would get increased volume, an issue that it feels much more strongly about. Depending on what type of strategy a negotiator is using, different types of tactics are appropriate and likely to be effective. These tactics are listed in Exhibit 12-4.

Apart from the issues directly under negotiation, there is often the long-term relationship between parties to consider. Most often during negotiations, the parties desire to remain friendly, trustful, and respectful of each other. For example, if a company was negotiating with an environmental group and the negotiations turned hostile, future relationships between the two groups would remain antagonistic. The company might do only what is absolutely required to meet the terms of negotiations and fail to develop new ways in which to protect the environment. The environmental group might then give only a weak endorsement to the company or refuse to work with it on environmental practices.

attitudinal structuring
Activities aimed at influencing the attitudes and relationships of the negotiating parties.

The activities aimed at influencing the attitudes and relationships of the negotiating parties are referred to as **attitudinal structuring**.[69] Examples of tactics to use for attitudinal structuring are also presented in Exhibit 12-4.

The Negotiation Process

There are generally four stages that a negotiation process should follow:[70]

1. *Preparation.* Prior to any negotiation, each party outlines the specific goals he or she hopes to achieve. At this point, negotiators must determine their best alternative to a negotiated agreement (BATNA). This is the least that the negotiator is willing to accept. Also, during the preparation stage, negotiators should engage in self-analysis and opponent analysis. It is important for negotiators to understand their own tendencies and behavior during negotiations as well as those of the other party. At this stage the following questions should be asked about the other party:
   a. What is the other party's position and power? Must the other party confer with other people to make concessions?

EXHIBIT 12-4   Negotiation Tactics

Distributive Tactics

- Convince the other that breaking off negotiations would be costly for him/her/it.
- Convince the other that you feel very committed to reaching your target outcome.
- Prevent the other from making a firm commitment to an outcome close to her target.
- Allow the other to abandon his position without loss of face or other cost.
- Convince the other that your own target outcome is fair.
- Convince the other that her target outcome is unfair.
- Convince the other that important third parties favor your own target outcome.
- Use nonhostile humor to build positive affect.
- Distract the other to impair his ability to concentrate.

Integrative Tactics

- Show the other that his/her/its concerns are important to you.
- Show the other that your target outcome is too important to compromise.
- Show the other that a win–win outcome is a possibility.
- Demonstrate that you are flexible with respect to various solutions.
- Insist on fair criteria for deciding among possible solutions.
- Make collaborative norms salient.
- Minimize use of behaviors or tactics that would cause negative emotions.
- Provide an emotionally supportive climate.
- Shield the other from emotional distractions.

Attitudinal Structuring Tactics

- Use language similar to the other party's.
- Dissociate oneself from others not liked by the opponent.
- Associate oneself with others the opponent likes.
- Reward opponent's behavior.
- Express appreciation.
- Remind opponent of role obligations.
- Assist opponent in working through negative attitudes.
- Return favors.
- Fight the antagonism, not the antagonist.

Sources: K.W. Thomas. 1992. "Conflict and Negotiation Processes," in M.D. Dunnette & L.M. Hough (Eds.), *Handbook of industrial and organizational psychology, Vol. 3* Palo Alto, CA: Consulting Psychologists Press, pp. 651–717; R.E. Walton, & R.B. McKersie. 1965. *A Behavioral Theory of Labor Negotiations* New York: McGraw-Hill.

    b. What does the other party consider a "win"?

    c. What is the history of the other party's negotiating style? Does she tend to focus on the distributive strategy or rely on the integrative strategy?

2. *Determining the negotiation process.* Determine the timeline, place, and structure of the negotiations. Also, agreements should be made about confidentiality, the sharing of information, and how agreements will be approved. At this point, who will be present during the negotiation process should be clarified.

3. *Negotiating the agreement.* During this stage the actual negotiation takes place and negotiation strategies and tactics are used.

4. *Closing the deal.* At this stage, both parties should be quite clear about the conclusion of the negotiations and the particulars of the final agreement. Final

agreements should be formalized and it should be made clear what each party's responsibility is in implementing the agreement.

The process outlined above appears to be quite formal. However, it should be followed in any form of negotiation, ranging from negotiating one's pay increase to negotiating major merger and acquisition deals. In the *Managerial Advice* feature, we explore a common type of negotiation scenario—that of negotiating one's salary when taking a new job.

MANAGERIAL ADVICE

A Costly Conflict Resolution: The Importance of Negotiation

Jane and Rob are very happy today. Both were offered jobs at ABSCO in the management trainee program. Because Jane and Rob had the same qualifications, ABSCO offered them the same salary of $40,000 per year. This was Rob's dream job, so he accepted right away. This was also Jane's dream job; however, she realized that she would be working in an area where the cost of living was high, and when this was taken into consideration, she would be making less than many of her colleagues in similar positions. So Jane negotiated her salary up to $42,500.

At ABSCO, pay increases are calculated as a percentage of salary. As can be seen in the chart, given the pay-raise schedule, Jane's initial increase over Rob of $2,500 will grow to nearly $3,500 at the end of a five-year period. Over that time, Jane will make almost $14,700 more than Rob. Should they both stay at ABSCO, Jane's salary will continue to grow faster than Rob's, even if they receive the same percentage increases. Thus, Rob's failure to negotiate a higher salary will mean that he is likely to receive less compensation than Jane for the rest of his career at ABSCO.

Salary negotiations are a classic case of conflict. The hiring organization wants to minimize its costs (lower compensation), whereas the applicant wants to earn as much as possible. This involves a distributive issue, as described earlier, in which two parties are contesting a limited resource. The conflict must be resolved. When you negotiate your salary, how can you participate effectively in this resolution? Advice abounds for how to negotiate your salary, but most experts agree on the fundamentals. Below are some commonly prescribed steps that you can take:

1. Do your homework. Know what you are worth on the job market and what the industry standards are for the position you are being offered. Numerous sources of information exist to help you with this task, including:

   • Salary survey information at your university's career services center.

   • Job listings that indicate salaries for similar positions.

	Raise	Rob's Salary	Jane's Salary
Year 1	—	$40,000.00	$42,500.00
Year 2	5%	42,000.00	44,625.00
Year 3	10%	46,200.00	49,087.50
Year 4	10%	50,820.00	53,996.25
Year 5	10%	55,902.00	59,395.88

As suggested in the *Managerial Advice* feature, the natural conflict over salary and its resolution are important to both the organization and the individual involved. Jane negotiated a higher salary before accepting the job offer, but Rob did not do so. Therefore, even though Rob and Jane had equal qualifications, they were compensated differently. Furthermore, assuming that they perform at equal levels over time and thus receive the same percentage pay increases, the gap between Jane's salary and Rob's will grow. Furthermore,

- Online salary surveys such as those found at JobStar.
- Friends, other students, and networking contacts.
- Websites that allow you to calculate the cost of living for various parts of the country; $40,000 goes a lot further in Houston than it does in New York City.

2. Determine your best alternative to a negotiated agreement (BATNA). This is the lowest offer you will consider; you will reject any offer lower than your BATNA. Your BATNA is a dynamic cutoff. You should always strive to increase it. One way to do this during salary negotiations is to have alternative job offers. The best current offer becomes your BATNA.

3. Know what salary you want—your target salary. Your BATNA is your least acceptable outcome. Your target salary is your preferred outcome.

4. Never make vague counteroffers, such as "I need more money." Be prepared to offer a specific salary range and a justification for the salary range. This is where your homework will come in handy. Ensure that the range you specify to the company does not limit your possibilities for negotiation. For example, if you specify your BATNA (say, $30,000) as the low end of your range, you may not be able to get more than your minimal acceptable amount. This does not mean you should communicate an unrealistically high figure, however. Suggesting unrealistically high figures leaves a bad impression with the organization.

5. Although you should not be vague, neither should you say, "I need X amount of dollars." This indicates that you are unwilling to negotiate. On the one hand, the organization can say no and withdraw the offer. On the other hand, if the

organization accepts immediately, you may experience "winner's remorse," whereby you feel that your suggested amount was too low.

6. Be realistic. Often, when organizations offer salaries for entry-level positions, they leave little room for negotiation. The higher you go in the organization, the more room there usually is for negotiation.

7. Be polite and direct during negotiations.

8. Never inflate your past salary or experience. Be honest in all aspects of the negotiation.

9. Remember to calculate benefits as part of the offer package. One offer may have a lower salary figure but a much more generous retirement plan. Again, do your homework.

10. Do not play "hard to get" when you have little bargaining power.

Sources: D. Gordon. 2004. "Suggested Salary Negotiation Guidelines for Recent College Graduates," at http://www.adguide.com/pages/articles/article257.htm; C. Krannich & R.L. Krannich. 2004. "30 Salary Negotiation Mistakes to Avoid," at http://www.washingtonpost.com/wl/jobs/Content?Content=/Career_Advic.../impactadvice8.html; L.L. Thompson. 2008. *The Mind and Heart of the Negotiator*, 4th ed. Upper Saddle River, NJ: Prentice Hall.

although the organization may save almost $14,700 over a five-year period, it may also lose a productive associate. Rob is likely to be unhappy about the difference in pay if he discovers it (which is likely). As we explained in Chapter 6, in the discussion of equity theory, Rob will feel that he is not being treated equitably. Consequently, he might search for a job with another organization. Unfortunately, if it leads to conflict between Rob and the organization, he is likely to depart for a job elsewhere. In this case, the organization loses valuable human capital.

Before closing this section on negotiation, it is important to point out that associates negotiate all the time in everyday work life. When we think of negotiations, we tend to think of formalized negotiations such as labor–management bargaining or merger-and-acquisition talks. However, negotiations take place whenever there are two or more parties who need to come to an agreement about a proposed course of action. Negotiation is just a means of trying to influence others to obtain outcomes that one desires. Thus, a major issue that underlies all negotiations as well as conflict situations is power.[71] When two parties try to influence each other to attempt to maximize their own outcomes or attain a target outcome, the issue of power can be critical to resolving the conflict.

Power

power
The ability to achieve desired outcomes.

The concept of power is one of the most pervasive in the study of organizational behavior.[72] **Power** is generally defined as the ability to achieve desired outcomes.[73] Power can also be thought of as the ability of one person to get another person to do something.[74] Thus, any time someone persuades another person to do something, he or she is exercising power. For example, a coach who requires players to do pushups is exercising power. A secretary who has the boss change her schedule to accommodate an associate is also exercising power.

Often, power is thought to be negative. However, little would be accomplished if power were not exercised on a regular basis.[75] Whether or not the exercise of power is harmful depends on the intent of the person holding the power. A manager who exercises power to meet organizational goals is using power in a positive, productive way. In contrast, a manager who exercises power to promote his personal interests, at the expense of others, is misusing power.

Power exists on different levels. Individuals and organizational units can have power. For example, a student body president can have power to influence university policy. Powerful units such as academic departments that bring in a great deal of external money can also influence university policy, as can the alumni association. It is generally easy to identify people in an organization or social unit who have power.[76] Think of an organization to which you belong, for example, and identify who has the power in that organization.

Bases of Individual Power

Power in organizations can come from many sources. John French and Bertram Raven developed one of the most commonly used typologies for describing the bases of power.[77] It includes five categories: legitimate power (formal authority), reward power, coercive power, expert power, and referent power.

Legitimate Power

People derive **legitimate power** (or formal authority) from the positions they hold in the organization. Legitimate power is narrow in scope because it can be applied only to acts that are defined as legitimate by everyone involved. For example, after being elected to a second term in 2004, President George W. Bush replaced many of the cabinet members from his first term. This was an exercise in legitimate power because the president has the formal authority to choose his cabinet members. However, when Attorney General Alberto Gonzales fired many U.S. attorneys, he came under fire because he was viewed as not having the legitimate authority to do so and his motives were questioned.[78]

legitimate power
Power derived from position; also known as formal authority.

Reward Power

Reward power results when one person has the ability or perceived ability to provide another with desired outcomes (i.e., the person controls or is believed to control desired resources). In the long run, reward power is limited by the person's actual ability to supply desired outcomes. For example, a supervisor may have power because she can assign pay raises to associates. However, if the company has a bad year, and the supervisor is not permitted to give pay raises, then she loses this source of power. Reward power is not limited to formal sources, such as the supervisor's power to give raises; it can also come from informal sources. For example, a secretary who often controls his boss's schedule may then reward associates with access to the boss.

reward power
Power resulting from the ability to provide others with desired outcomes.

Coercive Power

Coercive power exists when one person believes that another person has the ability or perceived ability to punish people. Coercive power is usually considered a negative form of power; thus, its use should be limited. Overuse or inappropriate application of this type of power can produce unintended results. For example, associates might respond with negative or undesired behaviors. Like reward power, coercive power can be derived from informal as well as formal sources. For example, an associate who spreads negative gossip about others may have coercive power because others fear that he will spread negative gossip about them.[79] Coercive power is limited by the fact that those being influenced must be highly dependent on the person wielding the power.[80]

coercive power
Power resulting from the ability to punish others.

Expert Power

Expert power arises from special expertise or technical knowledge that is valuable to others or the organization. Expert power is limited by the degree to which this expertise is irreplaceable. For example, an associate can gain power by becoming the only person in the unit who knows how to use certain software. However, if others learn to use the software, this person's power will be diminished.

expert power
Power resulting from special expertise or technical knowledge

Referent Power

People are said to have **referent power** when others are attracted to them or desire to be associated with them. For example, it has been found that executives who have prestigious reputations among their colleagues and shareholders have greater influence on strategic decision-making processes in their firms.[81] Referent power is the most resilient type of power because it is difficult to lose once it has been achieved. In addition, referent power can be used to influence a wide range of behaviors.[82]

referent power
Power resulting from others' desire to identify with the referent.

An Example of Power

The use of different power bases is not mutually exclusive. Associates and managers can use multiple bases at one time. The past CEO of Disney, Michael Eisner, is an example of someone who drew power from a variety of sources.[83] During the years of Eisner's reign at Disney (1984–2006), the entertainment giant went through a number of ups and downs. Owing to Eisner's efforts in his early years, the company's performance improved dramatically. In later years, Disney experienced a number of complex issues: hostile takeover threats; the acquisition of Miramax Studios and Capital Cities/ABC; conflict with Bob and Harvey Weinstein of Miramax; a successful alliance with Pixar Animation studios; the dissolution of the alliance with Pixar; the very public and contentious resignation of Jeffrey Katzenberg as president of Disney; constant battles with Disney family member Roy Disney; and the expensive hiring and resignation of Eisner's friend, Michael Ovitz.

For a long time, Eisner was incredibly successful in maintaining power over Disney, despite opposition from shareholders, other Disney companies, the Disney family, and even his own executives. How did he do it? Numerous reports exist about Eisner's strategies for increasing and holding his power.

First, Eisner had a great deal of legitimate power. He was both the chairman of the board of directors and the CEO. These positions allowed him to make managerial decisions while at the same time having the authority to evaluate those decisions. He also had the power to hire and fire executives and board members, almost guaranteeing that he was surrounded by people who supported him. This led to complaints by Eisner's detractors that he dominated the board by filling it with his own people, who often did not work in the best interests of other shareholders.

A second way in which Eisner obtained power was by lavishing attention on board members, important investors (like Warren Buffett and Sid Bass), members of the Disney family, and even the widows of former executives. In this way, he was able to curry favor with important Disney stakeholders.

Eisner was also a genius at using information. He wooed board members to support him by constantly supplying them with information. He stated "If I filled them in, made them my partner, if things didn't go so well, the likelihood of, 'I told you so' and those kind of reactions would not exist." At the same time, he controlled communication between executives and board members so that any disagreements, important discussions, or decisions had to go through him. When Eisner wanted to fire Michael Ovitz only months after hiring him, he went through elaborate procedures, talking to board members without Ovitz's knowledge and spreading the word that Ovitz wasn't working out.

Another way that Eisner maintained power was to divide those who might oppose him and to make himself indispensable. He encouraged and allowed rivalries between executives and board members to develop so that other important decision makers were unable to form a cohesive unit. He also refused to train or plan for who would succeed him in the chairman and CEO roles, thus making his departure a problem for Disney.

Finally, Eisner maintained power by restricting the power of others. One of the reasons that the Weinstein brothers wanted to separate Miramax from Disney was that Eisner tried to stop them from releasing the movie *Fahrenheit 911,* which was critical of the Bush administration. Ovitz's experiences seem to be parallel. According to Michael Ovitz, Eisner implied in the hiring process that the chief financial officer and the corporate operations chief would report to Ovitz. However, Ovitz soon learned at a dinner party that both of these men would report to Eisner.

By March 2004, Disney shareholders had become highly dissatisfied. Led by Roy Disney, among others, they participated in a 43 percent no-confidence vote to oust Eisner as the chairman of the Disney board. One of the major factors leading to this vote was the $140 million severance pay package that Eisner gave to Ovitz after Ovitz had been at Disney for only 15 months. Shareholders argued that they had not been given enough information about this deal and that the cost was detrimental to the company. They believed that Disney board members had buckled under Eisner's pressure at shareholders' expense. By December 2005, Eisner had stepped down as chairman; however, he stated that he planned to remain as CEO of Disney until his retirement in 2006.

It appears that Michael Eisner's use of power was sometimes inappropriate. This was a special concern because Eisner was both chairman and CEO of Disney. Thus, he already had significant legitimate power. Furthermore, his position also gave him reward power throughout the entire company. Because of his efforts in turning around Disney after he became CEO, many perceived him to have expert power. In addition, his prominent position afforded him referent power. His actions regarding Michael Ovitz suggest that he used coercive power as well. He fired Ovitz but only after conducting a negative campaign with members of the board of directors. He then gave Ovitz an exceptionally large severance pay package. It seems that Eisner may often have acted in his own best interests and not in the best interests of the company or its shareholders. This story perhaps suggests why Disney's performance suffered during the last years of Eisner's reign.

Strategic Contingencies Model of Power

Individuals and organizational units can also obtain power by being able to address the strategic problems that an organization faces. This is referred to as the **strategic contingencies model of power**.[84] For example, when an organization is in a highly innovative industry, where success depends on being able to develop new products, the research and development (R&D) department and its key people have a great deal of power. The R&D unit has the knowledge (human capital) critical for the success of the firm's strategy to produce innovations and compete effectively in its industry. Consider the pharmaceutical industry. Pharmaceutical firms must introduce valuable new drugs regularly, especially as their patents on their current drugs expire. Without new drugs, their revenues will decrease, and the firms will eventually die. The knowledge and expertise needed to develop new drugs is very important to the company strategy. Thus, the R&D units in pharmaceutical firms often have significant power. Essentially, these units control resources that are valuable to the organization.[85]

Units or individuals may obtain power, then, by identifying the strategic contingencies faced by an organization and gaining control over them. For example, in the United Airlines situation discussed earlier in this chapter, management (which controls the financial resources) gained more power by arguing that financial difficulties were critical and could be solved only by the unions' agreement to salary and pension concessions. However, the unions (which control the human capital in some ways) gained power by highlighting the importance and sensitivity of operations. They did this through disruptive work slowdowns. The most immediate problem for the organization, then, was to get its flights running on schedule again. The strategy of operating flights on time and satisfying customers was negatively affected by the union's exercise of its power. Thus, the unions controlled the most important resources for the strategy and had more power at that point.

If units or people are able to identify the contingencies important to the organization's strategy and performance and control them, they should be able to maintain their bases of

strategic contingencies model of power
A model holding that organizational units and people gain power by being able to address the major problems and issues faced by the organization.

power. They can then use that power to require the organization to act in ways that benefit them. Take, for example, an athletic department that brings a great deal of alumni money to its university. Because of its ability to provide the university with financial resources, the athletic department has power. The department then uses that power to demand that the university provide more resources to the athletic department. In so doing, the athletic department gains even more power.

Strategic contingency power is related to dependency.[86] Dependency occurs when a unit or person controls something that another unit/person wants or needs. For example, in the popular TV show *The Sopranos,* all the gangsters were dependent on Tony Soprano, the mob boss. Because Tony controlled all of the mob's "businesses" (such as phone-card fraud rings and truck-hijacking operations), the gangsters were able to make a living only if Tony allowed them to operate one of these businesses.

Beyond dependency, a key source of power in the structural contingencies model is the ability to cope with uncertainty.[87] Uncertainty creates threats for the organization. Anyone who can help reduce this uncertainty by addressing key issues will gain power. In the opening case, it was implied that environmental organizations have achieved greater power and influence with businesses. There are several reasons for this, including the uncertainties of tougher environmental regulations and the growing public concern with environmental issues. Environmental organizations gain power because they can help businesses deal with these uncertainties.

Another source of power involves being irreplaceable.[88] One of the power moves made by Michael Eisner at Disney was to avoid developing a succession plan. After all, if no one was prepared to replace him, the board would be unlikely to ask him to resign.[89] In contrast, Jack Welch, the former CEO of General Electric, announced 10 years before stepping down that finding a successor was the most important job he had to do.[90]

Finally, strategic contingency power can result from controlling the decision process, either by setting parameters on the types of solutions that are acceptable or by controlling the range of alternatives to be considered.[91] For example, consider a class project in which student project teams must choose a company to analyze. If a team member states that he knows what types of projects the professor prefers and what types of projects have received good grades in the past, he can gain a great deal of control over the group's decision making regarding the type of project on which they will work.

Organizational Politics

organizational politics
Behavior that is directed toward furthering one's own self-interests without concern for the interests or well-being of others.

When conflict is present in organizations, associates are likely to engage in political behavior. Indeed, politics are a fact of life in most organizations.[92] **Organizational politics** corresponds to behavior that is directed toward furthering one's own self-interests without concern for the interests or well-being of others.[93] The goal of political behavior is to exert influence on others. One survey of top-level executives and human resource managers indicated that organizational politics are on the rise.[94] Seventy percent of survey respondents said that they had been harmed by the political behavior of others and 45 percent said they had gained power and influence by acting politically. We now discuss the conditions under which political behavior is more likely to occur.[95]

Political behavior can occur at several levels. At the individual level, it involves an associate or manager who uses politics to suit his best interests, such as an individual who attempts to take sole credit for a project that was jointly completed. Political behavior at the group level often takes place in the form of coalitions. **Coalitions** are groups whose members act in an integrated manner to actively pursue a common interest. For example, when a new CEO must be chosen for an organization, groups of shareholders may act together to influence the board of directors' choice of a particular successor. Politics can also occur at the organizational level, such as when particular organizations hire lobbyists who try to influence congresspersons' votes on issues important to that organization.

Political tactics can also be aimed at any target. *Upward political influence* refers to individual or group influence on those in a superior position, such as their manager. *Lateral politics* refers to attempts to influence targets at the same hierarchical level. Finally, *downward influence* refers to attempts to influence those lower down in the hierarchy.

What do politics look like in organizations? In other words, what do people do to engage in political behavior? A great deal of research has examined the political tactics used within or by organizations.[96] These tactics include the following:

- *Rational persuasion.* A rational persuasion tactic involves using logical arguments or factual information to persuade targets that the persuader's request will result in beneficial outcomes. For example, a sales associate who is the number-one seller may tell her boss all the benefits of switching to a purely commission-based compensation system while ignoring the potential disadvantages.

- *Consultation.* A consultation tactic requires getting the target to participate in the planning or execution of whatever the politician wants accomplished. For example, a CEO who wants to implement a specific strategy would consult associates and managers at every relevant organizational level to gain their support for her plan. These consultations, though, may be quite cynical because the CEO is not really interested in anyone's input.

- *Personal appeal.* A personal appeal tactic often focuses on the target's loyalty or affection. For example, an associate may remind targets about how he has always supported their ideas and causes before asking them to support his idea.

- *Ingratiation.* An ingratiation tactic makes the target feel good by flattering or helping him. For example, a person may tell a colleague how valuable he is before asking for his support.

- *Inspirational appeal.* An inspirational appeal tactic is used to generate the enthusiasm and support of targets by appealing to their important values and ideals. For example, to obtain a target's support for her new web-based advertising plan, a person may appeal to an ecology-conscious target by explaining how electronic advertising saves trees as opposed to advertising in newspapers and magazines.

- *Exchange.* Using an exchange tactic, a person volunteers a favor in order to gain a favor in return. This is exemplified by the old axiom, "I'll scratch your back if you'll scratch mine."

- *Coalition.* As discussed above, a coalition tactic is used when people with common interests join together to pursue their interests. For example, a coalition is represented by ethnic and minority group members who band together to promote organizational diversity.

- *Legitimizing.* A legitimizing tactic involves making a request seem legitimate or official. For example, an associate who wants to complete a project in a certain manner will try to convince targets that this is "how management wants it done."

coalition
A group whose members act together to actively pursue a common interest.

- *Pressure.* A pressure tactic involves threats, nagging, or demands as a means of influencing targets. For example, an associate who threatens to expose a target's secret if the target does not comply with her wishes is using pressure tactics.

Events from a few years ago at Morgan Stanley, the large financial services firm, illustrate the use of some of these political tactics.[97] Over the five-year period ending in April 2005, Morgan Stanley stock lost one-third of its value, and the company was performing worse than its major competitors. In March 2005, a group of eight disgruntled Morgan Stanley ex-executives initiated a process intended to oust the CEO, Philip Purcell. Because they collectively owned only 1.1 percent of Morgan Stanley shares, they needed to convince other shareholders that Purcell should go.[98] One action they took involved sending a letter to other shareholders blaming the company's poor performance solely on Purcell's leadership. Because there are likely to be many causes for an organization's poor performance, this statement can be seen as a legitimizing tactic because they state the cause of the problem with assumed expertise (substantial experience in Morgan Stanley and the industry). The ex-executives also personally courted shareholders, displaying ingratiation. Another tactic involved speaking passionately about the future of Morgan Stanley. This was done by Robert Scott, who was the ex-president and would-be-CEO of the company. Unfortunately for Scott, many investors were concerned only with short-term profit, so his inspirational appeal held little sway over investors. As one independent analyst noted, "People who hold those shares are going to want something concrete before they give up their votes"[99]; he suggested that the ex-executives use an exchange tactic instead. As of late April 2005, Purcell continued as CEO, but the walls were beginning to crumble. Many important Morgan Stanley executives and senior analysts were deserting for competitors, and a large shareholder publicly expressed support for the disgruntled former ex-executives. In June of 2005, Purcell resigned.[100]

Research has examined the issue of who is better or more successful in behaving politically. One line of research has found that personality is related to the types of political tactics people are likely to use.[101] For example, extraverts are likely to use inspirational appeals and ingratiation, whereas people high on conscientiousness are most likely to use rational appeals. Also, people have varying abilities to engage in political behavior. Some people are quite good at it, but others are more transparent in their actions, thus alerting the target to their intentions. Research has identified an individual difference known as political skill that affects the successful use of political tactics. **Political skill** is the ability to effectively understand others at work and to use this knowledge to enhance one's own objectives.[102] People with strong political skills have the following qualities:[103]

political skill
The ability to effectively understand others at work and to use this knowledge to enhance one's own objectives.

- They find it easy to imagine themselves in others' positions or take another's point of view.
- They can understand situations and determine the best response. They can adjust their behavior to fit the situation.
- They develop large networks and are known by a great many people.
- They can easily gain the cooperation of others.
- They make others feel at ease.

Individuals with strong political skills can use them to the advantage of the organization (e.g., gaining the cooperation of diverse groups). Using political skills for one's own political gain, however, can harm the organization. Therefore, political skills can be positive, but only if used to achieve the appropriate goals.

THE STRATEGIC LENS

Managing conflict and power are important to the success organizations enjoy. As we learned in the chapter opener, companies such as Kimberly-Clark, Dell, and DuPont have learned to develop useful solutions with environmental organizations, which not only has had a positive impact on the companies' performance but will also benefit society. Most strategic leaders must deal with conflict while making decisions. Some of this conflict is functional; it produces better decisions because it forces consideration of a broader range of ideas and alternatives. Much of the conflict that occurs in organizations is dysfunctional, however. If the organization's strategy is to be effectively implemented, this conflict must be resolved, or at least managed. Negotiation is one way to resolve conflict.

Some conflict can be resolved through the exercise of power. In addition, people and units that have power because they control critical contingencies or resources can add a great deal of value to the organization. Most strategic leaders have considerable power, especially legitimate power, and their use of power is necessary for the achievement of their organizations' goals. Yet, they must exercise their power appropriately, or it could produce undesired consequences. Michael Eisner exercised his power primarily for his own benefit rather than for the best interests of the organization. By exercising power in this way, he created considerable internal politics (e.g., others vying for influence and working in their own best interests) throughout the organization. As a result, Disney's performance suffered. Similarly, the exercise of political behavior at Morgan Stanley cost the organization valuable human capital. The use of political tactics often has negative consequences for the organization. However, the attributes of people with political skills are not negative. These skills, such as easily gaining cooperation from others, can be especially helpful to managers. The skills are negative only if they are used for personal gain at the expense of others and the organization. They are especially bad when exercised in a negative way by the CEO or other top managers (e.g., at Morgan Stanley) because they tend to have significant effects on the organization.

Critical Thinking Questions

1. Can you describe a situation in which conflict was functional (i.e., it had positive outcomes)? If so, in what ways was the conflict functional?

2. A strategic leader must use power in many actions that she takes. In what ways can she exercise this power to achieve positive outcomes?

3. How can knowledge of conflict, negotiations, power, and politics in organizations help you be more successful in your career? Please be specific.

What This Chapter Adds to Your Knowledge Portfolio

This chapter has explored conflict, negotiation, power, and politics in organizations. It has covered the nature and types of conflict, causes of conflict, outcomes of conflict, responses to conflict, and how organizations can manage conflict. The chapter has also discussed various sources of power. In summary, we have made the following points:

- Conflict is a process in which one party perceives that its interests are being opposed or negatively affected by another party. Conflict can be either functional or dysfunctional for organizational effectiveness. Functional conflict leads to creativity and positive change. Dysfunctional conflict detracts from the achievement of organizational goals.
- Conflict can be classified as personal, substantive, or procedural. Personal conflict corresponds to relationship issues; substantive conflict concerns the work that is to be done; and procedural conflict concerns how work is to be accomplished.
- Causes of conflict include structural arrangements (e.g., specialization), communication problems, cognitive factors (e.g., differing expectations), individual characteristics

❓back to the knowledge objectives

1. Under what circumstances can conflict be functional? When is conflict dysfunctional? Which of the basic types of conflict are likely to be dysfunctional, and why?
2. Why does conflict often develop?
3. What is conflict escalation, and what conditions make it likely? What are other possible outcomes of conflict?
4. How do people respond to conflict, and under what circumstances is each type of response most effective?
5. What can organizations do to manage conflict?
6. Describe basic negotiating strategies and the tactics most likely to accomplish those strategies.
7. Why is the exercise of power necessary for organizations to operate effectively? What are some of the ways in which people gain power in organizations?
8. Why is political behavior common in organizations? How do people go about carrying out political behavior, and what makes them successful at it?

(e.g., personality), and the history of the parties (e.g., their previous interactions).

• Conflict escalation occurs when the conflict is not resolved and becomes worse. Possible resolution outcomes of conflict include lose–lose, win–lose/lose–win, compromise, and win–win.

• Parties to a conflict can adopt one of several responses to the conflict: competing, accommodating, avoiding, compromising, or collaborating. These responses vary in the degree to which they reflect assertiveness and cooperativeness on the part of conflicting parties.

• Often negotiations are required to resolve conflict. In some cases, managers act as a third party, using both mediator and, if necessary, arbitrator roles to achieve a negotiated settlement.

• Distributive and integrative negotiation strategies focus on either winning or reaching a mutually beneficial outcome. Attitudinal restructuring focuses on developing positive feelings and relationships between negotiating parties.

• Power is the ability of those who hold it to achieve the outcomes they desire. Nothing would be accomplished in organizations if individuals did not exercise power.

• Individuals can obtain power through several means. The bases of power include legitimate power, reward power, coercive power, expert power, and referent power. Referent power can influence a wider range of behaviors than the other four types of power.

• The strategic contingencies model of power suggests that units or individuals can obtain power by being able to address the important problems or issues facing the organization. Power can be obtained by identifying the critical contingencies facing an organization, creating dependency, being able to cope with uncertainty, being irreplaceable, and controlling the decision-making process.

• Organizational politics is a fact of life in most organizations. Political behavior can be carried out through a wide range of tactics. The extent to which a politician is successful in achieving his or her own goals depends on political skill.

Key Terms

conflict, p. 411
dysfunctional conflict, p. 411
functional conflict, p. 411
personal conflict, p. 412
substantive conflict, p. 413
procedural conflict, p. 413
conflict escalation, p. 419
negotiation, p. 423

distributive bargaining, p. 424
integrative bargaining, p. 424
attitudinal structuring, p. 424
power, p. 428
legitimate power, p. 429
reward power, p. 429
coercive power, p. 429

expert power, p. 429
referent power, p. 429
strategic contingencies model of power, p. 431
organizational politics, p. 432
coalition, p. 433
political skill, p. 434

Are You Ready to Manage with Power?

All types of managerial tasks require the exercise of power. After all, power is the ability to get others to do something you want them to do. Thus, any time you find yourself in a situation in which you need to get others to do something, you need to exercise power. However, many people are uncomfortable thinking about power and its use. The next time you find yourself in a situation in which you need to influence others, consider the following questions before acting:

1. What are your goals? What are you trying to accomplish?
2. Who will be influential in allowing you to achieve your goal? Who is dependent on you for certain outcomes?
3. How do you think others will feel about what you are trying to do? Do you think there will be resistance?
4. What are the power bases of those you wish to influence? For example, do they have reward power? Referent power?
5. What are your bases of power and influence? What rewards or valued outcomes can you control? What type of power can you exert to gain more control over the situation?

The Making of the Brooklyn Bluebirds

The Brooklyn Bluebirds is a professional baseball team. Years ago, it was the best team in professional baseball. Then it hit a period of almost 10 years without a pennant. Recently, though, things have been looking up. A new owner, Trudy Mills, acquired the Bluebirds and proclaimed that she intended to make them world champions again.

Trudy quickly began to use her wealth to rebuild the team by acquiring big-name players in the free-agent draft. She also signed a manager well known for his winning ways, Marty Bellman. Marty was also known for his "fighting ways" on and off the field. However, Trudy was more concerned with his winning record.

The first year of Trudy's and Marty's tenure, the Bluebirds came in second in the division, showing it was a team to be reckoned with. Trudy acquired even more big-name players in the free-agent draft. Everyone was predicting a pennant for the Bluebirds in the coming year.

The year began with great expectations. During the first month, the Bluebirds looked unstoppable. At the end of the month, the team was in first place with a record of 20 wins and 7 losses. But then problems began. Rumors of conflict between players were reported in the sports columns. Russ Thompson, a five-year veteran and starting first baseman, publicly stated that he wanted to renegotiate his contract. (He was unhappy that Trudy had brought in so many players at much higher salaries than his.) He and his lawyer met with Trudy and the Bluebirds' general manager, but the meeting ended in disagreement. Both Russ and Trudy were angry.

The team's record began to deteriorate, and by the All-Star Game at midseason, the Bluebirds had lost as many games as they had won and were back in fourth place. Right after the All-Star break, Marty decided he had to make a move. He benched both Russ Thompson and Mickey Ponds, a well-known player with a multimillion-dollar contract. Marty called them to his office and said, "You guys are not playing baseball up to your abilities. I think you've been loafing. When you decide to start playing baseball and quit counting your money or worrying how pretty you look on television, I'll put you back in the starting lineup. Until then, you can sit on the bench and cheer for your teammates."

Russ responded hotly, "The owner won't pay me what I'm worth, and now you won't play me. I don't want to play for the Bluebirds anymore. I'm going to ask to be traded." Mickey was no happier than Russ. "I'm going to Trudy. You can't bench me. You're the biggest jerk I've ever played for!"

At that, both players left his office, got dressed, and left the ballpark. Later, a few minutes before game time, Marty received a phone call in his office. It was Trudy, and she was upset. "Why did you bench Russ and Mickey? I hired you to manage the team, not create more problems. They're two of our best players, and the customers pay to see them play. I want you to apologize to them and put them back in the starting lineup."

Marty was not known for his diplomacy. "You hired me to manage, and that's just what I'm doing. Keep your nose out of my business. You may own the team, but I manage it. Russ and Mickey will stay benched until I say otherwise!" With that, Marty slammed the receiver down and headed for the field to get the game under way.

Discussion Questions

1. Describe the types of conflict that seem to exist within the Bluebirds organization. What are the causes?
2. Is the conflict functional, dysfunctional, or both? Explain.
3. Assume that Trudy has hired you as a consultant to help her resolve the conflict. Describe the steps that you would take.

---

team exercise

Managing Conflict

The purpose of this exercise is to develop a better understanding of the conflict-management process by examining three different conflict situations.

Procedure

1. With the aid of the instructor, the class will be divided into four- or five-person teams.
2. The teams should read each case and determine:
   a. Which conflict response should be used to manage the conflict (this may require starting with one style and moving to others as the situation changes).
   b. Which negotiation tactics should be used to resolve the conflict.
3. Each team should appoint a leader to explain its results to the class.
4. The instructor should call on the teams to explain the conflict response and negotiation tactics recommended. The information should be recorded on a board or flipchart for comparisons. The situations should be discussed one at a time.
5. The instructor will lead a general discussion regarding the application of conflict responses and negotiation tactics.

This exercise usually requires about 25 minutes for case analyses and another 20 to 30 minutes (depending on the number of teams) for class discussion.

Case Incident 1

You are James Whittington, manager of internal auditing. The nature of your position and of your unit's work often put you in conflict with managers of other units. Most of your audits are supportive of the actions taken in the audited units, although some are not. Nonetheless, the managers seem to resent what they consider an intrusion on their authority when the audits are conducted. You have come to accept this resentment as a part of your job, although you would prefer that it didn't occur. One case has been a particular problem. Bill Wilson, manager of compensation in the human resource department, has created problems every time your auditors have worked in his department. He has continually tried to hold back information necessary for the audit. Unfortunately, during the last year and a half, you have had to audit activities in his department several times.

Your department now has been assigned to audit the incentive bonus calculations for executives made by Bill's department. Bill was irate when he discovered that you were again going to audit his employees' work. When he found out about it, he called your office and left a message for you not to send your employees down, because he was not going to allow them access to the information. You are now trying to decide how to respond.

Case Incident 2

Irene Wilson is manager of corporate engineering and has a staff of 17 professional engineers. The group is project-oriented and thus must be flexible in structure and operation. Irene likes to hire only experienced engineers, preferably with division experience in the firm. However, during the past several years, the market for engineers has been highly competitive. Owing to shortages of experienced personnel, Irene has had to hire a few young engineers right after college graduation.

Robert Miller was one of those young engineers. Robert was considered a good recruit, but his lack of experience and arrogance have created some problems.

Irene has tried to work with him to help him gain the needed experience but has not yet discussed his arrogant attitude with him.

Last week, Robert got into an argument with several engineers from the International Division with whom he was working on a project. One of them called Irene, and she met with Robert and discussed it with him. Irene thought Robert would do better after their discussion. However, a few minutes ago, Irene received a call from the project manager, who was very angry. He and Robert had just had a shouting match, and he demanded that Robert be taken off the project. Irene did not commit to anything but said she would call him back. When Irene confronted Robert about the phone call that she had just received, he turned his anger on her. They also had an argument. Irene believes Robert has potential and does not want to lose him, but he has to overcome his problems.

Case Incident 3

Steve Bassett, a supervisor in the marketing research department, is scheduled to attend a meeting of the budget committee this afternoon at 1:30. Sarah McDonald, supervisor of budget analysis, is also a member of the committee. It has been a bad day for Steve; he and his wife argued about money as he left the house, one of his key employees called in sick, and the company's intranet went down at 9:00 this morning. Steve is not fond of being a member of this committee and really does not care to waste his valuable time listening to Sarah today. (He thinks that Sarah talks too much.)

Steve arrives at Sarah's office at 1:38 P.M. After glancing at her watch and offering a few harmless pleasantries, Sarah begins her assessment of the budget committee's agenda. Although not exciting, everything seems to be all right until she mentions how poorly Steve's unit has been responding to the budgeting department's requests for information. Steve becomes visibly irritated and tells Sarah that nothing good has ever come out of these committee meetings and that she places entirely too much emphasis on them. Sarah responds by noting that Steve has not followed company policy about preparing budget information. These failures, she reasons, are the causes of his inability to achieve positive results. Having heard this comment, Steve states, in a loud voice, that whoever designed the company's policy did not know a thing about the budgeting process.

Sarah realizes that she and Steve are in disagreement and that she should try to deal with it. How, she wonders, should she deal with Steve?

Endnotes

1. Dechant, K., & Altman, B. 1994. Environmental leadership: From compliance to competitive advantage. *Academy of Management Executive*, 8: 7–27; Porter, M.E., & Kramer, M.R., 2006. The link between competitive advantage and corporate social responsibility. *Harvard Business Review*, 84 (12): 78–92.
2. Porter & Kramer, The link between competitive advantage and corporate social responsibility.
3. Shatwell, J. 2007. The net loss of overfishing. At http:www.conservation.org/xp/frontlines/partners/06060601.xml.
4. Grayson, D., & Hodges, A. 2004. *Corporate social opportunity*. Sheffield, United Kingdom: Greenleaf.
5. Chatterji, A., & Levine, D. 2006. Breaking down the wall of codes: Evaluating non-financial performance measurement. *California Management Review*, 48(2): 29–51.

6. Orlitzky, F., Schmidt, F., & Rynes, S. 2003. Corporate social and financial performance: A meta-analysis. *Organizational Studies,* 24: 403–411.

7. Collier, J., & Esteban, R. 2007. Corporate social responsibility and employee commitment. *Business Ethics,* 16 (1): 12–31.

8. Turban, D.B., & Greening, D.W. 1997. Corporate social performance and organizational attractiveness to perspective employees. *Academy of Management Journal,* 40: 848–868.

9. Wall, J.A., Jr., & Callister, R.R. 1995. Conflict and its management. *Journal of Management,* 21: 515–558.

10. Bromiley, P. 1990. On the use of finance theory in strategic management. In P. Shrivastava and R. Lamb (Eds.), *Advances in strategic management (Vol. 6).* Greenwich, CT: JAI Press, pp. 71–98; Nixon, R.D., Hitt, M.A., Lee, H., & Jeong, E. 2004. Market reactions to announcements of corporate downsizing actions and implementation strategies. *Strategic Management Journal,* 25: 1121–1129; Orlitzky, Schmidt, & Rynes, Corporate social and financial performance.

11. Porter, & Kramer, The link between competitive advantage and corporate social responsibility.

12. Lippitt, G.L. 1982. Managing conflict in today's organizations. *Training and Development Journal,* 36: 66–72, 74.

13. Pelled, L.H. 1996. Demographic diversity, conflict, and work group outcomes: An intervening process theory. *Organizational Science,* 6: 615–631; Tjosvold, D. 1991. Rights and responsibilities of dissent: Cooperative conflict. *Employee Responsibilities and Rights Journal,* 4: 13–23.

14. Herbert, T.T. 1977. Improving executive decisions by formalizing dissent: The corporate devil's advocate. *Academy of Management Review,* 2: 662–667.

15. Eisenhardt, K., & Schoonhoven, C. 1990. Organizational growth: Linking founding team, strategy, environment, and growth among U.S. semiconductor ventures: 1978–1988. *Administrative Science Quarterly,* 35: 504–529.

16. Jehn, K.A. 1997. A qualitative analysis of conflict types and dimensions in organizational groups. *Administrative Science Quarterly,* 42: 530–557; Jehn, K.A., Greer, L., Levine, S., & Szulanski, G. 2008. The effects of conflict types, dimensions, and emergent states on group dynamics. *Group Decision and Negotiation,* 17: 465–495.

17. Ibid.

18. Jehn, K.A., & Mannix, E.A. 2001. The dynamic nature of conflict: A longitudinal study of intragroup conflict and group performance. *Academy of Management Journal,* 44: 238–251; Tekleab, A.G., Quigley, N.R., Tesluk, P.E. 2009. A longitudinal study of team conflict, conflict management, cohesion, and team effectiveness. *Group & Organizational Management,* 34: 170-205.

19. Deutsch, M. 1969. Conflicts: Productive and destructive. *Journal of Social Issues,* 25: 7–41.

20. Jehn, A qualitative analysis of conflict types and dimensions in organizational groups; Jehn, Greer, Levine, & Szulanski, The effects of conflict types, dimensions, and emergent states on group dynamics.

21. Smolowitz, I. 1998. Organizational fratricide: The roadblock to maximum performance. *Business Forum,* 23: 45–46.

22. Amason, A.C. 1996. Distinguishing the effects of functional and dysfunctional conflict on strategic decision making: Resolving a paradox for top management teams. *Academy of Management Journal,* 39: 123–148; Eisenhardt, & Schoonhoven, Organizational growth; Jehn, K.A. 1995. A multimethod examination of the benefits and detriments of intragroup conflict. *Administrative Science Quarterly,* 40: 256–282; Schweiger, D., Sandberg, W., & Rechner, P. 1989. Experiential effects of dialectical inquiry, devil's advocacy, and consensus approaches to strategic decision making. *Academy of Management Journal,* 29: 745–772; Tjosvold, D. 1991. Rights and responsibilities of dissent: Cooperative conflict. *Employee Responsibilities and Rights Journal,* 4: 13–23. For a different but contested view, see De Dreu, C.K.W., & Weingart, L.R. 2003. Task versus relationship conflict, team performance, and team member satisfaction. *Journal of Applied Psychology,* 88: 741–749.

23. Jehn, A qualitative analysis of conflict types and dimensions in organizational groups; Jehn, Greer, Levine, & Szulanski, The effects of conflict types, dimensions, and emergent states on group dynamics.

24. Jehn, K.A., Northcraft, G., & Neale, M. 1999. Why differences make a difference: A field study of diversity, conflict, and performance in workgroups. *Administrative Science Quarterly,* 44: 741–763.

25. Jones, G.R. 2009. *Organizational theory, design, and change.* Upper Saddle River, NJ: Prentice Hall; Lawrence, P.R., & Lorsch, J.W. 1967. *Organization and environment: Managing differentiation and integration.* Boston: Harvard University Press.

26. Morgan, C.P., & Hitt, M.A. 1977. Validity and factor structure of House—Rizzo's effectiveness scales. *Academy of Management,* 20: 165–169; Hitt, M.A., & Morgan, C.P. 1977. Organizational climate as a predictor of organizational practices. *Psychological Reports,* 40: 1191–1199.

27. Heneman, H.G. III, & Judge, T.A. 2003. *Staffing organizations.* Boston: McGraw-Hill/Irwin.

28. Wall & Callister, Conflict and its management.

29. Moline, A. 2001. Conflict in the work place. *Plants, Sites, and Parks,* 28: 50–52.

30. Ibid.

31. Filley, A.C. 1975. Interpersonal *conflict resolution.* Glenview, IL: Scott Foresman, p. 10.

32. Putnam, L.L., & Poole, M.S. 1987. Conflict and negotiation. In F.M. Jablin, L.L. Putnam, K.H. Roberts, & L.W. Porter (Eds.), *Handbook of organizational communication: An interdisciplinary perspective.* Newbury Park, CA: Sage, pp. 549–599.

33. Shafer, W.E., Park, L.J., & Liao, W.M. 2002. Professionalism, organizational-professional conflict, and work outcomes: A study of certified accountants. *Accounting, Auditing, and Accountability Journal,* 15: 46–68.

34. Kaplowitz, N. 1990. National self-images, perception of enemies, and conflict strategies: Psychopolitical dimensions of international relations. *Political Psychology,* 11: 39–81.

35. Wall, & Callister, Conflict and its management.

36. Kahn, R.L., & Byosiere, P. 1992. Stress in organizations. In M.D. Dunnette, & L.M. Hough (Eds.), *Handbook of industrial and organizational psychology (Vol. 3).* Palo Alto, CA: Consulting Psychologists Press, pp. 571–650.

37. Baron, R.A. 1990. Countering the effects of destructive criticism: The relative efficacy of four interventions. *Journal of Applied Psychology,* 75: 235–245.

38. Yamagishi, T. 1986. The provision of a sanctioning system as a public good. *Journal of Personality and Social Psychology,* 50: 110–116.

39. De Dreu, C.K.W., Geibels, E., & Van de Vliert, E. 1998. Social motives and trust in integrative negotiation: The disruptive effects of punitive capability. *Journal of Applied Psychology,* 83: 408–422.

40. Van Kleef, G.A., & De Dreu, C.K.W. 2006. Supplication and appeasement in conflict and negotiation: The interpersonal effects of disappointment, worry, guilt, and regret. *Journal of Personality and Social Psychology,* 91: 124–142.

41. Rousseau, D.M., Sitkin, S.B., Burt, R.S., & Camerer, C. 1998. Not so different after all: A cross-discipline view of trust. *Academy of Management Review,* 23: 393–404.

42. Augsberger, D.W. 1992. Conflict *mediation across cultures: Pathways and patterns.* Louisville, KY: Westminster/John Knox.

43. Leung, K. 1995. Negotiation and reward allocations across cultures. In P.C. Earley, & M. Erez (Eds.), *New perspectives on industrial/organizational psychology.* San Francisco: Jossey-Bass, pp. 640–675.

44. Fu, J.H., Morris, M.W., Lee, S., Chao, M., Chiu, C., & Hong, Y. 2007. Epistemic motives and cultural conformity: Need for closure, culture, and context as determinants of conflict judgments. *Journal of Personality and Social Psychology,* 92: 191–207.

45. Wall, & Callister, Conflict and its management.

46. Ibid.

47. Staw, B., Sandelands, L., & Dutton, J. 1981. Threat-rigidity effects in organizational behavior: A multi-level analysis. *Administrative Science Quarterly,* 26: 501–524.

48. Ibid.

49. Peterson, R.S., & Behfar, K.J. 2003. The dynamic relationship between performance feedback, trust and conflict in groups: A longitudinal study. *Organizational Behavior and Human Decision Processes,* 92: 102–112.

50. Wall, & Callister, Conflict and its management.

51. O'Connor, K.M., Arnold, J.A., & Burris, E.R. 2005. Negotiators' bargaining histories and their effects on future negotiation performance. *Journal of Applied Psychology,* 90: 350–362.

52. Pruitt, D.G., & Rubin, J.Z. 1986. *Social conflict: Escalation, stalemate, and settlement.* New York: McGraw-Hill.

53. Deutsch, M. 1990. Sixty years of conflict. *International Journal of Conflict Management,* 1: 237–263.

54. Fisher, R.J. 1990. *The social psychology of intergroup and international conflict resolution.* New York: Springer-Verlag.

55. Ember, C.R., & Ember, M. 1994. War, socialization, and interpersonal violence: A cross-cultural study. *Journal of Conflict Resolution,* 38: 620–646.

56. Pruitt, D.G., & Carnevale, P.J. 1993. *Negotiation in social conflict.* Pacific Grove, CA: Brooks/Cole.

57. Ibid.

58. Morrill, C., & Thomas, C.K. 1992. Organizational conflict management as disputing process. *Human Communication Research,* 18: 400–428.

59. Retzinger, S.M. 1991. Shame, anger, and conflict: Case study of emotional violence. *Journal of Family Violence,* 6: 37–59.

60. Brockner, J., Nathanson, S., Friend, A., Harbeck, J., Samuelson, C., Houser, R., Bazerman, M.H., & Rubin, J.Z. 1984. The role of modeling processes in the "knee deep in the big muddy"

61. phenomenon. *Organizational Behavior and Human Performance,* 33: 77–99.

61. Helyar, J. 2002. United We Fall. *Fortune,* 145 (4): 90–96; Skertic, M. 2004. United Asks Cuts in Pay of Up to 18%. *Chicago Tribune,* Nov. 6, at http://www.chicagotribune.com/classified/jobs/promo/chi-0411060211nov06,0,973948,print.stor.

62. Thomas, K.W. 1976. Conflict and conflict management. In M. Dunnette (Ed.), *Handbook of industrial and organizational psychology.* Chicago: Rand McNally, pp. 889–935.

63. Thomas, K.W. 1992. Conflict and negotiation processes. In M.D. Dunnette, & L.M. Hough (Eds.), *Handbook of industrial and organizational psychology (Vol. 3).* Palo Alto, CA: Consulting Psychologists Press, pp. 651–717.

64. Buller, P.F., Kohls, J.J., & Anderson, K.S. 2000. When ethics collide: Managing conflict across cultures. *Organizational Dynamics,* 28: 52–66.

65. Ibid.

66. Lippitt, G.L. 1982. Managing conflict in today's organizations. *Training and Development Journal,* 36: 66–72, 74.

67. Lewicki, R.J., Saunders, D.M., & Barry, B. 2009. *Negotiation* (6th ed.). Boston: McGraw-Hill/Irwin.

68. Walton, R.E., & McKersie, R.B. 1965. *A behavioral theory of labor negotiations.* New York: McGraw-Hill.

69. Ibid.

70. Cormack, G.W. 2005. *Negotiation skills for board professionals.* Mill Creek, WA: CSE Group; Dietmeyer, B. *Negotiation: A breakthrough four-step process for effective business negotiation.* Chicago: Dearborn Trade; Sperber, P. 1983. *Fail-safe business negotiating.* Englewood Cliffs, NJ: Prentice Hall; Thompson, L.L. 2008. *The mind and heart of the negotiator* (4th ed.). Upper Saddle River, NJ: Prentice Hall.

71. Somech, A., & Drach-Zahavy, A. 2002. Relative power and influence strategy: The effects of agent-target organizational power on superiors' choices of influence strategies. *Journal of Organizational Behavior,* 23: 167–181.

72. Dahl, R.A. 1957. The concept of power. *Behavioral Science,* 2: 201–215.

73. Salancik, G.R., & Pfeffer, J. 1977. Who gets power and how they hold on to it: A strategic contingency model of power. *Organizational Dynamics,* 5: 3–21.

74. Dahl, The concept of power.

75. Pfeffer, J. 1992. Understanding power in organizations. *California Management Review,* 34: 29–50.

76. Salancik & Pfeffer, Who gets power and how they hold on to it.

77. French, J.R.P., & Raven, B. 1959. The bases of social power. In D. Cartwright (Ed.), *Studies in social power.* Ann Arbor: University of Michigan Institute for Social Research, pp. 160–167.

78. Eggen, D. 2007. Deputy attorney general defends prosecutor firings. *Washington Post,* February 7, at http://washintonpost.com/wp-dyn/content/article/2007/02/06/AR2007020600732.htm.

79. Kurland, N.B., & Pelled, L.H. 2000. Passing the word: Toward a model of gossip and power in the workplace. *Academy of Management Review,* 25: 428–438.

80. Bacharach, S.B., & Lawler, E.J. 1980. *Power and politics in organizations.* San Francisco: Jossey-Bass.

81. Finkelstein, S. 1992. Power in top management teams: Dimensions, measurement, and validation. *Academy of Management Journal,* 35: 505–539.

82. French & Raven, The bases of social power.

83. Crawford, K. 2004. Eisner vs. Ovitz: This time in court, *CNN Money,* Oct 15, at http://money.cnn.com/2004/10/15/news/fortune500/ovitz; Levine, G. 2004. Eisner: Disney, Miramax talks staggered, *Forbes,* May 12, at http://www.forbes.com/2004/05/12/0512autofacescan03.html; McCarthy, M. 2004. Eisner foes keep up the pressure, *USA Today,* March 16, at usatoday.com/money/media/2004-03-16-eisner_x.htm; McCarthy, M. 2004. Disney strips chairmanship from Eisner, *USA Today,* March 3, at http://www.usatoday.com/money/media/2004-03-03disney-shareholder-meeting-x.htm; Orwall, B. 2004. Behind the scenes at Eisner's Disney: Beleaguered CEO, Ovitz, we're headed in opposite directions from the start, *Los Angeles Daily News,* November 23, at http://www.dailynews.com/cda/article/print/0,1674,200%257E20950%257E2554402,00.html; Smith, E., & Miller, S. 2009. Remembrances: A Namesake Who Reanimated Disney. *Wall Street Journal,* Dec. 17: A.22; Surowiecki, J. 2004. Good grooming, *The New Yorker,* October 4, at http://www.newyorker.com/talk/content/?011004ta_talk_surowiecki.

84. Salancik & Pfeffer. Who gets power and how they hold on to it.

85. Hillman, A.J., & Dalziel, T. 2003. Boards of directors and firm performance: Integrating agency and resource dependence perspectives. *Academy of Management Review,* 28: 383–396.

86. Pfeffer, J. 1981. *Power in organizations.* Marshfield, MA: Pitman Publishing.

87. Ibid.

88. Ibid.

89. Surowiecki, J. 2004. Good grooming. *The New Yorker,* October 4, at http://www.newyorker.com/talk/content/?011004ta_ talk_surowiecki.

90. Ibid.

91. Pfeffer, *Power in organizations.*

92. Mintzberg, H. 1985. The organization as political arena. *Journal of Management Studies,* 22: 133–154.

93. Kacmar, K.M., & Baron, R.A. 1999. Organizational politics: The state of the field, links to related processes, and an agenda for future research. In G.R. Ferris (Ed.), *Research in personnel and human resource management (Vol. 17).* Stamford, CT: JAI Press, pp. 1–39; Zivnuska, S., Kacmar, K.M., Witt, L.A., Carlson, D.S., & Bratton, V.K. 2004. Interactive effects of impression management and organizational politics on job performance. *Journal of Organizational Behavior,* 25: 627–640.

94. Anonymous. 2002. Politics at work: Backstabbing, stolen ideas, scapegoats. *Director,* 56: 74–80.

95. Poon, J.M.L. 2003. Situational antecedents and outcomes of organizational politics perceptions. *Journal of Managerial Psychology,* 18: 138–155.

96. Yukl, G., Kim, H., & Falbe, C.M. 1996. Antecedents of influence outcomes. *Journal of Applied Psychology,* 81: 309–317.

97. Popper, M. 2004. Morgan Stanley's board must end inaction, investor Matrix says. *Bloomberg.com,* April 21, at www.bloomberg.com/apps/news?pid=10000103&sid=aluJZFE02LOA&refer=us.

98. Martinez, M.J. 2005. Uphill fight for Morgan Stanley dissidents. *Associated Press,* April 8, at www.biz.yahoo.com/ap/0504080morgan_stanley.html.

99. Ibid.

100. Davis, A. 2005. Mack Takes Step to Clean House: Morgan Stanley CEO Bids Adieu to Crawford, but Move Will Cost Firm's Shareholders $32 Million. *Wall Street Journal,* July 12: C.1

101. Cable, D.M., & Judge, T.A. 2003. Managers' upward influence tactic strategies: The role of manager personality and supervisor leadership style. *Journal of Organizational Behavior,* 24: 197–214.

102. Ahearn, K.K., Ferris, G.R., Hochwater, W.A., Douglas, C., & Ammeter, A.P. 2004. Leader political skill and team performance. *Journal of Management,* 30: 309–327.

103. Ferris, G.R., Treadway, D.C., Kolodinsky, R.W., Hochwater, W.A., Kacmar, C.J., Douglas, C., & Frink, D.D. 2005. Development and validation of the political skill inventory. *Journal of Management,* 31: 126–152.

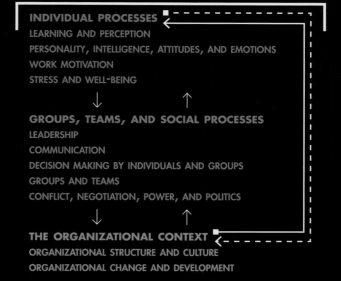

INDIVIDUAL PROCESSES
LEARNING AND PERCEPTION
PERSONALITY, INTELLIGENCE, ATTITUDES, AND EMOTIONS
WORK MOTIVATION
STRESS AND WELL-BEING

↓   ↑

GROUPS, TEAMS, AND SOCIAL PROCESSES
LEADERSHIP
COMMUNICATION
DECISION MAKING BY INDIVIDUALS AND GROUPS
GROUPS AND TEAMS
CONFLICT, NEGOTIATION, POWER, AND POLITICS

↓   ↑

THE ORGANIZATIONAL CONTEXT
ORGANIZATIONAL STRUCTURE AND CULTURE
ORGANIZATIONAL CHANGE AND DEVELOPMENT

PART **4**

the organizational context

In the final part of the book, we examine the organizational context for the individual and group processes discussed in Parts II and III. Thus, we began the book with a chapter that presented the strategic lens for managing behavior in organizations, and we end with two chapters that explain the organizational processes and context for that behavior.

In Chapter 13, we discuss structure and organizational culture. The organization's structure can have a significant effect on behavior. Organizational culture is based on shared values in the organization. Therefore, the fit between individual values and organizational values is important. Organizational

culture can significantly influence associates' and managers' behavior. It can affect individuals' motivation and attitudes as well as team processes such as leadership and conflict.

Chapter 14, the last chapter in the book, focuses on organizational change and development. Most organizations exist in dynamic environments requiring them to change regularly in order to adapt to environmental changes. Shifting environments also require that organizations develop flexibility in their strategies. Being flexible, however, necessitates taking an approach to change that associates and managers in the organization will accept. Most people dislike

and resist change because of the uncertainty involved. This chapter explains how managers can develop a change process that unfreezes associates' attitudes and allows them to accept change. The chapter also discusses organization development, a form of internal consulting aimed at improving communication, problem solving, and learning in the organization. The problem-solving process involves diagnosing the problem, prescribing interventions, and monitoring progress. The change processes and problem-resolution processes discussed in this chapter draw on many of the concepts explored in the previous chapters of this book.

organizational structure and culture

exploring behavior in action

Growth and Structure Provide an Integrated Portfolio of Services at FedEx

Many companies have goals designed to achieve growth and diversification of the markets they serve, both product and geographical. These long-term goals are often maintained even during economic recessions such as that experienced at the end of the first decade of the twenty-first century. Growth can be achieved by developing new products and services internally or by acquiring other organizations. Growth by external acquisition has been popular because it is often a faster and less risky means of achieving the desired growth. FedEx's corporate strategy involved both of these approaches.

In 1971, Federal Express Corporation was founded in Little Rock, Arkansas. Early in its history, FedEx used internal development to achieve rapid growth. In 1983, Federal Express achieved $1 billion in revenue; it made its first acquisition in 1984, Gelco Express International, launching its operations in the Asia Pacific region. Five years later, Federal Express purchased Flying Tigers to expand its international presence. That same year, Roberts Express (now FedEx Custom Critical) began providing services to Europe. In 1995, FedEx acquired air routes from Evergreen International with authority to serve China and opened an Asia Pacific Hub in Subic Bay, Philippines, launching the FedEx AsiaOne Network. By 1996, FedEx Ground achieved 100 percent coverage in North America. In 1998, FedEx acquired Caliber Systems, Inc. and created FDX Corporation. This series of acquisitions made FedEx a $16 billion transportation powerhouse. But the acquisitions and growth continued. In 1999, Federal Express Corporation acquired Caribbean Transportation Services. In January 2000, FDX Corporation was renamed

❓ knowledge objectives

After reading this chapter, you should be able to:

1. Define key elements of organizational structure, including both structural and structuring dimensions.
2. Explain how corporate and business strategies relate to structure.
3. Explain how environment, technology, and size relate to structure.
4. Define organizational culture, and discuss the competing values cultural framework.
5. Discuss socialization.
6. Describe cultural audits and subcultures.
7. Explain the importance of a fit between individual values and organizational culture.

446

FedEx Corporation. Also in 2000, FedEx Trade Networks was created with the acquisitions of Tower Group International and WorldTariff.

In 2001, FedEx acquired American Freightways; in 2004, it acquired Kinko's for $2.4 billion and also Parcel Direct; and it completed its acquisitions in 2007, with its purchase of Chinese shipping partner DTW Group in order to obtain more control over and access to services in secondary Chinese cities.

As suggested by the large list of acquisitions, FedEx's strategy to achieve growth was realized. It also diversified the company's portfolio of services. For example, it acquired Kinko's to expand the company's retail services through the 1,200-plus Kinko's stores.

©AP/Wide World Photos

In addition, by acquiring Parcel Direct, FedEx was able to expand services for customers in the e-tail and catalog segments. All of the companies acquired by FedEx Corp were carefully selected to ensure a corporate culture with a positive service-oriented spirit, thereby providing a good fit with FedEx. For example, in 2009, FedEx continued to be listed among *Fortune*'s 100 Best Companies to Work For and in the top ten of *Fortune*'s World's Most Admired Companies.

Because of the growth and additional services, FedEx adopted a multidivisional structure. FedEx Corporation provides strategic direction and consolidated financial reporting for the operating companies that are collectively under the FedEx name worldwide (FedEx Express, FedEx Ground, FedEx Freight, FedEx Kinko's Office and Print Services, FedEx Custom Critical, FedEx Trade Networks, and FedEx Services). Because of the growth in the size and scope of the company, FedEx delegated significant authority to the divisions. Together, the various divisions are FedEx, but independently, each division offers flexible, specialized services that represent an array of supply chain, transportation, and business and related information services. Operating independently, each FedEx company manages its own specialized network of services. The FedEx Corporation acts as the hub, allowing its decentralized divisions to work together worldwide. FedEx

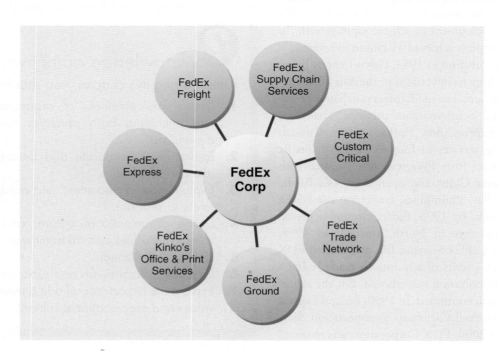

coordinates the activities of operating divisions in ways that integrate them to provide customers a unique and powerful portfolio of services globally.

Along with its competitive array of services, FedEx remains innovative and sensitive to its environment. For example, in 2010, it implemented a new service, Sense-aware, a sensor-enabled device that provides real-time data on the location and other important information (e.g., temperature) of a package. The device allows FedEx and

customers to monitor the condition and travel of highly important and sensitive packages. In addition, FedEx also has initiatives to promote a sustainable environment. In 2009, for example, it announced plans to install the largest rooftop solar power system in the United States at its major distribution facility in New Jersey. Therefore, despite an exceptionally difficult global economy in 2009, two analysts predicted that FedEx would "soar like an eagle" in 2010.

Sources: Associated Press. 2009. "FedEx Meets Estimates but Gives Cautious Forecast," *New York Times,* Dec. 17, www.nytimes.com; Paul Rubillo & Tom Reese. 2009. "FedEx Flies Like an Eagle," *Forbes,* Dec. 8, www.forbes.com; Cliff Kuang. 2009. "If the Delivery Guy Drops Your Package, Senseaware Updates You Online," *Fast Company,* Nov. 24, at http://www.fastcompany.com; Stephanie N. Metha. 2009. "Smart Phones. Smart networks. Smart Packages?" *Fortune,* Nov.17, at http://www.fortune.com; Ariel Schwartz. 2009. "FedEx to Build Largest Rooftop Solar Array in U.S.," *Fast Company,* July 30, at http://www.fastcompany.com; Mitch Jackson. 2009. "Is the Overnight Envelope Anti-green?" *Money,* May 1, at http://www.cnnmoney.com; "Best Big Companies to Work for," *Money,* April 27, 2009, www.cnnmoney.com; Associated Press. 2007. "FedEx Completes Acquisition of DTW Group," *BusinessWeek,* Feb. 28, at http://www.businessweek.com; Sarah Murray. 2006. "Putting the House in Order," *Financial Times,* Nov. 8, at http://www.ft.com; Dean Foust. 2006. "Taking Off Like 'a Rocket Ship,'" *BusinessWeek,* Apr. 3, at http://www.businessweek.com; 2007. "About FedEx," *FedEx Homepage,* at http://www.fedex.com.

organizational structure
Work roles and authority relationships that influence behavior in an organization.

organizational culture
The values shared by associates and managers in an organization.

the strategic importance of Organizational Structure and Culture

When considering the implementation of organizational strategies, we often focus on the roles of strong leaders, talented managers and associates, and effective processes such as communication and conflict management. Although all these factors are important, as emphasized in prior chapters, they provide only part of the support to implement an organization's strategy. The organization's structure and culture also play crucial roles in strategy implementation.

Organizational structure refers to the formal system of work roles and authority relationships that govern how associates and managers interact with one another.[1] To properly implement a strategy, an organization must build a structure ensuring that formal and informal activities and initiatives support strategic goals. Structure influences communication patterns among individuals and groups and the degree

to which they have the discretion to be innovative. If, for example, a strategy calls for rapid responses in several dynamic and different markets, it is important to create divisions around those markets and delegate authority to managers in those divisions so that they can act when necessary, similar to the decentralized divisions created by FedEx as described in the *Exploring Behavior in Action*. Firms that fail to design and maintain effective structures experience problems. FedEx also coordinates activities across its divisions in order to achieve synergies among its various services and geographical markets. Doing this enhances FedEx's performance.

An appropriate culture is also required to implement strategy effectively and achieve strong overall performance. **Organizational culture** involves shared values and norms that

influence behavior.[2] It is a powerful force in organizations. For example, Google's organizational culture has been touted as one reason for its phenomenal success. We examine the specific characteristics of Google's culture later in this chapter.

As one of the top companies to work for and one of the most admired companies in the world, FedEx is known to have a special culture as well. FedEx grew rapidly early in its existence by internally expanding its services and especially by reaching new geographical markets. It then began to expand into international markets, partly by acquisition (e.g., its acquisition of Flying Tigers). It also used acquisitions to diversify the services that it offered. An example of this expansion was the acquisition of Kinko's with its 1,200 retail outlets across the United States to support the diversification strategy and divisional structure. Over time, FedEx had to adopt a new structure in order to manage its diversified portfolio of services and geographical markets. The new divisional structure granted significant autonomy to each operating business (division) with corporate coordination across the divisions to achieve synergy in offering customers integrated services. FedEx was careful in its acquisitions to ensure that the acquired firms fit well with its positive customer-oriented culture. Both organizational structure and culture influence the behavior of managers and associates and therefore play a critical role in the success of an organization's strategy and its overall organizational performance.

In this chapter, we explore issues related to structure and culture. We open with a discussion of the fundamental elements of structure, emphasizing how they influence the behavior and attitudes of managers and associates. Next, we discuss the link between strategy and structure as well as the structural implications of environmental characteristics, internal technology, and organizational size. In the second part of the chapter, we focus on culture. Cultural topics include the competing values model of culture, socialization, cultural audits, and subcultures. We close with a discussion of person–organization fit.

Fundamental Elements of Organizational Structure

structural characteristics
The tangible, physical properties that determine the basic shape and appearance of an organization's hierarchy.

hierarchy
The reporting relationships depicted in an organization chart.

structuring characteristics
The policies and approaches used to directly prescribe the behavior of managers and associates.

height
The number of hierarchical levels in an organization, from the CEO to the lower-level associates.

span of control
The number of individuals a manager directly oversees.

The structure of an organization can be described in two different but related ways. First, **structural characteristics** refer to the tangible, physical properties that determine the basic shape and appearance of an organization's hierarchy,[3] where **hierarchy** is defined in terms of the reporting relationships depicted in an organization chart. Essentially, an organization's structure is a blueprint of the reporting relationships, distribution of authority, and decision making in the organization.[4] These characteristics influence behavior, but their effects are sometimes subtle. Second, **structuring characteristics** refer to policies and approaches used to directly prescribe the behavior of managers and associates.[5]

Structural Characteristics

Structural characteristics, as mentioned, relate to the basic shape and appearance of an organization's hierarchy. The shape of a hierarchy is determined by its height, spans of control, and type of departmentalization.

Height refers to the number of levels in the organization, from the CEO to the lower-level associates. Tall hierarchies often create communication problems, as information moving up and down the hierarchy can be slowed and distorted as it passes through many different levels.[6] Managers and associates can be unclear on appropriate actions and behaviors as decisions are delayed and faulty information is disseminated, causing lower satisfaction and commitment. Tall hierarchies also are more expensive, as they have more levels of managers.[7]

A manager's **span of control** is to the number of individuals who report directly to her. A broad span of control is possible when a manager can effectively handle many individuals, as is the case when associates have the skills and motivation they need to complete their tasks autonomously.

Broad spans have advantages for an organization. First, they result in shorter hierarchies (see Exhibit 13-1), thereby avoiding communication and expense problems.[8] Second, they promote high-involvement management because managers have difficulty micromanaging people when there are larger numbers of them. Broad spans allow for more initiative by associates.[9] In making employment decisions, many individuals take these realities into consideration.

Spans of control can be too broad, however. When a manager has too many direct reports, she cannot engage in important coaching and development activities. When tasks are more complex and the direct reports more interdependent, a manager often requires a relatively narrow span of control to be effective. It has been argued that a CEO's span of control should not exceed six people because of the complexity and interdependency of work done by direct reports at this level.[10]

Many older companies have removed layers of management and increased spans of control in recent years, whereas younger companies, such as AES, avoided unnecessary layers and overly narrow spans from the beginning.[11] Because of their profound effects on behavior and attitudes among associates and managers, spans of control are of concern to many organizations such as PricewaterhouseCoopers (PwC).[12] Through their Saratoga Institute, managers and consultants at PwC track spans of control in various industries and use the resulting insights in various reports and consulting engagements. They reported a few years ago that the median span for all managers in all industries was seven. An earlier *Wall Street Journal* report indicated an average span of nine. Yet, the Saratoga Institute reports that managerial spans of control have been increasing in recent years due to reductions in the number of managers in the recent global economic recession.[13]

Departmentalization describes the approach used in grouping resources within an organization. As highlighted in the opening case, one of the two basic options is the functional form of departmentalization, in which resources related to a particular functional area are grouped together (see Exhibit 13-2). The functional form provides several potential advantages, including deep specialized knowledge in each functional area (because functions are the focus of the firm) and economies of scale within functional areas (resources can be shared by all individuals working within each functional area).[14] This form, however, also has a potential major weakness: managers and associates in each functional department can become isolated from those who work in other departments, which harms coordinated action and causes slow responses to major industry changes that require two or more functional areas to work together.[15] Lateral relation mechanisms, discussed in a later section, can help to overcome this weakness.

If an organization has multiple products or services or operates in multiple geographical areas, it can group its resources into divisions (see Exhibit 13-3). The divisional form offers several benefits, such as better coordination among individuals in functional areas. Functional resources have been divided among the divisions, and associates and managers in the smaller functional departments within each division tend to coordinate with one another relatively easily. With smaller departments, people tend to be closer to one another, and there are fewer barriers (formal or informal) to direct communication. A second, related benefit is rapid response to changes in the industry that call for a cross-functional response. Because associates and managers in the various functional areas coordinate more effectively, response times are often faster. A third benefit is tailoring to the

©Gerard Fritz/Getty Images, Inc.

departmentalization
The grouping of human and other resources into units, typically based on functional areas or markets.

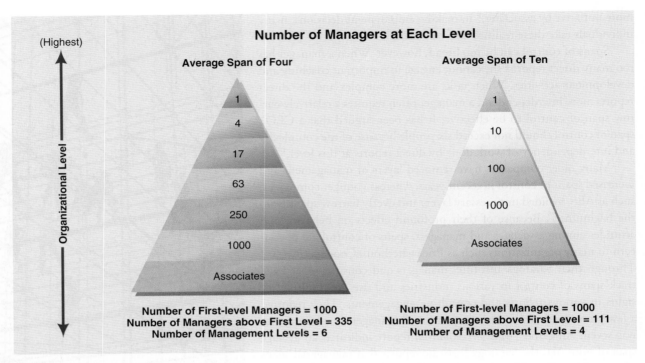

Exhibit 13-1 Average Span of Control: Effects of Height of the Hierarchy

different product/service or geographical markets. This occurs because the people in each division are dedicated to their own markets.[16]

The divisional form is not without its drawbacks, however. Two of the most important are (1) lack of collaboration across the product/service or geographic markets (individuals in one division can become isolated from those in other divisions) and (2) diseconomies of scale within functional areas (individuals in a given functional area but working on different markets cannot share resources as they can in the functional structure).[17] As described in the *Exploring Behavior in Action* feature, FedEx developed a diverse set of businesses offering a portfolio of services. To manage these businesses efficiently and to offer customers the most effective services, FedEx implemented a divisional structure.

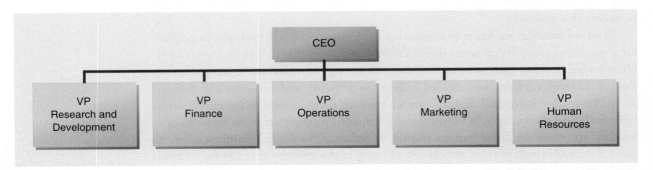

Exhibit 13-2 Simplified Functional Organization

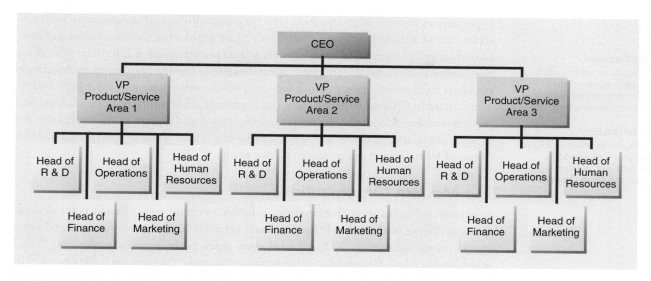

Exhibit 13-3 Simplified Divisional Organization

Hybrid forms also exist, with some functional areas divided across divisions, while others remain intact at the corporate level, often for cost reasons. *Network* organizations are another option, where many or most functional areas are outsourced to other organizations.[18] Home builders are usually network organizations, as they often do not complete their own architectural work and typically outsource to subcontractors much of the actual construction work. Nike is generally considered to be a network organization because it outsources manufacturing and other types of work.

The network approach has been emphasized by a number of firms in recent years, at least to some degree. Its chief benefit lies in allowing a firm to focus on what it does best while outsourcing the rest.[19] Quality control, however, is sometimes an issue, and coordination of internal and external efforts is often a substantial problem. Effective information technology that facilitates coordination across organizational boundaries is crucial.

Structuring Characteristics

Whereas structural characteristics indirectly affect behavior, *structuring* characteristics relate to policies and approaches used to directly prescribe the behavior of managers and associates. This second category of structure includes centralization, standardization, formalization, and specialization.

Centralization refers to the amount of decision-making authority that is held at the top of the organization.[20] In centralized organizations, top-level managers retain most authority, leaving less for mid- and lower-level managers and very little for associates. This is not consistent with high-involvement management, and research suggests that centralized organizations generally perform less well.[21] There are several conditions, however, that call for a significant degree of centralization. We discuss this issue in a later section.

Standardization refers to the existence of rules and standard operating procedures. When standardization is high, managers and associates are expected to follow prearranged approaches to their work. Under these circumstances, their behavior is very predictable. Although standardization is sometimes necessary for efficiency and safety, it reduces

centralization
The degree to which authority for meaningful decisions is retained at the top of an organization.

standardization
The degree to which rules and standard operating procedures govern behavior in an organization.

formalization
The degree to which rules and operating procedures are documented on paper or in company intranets.

specialization
The degree to which associates and managers have jobs with narrow scopes and limited variety.

opportunities for individual initiative, creativity, and self-directed collaboration with others inside and outside the organization. Thus, it can negatively affect motivation and satisfaction for many. **Formalization** is a closely related phenomenon; it is the degree to which rules and procedures are documented. **Specialization** is the degree to which managers and associates have narrow jobs that use focused skills; usually these jobs offer little variety. As discussed in Chapter 6, narrow jobs can negatively affect motivation, satisfaction, and performance for individuals who want to be challenged and to grow in the workplace. Yet, in some self-managed teams with associates having higher levels of specialization, some degree of formalization can produce positive results.[22]

The Modern Organization

Structural and structuring characteristics combine to create very different types of organizations. Some in the field of organizational behavior label the two fundamental types *organic* versus *mechanistic*.[23] Others label these types *learning* versus *nonlearning*.[24] Still others use the labels *boundaryless* versus *traditional* to make the same basic distinction.[25] In all cases, the more flexible empowering type of structure (i.e., organic, learning, or boundaryless) is associated with fewer management levels; broader spans of control; and lesser amounts of centralization, standardization, formalization, and specialization. Departmentalization at the top of the firm can be either functional or divisional. The flexible approach provides freedom for lower-level managers and associates to think for themselves, to communicate with anyone who could be helpful, and to try new ideas.

Although substantial freedom may exist, it is not unlimited, nor should it exist without alternative mechanisms designed to ensure that managers and associates are working for the common good of the organization. First, even in relatively organic firms there is some standardization, and some decisions are made by middle and senior-level managers. At Southwest Airlines, pilots and flight attendants have more freedom than at other airlines, but they still must follow applicable laws and safety rules.[26] Interestingly, research shows that new-venture firms need structure and thus often are more successful if their organization structure is less organic.[27] In addition, new-venture firms often are "boundaryless" in that they must operate in networks to gain access to needed resources. While these alliances may be critical to their survival, it can be difficult for them to break into an existing network of relationships. Working across these organizational boundaries requires that they not be too standardized or formalized. They need flexibility.[28]

Second, alternative mechanisms are used to ensure that individuals are working for the good of the organization. These mechanisms include selection systems, socialization schemes, and leadership processes. Selection systems should be designed to identify individuals who share the values of the organization. Socialization schemes, discussed later in this chapter, should be designed to further shape values and to promote a shared vision of the organization's future. Similarly, strong leadership at the top of the firm instills shared purpose among managers and associates. Shared values and vision act as guides to behavior, and reduce the chances of lower-level managers and associates acting in ways that are counterproductive. Reward systems also are used to promote appropriate behavior. Although lower-level managers and associates may not realize it, powerful forces guide their behavior in organizations characterized by relative freedom of thought and action.

Through the 1960s and into the 1970s, freedom in most organizations was severely limited. Over time, however, the value of unleashing human capital throughout an organization became widely recognized. Today, senior leaders in modern organizations tend to favor organic structures. Although this is positive, given that organic structures are closely aligned with high-involvement management, there are situations in which some aspects of this approach are not appropriate.

Factors Affecting Organizational Structure

Senior managers must choose the structures to use for their firms. Middle and lower-level managers often are involved in these choices and play a key role in the implementation of the choices. Factors that should be considered in designing the structure of the firm include strategy, external environment, internal technology, and organizational size.

The Role of Strategy

An organization's task environment is composed of customers, suppliers, competitors, government regulatory agencies, and perhaps unions. These are external components with which the organization frequently interacts and that have an effect on the organization.[29] Organizations adapt to their environments through formal strategies. In turn, these strategies affect the organization's structure.

Corporate Strategy

Corporate strategy is the overall, predominant strategy of the organization. It determines the direction for the total organization. Senior managers formulating corporate strategies focus on the organization's stockholders and other critical external constituents. Their strategies can be oriented toward growth, diversification, or both.[30]

Almost all types of organizations use **growth** as a measure of success. Awards are given for growth, such as the Growth Strategy Leadership Award given by the consulting firm Frost and Sullivan.[31] Under some circumstances, senior leaders are even willing to trade profits for increasing sales. Growth can be achieved through internal development or by external acquisition. Although the internal growth strategy is an attractive option, growth by external acquisition is popular with many companies.[32] Cisco Systems, a maker of telecommunication equipment, is known for its frequent acquisitions.[33] Acquisition is often a faster method of achieving growth, but it does carry some risk, in part because cultural differences between firms often cause difficulties in the post-acquisition integration of operations.[34] Some firms that have diversified through multiple acquisitions later retrenched and sold off prior acquisitions because of poor performance.[35]

Each of these two growth strategies has implications for structure. For example, firms using an internal-growth strategy are likely to have larger marketing and research and development (R&D) departments. It is also probable that authority for decisions is decentralized to the heads of these departments. In contrast, firms following an external acquisition strategy are likely to have the more well-developed financial and legal functions required to analyze and negotiate acquisitions. These firms may even have a separate specialized planning and acquisitions department. For example, given the number of acquisitions completed by FedEx over time, the company likely has enriched these functions.

Diversification has also been a common and popular corporate strategy. Diversification involves adding products or services different from those currently in the firm. Firms may diversify for several reasons, but the primary one is to reduce overall risk by decreasing dependency on one or a few product markets.[36] Thus, if demand for one of the firm's products falls, the other products may continue to sell.[37] Firms may also diversify the geographic markets they serve by entering new foreign markets.[38] Most companies start out

corporate strategy
The overall approach an organization uses in interacting with its environment. The emphasis is placed on growth and diversification.

growth
Relates to increases in sales as well as associates and managers.

diversification
Related to the number of different product lines or service areas in the organization.

EXHIBIT 13-4   Matches between Diversification Strategy and Structure

Diversification	Structure
Single product	Functional
Dominant product (few products)	Functional
Dominant product (several products)	Divisional
Related product	Divisional
Unrelated product	Divisional
Unrelated product	Holding company

as *single-product firms*, which are firms where more than 95 percent of annual sales come from one product. *Dominant-product firms* obtain 70 to 94 percent of their sales from one product. Most companies following a diversification strategy move on to become *related-product firms*, where less than 70 percent of annual sales come from one product and the various products are related to one another. The most diversified firms are classified as *unrelated-product firms*. In these firms, less than 70 percent of annual sales come from any one product, and the firm's various products are unrelated to the primary core business.[39]

As firms become more diversified, research suggests that they should adopt the divisional form.[40] In other words, they should develop divisions for each of their end-product businesses. Also, as firms become more diversified and divisionalized, authority should be delegated to the divisions.[41]

Matches between diversification and structure are shown in Exhibit 13-4. Single-product and most dominant-product firms should use a functional structure, where the major units of the organization are based on the functions performed (marketing, production, finance) rather than on products. Related-product and most unrelated-product firms should use a divisionalized structure. Large, highly diversified unrelated-product firms may use a *holding company* structure, in which the operating divisions are extremely autonomous.[42] Firms with functional structures are sometimes referred to as *U-form* (unitary) *organizations* and firms with divisionalized structures as *M-form* (multidivisional) *organizations*. Over time, FedEx changed from a single-product firm to a related-product firm. As such, it implemented the divisional structure and decentralized primary authority to make decisions to the heads of each division. Because the businesses are all related, the corporate office coordinated activities across the divisions to offer customers the full portfolio of FedEx's services (as described in the *Exploring Behavior in Action* feature).

Business Strategy

business strategy
How a firm competes for success against other organizations in a particular market.

Firms must formulate business strategies in addition to corporate strategies. A **business strategy** is developed for a particular product/service market and is a plan of action describing how the firm will operate in a particular market.[43]

Business strategies are necessary to ensure effective competitive actions in the different markets in which a firm intends to operate. One popular competitive strategy involves maintaining low internal costs as a basis for low prices offered to customers. Consumers interested in buying the least expensive goods in a particular market are targeted. To effectively implement this strategy, efficiency and control are important inside the firm or division utilizing this approach, and a somewhat more mechanistic structure is useful, if not taken to an extreme.[44] The structure used to implement a low-cost strategy often emphasizes functions, and the decisions are also centralized to maintain economies of scale in operations.[45] A second popular competitive strategy involves product/service differentiation. Consumers are targeted who are willing to pay more for a product/service that is different in some meaningful way (higher quality, superior technology, faster availability). To effectively implement this strategy, flexibility and initiative are useful for staying ahead of the competition, and a more organic structure can be helpful in supporting these needs.[46] To be effective, each strategy requires a unique set of internal resources (e.g., human capital as illustrated in the IDEO example) that can be used to effectively implement the strategy.[47]

In the *Experiencing Organizational Behavior* segment, IDEO illustrates four key points. First, this firm shows how a differentiation strategy can be used in the business of designing products and services. IDEO has distinguished itself through its unique approach to working with clients, and it promotes the innovation and initiative required to maintain its edge by using an organic structure. Second, the firm highlights the fact that companies occasionally supplement their internal human capital as they work to create a competitive advantage in the marketplace. All or most of IDEO's clients have talented associates and managers. Yet, on occasion they still need outside assistance. Third, IDEO promotes design thinking throughout their and their clients' organizations. In so doing, innovation is integrated into the organization's culture and DNA. Finally, the IDEO case again illustrates the value of teams with diverse members, as explained in Chapters 2 and 11. Teams provided invaluable help for IDEO and its client firms to implement a strategy of innovation designed to create or maintain a competitive advantage.

A more advanced form of the divisional structure, strategic business units (SBUs) are sometimes used for more complex firms. Large firms with multiple diversified businesses sometimes group their businesses into SBUs. At General Electric, for example, businesses are grouped into SBUs that include GE Advanced Materials, GE Commercial Finance, GE Consumer Finance, GE Consumer and Industrial Products, GE Energy, GE Healthcare, GE Infrastructure, GE Insurance Solutions, GE Transportation, and NBC Universal.[48] A business strategy is then formulated for each separate SBU, thus allowing the complex organization to be more effectively managed. The key to developing effective strategies for each SBU is the appropriate grouping of businesses. Each group must have commonalities among its businesses for a coherent strategy to be developed. These commonalities may correspond to market relatedness, shared technology, or common distinctive competencies.[49]

The Role of the Environment

Environmental forces account for many differences between organizations, and they have a marked effect on the way organizations conduct business.[50] Because organizations must obtain their inputs from the external environment, their relationships with suppliers and customers are critical. They also must satisfy governmental regulations, adapt to changes in the national and world economies, and react to competitors' actions.

Environment and Basic Structure

Managers must closely monitor their organization's external environment. However, some environments are more difficult to monitor than others because they are more uncertain (complex and changing). A number of researchers have found that the degree of

IDEO and the Differentiation Strategy

The computer mouse, stand-up toothpaste containers, Palm V, i-Zone cameras, patient-friendly waiting rooms, and shopper-friendly intimate apparel displays. Differentiation is not easy, but these products and services helped to differentiate Apple Computer, Procter & Gamble, Palm Inc., Kaiser Permanente, and Warnaco. In cooperation with IDEO, Shimano, a global company headquartered in Japan, developed an innovative new bicycle introduced in 2007. Ford is working closely with IDEO to design its new hybrid electric vehicle that will closely meet the needs of its customers. Ford refers to its project as SmartGauge with Eco-Guide to design a more-connected, fuel-efficient driving experience. IDEO is now the design firm that many organizations use to help design their new products and services. What is the secret of IDEO's success? It may have something to do with the associates and managers at IDEO, a design firm based in Palo Alto, California.

The people of IDEO have a long history of helping firms design award-winning products and services. More recently, IDEO has begun offering consulting and training in innovation and culture change. To make a difference, IDEO's associates and managers rely on a simple concept—empathy. Although this concept may not be conventional, IDEO's record of success is difficult to question. The purpose of this training and IDEO's approach more generally is to inculcate

"design thinking" even into the top leaders of the organization.

Empathy for the customer is created in clients through a set of time-tested, systematic research methods. First, IDEO forms a diverse team composed of client and IDEO members. Team members from IDEO may represent the disciplines of cognitive psychology, environmental psychology, anthropology, industrial design, interaction design, mechanical engineering, and business strategy. Team members from the client firm are key decision makers. With the team in place, observations in the real world are orchestrated. Team members observe how people use relevant products and services. For a project focused on intimate apparel, team members followed women as they shopped for lingerie, encouraging the shoppers to verbalize everything they were thinking. Team members may even act as customers themselves. For a health-care project, team members received care at various hospitals and documented their experiences by video and other media.

Second, team members engage in brainstorming. After some preliminary work, the designers, engineers, social scientists, and individuals from the client company engage in intense interactions to develop a rich understanding of an existing product/service design or of the needs in a novel product category. Unlike some group sessions, IDEO's brainstorming sessions have been compared to managed chaos.

Third, team members engage in rapid prototyping. This is one of the

characteristics that have made IDEO famous. IDEO associates and managers believe in the power of trying many different ideas rather than just talking about them. Rudimentary versions of products and services are quickly constructed and examined.

Finally, team members implement the fruits of their labor. Detailed design and engineering work is completed, and the team works closely with clients to ensure a successful launch. In many other design firms, team members simply turn over their work with little follow-up.

The critical component in this according to the president and one of the founders, Tim Brown, is design thinking. He suggests that all of these actions will not work effectively without this component. Innovation must be a part of the organization's DNA, Brown suggests. This thinking requires work across functions and combines creative confidence with analytic ability. This type of thinking is now used by Steelcase and Procter & Gamble, both of which have used it to become highly innovative companies.

IDEO has become so popular that many firms send their managers to the firm to observe the organic structure and to be trained in innovative thinking and action. These managers use what they have learned to enhance the operations and structures of their own firms. IDEO's approach continues to be highly successful. In 2009, it tied with Samsung for the most IDEA awards (eight) given for the top designs of the year.

Sources: IDEO. 2009. "Hybrid Electric Vehicle Dashboard Interaction for Ford Motor Company," at http://www. ideo.com, Dec. 29; V. Wong. 2009. "How to Nurture Future Leaders," *BusinessWeek, at* http://www.businessweek. com, Sept. 30; T. Brown. 2009. "Change by Design," *BusinessWeek, at* http://www.businessweek.com, Sept. 24; C. Kuang. 2009. "Big Awards for the Year's Best industrial Designs," *FastCompany, at* http://www.fastcompany. com, July 30; 2007. "Coasting Bicycle Design Strategy for Shimano," at http://www.ideo.com/ideo.asp, Apr. 16; B. Moggridge. 2006. *Designing Interactions,* Boston: MIT Press; IDEO. 2004. "About Us: Methods," at http://www. ideo.com/about/index.asp?x=3&y=3.

environmental uncertainty experienced by managers is related to the type of structure an organization utilizes. And, this is especially important today because of the high uncertainty of environments in which many organizations must operate.[51] Classic research indicated that effective organizations exhibit a match between environmental characteristics and organizational structures.[52] Although the evidence is not entirely consistent, a number of other researchers have found similar results, using mostly small organizations or units of larger ones.[53]

The classic study reported the following important findings:

- Effective organizations experiencing high environmental uncertainty tend to be more organic because lower-level managers and associates must be able to think for themselves. They must be able to respond to events quickly.
- Effective organizations experiencing low environmental uncertainty tend to be less organic. Mid and senior-level managers in conjunction with operations specialists can create efficient and effective rules and operating procedures. They can gain sufficient insight to understand and anticipate most situations that will arise and carefully create procedures to handle those situations.

It is important to understand the reasons for differences in functional departments within an organization. Because separate departments focus on different areas of the external environment, they often exhibit different types of structure. R&D, for example, is focused on technological advances and the changing pool of knowledge in the world. The relatively high level of uncertainty involved often requires a more organic structure with longer time horizons for decision making and planning and a greater emphasis on interpersonal relationships to promote important discussions and information sharing. In contrast, the accounting function is focused on more slowly evolving developments in accounting standards. The relatively low level of uncertainty generally supports use of a less organic structure, with shorter time horizons and lower emphasis on interpersonal relationships. In effective organizations, then, differences in the level of uncertainty in subenvironments create differences in functional departments.

Recent work suggests that environmental uncertainty also affects the way resources should be managed in organizations. For example, organizations operating in uncertain environments need to constantly enrich their current capabilities and even create new ones. Thus, they continuously train their managers and associates to upgrade their skills and are on the lookout for new associates with "cutting-edge" knowledge that can add to the organization's stock of knowledge. They also need to search for opportunities in the environment and to engage in entrepreneurial behavior to maximize the use of their capabilities to provide products and services that create value for their customers.[54] IDEO, as explained in the *Experiencing Organizational Behavior* feature, is helping firms to be more entrepreneurial and create products that are valued by their customers. All of the research then suggests that managers must continuously scan their firm's external environment to identify factors that may affect how the firm should act. Their scanning behavior is even more important in dynamic environments.[55]

Environment and Integration

Functional departments within a single-product firm or a division of a larger firm must be integrated. They must share information and understand one another in order to coordinate their work.[56] Thus, organizations must be structured to provide the necessary

environmental uncertainty
The degree to which an environment is complex and changing; uncertain environments are difficult to monitor and understand.

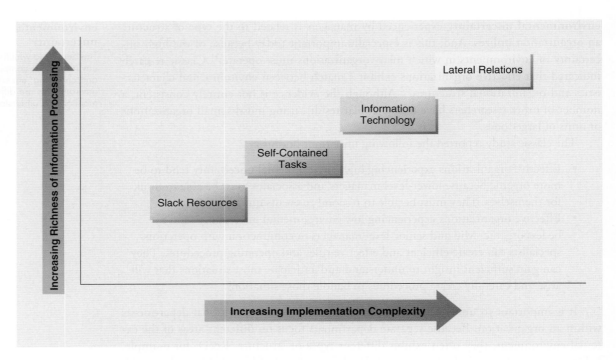

Exhibit 13-5   Integration in Organizations

information, or perhaps to reduce the need for it. Structural arrangements that address information needs are particularly important when the environment is uncertain. Useful arrangements include: (1) creation of slack resources, (2) creation of self-contained tasks, (3) investment in information technology, and (4) creation of traditional lateral relations.[57] Exhibit 13-5 shows the relationship of these elements of organizational structure and information processing needs.

The creation of **slack resources** reduces the need for interdepartmental information processing. Departments can operate more independently. Examples of slack resources include having extra time to complete tasks that other departments need as inputs and maintaining large inventories of raw materials provided by others. Although these extra resources reduce information exchange needs, they are costly.

The creation of **self-contained tasks** reduces the need for interdepartmental processing of information. This approach provides departments with more of the resources they need to do the job. For example, a department's tasks may require the help of a design engineer and a process engineer on a part-time basis. Instead of having a group of design engineers to which various departments would come when they need help, a design engineer is specifically assigned to each department, with nonengineering work used to fill any unused time. This method reduces the need for coordination between groups (e.g., the engineering group and other groups needing engineering services) and thereby reduces information-processing requirements.

Unlike the two elements of structure discussed above, **information technology** facilitates the processing of information rather than reducing the need to process it. This technology can help to transfer information up and down the hierarchy as well as horizontally from department to department. E-mail, web-based discussion boards, chat rooms, and Twitter

slack resources
An integration technique whereby a department keeps more resources on hand than absolutely required in order to reduce the need for tight communication and coordination with other departments.

self-contained tasks
An integration technique whereby a department is given resources from other functional areas in order to reduce the need to coordinate with those areas.

information technology
An overall set of tools, based on microelectronic technology, designed to provide data, documents, and commentary as well as analysis support to individuals in an organization.

are examples of simple tools that facilitate communication and coordination. An information repository is a more complex tool for integration. Such a repository requires individuals in various departments to deposit documents, data, and commentary in an open-access central database. An enterprise resource planning (ERP) system is an even more complex tool. ERP systems provide a common set of planning and analysis capabilities across departments, as well as a platform for electronically sharing evolving plans and analyses. This type of system has provided important benefits in the integration of departments,[58] particularly when the system has been explicitly designed to support the organization's strategy. An ERP system has even been used to coordinate the cross-functional curriculum of a business school.[59]

In addition to facilitating integration across existing departments in an organization, information technology has helped to flatten organizations and has promoted project-based structures.[60] Shorter hierarchies are consistent with high-involvement management because they push decision authority to the lowest levels of the organization and increase the speed and quality of decisions as a result. Such hierarchies would not be possible, however, without information technology to ensure that associates and lower-level managers have the information they need to make sound decisions. Project-based structures utilize individuals from various departments to work on complex projects requiring intense and integrated efforts. In some cases, these individuals are temporarily assigned to a project on a full-time basis. In other instances, individuals participate part-time as project members and part-time as members of their functional departments. In both cases, information technology ensures that project participants working on different aspects of the overall project understand the goals and activities of those working in other areas. Without sophisticated information technology, individuals could not integrate the various aspects of the project as effectively or as rapidly, resulting in some complex projects not being undertaken and others being handled more slowly through the traditional hierarchy.

Relations among departments are based on the need for coordinating their various tasks. Because **lateral relations** increase information flow at lower levels, decisions requiring interdepartmental coordination need not be referred up the hierarchy. Lateral relations are traditional elements of structure used to help organizations process more information. These relations may be facilitated by information technology but often are based on face-to-face communication. A number of alternative lateral processes can be used. Listed in order of least complex to most complex, they are as follows:

lateral relations
Elements of structure designed to draw individuals together for interchanges related to work issues and problems.

- *Direct contact* involves two individuals who share a problem and work directly with one another to solve it.
- *Liaison roles* are temporary coordination positions established to link two departments that need to have a large amount of contact.
- *Task forces* are temporary groups composed of members from several departments who solve problems affecting those departments.
- *Teams* are *permanent* problem-solving groups for continuous interdepartmental problems.
- *Integrating roles* are permanent positions designed to help with the coordination of various tasks.
- *Managerial linking roles* are integrative positions with more influence and decision-making authority.
- *Matrix designs* establish dual authority between functional managers (marketing manager, engineering manager) and project or product managers (leisure furniture manager, office furniture manager).

The Role of Technology

Within an organization, *technology* refers to the knowledge and processes required to accomplish tasks. It corresponds to the techniques used in transforming inputs into outputs. The relationship of technology and structure has been described in several ways, as discussed below.

Technology and Structure: A Manufacturing Framework

Early work on the relationship between technology and organization structure focused on manufacturing technology: small-batch production, mass production, and continuous-process production.[61]

This research found that technological complexity influenced structure and that effective organizations exhibited matches between technology and structure.[62]

Today, new types of technology are being used in smaller and larger manufacturing operations alike. Technology can equalize the competition between smaller and larger organizations. The use of advanced manufacturing technology (AMT), computer-aided design (CAD), and computer-aided manufacturing (CAM) helps firms of all sizes to customize their strategies by manufacturing products of high variety at lower costs and to commercialize new products in a shorter amount of time.[63] These technologies have been integrated to create forms of "mass customization." **Mass customization** is a process that integrates sophisticated information technology and management methods in a flexible manufacturing system with the ability to customize products in a short time.[64] Organizations using mass customization need a more flexible and organic structure.[65]

Technology and Structure: A Broader Framework

The link between technology and structure using a broader view of technology is useful in both manufacturing and service organizations. In this view, technology is defined as the number of different problem types that are encountered over time (*task variability*) and the degree to which problems can be solved using known steps and procedures (*task analyzability*).[66] Based on these two dimensions, he delineated four types of technology:

1. *Routine:* There is little variation in the fundamental nature of problems encountered over time, but any new problems can be solved using readily available methods.

2. *Craft:* There is little variation in the fundamental nature of problems encountered over time, but any new problems often require a novel search for unique solutions.

3. *Engineering:* There is significant variation in the fundamental nature of problems encountered over time, and new problems can be solved using readily available methods.

4. *Nonroutine:* There is significant variation in the fundamental nature of problems encountered over time, and new problems often require new methods to find unique solutions.

Exhibit 13-6 provides examples of organizations with these types of technologies. To be most effective, firms should match their structure to the technology used. Nonroutine organizations should adopt an organic structure; craft and engineering organizations should adopt a moderately organic structure; and routine organizations should adopt the least organic structure.[67] Essentially, as routineness increases, organic structures become somewhat less useful.

mass customization
A manufacturing technology that involves integrating sophisticated information technology and management methods to produce a flexible manufacturing system with the ability to customize products for many customers in a short time.

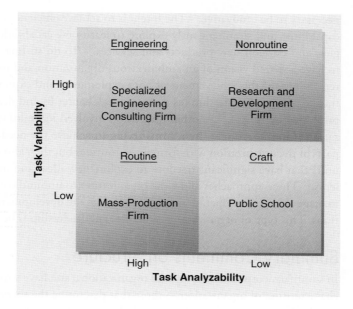

Exhibit 13-6 Organizations and Technology

These technology concepts can be applied to an organization as a whole or to units within the organization. For example, the technology of W. L. Gore, the maker of Gore-Tex fabric, can be described as a mixture of routine and craft technology at the firm level, but its R&D area can be described as nonroutine. Any unit can be assessed with respect to task variability and task analyzability and placed into one of the four technology categories. A number of studies have shown that technology influences structure at the unit level and that effective units exhibit a significant match between technology and structure.[68]

The Role of Organizational Size

It is not surprising that size has implications for organizational structure.[69] As an organization grows, it generally becomes taller; otherwise, the average span of control for managers becomes too large. As organizations increase in size, formalization also tends to increase to help maintain order. However, centralization tends to decrease, as senior managers cannot comprehend all of the organization's work and make all decisions.

The most important measure of size is the number of associates and managers. Research shows that managerial decisions regarding structure are based on the factors that are most salient to managers. Because people are highly important to most managers, managerial decisions on structure are often influenced by the number of people for whom the managers have responsibility.[70]

A common outcome of larger organizations and the heightened formalization and standardization that accompanies growing size is inertia.[71] Large formal organizations often have more standardized policies and routines for managers and associates to follow. These attributes often produce a resistance to change and thus lower innovation. Yet, innovation is a critical component of competitiveness for most organizations in our current global economic environment. The potential for inertia in large organizations and the need for innovation have led to the development of ambidextrous structures and practices.

Ambidextrous organizations balance the formalization and standardization that help to achieve efficiency and the flexibility required to explore new ideas and opportunities

ambidextrous organization
An organization structure that balances formalization and standardization to help to achieve efficiency and flexibility.

necessary to be innovative.[72] The intent is to achieve efficiency to exploit the firm's current capabilities and simultaneously explore to learn new capabilities, discover new technologies, and develop new products and services.[73] To do so first requires top management to have a shared vision of an ambidextrous organization and to develop an incentive system to reward the achievement of both exploitation and exploration. This often requires transformational leadership (as discussed in Chapter 8) and design thinking, such as that promoted by IDEO.[74] Another dimension involved in building an ambidextrous organization is the structure. Often, firms trying to achieve the needed balance maintain some parts of the organization with formalized routines but then also develop semi-autonomous units that have significant freedom to explore new ideas and unique approaches to problems.[75] These approaches allow the organization to unbundle operations and processes to manage the costs of operations but also pursue the development of technological innovations. This type of organization, structure, and leadership is becoming more common.[76]

Summary Comments on Structure

In summary, corporate strategy and organizational size have strong effects on the structural characteristics of organizations—those that determine the shape and appearance of the hierarchy. Corporate strategy is a particularly strong determinant of departmentalization, and size is an especially strong determinant of height and spans of control. Business strategy, environmental uncertainty, and technological nonroutineness have strong effects on unit structuring within organizations, as well as the overall structure of the organization.

An important study has shown how business strategy, environmental uncertainty, technological nonroutineness, and structure work together to influence performance in organizational units as well as in small organizations.[77] In this study, strong performance was associated with consistency among these factors:

- Uncertain environments led to strategies based on differentiation and innovation, which in turn led to nonroutine work, all of which were matched by organic structure.
- More certain environments led to strategies based on low costs and efficiency, which in turn led to routine work, all of which were matched by a less organic structure.

Other studies have provided similar results,[78] suggesting that managers in effective firms create consistency across strategy, environment, technology, and structure.

Organizational Culture

Culture is closely related to most other concepts in the field of organizational behavior, including structure, leadership, communication, groups, motivation, and decision making.[79] Culture is affected by and can also affect these other areas of organizational functioning and it is related to social, historic, and economic issues as well.[80] Thus, it is an important and encompassing concept.

Google's organizational culture is described in the *Experiencing Organizational Behavior* feature. Google's culture is highly informal, with a decentralized structure designed to enhance associates' creativity. Google must be doing something right because it is a highly successful company. Its culture and structure, along with its interrelated management model, have attracted significant human capital, which is one of the reasons for its success. Google's approach is highly similar to a high-involvement organization.

Google Culture Attracts High-Quality Associates

Larry Page and Sergy Brin graduated from Stanford University in 1995 with computer science degrees. They wanted to build a search engine that would retrieve selective information from the vast amount of data available on the Internet. In 1997, they named their search engine "Backrub," and in 1998 they renamed it "Google" (Google is a play on googol, the mathematical term for a + followed by 100 zeros—a reference to organizing the seemingly infinite Web). By 2003, it

©Kate Lacey/The New York Times/Redux Pictures

was the most preferred search engine in the world because of its precision and speed in delivering the desired data in searches. But their success can also be attributed to Google's organizational culture.

In organizing the firm, Page and Brin avoided unnecessary managerial hierarchies, creating a decentralized structure, and giving their engineers significant autonomy to encourage creative thinking. Google has a small management hierarchy and most engineers work in teams of three, with project leadership rotating among them. These teams had complete autonomy and freedom to create, reporting directly to the vice president. Open communication is encouraged and employees are free to approach top management as desired. They are allowed to communicate with

anyone in any department. Employees were also asked to eat in the cafeteria so they could meet others in the company and create opportunities for them to share and discuss technical ideas or issues. In addition, every Friday afternoon all employees are provided information about new products and the company's financial performance. Google's emphasis on innovation and commitment to cost containment requires each employee to be a contributor. The decentralized model of management and open lines of communication are essential parts of Google's organizational culture. And the organizational structure and culture have helped the firm attract and retain the most talented individuals in the field. Although still a young firm, Google's work culture has become legendary in Silicon Valley.

Larry and Sergy wanted to create a fun place to work and use incentives that could attract top talent. Google headquarters, known as the Googleplex, was decorated with lava lamps, giant plastic balls, and bright

colors. Employees are also allowed to bring their pets to work and are provided free snacks, lunch, and dinner, prepared by an award-winning former chef to the Grateful Dead. The founders said that the free, healthy meals came about after calculating the time saved from driving off-site and reduced health-care costs. They have even provided a Webcam that monitors the cafeteria lunch line, so employees can avoid a long wait. Employees are also provided recreational activities, which include workout gyms, assorted video games, pool tables, ping-pong tables, and roller-skater hockey. Additional benefits include flexible work hours, company-paid, midweek ski trips to Squaw Valley, and maternity/paternity leave with 75 percent pay. A benefit addition in 2008 was free afternoon tea service. The company reportedly has the best package of benefits available, even after some minor benefit cuts in 2009 due to the major economic recession.

A few people have criticized Google's organizational culture and management model. Some believe that Google has outgrown the informal culture and that it will not be able to sustain the growth and still maintain the informal lines of communication. Critics argue that even though engineers are free to pursue individual projects, the informality makes it difficult to coordinate and plan activities. Alternatively, as Google has grown much larger (from 1,000 to almost 15,000 managers and associates), sustaining its culture has been more challenging. A few associates have complained that they now feel a distance between them and management. They express concerns that the firm has become more bureaucratic. And, Google has begun losing some of its top talent, especially those who have increased their wealth with Google stock ownership and have departed to establish their own business. Yet, Google continues to be highly innovative. It was ranked as the second most innovative company in *BusinessWeek*'s 2009 rankings of the top 25 most innovative companies. In addition, Google continues to be ranked at the top of *Fortune*'s 100 best companies to work for.

But Google continues to engage its associates, involving them in addressing major issues, maintaining a flat organization, and striving to keep the entrepreneurial spirit alive. Thus, although it is losing some of the talent recruited in past years, it continues to attract some of the top talent in the industry. For example, in 2008, it received almost 1 million applications for the 3,000 positions it was trying to fill.

Google's culture and its talented associates have allowed it to continue to enhance its Internet search capabilities, maintaining its competitive advantage over formidable rivals such as Microsoft and Yahoo!. The culture and structure encourages and facilitates the development of innovative new services by associates, helping Google to remain one of the most successful companies in the world.

Sources: Staff of the Corporate Executive Board. 2009. "Involve Your Employees," Says Google, CEB, *Business Week*, Dec. 11, at http://www.businessweek.com; Andrzej Zwaniechi. 2009. "Google Aims to Retain Entrepreneurial Spirit as It Grows," America.gov, Oct. 28, at http://www.america.gov; "Google Hits Reset on Company Culture," Glassdoor, Oct. 8, 2009, at http:// www.glassdoor.com; Elizabeth Montailbano. 2009. "At 10-year mark, Google's glossy façade shows cracks," Macworld, Sept. 8, at http://www.macworld.com; "The 25 Most Innovative Companies," *Business-Week*, Apr. 20, 2009, at http://www.businessweek.com; Adam Lashinsky. 2008. "Can Google three-peat?" *Money*, Jan. 31, at http://www.cnnmoney.com; B-School News. 2006. "They Love it Here, and Here, and Here," *Business-Week*, June 4, at http://www.businessweek.com; Jade Chang. 2006. "Behind the Glass Curtain," *BusinessWeek*, July 18, at http://www.businessweek.com.

Organizational cultures are based on shared values, as described earlier.[81] As noted, culture begins with shared values, which then produce norms that govern behavior. Behavior produces outcomes that are reinforced or punished, thereby bolstering the culture. Thus, any culture, positive or negative, becomes self-reinforcing and difficult to change. The process of culture development and reinforcement is shown in Exhibit 13-7.

The strength of an organization's culture is based to some degree on the homogeneity of associates and managers and the length and intensity of shared experiences in the organization.[82] The longer a culture is perpetuated, the stronger it becomes because of its self-reinforcing nature. An organization's culture not only reinforces critical values but also important behaviors. For example, Google's culture could be described as a learning culture in which new knowledge is created, acquired externally, diffused internally,[83] and applied to create innovative services for Google's markets and customers. Organizational culture also affects an organization's ability to resolve problems and to create change. For example, in an open culture in which managers and associates are engaged (i.e., a high-involvement organization), more alternatives are likely to be generated and considered to resolve problems. Also, the open communication can help to resolve conflicts if they exist.[84] In addition, the openness of communications between managers and associates (exemplified by Google) and transparency because of the high involvement makes all participants more open to change. And, by participating in creating the change, managers and associates are more likely to be committed to it.[85]

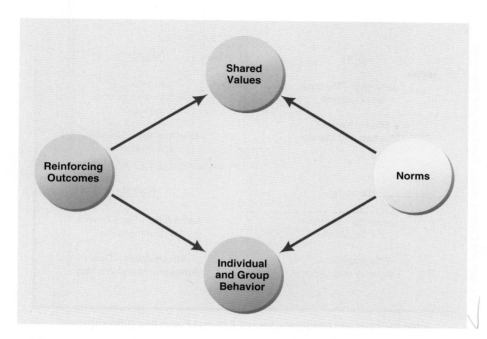

Exhibit 13-7 Process of Developing Organizational Culture

Competing Values Model of Culture

One of the most popular models of culture in business firms is the competing values model, in which two value dimensions are central.[86] The first dimension relates to the value placed on *flexibility and discretion* versus *stability and control.* In some organizations, managers and associates believe in the power and usefulness of flexibility and discretion, while in other organizations individuals believe in the power of a stable work situation where control is strongly maintained. Ambidextrous organizations, described earlier, achieve a balance in these values through the culture and structure. The second dimension relates to the value placed on an *internal focus* coupled with *integration* versus an *external focus* coupled with *differentiation* in the marketplace. In some organizations, associates and managers prefer to focus internally; in other organizations, individuals have an external orientation.

Four types of culture result from different combinations of these dimensions (see Exhibit 13-8):

1. *Clan*—strong value placed on flexibility and discretion with a focus inside the organization. Leaders tend to be mentors and coaches. Effectiveness is evaluated in terms of the cohesion and morale of individuals inside the firm and tacit knowledge held. Overall, the organization tends to be a friendly place to work, with a great deal of commitment and loyalty.

2. *Hierarchy*—strong value placed on control and stability with a focus inside the organization. Leaders tend to be monitors and organizers. Effectiveness is measured in terms of efficiency and orderly coordination. The organization tends to be a formal and standardized place to work, with emphasis on explicit knowledge.[87]

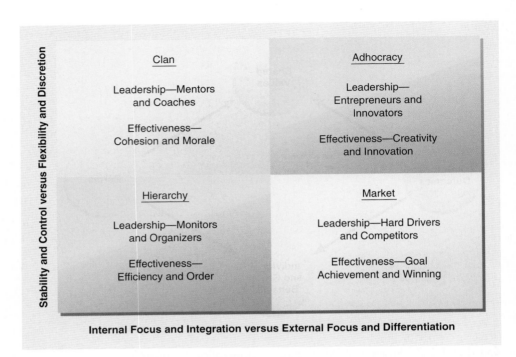

Exhibit 13-8 Competing Values Model of Organizational Culture

3. *Market*—strong value placed on control and stability with a focus outside the organization. Leaders tend be driven and competitive. Effectiveness is measured in terms of goal achievement and beating the competition in the marketplace. The organization can be a difficult place to work because there is a constant focus on results and doing better than colleagues.

4. *Adhocracy*—strong value placed on flexibility and discretion with a focus outside the organization. Leaders tend to be entrepreneurial and innovative, perhaps even visionary. Effectiveness is evaluated in terms of creativity and leading-edge innovation in the marketplace. The organization tends to be a vibrant place to work, with significant risk taking.

Organizations usually possess elements of all four cultural types. In fact, organizations need all four because morale, innovation, success relative to competitors in the market-place, and efficiency are all important for long-term performance and survival.[88] In most cases, however, an organization emphasizes one cultural type over another. Each culture can be useful as a point of emphasis, depending on circumstances. Hierarchy, for example, might be emphasized in an organization pursuing a low-cost business strategy in all of its product lines. In such an organization, however, managers must be careful not to allow the emphasis on hierarchy to become too great. If hierarchy is overemphasized, it will be difficult to incorporate the decision- and team-related aspects of high-involvement management.[89] Furthermore, research suggests that the hierarchy culture can reduce commitment and satisfaction. Market culture could be useful in industries that are highly competitive. Clan culture is often more useful for organizations operating in regulated industries or in small new-venture firms where working with good colleagues and positive working relationships are emphasized more than financial compensation. Google has used such a culture since its beginning. However, even as a large, more established organization, Google continues to use this culture successfully. Adhocracy might be emphasized in an organization pursuing the differentiation strategy in its product lines.

Clearly, organizational cultures affect managers' and associates' behaviors and thus organizational performance. The core values of an organization serve to attract new associates who share similar values or at least are comfortable with the organization's values.[90] For example, research has shown that organizational culture affects the extent to which associates are willing to accept changes in an organization. Specifically, associates who perceive an organizational culture that positively values human relations are more willing to participate in and accept changes made by the organization.[91] In addition, other studies have shown that when the organizational culture promotes respect for people, associates are more likely to view relationships with leaders more positively, to trust others, and to perceive that the organization treats associates fairly.[92] Therefore, such cultures are likely to support an organization's competitive advantage because of a motivated workforce and low turnover among associates.[93]

Cultural Socialization

Newcomers are taught an organization's culture through **socialization**—the imparting of the organization's values. Socialization can take several forms. Based on groundbreaking work by noted culture researchers John Van Maanen and Ed Schein, researchers have focused on three sets of issues: context, content, and social dynamics.[94]

Context refers to whether newcomers are exposed to key values through a collective or an individual process, and whether they experience a formal or an informal approach. In a collective process, all newcomers experience the same socialization events (videos, senior leadership greetings, exercises, receptions, stories, and so on). In an individual process, the experiences are unique. With a formal approach, newcomers learn about the organization away from the jobs they will be taking (off-the-job learning and training), whereas an informal approach puts them in their jobs immediately (on-the-job learning and training). To maximize absorption of an organization's values, a collective, formal approach may be best. This approach ensures that newcomers are exposed to a standard set of tactics in a focused manner away from the pressures of the new job. Bain and Company, a management consulting firm, illustrates this approach. It uses a formal standard induction program to provide specific training and to build cohesiveness and a sense of identity with the firm. This is supported by excellent materials on the Bain website that explain the company's culture and provide consultants' journals with valuable information on the jobs the new recruits will likely hold. In the program and on the website, information is provided to reinforce the idea that senior colleagues serve as mentors and coaches.[95]

Content refers to whether newcomers are provided information on the probable sequence of development activities and job rotations for the first year or two in the organization, and whether they are given specific information on the likely duration of each activity.

socialization
A process through which an organization imparts its values to newcomers.

©Goodshoot/Corbis

With detailed information on upcoming development activities, newcomers experience less uncertainty. They have a better sense of where they are going in the organization. When information provided to newcomers conveys a variable and random situation (no set sequence of development activities and no estimates of duration times), newcomers are less able to discern a clear path to success and advancement. This latter situation can create satisfaction and commitment issues.

Social dynamics refer to whether newcomers experience serial or disjunctive processes and whether they are exposed to an investiture or a divestiture approach. Newcomers experiencing a serial approach have experienced organizational members as role models. The disjunctive process does not formally establish contact with experienced associates and managers, forcing newcomers to make sense of the situation on their own. With the investiture approach, positive social support is provided from the beginning rather than negative information through a hazing process. The combination of serial and investiture techniques yields better socialization experiences.

In a high-involvement organization, socialization is usually an easier task, as the process begins before employment, during the selection process. Most applicants are rigorously screened with the purpose of discouraging those who may not fit the culture. For example, at Southwest Airlines, the socialization process begins well before the applicant is hired. Applicants are exhaustively screened by a number of interviewers. The interview team does not oversell Southwest but describes both the advantages and disadvantages of working for the firm. The purpose is to make sure that the applicant's values and objectives mesh with those of the airline.[96] The process has been highly effective, as Southwest's culture is often given credit for the company's success. In 2009, Southwest Airlines was ranked number 7 in *Fortune* magazine's list of the most admired corporations in the United States.[97]

Integrating new associates into the organization's culture is important, especially for maintaining the culture. Research has shown that organizations with highly integrative cultures, whether they are focused on associate development and harmony or customer orientation and innovation often perform better than organizations that pay less attention to their cultures.[98]

Cultural Audits

cultural audit
A tool for assessing and understanding the culture of an organization.

Managers must understand and monitor their organization's current culture to develop and effectively manage it.[99] Thus, a **cultural audit** should be conducted periodically. This type of audit is an analysis designed to uncover shared values and beliefs in an organization. It should identify the strengths and weaknesses of the current culture with respect to the support it provides for the achievement of the organization's goals.[100]

The following five steps may be used in conducting a cultural audit:[101]

1. Analyze the process and content of the socialization of new associates and managers (interview those directly involved in socialization).

2. Analyze responses to critical incidents in the organization's history (construct an organizational biography from documents and interviews of past and present associates and managers).

3. Analyze the values and beliefs of culture creators (founders) and carriers (current leaders) (observe and/or interview the founders and current leaders).

4. Explore anomalies or puzzling features discovered in other analyses (initiate joint problem-solving sessions with current leaders in the organization).

5. Examine the linkage of the current organizational culture to its goals.

A cultural audit is a complex and sometimes lengthy process that should be conducted only after careful planning and preparation. The results of an audit might indicate a culture that is not well developed or might disclose the presence of subcultures. An underdeveloped culture poses less of a problem than one that is dysfunctional, fully developed, and self-reinforcing, because the less-developed culture can be more easily influenced and its path altered if necessary.

Subcultures

It is possible for **subcultures** to develop in an organization, particularly when no dominant organizational culture exists or when the organization is diverse and geographically dispersed.[102] Subcultures are based on values shared by a group rather than by an organization as a whole. Some of the values of the subculture are similar to and others are dissimilar from the organization's values and the values of other groups. The existence of subcultures complicates the development and management of an organizational culture.

In large, diverse organizations, some researchers advocate viewing organizational culture as a system of integrated subcultures rather than a unified set of values.[103] In such cases, senior managers need to understand each subculture, ensure that it is appropriate for its market segment, and decide whether it fits with critical organizational values. Thus, a manager's purpose is to encourage the integration of critical organizational values in each subculture.

It is possible for a subculture to include values that are counter to those of the overall organization. Such a counterculture may be difficult to manage. Although a counterculture often creates problems, it can also produce positive outcomes. For example, a counterculture can induce a revolution, forcing change in a staid, outmoded culture. It also may encourage the development of new and creative ideas not allowed by existing norms of the organizational culture.[104]

It is also possible that some subcultures are related to national culture. This may be even more likely in large countries where there are several regional cultures that differ in some values (e.g., China, United States). Research has shown that attributes of national culture (e.g., extent of collectivism) interact with managerial actions such as rewards provided to affect how associates react to the organization (e.g., their commitment to the organization).[105] However, some research has found that national culture has only a small influence on organizational culture.[106]

The *Managerial Advice* segment provides an example of a misfit between a key manager and the company's culture. Bob Nardelli was hired as CEO of Home Depot to make some changes. He did so, but went further than desired by the board. His changes strongly revised the culture of the firm, making it control-oriented, thereby losing the entrepreneurial spirit among store managers and associates. While Home Depot likely needed better control systems, Nardelli's changes went too far. Although Home Depot has made several positive changes since Nardelli's departure, the effects of his tenure as CEO have been long lasting. This example shows the importance of a person–organization fit, discussed next.

subcultures
In the organizational context, groups that share values that differ from the main values of the organization.

Finding a Fit at Home Depot

Research indicates that similarity in values and goals attracts individuals to specific organizations. When an individual's management style and values are not congruent with the organization's culture, problems can develop. This is the reason why problems developed after Home Depot hired Bob Nardelli as CEO in 2000. Home Depot wanted to remain adaptive and make some necessary changes to increase stock prices by bringing in a key individual that the board of directors felt could accomplish these goals. In addition, the board believed that Nardelli's ideas might prompt reflection and help Home Depot make needed changes to impress investors and "pump up" its stock price.

In the early years, Home Depot founders Bernie Marcus and Arthur Blank took it personally if a customer left without buying something. Home Depot's culture was similar to a clan, as the founders placed strong value on flexibility, leaders tended to be mentors and coaches, and they worked to achieve group cohesion and high morale among the associates. The organization was known to be a friendly place to work, and they established a decentralized, entrepreneurial business model. Home Depot

©Scott Olson/Getty Images

was famous for its freewheeling, entrepreneurial spirit, with individual stores operated in a highly autonomous manner. All aspects of the store operations were the responsibility of local management. Using that model, it became the fastest-growing retailer in U.S. history, expanding from a three-store startup in 1979 to a $45 billion chain in 2000. The substantial growth caused the company to struggle with its internal systems and controls, and change was necessary in order to accommodate and manage additional growth.

However, Nardelli's changes were too significant and conflicted with the Home Depot culture. After five years with Nardelli as CEO, the company felt more like a military organization. He embarked on an aggressive plan to centralize control, and to support this change Home Depot invested more than $1 billion in new technology. To help generate the desired data, the company purchased self-checkout aisles and inventory management systems. Nardelli felt it was important to measure everything that occurred in the company and hold executives accountable for meeting "their numbers." He implemented a management model that imported ideas, people, and platitudes from the military, which was a key part of the move to reshape Home Depot into a more centralized organization. The culture he was trying to create was similar to a hierarchy culture, emphasizing control, and stability with leaders monitoring and organizing in an efficient manner. In making these changes, Nardelli failed to keep the entrepreneurial spirit alive in the company.

Some former executives said that Nardelli had created a "culture of fear" and a demoralized staff, which in turn caused customer service to wane. While some praised Nardelli for bringing greater discipline and structure, others blamed him for eroding the entrepreneurial culture at Home Depot. Many on Wall Street felt that Nardelli never understood the value of the previous organizational culture. Associates did not embrace the new culture and some feel this was the reason Home Depot struggled with customer satisfaction and performance in the stock market. Thus, the fit between an individual and the organization was unsuccessful and had debilitating effects on the company's performance.

In early 2007, it was announced that Nardelli departed the company in a disagreement with the board of directors. Home Depot has not fully recovered since, although it has made a number of positive changes. Because of its lost sales to rivals and poor stock market performance, it also sold its entire supply business in 2007. It also closed 15 underperforming stores in 2008 and closed 34 EXPO design stores in 2009. Along with these actions, 7,000 people were laid off, including 10 percent of the corporate officers. One of the first actions taken by the new CEO, Frank Blake, after assuming the position was to abolish the daily catered lunch for top executives. He encouraged his colleagues to eat in the cafeteria with the company's other home office managers and associates. In addition, in 2009, he promoted Marvin Ellison to executive vice president of U.S. stores because of his emphasis on customer service. Home Depot lost many customers to rivals such as Lowe's because of the poor customer service during Nardelli's tenure as CEO. But, the customers who have come back to Home Depot in recent times have had a positive experience.

Home Depot remains a large company, ranked 25th on *Fortune's* list of the largest 500 corporations. But it continues to struggle because of the poor fit between Nardelli and the company and perhaps the industry as well.

Sources: Jean Niemi. 2009. "The Home Depot to Launch Exclusive Martha Stewart Living Brand," Home Depot, Sept. 14, at http://www.phx.corporate-ir.net; Jena McGregor. 2009. "Smart Cost-Cutting: How Home Depot Built It in," *BusinessWeek*, Aug. 4, at http://www.businessweek.com; Jena McGregor. 2009. "Marvin Ellison: Home Depot's Mr. Fixit?" *BusinessWeek*, May 7, at http://www.businessweek.com; "25. Home Depot," *Fortune*, May 4, 2009, at http://www.cnnmoney.com; Michael Barbaro. 2007. "Home Depot Gets a Fresh Coat of Less-Glossy Paint," *The New York Times*, Feb. 8, at http://www.nytimes.com; Theresa Forsman. 2000. "The Maverick's Manual for Entrepreneurial Success," *BusinessWeek*, Dec. 5, at http://www.businessweek.com; Brian Grow. 2006. "Renovating Home Depot," *BusinessWeek*, Mar. 6, at http://www.businessweek.com; Julie Creswell & Michael Barbaro. 2007. "Home Depot Ousts Chief," *International Herald Tribune*, Jan. 4, at http://www.iht.com.

Person–Organization Fit

As suggested throughout this discussion of structure and culture, the fit between an individual and the organization has important implications for satisfaction, commitment, intent to turnover, and job performance.[107] **Values** are abstract ideals related to proper life goals and methods for reaching those goals. As such, individual values often underlie groups of attitudes. Although people may have thousands of attitudes, most likely they have only a few-dozen values.[108] Thus, values are more general than attitudes and form the basis for how we should behave. For example, we could have the underlying value that family time is highly important and a corresponding negative attitude toward a colleague who works most nights and many weekends.

Values emerge as individuals mature and as they develop the ability to form general concepts from their accumulated experiences. Also, during value formation, the value judgments of people we respect influence the nature of our values. Finally, as discussed in Chapter 2, national and ethnic culture affects the development of values.

Once formed, values serve as frames of reference that help guide people's behavior in many different contexts. Values can be modified or refined as a result of new experiences but are much more resistant to change than are attitudes. Thus, individuals will not change their values to join a particular organization. Rather, they make choices based on the agreement between their personal values and those of the organization. Many organizations try to select new associates who share the values consistent with their organizational culture. For example, the individuals who work at Southwest Airlines are likely to share values concerning equality, hard work and having fun at work, partly because of the

values
Abstract ideals that relate to proper life goals and methods for reaching those goals.

recruitment practices of Southwest and partly due to the choices made by individuals on where they prefer to work.

Values develop along two dimensions: (1) the types of personal goals that one ought to have and (2) the types of behaviors that one ought to use in reaching those goals.[109] These two dimensions are sometimes referred to as the end–means dimensions of values. Thus, individuals may develop an end value that they should seek a life of prosperity and a means value that they should be ambitious and hardworking to achieve that goal. These values complement each other by specifying a general goal in life and identifying acceptable behaviors for reaching it. A list of "end" values and "means" values is shown in Exhibit 13-9.

Research has shown that basic personal values affect individual reactions to job situations.[110] Our satisfaction with the type of work we do, the rules imposed by the organization, career advancement opportunities, and other organizational factors are evaluated in terms of our values. Workers' reactions to jobs in different cultures may vary because of differing basic value systems. For example, the basic value systems in the United States emphasize

EXHIBIT 13-9	Types of Personal Values
End (Goal) Values	**Means (Behavior) Values**
Prosperity	Ambition and hard work
Stimulating, active life	Open-mindedness
Achievement	Competence
World peace	Cheerfulness
Harmony in nature and art	Cleanliness
Equality	Courageousness
Personal and family security	Forgiving nature
Freedom	Helpfulness
Happiness	Honesty
Inner peace	Imagination
Mature love	Independence and self-reliance
National security	Intelligence
Pleasure and enjoyment	Rationality
Religion and salvation	Affection and love
Self-respect	Obedience and respect
Social respect	Courtesy
Friendship	Responsibility
Wisdom	Self-discipline

Source: Adapted from M. Rokeach. 1973. *The Nature of Human Values* (New York: The Free Press).

self-reliance and initiative, whereas in Japan basic value systems emphasize self-sacrifice, obedience, and cooperation. As explained in Chapter 3, this difference has implications for how high-involvement management systems should be developed in different cultures.

When an individual's values and preferences do not fit prevailing structural arrangements, she may be a less-satisfied and a less-positive contributor to the organization. Similarly, and perhaps more importantly, when an individual's values are not congruent with the

THE STRATEGIC LENS

We have emphasized that an organization's structure and culture play important roles in the implementation of its strategy. For example, if an organization's business strategy is to be a "first mover" in the market, it must be innovative in order to develop and introduce new products before competitors do so. To be entrepreneurial and innovative, the organization needs an organic structure, one that is flexible and decentralized. A centralized mechanistic structure would not allow managers and associates the freedom to be creative and take the risks necessary to identify market opportunities and develop innovative products. Similarly, the culture of the organization must allow for the use of intuition and risk-taking behaviors because associates and managers should not be afraid of making errors or failing. To be successful over time, most organizations must be ambidextrous.

In the chapter, we mentioned that Southwest Airlines has been highly successful because of its culture and its ability to hire new associates and managers who fit well with the culture. Southwest has followed an integrated low-cost/differentiation business strategy since its founding. Many airlines have tried to imitate this strategy but have been unable to reproduce Southwest's success. These competitors have failed to realize that Southwest uses not only low cost but also a differentiated high-quality service provided through its associates. Southwest's associates have fun at work and work together as a team. These attributes come through in the service provided and also help the airline to hold down its costs. Thus, Southwest Airlines' unique strategy, which integrates low cost and differentiation, is implemented effectively because of its culture and human resource management system.[116] Other airlines could not reproduce and effectively implement this integrated strategy because they could not imitate Southwest's culture.

A strategy will be only as effective as its implementation. If the strategy is well formulated, and the structure and the culture fit the strategy well, the organization will achieve higher performance. Congruence among strategy, structure, and culture is necessary to achieve the highest possible organization performance.

Culture's effects on strategy are also often evident in mergers and acquisitions. Many mergers between companies fail. Often these failures occur not because of financial or technical problems but because the companies involved have vastly different organizational cultures.[117] One company may be entrepreneurial and flexible, for example, whereas the other may be traditional and rigid. Merging these two cultures is problematic, at the least.

Therefore, senior managers who expect their firm to acquire another firm should understand the target firm's culture and what must be done to integrate it. They must also act immediately after the completion of the acquisition to merge the cultures. Doing so will require developing shared values between the two firms. Cisco Systems is well known for its ability to integrate acquisitions.[118] This firm assigns key people to preacquisition integration teams and carefully includes individuals from the firm being acquired.

Critical Thinking Questions

1. Consider an organization of which you are a member or an associate. What is the structure in this organization? Is it centralized or decentralized? Is it organic and flexible? How would you change the structure in this organization to make it more effective?

2. How would you describe the culture in the organization identified in your answer to question 1? How does the culture affect members' behavior in the organization?

3. When you become a manager, what type of culture will you establish in your unit? What values do you want to emphasize? Why?

organization's culture, problems are likely to develop. In fact, when the lack of fit is between the CEO and the organization's culture, the problems are likely to be more severe, as in the case of Home Depot and Bob Nardelli. The outcomes are consistent with a great deal of research suggesting that similarity in values and goals attracts individuals to one another and to organizations.[111] Job applicants as well as associates and managers in an organization should assess applicant fit with structure and culture prior to making final employment decisions. Selection for fit is a key aspect of high-involvement management, as discussed in Chapter 1.

Interestingly, socialization can bridge some differences between newcomer preferences and organizational structure and between newcomer values and organizational culture. Socialization achieves this function by highlighting how a person's preferences and values may fit in unseen or partial ways. To some small degree, socialization also may alter a newcomer's preferences. In one study based on the socialization framework presented earlier, individuals exposed to strong socialization efforts exhibited more congruence between their personal attributes and the organization's structure and culture. (This was true even after taking into account the initial level of congruence.)[112]

Although personal fit with structure and culture is important, two issues must be addressed. First, an organization that hires only those who fit existing organizational characteristics may find it difficult to make major changes when they become necessary.[113] With individuals throughout the organization sharing preferences and values, the organization may be resistant to change. To remain adaptive, an organization may want to hire a few key individuals who do not fit. Their ideas may prompt reflection and thereby help the organization to change if necessary. These issues are addressed more fully in Chapter 14. Second, an organization that hires only those who fit may inadvertently discriminate against minorities or foreign nationals.[114] Such an organization fails to experience the benefits from having a multicultural workforce, as discussed in Chapter 2. Perhaps the best advice is to hire for fit, but with a relatively broad definition of fit allowing exceptions and a specific plan for nurturing the exceptions, no matter what their differences.[115]

What This Chapter Adds to Your Knowledge Portfolio

In this chapter, we described several aspects of structure and explained how strategy, environment, technology, and firm size influence structure. We also discussed the competing values culture framework, as well as socialization, subcultures, and cultural audits. Person–organization fit has also been addressed. In summary, we have made the following points:

- Organizational structure is the formal system of work roles and authority relationships that govern how associates and managers interact with one another. Structure can be described using structural characteristics, which determine the shape and appearance of an organization's hierarchy. These characteristics include height, spans of control, and departmentalization (functional versus divisional grouping of resources). Structure can also be described using structuring characteristics, which directly prescribe behavior. These include centralization (the amount of decision authority held at the top of the organization), standardization (the existence of rules and standard operating procedures), formalization (the degree to which rules and procedures exist in written form), and specialization (the degree to which associates and managers have narrow jobs). Modern organizations tend to emphasize configurations of structural and structuring characteristics that yield a substantial amount of freedom for lower-level managers and associates.

- Strategy plays an important role in organizational structure. Corporate strategy corresponds to the emphasis placed on growth and diversification in a firm. An emphasis on growth through internal development suggests the need for substantial research and development and marketing departments. An emphasis on growth though acquisition suggests the need for well-developed financial and legal functions. Diversification must be matched by type of departmentalization, with a single business strategy and a dominant-product strategy calling for a functional structure and higher levels of diversification calling for a divisional structure. Business-level strategies represent the method of competing in a particular product or service market. Low-cost

back to the knowledge objectives

1. Compare and contrast the structural and structuring aspects of organizational structure.
2. Assume you manage a firm with three substantially different product lines. A differentiation strategy is used for each product line. What structure choices would you make, and why?
3. Assume you manage a small R&D department. When making choices concerning structure, would you be more concerned about the external environment, more concerned about technology, or equally concerned about the external environment and technology? Explain your answer.
4. What are the four types of culture in the competing values model? In which would you prefer to work, and why?
5. What is socialization? Describe a situation in which you were socialized into an organization (a club, a business firm, a church, or a volunteer organization).
6. What is a cultural audit? Why should organizations conduct cultural audits?
7. How does an organization ensure a fit between its associates' values and its organizational culture?

and differentiation are two popular strategies, with the low-cost strategy calling for a less organic structure and differentiation requiring a more organic structure.

- The external environment also plays a role in structure. Uncertain environments (those that are complex and changing) create a need for organic structure. They also increase the need for integration among functional departments focused on the same market. Elements of structure that address integration include slack resources, self-contained tasks, information technology, and lateral relations. Furthermore, different levels of uncertainty may be experienced by different functional departments, resulting in a need to differentiate the departments, with some being more organic than others.
- Technology, too, plays a role in structure. An early framework suggests that technological complexity determines the structure required in small manufacturing firms. More recent work demonstrates that mass customization can be used in manufacturing firms of all sizes and that organic structure facilitates this approach. Recent work has also focused on technological nonroutineness in manufacturing and service organizations, suggesting that high levels of nonroutineness in small organizations and units of larger ones should be matched with more organic structures.
- Finally, organizational size plays a role in structure. Large organizations must be taller and more formalized in order to ensure smooth functioning. Centralization

tends to decrease, however, because senior managers cannot make all decisions. However, as organizations grow in size, the potential increases that they will suffer from inertia. To avoid or overcome inertia, organizations must try to develop ambidextrous attributes. Ambidextrous organizations balance formalization and flexibility and thereby are able to maintain efficiency while also being innovative.

- Organizational culture represents shared values that influence behavior. The competing values culture model is an important and popular framework for analyzing cultural phenomena in organizations. The model is based on two value dimensions: (1) flexibility and discretion versus stability and control and (2) internal focus coupled with integration versus an external focus coupled with differentiation in the marketplace. Based on these two dimensions, four culture types emerge: clan, hierarchy, market, and adhocracy.

- Socialization involves imparting an organization's values to newcomers. Socialization is accomplished by exposing individuals to experiences that highlight the organization's values. In designing socialization activities, managers and associates should consider context (collective and formal versus individual and informal), content (sequential and fixed versus variable and random), and social dynamics (serial and investiture versus disjunctive and divestiture).

- Culture audits are formal analyses designed to uncover shared values in an organization. They involve: (1) analyzing the process and content of socialization, (2) analyzing how the organization has responded to critical incidents in its history, (3) analyzing the values and beliefs of founders and current leaders, and (4) exploring any puzzling findings from the earlier analyses.

- Subcultures can develop in an organization. In large, diverse organizations, the organizational culture can be seen as a system of integrated subcultures rather than a unified set of values. Although subcultures can sometimes cause problems when they are substantially inconsistent with the overall culture of the organization, they can also help to produce fresh insights and ideas.

- Individuals bring values to the organization. The fit between individual values and organization values can be important. If there is a misfit, individuals are likely to be unproductive or become dissatisfied and leave.

Key Terms

building your human capital

An Assessment of Creativity

Many organizations use a differentiation strategy that calls for initiative and creativity. Many of these same organizations have an adhocracy culture, where innovation and risk taking are valued. Not all individuals, however, are equally suited for these organizations. This assessment focuses on creativity. Although an individual's propensity to be creative can vary from situation to situation, his or her general tendencies provide useful insight.

Instructions

In this assessment, you will read 50 statements that describe people. Use the rating scale below to indicate how accurately each statement describes you. Rate yourself as you generally are now, not as you wish to be in the future; and rate yourself as you honestly see yourself. Read each item carefully, and then circle the number that corresponds to your choice from the rating scale.

1 Strongly Disagree	2 Disagree	3 In Between or Don't Know	4 Agree	5 Strongly Agree

1. I always work with a great deal of certainty that I am following the correct procedures for solving a particular problem.	1	2	3	4	5
2. It would be a waste of time for me to ask questions if I had no hope of obtaining answers.	1	2	3	4	5
3. I feel that a logical step-by-step method is best for solving problems.	1	2	3	4	5
4. I occasionally voice opinions in groups that seem to turn some people off.	1	2	3	4	5
5. I spend a great deal of time thinking about what others think of me.	1	2	3	4	5
6. I feel that I may have a special contribution to give to the world.	1	2	3	4	5
7. It is more important for me to do what I believe to be right than to try to win the approval of others.	1	2	3	4	5
8. People who seem unsure and uncertain about things lose my respect.	1	2	3	4	5
9. I am able to stick with difficult problems over extended periods of time.	1	2	3	4	5
10. On occasion I get overly enthusiastic about things.	1	2	3	4	5
11. I often get my best ideas when doing nothing in particular.	1	2	3	4	5
12. I rely on intuitive hunches and the feeling of "rightness" or "wrongness" when moving toward the solution of a problem.	1	2	3	4	5
13. When problem solving, I work faster analyzing the problem and slower when synthesizing the information I've gathered.	1	2	3	4	5

14. I like hobbies that involve collecting things.	1	2	3	4	5
15. Daydreaming has provided the impetus for many of my more important projects.	1	2	3	4	5
16. If I had to choose from two occupations other than the one I now have or am now training for, I would rather be a physician than an explorer.	1	2	3	4	5
17. I can get along more easily with people if they belong to about the same social and business class as myself.	1	2	3	4	5
18. I have a high degree of aesthetic sensitivity.	1	2	3	4	5
19. Intuitive hunches are unreliable guides in problem solving.	1	2	3	4	5
20. I am much more interested in coming up with new ideas than in trying to sell them to others.	1	2	3	4	5
21. I tend to avoid situations in which I might feel inferior.	1	2	3	4	5
22. In evaluating information, the source of it is more important to me than the content.	1	2	3	4	5
23. I like people who follow the rule "business before pleasure."	1	2	3	4	5
24. One's own self-respect is much more important than the respect of others.	1	2	3	4	5
25. I feel that people who strive for perfection are unwise.	1	2	3	4	5
26. I like work in which I must influence others.	1	2	3	4	5
27. It is important for me to have a place for everything and everything in its place.	1	2	3	4	5
28. People who are willing to entertain "crackpot" ideas are impractical.	1	2	3	4	5
29. I rather enjoy fooling around with new ideas, even if there is no practical payoff.	1	2	3	4	5
30. When a certain approach to a problem doesn't work, I can quickly reorient my thinking.	1	2	3	4	5
31. I don't like to ask questions that show my ignorance.	1	2	3	4	5
32. I can more easily change my interests to pursue a job or career than I can change a job to pursue my interests.	1	2	3	4	5
33. Inability to solve a problem is frequently due to asking the wrong questions.	1	2	3	4	5
34. I can frequently anticipate the solution to my problems.	1	2	3	4	5
35. It is a waste of time to analyze one's failures.	1	2	3	4	5
36. Only fuzzy thinkers resort to metaphors and analogies.	1	2	3	4	5
37. At times I have so enjoyed the ingenuity of a crook that I hoped he or she would go scot-free.	1	2	3	4	5
38. I frequently begin work on a problem that I can only dimly sense and cannot yet express.	1	2	3	4	5
39. I frequently tend to forget things, such as names of people, streets, highways, and small towns.	1	2	3	4	5

40. I feel that hard work is the basic factor in success.	1	2	3	4	5
41. To be regarded as a good team member is important to me.	1	2	3	4	5
42. I know how to keep my inner impulses in check.	1	2	3	4	5
43. I am a thoroughly dependable and responsible person.	1	2	3	4	5
44. I resent things being uncertain and unpredictable.	1	2	3	4	5
45. I prefer to work with others in a team effort rather than solo.	1	2	3	4	5
46. The trouble with many people is that they take things too seriously.	1	2	3	4	5
47. I am frequently haunted by my problems and cannot let go of them.	1	2	3	4	5
48. I can easily give up immediate gain or comfort to reach the goals I have set.	1	2	3	4	5
49. If I were a college professor, I would rather teach factual courses than those involving theory.	1	2	3	4	5
50. I'm attracted to the mystery of life.	1	2	3	4	5

Scoring Key

Combine the numbers you have circled, as follows:

Item 4 + Item 6 + Item 7 + Item 9 + Item 10 + Item 11 + Item 12 + Item 15 + Item 18 + Item 20 + Item 24 + Item 29 + Item 30 + Item 33 + Item 34 + Item 37 + Item 38 + Item 39 + Item 40 + Item 46 + Item 47 + Item 48 + Item 50 + [162 − (Item 1 + Item 2 + Item 3 + Item 5 + Item 8 + Item 13 + Item 14 + Item 16 + Item 17 + Item 19 + Item 21 + Item 22 + Item 23 + Item 25 + Item 26 + Item 27 + Item 28 + Item 31 + Item 32 + Item 35 + Item 36 + Item 41 + Item 42 + Item 43 + Item 44 + Item 45 + Item 49)]

Total scores can be interpreted as follows:

210–250	Very creative
170–209	Somewhat creative
130–169	Neither creative nor noncreative
90–129	Not very creative
50–89	Noncreative

Source: Adapted from D.D. Bowen, R.J. Lewicki, D.T. Hall, & F.S. Hall. 1997. *Experiences in Management and Organizational Behavior* (New York: John Wiley & Sons).

an organizational behavior moment
How Effective Is Hillwood Medical Center?

Sharon Lawson is the administrator of Hillwood Medical Center, a large hospital located in Boston, Massachusetts. She has been its administrator for almost five years. Although it has been a rewarding position, it has not been without its frustrations. One of Sharon's primary frustrations has been her inability to determine how she should measure the effectiveness of the hospital.

The chief medical officer, Dr. Ben Peters, thinks that the only way to measure the effectiveness of a hospital is the number of human lives saved, compared with the number saved in other, similar hospitals. But the board to which Sharon reports is highly concerned about the costs of running the hospital. Hillwood is nonprofit but has no outside sponsors, and so it must remain financially solvent without contributions from another major institution.

In order to be reimbursed for Medicare and Medicaid patients, the hospital must meet the licensing requirements of the state health department, as well as the requirements of the U.S. Department of Health and Human Services. Sharon finds that some of these requirements reflect minimum standards, whereas others are more rigid. She also finds that the demands of the administrative board and those of doctors on the staff frequently conflict. She must mediate these demands and make decisions to maximize the effectiveness of the hospital.

Sharon's day begins when she arises at 6:00 A.M., exercises, showers, has a quick breakfast, and heads for the office. She usually arrives at the office around 7:15 A.M. She likes to get there before others so that she can review and plan her day's activities without interruption. Today she sees that she has an appointment at 8:30 A.M. with a member of the state health department concerning its recent inspection. At 10:00 A.M., she has an administrative staff meeting. At 2:00 P.M., she has scheduled a meeting with the medical staff, and at 4:00 P.M. she has an appointment with the hospital's attorney. (She also has a luncheon appointment with an old college friend who is in town for a few days.) It looks as if her day is well planned.

At 8:15, Sharon receives a call from Dr. Ramon Garcia, chief of surgery.

"Sharon, I must see you. Do you have time now so that we could talk about an important matter?"

"Ramon, I have an appointment in fifteen minutes and probably won't be free until about eleven this morning. Would that be okay?"

"I guess so. I don't have much choice, do I?" With that, he hangs up.

At 8:30, Sharon ushers in Holly Wedman from the state health department. She learns that Hillwood has passed the general inspection but that some areas need to be improved. The kitchen meets only minimum standards for cleanliness, and some other areas are questionable. The inspectors also questioned hospital procedures that allow many people access to the drug supplies. (Sharon recalls that she tried to tighten up those procedures only two months ago, but the medical staff complained so strongly that she relented and made no change.) The state health department representative requests that appropriate changes be made and notes that these areas will be given especially rigorous scrutiny at the next inspection in six months. As the meeting ends, Sharon looks at her watch. It is 9:55—just enough time to make it to the conference room for her next meeting.

The administrative staff meeting begins normally, but after about 30 minutes, Helen Mathis, controller, asks to speak.

"Sharon, when are we going to get the new computer software we requested six months ago?"

"I don't know, Helen. I've discussed it with the board, but they've been noncommittal. We'll have to try to build it into next year's budget."

"But we need it now. We can't process our billing efficiently. Our accounts receivable are too large. We're going to run into a cash-flow problem soon if we don't find other ways to increase our billing efficiency."

Sharon thought, "Cash-flow problems. I wonder how those fit into Dr. Peters's definition of effectiveness."

It is finally decided that Sharon will make a new and stronger request to the board for the computer software.

At 11:00 sharp, Dr. Garcia comes stomping into Sharon's office, exhibiting his usual crusty demeanor. "Sharon, we have a serious problem on our hands. I've heard through the grapevine that a malpractice suit will be filed against one of our surgeons, Dr. Chambers."

"That's nothing new; we get several of those a year."

"Yes, but I think this one may have some merit, and the hospital is jointly named in the suit."

"What do you mean?"

"Well, I've suspected for several months that Dr. Chambers has been drinking a lot. He may have performed an operation while under the influence. I've talked to several people who were in the operating room at the time, and they believe that he was drunk."

"Oh, no! If you suspected this why didn't you do something?"

"What was I supposed to do? Accuse one of the oldest and most respected members of our surgical staff? You just don't accuse a person like that without proof. We've got to meet with Chambers now and confront him."

"Well, set up a meeting."

"I already have. His only free time was at lunch, so I took the liberty of scheduling a meeting with him for you and me at that time."

"I already have an engagement. I can't do it today. Try to set one up tomorrow."

Dr. Garcia, obviously feeling a great deal of stress, explodes, "You administrators are never available when we need you. Your only concern is holding down costs. We're talking about human lives here. Chambers may do it again before tomorrow."

Sharon seethes at his insinuation. "If that mattered to you, why did you wait until you heard of the malpractice suit to do something about it?"

Garcia leaves, slamming the door.

Sharon goes to lunch with her friend, but she can't enjoy it. Her mind is on problems at the hospital. She can hardly wait for the 2:00 P.M. medical staff meeting.

The meeting begins with only about half of the doctors in attendance, which is not unusual. Most of them will show up before the meeting is over. Much of the time is taken up discussing why the hospital has not purchased an upgraded piece of standard diagnostic equipment used in body scanning. Of course, it "only" costs $1 million. The meeting ends without resolving the problem. Sharon agrees to buy the equipment next year but does not have the money for it in this year's budget. The doctors do not fully understand why it cannot be purchased now if it can be purchased next year.

As soon as Sharon gets back to her office, her secretary gives her a message to call Terry Wilson, one of the third-floor pediatric nurses. Terry had said it was urgent.

"Terry, this is Sharon Lawson. What can I do for you?"

"Ms. Lawson, I thought you should know. The nurses in pediatrics are planning a walkout tomorrow."

"What? A walkout? Why?" Sharon is beginning to get a headache.

"Yes, a walkout. The nurses feel that Supervisor Tyson is a tyrant, and they want her replaced."

"Terry, can you get a group of those nurses together and meet me in my office in fifteen minutes? Be sure to leave several to cover the floor while you're gone."

"Okay. See you in a few minutes."

Sharon and the nurses meet and discuss the situation. The nurses are quite adamant but finally agree to give Sharon a week

to investigate the situation and attempt to resolve it. A meeting is scheduled for next week to review the situation.

The hospital's attorney has to wait for almost 20 minutes because Sharon's meeting with the nurses runs past 4:00 P.M. Finally they meet, and as Sharon feared, he brings news of the malpractice suit filed against Dr. Chambers and Hillwood. They discuss the steps that should be taken and how the situation with Dr. Chambers should be handled from a legal viewpoint. Obviously, some hard decisions will have to be made.

The attorney leaves at 5:30, and Sharon sits in her office pondering the day's problems. She also thinks of her original problem: how to measure Hillwood's effectiveness.

Discussion Questions

1. Describe the culture or cultures at Hillwood. Are there subcultures?
2. How would you recommend that Sharon measure effectiveness at Hillwood? What do you think some of the effectiveness criteria might be?

team exercise

Words-in-Sentences Company

In this exercise, you will form a "mini-organization" with several other people. You will also compete with other companies in your industry. The success of your company will depend on your planning and organizational structure. It is important, therefore, that you spend some time thinking about the best design for your organization.

Step 1: 5 Minutes

Form companies and assign workplaces. The total class should be divided into small groups of four or five individuals. Each group should consider itself a company.

Step 2: 10 Minutes

Read the directions below and ask the instructor about any points that need clarification. Everyone should be familiar with the task before beginning Step 3.

You are members of a small company that manufactures words and then packages them in meaningful (English-language) sentences. Market research has established that sentences of at least three words but not more than six words are in demand.

The "words-in-sentences" (WIS) industry is highly competitive in terms of price, and several new firms have recently entered the market. Your ability to compete depends on efficiency and quality control.

GROUP TASK

Your group must design and participate in running a WIS company. You should design your organization to be as efficient as possible during each 10-minute production run. After the first production run, you will have an opportunity to reorganize your company if you want to.

RAW MATERIALS

For each production run, you will be given a "raw material word or phrase." The letters found in the word or phrase serve as the raw materials available to produce new words in sentences. For example, if the raw material word is *organization,* you can produce the following words and sentence: "Nat ran to a zoo."

PRODUCTION RULES

Several rules must be followed in producing "words-in-sentences." If these rules are not followed, your output will not meet production specifications and will not pass quality-control inspection.

1. A letter may appear only as often in a manufactured word as it appears in the raw-material word or phrase; for example, *organization* has two *o*'s. Thus, *zoo* is legitimate, but *zoology* is not—it has too many *o*'s.
2. Raw-material letters can be used over again in new, different manufactured words.
3. A manufactured word may be used only once in a sentence and in only one sentence during a production run; if a word—for example, *zoo*—is used once in a sentence, it is out of stock.
4. A new word may not be made by adding s to form the plural of an already used manufactured word.
5. A word is defined by its spelling, not its meaning.
6. Nonsense words or nonsense sentences are unacceptable. All words must be in the English language.
7. Names and places are acceptable.
8. Slang is not acceptable.

MEASURING PERFORMANCE

The output of your WIS company is measured by the total number of acceptable words that are packaged in sentences in the available time. The sentences must be legible, listed on no more than two sheets of paper, and handed to the quality-control review board at the completion of each production run.

DELIVERY

Delivery must be made to the quality-control review board 30 seconds after the end of each production run.

QUALITY CONTROL

If any word in a sentence does not meet the standards set forth above, all of the words in the sentence will be rejected. The quality-control review board (composed of one member from each company) is the final arbiter of acceptability. In the event of a tie vote on the review board, a coin toss will determine the outcome.

Step 3: 15 Minutes

Design your organization's structure using as many group members as you see fit to produce your words-in-sentences. There are many potential ways of organizing. Since some are more efficient than others, you may want to consider the following:

1. What is your company's objective?
2. How will you achieve your objective? How should you plan your work, given the time allowed?
3. What degree of specialization and centralization is appropriate?
4. Which group members are more qualified to perform certain tasks?

   Assign one member of your group to serve on the quality-control review board. This person may also participate in production runs.

Step 4: 10 Minutes—Production Run 1

1. The instructor will hand each WIS company a sheet with a raw material word or phrase.
2. When the instructor announces "Begin production," you are to manufacture as many words as possible and package them in sentences for delivery to the quality-control review board. You will have 10 minutes.
3. When the instructor announces "Stop production," you will have 30 seconds to deliver your output to the quality-control review board. Output received after 30 seconds does not meet the delivery schedule and will not be counted.

Step 5: 10 Minutes

1. The designated members of the quality-control review board will review output from each company. The total output should be recorded (after quality-control approval) on the board.
2. While the review board is completing its task, each WIS company should discuss what happened during Production Run 1.

Step 6: 5 Minutes

Each company should evaluate its performance and organization. Companies may reorganize for Run 2.

Step 7: 10 Minutes—Production Run 2

1. The instructor will hand each WIS company a sheet with a raw-material word or phrase.
2. Proceed as in Step 4 (Production Run 1). You will have 10 minutes for production.

Step 8: 10 Minutes

1. The quality-control review board will review each company's output and record it on the board. The totals for Runs 1 and 2 should be tallied.
2. While the board is completing its task, each WIS company should prepare an organization chart depicting its structural characteristics for both production runs and should prepare a description of its structuring characteristics.

Step 9: 10 Minutes

Discuss this exercise as a class. The instructor will provide discussion questions. Each company should share the structure information it prepared in Step 8.

Source: Adapted from D.D. Bowen, RJ. Lewicki, D.T. Hall, & F.S. Hall. 1997. *Experiences in Management and Organizational Behavior* (New York: John Wiley & Sons).

Endnotes

1. Etzioni, A. 1964. *Modern organization.* Englewood Cliffs, NJ: Prentice Hall; Jones, G.R. 2010. *Organizational theory, design and change* (6th ed.). Englewood Cliffs, NJ: Pearson-Prentice Hall.
2. Ravashi, D. & Schultz, M. 2006. Responding to organizational identity threats: Exploring the role of organizational culture. *Academy of Management Journal,* 49: 433–458; Gerhart, B. 2009. How much does national culture constrain organizational culture? *Management and Organization Review,* 5: 241–259.
3. Campbell, J.P., Bownas, D.A., Peterson, N.G., & Dunnette, M.D. 1974. The measurement of organizational effectiveness: A review of the relevant research and opinion. Report Tr-71-1, San Diego, Navy Personnel Research and Development Center; Dalton, D.R., Todor, W.D., Spendolini, M.J., Fielding, G.J., & Porter, L.W.

1980. Organization structure and performance: A critical review. *Academy of Management Review*, 5: 49–64.

4. Keats, B. W. & O'Neill, H. 2001. Organizational structure: Looking through a strategy lens, in M.A. Hitt, R.E. Freeman, and J.S. Harrison (eds.), *Handbook of strategic management*, Oxford, United Kingdom: Blackwell Publishers, pp. 520–542.

5. Campbell, Bownas, Peterson, & Dunnette, The measurement of organizational effectiveness; Dalton, Todor, Spendolini, Fielding & Porter, Organization structure and performance.

6. Child, J. 1984. *Organization: A guide to problems and practices* (2nd ed.). London: Harper & Row; Larson, E.W., & King, J.B. 1996. The systematic distortion of information: An ongoing challenge to management. *Organizational Dynamics*, 24 (3): 49–61; Nahm, A.Y., Vonderembse, M.A., & Koufteros, X.A. 2003. The impact of organizational structure on time-based manufacturing and plant performance. *Journal of Operations Management*, 21: 281–306.

7. Child, *Organization: A guide to problems and practices*.

8. Ibid.

9. Bohte, J., & Meier, K.J. 2001. Structure and the performance of public organizations: Task difficulty and span of control. *Public Organization Review*, 1: 341–354; Worthy, J.C. 1950. Organizational structure and employee morale. *American Sociological Review*, 15: 169–179.

10. Jones, *Organizational theory, design and change*.

11. Paine, L.S., & Mavrinac, S.C. 1995. *AES Honeycomb*. Boston: Harvard Business School Publishing; AES Corporation 2005 Annual Report, at http://www.aes.com, March 3, 2007.

12. Davison, B. 2003. Management span of control: How wide is too wide? *The Journal of Business Strategy*, 24 (4): 22–29.

13. *The Saratoga Review*, 2009. Talent strategies for tough times: Reductions in force. PricewaterhouseCoopers, July 4–5.

14. Duncan, R. 1979. What is the right organization structure? Decision tree analysis provides the answer. *Organizational Dynamics*, 7 (3): 59–80.

15. Ibid.

16. Ibid.

17. Ibid.

18. Rank, O.N., Robins, G.L. & Pattison, P.E. 2010. Structural logic of intraorganizational networks. *Organization Science*, in press; Maria, J., & Marti, V. 2004. Social capital benchmarking system: Profiting from social capital when building network organizations. *Journal of Intellectual Capital*, 5: 426–442; Miles, R.E., Snow, C.C., Mathews, J.A., Miles, G., & Coleman, H.J. 1997. Organizing in the knowledge age: Anticipating the cellular form. *Academy of Management Executive*, 11 (4): 7–20.

19. Zhiang, L., Peng, M.W., Yang, H. & Sun, S.L. 2009. How do networks and learning drive an institutional comparison between China and the United States? *Strategic Management Journal*, 30: 1113–1132; Zhiang, L., Yang, H. & Arya, B. 2009. Alliance partners and firm performance: Resource complementarity and status association, *Strategic Management Journal*, 30: 921–940; Hitt, M.A., Ireland, R.D., & Hoskisson, R.E., 2011. *Strategic management: Competitiveness and globalization*. Cincinnati, OH: Cengage South-Western Publishing .

20. Mintzberg, H. 1993. *Structuring in fives: Designing effective organizations*. Englewood Cliffs, NJ: Prentice Hall; Zabojnik, J.

2002. Centralized and decentralized decision making in organizations. *Journal of Labor Economics*, 20: 1–21.

21. Huber, G.P., Miller, C.C., & Glick, W.H. 1990. Developing more encompassing theories about organizations: The centralization-effectiveness relationship as an example. *Organization Science*, 1: 11–40; Tata, J., & Prasad, S. 2004. *Journal of Managerial Issues*, 16: 248–265.

22. Bunderson, J.S., & Boumgarden, P. 2010. Structure and learning in self-managed teams: Why "bureaucratic" teams can be better learners, *Organization Science*, in press.

23. Burns, T., & Stalker, G.M. 1966. *The management of innovation*. London: Tavistock Institute; Jones, *Organization theory, design and change*.

24. The term "learning organization" has been defined in many different ways. As it stands, there is considerable confusion and disagreement concerning its proper definition. Many *users* of the term, however, focus on aspects of structure just as we do here. See, for example, Dodgson, M. 1993. Organizational learning: A review of some literatures. *Organization Studies*, 1: 375–394. Also see Goh, S.C. Toward a learning organization: The strategic building blocks. *S.A.M. Advanced Management Journal*, 63 (2): 15–22; For general insights, see Garvin, D.A. 1993. Building a learning organization. *Harvard Business Review*, 71 (4): 78–91.

25. The term "boundaryless organization" has been defined in various ways. Users of the term, however, generally refer to individuals having freedom and incentives to work across internal and external organizational boundaries. For a broad discussion, see Ashkenas, R., Ulrich, D., Jick, T., & Kerr, S. 1995. *The boundaryless organization*. San Francisco, CA: Jossey-Bass.

26. Freiberg, K., & Freiberg, J. 1996. *Nuts!: Southwest Airlines' crazy recipe for business and personal success*. Austin, TX: Bard Press.

27. Sine, W.D., Mitsuhashi, H., & Kirsch, D.A., 2006. Revisiting Burns and Stalker: Formal structure and new venture performance in emerging economic sectors, *Academy of Management Journal*, 49: 121–132.

28. Ahuja, G., Polidoro, F. & Mitchell, W. 2009. Structural homophily or social asymmetry? The formation of alliances by poorly embedded firms, *Strategic Management Journal*, 30: 941–956.

29. Thompson, J.P. 1967, *Organizations in action*. New York: McGraw-Hill; Hitt, M.A., Ireland, R.D., & Hoskisson, R.E. 2011. *Strategic management: Competitiveness and globalization*. Mason, OH: Cengage South-Western.

30. Hitt, M.A., Ireland, R.D., & Palia, K.A. 1982. Industrial firm's grand strategy and functional importance: Moderating effects of technology and uncertainty. *Academy of Management Journal*, 3: 265–298.

31. Anonymous. 2004, Dec. 19. Growth Strategy Leadership Award Given to Technology Company. *Medical Devices & Surgical Technology Week*, Atlanta, p. 25.

32. Hitt, M.A., Harrison, J.S., & Ireland, R.D. 2001. *Mergers and acquisitions: A guide to creating value for stakeholders*. New York: Oxford University Press; Hitt, M.A., King, D., Krishnan, H., Makri, M. Schijven, M. Shimizu, K. & Zhu, H. 2009. Mergers and acquisitions: Overcoming pitfalls, building synergy, and creating value. *Business Horizons*, 52: 523–529.

33. Holloway, C.A., Wheelwright, S.C., & Tempest, N. 1999. *Cisco Systems, Inc.: Acquisition integration for manufacturing.* Palo Alto, CA: Stanford Graduate School of Business.

34. Weber, Y., & Menipaz, E. 2003. Measuring cultural fit in mergers and acquisitions. *International Journal of Business Performance Management,* 5: 54–72.

35. Shimizu, K., & Hitt, M.A. 2005. What constrains or facilitates the divestiture of formerly acquired firms? The effects of organizational inertia. *Journal of Management,* 31: 50–72.

36. Palich, L.E., Cardinal, L.B., & Miller, C.C. 2000. Curvilinearity in the diversification-performance linkage: An examination of over three decades of research. *Strategic Management Journal,* 21: 155–174; David, P., O'Brien, J.P., Yoshikawa, T. & Delios, A. 2010. Do shareholders or stakeholders appropriate the rents from corporate diversification? The influence of ownership structure. *Academy of Management Journal,* in press.

37. Lim., E.N., Das, S.S. & Das, A. 2009. Diversification strategy, capital structure, and the Asian financial crisis (1997-1998): Evidence from Singapore firms. *Strategic Management Journal,* 30: 577–594.

38. Wiersema, M.F. & Bowen, H.P. 2008. Corporate diversification: The impact of competition, industry globalization and product diversification. *Strategic Management Journal,* 29: 115–132; Dastidar, P. 2009. International corporate diversification and performance: does firm self-selection matter? *Journal of International Business Studies,* 40: 71–85.

39. Hitt, Ireland & Hoskisson, *Strategic management.*

40. Galan, J.I. & Sanchez-Bueno, M.J. 2009. The continuing validity of the strategy-structure nexus: New findings, 1993–2003. *Strategic Management Journal,* 30: 1234–1243.

41. Hitt, Ireland, & Hoskisson, *Strategic management.*

42. Grinyer, P.H., Yasai-Ardekani, M. , & Al-Bazzaz, S. 1980. Strategy, structure, environment, and financial performance in 48 United Kingdom companies. *Academy of Management Journal,* 23:193–220; Hitt, & Ireland. Relationships among corporate level distinctive competence, diversification strategy, corporate structure and performance.

43. Porter, M.E. 1980. *Competitive strategy: Techniques for analyzing industries and competitors.* New York: The Free Press.

44. See, for example: Govindarajan, V. 1988. A contingency approach to strategy implementation at the business unit level: Integrating administrative mechanisms with strategy. *Academy of Management Journal,* 31: 828–853; Jones. *Organizational theory, design and change.*

45. Hoskisson, R.E., Hitt, M.A., Ireland, R.D., & Harrison, J.S. 2008. *Competing for advantage,* Cincinnati, OH: Thomson South-Western.

46. See, for example: Govindarajan, A contingency approach to strategy implementation at the business unit level: Integrating administrative mechanisms with strategy; Jones. *Organizational theory, design and change*; Vorhies, D.W., & Morgan, N.A. 2003. A configuration theory assessment of marketing organization fit with business strategy and its relationship with marketing performance. *Journal of Marketing,* 67: 100–115.

47. Holcomb, T.R., Holmes, Jr., R.M, & Connelley, B.L. 2009. Making the most of what you have: Managerial ability as a source of resource value creation. *Strategic Management Journal,* 30: 457–485.

48. General Electric. 2004. Our company: Business directory. At http://www.ge.com/en/company/ businesses/index.htm.

49. Bourgeois, L.J. 1980. Strategy and environment: A conceptual integration. *Academy of Management Review,* 5: 25–29.

50. Delmas, M.A. & Toffel, M.W. 2008. Organizational responses to environmental demands: Opening the black box, *Strategic Management Journal,* 29: 1027–1055.

51. Marren, P. 2009. Uncertainty cubed, *Journal of Business Strategy,* 30 (4): 52–54; Oriani, R. & Sobrero, M. 2008. Uncertainty and the market valuation of R&D within a real options logic, *Strategic Management Journal,* 29: 343–361.

52. Lawrence, P.R., & Lorsch, J.W. 1967. *Organization and environment.* Boston: Harvard Business School Press.

53. Naman, J.L., & Slevin, D.P. 1993. Entrepreneurship and the concept of fit: A model and empirical tests. *Strategic Management Journal,* 14: 137–153; Negandhi, A., & Reimann, C. 1973. Task environment, decentralization and organizational effectiveness. *Human Relations,* 26: 203–214; Priem, R.L. 1994. Executive judgement, organizational congruence, and firm performance. *Organization Science,* 421–437; Nadkarni, S. & Barr, P.S. 2008, Environmental context, managerial cognition, and strategic action: An integrated view, *Strategic Management Journal,* 29: 1395–1427.

54. Sirmon, D.G., Hitt, M.A., & Ireland, R.D. 2007. Managing firm resources in dynamic environments to create value: Looking inside the black box. *Academy of Management Review,* 32: 273–292.

55. Garg, V.K., Walters, B.A., & Priem, R.L. 2003. Chief executive scanning emphases, environmental dynamism, and manufacturing firm performance. *Strategic Management Journal,* 24: 725–744.

56. Jarzabkowski, P., & Balogun, J. 2009. The practice and process of delivering integration through strategic planning, *Journal of Management Studies,* 46: 1255–1288.

57. Galbraith, J. 1973. *Designing complex organizations.* Reading, MA: Addison-Wesley.

58. Al-Mudimigh, Z.M., & Al-Mashari, M. 2001. ERP software implementation: An integrative framework. *European Journal of Information Systems,* 10: 216–226; Davenport, T. 2000. *Mission critical: Realizing the promise of enterprise systems.* Boston: Harvard Business School Press.

59. Johnson, T., Lorents, A.C., Morgan, J., & Ozmun, J. 2004. A customized ERP/SAP model for business curriculum integration. *Journal of Information Systems Education,* 15: 245–253.

60. Huber, G.P. 2004. *The necessary nature of future firms: Attributes of survivors in a changing world.* Thousand Oaks, CA: Sage Publications.

61. Woodward, J. 1965. *Industrial organization: Theory and practice.* London: Oxford University Press.

62. Harvey, E., 1968. Technology and the structure of organizations. *American Sociological Review,* 33: 241–259; Zwerman, W.L. 1970. *New perspectives on organizational effectiveness.* Westwood, CT: Greenwood.

63. Hitt, M.A., Keats, B.W., & Demarie, S.M. 1998. Navigating in the new competitive landscape: Building strategic flexibility and competitive advantage in the 21st century. *Academy of Management Executive,* 12(4):22–42.

64. Kotha, S. 1995. Mass customization: Implementing the emerging paradigm for competitive advantage. *Strategic Management Journal*, 16: 21–42; Pine, B. 1993. *Mass customization*. Boston, MA: Harvard Business School Press.

65. Hitt, M.A. 2000. The new frontier: Transformation of management for the new millennium. *Organizational Dynamics*, 28 (3): 7–17.

66. Ibid.

67. Ibid.

68. See, for example: Argote, L. 1982. Input uncertainty and organizational coordination in hospital emergency units. *Administrative Science Quarterly*, 27: 420–434; Drazin, R., & Van de Ven, A.H. 1985. Alternative forms of fit in contingency theory. *Administrative Science Quarterly*, 30: 514–539; Schoonhoven, C.B. 1981. Problems with contingency theory: Testing assumptions hidden within the language of contingency theory. *Administrative Science Quarterly*, 26: 349–377.

69. Child, *Organization: A guide to problems and practices*.

70. Ford, J.D., & Hegarty, W.H. 1984. Decision makers' beliefs about the causes and effects of structure: An exploratory study. *Academy of Management Journal*, 27: 271–291.

71. Peli, G. 2009, Fit by founding, fit by adaptation: Reconciling conflicting organization theories with logical formalization, *Academy of Management Review*, 34: 343–360.

72. Luo, Y., & Rui, H. 2009. An ambidexterity perspective toward multinational enterprises from emerging economies. *Academy of Management Perspectives*, 23 (4): 49–70; Simsek, Z. 2009. Organizational ambidexterity: Towards a multilevel understanding, *Journal of Management Studies*, 46: 597–624.

73. Simsek, Z., Heavey, C., Veiga, J.F., & Souder, D. 2009. A typology for aligning organizational ambidexterity's conceptualizations, antecedents and outcomes. *Journal of Management Studies*, 46: 864–894.

74. Jansen, J.J.P., George, G., Van den Bosch, F.A.J., & Volberda, H.W. 2008. Senior team attributes and organizational ambidexterity: The moderating role of transformational leadership. *Journal of Management Studies*, 45: 982–1007.

75. Fang, C., Lee, J., & Schilling, M.A. 2009. Balancing exploration and exploitation through structural design: The isolation of subgroups and organizational learning. *Organization Science*, in press.

76. Taylor, A. 2010. The next generation: Technology adoption and integration through internal competition in new product development. *Organization Science*, 21: 23–41; Leiblein, M.J. & Madsen, T.L. 2009. Unbundling competitive heterogeneity: Incentive structures and capability influences on technological innovation. *Strategic Management Journal*, 30: 711–735.

77. Doty, D.H., Glick, W.H., & Huber, G.P. 1993. Fit, equifinality, and organizational performance: A test of two configurational theories. *Academy of Management Journal*, 36: 1196–1250.

78. See, for example: Burton, R.M., Lauridsen, J., & Obel, B. 2002. Return on assets loss from situational and contingency misfits. *Management Science*, 48: 1461–1485.

79. See, for example: Burton, R.M., Lauridsen, J., & Obel, B. 2002. Return on assets loss from situational and contingency misfits. *Management Science*, 48: 1461–1485.

80. Deetz, S. 1985. Critical-cultural research: New sensibilities and old realities. *Journal of Management*, 11: 121–136.

81. Chatman, J.A., & Cha, S.E. 2003. Leading by leveraging culture. *California Management Review*, 45 (4): 20–34; Keeley, M. 1983. Values in organizational theory and management education. *Academy of Management Review*, 8: 376–386.

82. Tetrick, L.E., & Da Silva, N. 2003. Assessing culture and climate for organizational learning. In S.E. Jackson, M.A. Hitt, & A. DeNisi (Eds.), *Managing knowledge for sustained competitive advantage*. San Francisco, CA: Jossey-Bass, pp. 333–359; Schein, E.H. 1984. Coming to a new awareness of organizational culture. *Sloan Management Review*, 25 (2): 3–16.

83. Joo, B.-K. & Lim, T. 2009. The effects of organizational learning culture, perceived job complexity, and proactive personality on organizational commitment and intrinsic motivation. *Journal of Leadership and Organizational Studies*, 16: 48–60.

84. Ren, H. & Gray, B. 2009. Repairing relationship conflict: How violation types and culture influence the effectiveness of restoration rituals. *Academy of Management Review*, 34: 105–126.

85. Latta, G.F. 2009. A process model of organizational change in cultural context (OC3 Model), *Journal of Leadership and Organizational Studies*, 16: 19–37.

86. Cameron, K.S., & Quinn, R.E. 1999. *Diagnosing and changing organizational culture: Based on the competing values framework*. Reading, MA: Addison-Wesley.

87. Turner, K.L., & Makhija, M.V. 2006. The role of organizational controls in managing knowledge. *Academy of Management Review*, 31: 197–217.

88. Bernard, C. 2009. Cultural innovation in software design: The new impact of innovation planning methods. *Journal of Business Strategy*, 30(2/3): 57–69; Quinn, R.E. 1988. *Beyond rational management*. San Francisco, CA: Jossey-Bass.

89. Goodman, E.A., Zammuto, R.F., & Gifford, B.D. 2001. The competing values framework: Understanding the impact of organizational culture on the quality of work life. *Organization Development Journal*, 19 (3): 59–68.

90. van Rekom, J., van Riel, C.B.M., & Wierenga, B. 2006. A methodology for assessing organizational core values. *Journal of Management Studies*, 43: 175–201.

91. Jones, R.A., Jimmieson, N.L., & Griffiths, A. 2005. The impact of organizational culture and reshaping capabilities on change implementation success: The mediating role of readiness for change. *Journal of Management Studies*, 42: 361–386.

92. Pech, R.J. 2009. Delegating and devolving power: A case study of engaged employees. *Journal of Business Strategy*, 30(1): 27–32.

93. Erdogan, B., Liden, R.C., & Kraimer, M.L. 2006. Justice and leader-member exchange: The moderating role of organizational culture. *Academy of Management Journal*, 49: 395–406.

94. Cable, D.M., & Parsons, C.K. 2001. Socialization tactics and person-organization fit. *Personnel Psychology*, 54: 1–23; Jones, G.R, 1986. Socialization tactics, self-efficacy, and newcomers' adjustments to organizations. *Academy of Management Journal*, 29: 262–279. Also see Van Maanen, J., & Schein, E.H. 1979. Toward a theory of organizational socialization. *Research in Organizational Behavior*, 1: 209–264.

95. Bain & Company. 2007. At http://www.bain.com, April 17.

96. Freiberg & Freiberg, *Nuts!*

97. Most admired companies. 2009. CNNMoney.com, at http://money.cnn.com/magazines/fortune/mostadmired/2009/full_list/index.html, Jan. 21, 2010.

98. Zander, U., & Zander, L. 2010. Opening the grey box: Social communities, knowledge and culture in acquisitions. *Journal of International Business Studies*, 41: 27–37; Tsui, A.S., Wang, H., & Xin, K.R. 2006. Organizational culture in China: An analysis of culture dimensions and culture types. *Management and Organization Review*, 2: 345–376.

99. Wilkins, A.L. 1983. The culture audit: A tool for understanding organizations. *Organizational Dynamics*, 12: 24–38.

100. Culture Audit. 2007. Smith Weaver Smith Accelerated Cultural Transformation, at http://www.smithweaversmith.com.

101. Schein, Coming to a new awareness.

102. Wilkins, A.L. 1983. Efficient cultures: Exploring the relationship between culture and organizational performance. *Administrative Science Quarterly*, 28: 468–481.

103. Riley, P. 1983. A structurationist account of political culture. *Administrative Science Quarterly*, 28: 414–437.

104. Martin, J., & Siehl, C. 1983. Organizational culture and counter-culture: An uneasy symbiosis. *Organizational Dynamics*, 12: 52–64.

105. Williamson, I.O., Burnett, M.F. & Bartol, K.M. 2009. The interactive effect of collectivism and organizational rewards on affective organizational commitment, *Cross Cultural Management*, 16: 28–43.

106. Gerhard, B. 2008. How much does national culture constrain organizational culture? *Management and Organization Review*, 5: 241–259.

107. Chatman & Cha, Leading by leveraging culture; Kristof, A.L. 1996. Person-organization fit: An integrative review of its conceptualizations, measurement, and implications. *Personnel Psychology*, 49: 1–48; O'Reilly, C.A., Chatman, J.A., & Caldwell, D.F. 1991. People and organizational culture: A profile comparison approach to assessing person-organization fit. *Academy of Management Journal*, 14: 487–516; Tziner, A. 1987. Congruency issue retested using Fineman's achievement climate notion. *Journal of Social Behavior and Personality*, 2: 63–78; Vandenberghe, C. 1999. Organizational culture, person-culture fit, and turnover: A replication in the health care industry. *Journal of Organizational Behavior*, 20: 175–184.

108. Ronen, S. 1978. Personal values: A basis for work motivation set and work attitude. *Organizational Behavior and Human Performance*, 21: 80–107.

109. Rokeach, M. 1973. *The nature of human values.* New York: The Free Press.

110. Ronen, Personal values.

111. Schneider, B. 1987. The people make the place. *Personnel Psychology*, 40: 437–453.

112. Cable & Parsons, Socialization tactics and person-organization fit.

113. See, for example, Bowen, D.E., Ledford, G.E., & Nathan, B.R. 1991. Hiring for the organization, not the job. *Academy of Management Executive*, 5 (4): 35–51.

114. See, for example, Lovelace, K., & Rosen, B. 1996. Differences in achieving person-organization fit among diverse groups of managers. *Journal of Management*, 22: 703–722.

115. For additional insights, see Powell, G. 1998. Reinforcing and extending today's organizations: The simultaneous pursuit of person-organization fit and diversity. *Organizational Dynamics*, 26 (3): 50–61.

116. Hitt, Ireland, & Hoskisson, *Strategic management: Competitiveness and globalization.*

117. Hitt, Harrison, & Ireland. 2001. *Mergers and acquisitions*; Cartwright, S., & Cooper, C.L. 1993. The role of culture compatibility in successful organizational marriage. *Academy of Management Executive*, 7 (2): 57–70.

118. Holloway, Wheelwright, & Tempest, Cisco Systems, Inc.

organizational change and development

Reinventing the Dream at Starbucks

Howard Schultz, the entrepreneurial force behind the organization, provided the guiding vision and a golden touch in building Starbucks into a huge company with 16,700+ stores at the beginning of 2010. Although Starbucks has achieved amazing success, it has experienced some "bumps in the road" along the way. In 2008, Starbucks began experiencing a reduction in its average sales per store for the first time in its history. The decline continued for 2008 and 2009. There are several reasons for the weakness in Starbucks's performance. Among them are increased competition (from national and local coffee wholesalers and retailers such as Green Mountain Coffee roasters and others introducing gourmet coffees, such as McDonald's) and the global recession's causing potential customers to reduce their discretionary purchases (Starbucks coffee is viewed by most as a luxury item). As a result there was a stock-price decline that became serious for Starbucks shareholders because it made its shares less attractive to potential investors.

In January 2010, Starbucks announced its first quarterly increases since 2008 in average sales per store open at least one year; and its quarterly profit tripled. The 4 percent increase was achieved through a series of major changes in Starbucks' operations. Prior to these changes, Howard Schultz stepped back in as the chief executive officer (CEO). One of his first actions as CEO was to announce the closing of several unprofitable stores. Eventually, Starbucks closed almost 800 stores and reduced the number of managers and associates by approximately 18,000 across its U.S. and international operations. Although, these actions were designed to stem the performance declines, Schultz felt that much more was needed to rejuvenate Starbucks and its performance.

A second action taken by Schultz was to conduct a thorough organizational analysis to identify the

knowledge objectives

After reading this chapter, you should be able to:

1. Describe three major internal pressures for change.
2. Identify and explain six major external pressures for change.
3. Describe the three-phase model of planned change.
4. Discuss important tactical choices involving the speed and style of a change effort.
5. Explain the four general causes of resistance to change and the tactics that can be used to address each cause.
6. Discuss the role of the DADA syndrome in organizational change.
7. Describe the basic organization development (OD) model and discuss OD interventions, including relationship techniques and structural techniques.

problems that precipitated the weak performance over recent years. This analysis identified several problems, chief among them was the lost focus on customers' desires. In becoming a large company with standardized products and store designs, customers thought Starbucks had also become sterile. Customers preferred coffee that was unique and customized to their tastes. Based on these findings, Schultz initiated other actions.

As described in Chapter 11, Starbucks has a strong team-based culture. Schultz engaged managers and associates to help redesign their local stores in ways that best fit with the local community and its interests. The structure was changed to include more geographic regional groups, allowing them to focus on the drinks desired most in their

©Scott Olson/Getty Images Inc.

areas (e.g., cold drinks in the southern U.S. region and espresso in the Pacific Northwest region). Starbucks has also increased its innovation of new products such as the new instant coffee, Via. The company is refocusing its attention on customer needs and service. Schultz asked the managers and associates (Starbucks refers to them as "partners") to invest energy in attentiveness to customers, providing them excellent service, and to be innovative in adapting their operations to local community values.

Howard Schultz recently expressed concerns that in the drive to increase its size and gain the economies of scale, the company may have compromised the "soul" of its original stores. He is now in the process of reinventing Starbucks to recapture that soul.

Sources: C.C. Miller. 2010. "Now at Starbucks: A Rebound," *The New York Times*, Jan. 21, at http://www.nytimes.com; M. Montandon. 2010. "Bean Counters No More: Starbucks Finding Success by Thinking Local," *Fast Company*, Jan. 21, at http://www.fastcompany.com; A.M. Heher. 2010. "Starbucks Rallies, Sets Sights Overseas," *The Seattle Times*, Jan. 21, at http://www.seattletimes.nwsource.com; M. Allison. 2010. "Starbucks Reports Strong First-Quarter Results as Via, International Sales Take Off," *The Seattle Times*, Jan. 21, at http://www.seattletimes.nwsource.com; J. Jargon. 2010. "Starbucks Growth Revives, Perked by Via," *The Wall Street Journal*, Jan. 21, at http://www.wsj.com; B.J. Barr. 2010. "Now Brewing Starbucks Gets a Makeover," *The New York Times Style Magazine*, Jan. 11, at http://www.tmagazine.blogs.nytimes.com; M. Bartiromo. 2008. "Howard Schultz on Reinventing Starbucks," *BusinessWeek*, Apr. 9, at http://www.businessweek.com; 2008. "Starbucks Makes Organizational Changes," Restaurant News Resource, Feb. 25, at http://www.restaurantnewsresource.com.

the strategic importance of Organizational Change and Development

Few, if any, organizations can remain the same for very long and survive. A classic case is Polaroid Corporation, which shows the outcome of being too slow to change. Polaroid introduced instant photography to the market and at one time was among the top 50 corporations in the United States.

However, in 2001, it declared bankruptcy, and in 2002, what was left

of the company was sold to Bank One's OEP Imaging Unit and then sold again in 2005 to the Petters Group. Polaroid's problem was its failure to adapt in a timely way to technological change. The company lost its market because it was too slow to recognize the importance of digital imaging technology and then too slow to change after competitors developed digital cameras.[1]

The development of a new technology created the need for change at Polaroid. Although top managers are responsible for instituting such changes, managers and associates lower in the organization must help because of their knowledge of the environment (markets, customers, competitors, technology, government regulations, and so forth). All managers should actively scan the environment for changes and help to identify external opportunities and threats. Unfortunately, Polaroid's managers did not perceive the threat to their existing business quickly enough to transform the firm. After learning of the need for a change, these managers began the difficult process of designing and implementing a new approach, but they were unable to do so in time to avoid failure. Competitors developed and introduced new cameras using digital technology before Polaroid could do so, causing Polaroid to lose a substantial share of its market.

In contrast, Starbucks has achieved considerable success since its founding. The company has been recognized for its high-involvement management practices (the manner in which it has valued and managed its human capital), environmentally conscious policies, accessibility to those with disabilities, and high-quality coffees. Yet, although Starbucks did change significantly over time, it had become rather predictable in store format and standardized coffee-product offerings. And it encountered significant competition from such unlikely sources as McDonald's and Dunkin Donuts, a recessionary economy, and disgruntled customers. Its sales per store began

declining, and its profits followed a similar path. Thus, Howard Schultz stepped back into the CEO position and instituted a number of changes. After downsizing the number of stores and the workforce, the firm made several other very important changes. The company reinstituted its strong focus on customer service and satisfaction. It began to remodel its stores, tailoring the décor to local community preferences. And it reinvigorated its focus on innovation, exemplified by its introduction of the new instant coffee, Via. Many of these changes were implemented by engaging managers and associates to gain their recommendations. Thus, Starbucks continued its commitment to high-involvement practices—effectively using the talents of associates and enhancing their motivation—which helped to reduce resistance to change by lower-level managers and associates. Some experts believe that effective management of human capital and developing effective ways of dealing with change have contributed significantly to Starbucks's ability to build and maintain a competitive advantage. Starbucks's leaders showed their concern by recapturing the soul that had made Starbucks successful. After experiencing two years of decline,

these changes began to pay dividends as the company's sales and profits began to increase again.

Change often involves an entire firm, as in the Starbucks case. In other instances, a single division or work group must change. To be prepared for either situation, managers must understand and appreciate change and possess the skills and tools necessary for implementing it. In high-involvement organizations, associates also play key roles in planning and implementing change, and they, too, must possess appropriate skills and tools.

In this chapter, we discuss organizational change and renewal. First, we examine internal and external pressures for change. Such pressures must be properly understood for effective change to occur. Next, we describe the basic process of planned change and consider important tactical decisions involved in a change effort. Building on this foundation, we then address the important topic of resistance to change. Individuals and groups often resist change, and the ability to diagnose causes of resistance and deal with them effectively is crucial. Finally, we discuss a set of assessment techniques and change tactics, collectively known as *organizational development*.

Pressures for Organizational Change

Organizations constantly face pressure for change; in order to cope, they must be agile and react quickly.[2] Organizations that understand and manage change well tend to be the most effective.[3] As suggested by Exhibit 14-1, pressures for change can be categorized as internal or external.

Internal Pressures for Change

Although many pressures for change exist in the external environments of organizations, some pressures are more closely identified with internal dynamics. Aspiration–performance

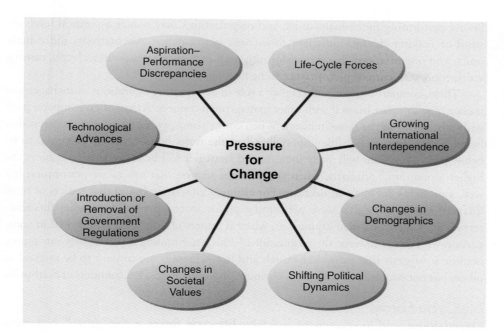

Exhibit 14-1   Internal
and External Pressures
for Organizational
Change

discrepancies, natural life-cycle forces, and changes in the CEO or top management team
are three of the most important pressures.

Aspiration–Performance Discrepancies

Perhaps the most fundamental pressure for change involves **aspiration–performance
discrepancies,** or differences between aspirations and current performance.[4] When an individual, work group, division, or organization is not meeting its expectations (often expressed
in goals), changes in tactics, strategies, and processes often follow. Failing to live up to expectations is an uncomfortable state that often motivates change. Some changes motivated
by failing to satisfy aspirations include divesting poorly performing units[5] or acquiring other
businesses to access resources that will hopefully allow the firm to achieve its aspirations.[6]

    To fully appreciate the role of aspirations, it is important to understand how they
develop. Research has identified three factors.[7] First, past aspirations play a role in current
aspirations. Thus, if an associate had high expectations of herself yesterday, she is likely to
have high expectations today as well. This point underscores an important phenomenon:
stickiness in aspirations. Stickiness exists when individuals, units, and organizations are
slow to revise their aspirations even when those aspirations appear to be too high or too
low. One study, for example, found that units of a company adjusted performance aspirations less than might be expected in the face of information suggesting that greater change,
either up or down, was warranted.

    Second, past performance plays an important role. If performance in the recent past
was below target levels, aspirations are likely to be reduced, although stickiness places
limits on the degree of adjustment in the short run. Conversely, if performance has been
above target levels, it is common for aspiration levels to be increased to some degree.
For example, in the early days, Starbucks executives learned that it was relatively easy to
perform well in a high-growth environment, and thus they increased the firm's aspiration
levels. Although such changes in aspiration levels may seem benign, they can be harmful.

**aspiration–performance
discrepancies**
Gaps between what
an individual, unit, or
organization wants to
achieve and what it is
actually achieving.

Poorly performing individuals, units, and organizations may reduce aspiration levels instead of making changes sufficient to increase performance. Alternatively, individuals, units, and organizations that are performing well may increase aspiration levels, causing satisfaction with current performance to be fleeting.

Third, comparisons with others play a role in determining aspirations. A management trainee may compare himself with other management trainees. A firm often compares itself with other firms in the same industry. When comparisons with similar others suggest that better performance is possible (especially when the firm's performance is perceived to be below par), aspirations will likely increase and strategies will be formulated to achieve the higher aspirations.[8] Similarly, when comparisons suggest that others are performing less well, aspirations are likely to decrease. For example, one study found that leaders of retail financial-service units that were performing poorly in comparison with other financial-service units increased their aspirations, whereas leaders of units performing well in comparison with others lowered their aspirations.[9] This latter finding is particularly intriguing, because it suggests that many individuals and business units are content to be as good as others but not necessarily better. This obviously did not apply to the founders of Starbucks.

Life-Cycle Forces

life-cycle forces

Natural and predictable pressures that build as an organization grows and that must be addressed if the organization is to continue growing.

Organizations tend to encounter predictable **life-cycle forces** as they grow.[10] Not every organization experiences the same forces in the same way as others, but most organizations face similar pressures. Although several models of the organizational life cycle have been proposed, an integrative model best highlights the key pressures that organizations experience. This model has four stages: entrepreneurial, collectivity, formalization and control, and elaboration (see Exhibit 14-2).

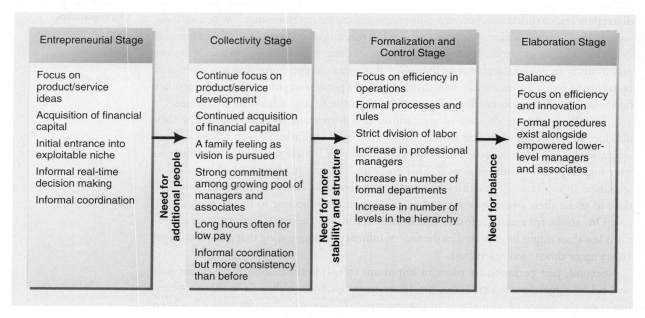

Exhibit 14-2 Integrative Life-Cycle Model

Source: Based on R.E. Quinn, & K. Cameron. 1983. "Organizational Life Cycles and Shifting Criteria of Effectiveness." *Management Science*, 24: 33–51.

In the *entrepreneurial stage,* founders and perhaps initially a few managers and associates develop ideas for products or services, acquire financial capital, and take actions to enter a niche in the marketplace. This is an exciting time, but after the market has been entered and success achieved, growth requires founders to add managers and associates. Processes must be introduced for selecting, training, and coordinating these individuals. In the *collectivity stage,* founders, managers, and associates continue to emphasize product or service development and fund-raising. Individuals in the young organization tend to feel like a family as they pursue the vision that attracted them to the firm. Individuals often work long hours for relatively low pay, and they tend to be highly committed. Informal communication and coordination are important, but founders often begin to handle more managerial responsibilities and fewer entrepreneurial responsibilities than they would like. As the firm continues to grow, professional managers and formal processes must be incorporated to resolve or prevent coordination and control problems.

In the *formalization and control stage,* managers and associates are guided by formal processes and rules, a strict division of labor, and a stable organizational structure. And they emphasize efficiency more than innovation. Functional disciplines such as accounting and operations management are elevated in status. As the firm continues to grow, more rules and procedures are often added, along with a greater number of management levels. Eventually, managers and associates can become alienated from the firm, partly because they lose discretion in decision making. Furthermore, in larger organizations, newer associates and managers do not have a connection to the original vision, and overall commitment may be lower. To prevent or overcome these problems, a renewed effort to empower both managers and associates should be considered. At Starbucks, Schultz and other leaders maintained their commitment to a high-involvement workplace, which helped the company postpone some of the negative side effects of the formalization stage. Starbucks grew rapidly and thus reached this stage more quickly than many firms. The firm continued to grow and eventually was unable to prevent the negative effects of this stage and thereby suffered performance declines. However, Schultz responded quickly with changes that now appear to be working, as evidenced in the *Exploring Behavior in Action* segment.

Unilever, a large multinational firm, began to experience declines in market share and profits largely due to more aggressive competitors such as Procter & Gamble and more innovative competitors such as Reckitt Benckiser. When the performance problems surfaced in 2005, top managers decided a change was in order. Its growth strategy appeared to have been unsuccessful. However, a thorough analysis showed that the strategy was correct but that Unilever had failed in its execution (implementation) of the strategy. To improve execution, the company streamlined its structure and developed a process referred to as "strategy in action," which involved mobilizing teams to implement the planned actions based on the strategies, and then a review process to monitor the results and make adjustments where needed to ensure success. This process was communicated to all 180,000 managers and associates. One of the outcomes was a significant increase in the amount of collaboration across teams and units. Unilever achieved its strategic vision in 2010 partly because of the changes implemented.[11]

In the *elaboration stage,* managers and associates experience a more balanced, mature organization. Formal rules and processes exist alongside empowered lower-level managers and associates. Efficiency concerns coexist with concerns for innovation and renewal. As discussed in Chapter 13, balancing these concerns is challenging but possible. Starbucks currently exemplifies this stage, especially with the changes it has implemented.

Overall, some firms handle life-cycle forces reasonably well; Starbucks and Unilever are examples of such firms. Other firms handle these issues less well. In these cases, there is often a change in the leadership of the organization that can trickle down through the organization. If effective leaders are chosen to replace the previous ones and the transition is handled in an orderly manner, the organization can experience positive outcomes from the change.[12]

Changes in Top Management

Changes in top management involve the replacement of top management team members who retire or depart the company for other reasons (e.g., resign). The changes often begin with the selection of a new CEO. When CEOs and other members of the top management team have been in their positions for some time, the organization can experience inertia. In these cases, it is more difficult to identify, develop, and implement changes. The reason for the inertia is an overly strong commitment to the current strategy and courses of action. Such commitment may be because of high performance in the past or because the managers feel personally invested in the approach they chose and implemented (e.g., feel their reputation is at stake).[13] To overcome the inertia caused by the unwillingness of top managers to make needed changes, a change in the CEO and perhaps other members of the top management team may be necessary.[14]

A new CEO and new members of the top management team, bring unique ideas on how to deal with problems the organization is experiencing. They also have no special commitment to the previous strategies and actions, unless they represent an inside succession. However, to make major changes, it is common for the new top managers to be chosen from outside the organization.[15] New top managers often select and implement new strategies that can turn around the organization's performance.[16]

Of course, not all new managers will be successful. Some may not make changes and others may make changes that do not adequately meet the challenges faced. As a result, some new managers may be replaced after a short tenure.[17] In particular, when an organization needs changes, perhaps they should search for specific types of individuals to undertake the top leadership roles. For example, managers with a strong belief in their capabilities have been found to be more entrepreneurial.[18] Thus, firms that require more innovation to be competitive may need such individuals in their top management team. Careful selection of a new leader can help an organization create the type of change needed.

External Pressures for Change

Along with internal pressures, organizations face external pressures for change. Organizations must be sensitive to these external pressures, or they may not survive. For example, if an organization does not react to changes in the market for its product, the demand for its product probably will decline. Such was the case for Polaroid, as discussed earlier. The new digital cameras introduced to the market by Polaroid's competitors greatly reduced the demand for Polaroid's products. When Polaroid was unable to respond quickly, it filed for bankruptcy and ceased to exist as an independent business.

External pressure for change comes from several sources, including technological advances, the introduction or removal of government regulations, changes in societal values, shifting political dynamics, changing demographics, and growing international interdependency (see Exhibit 14-1).

Technological Advances

Scientific knowledge, produced by both companies and universities, has been developing rapidly over the past 50 years.[19] For example, in 2007, there were 23,750 scientific journals that published 1.35 million pages.[20] With advances in research methods and a continuing need for answers to many important research questions, the rapid development of knowledge is expected to continue.

©Photodisc/Getty Images

Technological advances are based on advances in scientific knowledge. Such advances can lead to incremental or radical changes in how services and products are designed, produced, and delivered. Two facts illustrate the point that scientific knowledge drives technology. First, scientific knowledge is routinely cited in patent applications, with the number of scientific articles cited per patent on the increase in the United States, Germany, France, Britain, and other countries.[21] Second, the number of patents granted by the U.S. Patent Office is increasing at a growing rate, which matches the growth in science. In the first half of the twentieth century, patents granted increased by 50 percent.[22] In the second half of the twentieth century, they quadrupled.[23] These rapid changes can be seen in technologies of recent origin, such as advancements in wireless communications technologies, advanced manufacturing technologies, and nanotechnologies.[24] New technologies are being developed faster than they can be implemented. A prime example is provided by new developments in microelectronic technology, which occur before previous developments can be fully implemented.

Firms must adapt to technological advances or risk becoming outdated and ineffective.[25] Manufacturing firms, for example, must adopt new manufacturing technologies or suffer disadvantages in cost, quality, or speed relative to their competition in the marketplace.[26] Firms that failed, or were slow, to take advantage of computer-aided manufacturing, computer-aided design, and modern manufacturing resource planning experienced competitive disadvantages.

Changes in Government Regulations and Other Institutions

The U.S. government has the responsibility to regulate commerce for the common good. Much of the regulation is initiated because of societal pressures. Major regulation has been implemented over the years in areas such as civil rights and equal opportunity, environmental protection, and worker safety and health.

In recent times, regulations have been implemented that establish fuel-efficiency standards for automobile manufacturers, requirements for regional telephone companies to provide competitors access to their hardwired networks, and rules limiting telemarketers' ability to call people's homes.[27] The Drug-Free Workplace Act was passed to encourage employers to test associates for drugs and to implement employee assistance programs for substance abuse. Additional rules and regulations have been enacted since the original legislation to enhance effects. However, these regulations have been only partially effective in achieving the goals. For one thing, it covers only employers with federal contracts. In addition, the programs implemented by employers vary in their effectiveness.[28] Without question, however, organizations must adapt to regulatory changes.

Institutional changes such as in the rule of law can have a major effect on economic activity and especially on the willingness of foreign firms to enter markets.[29] Often firms are especially interested in the rule of law such as in relation to intellectual property rights (i.e., protection of copyrights and patents) and to corrupt practices (e.g., bribery).[30] Clearly, uncertainty related to regulations and the potential for changes may cause firms to postpone investments or to change their strategies.[31] Clearly, regulations can influence firm changes. For example, the U.S. government recently implemented new regulations on banks, and particularly those receiving funds from the government, to remain solvent. The banks are required to maintain ceilings on executive pay until they pay back all of the monies provided to them.[32]

The U.S. government also occasionally removes regulations created in earlier times. The airline, trucking, and communication industries, for example, have been largely deregulated. Such deregulation also requires changes. For example, firms in deregulated industries typically must adapt to a more competitive environment, which many firms in these industries have found difficult to do. Many airlines that prospered in the regulated era, such as Pan Am and Braniff, failed under deregulation.

Changes in Societal Values

Changes in societal values are normally seen in four ways. First, changing values influence consumer purchases, affecting the market for an organization's products or services. Second, society's values are evidenced in employee attitudes, behaviors, and expectations. Third, they affect potential investors in the company. Finally, society's values are represented in government regulations. The changing social values regarding environmental consciousness have had a major influence on organizational strategies and practices, as shown in the *Managerial Advice* segment.

Because of the increasing concerns about global warming, many people throughout the world have become sensitive to environmental issues. The importance of green issues is reflected by consumers' buying behaviors, by investors' purchases of stock in companies, and in other ways as well. The interest in green issues has encouraged Boeing, ExxonMobil, and Coca-Cola Enterprises to develop environmentally sensitive policies and practices as explained in the *Managerial Advice* segment. For example, ExxonMobil is developing a biofuel from algae that consumes carbon dioxide and thus helps to reduce emission of greenhouse gases.

The influence of societal values on consumer purchases can have a major effect on organizations. For example, Americans have become increasingly hostile to products manufactured by companies using questionable practices in foreign countries. Such practices include child labor, periods of intense overtime work, and very low wages. In past decades, individuals thought less about these issues, and firms could neglect them as well. Today, firms must be very careful.

Other influences of societal values are more indirect. They affect politicians who enact laws such as the Drug-Free Workplace Act. With over $200 billion in costs to organizations because of associates' substance abuse, the employee-assistance programs promoted by the Act are important to save lives and reduce costs to organizations from substance abuse.[33] Thus, societal values also influence government regulation, which in turn places external pressures on the organization.

Shifting Political Dynamics

Political pressures, both national and international, can influence organizational operations. The political philosophy of those elected to office affects legislation and the interpretation of existing legislation and government policies. For example, President Ronald

Social Pressures for "Green" Policies and Practices: The War against Carbon Emissions

While in times past, financing or regulatory approval were the most critical concerns for many major investments, in current times many investors are focused on the company's environmental sustainability policies and actions. Many companies have realized that changing their environmental policies—making them more green—will actually contribute to their bottom line, improve their public image, and make them more attractive to many investors. *Sustainability* in simple terms means meeting our current human needs without harming future generations. It is a major cause among environmentalists, human rights activists, and economic-development experts. And it has become important to many in the global society, such that companies are expected to be environmentally conscious. In the past, sustainability often meant higher costs for companies, but in current times, better environmental and social practices can yield strategic advantages. Customers are shifting their loyalties to companies that embrace the concept of sustainability.

The Boeing Company found that air used to cool its computers at its four-acre information technology processing site in Seattle was seeping out through openings in the floor. Those openings were plugged with insulation, thereby saving approximately 685,000 kilowatt-hours of electricity and $55,000 annually. Although the cost reduction is

meaningful, this action also reduced Boeing's carbon emissions. Boeing voluntarily reports its carbon emissions to the Carbon Disclosure Project. This project provides companies with information about ways to measure their emissions and compare them with their rivals (industry data). Scientists suggest that companies and energy providers produce 45 percent of the carbon emissions that contribute to global warming. Many companies are reporting these data and sharing information on their reductions in carbon emissions with the public to convince potential customers and investors that they are green.

©AP/Wide World Photos

Companies are beginning to make major investments in green projects. For example, ExxonMobil announced in 2009 that it will invest in a $600 million project to develop a new biofuel from algae. If the project is successful it could represent a major advancement in the sustainability war because algae can be grown using land and water unsuitable for other uses (e.g., food production) and algae consumes carbon dioxide, the major contributor to greenhouse gases. Likewise, GE announced a $1.4 billion contract to produce and provide maintenance service for 338 large wind turbines. The turbines are to be located

in Oregon and produce renewable energy for Southern California Edison. This is the largest order for wind turbines that GE has ever had.

Other companies are also investing in energy-saving projects. For example, Clorox is expanding its line of eco-friendly cleaners (Green Works), which have been highly successful in the market. In fact, sales have exceeded expectations by 600 percent. In addition, Coca-Cola Enterprises, the largest bottler of Coke drinks, announced plans to double the size of its fleet of hybrid trucks to 327 vehicles. McKinsey & Co. projected that the many efforts to reduce energy consumption will lead to a 17 percent decline in energy use in 2020 as compared with 2008. Although U.S. regulators do not require companies to quantify the effects of their environmental practices, these practices have become a powerful indicator of future market performance. Thus, responding positively to environmental pressures may help companies achieve long-term survival.

Sources: L. Kaufman. 2009. "NYT: Emissions Disclosure as Business Virtue," MSNBC, Dec. 29, at http://www.msnbc.msn.com; 2009. "GE Inks Largest Wind Turbine Contract Ever," MSNBC, Dec. 10, at http://www.msnbc.msn.com; A. Stone. 2009. "Honeywell: Green and Clean," *Forbes*, Nov. 2, at http://www.forbes.com; 2009. "Exxon Makes First Big Biofuel Investment," MSNBC, July 14, at http://www.msnbc.msn.com; J. Makower. 2009. "In Recession, Business Keeps Going Green," *BusinessWeek*, Feb. 2, at http://www.businessweek.com; J. Carey. 2007. "Hugging the Tree-Huggers," *BusinessWeek*, Mar. 12, at http://www. businessweek.com; Speeches. 2007. At http://www.thecoca-colacompany.com/presscenter; P. Engardio. 2007. "Beyond the Green Corporation," *BusinessWeek*, Jan. 29, at http://www.businessweek.com.

Reagan's views on U.S. defense spending created massive shifts in government expenditures that affected firms in several industries. These firms had to gear up to meet the government demand. International politics also influence organizational change. For example, the major changes in the former Soviet Union exemplified by the destruction of the wall separating East and West Germany led to a decline in the Cold War and thereby a reduction in U.S. defense spending (in turn leading to a downsizing of several industries). In addition, disagreements over proper tariffs between the European Union and the United States, for example, can cause uncertainty and perhaps higher costs for a firm if tariffs increase. Faced with increased tariffs in an important export market, a firm may need to enhance its efficiency to avoid being forced to raise prices to noncompetitive levels. Alternatively, it may need to shift exports to other markets.

Changes in Demographics

As discussed in Chapter 2, the average age of U.S. citizens has been increasing, along with the proportion of U.S. residents who belong to groups other than non-Hispanic whites. To deal with these changes, many organizations have altered internal practices to ensure fair treatment for people of all races and ages. Diversity programs designed to increase understanding across different groups have become common. Further changes in the demographic profile of the nation may require additional organizational changes.

Firms also have introduced products and marketing tactics designed to appeal to a broader mix of individuals or to a particular targeted niche that has grown in importance. In North Carolina, where the Hispanic population is growing rapidly as compared with most other states, auto dealers and service businesses have added Spanish-speaking associates; and Time-Warner Cable has created a special TV package targeting Hispanic viewers in the state.[34]

Age and income distribution are additional demographic characteristics of importance for workforce composition and marketplace opportunities. For example, Florida now has the largest percentage of citizens aged 65 or over (17.6 percent). This demographic has significant implications for the type of products and services likely to be in demand in that state. Incomes enjoyed by families are also important for the types of products and services likely important for particular geographic markets. The extent to which the income is produced by dual-career couples also has workforce implications. For example, dual-career couples are often less willing to accept international assignments because of the inability of the spouse to move with them.[35]

Growing International Interdependence

You have probably heard someone say that "the world is getting smaller." Or, in recent times a common statement is "the world is becoming flatter." Clichés such as this are frequently used to describe the growing interdependency among countries in the world today. The United States is no longer as self-sufficient as it once was. Growing interdependencies are created by many factors. At the national level, countries may have mutual national defense goals, which are implemented through organizations such as the North Atlantic Treaty Organization (NATO). At the organizational level, a company may need natural resources that it cannot obtain in its own country, or a firm from one country may establish operations in another.[36] One result of interdependency is that organizations must be concerned about what happens throughout the world, even if they have no operations outside the United States. As such, managers need to develop a global mindset whereby they are attentive to changes around the world, analyzing their potential influences on their organization.[37] For example, events in the Middle East have an effect on most major organizations in the United States in some way. International interdependencies provide both opportunities and constraints.[38] Many firms have found that international markets present more opportunities for sales growth than U.S. markets, as discussed in Chapter 3. Likewise, organizations have to remain flexible in their international activities, adapting to major events (e.g., acts of terror; major political changes in a country that likely will lead to changes in important policies) when they occur.[39]

Planned Change

How does an organization respond to pressures for change? One possibility is **planned change,** which involves deliberate efforts to transform an organization or a subunit from its current state to a new state. Planned change may be evolutionary over time, or can be more revolutionary, involving major changes in a shorter period of time.[40] To effectively move the organization from one state to another, those managing the change must consider a number of issues in three distinct parts of the change process.[41] Resistance to change may develop along the way, however.

planned change
A process involving deliberate efforts to move an organization or a unit from its current undesirable state to a new, more desirable state.

Process of Planned Change

Change is typically thought of as a three-phase process that transforms an organization from an undesirable state through a difficult transition period to a desirable new state. Although researchers tend to agree on the nature of these three phases,[42] different names for the phases have been used by different people.

Kurt Lewin, a noted social psychologist, provided the most commonly used labels: *unfreezing, transforming,* and *refreezing.*[43] That is, the change process involves unfreezing an organization from its current state, moving (changing) it to a new state, and refreezing it in the new state (see Exhibit 14-3).

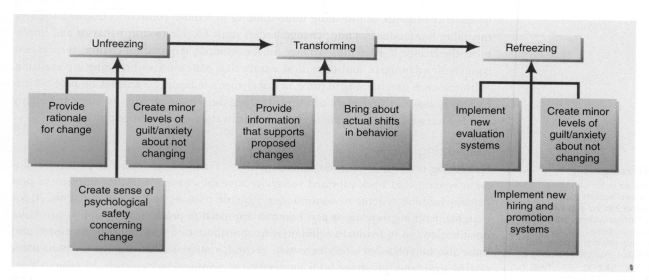

Exhibit 14-3   Process of Planned Change

Unfreezing

unfreezing
A phase in the change process in which leaders help managers and associates move beyond the past by providing a rationale for change, by creating guilt and/or anxiety about not changing, and by creating a sense of psychological safety concerning the change.

Unfreezing involves three activities.[44] First, change leaders provide a rationale—a reason why individuals in the organization should de-commit from the status quo. In particular, they need to motivate managers and associates to break out of the path dependence that currently exists;[45] instead of going down the same path, they need to select and start on a new path.[46] The leaders may accomplish this by providing information on poor financial performance, an impending regulatory change, or a new technological development. Second, leaders create at least minor levels of guilt or anxiety about not changing. Although causing undue negative emotion is not the intent, creation of psychological discomfort can be motivating. Leaders may create such a feeling by discussing the negative outcomes that the organization and its managers and associates will suffer if changes are not made. Third, leaders create a sense of psychological safety concerning the change. Managers and associates must believe they can successfully change.[47] Tactics that change leaders might use include the following:

- Reminding individuals that they have successfully changed in the past
- Communicating to individuals that managers and associates in other organizations in similar circumstances have successfully changed
- Explaining to individuals that support and training will be available for the specific changes to be made

Transforming

transforming
A phase in the change process in which leaders help to implement new approaches by providing information that supports proposed changes and by providing resources and training to bring about actual shifts in behavior.

Transforming involves three key activities.[48] First, change leaders must provide information and evidence that supports the proposed changes. Without supporting information, managers and associates may not have faith in what they are being asked to do, and they will not be committed. Pilot tests, outside experts, and data on how others have benefited from similar changes can be effective tactics. Furthermore, as noted in our discussion of transformational leaders in Chapter 8, a compelling vision of the future also can be useful in building commitment to proposed changes. Indeed, such a vision is likely to be crucial for creating change. Second, any potential constraints to making the change must be removed by the change leaders. This might require investing more money to reduce financial constraints or providing more training to remove constraints due to associates' capability limitations.[49] Third, change leaders must be able to shift behavior and implement the change.[50] They must arrange for the resources required for change, such as new equipment or budgets, and they must ensure that education and training are available. With resources and training in place, actual change can begin.[51] Feedback on progress can be used to make any necessary adjustments along the way. Small wins, or quick and highly visible successes, can be helpful in supporting this stage of the change process.

Refreezing

refreezing
A phase in the change process in which leaders lock in new approaches by implementing evaluation systems that track expected behaviors, by creating reward systems that reinforce expected behaviors, and by ensuring that hiring and promotion systems support the new demands.

Refreezing involves three interrelated activities.[52] First, change leaders implement evaluation systems that track expected behaviors after the change, and they implement permanent training systems to continuously upgrade relevant knowledge and skills. If, for example, working in teams is part of a new approach to production work in a particular organization, an individual's willingness to contribute to a team must be measured and must also be enhanced when necessary. Second, change leaders arrange for permanent reward structures, involving both monetary and nonmonetary rewards, to positively reinforce the new behaviors. Many managers suggest that, "You get what you reward."[53] Third, change leaders ensure that new hiring and promotion systems and other forms of support are designed to satisfy the altered demands.[54]

The Radical Transformation of Novartis

Several years after the pharmaceutical firm Novartis emerged from a merger, Dan Vasella, CEO, decided to make radical changes. Part of the reason for these changes was the lack of new "blockbuster" drugs in Novartis's pipeline. These new drugs were needed to replace major revenue-producing drugs in the firm's current portfolio that were scheduled to go off of patents and thus faced competition from makers of generic drugs (which would be marketed at a much lower price). In fact, the whole drug industry faces this problem, as few have new blockbuster drugs in their pipelines. Vasella decided that a major problem for Novartis and, indeed, all drug makers was that their research was not based strongly enough in science. Rather, the research targeted big diseases because of the opportunity to earn major returns. Vasella decided to include in the long and costly testing process required for the approval of new drugs only drugs that were backed by proven science. Often this means that the drugs are more targeted for very specific diseases, some of which may not affect large numbers of people. Thus, unless the drugs can help control multiple diseases, they promise only small returns. This approach changes the whole business model for drugs.

Vasella met resistance to this change from his marketing managers and others. He moved forward anyway. He hired a new person to head the R&D operations who was a strong academic scientist/researcher but did not have industry experience. He also moved the major research laboratories from Switzerland to Cambridge, Massachusetts, to be near Harvard and MIT. The research scientists were quite unhappy about the change in location, change in policy, and change in leadership. Thus, the changes were radical and also created uncertainty and concern among many of the managers and associates in the company.

His changes were praised by some management experts. For example, well-known management consultant, Ram Charan, said that Vasella was trying to change the existing paradigm in the industry rather than being a prisoner to it. Another management expert suggested that he had "the mind of a long-term strategist."

Vasella continued to make changes in the top executive ranks and finally in building a new and expensive corporate headquarters and research facilities. The new facilities were designed to be more open and to facilitate more communication among managers and associates, especially across units and functions. It is designed to promote cross-disciplinary perspectives and problem solving. A Harvard psychologist was consulted to help with the design and explain its value to people in the company. Yet, the change bothered people because it was dramatically different from what they had previously.

While many of the changes were based in logic and appeared to have the support of specialists who understood their value, Vasella

©AFP/Getty Images, Inc.

experienced significant resistance in the company. And, shareholders and analysts wanted better business performance to enhance the value of the firm's stock. Thus, in January 2010, it was announced that Vasella would depart the CEO position while remaining as chairman of the board. Joe Jimenez was promoted to be the new CEO. Jimenez had done a good job as head of the firm's dominant drug unit. Prior to his position with Novartis, Jimenez's experience was primarily in sales and marketing. He takes over the firm after a strong financial performance by Novartis in 2009. However, analysts are concerned about their lack of major drugs approved for the market and a recent and costly acquisition of the U.S. eye-care group, Alcon. Novartis paid $50 billion to acquire Alcon.

Thus, Jimenez has a full and challenging agenda in a highly competitive market and tough economic environment.

Sources: 2010. "New Novartis CEO: Cafepharma Reader, Former Heinz Exec," *The Wall Street Journal,* Jan. 26, at http://www.wsj.com; 2010. "Novartis Taps Joe Jimenez as CEO," *The New York Times,* Jan. 26, at http://www.nytimes. com; A. Jack & H. Simonian. 2010. "Novartis in Stealthy Pursuit of Change," *Financial Times,* Jan. 26, at http://www. ft.com; H. Plumridge. 2010. "New Novartis Chief Needs Surgery Skills," *The Wall Street Journal,* Jan. 26, at http:// www. wsj.com; N. Ouroussoff. 2009. "Many Hands, One Vision," *The New York Times,* Dec. 27, at http://www.nytimes.com; K. Capell. 2009. "Novartis: Radically Remaking its Drug Business," *BusinessWeek,* June 11, at http://www.businessweek. com; K. Capell. 2008. "Novartis Moves to the Next Stage," *BusinessWeek,* Oct. 20, at http://www.businessweek.com.

The *Experiencing Organizational Behavior* feature illustrates major changes implemented by Novartis. The changes described are substantial and represent a major departure from the way that research to identify major new drugs is commonly conducted in the industry. Overall, the changes implemented appear to be positive for the company and to hold value for future performance. They received praise from several management experts. However, the process used by the CEO to develop and implement the changes does not follow the process outlined herein. For example, rather than unfreezing the managers and associates in the organization, the CEO decided on the changes and announced them with little input from key managers. As a result, he encountered resistance from managers in the marketing unit (a very important function in the pharmaceutical industry) and from research scientists who not only had to change the focus of their research but also had to move from Switzerland to the United States, the new location of Novartis's research laboratories. The resistance likely produced less-effective changes or at least delayed the firm's ability to most effectively implement the changes. The end results were that the shareholders were unhappy with the financial performance of the firm and a new CEO was put in place to improve it. We conclude that Vasella appeared to have identified many positive changes for the company but followed a poor process to implement the changes in the company. Thus, they have not been as effective as they might have been.

The Novartis example emphasizes that the time and attention change leaders spend on the unfreezing phase can have a significant effect on the success of the change. When change leaders fail to treat unfreezing as a distinct and crucial phase, they often encounter problems, as Vasella obviously did. Without explicit attention to unfreezing, resistance to change is likely to be strong. Failure to focus attention on this phase, however, is common and is a source of failure in many change efforts. Two additional points are important. First, managers and associates should not expect all change activities to occur sequentially. Thus, activities important in one phase of the process may overlap activities necessary in the next phase.[55] For example, change leaders may engage in various activities in the moving phase while continuing to convince people of the need to change, an activity associated with the unfreezing phase. Although it is very useful to think in terms of three distinct phases, a measure of flexibility is required in actually creating change.

Second, a team of change leaders, rather than a single individual, should guide an organization through a major change effort. Relying on a single leader is risky because there is too much work required for one person to handle.[56] Deciding how best to unfreeze people, developing a vision, communicating a vision, generating small wins, and overseeing numerous change projects require more than one key change leader.[57]

In constructing the team, several factors should be considered. According to a well-known researcher and business consultant, John Kotter, four factors are crucial:[58]

1. *Position power* plays a role. Individuals with power based on their formal positions can block change or at least slow it down. Including some of these individuals on the team will leave fewer potential resisters who have the power to slow or resist the change.
2. *Informal credibility* is important. Individuals who have credibility are admired and respected and can be effective in selling change. Associates often are selected as change leaders based on this criterion.

3. *Expertise* is a relevant factor. Individuals on the team should possess knowledge related to the problems requiring the change effort and should have diverse points of view on potential solutions.
4. *Proven leadership* is crucial. The team needs individuals who can lead other managers and associates through the transition.

The size of the team is also a concern. There is little agreement on how large or small the team of change leaders should be, but the size of the organization that will be changed plays a role.[59] Six may be sufficient in a smaller organization or in a division of a larger organization. Fifteen or more may be required in a larger organization. However, as the team grows, it will be more difficult to coordinate and manage.

Important Tactical Choices

Change leaders must make many decisions. Among these are two important tactical decisions, the first involving speed and the second involving style.[60] Although these issues have no right or wrong answers, certain criteria must be considered when making informed choices.

Speed of Change

A fundamental decision in any change effort involves speed. A fast process, where unfreezing, moving, and refreezing occur quickly, can be useful if an ongoing problem will cause substantial damage in the near term.[61] Senior managers, for example, often initiate rapid change when they realize that organizational strategies or structure no longer provide value to customers. When Charlotte Beers became CEO of Ogilvy and Mather, a global advertising firm, the firm was out of step with the needs of the advertising industry, was losing important customers, and was suffering from declining overall performance. To save the firm, she and her circle of senior advisors created a vision, designed transformational change, and orchestrated its implementation in a matter of months.[62]

Overall, criteria that can be usefully considered when deciding on speed include:[63]

- *Urgency:* If the change is urgent, a faster pace is warranted.
- *Degree of support:* If the change is supported by a wide variety of people at the outset, a faster pace can be used.
- *Amount and complexity of change:* If the change is small and simple, a faster pace often can be used; but if the change is large, more time may be required.[64]
- *Competitive environment:* If competitors are poised to take advantage of existing weaknesses, a faster pace should be considered.
- *Knowledge and skills available:* If the knowledge and skills required by the new approach exist in the firm or can be easily acquired, a faster pace can be used.
- *Financial and other resources:* If the resources required by the change are on hand or easily acquired, a faster pace can be considered.

Style of Change

A second fundamental decision involves style. When using a top-down style, change leaders design the change and plan its implementation with little participation from those below them in the hierarchy. In contrast, when using a participatory style, change leaders seek the ideas and advice of those below them and then use many of those ideas.

Unfortunately, the Novartis CEO did not use a participatory style, and his top-down approach likely dulled the effectiveness of the changes he desired to implement. A transformational leadership style would have been more successful in this case.[65]

In a high-involvement organization, leaders use a participatory style whenever possible. Participation can be useful in generating ideas and developing commitment among those who will be affected by a change.[66] Participation, however, can be time-consuming and expensive, as meetings, debates, and synthesis of multiple sets of ideas take significant time. Overall, the following criteria are useful in evaluating the degree to which a participatory approach should be used:[67]

- *Urgency:* If the change is urgent, a participatory approach should not be used, as it tends to be time-consuming.
- *Degree of support:* If the idea of changing is supported initially by a wide variety of people, a participatory approach is less necessary.
- *Referent and expert power of change leaders:* When change leaders are admired and are known to be knowledgeable about pertinent issues, a participatory approach is less necessary.

Resistance to Change

resistance to change
Efforts to block the introduction of new approaches. Some of these efforts are passive in nature, involving tactics such as verbally supporting the change while continuing to work in the old ways; other efforts are active in nature, involving tactics such as organized protests and sabotage.

Although organizations experience both internal and external pressures to change, they frequently encounter strong resistance to needed changes. **Resistance to change** involves efforts to block the introduction of new ways of doing things. Dealing with resistance is one of the most important aspects of a manager's job. In a high-involvement organization, associates also must take responsibility for helping to motivate change among their peers.

Resistance may be active or passive.[68] Individuals may actively argue and use political connections in the firm to stop a change. In extreme cases of active resistance, resisters may sabotage change efforts through illegal means. In other cases, individuals passively resist change, which is more difficult to detect. Resisters may act as though they are trying to make the change a success, but in reality they are not. This often occurs in organizations that have attempted to change too frequently in the recent past, because individuals in these organizations have become tired of change.[69]

Resistance to change can usually be traced to one or more of the following four causal factors: lack of understanding, different assessments, self-interest, and low tolerance for change.[70]

Lack of Understanding

The first possible cause is lack of understanding. In some cases, individuals are unsure of what a change would entail. They resist because they do not understand the change.[71] For example, change leaders may decide to redesign jobs in a manufacturing facility using job enrichment. Such a redesign can result in substantial benefits to associates in the affected jobs, as discussed in Chapter 6. If, however, change leaders fail to explain the expected changes, some associates may begin to make false assumptions. They may, for example, believe that if job enrichment is implemented, their pay status will change from hourly wages to established salaries (with no overtime or incentive pay provided). Thus, they resist the change.

The key to avoiding or handling resistance to change based on lack of understanding is to communicate clearly what the change entails.[72] Many organizational researchers have emphasized the importance of rich communication for successful change. Meetings, articles in newsletters, and articles on company intranets are examples of possible communication tools.

Different Assessments

A second possible cause of resistance involves differing assessments of the change. Associates and managers who resist on this basis believe that the change would have more costs and fewer benefits than claimed by those who desire the change.[73] In this case, it is often not that the resisters have inaccurate or insufficient information, but rather that they understand the change but disagree with change leaders about the likely outcome. For example, a midlevel manager may resist an increase in product diversification because she sees more costs from the loss of focus than do those who are encouraging the change. Furthermore, she may see less potential for synergy across product lines than others do. Increased diversification may or may not be beneficial to a firm. Many factors are involved, and the situation is usually quite complex. Thus, honest disagreements are common when a firm is considering product-line expansion. Obviously, this is true for many other changes as well.

To prevent or deal with resistance based on different assessments, change leaders should consider including potential or actual resisters in the decision-making process.[74] This focus on participation serves two purposes. First, change leaders can ensure that they have all of the information they need to make good decisions.[75] Individuals resisting on the basis of different assessments may have more and better information than change leaders, making their resistance to change positive for the organization. Change leaders must explore why resisters feel the way they do.

Second, by emphasizing participation, change leaders can help to ensure procedural justice for actual or potential resisters.[76] In the context of organizational change, **procedural justice** is defined as perceived fairness in the decision process. Individuals are more likely to believe the process is fair and are more likely to trust the organization and change leaders if they are included in the decision process. One study showed the potential power of procedural justice. Associates in two U.S. power plants who believed they had input into change-related decisions felt more obligated to treat the organization well, trusted management to a greater degree, and expressed an intention to remain with the organization.[77]

procedural justice
In the context of organizational change, the perceived fairness of the change process.

Self-Interest

Individuals who resist change because of self-interest believe that they will lose something of value if the change is implemented.[78] Power, control over certain resources, and a valued job assignment are examples of things that could be lost. For example, the head of marketing in a small, rapidly growing firm might resist the establishment of a unit devoted to new-product development. If such a unit were established, he would lose his control over product development. Another example of self-interest is when individuals oppose an appointment to a higher-level position on the basis of gender or ethnicity.[79] Finally, managers and associates may resist change when they have no incentives to support it and could actually lose resources if changes are made such as in the current U.S. health care system (i.e., government payments are tied to specific actions and may not be made if innovations changing the treatments are made).[80]

To combat this type of resistance, change leaders can try to reason with resisters, explaining that the health of the organization is at stake. Leaders can also transfer resisters or, in extreme cases, ask them to leave the organization. Another option is to adopt a more coercive style and insist on compliance. In rare cases, when the resisters are extremely valuable to the organization and other tactics have failed or are unavailable, change leaders can negotiate in an effort to overcome the resistance.[81] Valuable resisters who are managers can be offered larger budgets or a valued new assignment for favored subordinates, for example. In the case of associates, additional vacation time might be offered. These actions, however, should be undertaken only under exceptional circumstances because they may create expectations on the part of other managers or associates.

Low Tolerance for Change

Associates and managers who resist on the basis of low tolerance for change fear the unknown. They have difficulty dealing with the uncertainty inherent in significant change. Such resistance leads to higher commitment to the current activities and thus organizational inertia (very slow or no change).[82] A manager, for example, may resist a change that seems good for the organization but that will disrupt established patterns. He may not be able to cope emotionally with the uncertainty and be concerned about having the capability to perform in the new situation.[83] Change leaders should offer support to these resisters.[84] Kind words, emotional support, and attention to training and education that properly prepare the individuals for the planned changes are appropriate tactics.

Research has shown that certain individual characteristics are associated with low tolerance for change. Lack of self-efficacy is perhaps the most important of these characteristics.[85] An associate or manager low in self-efficacy does not believe that he or she possesses or can mobilize the effort and ability needed to control events in his or her life. In the workplace, this translates into uncertainty about the capacity to perform at reasonable levels.[86] Another factor is low risk tolerance.[87] Individuals who do not tolerate risk very well often dislike major change. In a study of 514 managers from companies headquartered in Asia, Australia, Europe, and North America, poor views of self and low risk tolerance were found to harm the ability to deal with change.[88] In particular, openness to change is critical for organizations to be innovative.[89]

The DADA Syndrome

DADA syndrome
A sequence of stages—denial, anger, depression, and acceptance—through which individuals can move or in which they can become trapped when faced with unwanted change.

Beyond the resistance to change discussed above, change leaders must realize that associates and managers can become trapped in the so-called **DADA syndrome**—the syndrome of denial, anger, depression, and acceptance.[90] This syndrome highlights what can occur when individuals face unwanted change. In the denial stage, individuals ignore possible or current change; in the anger stage, individuals facing unwanted change become angry about the change; and in the depression stage, they experience emotional lows. Finally, in the acceptance stage, they embrace the reality of the situation and try to make the best of it. Not all individuals who experience this syndrome move through all of the stages sequentially, but many do. Some, however, remain in the anger or depression stage, resulting in negative consequences for them and the organization.

In a well-known incident, Donna Dubinsky at Apple Computer experienced the DADA syndrome.[91] Dubinsky headed the distribution function at Apple in the mid-1980s. She had performed well in her time at Apple and was considered to be a valuable part of the organization. Even so, Steve Jobs, chairman of the board at the time, began to criticize distribution and called for wholesale changes in the way this unit functioned. Dubinsky, incredulous that her unit was being questioned, decided the issue would go away on its own (denial stage). But the issue did not go away. Instead, Jobs asked the head of manufacturing in one of the operating divisions to develop a proposal for a new approach to distribution. Dubinsky still could not believe her unit would be changed, particularly without her input. Over time, however, she became defensive and challenged the criticisms (anger stage).

Transforming Cisco into a Recession-Proof Growth Machine

Cisco experienced its share of problems during the first decade of the twenty-first century. The two recessions during this time were especially unkind to technology-based firms. Yet, John Chambers, CEO of Cisco, has designed and implemented substantial changes in the organization. In his view, he is positioning the firm to be a growth machine for many years to come. To do so has required that he take several aggressive actions to transform the firm and to take these actions during a significant recession. However, because the firm has been well managed over the years, Chambers has $40 billion in cash that can be invested in aggressive actions.

First, Cisco has made a number of acquisitions and formed strategic alliances, both of which have the purpose of broadening Cisco's reach in attractive markets. For example, Cisco recently acquired companies with products and capabilities in the Internet videoconferencing, web security, and large-data-management markets. It also recently formed a joint venture, partnering with EMC, which expands Cisco's networking capabilities. These actions have special significance for Cisco's future. For example, Cisco predicts that 80 percent of the Internet data traffic will be in video form within four years.

©Steve Marcus/Reuters/Corbis

This could be especially important because Cisco is currently the largest seller of networking equipment in the world.

Cisco managers believe that collaboration will play a major role in business operations in the future, particularly to take advantage of human capital in the organization. As such organizations are likely to be decentralized networks of managers and associates working to accomplish the broad goals of the organization. The expectation is that the collaboration fostered by this environment will lead to more innovation and enhanced operational effectiveness. Some refer to this approach as collaborative social networking. And these networks will require tools that facilitate the communication and collaboration. The tools focus on video, collaboration, and virtualization.

In addition, Cisco has made substantial changes in its structure and mode of operation. The

reorganization has produced a much flatter structure, with people and managers organized in teams. The teams are empowered to make decisions that commit resources and act without central management approval. Managers and teams have compensatory incentives to work with other teams (i.e., collaborate) to develop new products and take advantage of new market opportunities. The structure then represents a distributed network with the hope of making fast decisions to move into new markets shortly after the market opportunity is identified. The bold promise is, "Power to the people and profits to the company."

Chambers suggests that with these changes, his company should be able to achieve annual sales growth of 12 to 15 percent. For a company with annual sales of $36 billion, this amount of increase per year is not trivial. Given Cisco's positive record and the changes made to resemble more of a high-involvement organization, many believe that this level of growth is achievable.

Cisco made major changes in its organization largely by acquiring products and capabilities to enter markets new to the firm and by dramatically changing the organizational structure and approach to management. The decentralized and distributed social networks of managers and associates help to produce greater innovation and to act quickly to exploit opportunities after they are identified. Chambers has been more successful in making changes and in producing positive results than the

CEO of Novartis. As noted previously, although the changes made by the Novartis CEO appeared to be good ones, the process used to create the change and implement it was ineffective. The CEO at Cisco encountered

less resistance than the changes in Novartis, because Cisco empowered managers and associates who in turn helped implement the change. As a result one could predict greater future success for Cisco than for Novartis.

Sources: A. Greenberg. 2010. "Cisco Aims Telepresence at Consumers' TVs," *Forbes*, Jan. 6, at http://www.forbes.com; D. Clark. 2009. "Tech Firms Jockey Ahead of Recovery," *The Wall Street Journal*, Dec. 31, at http://www.wsj.com; J. Fortt. 2009. "Cisco: We're a Growth Machine," *Fortune*, Dec. 9, at http://www.cnnmoney.com; A. Dugdale. 2009. "Cisco's Collaboration Platform: Facebook for Business?" *Fast Company*, Nov. 9, at http://www.fastcompany.com; A.S. Cohen. 2009. "The Latest Tech Tool? People Power," *Fortune*, Nov. 9, at http://www.cnnmoney.com; A. Greenberg. 2009. "Cisco Preps for Recovery," *Forbes*, Nov. 2, at http://www.forbes.com; E. McGirt. 2008. "How Cisco's CEO John Chambers Is Turning the Tech Giant Socialist," *Fast Company*, Nov. 25, at http://www.fastcompany.com.

Concerned with the process through which Jobs was attempting to change distribution, senior management in the company protested, which led to the creation of a task force to examine distribution issues. Dubinsky continued to be defensive as a member of this task force. As it became clear that the task force would endorse Jobs's proposed changes, however, Dubinsky reached an emotional low (depression stage). She was eventually revived by conversations at a retreat for executives. There, Dubinsky realized she had not invested her considerable talents in effectively handling the criticisms and plans for change in the distribution function. She went on the offensive and asked that she be allowed to develop her own proposal for change (acceptance). She was allowed to do so, and after examining the concerns and alternatives, she recommended major changes—changes that were different from Jobs's original ideas. Dubinsky's ideas were incorporated in the final plan.

Change leaders should be sensitive to the potential for the DADA syndrome. To prevent associates and managers from entering the DADA stages or to ensure they do not become mired in the anger or depression stage, leaders must monitor their organizations for actual or potential resistance to change. If resistance is discovered, its cause must be diagnosed and addressed.

Organization Development

Leaders must recognize internal and external pressures for change and introduce initiatives designed to cope with them. In addition, leaders can proactively position their organizations to better recognize the need for change and to more easily implement change when necessary. In other words, leaders can develop their organizations so that communication, problem solving, and learning are more effective.

organization development (OD)
A planned organization-wide continuous process designed to improve communication, problem solving, and learning through the application of behavioral science knowledge.

To achieve these goals, **organization development (OD)** is useful. Although researchers have not always agreed on the specific features of organization development, they agree that its purpose is to improve processes and outcomes in organizations.[92] OD has had its share of critics in recent years but it has produced some worthwhile results.[93]

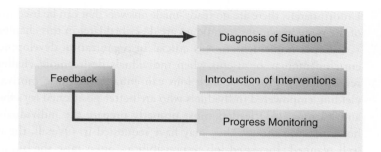

OD can be defined as a planned, organization-wide, continuous process designed to improve communication, problem solving, and learning through the application of behavioral science knowledge.[94] With its roots in humanistic psychology, OD is grounded in values of individual empowerment and interpersonal cooperation.[95] Thus, it is consistent with the high-involvement management approach.

The Basic OD Model

The basic OD model uses a medical approach, in which organizations are treated when they suffer ill health. OD researchers and practitioners diagnose the illness, prescribe interventions, and monitor progress.[96] Exhibit 14-4 provides an overview.

Diagnosis

Diagnosis is an important step in organization development. Without effective diagnosis, managers will not understand what their organization really needs, and the chosen course of action will likely be ineffective.

Although the diagnostic approaches used by physicians and managers are similar, the tools they use vary. Over the years, physicians' diagnostic tools have become quite sophisticated (laboratory tests, CT scans, MRIs, electrocardiograms, and so on). Those of the manager, though useful, are less precise. Even so, our knowledge of diagnostic tools has increased rapidly in recent years.

Diagnostic devices for managers include interviews, surveys, group sociometric devices, process-oriented diagnosis, and accurate records (e.g., performance records). Of these tools, the most frequently used are surveys and individual and group interviews.[97] Managers can conduct many different surveys, including job-satisfaction surveys (such as the Job Description Index), organization climate or culture surveys (such as the Organizational Practices Questionnaire), job design measures (such as the Job Diagnostic Survey), and assessments of leaders (such as the Leadership Practices Inventory). In many cases, standard survey forms can be used; in other cases, surveys may need to be custom-designed for the situation. These diagnostic tools can be useful in determining needed interventions. Some organizations administer surveys to employees on a regular basis, such as annually, to identify problems.

Interventions

After the situation has been diagnosed, interventions can be prescribed. Organization development interventions include different forms of group training, team building, and job redesign.[98] The most appropriate technique will vary with the situational factors involved.

Unfortunately, there are no ready-made answers that can be used for all situations. Several of the more important techniques are described later in this chapter.

Proper implementation is crucial in organization development. For example, job enrichment may be useful when individuals desire more challenging jobs and more responsibility. Providing such jobs can enhance intrinsic motivation and satisfaction, yielding empowered individuals who are better positioned for effective problem solving and learning. OD leaders must properly prepare the individuals for job enrichment, however, even though they may have requested it. Overall, the interventions must be well planned. Increased job responsibilities often raise the question, "Don't I deserve more pay if I'm performing a more responsible job?" OD leaders must be prepared to answer such questions.

A well-trained OD specialist should play an important role in any intervention.[99] Often, managers who understand only one or two specific OD techniques attempt to use these approaches to solve whatever problem exists. But the techniques must match the situation, or the likelihood of failure is high. Furthermore, people who are not fully knowledgeable about organization development frequently have problems implementing a successful program. For example, only experts in group training, team building, or conflict resolution should implement those particular OD change techniques.

Progress Monitoring

The effects of the interventions must be evaluated after an appropriate interval.[100] The evaluation is important to ensure that the objectives have been met.[101] A common evaluation technique is the survey, which may be used to diagnose a problem and then reused after an OD technique has been implemented to determine what progress has been made toward resolving the problem. Other evaluation tools may be used as well. In any case, the main criterion for evaluation is to determine whether the original objectives have been accomplished. Some OD tools such as process consultation have evaluation processes built into them.[102]

If the evaluation shows that objectives have not been accomplished, further efforts may be necessary. A new or modified approach may be designed and implemented. The type and degree of these actions depend on why the objectives were not reached and by how far they were missed. Questions such as "Was the original process correct?" and "Was it correctly implemented?" must be answered.

Frequently, some modifications are needed to increase the positive benefits of OD work, but if care has been taken in the OD process, wholesale changes are unnecessary at this stage. Because a comprehensive OD program is continuous, the process of sensing the organization's need for development is continuous. In this way, an organization is in a constant state of renewal and regularly checks its health.

Organization Development Interventions

The interventions used to create organizational change are at the heart of organization development. Here, we describe several of the more important OD intervention techniques. Research suggests that using more than one technique is generally superior to using a single technique.[103] For convenience of discussion, we have placed the interventions into two groups: techniques directly focused on how individuals relate to one another[104] and techniques focused on structure and systems[105] (see Exhibit 14-5).

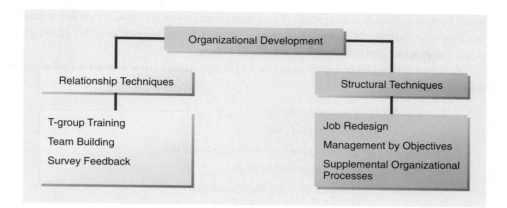

Exhibit 14-5
Organization Development Interventions

Relationship Techniques

Relationship techniques focus on how individuals perceive and respond to one another. T-group training, team building, survey feedback, and more general training are among the most important techniques in this category.

In **t-group training,** individuals participate in various interpersonal and group situations to better understand how they act, how others perceive their actions, and how others react to them.[106] In many cases, individuals involved in this type of training do not know one another before the group experience. Participating with strangers rather than work colleagues helps to promote honest behavior. T-group training is aimed at helping individual associates and managers learn about themselves in a group setting and then transfer that learning to the workplace. An individual often is able to learn about unintended negative effects created by certain types of behavior, for example, and then change that behavior, resulting in a positive effect on the workplace environment.

T-group training must be used carefully and only with a trained, qualified facilitator. The facilitator plays an important role in increasing the chances of success. The use of this technique is declining because it can produce negative outcomes for some people (e.g., those who are insecure). Thus, group participants must be chosen with great care. Neglecting to take such care is one reason that OD efforts fail.

Team building, a cornerstone of organization development, is a technique that requires members of a team to work together to understand their problems and implement solutions.[107] A team is any group of associates and/or managers who work together to accomplish a task (see Chapter 11 for additional details). The problems faced by teams usually involve substantive team tasks (e.g., technical design problems for a new-product-development team), the processes of the team (e.g., weaknesses in problem solving), and interpersonal relationships among team members (e.g., difficulties based on differences in personality).

In successful applications of team building, team members focus mostly on substantive tasks rather than on process and interpersonal issues.[108] While team members concentrate on substantive problem solving, a skilled leader can introduce interpersonal and other process guidance as needed.[109]

Overall, the team-building process can help to positively reinforce relations among team members and may be particularly useful for teams experiencing conflict, lack of cohesiveness, or ambiguous goals. Team building can be important for self-managed teams and teams that have new leaders.[110] New leaders taking over the responsibility for a team

t-group training
Group exercises in which individuals focus on their actions, how others perceive their actions, and how others generally react to them; participants often learn about unintended negative consequences of certain types of behavior.

team building
A process in which members of a team work together and with a facilitator to diagnose task, process, and interpersonal problems within the team and create solutions.

often find that team building reduces suspicion, increases trust, and promotes a healthy working relationship. At times, the use of a third-party consultant may be necessary to guide the process, particularly when conflict is present.

In summarizing their experiences, two OD researchers have offered a useful list of team-building tips:[111]

1. Get the *right people together* for
2. a large *block of uninterrupted time*
3. to work on *high-priority problems or opportunities* that
4. *they have identified* and have them work
5. in *structured ways* to enhance the likelihood of
6. *realistic solutions and action plans,* which are then
7. *implemented* enthusiastically and
8. *followed up to assess* actual versus expected results.

survey feedback
Data obtained from questionnaires; managers receive the data for their units and are expected to hold unit meetings to discuss problems.

The **survey feedback** technique emphasizes the collection and use of data from questionnaires.[112] Although all OD efforts involve collecting data through surveys and interviews as part of diagnosing the organization's situation, surveys can also be used as an intervention following diagnosis. If, for example, the diagnosis suggests that poor motivation among associates is driven partly by a feeling of lack of input, using surveys more frequently may be helpful in changing this feeling.

The first step in the survey feedback technique involves collecting data on how individuals feel about various aspects of leadership and interpersonal relations within the unit, as well as broader organizational issues. Each manager in the organization receives a summary of the survey results for her unit. An internal or external OD consultant meets with the manager to discuss the results. A second meeting is then arranged for the manager to present the findings to associates and lower-level managers. The OD consultant often attends this unit meeting to explain any technical aspects of the data. The unit members then work together to interpret the findings, understand problems, and find solutions.

It is important that all information from a survey be discussed. Positive information is crucial in helping to build and maintain a positive climate. Negative information is critical for understanding problems.

training
A process used in OD to help managers and associates to gain skills and capabilities needed to accomplish tasks in their jobs.

Training is a process used in OD to help managers and associates to gain skills and capabilities needed to accomplish tasks in their jobs.[113] It is common, for example, to provide managers leadership training to help them become more effective leaders. Training can also enrich managers' and associates' capabilities that help prepare them for future positions in the organization. Such training provides the organization with more flexibility, allowing it take advantage of new opportunities that are identified.[114] Training is a common tool used universally by all types of organizations. In addition, training is a global phenomenon. For example, most multinational enterprises have their managers and associates participate in training in their subsidiaries throughout the world. However, they do have to adjust their processes and content to adapt to local cultural values.[115]

Structural Techniques

Structural OD techniques, as the name implies, involve adjustments in the organization's structure. In the field of organization development, some structural interventions are focused on changing tasks; others are focused on changing the method of setting task objectives; and still others are broadly focused on communication, problem solving, and learning. Commonly used techniques include job redesign, management by objectives (MBO), and supplemental organizational elements.

The **job redesign** technique may include job enlargement, job enrichment, or both.[116] As discussed in Chapter 6, job enlargement involves adding tasks that offer more variety and that may require the use of different skills. The additional tasks, however, are not of greater complexity. Some refer to this as horizontal loading. Job enrichment involves adding more complex tasks, generally by incorporating tasks formerly handled by managers (e.g., scheduling of maintenance on a production machine) and staff specialists (e.g., making quality-control decisions). Thus, associates whose jobs are enriched have greater responsibility because they begin to manage their own jobs individually or as members of self-managing teams.

Much of the emphasis on the redesign of jobs in organization development grew out of controversy surrounding boring, repetitive tasks often seen in mass-production systems. Many observers, believing that repetitive tasks led to an alienated workforce, proposed to enrich jobs by providing more challenging tasks. Through enrichment, associates become more engaged problem solvers. Because managers no longer need to closely supervise the routine activities of associates, they can focus more of their attention on helping to solve key organizational problems and helping to establish a learning orientation in their units. In current organizations, jobs are often enriched by assigning coordination responsibilities related to interdependent tasks. And, these tasks frequently require collaboration with people and units based in other countries.[117]

When an organization uses **management by objectives (MBO)**, individuals negotiate task objectives with their managers at each level in the organization. (See Chapter 6 for a more detailed discussion of participation in setting goals and the motivational properties of goals.) This technique changes the objective-setting structure from one determined by the supervisor to one in which both supervisor and subordinates participate. Once set, objectives are used in performance assessments.

As an OD technique, MBO involves several specific steps.[118] First, information collected from organization members, senior managers, and perhaps others is used to diagnose organizational problems. This diagnosis provides a focus for MBO efforts. After diagnosis, senior managers and others can define major organizational objectives. Next, workshops about the MBO process generally are conducted for all managers to help them understand and use the technique correctly.

Objectives for middle managers are then defined by teams of middle and senior managers. Objectives for lower-level managers are set by teams of lower-level and middle managers, with senior managers also possibly involved. Finally, objectives for associates are established by teams of associates and managers. The participatory approach embedded in MBO often yields associates and managers who are more satisfied with and committed to the organization. As a result, they are more likely to be enthusiastic problem solvers who are open to learning.

Management by objectives can be a useful technique, but it does carry risks.[119] First, objectives can be rather static and inflexible, while the environment is constantly changing. People may have to change their focus and what they do in order to meet changing environmental demands. Second, an associate's accomplishments are often influenced by factors outside of his control. Thus, performance assessments tied to meeting objectives can be unfair. Third, a strong focus on objective attainment may mean that intangible aspects of the job for which objectives have not been set are ignored.

Finally, senior managers can create **supplemental organizational** processes to enhance communication, problem solving, and learning. Examples of such processes include

job redesign
Enlargement or enrichment of jobs; enrichment is the better method to enhance motivation for effective problem solving, communication, and learning.

management by objectives (MBO)
A management process in which individuals negotiate task objectives with their managers and then are held accountable for attainment of those objectives.

supplemental organizational processes
Processes in which associates and/or managers have ongoing meetings for the purpose of understanding and addressing important problems.

quality circles, safety councils, regular union-management meetings, and periodically scheduled management retreats. At the core, these supplemental processes involve ongoing meetings of associates and/or managers for the purpose of understanding and addressing important problems. Team building, with its attention to process and interpersonal issues, sometimes is involved.

Senior managers at General Electric used a number of OD interventions to improve honest communication, problem solving, and learning. Their efforts had remarkable results.[120] The management–union meetings implemented in the transportation division constituted a supplemental organizational process. Work-out was also a supplemental process, and it involved aspects of team building as well. The boundaryless organization involved job redesign, as individuals were expected to search across unit lines for ideas— an activity formerly outside their domain. Many analysts believe that the work-out and boundaryless organization concepts contributed to GE's phenomenal performance during the 20 years of Jack Welch's tenure as CEO. During this time, GE created more value for shareholders than any other company in the world.[121]

Beginning with the efforts of Thomas Edison, over the years GE has provided significant advances in many useful products, including the incandescent light bulb, x-ray equipment, the electric fan, radios, TVs, and turbines. But despite GE's history of innovation in product development and its overall success, the company had become stale and out of step with its environment by the time Welch took over as CEO in 1981. Many associates and managers were unhappy and unproductive, and financial performance was beginning to decline. Internal processes and structures were hindering rather than helping. But, OD interventions helped to create a healthier company. Through these interventions, associates and lower-level managers became more motivated to help identify needed changes, middle and senior managers had better forums for information exchange, and everyone had greater incentives to develop, borrow, and share ideas. The outcome was highly positive for GE's shareholders, managers, and associates.

Organizational Learning

Most organizational development and change require learning. The changes may be based on learning new capabilities, new processes, or adding new knowledge that helps the organization more effectively use its current capabilities and processes. Thus, managing organizational change entails managing knowledge transfers and development.[122] Learning how to more effectively use current knowledge is referred to as **exploitative learning**. Alternatively, **exploratory learning** involves creating new knowledge and being innovative.[123]

exploitative learning
Learning how to more effectively use current knowledge.

exploratory learning
Creating new knowledge and being innovative.

As explained earlier, some of the OD techniques also involve learning about relationships and building relationship skills.[124] Some of this learning can eventually be integrated into and enrich current organizational routines (e.g., regular processes and approaches for problem solving) or create new ones.[125] But, it is critical to emphasize that organizational change is successful in the long term only if learning occurs. For example, the changes that enhanced GE's phenomenal performance during Jack Welch's tenure as CEO were based on managers learning how to make effective decisions that created value for the organization. And, in turn, managers must help the associates who work with her to learn as well.[126] Individual learning is important to solicit creative ideas from associates and to build their capabilities to participate in problem-solving activities important in high-involvement organizations.[127]

Organization Development across Cultures

The growth of multinational corporations and the global marketplace requires that the cultural implications of OD programs be considered. Behavioral science techniques may not work the same way in different cultures, and methods of managing successful organizations can vary across cultures. Managers hoping to implement an OD program in a culture different from their own must avoid an ethnocentric attitude (assuming that everyone is similar to those back home) as well as stereotyping.

To implement OD successfully in different cultures, those involved should demonstrate the following qualities:

- *Flexibility*—openness to new approaches, ideas, and beliefs and willingness to change one's own behavior
- *Knowledge of specific cultures*—understanding of the beliefs and behavior patterns of different cultures (see Chapter 3 for a discussion of cultural differences)
- *Interpersonal sensitivity*—the ability to listen to and resolve problems with people from different cultures[128]

THE STRATEGIC LENS

Organizations must adapt to their external environments in order to survive, grow, and achieve financial success. Organizations design their strategies to engage in actions that give them an advantage over their competitors. Because most organizations exist in dynamic environments, they have to adjust their strategies regularly. Implementing strategies and adjustments to them requires the involvement and support of all managers and associates in the organization. Therefore, identifying the need for major changes and implementing those changes are critical determinants of organizational success. Managers must overcome resistance to change and effectively use the human capital in the organization to achieve and sustain a competitive advantage. Yet, the largest challenge in creating organizational change is in changing the behavior of people. This conclusion is supported by research showing that 90 percent of people who have serious heart disease find it highly difficult to change their lifestyle even though they understand the importance of doing so for their personal health.[129] One can easily surmise that if people cannot change their lifestyle when it affects their health, changing their behavior for the good of the organization is likely to be even more difficult. Research also shows that events creating a need for substantial change (often referred to as "discontinuous change") rarely trigger a response until they are perceived as a threat to survival.[130]

The examples of major changes implemented at Starbucks, Cisco, and GE show the importance of managing organizational change, as well as the potential importance of OD interventions. The major organizational changes implemented at GE are reportedly the primary reason that Jack Welch enjoyed so much success as CEO during his 20-plus years in that role. Alternatively, the major changes recently implemented at Starbucks and Cisco are positioning them to be successful in the future. Developing and implementing effective organizational strategies and managing organizational change are interdependent.

Critical Thinking Questions

1. Why do organizations need to make changes on a regular basis? What are the major causes of these changes?

2. Why is it so difficult for people to change their behavior, even when they know it is important to do so?

3. If you were in a managerial position and believed that a major change in your unit's structure was needed, what actions would you take to ensure that the change was made effectively?

What This Chapter Adds to Your Knowledge Portfolio

In our final chapter, we have discussed change in organizations. More specifically, we have discussed pressures for change, a three-phase change model, two critical tactical decisions, and resistance to change. We have also examined organization development, offering a definition and basic model, along with a set of techniques. In summary, we have made the following points:

- Organizations experience pressures for change, some of which are internal. Aspiration–performance discrepancies constitute one internal source of pressure. These discrepancies are simply differences between desired and actual performance. Past aspirations, past performance, and comparisons with others affect today's aspirations. Life-cycle forces constitute a second internal source of pressure. When organizations grow, pressure tends to build at certain predictable points, forcing organizations to respond. If an organization responds effectively, it tends to move through several stages: entrepreneurial, collectivity, formalization, and elaboration. Changes in the persons occupying top management positions often produce broader organizational changes. First, new managers are not committed to previous strategies and decisions made. Second, new managers bring unique ideas and perhaps a different vision for the organization. In turn, these reduce resistance to change and provide directions for change.
- Organizations experience a host of external pressures for change. Such pressures originate with technological advances, the introduction or removal of government regulations, changes in societal values, shifting political dynamics, changes in demographics, and growing international interdependencies.
- Planned change entails deliberate efforts to move an organization or a subunit from its current state to a new state. Such change is typically thought of as a three-phase process comprising unfreezing, transforming, and refreezing. Unfreezing involves providing a rationale for change, producing minor levels of guilt or anxiety about not changing, and creating a psychological sense of safety concerning the change. Transforming involves providing information that supports the proposed change and creating actual change. Refreezing focuses on implementing evaluation systems to track expected new behaviors and training systems to ensure continuous upgrading of relevant knowledge and skills. It also involves creating permanent reward structures to reinforce the new behaviors, as well as hiring and promotion systems that support the new approaches.
- Decisions related to speed and style must be made in all planned change projects. Whether movement toward change should be fast or slow depends on the urgency of the change, the degree of support for changing, the amount or complexity of the change, the competitive environment, the knowledge and skills available to support the change, and the availability of financial and other resources necessary to implement the change. Style involves using a top-down or participatory approach. Key criteria for this decision are the urgency of the change, the degree of support for changing, the referent and expert power of change leaders, and organizational norms.
- Resistance to change can be traced to a general set of causes: lack of understanding, different assessments, self-interest, and/or low tolerance for change. To address lack of understanding, change leaders should ensure proper communication about proposed

changes. To address different assessments, leaders should include actual or potential change resisters in the decision-making process in order to learn as much as possible about their thinking and to create a sense that all voices are being heard. To address self-interest, leaders must consider a host of tactics, including transferring resisters or even terminating their employment, using a coercive style to ensure compliance, and in rare situations, negotiating compliance. Finally, to address low tolerance for change, change leaders should offer emotional support and ensure proper education and training to break the inertia.

- Individuals facing unwanted change may move through a series of stages known as denial, anger, depression, and acceptance. Change leaders must understand this so-called DADA syndrome. To prevent associates and others from experiencing it, they must monitor their organizations for potential and actual resistance to change and deal effectively with resistance when it is identified.
- Organization development is an applied field of study focused on improving processes and outcomes in organizations. It can be formally defined as a planned, organization-wide, continuous process designed to improve communication, problem solving, and learning. Because it has roots in humanistic psychology, it is grounded in values of individual empowerment and interpersonal cooperation. The basic OD

model has three steps: diagnosis, intervention, and progress monitoring.

- The various interventions used in organization development can be classified as either relationship techniques or structural techniques. Relationship techniques, which focus on how individuals perceive and respond to one another, include t-group training, team building, survey feedback, and more general skills training. Structural techniques, which involve adjustments to the structural aspects of an organization, include job redesign, management by objectives, and supplemental structural elements. OD techniques involve organizational learning in order to create the desired change.
- Cultural differences must be considered when organization development techniques are being used. Techniques must be chosen in light of the prevailing culture. To implement OD successfully in different cultures, those involved should be flexible, understand the various cultures, and possess interpersonal sensitivity.

back to the knowledge objectives

1. What are the three major sources of internal pressure for organizational change? In your opinion, which of these three is most difficult to handle? Why?
2. What are the six major sources of external pressure for organizational change? In your opinion, which of these is most difficult to handle? Why?
3. What is involved in each phase of the unfreezing–transforming–refreezing model of planned change?
4. What are the factors to consider in deciding whether a fast or slow approach to change is best? What are the factors to consider in deciding whether a top-down or participatory approach to change is best? Describe a situation in which you were either a change recipient or a change leader and a poor choice was made for at least one of these two decisions (use an example from an organization in which you currently work or formerly worked, or use a voluntary organization, a church, a sports team, or a fraternity/sorority).
5. Compare the four basic causes of resistance to change. If you had to choose one, which would you prefer to deal with as a manager, and why?
6. What is the DADA syndrome?
7. What is organization development? Provide a definition as well as a basic model. A number of interventions can be used in organization development. As a manager, which of these interventions would you prefer to use, and why?

Key Terms

aspiration–performance
  discrepancies, p. 491
life-cycle forces, p. 492
changes in top management,
  p. 494
planned change, p. 499
unfreezing, p. 500
transforming, p. 500
refreezing, p. 500

resistance to change, p. 504
procedural justice, p. 505
DADA syndrome, p. 506
organization development
  (OD), p. 508
t-group training, p. 511
team building, p. 511
survey feedback, p. 512
training, p. 512

job redesign, p. 513
management by objectives
  (MBO), p. 513
supplemental organizational
  processes, p. 513
exploitative learning, p. 514
exploratory learning, p. 514

---

building your human capital

An Assessment of Low Tolerance for Change

People differ in their tolerance for change. Low self-efficacy and low risk tolerance are two important factors that affect tolerance for change. Although an individual's self-efficacy and risk tolerance may vary from situation to situation, overall scores on these factors provide insight into general tendencies. Understanding these tendencies can help you to understand how and why you behave as you do. In this installment of Building Your Human Capital, we present an assessment tool for efficacy and risk.

Instructions

In this assessment, you will read 19 phrases that describe people. Use the rating scale below to indicate how accurately each phrase describes you. Rate yourself as you generally are now, not as you wish to be in the future, and rate yourself as you honestly see yourself. Keep in mind that very few people have extreme scores on all or even most of the items (a "1" or a "5" is an extreme score); most people have midrange scores for many of the items. Read each item carefully, and then circle the number that corresponds to your choice from the rating scale that follows.

1	2	3	4	5
Not at all like me	Somewhat unlike me	Neither like nor unlike me	Somewhat like me	Very much like me

1. Enjoy being reckless	1	2	3	4	5
2. Become overwhelmed by events	1	2	3	4	5
3. Would never go hang-gliding or bungee-jumping	1	2	3	4	5
4. Readily overcome setbacks	1	2	3	4	5
5. Take risks	1	2	3	4	5
6. Am often down in the dumps	1	2	3	4	5
7. Would never make a high-risk investment	1	2	3	4	5
8. Can manage many things at the same time	1	2	3	4	5
9. Seek danger	1	2	3	4	5
10. Feel that I am unable to deal with things	1	2	3	4	5
11. Stick to the rules	1	2	3	4	5

12. Can tackle anything	1	2	3	4	5
13. Know how to get around rules	1	2	3	4	5
14. Am afraid of many things	1	2	3	4	5
15. Avoid dangerous situations	1	2	3	4	5
16. Think quickly	1	2	3	4	5
17. Am willing to try anything once	1	2	3	4	5
18. Need reassurance	1	2	3	4	5
19. Seek adventure	1	2	3	4	5

Scoring Key

To determine your score, combine your responses to the items above as follows:

Self-efficacy = (Item 4 + Item 8 + Item 12 + Item 16) + (30 − (Item 2 + Item 6 + Item 10 + Item 14 + Item 18))

Tolerance for risk = (Item 1 + Item 5 + Item 9 + Item 13 + Item 17 + Item 19) + (24 − (Item 3 + Item 7 + Item 11 + Item 15))

Scores for self-efficacy can range from 9 to 45. Scores of 36 or above may be considered high, while scores of 18 or below may be considered low. Scores for risk tolerance can range from 10 to 50. Scores of 40 or above may be considered high, while scores of 20 or below may be considered low.

Source: International Personality Item Pool. 2001. A Scientific Collaboration for the Development of Advanced Measures of Personality Traits and Other Individual Differences, at http://ipip.ori.org.

an organizational behavior moment

Organization Development at KBTZ

KBTZ is a large television station located in a major metropolitan area in the United States. The station is one of the largest revenue producers in its market and employs more than 180 people, considerably more than its closest competitors. It is a subsidiary of a large corporation that has diversified interests in other businesses as well as the communications field. KBTZ represents a significant portion of the corporation's profit base.

Over the past few years, substantial investments have been made in the television station by the parent corporation. These investments have not only resulted in significant tax advantages but also have established KBTZ as the local television leader in the use of sophisticated electronic equipment. The station's physical plant was remodeled at considerable expense to accommodate the new equipment and to boost its image as the leader in the market. KBTZ is a successful business and a respected member of the metropolitan community. However, in part because of the recent changes in the station and in part because of its desire to maintain its established success, the station has requested that a consultant examine important problems. You are the consultant.

In your initial meeting with Valerie Diaz, the president and general manager of KBTZ, she explained her perceptions of key problems facing the station.

One of our biggest problems is the high stress to which our managers and associates are exposed. This is especially true with respect to time deadlines. There is no such thing as slack time in television. For example, when it is precisely six o'clock, we must be on the air with the news. All of the news material, local reporting, news interviews, and so on must be processed, edited, and ready to go at six. We can't have any half-prepared material or extended deadlines, or we lose the audience and, most likely, our sponsors. I believe this situation causes a great deal of conflict and turnover among our employees. We have a number of well-qualified and motivated employees, some of whom work here because of the glamour and excitement. But we also have a lot of problems.

Valerie concluded by saying, "I've asked you here because I believe the station needs an outside viewpoint. Our employee turnover is about 35 percent, which is too high. We are having trouble hiring qualified people who fit our culture and who can help us deal with the challenges. We must eliminate the conflicts and develop a cohesive organization to retain our profit and market-leading positions. I would like to hire you as a consultant for this job. I want you to monitor our operations and diagnose our problems."

You have now collected data within each department (there are seven departments based on function, as discussed below).

All department heads have been interviewed, while other employees have responded to questionnaires concerning organizational culture and job satisfaction. The information collected during this diagnosis phase has been summarized as follows.

Interviews with Department Heads

Business Manager: "I'm very new in this job and haven't really learned the ropes yet. I previously worked in sales and in the general manager's office. This is my first managerial position, and I need help in managing my department, because I don't have any management training."

News Director: "Let me be frank with you. I've worked for the big network, and the only reason I'm here is because I wanted to come back home to live. I don't think we need you here. We don't need any new 'management programs.' My department functions smoothly, my people are creative, and I don't want you messing us up with the latest fad program."

Operations Manager: "We truly have the best department in the station. I believe in Valerie's management of the station. I also believe in working my people hard. Nobody lags in this department, or out they go. Our only problems are with the news director's people, who are confused all of the time, and the engineering group, which is lazy and uncooperative. Our effectiveness depends on these groups. I think the chief engineer is incompetent. Get rid of him, shape up the news group and the engineers, and you'll have done a great job."

Chief Engineer: "Things go pretty well most of the time, except for the unreasonableness of certain people in other departments. Some people expect us to drop whatever we're doing and immediately repair some malfunctioning equipment in their area. This is sophisticated equipment, and it can take several hours just to determine the cause of the failure. The news people just have to treat their equipment better, and the operations manager—he's up here nearly every day screaming about something. One of these days I'm going to punch his lights out!"

Program Director: "My department is okay, but the station is missing a lot of opportunities in other areas. We have a lot of people problems in some departments, especially news and sales. The chief engineer is incompetent, and the operations manager pushes his lower-level managers and associates too hard—never lets them make any decisions or take any responsibilities. The general manager, Valerie Diaz, doesn't want to face up to these problems."

Promotion Manager: "We're a small, friendly group. We have few problems—except with the news group people, who think they know more than we do. But that's just a small problem. I would like a little training in how to deal with people—motivation, communication, and that sort of stuff."

Sales Manager: "Things are just great in our department. To be sure, the sales reps complain sometimes, but I just remind them that they're the highest-paid people in the station. I think Mom [Valerie Diaz] is doing a great job as general manager of the station."

Survey of Departments

Business Office and Programming Departments. The survey showed individuals in these departments to have generally positive attitudes. Job satisfaction was somewhat mixed but still positive. These individuals did, however, have two important negative perceptions of their task environment. First, they thought that their department heads and the general manager could handle downward communication better. Second, there were several unsolicited comments about being underpaid relative to other station employees.

News Department. Managers and associates in the news department reported very high satisfaction with their jobs but extreme dissatisfaction with the department head (the news director) and very negative attitudes toward their overall work environment. Communication between managers and associates was perceived to be almost nonexistent. Associates complained of very low rewards, including pay, promotion opportunities, and managerial praise. They also complained of constant criticism, which was the only form of managerial feedback on performance. In addition, in spite of their high job satisfaction, they believed that the negative factors led them to be poorly motivated.

The severity of the problems in this department was highlighted when some associates reported that they weren't certain who their immediate manager was, because both the assignments editor and the assistant news director gave them assignments. They also reported that creativity (thought to be important in their jobs) was discouraged by the director's highly authoritarian and structured style. Many employees resented the news director, referring to him as erratic, caustic, and alcoholic.

Operations Department. Most of the operations associates were satisfied with their jobs and reported pride in their department. However, satisfaction with immediate managers was mixed. Furthermore, some associates had very positive feelings about the department head, but most held him in low regard. The associates tended to feel overworked (reporting an average 74-hour work week) and thought the department head expected too much. They also thought they were underpaid relative to their task demands, and they criticized managerial feedback on their performance. They noted that the department head never praised positive performance—he only reprimanded them for poor performance. They also reported concern over the conflict with engineering, which they believed should and could be resolved.

Engineering Department. The survey revealed that members of this department were very dissatisfied with their jobs and immediate managers. Responses also showed that department members perceived a high level of conflict between themselves and the operations and news departments, especially the operations department. They also believed the department head did not support them and that managers and associates in other departments held them in low regard. They noted that they never had department meetings and that they rarely received feedback on their performance from the chief engineer.

Promotions Department. The survey showed this department to have very positive attitudes. Job satisfaction was high, and everyone viewed their work environment positively. The few negative comments were primarily directed toward the "ineffectiveness" of the news department.

Sales Department. Very few individuals from the sales department responded to the survey. To find out why they hadn't received responses, the consultant approached several salespersons for private discussions. Nearly all of them indicated that they couldn't complete the survey honestly. As one stated, "My attitudes about this place are largely negative, and my department head is the station manager's son. I'd lose my job today if he knew what I really thought about him."

Discussion Questions

1. Identify the basic problems at KBTZ.
2. Which OD techniques would you consider using, and why?

team exercise

Identifying Change Pressures and Their Effects

Procedure

1. With the aid of the instructor, the class will be divided into four- or five-person groups.
2. The groups will be assigned several tasks:

   - Each group should identify several specific change pressures that are acting on their institution (e.g., college, university). The group should record these pressures as external or internal.

   - Once the change pressures have been identified, the group should determine and record the effects of each change pressure on the institution.

   - Each group should prepare a list of recommendations concerning what the institution should do to deal with these change pressures.

   - Finally, each group should conduct an analysis of possible resistance to change. Who or what groups might resist each recommendation and why? How should the possible resistance be handled?

3. The instructor will call on each group in class, asking it to present its lists of (1) change pressures, (2) effects of change pressures, (3) recommendations, and (4) people/groups that might resist change.
4. The instructor will guide a discussion of this exercise.

Endnotes

1. Hitt, M.A., Ireland, R.D., & Hoskisson, R.E. 2009. *Strategic management: Competitiveness and globalization* (8th ed). Mason, OH: South-Western.
2. Walsh, J.P., Meyer, A.D., & Schoonhoven, C.B. 2006. A future for organization theory: Living in and living with changing organizations. *Organization Science*, 17: 657–671; Fiss, P.C., & Zajac, E.J. 2006. The symbolic management of strategic change: Sensegiving via framing and decoupling. *Academy of Management Journal*, 49: 1173–1193.
3. Huber, G.P. 2004. *The necessary nature of future firms: Attributes of survivors in a changing world.* Thousand Oaks, CA: Sage Publications.
4. Chen, W.-R., & Miller, K.D. 2007. Situational and institutional determinants of firms' R&D search intensity. *Strategic Management Journal*, 28: 368–381; Cyert, R.M., & March, J.G. 1963. *A behavioral theory of the firm.* Englewood Cliffs, NJ: Prentice Hall.
5. Berry, H. 2010. Why do firms divest? *Organization Science*, in press.
6. Rao, S.K. 2009. Re-engineering a product portfolio: Case study of a pharmaceutical merger, *Journal of Business Strategy*, 30 (6): 52–62; Wan, W.P., & Yui, D.W. 2009. From crisis to opportunity: Environmental jolt, corporate acquisitions, and firm performance. *Strategic Management Journal*, 30: 791–801.
7. Cyert & March, *A behavioral theory of the firm*; Mezias, S.F., Chen Y.-R., & Murphy, P.R. 2002. Aspiration level adaptation in an American financial services organization: A field study. *Management Science*, 48: 1285–1300.
8. Morrow, J.L., Jr., Sirmon, D.G., Hitt, M.A., & Holcomb, T.R. 2007. Creating value in the face of declining performance: Firm strategies and organizational recovery. *Strategic Management* Journal, 28: 271–283.

9. Mezias, Chen, & Murphy, Aspiration level adaptation in an American financial services organization.

10. de Figueiredo, J.M., & Kyle, M.K. 2006. Surviving the gales of creative destruction: The determinants of product turnover. *Strategic Management Journal*, 27: 241–264; Greiner, L.E. 1998. Evolution and revolution as organizations grow. *Harvard Business Review*, 76(3): 55–68; Flamholtz, E., & Hua, W. 2002. Strategic organizational development, growing pains and corporate financial performance: An empirical test. *European Management Journal*, 20: 527–536; Lynall, M.D., Goleen, B.R., & Hillman, A.J. 2003. Board composition from adolescence to maturity: A multitheoretic view. *Academy of Management Review*, 28: 416–431.

11. Smith, W.S. 2009. Vitality in business: Executing a new strategy at Unilever. *Journal of Business Strategy*, 30 (4): 31–41.

12. Arthaud-Day, M.L., Certo, S.T., Dalton C.M., & Dalton, D.R. 2006. A changing of the guard: Executive and director turnover following corporate financial restatements. *Academy of Management Journal*, 49: 1119–1136.

13. Shimizu, K., & Hitt, M.A. 2005. What constrains or facilitates divestitures of formerly acquired firms? The effects of organizational inertia. *Journal of Management*, 31: 50–72.

14. Hayward, M., & Shimizu, K. 2006. De-commitment to losing strategic action: Evidence from divestiture of poorly performing acquisitions. *Strategic Management Journal*, 27: 541–557.

15. Yokota, R., & Mitsuhashi, H. 2008. Attributive change in top management teams as a driver of strategic change. *Asia Pacific Journal of Management*, 25: 297–315.

16. Boyne, G.J., & Meier, K.J. 2009. Environmental change, human resources and organizational turnaround. *Journal of Management Studies*, 46: 835–863.

17. Zhang, Y. 2008. Information asymmetry and the dismissal of newly appointed CEOs: An empirical investigation. *Strategic Management Journal*, 29: 859–872.

18. Simsek, Z., Heavey, C., & Veiga, J.F. 2010. The impact of CEO core self-evaluation on the firm's entrepreneurial orientation. *Strategic Management Journal*, 31: 110–119.

19. Huber, *The necessary nature of future firms.*

20. Bjork, B.-C., Roos, A., & Lauri, M. 2009. Scientific journal publishing: Yearly volume and open access availability. *Informationresearch*, at http://informationr.net, March.

21. Narin, F., & Olivastro, D. 1998. Linkage between patents and papers: An interim EPO/U.S. Comparison. *Scientometrics*, 41: 51–59.

22. U.S. Patent and Trademark Office. 2000. U.S. patent studies report. Washington, DC: Government Printing Office.

23. U.S. Patent and Trademark Office, U.S. patent statistics report.

24. Sinha, R., & Noble, C.H. 2008. The adoption of radical manufacturing technologies and firm survival. *Strategic Management Journal*, 29: 943–962.

25. Benner, M.J. 2010. Securities analysts and incumbent response to radical technological change: Evidence from digital photography and internet telephony. *Organization Science*, 21: 42–62; Lin, Z., Zhao, X., Ismail, K.M., & Carley, K.M. 2006. Organizational restructuring in response to crises: Lessons from computational modeling and real-world cases. *Organization Science*, 17: 598–618.

26. Taylor, A. 2010. The next generation: Technology adoption and integration through internal competition in new product development. *Organization Science*, 21; 23–41.

27. Bell, J., & Power, S. 2004. Nissan is seeking U.S. exemption on fuel efficiency. *Wall Street Journal*, March 10, p. D.12; Draper, H. 2004. "Do not call" list forces marketers to seek new ways to get attention. *Wall Street Journal*, July 7, p. 1; Latour, A., & Squeo, A.M. 2004. FCC to urge telecoms to settle on local network-access issue. *Wall Street Journal*, March 31, p. D.4.

28. Spell, C.S., & Blum, T.C. 2006. Adoption of workplace substance abuse prevention programs: Strategic choice and institutional perspectives. *Academy of Management Journal*, 49: 1125–1142.

29. Coeurderoy, R., & Murray, G. 2008. Regulatory environments and the location decision: Evidence from early foreign market entries of new-technology-based firms. *Journal of International Business Studies*, 39: 670–687; Peng, M.W., Wang, D.Y.L., & Jiang, Y. 2008. An institution-based view of international business strategy: A focus on emerging economies. *Journal of International Business Studies*, 39: 920–936.

30. Cuervo-Cazurra, A. 2008. The effectiveness of laws against bribery. *Journal of International Business Studies*, 39: 634–651.

31. Hoffmann, V.H., Trautmann, T., & Hamprecht, J. 2009. Regulatory uncertainty: A reason to postpone investments? Not necessary. *Journal of Management Studies*, 46: 1225–1253.

32. Rajagopalan, N., & Zhang, Y. 2009. Recurring failures in corporate governance: A global disease? *Business Horizons*, 52: 545–552.

33. Spell & Blum, Adoption of workplace substance abuse prevention programs.

34. Spanish Resources: Overview—Hispanics in North Carolina, 2007. CarolinasAGC, at http://www.cagc.org/spanish_res/hisp_nc.cfm, May 21; Hummel, M. 2004. Speaking the language: Booming Spanish-speaking population alters business strategies. *Greensboro News Record*, May 16, p. E.1.

35. Hitt, M.A., Ireland, R.D., & Hoskisson, R.E. 2011. *Strategic management: Competitiveness and globalization* (9th ed). Mason, OH: Cengage South-Western.

36. Hitt, M.A., Tihanyi, L., Miller T., & Connelly, B. 2006. International diversification: Antecedents, outcomes and moderators. *Journal of Management*, 32: 831–867; Meyer, K.E. 2006. Globalfocusing: From domestic conglomerates to global specialists. *Journal of Management Studies*, 43: 1109–1144.

37. Bowen, D.E., & Inkpen, A.C. 2009. Exploring the role of "global mindset" in change in international contexts, *Journal of Applied Behavioral Science*, 45: 230–260.

38. Mathews, J.A., & Zander, I. 2007. The international entrepreneurial dynamics of accelerated internationalisation. *Journal of International Business Studies*, 38: 387–403; Szulanski, G., & Jensen, R.J. 2006. Presumptive adaptation and the effectiveness of knowledge transfer. *Strategic Management Journal*, 27: 937–957.

39. Lee, S.-H. & Makhija, M. 2009. Flexibility in internationalization: Is it valuable during an economic crisis? *Strategic Management Journal*, 30: 537–555.

40. Koka, B.R., Madhavan, R., & Prescott, J.E. 2006. The evolution of interfirm networks: Environmental effects on patterns of network change. *Academy of Management Review*, 31: 721–737.

41. Latta, G. 2009. A process model of organizational change in cultural context (OC3 Model). *Journal of Leadership and Organizational Studies*, 16: 19–37.

42. See, for example, Kanter, R.M., Stein, B.A., & Jick, T.D. 1992. *The challenge of change: How companies experience it and leaders guide it*. New York: The Free Press.

43. Ford, M.W. 2006. Profiling change. *Journal of Applied Behavioral Science*, 42: 420–446; Hayes, J. 2002. *The theory and practice of change management*. New York: Palgrave; Lewin, K. 1951. Field theory in social science. New York: Harper & Row; Lewin, K. 1958. Group decisions and social change. In E.E. Maccobby, T.M. Newcomb, & E.L. Hartley (Eds.), *Readings in social psychology* (3rd ed.). Austin, TX: Holt, Rinehart & Winston.

44. Based on Goodstein, L.D., & Burke, W.W. 1993. Creating successful organizational change. *Organizational Dynamics*, 19(4): 5–18; Kanter, Stein, & Jick, *The challenge of change*; Lewin, *Field theory in social science*; Lewin, Group decisions and social change; Schein, E.H. 1987. *Process consultation (Vol. II)*. Boston: Addison-Wesley; Sitkin, S. 2003. *Notes on organizational change*. Durham, NC: Fuqua School of Business.

45. Sydow, J., Schreyogg, G. & Koch, J. 2009. Organizational path dependence: Opening the black box. *Academy of Management Review*, 34: 689–709.

46. Geiger, D. 2009. Narratives and organizational dynamics. *Journal of Applied Behavioral Science*, 45: 411–436.

47. Reay, T., Golden-Biddle, K., & Germann, K. 2006. Legitimizing a new role: Small wins and microprocesses of change. *Academy of Management Journal*, 49: 977–998.

48. Based on Goodstein & Burke, Creating successful organizational change; Kanter, Stein, & Jick, *The challenge of change; Lewin, Field theory in social science*; Lewin, Group decisions and social change; Schein, *Process consultation (Vol. II)*; Sitkin, *Notes on organizational change*.

49. Filatotchev, I., & Toms, S. 2006. Corporate governance and financial constraints on strategic turnarounds. *Journal of Management Studies*, 43: 407–433.

50. Lavie, D. 2006. Capability reconfiguration: An analysis of incumbent responses to technological change. *Academy of Management Review*, 31: 153–174.

51. Furuya, N., Stevens, M.J., Bird, A., Oddou, G., Mendenhall, M. 2009. Managing the learning and transfer of global management competence: Antecedents and outcomes of Japanese repatriation effectiveness. *Journal of International Business Studies*, 40: 200–215.

52. Based on Goodstein & Burke, Creating successful organizational change; Kanter, Stein, & Jick, *The challenge of change*; Lewin, Field theory in social science; Lewin, Group decisions and social change; Schein, *Process consultation (Vol. II)*. Sitkin, Notes on organizational change.

53. See, for example, Schuster, J.R. 2004. Total rewards. *Executive Excellence*, 21 (1): 5.

54. Anand, N., Gardner, H.K., & Morris, T. 2007. Knowledge-based innovation: Emergence and embedding of new practice areas in management consulting firms. *Academy of Management Journal*, 50: 406–428.

55. See, for example, Kotter, J.P. 1996. *Leading change*. Boston: Harvard Business School Publishing.

56. Gilley, A., McMillan, H.S., & Gilley, J.W. 2009. Organizational change and characteristics of leadership effectiveness, *Journal of Leadership and Organizational Studies*, 16: 38–47.

57. See, for example, Kotter, *Leading change*

58. Ibid.

59. Ibid.

60. See Hailey, V.H., & Balogun, J. 2002. Devising context sensitive approaches to change: The example of Glaxo Wellcome. *Long Range Planning*, 35: 153–178; Kanter, Stein, & Jick, *The challenge of change*; Nohria, N., & Khurana, R. 1993. *Executing change: Seven key considerations*. Boston: Harvard Business School Publishing.

61. See Hailey & Balogun, Devising context sensitive approaches to change; Kanter, Stein, & Jick, *The challenge of change*.

62. Ibarra, H., & Sackley, N. 1995. *Charlotte Beers at Ogilvy and Mather (A)*. Boston: Harvard Business School Publishing.

63. Kanter, Stein, & Jick, *The challenge of change*.

64. Durand, R., Rao, H., & Monin, P. 2007. Code and conduct in French cuisine: Impact of code changes on external evaluations. *Strategic Management Journal*, 28: 455–472.

65. Jansen, J.J.P., George, G., Van den Bosch, F.A.J., & Volberda, H.W. 2008. Senior team attributes and organizational ambidexterity: The moderating role of transformational leadership, *Journal of Management Studies*, 45: 982–1007.

66. Marrow, A.J., Bowers, D.F., & Seashore, S.E. 1967. *Management by participation*. New York: Harper & Row.

67. Kanter, Stein, & Jick, *The challenge of change*.

68. Judson, A.S. 1991. *Changing behavior in organizations: Minimizing resistance to change*. Cambridge, MA: Basil Blackwell.

69. Abrahamson, E. 2004. Avoiding repetitive change syndrome. *Sloan Management Review*, 45 (2): 93–95.

70. Kotter, J.P., & Schlesinger, L.A. 1979. Choosing strategies for change. *Harvard Business Review*, 57 (2): 106–114.

71. Elliott, D., & Smith, D. 2006. Cultural readjustment after crisis: Regulation and learning from crisis within the UK soccer industry. *Journal of Management Studies*, 43: 290–317.

72. Kotter & Schlesinger, Choosing strategies for change.

73. David, P., Bloom, M., & Hillman, A.J. 2007. Investor activism, managerial responsiveness, and corporate social performance. *Strategic Management Journal*, 28: 91–100.

74. Kotter & Schlesinger, Choosing strategies for change.

75. See Vroom, V.H., & Yetton, P.W. 1973. *Leadership and decision making*. Pittsburgh: University of Pittsburgh Press.

76. Korsgaard, M.A., Sapienza, H.J., & Schweiger, D.M. 2002. Beaten before begun: The role of procedural justice in planning change. *Journal of Management*, 28: 497–516; Saunders, M.N.K., & Thornhill, A. 2003. Organizational justice, trust, and the management of change: An exploration. *Personnel Review*, 32: 360–375.

77. Korsgaard, Sapienza, & Schweiger, Beaten before begun.

78. Matta, E., & Beamish, P.W. 2008. The accentuated CEO career horizon problem: Evidence from international acquisitions. *Strategic Management Journal*, 29: 683–700.

79. Ryan, M.K., & Haslam, S.A. 2007. The glass cliff: Exploring the dynamics surrounding the appointment of women to precarious leadership positions. *Academy of Management Review*, 32: 549–572.

80. Duncan, A.K., & Breslin, M.A. 2009. Innovating health care delivery: The design of health services. *Journal of Business Strategy*, 30 (2.3): 13–20.

81. See Kotter & Schlesinger, Choosing strategies for change.

82. Elias, S. 2009. Employee commitment in times of change: Assessing importance of attitudes toward organizational change. *Journal of Management*, 35: 37–55.

83. Henderson, A.D., Miller, D., & Hambrick, D.C. 2006. How quickly do CEOs become obsolete? Industry dynamism, CEO tenure and company performance. *Strategic Management Journal*, 27: 447–460.

84. Kotter & Schlesinger, Choosing strategies for change.

85. Judge, T.A., Thoresen, V.P., & Welbourne, T.M. 1999. Managerial coping with organizational change: A dispositional perspective. *Journal of Applied Psychology*, 84: 107–122; Malone, J.W. 2001. Shining a new light on organizational change: Improving self-efficacy through coaching. *Organizational Dynamics*, 19(2): 27–36; Morrison, E.W., & Phelps, C.C. 1999. Taking charge at work: Extrarole efforts to initiate workplace change. *Academy of Management Journal*, 42: 403–419; Bandura, A. 1977. Self-efficacy: Toward a unifying theory of behavioral change. *Psychological Review*, 84: 191–215.

86. Cassar, G., & Friedman, H. 2009. Does self-efficacy affect entrepreneurial investment? *Strategic Entrepreneurship Journal*, 3: 241–260.

87. Judge, Thorenson, & Welbourne, Managerial coping with organizational change.

88. Ibid.

89. Laursen, K., & Salter, A. 2006. Open for innovation: The role of openness in explaining innovation performance among U.K. manufacturing firms. *Strategic Management Journal*, 27: 131–150.

90. Jick, T.D. 1991. *Donna Dubinsky and Apple Computer* (A) (B) (C): Note. Boston: Harvard Business School Publishing. For the original basis of these ideas, see Kubler-Ross, E. 1969. *On death and dying*. New York: Macmillan.

91. Ibid.

92. French, W.L., & Bell, C.H. 1999. *Organization development: Behavioral science interventions for organization improvement* (6th ed.). Upper Saddle River, NJ: Prentice Hall.

93. Worley, C.G., & Feyerherm, A.E. 2003. Reflections on the future of organization development. *Journal of Applied Behavioral Science*, 39: 97–115; Robertson, P.J., Roberts, D.R., & Porras, J.I. 1993. An evaluation of a model of planned organizational change: Evidence from a meta-analysis. In R.W. Woodman & W.A. Passmore (Eds.), *Research in organizational change and development (Vol. 7)*. Greenwich, CT: JAI Press.

94. See Egan, T.M. 2002. Organization development: An examination of definitions and dependent variables. *Organization Development Journal*, 20(2): 59–70; French & Bell, *Organization development: Behavioral science interventions for organization improvement* (6th ed.); Schifo, R. 2004. OD in ten words or less: Adding lightness to the definitions of organizational development. *Organization Development Journal*, 22(3): 74–85; Worley & Feyerherm, Reflections on the future of organization development.

95. Paz, A.E. 2009. Transplanting management. *Journal of Applied Behavioral Science*, 45: 280–304.

96. See Beckhard, R. 1969. *Organization development: Strategies and models*. Reading, MA: Addison-Wesley.

97. See French & Bell, *Organization development*.

98. Ibid.

99. Worley & Feyerherm, Reflections on the future of organization development.

100. French & Bell, Organization development.

101. Luscher, L.S., & Lewis, M.W. 2008. Organizational change and managerial sensemaking: Working through paradox. *Academy of Management Journal*, 51: 221–240.

102. Lambrechts, F., Grieten, S., Bouwen, R., & Corthouts, F. 2009. Process consultation revisited. *Journal of Applied Behavioral Science*, 45: 39–58.

103. Guzzo, R.A., Jette, R.D., & Katzell, R.A. 1985. The effects of psychologically based intervention programs on worker productivity. *Personnel Psychology*, 38: 461–489; Neuman, G.A., Edwards, J.E., & Raju, N.S. 1989. Organization development interventions: A meta-analysis of their effects on satisfaction and other attitudes. *Personnel Psychology*, 42: 461–489.

104. See the "human processual" approaches in Friedlander, F., & Brown, D. 1974. Organization development. *Annual Review of Psychology*, 25: 313–341; Also see Porras, J.I., & Berg, P.O. 1978. The impact of organization development. *Academy of Management Review*, 3: 249–266.

105. See structural interventions in French & Bell, *Organization development*.

106. Argyris, C. 1964. T-groups for organizational effectiveness. *Harvard Business Review*, 42 (2): 60–74; French & Bell, *Organization development*.

107. Porras & Berg, The impact of organization development.

108. See team-building interventions in French & Bell, *Organization development*; also see Hackman, J.R. 2002. *Leading teams: Setting the stage for great performances*. Boston: Harvard Business School Press.

109. Morgeson, F.P., DeRue, D.S., & Karam, E.P. 2010. Leadership in teams: A functional approach to understanding leadership structures and processes. *Journal of Management*, 36: 5–39.

110. Solansky, S.T. 2008. Leadership style and team processes in self-managed teams. *Journal of Leadership and Organization Studies*, 14: 332–341.

111. Bell, C., & Rosenzweig, J. 1978. Highlights of an organization improvement program in a city government. In W.L. French, C.H. Bell, Jr., & R.A. Zawacki (Eds.), *Organization development theory, practice, and research*. Dallas: Business Publications.

112. Bowers, D.G., & Franklin, J.L. 1972. Survey-guided development: Using human resources management in organizational change. *Journal of Contemporary Business*, 1: 43–55.

113. Mabey, C. 2008. Management development and firm performance in Germany, Norway, Spain and the UK. *Journal of International Business Studies*, 39: 1327–1342.

114. Berk, A., & Kase, R. 2010. Establishing the value of flexibility created by training: Applying real options methodology to a single HR practice. *Organization Science*, in press.

115. Beck, N., Kabst, R., & Walgenbach, P. 2009. The cultural dependence of vocational training, *Journal of International Business Studies*, 40: 1374–1395.

116. Hackman, J.R., Oldham, G., Janson, R., & Purdy, K. 1975. A new strategy for job enrichment. *California Management Review*, 17(4): 57–71.

117. Kumar, K., van Fenema, P.C., & Glinow, M.A. 2009. *Journal of International Business Studies*, 40: 642–667.

118. Steps based on French, W., & Hollman, R. 1975. Management by objectives: The team approach. *California Management Review*, 17(3): 13–22.

119. Levinson, H. 2003. Management by whose objectives? *Harvard Business Review*, 81(1): 107–116.

120. Bartlett, C.A., & Wozny, M. 2004. *GE's two-decade transformation: Jack Welch's leadership*. Boston: Harvard Business School Publishing.

121. Hitt, M.A., Ireland, R.D., & Hoskisson, R.E. 2003. *Strategic management: Competitiveness and globalization* (5th ed.). Mason, OH: South-Western.

122. Song, J., & Shin, J. 2008. The paradox of technological capabilities: A study of knowledge sourcing from host countries of overseas R&D operations. *Journal of International Business Studies*, 39: 291–303; Meyer, K. 2007. Contextualizing organizational learning: Lyles and Salk in the context of their research. *Journal of International Business Studies*, 38: 27–37.

123. Gupta, A., Smith, K.G., & Shalley, C.E. 2006. The interplay between exploration and exploitation. *Academy of Management Journal*, 49: 693–706.

124. Kang, S.-C., Morris, S.S. & Snell, S.A. 2007. Relational archetypes, organizational learning and value creation: Extending the human resource architecture. *Academy of Management Review*, 32: 236–256.

125. Espedal, B. 2006. Do organizational routines change as experience changes? *Journal of Allied Behavioral Science*, 42: 469–490.

126. Bezuijen, X.M., van den Berg, P.T., van Dam, K & Thierry, H. 2009. Pygmalion and employee learning: The role of leader behaviors. *Journal of Management*, 35: 1248–1267.

127. Hirst, G., Knippenberg, D.V., & Zhou, J. 2009. A cross-level perspective on employee creativity, goal orientation, team learning behavior and individual creativity. *Academy of Management Journal*, 52: 280–293.

128. Son & Shin. The paradox of technological capabilities; Beck, Kabst, & Wallenbach. The cultural dependence of vocational training.

129. Deutschman, A. 2005. Change or die. *Fast Company*, May: 52–62.

130. Gilbert, C.G. 2006. Change in the presence of residual fit: Can competing frames coexist? *Organization Science*, 17: 150–167.

glossary

achievement motivation The degree to which an individual desires to perform in terms of a standard of excellence or to succeed in competitive situations.

achievement-oriented leadership Leadership behavior characterized by setting challenging goals and seeking to improve performance.

acute stress A short-term stress reaction to an immediate threat.

affective commitment Organizational commitment due to one's strong positive attitudes toward the organization.

agreeableness The degree to which an individual is easy-going and tolerant.

ambidextrous organization An organization structure that balances formalization and standardization to help to achieve efficiency and flexibility.

anchoring bias A cognitive bias in which the first piece of information that is encountered about a situation is emphasized too much in making a decision.

approval motivation The degree to which an individual is concerned about presenting himself or herself in a socially desirable way in evaluative situations.

ascribed status Status and power that is assigned by cultural norms and depends on group membership.

aspiration–performance discrepancies Gaps between what an individual, unit, or organization wants to achieve and what it is actually achieving.

associates The workers who carry out the basic tasks.

attitude A persistent tendency to feel and behave in a favorable or unfavorable way toward a specific person, object, or idea.

attitudinal structuring Activities aimed at influencing the attitudes and relationships of the negotiating parties.

authoritarianism The degree to which an individual believes in conventional values, obedience to authority, and legitimacy of power differences in society.

brainstorming A process in which a large number of ideas are generated while evaluation of the ideas is suspended.

burnout A condition of physical or emotional exhaustion generally brought about by stress; associates and managers experiencing burnout show various symptoms, such as constant fatigue, or lack of enthusiasm for work, and increasing isolation from others.

business strategy How a firm competes for success against other organizations in a particular market.

centralization The degree to which authority for meaningful decisions is retained at the top of an organization.

centralized networks A communication network in which one or a few network members dominate communications.

changes in top management Involve the replacement of top management team members who retire or depart the company for other reasons.

charisma A leader's ability to inspire emotion and passion in his followers and to cause them to identify with the leader.

chronic stress A long-term stress reaction resulting from ongoing situations.

coalition A group whose members act together to actively pursue a common interest.

coercive power Power resulting from the ability to punish others.

cognitive biases Mental shortcuts involving simplified ways of thinking.

cognitive dissonance An uneasy feeling produced when a person behaves in a manner inconsistent with an existing attitude.

common information bias A bias in which group members overemphasize information held by a majority or the entire group while failing to be mindful of information held by one group member or a few members.

communication audit An analysis of an organization's internal and external communication to assess communication practices and capabilities and to determine needs.

527

communication climate Associates' perceptions regarding the quality of communication within the organization.

communication medium or communication channel The manner in which a message is conveyed.

communication The sharing of information between two or more people to achieve a common understanding about an object or situation.

competitive advantage An advantage enjoyed by an organization that can perform some aspect of its work better than competitors can or in a way that competitors cannot duplicate, such that it offers products/services that are more valuable to customers.

confirmation bias A cognitive bias in which information confirming early beliefs and ideas is sought while potentially disconfirming information is not sought.

conflict escalation The process whereby a conflict grows increasingly worse over time.

conflict A process in which one party perceives that its interests are being opposed or negatively affected by another party.

conscientiousness The degree to which an individual focuses on goals and works toward them in a disciplined way.

consideration A behavioral leadership style demonstrated by leaders who express friendship, develop mutual trust and respect, and have strong interpersonal relationships with those being led.

contingency theory of leadership effectiveness A theory of leadership that suggests that the effectiveness of a leader depends on the interaction of his style of behavior with certain characteristics of the situation.

continuance commitment Organizational commitment due to lack of better opportunities.

continuous reinforcement A reinforcement schedule in which a reward occurs after each instance of a behavior or set of behaviors.

corporate strategy The overall approach an organization uses in interacting with its environment. The emphasis is placed on growth and diversification.

cultural audit A tool for assessing and understanding the culture of an organization.

cultural fluency The ability to identify, understand, and apply cultural differences that influence communication.

cultural intelligence The ability to separate the aspects of behavior that are based in culture from those unique to the individual or all humans in general.

culture shock A stress reaction involving difficulties coping with the requirements of life in a new country.

culture Shared values and taken-for-granted assumptions that govern acceptable behavior and thought patterns in a country and give a country much of its uniqueness.

DADA syndrome A sequence of stages—denial, anger, depression, and acceptance—through which individuals can move or in which they can become trapped when faced with unwanted change.

decentralized networks A communication network in which no single network member dominates communications.

decisions Choices of actions from among multiple feasible alternatives.

decoding The process whereby a receiver perceives a sent message and interprets its meaning.

Delphi technique A highly structured decision-making process in which participants are surveyed regarding their opinions or best judgments.

demand–control model A model that suggests that experienced stress is a function of both job demands and job control. Stress is highest when demands are high but individuals have little control over the situation.

dense networks A communication network in which most or all network members communicate with many other members.

departmentalization The grouping of human and other resources into units, typically based on functional areas or markets.

destructive individual roles Roles involving self-centered behaviors that put individual needs and goals ahead of the team.

devil's advocacy A group decision-making technique that relies on a critique of a recommended action and its underlying assumptions.

dialectical inquiry A group decision-making technique that relies on debate between two subgroups that have developed different recommendations based on different assumptions.

directive leadership Leadership behavior characterized by implementing guidelines, providing information on what is expected, setting definite performance standards, and ensuring that individuals follow rules.

discrimination Behavior that results in unequal treatment of individuals based on group membership.

distributive bargaining A strategy that: (1) involves a competing, win–lose approach and (2) tends to be used when one party's goals are in direct conflict with the goals of another party.

distributive justice The degree to which people think outcomes are fair.

diversification Related to the number of different product lines or service areas in the organization.

diversity A characteristic of a group of people where differences exist on one or more relevant dimensions such as gender.

diversity-based infighting A situation in which group members engage in unproductive, negative conflict over differing views.

divisible tasks Tasks that can be separated into subcomponents.

downward communication Communication that flows from superior to subordinate.

dysfunctional conflict Conflict that is detrimental to organizational goals and objectives.

dystress Negative stress; often referred to simply as stress.

ease-of-recall bias A cognitive bias in which information that is easy to recall from memory is relied upon too much in making a decision.

effort–reward imbalance model A model that suggests that experienced stress is a function of both required effort and rewards obtained. Stress is highest when required effort is high but rewards are low.

emotional contagion Phenomenon where emotions experienced by one or a few members of a work group spread to other members.

emotional intelligence The ability to accurately appraise one's own and others' emotions, effectively regulate one's own and others' emotions, and use emotion to motivate, plan, and achieve.

emotional labor The process whereby associates must display emotions that are contrary to what they are feeling.

emotional stability The degree to which an individual easily handles stressful situations and heavy demands.

emotions Complex subjective reactions that have both a physical and mental component.

emotions States corresponding to specific feelings, such as anger, that tend to be associated with particular events, people, or other stimuli.

employee-centered leadership style A behavioral leadership style that emphasizes employees' personal needs and the development of interpersonal relationships.

encoding The process whereby a sender translates the information he or she wishes to send in a message.

environmental uncertainty The degree to which an environment is complex and changing; uncertain environments are difficult to monitor and understand.

equity theory A theory that suggests motivation is based on a person's assessment of the ratio of outcomes she receives (e.g., pay, status) for inputs on the job (e.g., effort, ability) compared to the same ratio for a comparison other.

ERG theory Alderfer's theory that suggests people are motivated by three hierarchically ordered types of needs: existence needs (E), relatedness needs (R), and growth needs (G). A person may work on all three needs at the same time, although satisfying lower-order needs often takes place before a person is strongly motivated by higher-level needs.

ethnocentrism The belief that one's culture is better than others.

eustress Positive stress that results from facing challenges and difficulties with the expectation of achievement.

expatriate An individual who leaves his or her home country to live and work in a foreign land.

expectancy theory Vroom's theory that suggests that motivation is a function of an individual's expectancy that a given amount of effort will lead to a particular level of performance, instrumentality judgments that indicate performance will lead to certain outcomes, and the valences of outcomes.

expectancy The subjective probability that a given amount of effort will lead to a particular level of performance.

expert power Power resulting from special expertise or technical knowledge

exploitative learning Learning how to more effectively use current knowledge.

exploratory learning Creating new knowledge and being innovative.

extinction A reinforcement contingency in which a behavior is followed by the absence of a previously encountered positive consequence, thereby reducing the likelihood that the behavior will be repeated in the same or similar situations.

extraversion The degree to which an individual is outgoing and derives energy from being around other people.

feedback The process whereby a receiver encodes the message received and sends it or a response to it back to the original sender.

feeling A decision style focused on subjective evaluation and the emotional reactions of others.

formal communication Communication that follows the formal structure of the organization (e.g., superior to subordinate) and entails organizationally sanctioned information.

formal groups Groups to which members are formally assigned.

formalization The degree to which rules and operating procedures are documented on paper or in company intranets.

functional conflict Conflict that is beneficial to organizational goals and objectives.

fundamental attribution error A perception problem in which an individual is too likely to attribute the behavior of others to internal rather than external causes.

glass border The unseen but strong discriminatory barrier that blocks many women from opportunities for international assignments.

global strategy A strategy by which a firm provides standard products and services to all parts of the world while maintaining a strong degree of central control in the home country.

globalization The trend toward a unified global economy where national borders mean relatively little.

goal-setting theory A theory that suggests challenging and specific goals increase human performance because they affect attention, effort, and persistence.

gossip Information that is presumed to be factual and is communicated in private or intimate settings.

group Two or more interdependent individuals who influence one another through social interaction.

groupthink A situation in which group members maintain or seek consensus at the expense of identifying and debating honest disagreements.

growth Relates to increases in sales as well as associates and managers.

halo effect A perception problem in which an individual assesses a person positively or negatively in all situations based on an existing general assessment of the person.

hardiness A personality dimension corresponding to a strong internal commitment to activities, an internal locus of control, and challenge seeking.

height The number of hierarchical levels in an organization, from the CEO to the lower-level associates.

hierarchy of needs theory Maslow's theory that suggests people are motivated by their desire to satisfy specific needs, and that needs are arranged in a hierarchy with physiological needs at the bottom and self-actualization needs at the top. People must satisfy needs at lower levels before being motivated by needs at higher levels.

hierarchy The reporting relationships depicted in an organization chart.

high-context cultures A type of culture where individuals use contextual cues to understand people and their communications and where individuals value trust and personal relationships.

high-involvement management Involves carefully selecting and training associates and giving them significant decision-making power, information, and incentive compensation.

horizontal communication Communication that takes place between and among people at the same level.

human capital imitability The extent to which the skills and talents of an organization's people can be copied by other organizations.

human capital rareness The extent to which the skills and talents of an organization's people are unique in the industry.

human capital value The extent to which individuals are capable of producing work that supports an organization's strategy for competing in the marketplace.

human capital The sum of the skills, knowledge, and general attributes of the people in an organization.

hygienes Job factors that can influence job dissatisfaction but not satisfaction.

identity groups Groups based on the social identities of members.

implicit person theories Personal theories about what personality traits and abilities occur together and how these attributes are manifested in behavior.

incivility Slightly deviant behavior with ambiguous intent to harm another person.

informal communication Communication that involves spontaneous interaction between two or more people outside the formal organization structure.

informal groups Groups formed spontaneously by people who share interests, values, or identities.

information technology An overall set of tools, based on microelectronic technology, designed to provide data, documents, and commentary as well as analysis support to individuals in an organization.

initiating structure A behavioral leadership style demonstrated by leaders who establish well-defined patterns of organization and communication, define procedures, and delineate their relationships with those being led.

instrumentality Perceived connections between performance and outcomes.

integrative bargaining A strategy that: (1) involves a collaborative, win–win approach and (2) tends to be used when the nature of the problem permits a solution that is attractive to both parties.

intelligence General mental ability used in complex information processing.

intermittent reinforcement A reinforcement schedule in which a reward does not occur after each instance of a behavior or set of behaviors.

international ethics Principles of proper conduct focused on issues such as corruption, exploitation of labor, and environmental impact.

interpersonal cohesion Team members' liking or attraction to other team members.

interpersonal communication Direct verbal or nonverbal interaction between two or more active participants.

intuition A decision style focused on developing abstractions and figurative examples for use in decision making, with an emphasis on imagination and possibilities.

job enlargement The process of making a job more motivating by adding tasks that are similar in complexity relative to the current tasks.

job enrichment The process of making a job more motivating by increasing responsibility.

job redesign Enlargement or enrichment of jobs; enrichment is the better method to enhance motivation for effective problem solving, communication, and learning.

job stress The feeling that one's capabilities, resources, or needs do not match the demands or requirements of the job.

job-centered leadership style A behavioral leadership style that emphasizes employee tasks and the methods used to accomplish them.

lateral relations Elements of structure designed to draw individuals together for interchanges related to work issues and problems.

leader–member exchange A model of leadership focused on leaders developing more positive relationships with some individuals and having more positive exchanges with these individuals.

leader–member relations The degree to which a leader is respected, is accepted as a leader, and has friendly interpersonal relations.

leadership The process of providing general direction and influencing individuals or groups to achieve goals.

learning A process through which individuals change their relatively permanent behavior based on positive or negative experiences in a situation.

legitimate power Power derived from position; also known as formal authority.

life-cycle forces Natural and predictable pressures that build as an organization grows and that must be addressed if the organization is to continue growing.

locus of control The degree to which an individual attributes control of events to self or external factors.

low-context cultures A type of culture where individuals rely on direct questioning to understand people and their communications and where individuals value efficiency and performance.

management by objectives (MBO) A management process in which individuals negotiate task objectives with their managers and then are held accountable for attainment of those objectives.

managing organizational behavior Actions focused on acquiring, developing, and applying the knowledge and skills of people.

mass customization A manufacturing technology that involves integrating sophisticated information technology and management methods to produce a flexible manufacturing system with the ability to customize products for many customers in a short time.

maximization tasks Tasks with a quantity goal.

modern racism Subtle forms of discrimination that occur despite people knowing it is wrong to be prejudiced against other racial groups and despite believing they are not racist.

monochronic time orientation A preference for focusing on one task per unit of time and completing that task in a timely fashion.

monolithic organization An organization that is homogeneous.

moods States corresponding to general positive or negative feelings disconnected from any particular event or stimulus.

motivation Forces coming from within a person that account for the willful direction, intensity, and persistence of the person's efforts toward achieving specific goals, where achievement is not due solely to ability or to environmental factors.

motivators Job factors that can influence job satisfaction but not dissatisfaction.

multicultural organization An organization in which the organizational culture values differences.

multidomestic strategy A strategy by which a firm tailors its products and services to the needs of each country or region in which it operates and gives a great deal of power to the managers and associates in those countries or regions.

need for achievement The need to perform well against a standard of excellence.

need for affiliation The need to be liked and to stay on good terms with most other people.

need for power The desire to influence people and events.

negative reinforcement A reinforcement contingency in which a behavior is followed by the withdrawal of a previously encountered negative consequence, thereby increasing the likelihood that the behavior will be repeated in the same or similar situations.

negotiation A process through which parties with different preferences and interests attempt to agree on a solution.

nominal group technique A process for group decision making in which discussion is structured and the final solution is decided by silent vote.

nonverbal communication Communication that takes place without using spoken or written language, such as communication through facial expressions and body language.

normative commitment Organizational commitment due to feelings of obligation.

norms Informal rules or standards that regulate the team's behavior.

OB Mod A formal procedure focused on improving task performance through positive reinforcement of desired behaviors and extinction of undesired behaviors.

openness to experience The degree to which an individual seeks new experiences and thinks creatively about the future.

operant conditioning theory An explanation for consequence-based learning that assumes learning results from simple conditioning and that higher mental functioning is irrelevant.

optimization tasks Tasks with a quality goal.

organization development (OD) A planned organization-wide continuous process designed to improve communication, problem solving, and learning through the application of behavioral science knowledge.

organization A collection of individuals forming a coordinated system of specialized activities for the purpose of achieving certain goals over an extended period of time.

organizational behavior The actions of individuals and groups in an organizational context.

organizational culture The values shared by associates and managers in an organization.

organizational politics Behavior that is directed toward furthering one's own self-interests without concern for the interests or well-being of others.

organizational structure Work roles and authority relationships that influence behavior in an organization.

participative leadership Leadership behavior characterized by sharing information, consulting with those who are led, and emphasizing group decision making.

path–goal leadership theory A theory of leadership based on expectancy concepts from the study of motivation, which suggests that leader effectiveness depends on the degree to which a leader enhances the performance expectancies and valences of her subordinates.

perception A process that involves sensing various aspects of a person, task, or event and forming impressions based on selected inputs.

personal conflict Conflict that arises out of personal differences between people, such as differing values, personal goals, and personalities.

personality A stable set of characteristics representing internal properties of an individual, which are reflected in behavioral tendencies across a variety of situations.

planned change A process involving deliberate efforts to move an organization or a unit from its current undesirable state to a new, more desirable state.

plural organization An organization that has a diverse workforce and takes steps to be inclusive and respectful of differences, but where diversity is tolerated rather than truly valued.

political skill The ability to effectively understand others at work and to use this knowledge to enhance one's own objectives.

polychronic time orientation A willingness to juggle multiple tasks per unit of time and to have interruptions, and an unwillingness to be driven by time.

position power The degree to which a leader can reward, punish, promote, or demote individuals in the unit or organization.

positive organizational behavior An approach to managing people that nurtures each individual's greatest strengths and helps people use them to their and the organization's advantage.

positive reinforcement A reinforcement contingency in which a behavior is followed by a positive consequence, thereby increasing the likelihood that the behavior will be repeated in the same or similar situations.

power The ability to achieve desired outcomes.

prejudice Unfair negative attitudes we hold about people who belong to social or cultural groups other than our own.

procedural conflict Conflict that arises over how work should be completed.

procedural justice The degree to which people think the procedures used to determine outcomes are fair.

process loss The difference between actual and potential team performance that is caused by diverting time and energy into maintaining the team as opposed to working on substantive tasks.

projecting A perception problem in which an individual assumes that others share his or her values and beliefs.

punctuated equilibrium model (PEM) A model of team development that suggests that teams do not go through linear stages but that team formation depends on the task at hand and the deadlines for that task.

punishment A reinforcement contingency in which a behavior is followed by a negative consequence, thereby reducing the likelihood that the behavior will be repeated in the same or similar situations.

reference point A possible level of performance used to evaluate one's current standing.

referent power Power resulting from others' desire to identify with the referent.

refreezing A phase in the change process in which leaders lock in new approaches by implementing evaluation systems that track expected behaviors, by creating reward systems that reinforce expected behaviors, and by ensuring that hiring and promotion systems support the new demands.

resistance to change Efforts to block the introduction of new approaches. Some of these efforts are passive in nature, involving tactics such as verbally supporting the change while continuing to work in the old ways;

other efforts are active in nature, involving tactics such as organized protests and sabotage.

reward power Power resulting from the ability to provide others with desired outcomes.

risk-taking propensity Willingness to take chances.

risky shift A process by which group members collectively make a more risky choice than most or all of the individuals would have made working alone.

role ambiguity A situation in which goals, expectations, and/or basic job requirements are unclear.

role conflict A situation in which different roles lead to conflicting expectations.

roles Expectations shared by group members about who is to perform what types of tasks and under what conditions.

rumors Unsubstantiated information of universal interest.

satisficing decisions Satisfactory rather than optimal decisions.

self-contained tasks An integration technique whereby a department is given resources from other functional areas in order to reduce the need to coordinate with those areas.

self-efficacy An individual's belief that he or she will be able to perform a specific task in a given situation.

self-monitoring The degree to which an individual attempts to present the image he or she thinks others want to see in a given situation.

self-serving bias A perception problem in which an individual is too likely to attribute the failure of others to internal causes and the successes of others to external causes, whereas the same individual will be too likely to attribute his own failure to external causes and his own successes to internal causes.

sensing A decision style focused on gathering concrete information directly through the senses, with an emphasis on practical and realistic ideas.

servant leadership An approach to leadership focused on serving others.

simulation A representation of a real system that allows associates and managers to try various actions and receive feedback on the consequences of those actions.

slack resources An integration technique whereby a department keeps more resources on hand than absolutely required in order to reduce the need for tight communication and coordination with other departments.

social dominance orientation A general attitudinal orientation concerning whether one prefers social relationships to be equal or to reflect status differences.

social facilitation effect Improvement in individual performance when others are present.

social identity A person's knowledge that he or she belongs to certain social groups, where belonging to those groups has emotional significance.

social learning theory An explanation for consequence-based learning that acknowledges the higher mental functioning of human beings and the role such functioning can play in learning.

social loafing A phenomenon wherein people put forth less effort when they work in teams than when they work alone.

socialization model A model proposing that all leaders in a particular organization will display similar leadership styles, because all have been selected and socialized by the same organization.

socialization A process through which an organization imparts its values to newcomers.

socioemotional roles Roles that require behaviors that support the social aspects of the organization.

span of control The number of individuals a manager directly oversees.

sparse networks A communication network in which most or all network members communicate with only a few other members.

specialization The degree to which associates and managers have jobs with narrow scopes and limited variety.

standardization The degree to which rules and standard operating procedures govern behavior in an organization.

stereotype A generalized set of beliefs about the characteristics of a group of individuals.

stereotyping A perception problem in which an individual bases perceptions about members of a group on a generalized set of beliefs about the characteristics of a group of individuals.

strategic contingencies model of power A model holding that organizational units and people gain power by being able to address the major problems and issues faced by the organization.

strategic OB approach An approach that involves organizing and managing people's knowledge and skills effectively to implement the organization's strategy and gain a competitive advantage.

stress response An unconscious mobilization of energy resources that occurs when the body encounters a stressor.

stress A feeling of tension that occurs when a person perceives that a situation is about to exceed her ability to cope and consequently could endanger her well-being.

stressors Environmental conditions that cause individuals to experience stress.

structural characteristics The tangible, physical properties that determine the basic shape and appearance of an organization's hierarchy.

structural–cultural model A model holding that because women often experience lack of power, lack of respect, and certain stereotypical expectations, they develop leadership styles different from those of the men.

structuring characteristics The policies and approaches used to directly prescribe the behavior of managers and associates.

subcultures In the organizational context, groups that share values that differ from the main values of the organization.

substantive conflict Conflict that involves work content, tasks, and task goals.

sunk-cost bias A cognitive bias in which past investments of time, effort, and/or money are heavily weighted in deciding on continued investment.

supplemental organizational processes Processes in which associates and/or managers have ongoing meetings for the purpose of understanding and addressing important problems.

supportive leadership Leadership behavior characterized by friendliness and concern for individuals' well-being, welfare, and needs.

survey feedback Data obtained from questionnaires; managers receive the data for their units and are expected to hold unit meetings to discuss problems.

swift trust A phenomenon where trust develops rapidly based on positive, reciprocated task-related communications.

synergy An effect wherein the total output of a team is greater than the combined outputs of individual members working alone.

task cohesion Team members' attraction and commitment to the tasks and goals of the team.

task roles Roles that require behaviors aimed at achieving the team's performance goals and tasks.

task structure The degree to which tasks can be broken down into easily understood steps or parts.

team building A process in which members of a team work together and with a facilitator to diagnose task, process, and interpersonal problems within the team and create solutions.

team orientation The extent to which an individual works well with others, wants to contribute to team performance, and enjoys being on a team.

team Two or more people with work roles that require them to be interdependent, who operate within a larger social system (the organization), performing tasks relevant to the organization's mission, with consequences that affect others inside and outside the organization, and who have membership that is identifiable to those on the team and those not on the team.

t-group training Group exercises in which individuals focus on their actions, how others perceive their actions, and how others generally react to them; participants often learn about unintended negative consequences of certain types of behavior.

thinking A decision style focused on objective evaluation and systematic analysis.

training A process used in OD to help managers and associates to gain skills and capabilities needed to accomplish tasks in their jobs.

transactional leadership A leadership approach that is based on the exchange relationship between followers and leaders. Transactional leadership is characterized by contingent reward behavior and active management-by-exception behavior.

transformational leadership A leadership approach that involves motivating followers to do more than expected, to continuously develop and grow, to increase self-confidence, and to place the interests of the unit or organization before their own. Transformational leadership involves charisma, intellectual stimulation, and individual consideration.

transforming A phase in the change process in which leaders help to implement new approaches by providing information that supports proposed changes and by providing resources and training to bring about actual shifts in behavior.

transnational strategy A strategy by which a firm tailors its products and services to some degree to meet the needs of different countries or regions of the world but also seeks some degree of standardization in order to keep costs reasonably low.

two-factor theory Herzberg's motivation theory that suggests that job satisfaction and dissatisfaction are not opposite ends of the same continuum but are independent states and that different factors affect satisfaction and dissatisfaction.

Type A personality A personality type characterized by competitiveness, aggressiveness, and impatience.

unfreezing A phase in the change process in which leaders help managers and associates move beyond the past by providing a rationale for change, by creating guilt and/or anxiety about not changing, and by creating a sense of psychological safety concerning the change.

unitary tasks Tasks that cannot be divided and must be performed by an individual.

upward communication Communication that flows from subordinate to superior.

valence Value associated with an outcome.

values Abstract ideals that relate to proper life goals and methods for reaching those goals.

virtual electronic teams Teams that rely heavily on electronically mediated communication rather than face-to-face meetings as the means to coordinate work.

virtual teams Teams in which members work together but are separated by time, distance, or organizational structure.

organization index

name index

Martorana, P. V., 190
Maslow, A. H., 198–200, 228
Mason, R. O., 373
Massey, A. P., 374
Massimillian, D., 44
Massini, S., 45, 115
Master, M., 152
Mathews, J. A., 484, 522
Mathis, A., 47
Matteson, M. T., 259
Matthews, J., 333
Mausner, B., 228
Mavrinac, S. C., 484
May, K. E., 406
Mayer, R. C., 45
Mead, F., 227
Meade, G., 362
Medsker, G. J., 406
Medsker, K. L., 151
Meglino, B. M., 229
Mehl, M. R., 153
Mehra, A., 191
Mehrabian, A., 334
Meier, K. J., 484, 522
Meili, R., 190
Mendenhall, M., 115
Menipaz, E., 485
Meschi, P.-X., 116
Mesmer-Mangus, J. R., 45
Messe, L. A., 152
Meyer, A. D., 521
Meyer, J. P., 192, 193
Meyer, K., 113
Meyer, K. E., 114, 522, 525
Meyerson, D., 70
Mezias, S. J., 522
Michael, J. H., 333
Michaelson, L. K., 406
Michailova, S., 116
Michela, J., 153
Michelson, G., 334
Miles, E. W., 229
Miles, G., 231, 484
Miles, R. E., 484
Miller, C. C., 373, 406, 484, 485
Miller, C. E., 374
Miller, D., 44, 190, 334, 524
Miller, K. D., 5, 191, 521
Miller, K. I., 333, 335
Miller, N., 79
Miller, P., 231
Miller, S., 442
Miller, T., 113
Miners, C. T. H., 194
Mintzberg, H., 442, 484
Mishra, A. K., 258

Mishra, K. E., 258
Mitchell, T. R., 153, 192, 299, 405
Mitchell, W., 484
Mitroff, I. I., 373
Mitsuhashi, H., 484, 522
Mittleman, D., 405
Mizra, P., 230
Moag, J. F., 230
Mohammed, S., 374, 405
Mohler, C. J., 229
Mohrman, S. A., 45, 404
Moline, A., 440
Molleman, E., 78
Mollica, K. A., 78
Monaco, G., 77
Monge, P. R., 333, 335
Monin, P., 523
Monroe, G. S., 372
Montagno, R. V., 300
Monterosso, J., 370
Montibello, E., 316
Montoya-Weiss, M. M., 374
Moore, D., 63
Moore, D. A., 370, 371
Moran, P., 43
Morgan, C. P., 335, 440
Morgan, J., 485
Morgan, N. A., 485
Morgeson, F. P., 300, 524
Morrill, C., 407, 441
Morris, J. H., 333
Morris, M. E., 153
Morris, M. W., 114, 441
Morris, R., 259
Morris, S. S., 525
Morris, T., 523
Morrison, A., 113
Morrison, E. W., 524
Morrow, J. L., Jr., 521
Morse, G., 230
Mossholder, K. W., 260
Motowidlo, S. J., 229
Mouly, V. S., 334
Mount, M. K., 189, 190, 191, 406
Moynihan, L. M., 191, 193
Muhonen, T., 260
Mulcahy, A., 64
Mullen, B., 373, 406, 407
Mullen, K., 259
Mumford, M. D., 333
Munoz, A. R., 260
Munter, M., 115
Murnighan, J. K., 406
Murphy, J., 334
Murphy, K. R., 194, 300
Murphy, L., 258

Murphy, P. R., 521
Murthy, U. S., 373
Murray, B., 231
Murray, G., 522
Murray, H. A., 152
Myers, I. B., 371
Mynatt, C., 373
Myrowitz, J., 298, 300

N
Nadkarni, S., 485
Nahm, A. Y., 484
Nahrgang, J. D., 300
Naman, J. L., 485
Nardelli, R., 470–471, 474
Narin, F., 522
Natera, N. I. M., 260
Nathan, B. R., 487
Nathans, A., 5
Nathanson, S., 441
Neale, M. A., 77, 78, 440
Nebeker, D. M., 298
Neck, C. P., 43, 45, 260, 261
Neeleman, D., 315
Negandhi, A., 485
Nelson, D. L., 258, 260
Nelson, M. C., 43
Nelson, R., 32
Nelson, T., 119
Nemanich, L. A., 300
Netterstrøm, B., 258
Neubert, M. J., 406
Neuman, G. A., 190, 406
Newbert, S. L., 44
Newburry, W., 116
Ng, K. Y., 78
Ng, T. W. H., 45, 191
Ngo, H.-Y., 229
Nicholls-Nixon, C. L., 152
Nieva, V. F., 406
Nijstad, B. A., 373
Nisbett, R. D., 153
Nixon, R. D., 177, 258, 407, 440
Noble, C. H., 522
Noe, R. A., 151
Nohria, N., 298, 523
Nooderhaven, N., 115
Nooyi, Indra, 92
Nordstrom, R., 152
Northcraft, G., 77, 78, 440
Novak, M., 300
Nowicki, G. P., 193

O
Obama, B., 58–59, 244, 350–351
Obama, M., 58

subject index

Organizational structure (*continued*)
  organizational size and, 461–462
  structural characteristics and, 448–451
  structuring characteristics and, 448, 451–452
  technology and, 460–461
Organizational success, 14
Outcome criteria (teams), 383
Overload, work, 240–242

P

Palestine, 93
Paralanguage, 317
Participative leadership, 278
Passive-avoidant leadership, 282
Past performance:
  and aspiration—performance discrepancies, 491–492
  and conflict, 418–419
Patent applications, 495
Path—goal leadership theory, 277–280
Pearl Harbor, 354
PEM (punctuated equilibrium model), 395–396
People, perceptions of, 137–141
Perception(s), 136–146
  attributions of causality and, 141–145
  conflict and, 417
  defined, 136
  differing, 323–324
  importance of, 119–121
  and nature of perceiver, 137–139
  and nature of situation, 139
  of people, 137–141
    problems in, 139–141
  self-perception, 141
  stages of, 137
  task, 145–146
Perceptual speed, 168
Performance:
  and aspiration—performance discrepancies, 491–492
  effect of conflict on, 412
  motivation and, 198
  rewards tied to, 217–219
Performance goals. see Goal-setting theory
Performance management, 130
Performance orientation, 100
Performing stage (of team development), 395
Personal appeal tactic, 433
Personal conflicts, 392, 412
Personal growth, and decision making, 364
Personality, 154–168. *See also* Big Five personality traits
  Big Five traits, 159–163

cautions about, 166–168
cognitive concepts of, 163–165
conflict and, 417–418
defined, 157
determinants of, 157–159
environment and, 158–159
fundamentals of, 157–168
heredity and, 158
importance of, 154–156
motivational concepts of, 165–166
person-organization fit, 167
in teams, 385–386
Type A, 245, 417
usefulness of measuring, 156
Personality testing, 155, 156
Personality traits, 157, 159–163
Personal power, 203
Personal space, 324–325
Personal theories, 140
Personal values, 472
Person-organization fit, 471–474
Persuasive communication, 177–178
Philippines, 92, 100, 291
Physical layout (of work environment), as source of conflict, 415
Physiological consequences (of stress), 248–249
"Pink-collar ghetto," 66
Planned change, 499–508
Plural organizations, 50–51
Political dynamics, shifting, 496–498
Political risks, with international markets, 87
Political skill, 434
Politics, organizational, 432–434
Polychronic time orientation, 94–95
Position power, 275, 502
Positive organizational behavior, 25–26
Positive reinforcement, 123
Power, 428–432
  bases of, 428–429
  defined, 428
  at Disney, 430–431
  and diversity, 65–66
  example of, 430–431
  managing, 435
  need for, 203
  position, 275, 502
  strategic contingencies model of, 431–432
  types of, 429
Power distance, 99
Practice, and learning, 129
Prejudice, 60–61
Prepotency, 200
Presentation dos and don'ts, 329–331
Pressure (in groupthink), 353
Pressure tactic, 434
Procedural conflicts, 392, 413

Procedural justice, 210–211, 505
Process loss, 384
Production teams, 380
Productivity, 14
Progress monitoring (in OD model), 510
Projecting, 140
Project teams, 380
Proven leadership, 503
Psychological consequences (of stress), 247–248
Public-sector organizations, 17–19
Punctuated equilibrium model (PEM), 395–396
Punishment, 123–124, 125

Q

Qatar, 290

R

Racism, modern, 60
Rareness, human capital, 21–22
Rationalization (in groupthink), 354
Rational persuasion tactic, 433
Reference point, 346
Referent power, 429, 504
Refreezing, 500
Reinforcement, 122–128
  contingencies of, 122–126, 130
  continuous, 126, 128
  and extinction, 124–126
  intermittent, 126–127, 128
  positive vs. negative, 123
  and punishment, 123–124
  schedules of, 126–128
Related-product firms, 454
Relationship OD techniques, 511–512
Relationship-oriented leadership, 276–277
Research and development (R&D), 431, 453, 457
Resistance to change, 504–506
Resource inadequacy, as stressor, 242
Reward power, 429
Rewards:
  contingent, 281
  in effort—reward imbalance model, 238–239
  leadership and, 278, 281, 294, 295
  motivation and, 216–219
  performance and, 217–220, 278
  for teams, 398
Risk(s):
  and aspiration—performance discrepancies, 491–492
  degree of acceptable, in decision making, 346–347
  with international markets, 87